# Economic Analysis and Infrastructure Investment

NATIONAL BUREAU *of* ECONOMIC RESEARCH

A National Bureau of Economic Research Conference Report

NBER

NATIONAL BUREAU *of* ECONOMIC RESEARCH

# Economic Analysis and Infrastructure Investment

Edited by

**Edward L. Glaeser and James M. Poterba**

**The University of Chicago Press**

Chicago and London

The University of Chicago Press, Chicago 60637
The University of Chicago Press, Ltd., London

Published 2021
Printed in the United States of America

30 29 28 27 26 25 24 23 22 21     1 2 3 4 5

ISBN-13: 978-0-226-80058-5 (cloth)
ISBN-13: 978-0-226-80061-5 (e-book)
DOI: https://doi.org/10.7208/chicago/9780226800615.001.0001

Library of Congress Cataloging-in-Publication Data

Names: Glaeser, Edward L. (Edward Ludwig), 1967– editor. | Poterba, James M., editor.
Title: Economic analysis and infrastructure investment / Edward L. Glaeser and James M. Poterba [editors].
Description: Chicago : The University of Chicago Press, 2021. | Series: National Bureau of Economic Research conference reports | Includes bibliographical references and index.
Identifiers: LCCN 2021010981 | ISBN 9780226800585 (cloth) | ISBN 9780226800615 (ebook)
Subjects: LCSH: Infrastructure (Economics)—United States. | Government spending policy—United States. | Economic development—United States. | United States—Economic conditions—21st century.
Classification: LCC HC110.C3 E26 2021 | DDC 363.0973—dc23
LC record available at https://lccn.loc.gov/2021010981

⊗ This paper meets the requirements of ANSI/NISO Z39.48-1992 (Permanence of Paper).

## Relation of the Directors to the Work and Publications of the NBER

1. The object of the NBER is to ascertain and present to the economics profession, and to the public more generally, important economic facts and their interpretation in a scientific manner without policy recommendations. The Board of Directors is charged with the responsibility of ensuring that the work of the NBER is carried on in strict conformity with this object.

2. The President shall establish an internal review process to ensure that book manuscripts proposed for publication DO NOT contain policy recommendations. This shall apply both to the proceedings of conferences and to manuscripts by a single author or by one or more co-authors but shall not apply to authors of comments at NBER conferences who are not NBER affiliates.

3. No book manuscript reporting research shall be published by the NBER until the President has sent to each member of the Board a notice that a manuscript is recommended for publication and that in the President's opinion it is suitable for publication in accordance with the above principles of the NBER. Such notification will include a table of contents and an abstract or summary of the manuscript's content, a list of contributors if applicable, and a response form for use by Directors who desire a copy of the manuscript for review. Each manuscript shall contain a summary drawing attention to the nature and treatment of the problem studied and the main conclusions reached.

4. No volume shall be published until forty-five days have elapsed from the above notification of intention to publish it. During this period a copy shall be sent to any Director requesting it, and if any Director objects to publication on the grounds that the manuscript contains policy recommendations, the objection will be presented to the author(s) or editor(s). In case of dispute, all members of the Board shall be notified, and the President shall appoint an ad hoc committee of the Board to decide the matter; thirty days additional shall be granted for this purpose.

5. The President shall present annually to the Board a report describing the internal manuscript review process, any objections made by Directors before publication or by anyone after publication, any disputes about such matters, and how they were handled.

6. Publications of the NBER issued for informational purposes concerning the work of the Bureau, or issued to inform the public of the activities at the Bureau, including but not limited to the NBER Digest and Reporter, shall be consistent with the object stated in paragraph 1. They shall contain a specific disclaimer noting that they have not passed through the review procedures required in this resolution. The Executive Committee of the Board is charged with the review of all such publications from time to time.

7. NBER working papers and manuscripts distributed on the Bureau's web site are not deemed to be publications for the purpose of this resolution, but they shall be consistent with the object stated in paragraph 1. Working papers shall contain a specific disclaimer noting that they have not passed through the review procedures required in this resolution. The NBER's web site shall contain a similar disclaimer. The President shall establish an internal review process to ensure that the working papers and the web site do not contain policy recommendations, and shall report annually to the Board on this process and any concerns raised in connection with it.

8. Unless otherwise determined by the Board or exempted by the terms of paragraphs 6 and 7, a copy of this resolution shall be printed in each NBER publication as described in paragraph 2 above.

# Contents

# Acknowledgments

This volume is the culmination of a three-year project on the economics of infrastructure investment that was carried out under the auspices of the National Bureau of Economic Research (NBER). This project was made possible by a generous research grant from the Smith Richardson Foundation. We are very grateful to Mark Steinmeyer of the foundation for his interest in these important issues and for his ongoing engagement and support.

This project drew together researchers from many subfields within economics, including international trade, macroeconomics, public finance, and urban economics. Together they formed a study group on infrastructure economics, the members of which were linked by an interest in understanding the process by which infrastructure investment takes place and the economic effects of infrastructure projects. We thank the participants in the three study group meetings that helped to expand the network of scholars who were working on infrastructure-related issues. The papers in this volume were presented and discussed at the study group's capstone research conference in Cambridge, Massachusetts, in November 2019.

We especially thank Lawrence Summers of Harvard University, who delivered a keynote presentation at the first meeting of our study group, for drawing both research and policy attention to infrastructure-related issues. Steve Poftak, general manager of the Massachusetts Bay Transportation Authority (MBTA), provided an overview of the challenges of managing transportation infrastructure. Stephen Redding of Princeton University played a key role in connecting researchers from the fields of trade and spatial economics to this project. He has also collaborated with us on a related NBER project on the economics of transportation in the twenty-first century. Clifford Winston of the Brookings Institution helped to connect the discussion of infrastructure policy to broader themes in transportation economics and emphasized that pricing and maintenance decisions can be as important as infrastructure construction.

Many NBER staff members contributed in important ways to the success of this project. Denis Healy did a superb job of grant administration and served as liaison to the Smith Richardson Foundation. Carl Beck and the NBER conference staff delivered flawless meeting logistics and made it easy to convene the study group participants. Helena Fitz-Patrick did a terrific job of overseeing the process by which a collection of papers becomes a volume, and her editorial assistance has been invaluable. We are very grateful to all of them.

All of the authors and discussants whose papers and comments appear in this volume contributed to the project's overall coherence. Two reviewers, Robert Inman and another anonymous referee, provided comments and suggestions on the entire manuscript. This volume is far stronger as a result of their input, and we appreciate all of their suggestions.

Finally, it has been an unalloyed pleasure to work with the members of the University of Chicago Press editorial and production teams, who have worked hard to accelerate the production of this volume at a time of rising interest in infrastructure policy in the United States and many other nations.

# Introduction

Edward L. Glaeser and James M. Poterba

In 2017, according to the US Congressional Budget Office (2018), the federal government spent \$98 billion on transportation and water infrastructure. State and local governments spent another \$342 billion—a total of \$440 billion, or about 2.3 percent of gross domestic product (GDP). Although substantial, as a share of GDP this outlay is less than it has been at any time since President Dwight D. Eisenhower launched the Interstate Highway System in 1956. Diverse voices clamor to raise spending. Early in his term, President Donald Trump proposed increasing infrastructure spending by \$1.5 trillion, in substantial part using private funding. Advocates of the Green New Deal, which includes a plan to overhaul the transportation system, call for spending more than \$10 trillion over an extended period. The American Society of Civil Engineers (ASCE) has a long tradition of assigning weak grades to the state of US infrastructure and claiming that additional spending on infrastructure will yield substantial economic benefits.

In contrast to these calls, transportation economists are likely to call for better use of existing infrastructure before advocating greater spending overall. Pigou (1920) and Vickrey (1952) proposed congestion pricing, which could allow road traffic to flow more quickly during peak periods by requiring travelers to recognize the time-varying congestion externality that they

Edward L. Glaeser is the Fred and Eleanor Glimp Professor of Economics at Harvard University and a research associate and director of the working group on urban economics at the National Bureau of Economic Research.

James M. Poterba is the Mitsui Professor of Economics at Massachusetts Institute of Technology (MIT) and president of the National Bureau of Economic Research.

For acknowledgments, sources of research support, and disclosure of the authors' material financial relationships, if any, please see https://www.nber.org/books-and-chapters/economic-analysis-and-infrastructure-investment/introduction-economic-analysis-and-infrastructure-investment.

impose on others. Meyer, Kain, and Wohl (1965) emphasized the economic advantages of buses over urban rail for passenger travel. Winston (2010, 2020) identified substantial costs associated with inefficient highway policies and urged experimentation with private roads along with expedited adoption of autonomous vehicles, which use highway capacity more efficiently than driver-driven cars.

This essay frames the economic issues associated with infrastructure investment and introduces a collection of studies that offer new economic insights on this investment. The first section discusses three reasons—limited private capital markets, externalities, and potential natural monopolies—responsible for drawing the public sector into the ownership and operation infrastructure projects. Although some of the historic rationales for public investment in infrastructure have diminished over time, many remain, including the presence of externalities related to public health and macroeconomic conditions, and the fear of monopoly power.

The next section considers the forces that determine optimal spending on infrastructure, recognizing that there are both macroeconomic and microeconomic approaches to this question. The microeconomic approach emphasizes the direct benefits to users and a careful consideration of optimal spending mix across modes and infrastructure types. The macroeconomic approach focuses on interest rates, the alleged counterrecessionary benefits of infrastructure spending, and the role that infrastructure capital plays in contributing to economic growth. While Valerie A. Ramey's contribution to this volume casts doubt on the efficacy of infrastructure as a stimulus for growth, there is a need for a unified approach that better integrates the microeconomic and macroeconomic approaches to optimal infrastructure spending. The natural way forward is to quantify the macroeconomic externalities that come from various forms of infrastructure and to incorporate them into standard microeconomic cost-benefit analysis.

After this discussion of optimality conditions, we turn to the management and funding of infrastructure. The two issues are linked because, as the chapter written by Eduardo Engel, Ronald D. Fischer, and Alexander Galetovic emphasizes, some of the incentive problems that arise in private-public partnerships can be attenuated when infrastructure is paid for with user fees that roughly cover its average cost. Funding infrastructure in this way can avoid debates over redistribution and helps anchor project selection. There is less risk of "white elephants" when infrastructure projects are funded only when they are expected to generate revenues that will cover project costs. Such user charges create inefficiencies, however, if the average cost of the infrastructure is far above its marginal cost. This is likely to be the case for many projects, and in this setting, funding mechanisms that rely on other revenue sources to cover part or all of the fixed cost can lead to more efficient outcomes. One particularly interesting funding approach is to exploit revenue tools that capture part of the increase in local property values that flows from infrastructure provision, such as through so-called tax increment financing. Gupta, Van Nieuwerburgh, and Kontokosta (2020) provide an illustration of the potential revenue yield of such instruments in the context of New York City's recent Second Avenue subway project. Revenue instruments like this can get closer to an efficient two-part tariff than average-cost user charges.

While the privatization of infrastructure is currently attracting substantial attention, for the US, the intergovernmental allocation of responsibility for infrastructure is at least as important. Since the 1950s, the federal government has been responsible for paying for highways, but the allocation of funds is largely done at the state level. Public transit authorities are typically governmental agencies, but even those that work within a single locality typically answer to the state government as well. The Port Authority of New York and New Jersey, which is among the largest governmental infrastructure authorities in the world, answers to two state governors. What level of government should provide and control infrastructure, and whether the infrastructure should be controlled directly by the executive branch of government or through an independent public authority, are therefore important questions. The usual fiscal federalism argument suggests that higher levels of government are better able to internalize externalities, while local governments are more accountable. But the move toward federal funding is particularly driven by the federal government's greater comfort with large-scale borrowing, especially during a recession. At their best, independent public authorities have more flexibility and are free from short-term political concerns. At their worst, these authorities operate with little oversight and less accountability than an elected executive.

The next section asks whether infrastructure spending and utilization could be made more efficient in three areas: procurement, management, and mitigation spending. With regard to procurement, a growing literature, exemplified by Bajari, Houghton, and Tadelis (2014) and Bolotnyy and Vasserman (2019), estimates structural auction models using data on infrastructure procurement. This research can address, for example, the choice between fixed-price and cost-plus contracts and may ultimately provide lessons on how to raise the cost-effectiveness of infrastructure procurement. With regard to management, many of the most expensive infrastructure investments in the US, including Boston's Big Dig and New York's Second Avenue Subway, cost a multiple of their original estimates because new events led to renegotiations with contractors during the construction process. When cancellation of the project is not an option, contractors have a strong position in the negotiations. Even when the original bid process is a competitive auction, renegotiation is often a one-on-one bargaining process that may put governments at a disadvantage. Since renegotiation is likely to be a constant in future large infrastructure projects as well, we discuss the ways management affects project outcomes and underscore the potential returns to making renegotiation less expensive. The essay by Leah Brooks and Zachary Liscow in this volume suggests that mitigation spending, which in the highway context includes sound walls, the curving of roads, and related features, accounts for a significant part of the increase in the cost of highways between the 1950s and 1980s. Whether a more stringent cost-benefit criterion should be applied to these outlays is an open question.

The next section summarizes each chapter in this volume and explains the interconnections that knit the chapters into a single coherent volume. A final section just before the brief conclusion considers how the COVID-19 pandemic and its aftermath could impact the demand for infrastructure services and the government's role in providing them.

## Why Have Governments Invested in Infrastructure? Perspectives from US History

This section reviews three standard arguments for public provision of infrastructure and illustrates each with an episode from US history. Broadly speaking, the public sector has built and managed infrastructure when (1) the scale of investment was thought to be too large for private investors; (2) the infrastructure generated positive externalities including health benefits, nation-building benefits, or counterrecessionary macroeconomic benefits that would not be considered by private investors; and (3) the infrastructure capital could be used by a monopolistic owner to exploit those who need its services. The relative importance of these arguments today helps to shape our discussion of the later questions. For example, if public spending on infrastructure is motivated primarily by the inability to secure sufficient private sector credit, public-private partnerships may be attractive and should be considered when user-fee financing is appropriate. If the public sector's engagement with infrastructure reflects a large gap between average cost and marginal cost of infrastructure services, which will occur when infrastructure is a natural monopoly, then charging user fees dictated by average costs is less appropriate.

### The Erie Canal and the Limits of Private Funding

Before George Washington became president of the United States, he served as president of the Patowmack Canal Company. Limited financing slowed the canal's construction. The company tried to build a connection to the Ohio River, but engineering and financial difficulties led the company to embrace a far narrower vision. The link between the Eastern Seaboard and western waterways would be achieved far to the north through the publicly funded Erie Canal.

New York governor DeWitt Clinton was aware of the difficulties of securing enough private funding to create a massive infrastructure project. He therefore established the Erie Canal Commission, which used public funds and public borrowing power to link the Hudson to the Great Lakes. The commission was an early example of an independent public entity overseeing an infrastructure project that relied on public financing. The most famous nineteenth-century canals, such as the Erie, the Erie and Ohio, and the Illinois and Michigan, were funded by states, not the federal government. Although Congress passed an act to provide federal support for the Erie Canal, the legislation was vetoed by President Madison.

The Erie Canal was enormously successful, and user fees quickly funded its costs. In *The Wealth of Nations*, published nearly 50 years before the canal was built, Adam Smith extolled the virtues of user-funded infrastructure projects: "When high roads, bridges, canals, &c. are in this manner made and supported by the commerce which is carried on by means of them, they can be made only where that commerce requires them, and consequently where it is proper to make them" (1776, book V, chap. I, part iii). Smith's remarkable analysis even included recommendations for weight-based user charges for carriages and wagons, to cover the greater maintenance induced by heavier vehicles.

The Erie Canal remains synonymous with infrastructure spending at its best, and the canal surely yielded benefits that went beyond the value paid for by its direct users. Yet the public sector was involved largely because private capital markets were underdeveloped in 1810, and the public sector was the only plausible source of so much funding. Cutler and Miller (2005) document a strong link between public borrowing capacity and the construction of urban water and sewerage infrastructure during the late nineteenth century. America's cities and towns were spending as much on water at the start of the twentieth century as the federal government was spending on everything except the Post Office and the Army. The ability of cities and towns to borrow large sums enabled these massive sanitary investments.

This American story contrasts with pre-1800 English canal building, which involved smaller, flatter distances and private funds. For example, the original Mersey and Irwell Navigation linking Manchester and the Irish Sea was funded and built privately in 1734. When the much larger Caledonian Canal was dug in Great Britain in 1804, public funding was used, but by the end of the nineteenth century, financial markets were sufficiently well developed that the Manchester Ship Canal was a private enterprise.

Some recent calls for infrastructure spending have envisioned a small public subsidy that could encourage a much larger volume of private investment. Such calls assume that global financial markets are robust enough to fund almost any feasible piece of infrastructure that can be reasonably expected to pay for itself at the appropriate discount rate. Whether that vision is correct is an open issue. Andonov, Kräussl, and Rauh (2018) report that investment funds that focus on infrastructure projects have cash flow and distribution profiles similar to venture capital funds, seeking to exit investments in 5–10 years, rather than after the decades-long life spans of many infrastructure projects.

### Local Externalities and Public Ownership: The Case of Water Supply

In 1793, refugees from the Haitian revolution brought yellow fever to the port of Philadelphia. Dr. Benjamin Rush saw the symptoms and tried to impose a quarantine on ships arriving from the tropics, but limited state capacity made enforcing the regulation impossible. Thousands died from the disease in Philadelphia and across America's Eastern Seaboard. Yellow fever returned to Philadelphia in 1797, 1798, and 1799. Although yellow fever is actually carried by mosquitoes, many at the time suspected unclean water, which was indeed responsible for spreading many other diseases. Philadelphia formed a "Watering Committee," which commissioned Benjamin Latrobe to design a waterworks system. The system was finally completed in 1815. Cutler and Miller (2005) find that the creation of public water systems, like Philadelphia's, during the nineteenth century led to dramatic decreases in mortality across America's cities.

Cholera became an even deadlier scourge of America's cities after 1830, and its epidemiology was discovered by Dr. John Snow in London. Snow's geographic investigation of the 1854 Bond Street cholera epidemic found that a poisoned water pump was at the center of the outbreak. Gradually, the medical profession came to argue that investing in water infrastructure was necessary to prevent the spread of disease. New York City followed a different path after the yellow fever epidemics of the 1790s. Instead of a public waterworks system, the city established the Manhattan Water Company to provide clean water for city residents. The company was subsidized with a franchise to run a bank, a rare privilege at the time. It transpired that the company earned far higher returns by banking than by pumping water, and the Bank of the Manhattan Water Company eventually evolved into Chase Manhattan Bank and then J.P. Morgan Chase.

There were two key market failures related to water production during the nineteenth century. First, an individual who consumed dirty water did not internalize the health consequences to his neighbors of becoming infected with a waterborne disease. Second, consumers could not directly observe whether privately sold water was clean or dirty. Both factors limited the demand for the Manhattan Company's water. After New York City's 1832 cholera epidemic, the city embraced the option of investing in clean public water. The city's leaders created an independent public authority as a way to limit municipal corruption. Work on the Croton Aqueduct began in 1837, and water began to flow in 1842. While the aqueduct provided free hydrants, most users were expected to pay for water connections, and many low-income New Yorkers thought that the price of a water connection exceeded the private benefit of access to clean water. Poorer parts of the city continued to rely on shallow wells, and cholera continued to kill city residents. In 1866, a Metropolitan Board of Health was established; it could fine tenement owners who did not connect to the water and sewer system. This Pigouvian tax (before Arthur C. Pigou) seems to have had an effect; after 1866, death tolls from waterborne diseases in New York City began to decline.

If anything, public sewerage has an even higher ratio of public benefits to private benefits than public water supply. If sewage is dumped on a neighbor's property, the neighbor pays most of the cost, making the need for public subsidies with sewerage even more extreme than with water. Alsan and Goldin (2019) find that early twentieth-century investments in sewers in greater Boston complemented the earlier provision of clean water to reduce death rates.

The saga of the Manhattan Water Company provides a warning against private provision of health-related infrastructure, at least without a robust testing technology that enables consumer quality verification. Troesken's (2004) work on later nineteenth-century water systems finds that the death rates of African Americans declined substantially when cities switched from private to public water provision, which is consistent with the view that private companies skewed their service toward wealthier customers who could pay more. Despite this skew, even the rich were at risk from cholera epidemics that began in poorer neighborhoods.

Local externalities are still a potent justification for public investment in water infrastructure, yet we may question whether financially strapped communities are doing enough to maintain old water systems. Flint, Michigan, famously cut its water spending for budgetary reasons, and the city's emergency manager overruled the city council's vote to pay for cleaner, more expensive water. The poor quality of Flint water expressed itself both in highly elevated lead levels and in the spread of Legionnaires' disease, with associated reductions in the health status of residents. Yet the Flint story is a shocking aberration rather than a sign that communities are seriously debating the pros and cons of investing in clean water. There are still considerable debates about private versus public water provision, but these controversies concern costs more than cleanliness, because private water quality can now be easily monitored.

The local externalities associated with public provision of water supply and sewerage have parallels in the case of transportation infrastructure, notably when there are congestion externalities associated with road overcrowding. One common justification for public subsidies to metropolitan transportation systems is that they may reduce road congestion. Taxing driving is a more direct and efficient means of reducing congestion externalities than subsidizing alternative modes of transportation. Baum-Snow and Kahn (2000) found that newer metro systems in the US have had limited impact on commuting patterns. Declining ridership and chronic budget deficits are important challenges for public transit more generally.

If congestion pricing is politically infeasible, then whether it is appropriate to subsidize public transit becomes an empirical question. The appropriate subsidy for each public transit trip equals the reduction in driving caused by that trip multiplied by the external benefits of reducing the number of drivers, including both congestion and deaths from traffic accidents. If public transit takes the form of buses, then this optimal subsidy can be estimated using experiments with bus service to determine the impact on rides, traffic, and accidents. The number of buses can then be scaled up or down depending on the appropriate subsidy. If public transit means a fixed rail system, however, then ex post alterations to pricing can still be made, but it is difficult to change the quantity of subway lines after building finishes.

Congestion externalities also potentially justify building more highways, but any new construction must recognize that more highways often generate more driving. Indeed, a fundamental law of highway traffic, suggested by Downs (1962) and supported by Duranton and Turner's (2011) empirical analysis, suggests that the level of traffic may be roughly independent of the number of roads, since vehicle miles traveled seem to scale up roughly one-for-one with highway miles built. If that law holds, then new highway construction raises welfare by allowing more trips but does not materially reduce congestion on existing highways.

Nation Building

In the nineteenth century, Henry Clay and the Whig Party advanced a program called the "American System," which was meant to strengthen the nation by imposing tariffs on imports and subsidizing internal improvements such as transportation infrastructure. The Cumberland or National Road was the most visible example. That macadamized road ran from the Potomac to Illinois. The Whig's Republican successors used federal land grants to subsidize a privately built intercontinental railroad, also with the hope of binding the nation together.

Nation building has at least three coherent economic interpretations. First, it may refer to general equilibrium impacts of transportation that are not internalized by railroad builders. Building new infrastructure may raise land values. Firms may benefit from cheaper inputs. Donaldson and Hornbeck (2016) and Hornbeck and Rotemberg (2019) document that the US railroad system yielded significant and far-flung benefits. This finding is not inconsistent with Fogel's (1962) claim that American economic development could have proceeded without the railroads; Fogel focused exclusively on the cost saving for users of prerail transportation modes, thereby neglecting gains in productivity and innovation in other sectors.

Second, nation building may refer to protecting or expanding a nation's territory. In the nineteenth century, the US had border disputes with Mexico, Great Britain, and Native Americans. A more developed transportation network, and the migration that the network would induce, could have been viewed as strengthening the nation's political hold over the central North American land mass. In this case, nation building would be associated with political benefits for the US that come at a cost to other nations and peoples.

Third, nation building may mean creating a coherent sense of national unity. By increasing economic interdependence between regions, transportation infrastructure could potentially limit future secession movements and reduce the interregional strife that led to the Civil War. There is some evidence, for example, that the strong transportation linkages between New York City and the US South made some New York merchants more sympathetic to the Southern cause during the Civil War. While the benefits of national coherence are hard to quantify, the costs of fighting over national dissolution were enormous and many leaders, including Abraham Lincoln, saw the cause of preserving the Union as paramount.

Today, the second nation-building motive, defending borders, is no longer relevant for the US. The nation's borders have been essentially fixed for 150 years. The other two motives still matter. Trade economists build general equilibrium models to quantify the national economic gains from better connections. In addition, infrastructure's role in national cohesion has evolved. While nineteenth-century infrastructure advocates argued that simply connecting to dispersed areas would help build the country, twenty-first-century advocates emphasize that infrastructure can help bring prosperity to poorer regions and allow residents of those regions to feel like fuller partners in the national economy.

While arguments for infrastructure-led economic development are often made, whether new infrastructure projects can substantially increase economic activity in poorly performing regional economies is uncertain. In the context of US regional policies, two studies find that infrastructure improvements, notably low-cost electricity and an expanded highway network, have had positive effects in the low-income southeastern United States. Kline and Moretti (2014) find that the infrastructure projects associated with the Tennessee Valley Authority raised average incomes, largely by shifting employment from agriculture to manufacturing. Jaworski and Kitchens (2019) estimate that the Appalachian Highway Development System, which built about 2,500 miles of highways, raised income in Appalachia by about $22 billion. This translates to an income gain of nearly $10,000 per road mile. Even with such initiatives, however, Appalachia is still quite poor after 50 years of extra investment. It is particularly difficult to assess the long-run effects of infrastructure projects, given the potential range of confounding factors.

### Macroeconomic Externalities

Another potential rationale for national spending on infrastructure is the provision of macroeconomic externalities. Herbert Hoover pioneered the view that public infrastructure investment can offset downturns in the national business cycle. In 1921, as commerce secretary, Hoover organized the President's Conference on Unemployment, which urged state and local governments to undertake construction projects during the downturn. Hoover, a mining engineer by training, believed that the costs of such construction would be lower during the recession because labor was cheap and that such projects would reduce unemployment by boosting the demand for labor. As president, Hoover wanted an infrastructure act as early as 1930; he eventually signed the Emergency Relief and Construction Act of 1932. Hoover's early efforts were expanded by Franklin Roosevelt, and infrastructure spending was a significant part of the New Deal. President Obama's American Recovery and Reinvestment Act of 2009 followed this path and included $105 billion of infrastructure spending, split equally between transportation and energy projects. Proposals to increase infrastructure spending are frequently offered during economic downturns as a potential tool to reduce unemployment and boost aggregate demand.

Ramey's contribution to this volume calls into question the efficacy of infrastructure as antirecessionary spending. Other studies, analyzing historical experience, reach similar conclusions. Garin (2019) found that transportation spending generated only small increases in employment. The macroeconomic case for infrastructure remains among the most important and least well-developed aspects of the economic analysis of infrastructure spending.

### Monopoly Power and the Regulation of Railroads

Intercity railroads in the US were built by private companies, many of which received subsidies for nation-building purposes. Although in some markets multiple railroads competed actively, this competition often gave way to consolidation. In other markets, the railroads had local monopolies. Over time, the railroads were criticized for alleged abuse of their monopoly power. The public policy response to natural monopolies in industries like railroads has taken one of two forms in most countries: regulation of private operators or public ownership. The US initially followed the regulatory approach.

In 1887, the Interstate Commerce Commission (ICC) was created and given authority to regulate the rates charged by railroads. The 1893 Railroad Safety Appliance Act gave the ICC further control over safety issues; Glaeser and Shleifer (2003) argue that the motive for the legislation was in part the belief that traditional tort remedies for damages were insufficient given the railroads' legal muscle. Subsequent legislation, the Hepburn Act of 1906 and the Mann-Elkins Act of 1910, strengthened the ICC's controls over rate setting. In 1917, as part of the World War I mobilization effort, President Woodrow Wilson nationalized all US railroads. The US Railroad Administration oversaw all railroad operations, including scheduling, investment, labor compensation, and locomotive design. Railroads were returned to private control in March 1920. The Esch-Cummins Act, enacted that year, further expanded the ICC's regulatory powers.

Changes in the passenger and freight transportation industry over the subsequent 50 years, culminating in the bankruptcy of the Penn Central railroad in 1970, combined with a broader trend toward deregulation in the 1970s, led to a rollback of the ICC's authority. Starting in 1976, with the passage of the Railroad Revitalization and Regulatory Reform Act, the ICC's role in regulating railroads was restructured and reduced. It was finally eliminated in 1995. By the mid-1970s, concerns regarding railroad monopoly power had been replaced by the prospects of railroad insolvency. The ICC had restricted railroads' ability to abandon unprofitable routes and to adjust to competitive realities. In the early decades of ICC regulation, many farmers had few alternatives to shipping their harvest by rail. By the 1970s, the relatively competitive trucking industry provided a viable alternative for many shippers. Deregulation allowed the remaining railroads to focus on their profitable lines of business, to close poorly performing ones, and in some cases to focus on moving goods rather than moving people.

Penn Central's bankruptcy was one of the events that led to the consolidation of US passenger rail into Amtrak, a quasi-public entity subsidized by tax dollars, and to the creation of Conrail as the provider of rail freight services in the Northeast Corridor. The lightening of regulatory rules allowed Conrail to limit route structure and to innovate in ways that ultimately restored profitability and supported Conrail's sale to CSX and Norfolk Southern. In addition to loosening ICC regulation, the 1976 legislation also provided funds for Amtrak to acquire railroad assets in the Northeast Corridor. The evolution of passenger railroads from private companies to public entities repeats the movement, beginning before World War II, of municipal transit systems from private to public ownership as once profitable local transit companies lost ridership to automobiles. Public ownership of transit companies became a means of avoiding bankruptcy.

The economic cases for Amtrak, which today provides nationwide intercity rail service, and for local public transit systems are rarely articulated. The standard argument for public subsidy reflects the congestion externalities associated with driving. Yet that argument can hardly explain why Amtrak continues to provide service with relatively low ridership in areas other than California and the Eastern Seaboard. Another argument holds that rail and bus service are natural monopolies with marginal costs of use below their average costs, which implies that charging below average cost is efficient and requires subsidies. Winston (2013) presents some evidence that the social benefits of these services may fall short of current taxpayer support; this issue warrants further analysis.

### What Determines the Optimal Level of Public Infrastructure Spending?

Calls from politicians for increased spending on infrastructure are sometimes echoed by macroeconomists who see countercyclical benefits of spending on infrastructure and perhaps also benefits for long-term growth. Transportation economists, in contrast, are generally more skeptical of these calls. This section contrasts the microeconomic and macroeconomic approaches to determining optimal infrastructure spending. We do not develop a grand synthesis of the two approaches, but we sketch a research agenda that might lead to one. We then turn to microeconomic concerns that shape the optimal level of infrastructure spending, discussing both engineering reports and optimal allocation across modes, a topic explored further in this volume's chapter by Gilles Duranton, Geetika Nagpal, and Matthew A. Turner. We end with a discussion of macroeconomic issues that shape optimal infrastructure spending.

### Macroeconomic versus Microeconomic Approaches to Optimal Infrastructure Spending

Microeconomists approach infrastructure spending project by project with the well-worked tools of cost-benefit analysis. Benefits are determined primarily by effects on infrastructure users, although sometimes the analyses incorporate rising local property values or business profits. Costs are largely construction costs. This approach typically yields only modest returns for most new large-scale infrastructure projects. Returns for maintenance of existing infrastructure are typically much higher.

These arm's-length analyses often differ from the cost-benefit calculations that are provided for policy purposes, sometimes by entities that stand to gain financially through the construction of new infrastructure. For example, Parsons Brinckerhoff prepared an optimistic cost-benefit analysis for high-speed rail in California in 2014 and received a $700 million contract to manage the program the next year. Cost projections for this ongoing initiative have already moved far beyond those included in the report. Kain (1990) and others have also argued that skewed cost-benefit analyses often radically overstate reasonable projections of future ridership of rail projects. The relatively low returns to many projects reflect, in part, the advanced level of infrastructure in the US today. In 1816, it cost as much to move goods 30 miles overland as it did to cross the Atlantic Ocean; consequently, the Erie Canal provided a stunning reduction in transportation costs. Today, passengers can fly or drive from Los Angeles to San Francisco, and so the benefits of rail are far more muted.

The most exciting recent development in cost-benefit analysis for transportation projects has been the introduction of general equilibrium models from trade theory. Allen and Arkolakis (2019) provide an excellent example of this work. Their estimates suggest that the benefits from expanding some highway corridors, especially around New York City, are particularly high. Yet, the political and financial costs of such expansions may also be very high. Infrastructure projects in dense urban areas, such as the Big Dig in Boston, have proved particularly expensive in recent decades.

In contrast to the microeconomic approach, the macroeconomic approach to infrastructure starts with objectives linked to either stabilization or growth. Keynes (1936) wrote, "I expect to see the State, which is in a position to calculate the marginal efficiency of capital-goods on long views and on the basis of the general social advantage, taking an ever-greater responsibility for directly organizing investment" (164). Keynes feared both excessive speculation and "crises of confidence," which would lead private markets to either overinvest or underinvest in capital. He distrusted the ability of private markets to get the overall level of investment right or to target that investment toward its most productive use. He did not specifically mention infrastructure, but he saw public sector investment as an antidote for the vagaries of financial markets.

Keynes's general skepticism about private investment has had less impact than his advocacy of public spending during a recession: "The employment of a given number of men on public works will (on the assumptions made) have a much larger effect on aggregate employment at a time when there is severe unemployment, than it will have later on when full employment is approached." He goes on to provide a numerical example in which adding 100,000 workers on public works projects leads total employment to rise from 5.2 million to 6.4 million because of the multiplier.

While Herbert Hoover's enthusiasm for countercyclical spending predates Keynes's work, the latter's writing inspired subsequent generations of economists and policy makers to consider spending on public works as a way to reduce unemployment. Aschauer (1989a) added a longer-term macroeconomic rationale for infrastructure spending by empirically linking public infrastructure spending and economic growth in US economic time series. Aschauer (1989b) showed the connection between public infrastructure and growth across the G7 nations between 1965 and 1985. Gramlich's (1994) skeptical response to Aschauer's work is widely embraced by microeconomists, but Aschauer's views retain considerable currency among many policy-oriented macroeconomists. The reason may be that the difficult-to-explain decline in aggregate US productivity growth is roughly contemporaneous with the decline in infrastructure spending relative to GDP.

While the microeconomic approach yields clear policy tools for selecting infrastructure projects, the macroeconomic approach often yields only general advice to spend more on infrastructure during a downturn. A much-needed reconciliation of the two approaches could start with a clear quantification of the macroeconomic externalities associated with providing different forms of infrastructure. This might be accomplished using any of a number of standard macroeconomic models. There is probably more debate about the choice of the right model for the macroeconomic externality analysis than about the choice of discount rate and other parameters for the microeconomic approach. While both calculations rely on various assumptions, by unifying the two and acknowledging the resulting uncertainties it should be possible to move forward in evaluating the total return to infrastructure projects.

The most obvious employment-related externality is the fiscal externality. Employed workers pay taxes. Unemployed workers receive benefits. Any infrastructure that moves workers from being unemployed to being employed generates fiscal benefits equal to the sum of the benefits saved and the tax payments collected. The fiscal benefit from each employed worker is easier to estimate than the employment impact of infrastructure spending. The tax and benefit payments can be plausibly estimated, and so it is relatively easy to multiply the change in employment by that number.

Ramey's contribution in this volume makes clear that no consensus has been reached in the empirical literature on the employment effects of infrastructure. Many researchers doubt that most forms of infrastructure spending affect aggregate employment. An added challenge is that infrastructure spending is slow to plan and implement. Even if an infrastructure spending package is pushed at the start of the recession, the money may not flow until after the recession is over, when the employment benefits of the spending package will no longer be as valuable. Counterrecessionary maintenance spending is easier to manage than outlays on new projects, but even then there may be some social losses from basing maintenance schedules on the state of aggregate employment rather than the condition of the infrastructure capital stock. New large-scale projects are particularly hard to initiate during downturns. Planning for California's high-speed rail began with federal funds spent during the Great Recession, but continuous construction activity began only in 2015, and further work on most of the system was indefinitely postponed in 2019.

Growth-related benefits are harder to conceptualize and quantify than short-run macroeconomic effects. Aschauer (1990) treats government capital as a form of productive capital, and he estimates high economic returns to it. Leaving aside a number of empirical issues surrounding the measurement of the government capital stock as well as concerns about measuring the rate of return that government capital generates, such as the correlation of government spending with unobserved determinants of productivity, this approach yields little clarity about which forms of infrastructure are likely to yield the most benefit.

At some point, it may be possible to combine the estimated macroeconomic effects with the network and other microeconomic effects of particular projects. If the connection between firms and transportation infrastructure is directly incorporated in a spatial equilibrium model, then the model could be expected to match any observed relationship between the level of public infrastructure and overall economic activity. This model could then generate an empirically grounded estimate of the productive benefits of different road segments that incorporates the larger growth estimates, permitting welfare statements about different forms of infrastructure investment.

The most difficult macroeconomic concern to include within infrastructure planning may be Keynes's skepticism about the rationality of private investment. If the market misperceives the value of additions to the capital stock, private spending could be stimulated or taxed through the tax code, or public planners could raise or lower the level of infrastructure spending. It is not clear whether these planners can outguess the private sector and correctly compute the long-run marginal efficiency of public sector capital.

### Microeconomic Analyses of Optimal Infrastructure Spending

The microeconomic approach to infrastructure investment generally proceeds on a project-by-project basis and correspondingly yields results on whether an investment should be undertaken at this disaggregate level. There are at least two major aggregate scorecards, however, that adopt a microeconomic approach to infrastructure assessment and provide widely followed assessments of the infrastructure capital stock. One report, the *Infrastructure Report Card*, is prepared by the American Society of Civil Engineers (ASCE). The other, prepared by the World Economic Forum, is *The Global Competitiveness Report*. The ASCE's *Infrastructure Report Card* is the work of 28 civil engineers who assign grades based on their assessment of the current state of infrastructure. *The Global Competitiveness Report* is based on surveys of business leaders.

The overall grade for the US in the ASCE's 2017 report card is a D+, which implies that infrastructure is "poor" and "at risk." Roads received a straight D; bridges received a C+, which indicates that they are "mediocre" and "need attention"; and drinking water received a D. The ASCE methodology is often misinterpreted as an engineering assessment of the physical condition of existing infrastructure, and the language may cause confusion. A bridge that is "structurally deficient" need not be unsafe, but it may not meet all current standards for bridge construction. Moreover, while assessments of the structural status of existing infrastructure capital are a component of the grade, there are also a number of other elements, such as funding, future need, and innovation, that include either forecasts or subjective elements. One consideration is "what is the cost to improve the infrastructure, [and] will future funding prospects address the need?" Another is "what new and innovative techniques . . . are being implemented to improve the infrastructure?" Both questions go well beyond current physical condition. The score for an infrastructure category could be pulled down by limited current public funding relative to anticipated future needs or by the absence of the latest technology, even if the capital's current physical condition is satisfactory.

An important limitation of the grading rubric is the assumption that the only way to address projected growth in infrastructure demand is to build more of it. Alternative approaches, such as adopting congestion pricing to use existing infrastructure more efficiently, do not feature in the analysis.

The ASCE's approach is likely to overstate the potential shortfalls in future infrastructure capacity and to bias the grades for existing infrastructure downward.

Taken at face value, these grades suggest that the US needs to spend more on its infrastructure, although some might observe that civil engineers might have a financial interest in making the case for more spending on such projects. Moreover, it is hard to reconcile a grade of D for drinking water given the rarity of outbreaks of waterborne diseases. The catastrophe in Flint, Michigan, is correctly seen as terrible disaster, not the routine state of affairs. Duranton, Nagpal, and Turner's chapter in this volume shows that Interstate Highways in the US have become smoother over time, which makes the grade of D for roads difficult to understand, especially since the report card gave the much rougher highways of 1988 a grade of C+. While there may be challenges reconciling the ASCE grades with some data on the service flow from infrastructure capital, the engineers are most likely to know whether bridges are in danger of imminent collapse or whether other components of infrastructure have reached the end of their design lifetimes and need to be repaired or replaced.

The heterogeneous grades by sector and state offer the hope of incorporating more engineering into public infrastructure decisions. To make these estimates usable, they need to be combined with estimates of the harm of failing to maintain particular assets. Estimates of the current state of infrastructure need to be turned into assessments of the risk of various failures, and these can in turn be multiplied by the social costs of an infrastructure failure. For example, bridges may be in better shape than roads, but if bridges fail, the loss of life may be far more terrible than anything that would result from a failure to maintain roads. That comparison should feature in the calculation of replacement or maintenance expenditures on bridges versus roads.

*The Global Competitiveness Report* does not claim to utilize the civil engineering expertise embedded in the ASCE report card, but the World Economic Forum's report does have the virtue of global compatibility. The report contains a significant section on infrastructure and splits the infrastructure scores into transportation and utilities. Overall, the US score on infrastructure in 2019 was 87.9, which placed 13th in the world. While this score (a high B?) is considerably higher than the ASCE's D+, many are still troubled that infrastructure in the US no longer rates as among the best in the world.

The two worst infrastructure scores for the US appear in the railroad sector: 41.3 in railroad density—48th in the world—and 69.2 in the efficiency of rail services. These low scores reflect the reality that since the deregulation of rail services in the 1970s, the US has not significantly invested in passenger rail. Yet generations of transportation economists since Meyer, Kain, and Wohl (1965) have argued that passenger rail is relatively inefficient both within and across cities. A low score in the rail categories may well be optimal.

In other areas, connectivity in the US is superb, but maintenance is less good. The US is the global leader in road and airport connectivity. One hundred percent of the US population has access to electricity, and the nation ranks eighth in "liner shipping connectivity." The quality of road infrastructure, however, is rated only 74.5, 17th in the world. The efficiency of airport and port services ranks 10th. *The Global Competitiveness Report* gives the US a 100 for water safety, somewhat belying the ASCE Report Card's D, but only an 86.1 for water reliability.

The World Economic Forum's report lends support to Gramlich's (1994) conclusion that the US invested in the most productive forms of infrastructure first. Subsequent investments yielded lower economic returns. Consequently, for the US, the highest social returns come from maintaining existing infrastructure rather than from new projects. This has been a mantra for microeconomic transportation economists ever since. Winston (2013) calls attention to the inefficiencies in road maintenance policies, suggesting that public expenditures to achieve improvements in road quality have been larger than needed.

Decisions about new infrastructure can be divided into within-mode choices and choices across modes. Tools similar to those that are used to explore expanding network capacity can be used to estimate the returns to adding capacity in different airports. Duranton, Nagpal, and Turner provide a simple framework for optimal investment across modes. They maintain that the marginal benefit of public spending needs to be equalized across modes of travel. If the marginal benefit is proportional to the average cost of each mile of travel, public spending per mile traveled should be equalized across modes. While Duranton, Nagpal, and Turner's assumed relationship between marginal benefit and average spending is unlikely to be literally correct, they find that the marginal product of spending on Interstate Highways is three times the marginal benefit of spending on buses and more than twice the marginal benefit of spending on rails. While Duranton, Nagpal, and Turner do not incorporate any redistributive benefits of favoring transit for lower-income individuals, their work highlights the fact that the US currently spends far more per passenger mile on rail and buses than on highways. This pattern may in part reflect historical path dependence: many components of the rail network were built before auto, truck, and air competition constituted a viable alternative to rail travel.

While rail and buses look similar in the calculations of Duranton, Nagpal, and Turner, there are two major differences between these modes. Buses are particularly skewed toward the poor and are also a flexible mode of transportation. Consequently, providing extensive bus service may impact individuals on the margins of employment, which can encourage working and generate fiscal externalities. The flexibility of bus transportation also means that bus service can be scaled up or down in response to new information. Such adjustments are much harder with fixed rail investments.

Macroeconomic Determinants of Optimal Infrastructure Investment

The macroeconomic approach to infrastructure typically emphasizes two measurable variables: the interest rate and joblessness. This approach could also include the effects of infrastructure spending on economic growth, but there is little evidence on these effects for different types of projects. The benefits of infrastructure investment occur over time; consequently, the discount rate determines the net present value of the flow of these investments. Lower interest rates mean that the future benefits are valued more highly. All else being equal, a decline in the discount rate implies that the optimal level of infrastructure investment should rise. Equivalently, if the repayment of infrastructure debt is timed to coincide with future usage and user fees, then lower long-term interest rates imply that future taxpayers will have a lower tax or user-fee burden for any fixed level of infrastructure spending.

This logic, which is true for any form of capital investment, lies behind the calls from Furman and Summers (2019) and many others for spending more on infrastructure in the current environment of low interest rates than in previous higher-interest-rate settings. The basic logic of these calls is unassailable, since many infrastructure projects have up-front costs and future benefits that must be discounted. However, even when the interest rate is zero, it does not make sense to invest in a project with a negative undiscounted sum of net benefits. In addition, some forms of infrastructure involve future costs as well as benefits; lower rates raise, rather than lowering, the present value of those costs.

The chapter by Deborah Lucas and Jorge Jimenez Montecinos addresses the issue of risk adjustment when discounting the stream of net benefits from public infrastructure projects. The widely referenced Arrow-Lind (1970) theorem proves that the benefits of public projects should be discounted at the risk-free rate when the benefits of each project are independent of one another and of overall macroeconomic risk and when the number of projects is large. In this case, the overall portfolio of projects becomes risk-free, and the risk-free rate is appropriate.

The Arrow-Lind conditions seem unlikely to hold in most cases. Many projects, including roads and bridges, yield benefits that increase with the overall level of economic activity. Many projects, including roads, have benefits that are correlated across projects. Improvements in the quality of cars will cause the benefits of all roads to rise together. Increasing costs of fossil fuel emissions will cause the benefits of all roads, and many other forms of infrastructure as well, to decline together. The issue of risk adjustment for discounting the benefits of infrastructure projects is far from settled.

There is similar controversy about the connection between the level of unemployment and optimal infrastructure investment. Keynes argued that the employment-related benefits of public works spending were greater when employment was low, and macroeconomic advocates of countercyclical infrastructure spending echo his line. Ramey's chapter casts doubt on this view, noting that both empirical work and theory suggest that infrastructure is a weak tool for fighting unemployment. The changing nature of infrastructure investment lends support to her perspective. When Keynes wrote, public works were labor-intensive. New Deal projects often featured large numbers of unskilled laborers. Today, infrastructure is far more capital-intensive and far more likely to use skilled laborers who would be employed in any case. If infrastructure requires machines more than less-skilled people, then the scope for infrastructure policy to exert short-run effects on employment will be limited.

## Pricing, Provision, and Maintenance

We now turn from a discussion of the optimal level of infrastructure capital to questions about the management of this capital. We begin with optimal pricing, and then turn to whether it should be provided by the public or private sector, a topic addressed in the chapters by Engel, Fischer, and Galetovic and by Lucas and Montecinos. We also consider the optimal allocation of infrastructure responsibilities between the federal and local governments. We conclude by discussing maintenance and repair, highlighting cases in which the answers about optimal funding and provision may differ between maintenance and new construction.

### Efficient Infrastructure Pricing and Funding

Pricing determines the level of infrastructure usage conditional upon the infrastructure's level of maintenance. Pricing can also play a role in determining infrastructure investment decisions, shape incentives for maintenance, and affect the distribution of net benefits from infrastructure. Higher prices for some infrastructure services, such as bus trips, can particularly impact the poor.

The starting point for pricing any service is the principle that efficient use results if price equals marginal cost. On a road, that cost includes the depreciation, congestion, and lost safety to other drivers created by an extra driver. Historically, these costs have often been treated as minimal; consequently, free roads seemed like a reasonable benchmark. Indeed, the Interstate Highway System was originally intended to be without tolls, partly because tolls were seen as largely as a way to raise revenues rather than to ration use. Traditionally, the perceived marginal cost of public transit use was also thought to be quite low, at least up to the point where additional buses or cars need to be run. The gap between marginal and average cost was also invoked in support of tax subsidies for infrastructure construction, such as exempting the interest on bonds issued to finance such projects from income taxation.

In dense metropolitan regions today, the marginal costs of both transit use and driving can be high. Subways, buses, and roads can be quite crowded. For roads, optimal congestion pricing could lead to charges that significant exceed the average cost of provision, especially if the opportunity cost of the land under the road is ignored. Efficient pricing in this setting would mean that road systems break even or generate surpluses instead of requiring subsidies. Small, Winston, and Evans (1991) present calculations in which a system of congestion charges for both cars and trucks, coupled with pavement damage charges for trucks, roughly covers the road system's operating costs.

We have considered externalities within the transit system together with other costs, but if there are other externalities associated with infrastructure use then they should also be included in pricing. If carbon use generates negative environmental externalities, then the price of fuel-intensive infrastructure should be increased to reflect this. If water use in dry states exacerbates fire risks, then the price charged to users of water-intensive infrastructure should include the cost of remediating or insuring those risks.

The optimal pricing for one transport mode, using one type of infrastructure, depends on the pricing or mispricing of other modes. If driving creates negative externalities that are not priced, then reducing the cost of public transit provides one tool for mitigation. This second-best solution will always be less efficient, absent administration costs, than directly taxing the negative externality.

The consequences of pricing decisions can extend beyond rationing use. In public-private partnerships, Engel, Fischer, and Galetovic (2014) point out, charging users for infrastructure access creates incentives for better maintenance, because the private provider does not get paid unless the roads are used, and the roads are not used if they are in bad shape. Ashraf and colleagues (2017) find that water pipes in Zambia are repaired more rapidly when consumers pay by the liter of water consumed rather than by the month. Public providers may be less sensitive to revenues than private providers, but public providers may also deliver better maintenance if they are concerned about losing users. User-fee financing can also be quite helpful when selecting infrastructure projects. If projects are funded primarily through subsidies, then there is little financial reason to choose better projects. If infrastructure is expected to pay for itself, then there is more discipline in the project selection process. Projects will be more likely to be selected when they are expected to generate revenues; this likelihood helps make sure that the projects will actually be used. Typically, equity concerns are used to argue for prices that are lower than marginal cost for services like buses, but equity concerns can also push for higher prices. Airport users are, on average, better off than nonusers. If airports are funded by general tax revenues, and the revenue burden is spread more broadly than airport utilization, then this represents a transfer from the poor to the rich. Setting user fees to cover the cost of an airport project eliminates the possibility of redistribution via pricing.

When there is a gap between the user fee and average cost, then infrastructure requires other forms of financing. In rare cases, infrastructure is priced through a classic two-part tariff, which causes users to pay a flat fee for accessing the infrastructure and then face a low cost of using the infrastructure on a daily basis. Commuter trains sometimes offer monthly passes that have this structure. In other cases, local property taxes serve as form of two-part tariff. If the beneficiaries of infrastructure live in a particular locale, then a combination of low user fees and property-tax financing can still charge those who use the infrastructure but not distort usage decisions.

Tax-increment financing envisions using the increases in property values associated with new infrastructure to help pay for that infrastructure. Hong Kong's Mass Transit Railway uses a particularly creative means of financing in this spirit. The company finances its railways with dense building around new subway stops. The real estate value created by the rail system is therefore captured by the rail builder.

Much US highway financing occurs through the federal Highway Trust Fund, which has historically been financed largely by gasoline taxes. These taxes are a form of user fee, since drivers who use the roads buy gasoline. Over the past 15 years, as gasoline consumption per mile driven has declined and vehicles that do not require gasoline have emerged, a greater share of the trust fund has come from general tax revenues, which means that ordinary taxpayers are subsidizing highway drivers. The highway trust fund also redistributes from high-density states to low-density states that have a large number of highways per capita. In some cases, goods bought in high-density states travel through low-density states, and therefore high-density states benefit from highways in low-density states. Standard economic analysis suggests that directly charging shippers for their highway use is likely to be a more efficient funding mechanism than the current use of Highway Trust Fund subsidies. Beyond shipping and occasional recreational use, it is unclear how higher-density parts of the US benefit from highways in more open areas.

### Public versus Private Provision of Infrastructure

Privatization of infrastructure may seem to some to be a recent innovation, but in fact, debates over private versus public infrastructure are centuries old. Private canals and turnpikes were a common feature of the eighteenth century; private transit systems were ubiquitous in the nineteenth century.

The classic analysis of Hart, Shleifer, and Vishny (1997) presents the choice between private and public ownership as a choice between good and bad incentives. Private managers have stronger incentives to cut costs, which can both reduce waste and reduce quality, especially when quality reductions do not lead to losses in revenues. Consequently, there may be some services, such as providing airport safety or prisons, for which the welfare losses from lost quality exceed the benefits from lower expenses.

Engel, Fischer, and Galetovic (2014) turn this logic on its head for public-private partnerships (PPPs) by arguing that private providers have stronger incentives to deliver quality, especially for roads, when the number of riders depends on the maintenance of the road. Singh (2018) shows that private road providers in India deliver smoother roads. The primary difference between public and private road providers appears to be that private ones share responsibility both for initial construction and later maintenance. Because private providers do not cut corners at the initial construction phase, they provide better road services later on.

For many PPPs, the problem is not cutting quality but subverting the government. Glaeser (2004) presents a model in which private companies that supply public services bribe the government to overpay the companies for their effort. In weak institutional environments, the combination of highly incentivized private companies and public officials facing weak oversight can lead to a drain on public funds. Engel, Fischer, and Galetovic (2014) discuss the many problems of this nature created by PPPs in the developing world. While explicit bribery is less common in the US than in emerging markets, private companies still have the capacity to influence the politicians and bureaucrats who determine contract terms.

Several factors bear on whether private or public provision is optimal. If the service is to be funded by user fees and quality is observable to users, then private ownership creates incentives for maintenance. If quality is unobservable, or if there is no link between the number of users of the facility and the private owner's financial return, this effect is not operative. In such cases, private management can lead to lower quality. Roads may be more natural candidates for privatization than prisons, because their output is more observable and the advantage of private rather than public management may therefore be greater. If the procurement process is well designed and relatively immune to subversion or collusion, then private ownership should reduce financial costs. If the number of bidders is small or the institutional environment is weak, then public ownership may be a more attractive option. If public management must be combined with private construction, then private ownership may be a better option since it may be difficult to monitor the quality of initial construction.

Another consideration is the relative quality of lawyers and engineers in the public sector. Public management is engineering intensive. Private management is contract intensive, at least for the public sector. If the legal capacity of government is strong, then contracting with a private provider is relatively more attractive than otherwise. If the engineering capacity of the government is strong, then public management may be relatively more appealing.

A final consideration in the choice between public and private provision is resilience to economic downturns and other adverse demand shocks. In some settings, such as railroads in the US in the 1950s and 1960s and urban bus service providers in earlier decades, private infrastructure providers were unable to weather periods of adversity and the public sector stepped in to ensure continuing service. Enhancing the resilience of private providers, perhaps with new insurance schemes that involve government support but not takeover during periods of adversity, could improve the long-run viability of the private sector in the infrastructure sphere.

This discussion has focused on public versus private provision, but two other distinctions are worth making. First, private provision can be done by nonprofit firms or for-profit entities. The former have weaker incentives to make quality reductions that reduce costs and weaker incentives to subvert the government. Turnpike trusts were essentially local nonprofits that managed roads in eighteenth-century England. Unfortunately, many infrastructure projects today require outlays that are too large for most nonprofits to handle.

Second, there is a question about the choice of public management. When is it optimal for public control of infrastructure to be embedded in the executive branch of government rather than and when is it optimal for that control to be in the hands of a public authority? In the nineteenth-century US, independent authorities were thought to provide freedom from widespread corruption. Yet in many developing countries today, independent authorities or parastatal enterprises are seen as being even more corrupt and unaccountable than the elected executive branch of government. A key question is whether the independent authority will be led by someone whose future depends more on support by local politicians or on the individual's reputation for excellence. If the leader of the authority is beholden to local politicians, then independent authorities only provide an excuse for poor quality. If the leader cares about his or her reputation, then the authority is more likely to deliver quality and cost improvements.

### Infrastructure in a Federal System

In the US, infrastructure is provided by national, state, and local governments. Water and sewer infrastructure have primarily been handled at the local level. In some cases, the city government directly owns the waterworks. Local roads similarly are handled by towns and municipalities. Major roads and large public transit systems are overseen by state governments, even when the funding is provided by the federal government. The federal government is extensively involved in most forms of transportation, especially air. Most of these divisions are natural outcomes of network size. Air travel often crosses state boundaries, and so national management is appropriate.

Local streets have fewer externalities across place boundaries. The most basic model of local public finance would allocate control of infrastructure to the lowest level of government that includes all or most of the network. The benefit of local control would come, as Tiebout (1956) suggested, from better local information and stronger incentives to cater to local voters.

The US also presents some interesting hybrid cases. Highways are an example. The federally funded Highway Trust Fund provides resources, but the resources are directed at the state level. The national government has some ability to place requirements on state governments, such as tying funding to raising the drinking age or lowering speed limits. Typically, though, federal funding does not come with any attempt to manage the highway network.

The federal role in highway spending reflects both historical precedent and federal willingness to borrow, especially during a recession. Indeed, if infrastructure spending plays a countercyclical role that spills over state boundaries, then federal funding may be appropriate. States and localities will not fully internalize the impact that their spending has on national aggregate demand and unemployment during a recession and so will underinvest in infrastructure during a downturn. The case for federal funding is weaker if the macroeconomic stimulus associated with infrastructure spending is limited. Whether the current federal funding of highways is optimal, or whether more state and local financial responsibility would lead to more efficient outcomes, is an open question. The redistribution of highway funds to low-density states is done with little cost-benefit analysis. The reliance on general federal tax revenues rather than local taxes and user fees is an interesting topic for future research.

There are also important questions about the division of control between states and localities. In most cases, localities have better incentives than a state regulator does to monitor and maintain local infrastructure, but localities may also be more subject to capture by connected contractors than the state government. The optimal level of local control must weigh the state's superiority at contracting with the local edge in directing that contracting efficiently.

### Efficient Maintenance Policy

Economic analysis and data on the condition of infrastructure assets can help to guide investments in maintenance. For example, the international roughness index (IRI) provided by the Department of Transportation is created by measuring the vertical acceleration of official road surveyors who drive at a fixed speed. Big data provided by private companies can supplement this data by providing more up-to-date information on road quality and by estimating the links between road quality and road speeds and accidents. Both Uber and Lyft have real-time data on the vertical acceleration of their drivers during every trip. Data from these sources mimic the IRI data and are available more frequently and more widely. These data sources can be combined with Google Maps data on road speeds to estimate the time losses due to undermaintained roads, and with data from the American Automobile Association (AAA) to link road roughness to breakdowns and flat tires. If merged with police information, these data could be used to test whether road roughness leads to accidents. Such estimates could be improved by using natural experiments—for example, by looking at the temporal discontinuity in road quality before and after road repaving.

Armed with estimates of the costs of poor road quality, researchers could estimate the optimal time, or road quality level, for repaving. This is a standard optimal control exercise, and it has been solved with a variety of different assumptions about the nature of road depreciation and repair costs, as in studies by Worm and Van Harten (1996) and Gao and Zhang (2013). New estimates using big data like cell phone geolocation information can also contribute to our knowledge of the causes and speed of road deterioration. Other maintenance decisions are less amenable to analysis, especially when maintenance is needed to avoid catastrophic risk. At this point, engineering estimates of the risk of bridge collapse seem far more reliable than anything that can be gleaned from cars driving on the bridge. Similarly, the risks of rail disaster are much harder to meaningfully estimate.

### Maintenance, New Construction, and Infrastructure Operation

The foregoing discussion of the appropriate ownership of infrastructure did not differentiate between initial construction and maintenance. In many cases, however, the problems are quite different, and it may well be optimal to split these roles between federal and local government or between public and private entities. Splitting the tasks is easier when monitoring initial construction quality is easier, because otherwise the initial builder may cut quality to save costs, thereby placing greater burdens on the actors responsible for maintenance.

Planning the construction of interstate systems, such as highways and air traffic systems, seems to merit significant federal engagement. The choice of where to put the roads involves the greatest amount of interjurisdictional spillovers. By contrast, the maintenance problem may be more likely to benefit from local attention. Local maintenance is more problematic when the costs of poor maintenance are borne mainly by drivers outside of the community. Indeed, a locality may even have incentives to let roads remain rough in some cases to deter crosstown traffic. In the case of rail, ownership of the rails themselves may generate a local monopoly. In that case, the appropriate model may be public ownership of the rail lines along with competitive private access. That model is followed with private roads, which effectively rent out access to their blacktop to private drivers and truckers. Typically, the monopoly problem in that case is moderated by rules that limit the size of tolls. This same model is typically followed by US airports. They are usually publicly owned entities that contract with private airline companies, which then negotiate rights over gates while the public entity manages the common space. Outside the US, private airport ownership is more common and is often combined with some regulation to reduce monopoly rent extraction. This model is worthy of more study.

In many infrastructure projects, distinctions between new construction (capital costs) and ongoing operations (variable costs) are somewhat artificial. Department of Transportation grants often privilege new purchases, when leasing might be more appropriate. There is no obvious reason why public transit authorities should be expected to cover their variable costs but not their capital costs, but that expectation is quite common. If these entities are pricing at marginal cost, then operating deficits may be entirely appropriate. If fiscal discipline is a primary concern, presumably this discipline should focus on overall deficits, not merely operating deficits.

## Can US Infrastructure Spending Become More Efficient?

There are three potential areas for improving the efficiency of infrastructure construction and use: procurement, project management, and cost-benefit analysis of expenditures on mitigation of potentially adverse project externalities. A concern that motivates the efficiency discussion is that US infrastructure costs on a per-unit basis are high from an international perspective. Some policies—such as the Davis-Bacon Act, which requires contractors to pay prevailing wages, and Buy American Act contract provisions—are likely to raise input costs, but their net impact is not clear. While existing research does not provide a to-do list for making US infrastructure spending more cost-effective, additional study of the cost of building and maintaining infrastructure may yield conclusions relevant to policy.

### Procurement

In the US, procurement rules were established in the shadow of corruption. Nineteenth-century procurement often involved high costs that were compensated by kickbacks to politicians. A strict set of rules about procurement evolved to limit corrupt practices, but in many cases those rules do not seem to deliver low costs. The rules typically require open bidding on projects and provide frameworks for vendor choice that lead to the selection of the low-cost bidder or the choice of higher-cost bidders only with some justification.

Researchers have identified several ways in which existing first-price auctions can fail to deliver low costs. Most obviously, bidders can collude and agree to bid only high prices or agree that some contractors will sit out the auction. When bids involve specifying a cost for each service and a projected number of services, Bolotnyy and Vasserman (2019) show that savvy contractors can deliver low bids on services where predicted use is too high and high bids on services where predicted use is too low. Finally, highly regulated auctions do not perform well when only one bidder shows up.

The first major procurement choice involves the decision between the use of auctions or negotiation. Bulow and Klemperer (1996) argue that any advantages provided by negotiation are small relative to the benefits that come from adding more bidders to an auction. While correct, this argument ignores the fact that a highly regulated auction may end up with only one bidder. A smart negotiator can keep on calling until he or she gets a reasonable bid.

The downside of flexible negotiation is that it is more prone to corruption than an arms'-length sealed-bid auction. While some countries, such as Singapore and Denmark, appear to give their procuring entities substantial independence, it is unclear whether that approach would produce efficiency or corruption in the US setting. Flexible procurement will work only if procuring entities have strong incentives to keep costs down; US bureaucracy is not known for strong incentives.

The contribution to this volume by Dejan Makovšek and Adrian Bridge considers the choice between strong incentive systems, such as fixed-price contracts, and weak incentive systems. The authors point out that strong incentive systems generally come at a higher cost, which can be explained if contractors are risk averse. In many cases, Byzantine regulations serve to restrict entry into an auction rather than to promote competition. These restrictions may ensure high quality levels but warrant further analysis. One reliable message of both theory and empirical work on procurement auctions is that attracting more bidders is important for keeping costs low.

### Project Management

The initial bidding phase of procurement typically features competition among contractors, but inevitably, once work has begun, renegotiation becomes bilateral. Consequently, midstream renegotiation during the course of a contract is a chance for costs to rise enormously. The perils of renegotiation provide one reason so many megaprojects end up costing far more than initially planned or bid. For smaller well-defined projects, the renegotiation process can be regulated ex ante. For example, the auction process described by Bolotnyy and Vasserman (2019), in which bidders specify costs for specific services, is meant to accommodate changes in services over time. The procurer has the right to change the services needed as the work develops, and the contractor must provide those services at the auction-specified price. If the contractor has some predictive power beyond the estimates provided by the procurer, then the system can be gamed, but at least it is less subject to wholesale abuse ex post. In a large megaproject, this renegotiation process is far more complex. When tunneling hits an unexpected barrier, resolving the problem is not simply a matter of adding an extra ton of concrete. The costs must be renegotiated, and there is no competition to keep costs down.

There is a robust literature, illustrated by Hart and Moore (1988), on contracts and renegotiation. The models, typically formulated with private sector settings in mind, can be used to analyze the renegotiation of infrastructure projects. The complexity of these projects nevertheless limits the application of any simple model. Unless the work can be partitioned so that any new requirement for renegotiation can be handled competitively, the difficulties of bilateral bargaining reappear. Renegotiation appears to be a much greater generator of cost overruns for infrastructure in the US than elsewhere. Further research on this issue is needed. It could take the form of more qualitative comparisons of the US with other countries in which renegotiation is less difficult, or of a detailed study of renegotiation across many US contracts. While painstaking, such work seems necessary if we are to make any progress on understanding how to limit the extra costs that are added to projects after they are awarded.

### Externality Mitigation and Infrastructure Costs

In the 1950s, Altshuler and Luberoff (2003) explain, infrastructure projects often ignored the concerns of local residents. The projects were cheaper, but many of those who were harmed went largely uncompensated. After the neighborhood organization and freeway revolts of the 1960s, projects were far more carefully selected and planned. They were also far more expensive, as Brooks and Liscow (2019) document. Glaeser and Ponzetto (2018) present a simple model in which rising education levels lead to more mitigation expenditures, especially if the federal government is paying for much of the cost.

This combination of well-organized community residents and federal funding lies behind the planning and expense of Boston's Central Artery/Tunnel Project, the Big Dig. Although the enormous cost of the project was largely paid for ex post by Massachusetts, ex ante voters were told that the costs would be covered by federal funding. The project was planned so that not a single house would have to be moved. A key question is how much could have been saved if a somewhat less sensitive planning procedure had been followed.

Other countries that pay less attention to community concerns have much lower infrastructure costs. China is an extreme example; infrastructure is built with a focus on low cost and speed, not compliance with local desires. It would be helpful to better understand the sources of cost differences between China and the US. France, Japan, and Spain might provide more natural comparisons. Gordon and Schleicher (2015) report that the per-mile cost of building the Second Avenue Subway line in New York City was eight times higher than a recent subway project in Japan and 36 times more expensive than one in Madrid. Even Paris's Metro Line 7, a particularly tricky building project, was much less costly than recent US projects.

Gordon and Schleicher suggest that potential litigation, standard in common-law countries, may explain some of the difference. The threat of litigation is one reason US infrastructure builders spend so much on mitigation. The Big Dig, for example, made numerous concessions because of environmental lawsuits. Concern for local harm is appropriate, and mitigation expenses can be well justified. Yet if mitigation explains a sizable fraction of the relatively high infrastructure construction costs in the US, some assessment of the efficiency of mitigation spending may be warranted.

Two types of research seem necessary. First, there must be more testing of whether mitigation expenses are responsible for high costs. This research could compare environments in which mitigation is more or less necessary. Alternatively, mitigation effects can be directly estimated for particularly projects, with engineering cost estimates used to determine the impact. Second, there is a need for better cost-benefit tools for examining mitigation actions. How should we value the losses to neighbors who are harmed by an infrastructure project? Do those neighbors value the expensive forms of mitigation that now exist? Are there less costly tools for compensating those neighbors? The call to improve US infrastructure currently collides with the very high cost of building that infrastructure. Strategies for reducing costs while still sheltering impacted communities could lead to welfare improvements for all.

### A Road Map of This Book

The essays in this volume collectively survey much of the economic research on infrastructure. While this volume is not comprehensive—some important issues that have been actively studied have been omitted, and a number of key issues warrant future research—the book nevertheless introduces several core streams of investigation.

The volume begins with a chapter by Jennifer Bennett, Robert Kornfeld, Daniel Sichel, and David Wasshausen that describes the measurement of infrastructure in the Bureau of Economic Analysis's National Income and Product Accounts. Two difficult issues are determining the rate of depreciation for infrastructure and computing a price index for new infrastructure projects. The empirical work used to establish infrastructure depreciation rates is dated and might benefit from updating. The chapter provides basic facts about the stocks of infrastructure and the flow of infrastructure spending over time, including an experimental new data series on highway investment at the state level. One finding is that real net infrastructure investment per capita has fallen since the Great Recession (2007–2009) and that it is currently at its lowest level since 1983. The only significant infrastructure growth since the 1990s has been in digital infrastructure. The stock of basic infrastructure has grown by only 0.6 percent per year over the past 20 years. State-level variation in highway infrastructure investment per capita is particularly illuminating. Throughout the period from 1992 to 2017, states such as the Dakotas and Wyoming have led the nation in per capita highway investment. Between 1992 and 2017, spending on infrastructure investment in northeastern states, such as Pennsylvania and New York, rose dramatically relative to other states, which may reflect the extremely high cost of building in those areas. Southern states have seen their highway investment decline relative to northern states.

The second chapter, by Brooks and Liscow, focuses on the cost of building highways in the US. This paper and their related work (Brooks and Liscow 2019) suggest that the per-mile cost of building highways rose dramatically between the 1950s and the 1980s. This fact does not appear to reflect changing highway locations, such as a switch to more urban environments, or rising input costs. Rather, the cost of mitigating environmental or other local externalities appears to be an important factor. The rise in highway costs occurred largely after environmental concerns associated with highways began appearing in the media in the late 1960s. The rise is associated with increasingly wiggly roads, which may arise from attempts to avoid disturbing existing residents.

The chapter also documents large differences across states in construction costs. Connecticut and New Jersey spend much more per mile than the national average, even controlling for geography, while Wyoming and the Dakotas spend much less. Once the researchers control for geography, Delaware and Rhode Island appear to be areas with particularly low construction costs. Differences in construction costs after 1970 appear to be correlated with other measures of local spending. For example, while highway costs are correlated with average construction costs, there is also a strong correlation between highway costs and both Medicare spending per enrollee and per capita local government spending. These correlations suggest that some states may exercise less restraint than others with their budgets. The correlation with construction costs may mean that states that regulate housing supply more, and therefore drive up building costs, also impose more mitigation requirements on highway construction.

The third chapter, by Duranton, Nagpal, and Turner, presents evidence on the output of the infrastructure capital stock, rather than the flow of new investment. The chapter shows that according to Department of Transportation IRI measures, US roads are in much better shape today than in the past. This fact challenges the prevailing view of national infrastructure decline, primarily by dispelling the view that in some distant past the nation had pristine roads. Bridge quality also shows no clear downward trend. The US subway fleet did get older between the 1980s and the early 2000s, but average subway car age has remained constant since that point.

Duranton, Nagpal, and Turner, like Brooks and Liscow, find rising highway construction costs. One consequence of rising costs is a lower optimal level of highway capital and construction. Chapter 3 does not dispute the decline of investment levels, but rather suggests that this decline represents diminishing returns to expanding traditional transportation infrastructure. These facts suggest the value of grounding infrastructure investment decisions in data on performance and quantified risks rather than opaque letter grades.

The chapter also includes an interesting theoretical contribution on how to assess the optimal level of infrastructure investment across different modes. The logic of the model is that the incremental cost, including public and private spending, of providing a given level of mobility—think "move a person a mile"—should be equalized across modes. Duranton, Nagpal, and Turner apply this framework to highways, buses, and subways and find that current spending patterns generate less transportation services per dollar from spending on subways and buses than from spending on highways.

The fourth chapter, Ramey's analysis of the macroeconomic effects of infrastructure spending, begins with a standard neoclassical macroeconomic model that generates multipliers from government investment and consumption. The multiplier for government investment is typically higher than the multiplier from consumption. While Ramey's baseline model generates a multiplier between 2.2 and 4.4, she also presents results from a number of more complicated models that generate lower multipliers, some even below 1. This chapter summarizes the large empirical literature on infrastructure multipliers and presents estimates of the impact of American Recovery and Reinvestment Act (ARRA) spending. ARRA seems to have generated a modest increase in highway spending but little rise in long-term highway-related employment. The findings of Garin (2019), and Ramey's summary of related empirical work, suggest relatively low multipliers from ARRA-related spending, casting doubt on the use of infrastructure spending as a countercyclical policy tool.

The next chapter, by Makovšek and Bridge, addresses infrastructure procurement. The chapter adopts a global perspective and describes differences in the structure of procurement contracts that are used in different nations. Some contracts bundle the design and build phases together, while others proceed linearly, going from design to bid to build. Contracts also differ in whether they have high-powered incentives, such as a fixed price, or more flexible cost-plus structures. Prior research is not clear about whether bundling designing and building together is optimal, but chapter 5 suggests that fixed-price contracts generally lead to higher costs, perhaps because risk-averse builders require high payments to bear the risk of unknown cost shocks. The chapter presents a typology of procurement contracts, which is interpreted through the theoretical lens developed by Laffont and Tirole (1993) and others. The essay ends with a summary of the empirical work on the efficiency of different procurement contracts and a case study that illustrates many of the points about procurement that are developed in the chapter.

Chapter 6, an assessment of public-private partnerships (PPPs) by Engel,

Fischer, and Galetovic, builds on the authors' previous criticism of many standard arguments for PPPs. The public case for PPPs often claims that private provision reduces the need for public outlays. The authors note that this argument often is only a reflection of artificial accounting practices. If the project will cost more than it earns, in net present value terms, then the government will need to pay for that difference, whether the provision is private or public. The PPP may enable the government to pay the costs in the future, but the same benefit could be achieved by borrowing.

Instead, these authors argue, the potential gains from PPPs must arise from better incentives in some part of the infrastructure procurement or management process. For example, while public managers may not be interested in revenues from tolls, for a PPP those tolls determine profits and losses. Tolls give the PPP strong incentives to maintain roads or other infrastructure and to generate future revenues. The PPP may also have stronger incentives to cut construction costs.

The downside of PPPs is that they must be monitored by the government. Failures to monitor may mean that the PPP delivers lower-quality infrastructure or extracts too much in payments from the public, either through excessive prices or excessive contributions from the public sector. The downsides can be particularly large when the public sector can be easily corrupted.

The next chapter, by Lucas and Montesinos, addresses the role of risk in assessing the fair value of infrastructure investments. This is often a particularly important consideration in valuing PPPs. The authors question the claim that the benefits of public projects should be discounted at the risk-free rate because project risks are largely idiosyncratic, suggesting instead that both public and private investments should be evaluated using a market rate that will differ from the risk-free rate based on the covariance between the project's future benefits and aggregate consumption, which is its "beta." A high-beta public project should be discounted just as much as a high-beta private project. Using the risk-free rate or the rate on government bonds to discount the benefits of infrastructure will generally lead to inefficient overinvestment.

A novel aspect of this study is its proposed approach to analyzing minimum revenue guarantees that are often promised by the public sector to PPPs. These guarantees are options that are transferred to the PPP; their cost to the government can be evaluated using a variant of the Black-Scholes options pricing formula. The authors point out that when options change the incentives of the PPP—for example, when guarantees reduce the incentive to maintain infrastructure—these options may have other costs that also need to be considered.

The volume concludes with Shane Greenstein's analysis of digital infrastructure, which is the category of infrastructure investment that has grown most significantly over the last 25 years. The discussion in this chapter is divided into three parts. The first addresses the expansion of digital access for both consumers and businesses. The adoption of broadband followed an S-shaped curve: richer consumers adopted first. Later in the adoption cycle, it was not lower prices but rising broadband speeds and the proliferation of broadband-intensive content that attracted initially reluctant adopters. This part of the chapter reviews measures of the productivity gains that broadband produced for businesses.

The second part focuses on the growth of network-related services that did not exist in the 1990s. For example, content delivery networks (CDNs) that deliver video and gaming experiences online have proliferated since 2000. The rise of data centers in the "cloud" is another example of new businesses that are made possible because of improved digital infrastructure. In a sense, this process is repeating the business transformations that followed the earlier transportation revolutions around sea shipping, railroads, and highways. The mass production of cotton in the nineteenth century, for example, was far more attractive because recent advances in transportation made it possible to ship cotton worldwide at relatively low cost.

The third section focuses on governance of the digital world. Protocols that shape the efficiency of digital connections were largely developed by public and nonprofit entities. This part of the chapter raises questions about whether current institutions are designed to maximize the efficiency of future protocol innovation and about the appropriate governance institutions for software, mapping, and entities such as Wikipedia.

## COVID-19 and the Economic Analysis of Infrastructure

Four months after the symposium at which the research papers in this volume were presented, the US was struck by the COVID-19 pandemic. The pandemic has affected virtually every aspect of the economy, and it is likely to have long-term effects as well as short-term consequences. Many of the most notable short-run effects, such as the collapse of public transit use in large metropolitan areas and the drop in air travel, are related to infrastructure. This section offers a postscript to the chapters in this volume by describing some of the ways the pandemic has affected the demand for some types of infrastructure. This section also identifies key questions about the future role of infrastructure that have been raised by the pandemic.

Mobility declined radically over the course of a single week in March 2020. As the pandemic raged, international air travel was often impossible. Roads that had been clogged were empty. Many saw public transportation as a source of potential contagion, and millions avoided subway cars and buses. By May 2020, 49 million Americans were telecommuting, placing extraordinary demands on the country's digital infrastructure. How the demand for public transportation infrastructure will evolve after a vaccine or other public health measures make it possible to return to most prepandemic activities is an important but open question, and it is too soon to offer long-run predictions.

Nonetheless, it seems sure that existing public transit systems will face enduring challenges and that the impact of future pandemic risk will need to be considered as future investments in public transit are made. Public transit is particularly vulnerable to the effects of contagion, both because travel in this mode entails human proximity and because the costs of public transit scale down less readily when use declines. Drivers do not pay for gas when they do not drive, but public transit systems continued to run throughout 2020 with only a small fraction of their pre-COVID ridership. These systems are incurring large operating costs even with very low levels of use.

Reduced ridership levels seem likely to persist until there is widespread access to a COVID-19 vaccine and even perhaps beyond that time. All mobility declined substantially because of COVID-19, but transit particularly suffered because of fear that shared travel can lead to infection. In one May 2020 poll, 57 percent of all Massachusetts residents said that they would avoid taking public transit even if COVID-19 could be effectively treated. Rules about wearing masks have proved difficult to enforce on buses, and this difficulty may further reduce public confidence in shared vehicular transit.

Reduction in ridership leaves a fiscal hole in the system that will persist for many years without a state or federal bailout. If systems are left to cover their COVID-related fiscal shortfalls, then they will reduce their service further even after the disease has disappeared. The fiscal problems will create pressure to increase fares, which will reduce ridership further.

The extreme vulnerability of public transit to pandemics has rarely been incorporated into past cost-benefit analyses of system extensions, yet the COVID-19 pandemic is a reminder that public health shocks are a nontrivial risk. Similar disease outbreaks could have potentially occurred with SARS, MERS, and H1N1 during just the past two decades. Going forward, there is value in research that examines how to make systems more resilient during disease outbreaks and how to incorporate the risks of future pandemics in transit planning.

The US Bureau of Labor Statistics (2020) reports that nearly 50 million US workers stopped commuting and switched to working from home in spring 2020. If this massive shift from physical transportation to digital mobility persists, it would require an associated shift of investment in digital infrastructure. The rise of videoconferencing has led many to suspect that decades-old predictions that a vast fraction of the American economy would no longer meet face-to-face might come to pass, creating a massive decrease in demand for cities and urban space. Bartik et al. (2020) find that more than 40 percent of small businesses predict that more than one-third of their workers who switched to remote work during the pandemic will remain at home after the pandemic. That prognosis does not mean that office towers will be vacant in the future; rents may decline. Some commercial space may convert into residential usage. Still, if predictions for increased telecommuting prove accurate, the demand for urban real estate will decline along with demand for access to the highways that facilitate commuting.

The long-run postpandemic changes in economic activity are difficult to predict. Surges in entertainment-related mobility that followed the end of lockdowns in the Sunbelt in June and July 2020 are reminders that the demand for face-to-face contact is likely to be robust, especially for younger consumers. Younger workers and consumers seem likely to still pursue the pleasures of proximity. A switch from older urbanites to younger urbanites, and from established urban businesses to new firms, would have important implications for transportation infrastructure. Some suburban office parks may actually see an increase in demand, especially if firms attempt to provide their workers with more square footage to reduce the risk of disease spread. Some telecommuting professionals may relocate to high-amenity, medium-density locales such as Vail or Boulder. These areas have experienced rapid growth in recent decades and seem likely to continue to present robust demand for future infrastructure investments.

The pandemic should stimulate new research not just on public transit and air travel, but also on digital infrastructure. The switch to remote work occurred disproportionately among better-educated and better-paid workers, who had presumably acquired access to digital connections long ago. The switch to remote schooling, however, was universal and the lack of access to digital infrastructure imposed particular costs on poorer children. While the effects of the switch to digital learning is sure to be extensively studied, one important realization is that if online classes are going to feature more prominently in the education sector going forward, digital infrastructure requires heightened attention. Children without reliable Wi-Fi access will lose out in any such transition, even if they are motivated learners.

The pandemic has renewed calls for the use of infrastructure spending as a tool of macroeconomic stabilization, while also highlighting some of the limitations of such policy levers. The Ramey chapter in this volume discusses the evidence on the capacity of infrastructure spending to improve macroeconomic outcomes. One of the traditional arguments for funding infrastructure investment during a downturn is that there are jobless workers available. Employment in the construction industries dropped substantially during 2020, but it has already begun to rebound, without an infrastructure spending plan, in part because of the robust demand for housing. The brunt of the labor market decline during the pandemic was felt by workers in urban services industries, like leisure and hospitality. It is not clear that expanding spending on infrastructure projects would support a stronger labor market for these workers, particularly if public health concerns still discourage visits to restaurants, bars, and sporting events.

## Conclusion

Taken together, the essays in this volume highlight many important economic insights about infrastructure and also show that much is still to be learned. We need to know more about improving procurement, and to better understand why US infrastructure costs are so high. We hope that future research will address these topics and that the economic analysis of infrastructure will receive the attention that its enormous importance merits.

## References

Allen, Treb, and Costas Arkolakis. 2019. "The Welfare Effects of Transportation Infrastructure Improvements." NBER Working Paper 25487. Cambridge, MA: National Bureau of Economic Research.

Alsan, Marcella, and Claudia Goldin. 2019. "Watersheds in Child Mortality: The Role of Effective Water and Sewerage Infrastructure, 1880–1920." *Journal of Political Economy* 127 (2): 586–638.

Altshuler, Alan, and David Luberoff. 2003. *Mega-Projects*. Washington: Brookings Institution.

American Society of Civil Engineers. 2017. *2017 Infrastructure Report Card*. Reston, VA: ASCE. https://www.infrastructurereportcard.org/.

Andonov, Aleksandar, Roman Kräussl, and Joshua Rauh. 2018. "The Subsidy to Infrastructure as an Asset Class." NBER Working Paper 25045. Cambridge, MA: National Bureau of Economic Research.

Arrow, Kenneth J., and R. C. Lind. 1970. "Uncertainty and the Evaluation Decisions of Public Investment." *American Economic Review* 60 (3): 364–78.

Aschauer, David. 1989a. "Is Public Expenditure Productive?" *Journal of Monetary Economics* 23 (2): 177–200.

———. 1989b. "Public Investment and Productivity Growth in the Group of Seven." *Federal Reserve Bank of Chicago Economic Perspectives* 13 (5): 17–25.

———. 1990. "Is Government Spending Stimulative?" *Contemporary Policy Issues* 8 (4): 30–46.

Ashraf, Nava, Edward Glaeser, Abraham Holland, and Bryce Millett Steinberg. 2017. "Water, Health and Wealth." NBER Working Paper 23807. Cambridge, MA: National Bureau of Economic Research.

Bajari, Patrick, S. Houghton, and S. Tadelis. 2014. "Bidding for Incomplete Contracts: An Empirical Analysis." *American Economic Review* 104 (April): 1288–319.

Bartik, Alexander W., Zoe B. Cullen, Edward L. Glaeser, Michael Uca, and Christopher Stanton. 2020. "What Jobs Are Being Done at Home during the COVID-19 Crisis? Evidence from Firm-Level Surveys." NBER Working Paper 27422. Cambridge, MA: National Bureau of Economic Research.

Baum-Snow, Nathaniel, and Matthew E. Kahn. 2000. "The Effects of New Public Projects to Expand Urban Rail Transit." *Journal of Public Economics* 77 (2): 241–63.

Bolotnyy, Valentin, and Shoshana Vasserman. 2019. "Scaling Auctions as Insurance: A Case Study in Infrastructure Procurement." Working paper, Harvard Economics Department.

Brooks, Leah, and Zachary Liscow. 2019. "Infrastructure Costs." Working paper, Yale Law School.

Bulow, Jeremy, and Paul Klemperer. 1996. "Auctions versus Negotiations." *American Economic Review* 86: 180–94.

Cutler, David, and Grant Miller. 2005. "The Role of Public Health Improvements in Health Advances: The Twentieth-Century United States." *Demography* 42 (1): 1–22.

Donaldson, Dave, and Richard Hornbeck. 2016. "Railroads and American Economic Growth: A 'Market Access' Approach." *Quarterly Journal of Economics* 131 (2): 799–858.

Downs, Anthony. 1962. "The Law of Peak-Hour Expressway Congestion." *Traffic Quarterly* 16 (3): 393–409.

Duranton, Gilles, and Matthew A. Turner. 2011. "The Fundamental Law of Road Congestion: Evidence from US Cities." *American Economic Review* 101 (6): 2616–52.

Engel, Eduardo, Ronald Fischer, and Alexander Galetovic. 2014. *The Economics of Public-Private Partnerships: A Basic Guide.* Cambridge: Cambridge University Press.

Fogel, Robert. 1962. "A Quantitative Approach to the Study of Railroads in American Economic Growth: A Report of Some Preliminary Findings." *Journal of Economic History* 22 (2): 163–97.

Furman, Jason, and Lawrence H. Summers. 2019. "Who's Afraid of Budget Deficits?" *Foreign Affairs.* March/April.

Gao, Hui, and Xueqing Zhang. 2013. "A Markov-Based Road Maintenance Optimization Model Considering User Costs." *Computer-Aided Civil and Infrastructure Engineering* 28 (6): 451–64.

Garin, Andrew. 2019. "Putting America to Work, Where? Evidence on the Effectiveness of Infrastructure Construction as a Locally Targeted Employment Policy." *Journal of Urban Economics* 111: 108–31.

Glaeser, Edward. 2004. "Public Ownership in the American City." In *Urban Issues and Public Finance: Essays in Honor of Dick Netzer*, edited by A. E. Schwartz. Northampton, MA: Edward Elgar.

Glaeser, Edward, and Giacomo Ponzetto. 2018. "The Political Economy of Transportation Investment." *Economics of Transportation* 13: 4–26.

Glaeser, Edward, and Andrei Shleifer. 2003. "The Rise of the Regulatory State." *Journal of Economic Literature* 41 (2): 401–25.

Gordon, Tracy, and David Schleicher. 2015. "High Costs May Explain Crumbling Support for U.S. Infrastructure." *Real Clear Policy*. https://www.realclearpolicy.com/blog/2015/03/31/high_costs_may_explain_crumbling_support_for_us_infrastructure_1249.html.

Gramlich, Edward. 1994. "Infrastructure Investment: A Review Essay." *Journal of Economic Literature* XXXII (September): 1176–96.

Gupta, Arpit, Stijn Van Nieuwerburgh, and Constantine Kontokosta. 2020. "Take the Q Train: Value Capture of Public Infrastructure Projects." NBER Working Paper 26789. Cambridge, MA: National Bureau of Economic Research.

Hart, Oliver, and John Moore. 1988. "Incomplete Contracts and Renegotiation." *Econometrica* 56 (4): 755–85.

Hart, Oliver, Andrei Shleifer, and Robert W. Vishny. 1997. "The Proper Scope of Government: Theory and an Application to Prisons." *Quarterly Journal of Economics* 112 (4): 1127–61.

Hornbeck, Richard, and Martin Rotemberg. 2019. "Railroads, Reallocation, and the Rise of American Manufacturing." NBER Working Paper 26594. Cambridge, MA: National Bureau of Economic Research.

Jaworski, Taylor, and Carl T. Kitchens. 2019. "National Policy for Regional Development: Historical Evidence from Appalachian Highways." *Review of Economics and Statistics* 101 (5): 777–90.

Kain, John. 1990. "Deception in Dallas: Strategic Misrepresentation in Rail Transit Promotion and Evaluation." *Journal of the American Planning Association* 56 (2): 184–96.

Keynes, John Maynard. 1936. *The General Theory of Employment, Interest, and Money*. New York: Harcourt Brace.

Kline, Patrick, and Enrico Moretti. 2014. "Local Economic Development, Agglomeration Economies, and the Big Push: 100 Years of Evidence from the Tennessee Valley Authority." *Quarterly Journal of Economics* 129 (1): 275–331.

Laffont, Jean-Jacques, and Jean Tirole. 1993. *A Theory of Incentives in Procurement and Regulation*. Cambridge, MA: MIT Press.

Meyer, John, John Kain, and Martin Wohl. 1965. *The Urban Transportation Problem*. Cambridge, MA: Harvard University Press.

Pigou, Arthur C. 1920. *The Economics of Welfare*. London: Macmillan.

Singh, Ram. 2018. "Does Choice of Procurement Contract Matter for Cost and Quality of Infrastructure?" International Growth Center Working Paper S-89209-INC2.

Small, Kenneth A., Clifford Winston, and Carol A. Evans. 1991. *Road Work: A New Highway Pricing and Investment Policy.* Washington, DC: Brookings Institution.

Smith, Adam. 1776. *The Wealth of Nations.* https://www.adamsmithworks.org/documents/chapter-i-of-the-expences-of-the-sovereign-or-commonwealth.

Tiebout, Charles M. 1956. "A Pure Theory of Local Expenditures." *Journal of Political Economy* 64 (5): 416–24.

Troesken, Walter. 2004. *Water, Race, and Disease.* Cambridge, MA: MIT Press.

US Bureau of Labor Statistics. 2020. *Labor Force Statistics from the Current Population Survey: Supplemental Data Measuring the Effects of the Coronavirus (COVID-19) Pandemic on the Labor Market.* Accessed November 26, 2020. https://www.bls.gov/cps/effects-of-the-coronavirus-covid-19-pandemic.htm#data.

US Congressional Budget Office (CBO). 2018. *Public Spending on Transportation and Water Infrastructure, 1956 to 2017*. Washington, DC: CBO. https://www.cbo.gov/system/files/2018-10/54539-Infrastructure.pdf.

Vickrey, William. 1952. *The Revision of the Rapid Transit Fare Structure of the City of New York.* Technical Monograph 3, Finance Project, New York City Mayor's Committee for Management Survey.

Winston, Clifford. 2010. *Last Exit: Privatization and Deregulation of the US Transportation System.* Washington, DC: Brookings Institution.

———. 2013. "On the Performance of the U.S. Transportation System: Caution Ahead." *Journal of Economic Literature* 51 (3): 773–824.

———. 2020. *Autonomous Vehicles: The Road to Economic Growth?* Washington, DC: Brookings Institution.

World Economic Forum. 2019. *The Global Competitiveness Report.* Geneva: World Economic Forum.

Worm, J. M., and A. Van Harten. 1996. "Model Based Decision Support for Planning of Road Maintenance." *Reliability Engineering & System Safety* 51 (3): 305–16.

1

# Measuring Infrastructure in BEA's National Economic Accounts

Jennifer Bennett, Robert Kornfeld, Daniel Sichel, and David Wasshausen

## 1.1 Introduction

Infrastructure provides critical support to the economy and contributes in an important way to living standards; assessing the economic role of infrastructure requires defining and measuring it.[1] That task is the topic of this chapter. We focus on the measurement of infrastructure in the US National Economic Accounts to highlight the availability of these data and to gauge trends in recent decades; in particular, has investment in infrastructure by the public and private sectors (and the associated capital stocks) kept up

Jennifer Bennett is an economist at the Bureau of Economic Analysis.

Robert Kornfeld is an economist at the Bureau of Economic Analysis.

Daniel Sichel is a professor of economics at Wellesley College and a research associate of the National Bureau of Economic Research.

David Wasshausen is an economist at the Bureau of Economic Analysis.

This paper is part of the National Bureau of Economic Research's Economics of Infrastructure Project, supported by the Smith Richardson Foundation. The views expressed in this chapter are solely those of the authors and not necessarily those of the US Bureau of Economic Analysis, the Department of Commerce, or the NBER. For useful comments and discussions, we thank the editors of this volume, Peter Henry, Shane Greenstein, other participants in the NBER's Economics of Infrastructure Conference in November 2019, and Barbara Fraumeni. We also thank Michael Cusick at BEA for assistance. For acknowledgments, sources of research support, and disclosure of the authors' material financial relationships, if any, please see https://www.nber.org/books-and-chapters/economic-analysis-and-infrastructure-investment/measuring-infrastructure-beas-national-economic-accounts.

1. In a classic paper, Aschauer (1989) argued that government infrastructure was a key determinant of aggregate productivity growth in the US from 1949 to 1985. While the empirical magnitude of the effect has been a subject of debate (see Fernald 1999), the basic idea stands that infrastructure is an important economic input. Munnell (1992) also highlights the important role of infrastructure.

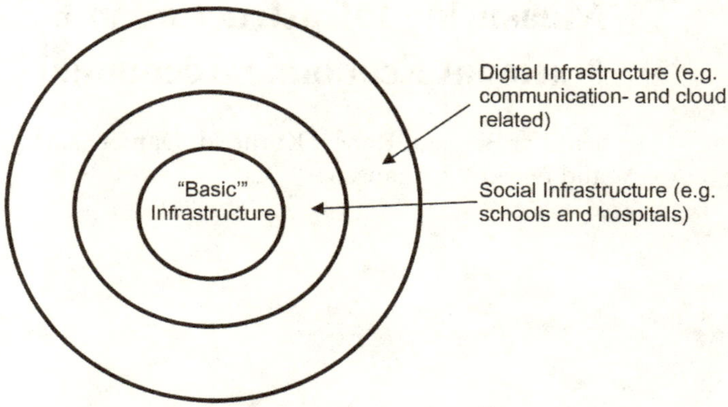


**Fig. 1.1 Basic, social, and digital infrastructure**

with key measures such as population and gross domestic product (GPD)?[2] Assessing these trends is particularly valuable given ongoing changes in the nature of infrastructure, as networks, connectivity, alternative-energy infrastructure, and digital and intangible infrastructure have become increasingly important and the focus of policy debates.

We begin with the challenging question of how to define "infrastructure." Defining the economic boundaries of infrastructure is imprecise and somewhat subjective. We consider three broad categories of infrastructure that can gauge different aspects of infrastructure from a National Economic Accounts standpoint. "Basic" infrastructure (such as transportation and utilities) reflects a traditional definition of infrastructure. From there, we expand that core to include additional economic activity that would potentially be included in infrastructure, including social and digital infrastructure.[3] Figure 1.1 illustrates this idea of basic or core infrastructure surrounded by broader concepts of infrastructure. Moreover, within each of these types, some infrastructure is owned by the public sector and some by the private sector.

After providing details on this framework for defining infrastructure, we describe the methodologies and the source data used by the Bureau of Economic Analysis to estimate US infrastructure investment, depreciation, and net stocks.

With definitions in hand, we consider different metrics for gauging levels

2. The data developed and discussed in this chapter are available in downloadable spreadsheets to enhance opportunities for further research.

3. As noted later, an interesting further extension would include a wide range of intangible infrastructure. R&D and more extensive coverage of software could be contemplated within the current asset boundary of the National Economic Accounts, while extensions to a wider set of intangible assets would require expanding the asset boundary in the Accounts. For a discussion of public intangibles, see Corrado, Haskel, and Jona-Lasinio (2017).

and trends of US infrastructure. In addition to measures for overall infrastructure, we will consider infrastructure by broad category, by detailed type, and by public or private ownership. Our data analysis covers the following topics, with our main conclusions briefly summarized here as well.

### 1.1.1 Investment and Capital Stocks

In terms of the composition of infrastructure stocks, the share of gross investment in basic infrastructure out of all infrastructure has fallen since the late 1950s, while the shares of social and digital infrastructure have increased. For net capital stocks, the share of basic infrastructure has fallen while the share of social has risen.

In terms of ownership, the share of the infrastructure capital stock that is publicly owned (both state and local ownership) has increased since the late 1950s, while the privately owned share has fallen. An important contributor to the decline in the private share is the huge drop in the investment share of privately owned railroads.

Gross real investment in infrastructure has trended up for most types of infrastructure, though patterns are widely mixed across asset types. These data highlight the resources devoted to different types of infrastructure each year and provide a useful overview of trends. These data also are closest to the source data before translation into net investment or capital stock measures (which rely on estimates and assumptions about depreciation).

Regarding trends in the budget resources devoted to infrastructure, gross real investment per capita has gently drifted up since the early 1980s. However, depreciation has absorbed a rising share of that investment, and real net investment per capita has barely risen.

Growth rates of real net capital stocks per capita also provide a metric for assessing how well infrastructure investment has kept up. This metric is particularly interesting because of its connection to measures of the contribution of capital to productivity growth. For this metric, the real net stock of basic infrastructure per capita has been soft for a long time, running below a 1 percent pace. For social infrastructure, this metric rose at more than a 2 percent pace during the 2000s, but since the financial crisis its growth rate has been around just 1 percent. The growth rate of the real net stock of digital infrastructure per capita has been much higher than that of other types of infrastructure, though that rate has been quite volatile. It is difficult to draw strong conclusions from these figures, but infrastructure investment certainly has, in general, not been growing rapidly (with the exception of digital infrastructure, some categories of electric power, medical equipment, and a few other categories).

### 1.1.2 State-Level Data

As interesting as national measures of infrastructure are, infrastructure is built in a particular region and has particular benefits for that region. In addition, to state the obvious, the geographic distribution of infrastructure carries considerable political salience. However, the National Economic Accounts do not, in general, include information on regional breakdowns of infrastructure. To get some visibility into the geographic distribution of infrastructure, we present new prototype measures on highway investment by state.[4] These estimates show that investment per capita and as a share of GDP has varied dramatically across states. Interestingly, the state-by-state rankings have tended to be relatively stable since 1992 (when our state-level data begin).

### 1.1.3 Depreciation Rates, Service Lives, and the Age of the Infrastructure Stock

This chapter also reviews the methodology and estimates used for calculating depreciation rates, service lives, ages, and remaining service life for infrastructure assets. Regarding depreciation, the rates used in National Economic Accounts for infrastructure assets were developed about 40 years ago. In addition, even at that time, the information set used for developing estimates of depreciation was relatively thin. Whether depreciation rates have changed over that period is an interesting question, although international comparisons raise the possibility that new research would generate different estimates.

The average age of the publicly owned basic and social infrastructure stock in the US has increased quite noticeably in recent decades, and the remaining service life of infrastructure assets has been falling. Moreover, average ages of infrastructure stock in the US are often greater than those in Canada and have followed a different trend. While ages have increased in the US, the average ages of comparable types of infrastructure in Canada have decreased during the past 10 years.

### 1.1.4 Maintenance Expenditures

Regarding depreciation and maintenance, a host of interesting issues are raised by the fact that maintenance expenditures and new investment can sustain the service flow from some types of infrastructure for many years.[5] To push forward on issues related to maintenance expenditures, we present new prototype data for maintenance expenditures for highways. These maintenance expenditures have amounted to about 15 percent of gross investment in highways, running a bit below that figure from the late 1990s through about 2011 and above that figure since then.

4. We use the term "prototype" here to denote that neither these estimates, nor the methods used to prepare them, have been approved by BEA for official publication. The same qualification applies to new data on maintenance expenditures described later.

5. See Diewert (2005) for a model in which maintenance expenditures sustain the service flow from an asset.

### 1.1.5 Prices

This chapter also reviews trends in price deflators and quality change for infrastructure assets. Prices of infrastructure increased more rapidly than GDP prices in the first part of the sample (1947–1987), but more slowly than GDP prices since 2000. Since 2010, overall infrastructure prices have changed little, a pace noticeably below that for GDP prices. The softness in infrastructure prices since the financial crisis reflects a step-down in rates of increase for basic and social infrastructure. Within social infrastructure, prices for health care infrastructure actually have fallen since 2010, largely because of declines in quality-adjusted prices for medical equipment.

Our final conclusions focus on methodology and directions for future research. First, as we highlight later, estimates of depreciation rates warrant a fresh look. Second, price deflators for some categories of infrastructure are based on cost indexes, which may not fully reflect quality improvements and productivity gains. Third, we note that, in some cases, relevant data are not granular enough to isolate digital infrastructure assets of interest, suggesting that greater granularity would be valuable. Fourth, we believe that development of additional data on regional estimates and for maintenance expenditures would be valuable. Finally, we believe much could be gained from additional international comparisons. The United Kingdom's Office for National Statistics is actively engaged in international comparisons of infrastructure across Europe and has issued a series of interesting reports presenting the results.[6] Of course, we are not the first to make these methodological observations, and the problems are challenging. Some creativity and novel data likely are the key to progress in these areas.

This chapter is organized as follows. Section 1.2 describes our definitions of basic, social, and digital infrastructure, and section 1.3 describes the methodologies and data used by the Bureau of Economic Analysis in its estimates of infrastructure investment, net capital stocks, depreciation rates, and prices. Section 1.4 turns to analysis of the data, highlighting both recent and longer-term trends. At the beginning of section 1.4, we provide a road map of the different metrics we examine and the broad questions our analysis addresses. Section 1.5 concludes and offers our thoughts on directions for future research.

6. These reports prepared by United Kingdom's Office for National Statistics are available online: first article (July 2017), https://www.ons.gov.uk/economy/economicoutputandproductivity/productivitymeasures/articles/developingnewmeasuresofinfrastructureinvestment/july2017; second article (August 2018), https://www.ons.gov.uk/economy/economicoutputandproductivity/productivitymeasures/articles/developingnewmeasuresofinfrastructureinvestment/august2018; third article (May 2019), https://www.ons.gov.uk/economy/economicoutputandproductivity/productivitymeasures/articles/experimentalcomparisonsofinfrastructureacrosseurope/may2019.

## 1.2 Defining Infrastructure

Defining infrastructure is not a precise science and is prone to subjective analysis. Henry Cisneros, former secretary of Housing and Urban Development (HUD), defined infrastructure capital as the structures and equipment that comprise "the basic systems that bridge distance and bring productive inputs together" (Cisneros 2010). These systems, or elements of them, often are shared and can have characteristics of public goods—for example, the Interstate Highway System—though infrastructure also can be excludable and rival public goods (a toll road suffering from congestion).

One preliminary issue for implementing any definition of infrastructure is deciding whether to categorize by type of asset or by private industry or government function. In this chapter, we categorize by asset type; for example, we consider specific assets providing transportation rather than the total capital stocks used in various industries providing transportation services. We believe this classification provides sharper focus for analyzing recent trends in infrastructure by keying in on specific assets that may have grown rapidly or slowly relative to other economic trends. In addition, this asset-type approach lines up more closely with available estimates of depreciation rates and prices in the National Economic Accounts.

Turning to our specific definitions, our "basic" measure of infrastructure is largely consistent with Cisneros's concept. In particular, we define basic infrastructure to include those asset types, both structures and equipment, related to power, transportation, water supply, sewage and waste disposal, and conservation and development (dams, levees, sea walls, and related assets). Expanding our definition from basic (or core) infrastructure, we consider social infrastructure, including assets such as public safety facilities, schools, and hospitals. Our final expansion from basic infrastructure brings in digital infrastructure, assets that enable the storage and exchange of data through a centralized communication system.

Digital infrastructure is particularly challenging to define, both because much of it represents new and evolving technologies and because, in some cases, the National Economic Accounts data are not sufficiently granular to separately identify assets of interest. Moreover, deciding what portion of specific assets to allocate to digital infrastructure raises challenging issues. For example, the equipment and software providing wireline and wireless access to the internet could, in principle, be counted as part of cloud computing infrastructure and therefore included in a measure of digital infrastructure. However, these assets also are used for other purposes. Perfectly dividing these assets and sorting out these issues may be impossible.

Despite these difficulties, we forge ahead and propose a definition of digital infrastructure, with the understanding that it likely will evolve as additional research and data work allow further refinement. Our definition includes pieces that are identifiable in the National Economic Accounts

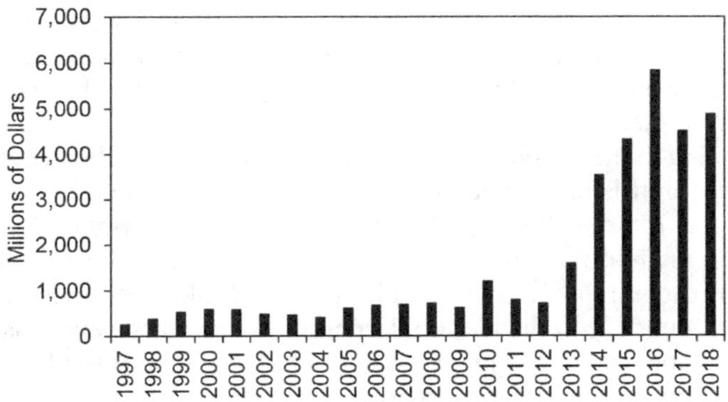


**Fig. 1.2 Office buildings construction, owned by NAICS 518 and 519**

and that we believe would unambiguously be considered infrastructure. In particular, we include all private communication structures—for example, cell towers—as well as computers, communications equipment, and software owned by the broadcast and telecommunications industries (North American Industry Classification System [NAICS] 515 and 517) and by the data processing, internet publishing, and information services industries (NAICS 518 and 519).[7] This latter category should include the equipment and software within data centers.

The assets described in the previous paragraph cover an important part, but by no means all, of what would be thought of as the infrastructure supporting the internet and cloud computing. One important category that is missing is the structures component of data centers (as mentioned, we believe we are capturing the equipment and software within data centers). As strange as this may sound, these structures likely fall within the "office" category of commercial construction but are not currently broken out as a separate line item so cannot be directly quantified. That being said, collateral evidence points to extremely rapid growth in these types of structures. As shown in figure 1.2, "office" construction for establishments classified in NAICS 518 and 519 (Data Processing, Hosting, and Related Services and Other Information Services) surged dramatically after 2012, timing that is roughly consistent with a boom in data center construction. While this category includes office structures unrelated to data centers, which we would

7. Our definition of digital infrastructure explicitly excludes servers owned by private firms outside of NAICS 518 and 519. If such a firm in, say, the auto industry transitioned most of its computing from private servers to Amazon Web Services, then the private server that is being transitioned away from (and not replaced) would be out of scope in our definition while the server run by Amazon would, in principle, be in scope in our definition. The logic of this outcome is that the firm is transitioning from utilizing a privately used asset to a shared digital "infrastructure" asset.

not want to include in our definition, the surge strongly suggests that data centers are a big growth category. With some further work, it may be possible to isolate the data center piece of this category and include it in a definition of digital infrastructure.

Returning to the big picture, note that one category of infrastructure that we largely omit is intangible infrastructure (except for selected software). Within the framework of the National Economic Accounts, we did not develop a methodology for splitting R&D into infrastructure and noninfrastructure components. In principle, this split could be done. Moreover, if the asset boundary in the National Economic Accounts were expanded to include a wider set of intangible assets, then it would be possible to include a wider set of intangible infrastructure in a definition.[8]

To provide some quick intuition for the size of our defined categories, the right three columns of table 1.1 report net capital stock shares for types of basic, social, and digital infrastructure (and components) out of total infrastructure for 1957, 1987, and 2017.[9] These shares demonstrate the declining role of basic infrastructure and the greater role of social and digital infrastructure over the past 60 years. Table 1.2 provides detailed examples for the components of infrastructure.

## 1.3 Source Data and Methodology Used for Estimating Investment, Net Capital Stocks, and Depreciation

The data for this chapter are from BEA's capital accounts, also known as the fixed assets accounts (FAAs).[10] BEA produces the US National Income and Product Accounts (the NIPAs) and is perhaps best known for the estimates of current production income—GDP and gross domestic income (GDI).[11] As part of its work to produce GDP and GDI, BEA also produces the FAAs, which provide estimates of depreciation and capital stocks for many types of private and government fixed assets used in production. These data exist from 1925 to the present.

More specifically, "private and government gross investment" (also known as capital investment or gross fixed capital formation) in the NIPAs

8. See Corrado, Haskel, and Jona-Lasinio (2017) for an examination of public intangibles.

9. We report shares starting in 1957 even though our data reach back earlier. We begin in 1957 to avoid volatility related to the aftermath of World War II.

10. BEA's main web page is www.bea.gov. For the FAAs, see https://apps.bea.gov/iTable/index_FA.cfm.

11. GDP, a measure of current period production, is the sum of personal consumption expenditures (spending by households and nonprofits), gross private domestic investment, the change in private inventories, net exports of goods and services, and government consumption expenditures and gross investment. GDI, which is theoretically equal to GDP but can differ because of measurement challenges, equals the sum of employee compensation, corporate profits, the income of sole proprietors and partnerships, net interest, and some other income sources from current production. For more information see the NIPA handbook, https://www.bea.gov/resources/methodologies/nipa-handbook.

**Table 1.1** **Real net stocks and nominal net stock shares of infrastructure**

| | Real net stocks | | | Nominal net stock shares (%) | | |
|---|---|---|---|---|---|---|
| | Millions of 2012 dollars | | | | | |
| | 1957 | 1987 | 2017 | 1957 | 1987 | 2017 |
| Total | 3,603,208 | 8,456,642 | 15,359,512 | 100.0 | 100.0 | 100.0 |
| *Basic* | 2,785,755 | 5,876,110 | 9,208,860 | 77.0 | 65.4 | 60.9 |
| Water | 130,776 | 316,322 | 576,355 | 3.8 | 3.7 | 4.0 |
| Sewer | 160,315 | 473,080 | 759,160 | 4.5 | 5.5 | 5.2 |
| Conservation and development | 196,343 | 352,276 | 433,687 | 5.2 | 4.2 | 2.8 |
| Power | 780,243 | 1,821,224 | 2,937,757 | 23.3 | 21.6 | 19.1 |
| Electric | 521,995 | 1,377,501 | 2,349,967 | 16.3 | 17.5 | 15.5 |
| Wind and solar structures | 0 | 0 | 205,699 | 0.0 | 0.0 | 1.3 |
| Other structures | 428,040 | 1,079,038 | 1,500,997 | 11.1 | 12.5 | 10.3 |
| Equipment | 65,784 | 238,263 | 514,875 | 4.2 | 4.1 | 3.1 |
| Turbines/steam engines | 28,171 | 60,200 | 128,396 | 1.1 | 0.8 | 0.7 |
| Petroleum | 84,184 | 103,073 | 162,524 | 2.3 | 1.0 | 1.0 |
| Natural gas | 174,064 | 340,650 | 425,266 | 4.7 | 3.2 | 2.7 |
| Transportation | 1,518,077 | 2,913,208 | 4,501,901 | 40.2 | 30.4 | 29.8 |
| Highways and streets | 900,093 | 2,178,097 | 3,311,203 | 19.5 | 20.9 | 21.8 |
| Air transportation | 31,182 | 121,449 | 327,523 | 0.7 | 1.2 | 2.2 |
| Rail transportation | 504,227 | 399,894 | 369,996 | 17.5 | 5.9 | 2.5 |
| Transit | 54,001 | 135,363 | 366,522 | 1.8 | 1.5 | 2.5 |
| Water transportation | 16,065 | 51,983 | 89,113 | 0.4 | 0.5 | 0.6 |
| Other transportation | 12,509 | 26,421 | 12,787 | 0.3 | 0.3 | 0.1 |
| *Social* | 728,874 | 2,211,426 | 4,786,118 | 18.0 | 26.7 | 32.0 |
| Public safety | 29,608 | 140,062 | 254,038 | 0.8 | 1.9 | 1.9 |
| Education | 532,071 | 1,323,417 | 2,774,969 | 12.0 | 14.1 | 18.9 |
| Health care | 167,194 | 747,947 | 1,757,111 | 5.1 | 10.8 | 11.2 |
| Structures | 163,227 | 685,446 | 1,265,156 | 4.8 | 9.2 | 8.5 |
| Equipment | 3,967 | 62,501 | 491,956 | 0.3 | 1.6 | 2.7 |
| *Digital* | 88,579 | 369,106 | 1,364,534 | 5.0 | 7.9 | 7.1 |
| Structures | 84,682 | 327,975 | 639,499 | 3.5 | 4.0 | 3.9 |
| Equipment and software in NAICS 513 and 514 | 3,897 | 41,131 | 725,035 | 1.5 | 3.9 | 3.1 |

and FAAs refers to additions and replacements to the stock of fixed assets without deduction of depreciation.[12] "Fixed assets" are produced assets that are used repeatedly in production for more than one year. Fixed assets include structures (buildings and other generally immobile assets such as cables, pipelines, and roads), equipment (such as computers and communications, industrial, and transportation equipment), and intellectual prop-

12. Estimates of fixed investment in the FAAs and in GDP are very similar; minor differences are presented at https://apps.bea.gov/iTable/index_FA.cfm; see "Relation of the NIPAs to the Corresponding Items in the FAAs."

**Table 1.2** **Infrastructure component examples**

| | |
|---|---|
| *Basic* | |
| Water | Plant, wells, water transmission pipelines, tunnels and water lines, pump stations, reservoirs, tanks and towers |
| Sewer | Solid waste disposals (incinerator or burial), sewage treatment plants, sewage disposal plants, wastewater disposal plants, recycling facilities, sanitary sewers, sewage pipeline, interceptors and lift/pump stations, water collection systems (nonpotable water), and storm drains |
| Conservation and development | Dam/levees—includes nonpower dams, dikes, levees, locks and lock gates; breakwater/jetty—includes breakwaters, bulkheads, tide gates, jetties, erosion control, retaining walls, and seawalls; dredging |
| Power | |
| Electric | |
| Structures | Power plants (nuclear, oil, gas, coal, wood), nuclear reactors, hydroelectric plants, dry-waste generation, thermal energy facilities, electric distribution systems, electrical substations, switch houses, transformers, and transmission lines |
| Equipment | Power, distribution, and specialty transformers; electricity and signal testing instruments |
| Gas | Buildings and structures for the distribution, transmission, gathering, and storage of natural gas |
| Transportation | |
| Highways and streets | Pavement, lighting, retaining walls, tunnels, bridges and overhead crossings (vehicular or pedestrian), toll/weigh stations, maintenance buildings, and rest facilities |
| Air transportation | Passenger terminals, runways, as well as pavement and lighting, hangars, air freight terminals, space facilities, air traffic towers, aircraft storage and maintenance buildings |
| Water transportation | Docks, piers, wharves, marinas, boatels, and maritime freight terminals |
| Rail transportation | Track and bridges |
| Transit | Maintenance facilities, passenger/freight terminals for buses and trucks |
| *Social* | |
| Public safety | Detention centers, jails, penitentiaries, prisons, police stations, sheriffs' offices, fire stations, rescue squads, dispatch and emergency centers |
| Education | In addition to all types of schools, includes zoos, arboreta, botanical gardens, planetariums, observatories, galleries, museums, libraries, and archives |
| Health care | |
| Structures | Hospitals, mental hospitals, medical buildings, and infirmaries |
| Equipment | Electromedical machinery and medical instruments |
| *Digital* | |
| Structures | Telephone, television, and radio distribution and maintenance buildings and structures; includes fiber optic cable |
| Equipment | Internet switches, routers, and hubs; cloud computing hardware and software |

erty (software, research and development, and entertainment originals). The FAAs report investment (as a component of GDP) as well as economic depreciation or "consumption of fixed capital" (as components of GDP and GDI). Economic depreciation is defined as the decline in the value of stock of these fixed assets due to normal physical deterioration and obsolescence. The FAAs also report net capital stocks of fixed assets, reflecting the accumulation of previous investment less accumulated depreciation. These statistics are reported in nominal and in inflation-adjusted (real, or chain) dollars for more than 100 types of government and private fixed assets; for the entire economy; for about 70 industries; and for several "legal forms of organization," such as corporations, partnerships, sole proprietorships, and nonprofits.

The FAAs' comprehensive national statistics on investment, depreciation, and capital stocks are widely cited and have several purposes. Net investment—investment less depreciation—is a useful measure of the extent to which investment adds to the capital stock rather than merely replacing stock lost to depreciation.

The FAAs are used in several ways. In the Integrated Macroeconomic Accounts (IMAs), produced jointly by the BEA and the Federal Reserve Board, the value of stocks of fixed assets are entries in the balance sheets of major sectors of the US economy, such as households, government, and nonfinancial corporations. Rates of return of capital investment and Q ratios presented by BEA and others are based on BEA's estimates of net stocks.[13] The FAAs also are used for the estimates of multifactor productivity (MFP) produced by the Bureau of Labor Statistics (BLS) and BEA's industry-level production account.[14] Finally, and most germane to this chapter, because a subset of the assets in the FAAs are within our definition of "infrastructure," these data can be used to gauge investment and capital stocks of different types of infrastructure and to examine their long-term trends.

13. See the NIPA handbook (https://www.bea.gov/resources/methodologies/nipa-handbook) for more information on the uses of consumption of fixed capital (CFC) in the NIPAs. For a description of the Integrated Macroeconomic Accounts, see Yamashita (2013). The IMAs can be found https://www.bea.gov/data/special-topics/integrated-macroeconomic-accounts. Rates of return may be calculated as net operating surplus (a measure of business income net of depreciation) as a share of the stock of fixed assets. Q ratios are calculated as the ratio of financial-market valuation of corporate assets to the current-cost value of fixed assets. BEA produces an annual article on rates of return of fixed investment and Q ratios; see Sarah Osborne and Bonnie A. Retus, "Returns for Domestic Nonfinancial Business," *Survey of Current Business* (December 2018), https://apps.bea.gov/scb/2018/12-december/1218-domestic-returns.htm.

14. For estimates of and background on the BLS MFP estimates, see https://www.bls.gov/mfp/. Note that these estimates rely on BEA's investment data but the BLS estimates its own measures of capital stocks, which are generally similar to BEA's FAAs but use slightly different depreciation rates. For the BEA industry-level production account, see https://www.bea.gov/data/special-topics/integrated-industry-level-production-account-klems.

### 1.3.1 Methodology

In the FAAs, inflation-adjusted (real) net stocks and depreciation of fixed assets, including infrastructure, are calculated for each type of asset using the perpetual inventory method (PIM). Under the PIM, the real net stock of each asset type in a year equals last year's real net stock plus the cumulative value of real fixed investment through that year, less the cumulative value of real depreciation through that year, less "other changes in the volume of assets" (mainly damage from major disasters). Real economic depreciation (consumption of fixed capital) for most assets is estimated as a fixed percentage of the net stock (geometric depreciation).[15] The PIM can be expressed as

$$K_{jt} = K_{j(t-1)}(1 - \delta_j) + I_{jt}(1 - \delta_j/2) - O_{jt},$$

where

$K_{jt}$ = real net stock for year $t$ for asset type $j$,
$\delta_j$ = annual depreciation rate for asset type $j$,
$I_{jt}$ = real investment for year $t$ for asset type $j$, and
$O_{jt}$ = other changes in volume of assets for year $t$ for type $j$ (often small or zero).

The PIM can be rewritten as

$$K_{jt} = K_{j(t-1)} + I_{jt} - O_{jt} - M_{jt},$$

where

$$M_{jt} = K_{j(t-1)}\delta_j + I_{jt}\delta_j/2$$

= real depreciation for year $t$ for asset type $j$

(also known as consumption of fixed capital, or CFC).

Real estimates of fixed investment are, for almost all assets, obtained by dividing estimates of nominal investment by a price index. The prices used for the FAAs are generally the same prices used for estimates of fixed investment in GDP. Once the real net stocks are estimated using the PIM, current-cost net stocks are estimated by multiplying real net stocks by corresponding end-of-year price indexes (we refer to this as "reflating"). For example, the current-cost estimate of the net stock for 2018 is an estimate of the replacement cost or market value of the stock at the end of 2018. Similarly, current-cost depreciation or CFC is estimated by reflating real

15. Investment in the current year is depreciated using half the annual depreciation rates, under the assumption that investment occurs throughout the year. Price indexes used for investment and depreciation reflect the average price of the asset over the investment period, whereas price indexes used for stocks reflect the price of the asset at the end of the period. BEA constructs end-of-period prices using moving averages of the average period prices.

CFC with corresponding average year price indexes. At the end of 2018, the estimated current-cost value of total private and government net stocks of fixed assets was about $63 trillion, and depreciation was about $3.3 trillion.

The accuracy of these estimates depends, as the equation implies, on the accuracy of estimates of investment, depreciation, and prices. The FAAs may, for example, overstate net stocks if the NIPAs overstate fixed investment or understate depreciation. For many types of structures, annual depreciation rates can be well below 5 percent, so that the current stock includes slices of investment from decades earlier, and errors in depreciation rates can result in significant biases in the amount of older assets included in the net stock.

Regarding the role of prices, estimates of both real and current-cost net stocks of assets in any year are sensitive to changes in these prices and to any errors in price measurement. For example, if price indexes fail to accurately capture quality change and are biased, then real investment would be misstated, and therefore estimates of real stocks built up from these investment flows would be biased. In addition, given the reflation procedure used to estimate current-cost net stocks, mismeasurement of prices also will bias estimates of the current-cost stocks.[16]

Despite these challenges, the FAAs provide perhaps the best available comprehensive estimates of investment and stocks of US infrastructure-related assets. The rest of this section of the chapter describes the methodology for estimating fixed investment, depreciation rates, and prices in greater detail.

### 1.3.2 Data Sources for Investment

In BEA's FAAs, the current-dollar fixed investment statistics that serve as the foundation for the net stock estimates are generally the same as the fixed investment statistics that are part of BEA's estimates of GDP. These estimates rely on a wide and comprehensive range of source data. Most infrastructure assets in this chapter are classified as structures. For structures, current-dollar investment in private and federal government nonresidential fixed investment is primarily based on detailed data on the value of construction put in place (VIP) from the Census Bureau's monthly survey of construction spending.[17] Investment in state and local government structures is largely based on the five-year Census of Governments (COG) and the Annual Surveys of State and Local Government Finances (GF), with

16. The effects of price mismeasurement on real investment and current-cost stock reflation generally will not be exactly offsetting. The effect on real net stocks via real investment reflects mismeasurement of prices in past years, while the effect on current-cost stocks via reflation reflects mismeasurement of prices in the single year of prices used for reflation.

17. For more information on the Census Bureau's construction statistics, see https://www.census.gov/construction/c30/definitions.html.

the Census VIP data used to extrapolate estimates for the months and years before the next round of GF data are available.[18]

In these surveys of investment in structures, the "value of construction put in place" is defined as the value of construction installed at the construction site during a given period, regardless of when the overall project was started or completed, when the structure was sold or delivered, or when payment for the structure was made. For an individual project, construction costs include materials installed or erected; labor (both by contractors and in-house); a proportionate share of the cost of construction equipment rental; the contractor's profit; architectural and engineering services; miscellaneous overhead and office costs chargeable to the project on the owner's books; and interest and taxes paid during construction. This "sum of costs" estimate of investment does not reflect the eventual selling price of the asset, which may be above cost in a strong market or below cost in a weak market.

The category "construction" includes the following items:

- New buildings and structures
- Additions, alterations, conversions, expansions, reconstruction, renovations, rehabilitations, and major replacements (such as the complete replacement of a roof or heating system)
- Mechanical and electrical installations, such as plumbing, heating, elevators, and central air-conditioning equipment
- Site preparation and outside construction of fixed structures or facilities

Construction costs and BEA's estimates of fixed investment in structures exclude the cost of land and the cost of routine maintenance and repairs. Investment reflects only the construction of new assets and excludes the purchase of already existing assets.[19]

Our definitions of infrastructure also include some equipment and software categories. For private equipment, such as computers and communications, medical, and electrical transmission and distribution equipment, BEA's estimates are prepared using the "commodity-flow method." This method begins with a value of domestic output (manufacturers' shipments) based on data from the five-year Economic Census and the Annual Surveys of Manufacturers (ASM). Next, the domestic supply of each commodity—the amount available for domestic consumption—is estimated by adding imports and subtracting exports, both based on the Census Bureau's international trade data. The domestic supply is then allocated among domestic

18. For more information on NIPA measures of fixed investment, see Bureau of Economic Analysis (2019), chaps. 6 and 9.

19. One complication to the exclusion of sales and purchases of existing assets is the transfer of assets between the private sector and the government. For example, if the government sells a building to a private business, that transaction would count as an addition to the private-sector capital stock and a subtraction from the government's capital stock. BEA estimates the net value of these purchases or sales using data from other government sources.

purchasers—business, government, and consumers—based on Economic Census data. Investment in equipment by state and local governments is also based on the commodity-flow method, relying on these same data sources and also the COG and GF data. Investment in equipment by the federal government is based on data from federal agencies.

Estimates of investment in private purchased software are based on industry receipts data from the Economic Census and Census Bureau's Service Annual Survey. The estimates for own-account software are measured as the sum of production costs, including the value of capital services (which includes depreciation). The estimates are based on BLS data on occupational employment and wages, on Economic Census data, and on BEA-derived measures of capital services. For the estimates of infrastructure for the digital economy, the share of investment allocated to the relevant subset of industries we identified earlier is based on industry shares of purchases of fixed investment reported by the Census Bureau's Annual Capital Expenditures Survey (ACES) and the Information and Communication Technology Survey.

### 1.3.3 Capital Improvements versus Maintenance and Repairs

One of the challenges of measuring fixed investment is distinguishing between "capital improvements" (which are part of investment) and "maintenance and repairs" (which are not). The 2008 System of National Accounts (SNA)[20] defines "fixed assets" as produced assets that are used repeatedly or continuously in production processes for more than one year. Moreover, fixed investment (gross fixed capital formation in the SNA) may take the form of improvements to existing fixed assets that increase their productive capacity, extend their service lives, or both.

Distinguishing between capital improvements and maintenance and repairs can be particularly difficult in practice, and the SNA acknowledges that "the distinction between ordinary maintenance and repairs that constitute intermediate consumption and those that are treated as capital formation is not clear cut." According to the SNA, ordinary maintenance and repairs are distinguished by two features:

- They are activities that must be undertaken regularly in order to maintain a fixed asset in working order over its expected service life. The owner or user of the asset has no choice about whether or not to undertake ordinary maintenance and repairs if the asset in question is to continue to be used in production.
- Ordinary maintenance and repairs do not change the fixed asset's performance, productive capacity or expected service life. They simply

20. The SNA refers to an agreed-upon set of international standards for National Economic Accounts. For more information on the 2008 System of National Accounts, see https://unstats.un.org/unsd/nationalaccount/sna2008.asp.

maintain it in good working order, by replacing defective parts with new parts of the same kind.

On the other hand, improvements to existing fixed assets that constitute fixed investment must go well beyond the requirements of ordinary maintenance and repairs. Such improvements must bring about significant changes in the characteristics of existing asset and may be distinguished by the following features:

- The decision to renovate, reconstruct, or enlarge a fixed asset is a deliberate investment decision that may be taken at any time, even when the good in question is in good working order and not in need of repair. Major renovations of ships, buildings or other structures are frequently undertaken well before the end of their normal service lives.
- Major renovations, reconstructions, or enlargements increase the performance or productive capacity of existing fixed assets or significantly extend their previously expected service lives, or both. Enlarging or extending an existing building or structure constitutes a major change in this sense, as does the refitting or restructuring of the interior of a building or ship or a major extension to or enhancement of an existing software system.

BEA's and the Census Bureau's definitions of fixed investment in new construction, improvements, and maintenance and repairs are generally consistent with the definitions prescribed in the SNA and, as well as possible, classify capital improvements as investment and maintenance and repairs as current spending. As noted, these criteria are sometimes difficult to implement in practice. Currently, the Census Bureau's nonresidential construction statistics do not separately report spending for new construction and for improvements, complicating efforts to separately track these expenditures. That being said, we develop estimates of maintenance and repair expenditures for highways later in this chapter.

### 1.3.4 Price Measures

As noted, BEA's estimates of real infrastructure investment (quantities) are derived by deflating nominal investments with corresponding price indexes. BEA's price indexes are chosen to be as consistent as possible with the categories of current-dollar investment, reflecting prices of new investment and improvements and excluding prices of maintenance and repair and land.

Given the heterogenous nature of many infrastructure-related structures (for example, bridges, tunnels, power plants, hospitals), constructing accurate, constant-quality price indexes for these types of assets presents challenges. When possible, BEA uses producer price indexes (PPI) published by the Bureau of Labor Statistics. However, for many of the infrastructure asset types, PPIs do not exist, and BEA instead uses combinations of input-cost measures and output-cost measures from trade sources and government agencies in an effort to capture productivity and quality changes.[21] Naturally, cost indexes are a second-best approach for estimating prices as cost indexes potentially exclude changes in productivity and margins. For infrastructure-related structures, key source data for price indexes are as follows:

- Electric power structures: weighted average of Handy-Whitman construction cost indexes for electric light and power plants and for utility building
- Other power structures: Handy-Whitman gas index of public utility construction costs
- Communications structures: AUS Consultants Incorporated telephone plant cost index
- Highways: Federal Highway Administration composite index for highway construction costs
- Water transportation: Handy-Whitman water index of public utility construction costs
- Health care structures: PPI for health care building construction
- Educational and vocational structures: PPI for new school construction
- Land transportation structures, railroad: weighted average of BLS employment cost index for the construction industry, of Bureau of Reclamation construction cost trends for bridges and for power plants, of PPI for material and supply inputs to construction industries, and of PPI for communications equipment
- Air transportation, land transportation other than rail, all other structures: unweighted average of Census Bureau price index for new one-family houses under construction and of Turner Construction Company building-cost index

For most equipment categories that we include in infrastructure, BEA relies on detailed PPIs and import price indexes (IPIs) from BLS. These measures control for quality change just as in the noninfrastructure parts of the National Economic Accounts. Of particular note for purposes of capturing digital infrastructure, the prices for computers, communications equipment, and medical equipment are quality adjusted based on recent research. The price for communications equipment uses the Federal Reserve Board quality-adjusted price indexes for data networking equipment, voice network equipment, data transport equipment, and a weighted composite of wireless networking equipment and cellular phone equipment, in addition to several PPIs and IPIs. The price for medical equipment and instruments uses

21. For more information, see Lally (2009).

BEA's own quality-adjusted price indexes for medical imaging equipment and for medical diagnostic equipment, along with several PPIs and IPIs.

The price measures for software also reflect recent research on quality adjustment. The price index for prepackaged software is based on the PPI for software publishing (except games) and quality adjustments by BEA. The price index for custom and own account software is a weighted average of the prepackaged software price and of a BEA input-cost index. The input-cost index is based on BLS data on wage rates for computer programmers and systems analysts and on intermediate input costs associated with the production of software. This input-cost index also reflects a modest adjustment for changes in productivity based on BEA judgment.

### 1.3.5 Depreciation Rates and Service Lives

Intuitively, the concept of depreciation is easy to understand: depreciation captures the loss in value as a tangible (or intangible) asset ages. In practice, the measurement of depreciation can be complicated by differences in concepts, terminology, and implementation, as reflected in active debates over the years.[22]

The basic underlying idea is that, over time, an asset's value typically will decline, reflecting depreciation and revaluation. Depreciation is the loss in value arising from aging, and revaluation is the change in value arising from all factors other than aging. Fraumeni (1997) nicely illustrates the distinction with an example of the price over time of a used car. The price difference between a one-year-old car of a specific make and model in 2018 and the same make and model car in 2019, when the vehicle is now two years old, reflects depreciation. The price difference between a one-year-old car of a specific make and model in 2018 and a one-year-old car of the same make and model in 2019 reflects revaluation. (Perhaps gas prices changed, making a particular vehicle more or less attractive to buyers.)

For the National Economic Accounts, BEA conceptualizes depreciation as the consumption of fixed capital or a cost of production. Specifically, BEA defines depreciation as "the decline in value due to wear and tear, obsolescence, accidental damage, and aging" (Katz and Herman 1997). Assets withdrawn from service (retirements) also count within BEA's definition of depreciation. This definition draws in the pure concept of depreciation described in the preceding paragraph as well as a part of revaluation (specifically, obsolescence related to factors other than age).

Prior to 1997, depreciation in the National Economic Accounts was calculated on a straight-line basis. Starting in that year, BEA adopted geometric depreciation rates for most assets, including most infrastructure assets. This

22. See Fraumeni (1997) and Diewert (2005) for an introduction to and discussion of the issues.

choice and the estimates adopted were influenced heavily by the work of Hulten and Wykoff (1981a, 1981b) and their analysis of age-price profiles. This work pointed to geometric depreciation for most assets and provided estimates of depreciation rates.[23]

### 1.3.6 Alternative Ways to Prepare Capital Measures

Although BEA's measures of capital for infrastructure-related assets are of high quality and largely follow international guidelines, there are alternative methods that would likely yield different results. As described in section 1.3.1, BEA uses the perpetual inventory method to derive net stocks. In order for this method to yield high-quality, accurate measures, the price indexes, nominal investment estimates, and depreciation profiles must all be of high quality. An alternative to the perpetual inventory method that is also used by BEA for selected assets is the physical inventory method. The physical inventory method applies independently estimated prices to a direct count of the number of physical units of each type of asset. The physical inventory method is a more direct approach, but it does require robust, detailed statistics on prices and number of units of new and used assets in the stock of each vintage available. Preparing measures of net stock using this method typically is extremely costly and time-consuming. BEA currently uses this method only for automobiles and light trucks, using detailed data on motor vehicle prices and units purchased from private vendors.

Some other alternative measures of capital stock and the services that it provides are estimated by other government agencies. The Bureau of Labor Statistics estimates a capital services index, and a corresponding productive capital stock, that is used as a measure of capital input in the estimation of multifactor productivity.[24] The BLS measure of capital services is designed to measure the flow of services provided by capital assets in the production process, similar to the flow of labor hours. BLS estimates the capital service flow using data on investment, rates of deterioration and depreciation of capital, and data on the income of firms utilizing capital. Although BLS uses formulas for deterioration that are not strictly consistent with formulas used by BEA for depreciation, the investment, income, and service-life data used by BLS are similar to the estimates presented by BEA, resulting in depreciation rates that are generally consistent with BEA's estimates. Exploring alternative measures of capital services provided by infrastructure-related assets and their effect on multifactor productivity, rates of return, and Q ratios is a rich field for future research.[25]

23. BEA deviates from geometric depreciation for assets for which empirical studies have provided evidence of nongeometric depreciation.

24. See US Bureau of Labor Statistics, *Handbook of Methods*, chap. 11, "Industry Productivity Measures," https://www.bls.gov/opub/hom/inp/home.htm.

25. See Diewert (2005) for a discussion of some alternatives.

Additional alternative methods exist specifically with respect to how to depreciate these assets. Several models of depreciation are available, including geometric depreciation, straight-line depreciation, and one-hoss shay.[26] As noted earlier, BEA primarily uses geometric depreciation rates, although alternative methods are used for selected assets.

## 1.4 Data Trends and Analysis

In this section, we highlight broad trends in the data and discuss underlying details and methodological questions that are of particular interest for infrastructure assets. For our main categories of infrastructure—basic, social, and digital—many metrics are available, including gross and net investment in both real and nominal terms, net capital stocks in real and nominal terms, and measures of depreciation. Each of these variables also can be scaled by population, GDP, or some other variable. These different metrics are useful for answering different questions. We are particularly interested in several broad questions that guide our choice of metrics to present in the chapter.

Because we consider a number of metrics, the following road map highlights the subsections that discuss different metrics and focus on different broad questions.

- Section 1.4.1: What are recent and long-term trends in investment for different types of infrastructure?
- Sections 1.4.1 and 1.4.2: Has the infrastructure stock kept up with growth in the US population?
- Section 1.4.3: What do we know about infrastructure investment by state? The short answer is not so much; to begin to fill this lacuna, we provide new prototype measures of investment in highways by state for 1992, 2002, 2012, and 2017.
- Section 1.4.4: How do US estimates of depreciation rates and service lives compare with those in other countries? This analysis provides one way of gauging whether US estimates of depreciation and service lives of infrastructure would benefit from additional research.
- Section 1.4.5: What is the age profile of infrastructure?
- Section 1.4.6: What do we know about the interplay between stocks of infrastructure and maintenance and repair expenditures? This is a difficult question to answer. To provide some basic insights, we present new prototype estimates of maintenance and repair expenditures for highways.
- Section 1.4.7: What has happened to prices of infrastructure?

26. For information on differing measures of depreciation under alternative assumptions, see Diewert (2005).

### 1.4.1 Investment in Infrastructure

We begin by focusing on trends in real investment.

#### *1.4.1.1 Investment*

Gross investment highlights the resources (in inflation-adjusted dollars) set aside each year for infrastructure. Net investment indicates how much actually is being added to capital stock each year after accounting for depreciation. We begin with investment measures because these figures represent the raw data that feed into estimates of net investment and capital stocks; accordingly, these estimates provide a broad overview of the National Economic Accounts infrastructure data. (For a broad overview of the data from another perspective, the first three columns of table 1.1 report real net capital stocks for basic, social, and digital infrastructure and their components for 1957, 1987, and 2017.)

As shown in figure 1.3 on a ratio scale, real gross investment in total infrastructure rose to about $340 billion in 1968, declined somewhat afterward, and then began to rise again in mid-1980s, to nearly $800 billion in

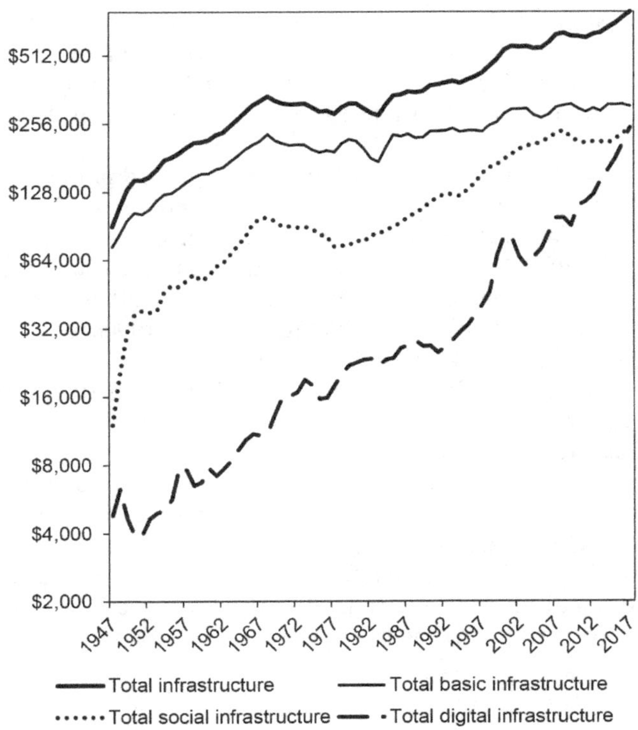


**Fig. 1.3 Real infrastructure investment, millions of chained 2012 dollars**

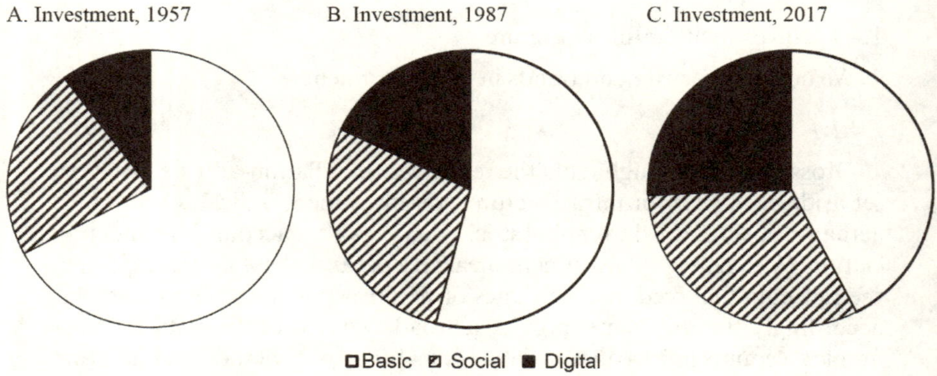


**Fig. 1.4 Infrastructure shares by type: Investment**

2017.[27] Real investment generally dipped or flattened out during recessions. The overall pattern exhibited by total infrastructure investment is roughly mirrored for real investment in many (but not all) other broad categories of infrastructure.

Real investment in basic infrastructure exhibited a pattern similar to that for the total category, as shown in figure 1.3. Investment peaked in the late 1960s, at about $230 billion, and fell in the 1970s and early 1980s. It did not rise appreciably above its late-1960s level until the early 2000s and has remained fairly flat since then.

Real investment in social infrastructure also peaked in the late 1960s at about $100 billion. Investment fell afterward, resumed rising in the 1980s to about $240 billion in 2008, then fell with the financial crisis but rose to precrisis levels by 2017. Real investment in digital infrastructure displayed a different pattern. It has increased more rapidly than the other categories, with the faster growth particularly notable from the mid-1990s to the present.

To illustrate these broad trends another way, figure 1.4 shows nominal gross investment shares for basic, social, and digital infrastructure for 1957, 1987, and 2017. Gross investment has shifted away from basic and toward social infrastructure since 1957 and, more recently, toward digital infrastructure. Despite this shift in investment shares, figure 1.5 shows that the shift in nominal net capital stocks has been somewhat less dramatic, with a much smaller rise in the net stock share of digital infrastructure than is evident in investment shares. This pattern reflects the fact that while gross investment has risen dramatically for digital infrastructure, depreciation for these assets is high, so stock accumulation has not been as noticeable.

27. Fair (2019) also examined trends in infrastructure, highlighting a slowdown after the early 1970s.

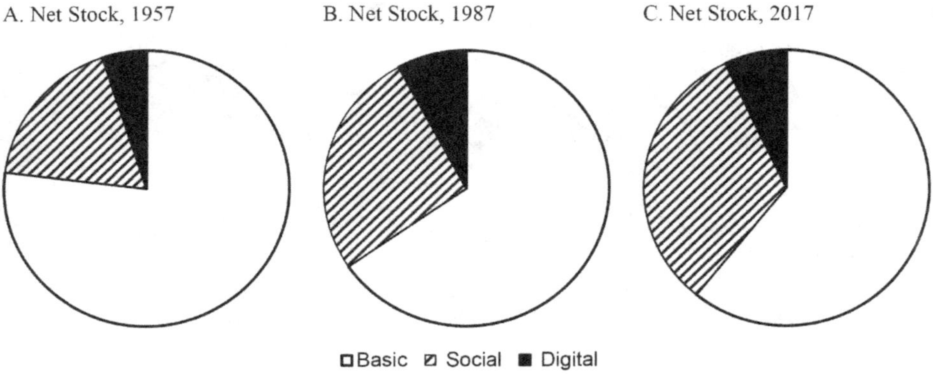


**Fig. 1.5 Infrastructure shares by type: Net stocks**

We now turn to a more detailed analysis of trends in real investment in infrastructure.

*1.4.1.2 Basic Infrastructure*

Trends in the basic category are mainly determined by trends in transportation and power (figure 1.6). Investment in transportation infrastructure and in highways and streets (by far the biggest part of transportation investment) shows similar patterns (figure 1.7). Investment in highways and streets mostly rose after the end of World War II, reaching $94 billion in 1968, and then fell afterward to about $52 billion in 1982 (except for a brief increase in the late 1970s). Investment in highways then generally rose through 2001, declined through 2013, and since that time has risen slightly. Figure 1.8 provides detail on investment in other components of transportation infrastructure.

Investment in all forms of power-related infrastructure (figure 1.6) rose to $84 billion in 1973, fluctuated over the next 25 years, and then began rising more noticeably in the late 1990s. Electric power is the largest category, with its details plotted in figure 1.9. Overall investment in electric power peaked at about $67 billion in 1973, fluctuated unevenly through the late 1990s, and rose very unevenly again, reaching a level of $124 billion by 2016. Investment in electric power structures (other than wind and solar) displays similar trends. The increase in electric power investment since 2000 comes partly from investment in wind and solar electric power structures, which rose sharply since the early 2000s, though the pace of this increase has slowed more recently.

Investment in petroleum and natural gas structures and components (figure 1.10) is considerably less than investment in electric power. Investment in private petroleum pipelines exhibited a sharp peak in the mid-1970s with the energy crisis and then rose in the mid-2000s as fracking got going. Invest-

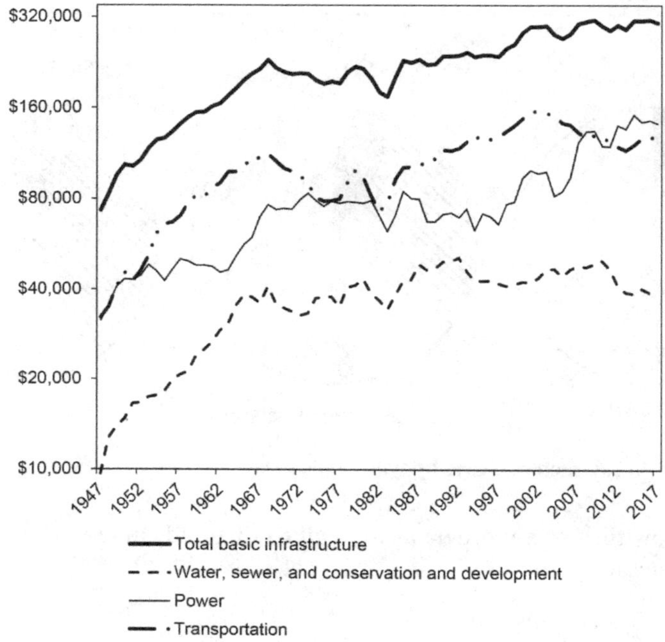


**Fig. 1.6 Real basic infrastructure investment, millions of chained 2012 dollars**

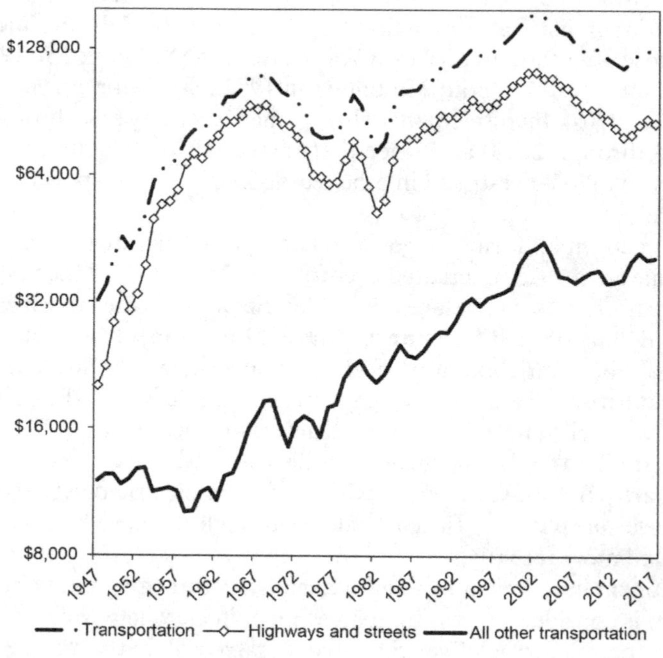


**Fig. 1.7 Real basic infrastructure investment: Transportation, millions of chained 2012 dollars**

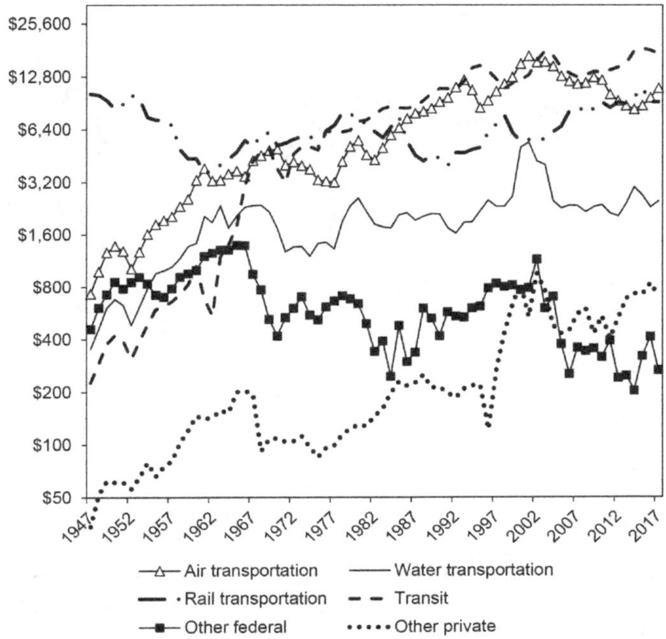


**Fig. 1.8 Real basic infrastructure investment: All other transportation, millions of chained 2012 dollars**

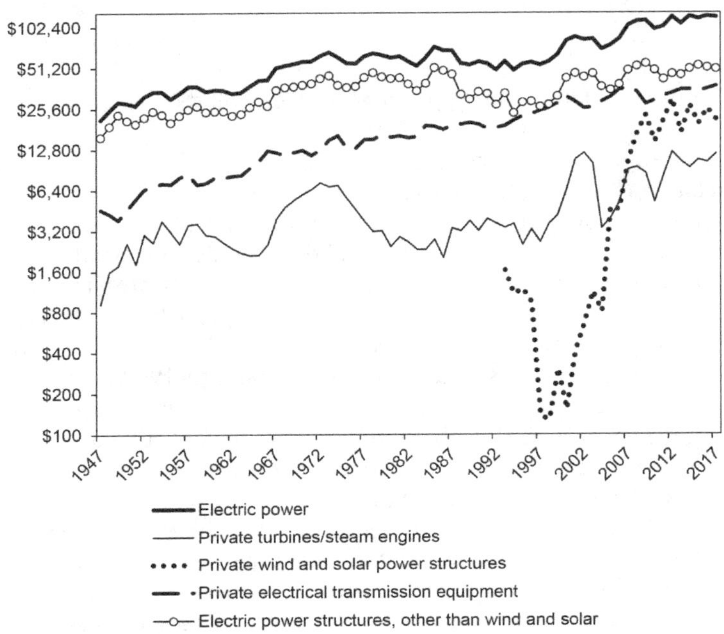


**Fig. 1.9 Real basic infrastructure investment: Electric power, millions of chained 2012 dollars**

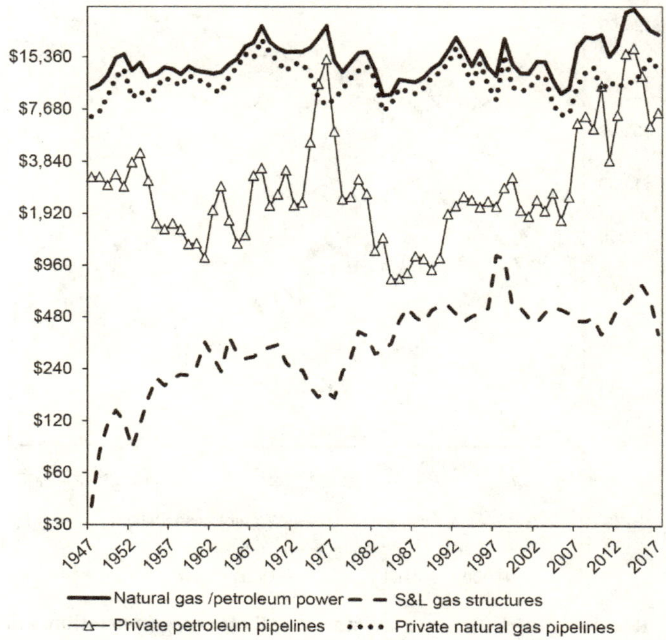


**Fig. 1.10 Real basic infrastructure investment: Petroleum and natural gas, millions of chained 2012 dollars**

ment in private natural gas pipelines has been volatile, but the underlying trend has been relatively flat since the 1960s.

Water, sewer, and conservation and development (dams, levees, seawalls, and related assets) make up a relatively small share of basic infrastructure. Conservation and development (figure 1.11) peaked in 1966 and then declined, and this category has remained quite modest in recent years. This will be an interesting category to watch as efforts to mitigate climate change gain traction. Water treatment rose rapidly through the late 1960s, fell back, rose by fits and starts through the early 2000s, and has moved lower since then. Sewer investment rose unevenly through the early 1990s, fell until 2000, and has bounced around since then, recently at a level about equal to where it was in the early 1970s. The flat trends during the past two decades in the water and sewer categories seem broadly consistent with the narrative of decaying systems in many municipalities.

These different trends in investment have led to shifts in the composition of capital stocks of basic infrastructure over time (table 1.1). Generally, net stocks of most types of infrastructure have risen over time; even with periods of flat and declining investment, stocks tend to increase because depreciation rates for these assets (mostly structures) are low. One notable exception

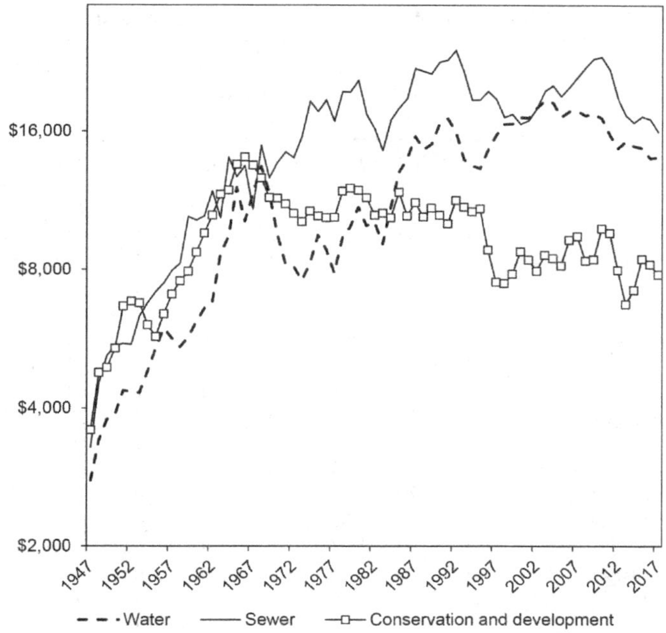


**Fig. 1.11 Real basic infrastructure investment: Water supply, sewer and waste, conservation and development, millions of chained 2012 dollars**

is railroad transportation: the US had substantial stocks of rail assets at the end of World War II but limited additional investment since then as the nation turned to roads, airplanes, and other forms of transportation. As a result, net stocks of railroad assets decreased markedly over these decades. Over time, the largest increases in real net stocks of basic infrastructure were in highways and streets, electric power structures and equipment, and water and sewer.

These changes in the composition of basic infrastructure also imply changes in the public-private mix of ownership. Trends in the ownership mix depend on trends in total stocks by asset type and on ownership patterns for each type of asset. For many assets, the ownership mix is stable. Highways and water and sewer assets are mostly or entirely owned by state and local governments. Air and water transportation assets are also mostly owned by state and local governments, and the private share actually has declined over time. The conservation and development category is mostly federal, although the state and local share has grown over time. Power and railroad assets are, on the other hand, mostly or entirely owned by private companies.

Putting these pieces together, the state and local government share has risen over time while the private share has declined, as reported in table 1.3.

**Table 1.3** **Private and public ownership shares of nominal net stocks**

| | Private (%) | | | Federal government (%) | | | State and local government (%) | | |
|---|---|---|---|---|---|---|---|---|---|
| | 1957 | 1987 | 2017 | 1957 | 1987 | 2017 | 1957 | 1987 | 2017 |
| *Total* | 52 | 45 | 41 | 6 | 5 | 3 | 42 | 50 | 56 |
| *Basic* | 54 | 40 | 34 | 7 | 5 | 4 | 39 | 54 | 62 |
| Water | 10 | 12 | 9 | 0 | 0 | 0 | 90 | 88 | 91 |
| Sewer | 8 | 9 | 7 | 0 | 0 | 0 | 92 | 91 | 93 |
| Conservation and development | 4 | 7 | 7 | 85 | 71 | 62 | 10 | 22 | 31 |
| Power | 92 | 86 | 87 | 0 | 0 | 1 | 7 | 13 | 12 |
| Electric | 90 | 84 | 85 | 0 | 0 | 1 | 10 | 16 | 14 |
| Petroleum/natural gas | 99 | 98 | 97 | 0 | 0 | 0 | 1 | 2 | 3 |
| Transportation | 48 | 22 | 10 | 2 | 2 | 1 | 50 | 77 | 89 |
| Highways and streets | 0 | 0 | 0 | 3 | 2 | 1 | 97 | 98 | 99 |
| Air transportation | 21 | 20 | 12 | 0 | 0 | 0 | 79 | 80 | 88 |
| Rail transportation | 100 | 100 | 100 | 0 | 0 | 0 | 0 | 0 | 0 |
| Transit | 88 | 20 | 3 | 0 | 0 | 0 | 12 | 80 | 97 |
| Water transportation | 9 | 7 | 6 | 0 | 0 | 0 | 91 | 93 | 94 |
| *Social* | 28 | 40 | 40 | 6 | 6 | 4 | 66 | 54 | 56 |
| Public safety | 23 | 9 | 8 | 19 | 37 | 24 | 58 | 54 | 68 |
| Education | 18 | 16 | 18 | 4 | 3 | 2 | 78 | 81 | 80 |
| Health care | 53 | 76 | 83 | 9 | 5 | 4 | 38 | 19 | 13 |
| *Digital* | 100 | 100 | 100 | 0 | 0 | 0 | 0 | 0 | 0 |

The biggest change in ownership occurs for transportation investment, with the state and local government share rising over time and the private share falling. This pattern reflects the decline in stocks of private railroad assets, the shift in transit from private to state and local governments, and the growth in mostly public air transportation infrastructure. All told, in 2017, state and local governments owned 62 percent of basic infrastructure, while the federal government owned 4 percent and private companies owned 34 percent.

#### *1.4.1.3 Social Infrastructure*

Trends in social infrastructure are mainly determined by trends in health and education and public safety (figure 1.12). Health-related infrastructure investment rose steadily over time, with occasional pauses in recessions; after the financial crisis, investment continued to rise, reaching about $152 billion in 2017. Most of the rise in health investment resulted from increases in investment in equipment, as shown in figure 1.13, although increases in investment in hospitals and other structures also played a role. The increases in real equipment spending partly reflect BEA's quality-adjusted, declining prices for medical equipment.

Investment in education-related infrastructure (figure 1.14) has fol-

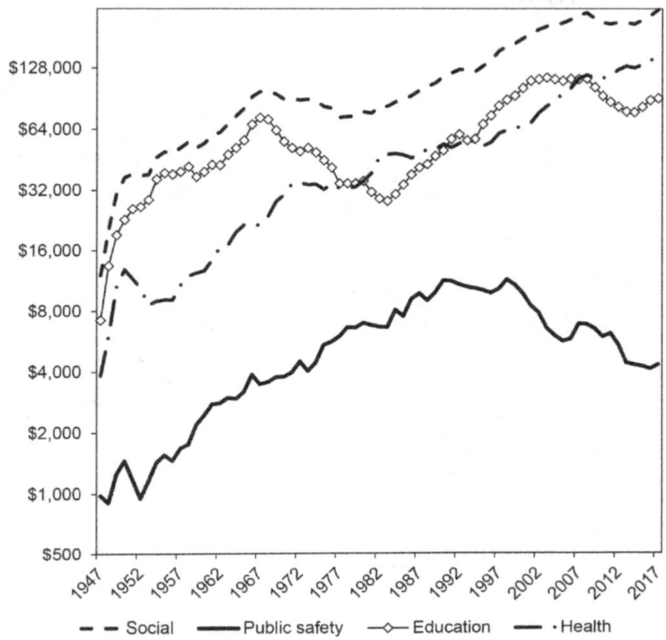


**Fig. 1.12 Real social infrastructure investment, millions of chained 2012 dollars**

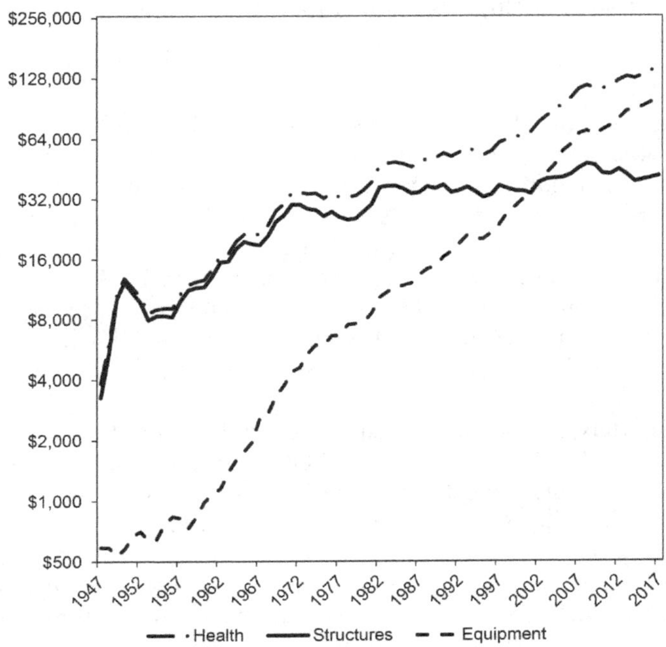


**Fig. 1.13 Real social infrastructure investment: Health, millions of chained 2012 dollars**

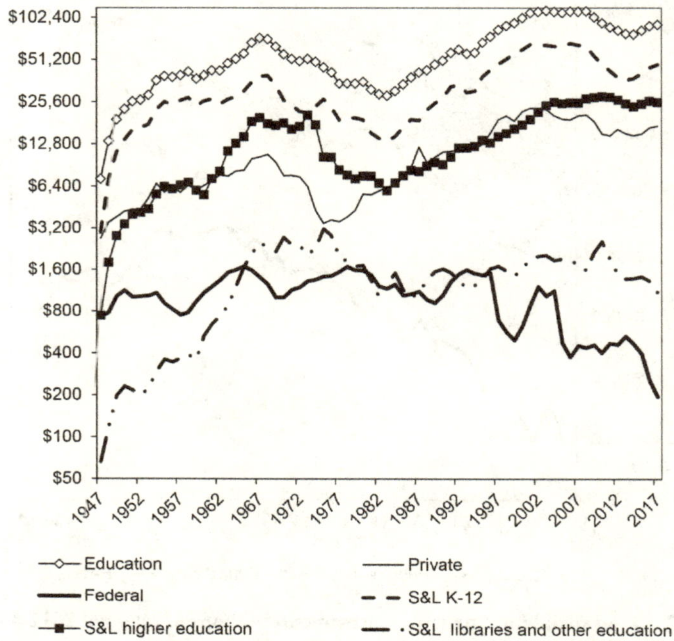


**Fig. 1.14 Real social infrastructure investment: Education, millions of chained 2012 dollars**

lowed long up-and-down waves, rising through the late 1960s, falling back through the early 1980s, rising again through the early 2000s, and then generally drifting lower. The pattern mainly results from trends in investment in K-12 school structures by state and local governments, which presumably reflect demographic and budgetary trends. State and local government investment in higher education peaked in 1973, fell afterward, resumed rising in the early 1980s, but has flattened out since then. Private education investment (all grades) reached $11 billion in 1968, then fell and resumed rising in the late 1970s, but began moving lower, on balance, in the early 2000s.

Public safety, a much smaller part of social infrastructure, rose through the 1990s to $11 billion in 1998, but then declined afterward (figure 1.15). This decline resulted mostly from declines in investment in correctional facilities by state, local, and federal government and by private companies.

Real net stocks of social infrastructure rose substantially over these years, and most of the increase occurred because of increases in education (especially K-12) and health-related stocks (equipment and structures, table 1.1).

For social infrastructure, the share of privately owned net stock grew

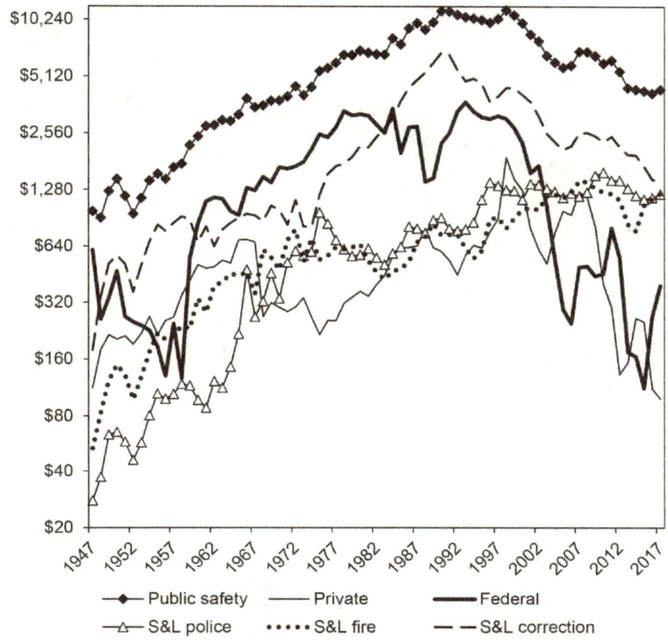


**Fig. 1.15 Real social infrastructure investment: Public safety, millions of chained 2012 dollars**

over time, while the share of stock owned by state and local government fell (table 1.3). The main driver of this shift is the growth of the stock of health infrastructure, which is mostly owned by the private sector.

### *1.4.1.4 Digital Infrastructure*

Investment in digital infrastructure rose from about $25 billion annually in the 1980s to almost $250 billion in 2017 (figure 1.16). The sharp increase in digital infrastructure since the 1990s came about because of increases in investment in private communications equipment in NAICS 513 and 514 as well as investment in software and computers in these industries. These increases in real investment partly reflect work by BEA and others to quality-adjust the prices of these assets. Interestingly, the pattern of investment in communications structures since the 1990s has been more mixed. This category—which accounted for a modest share of digital investment—includes cell towers but also includes old-fashioned telephone switching structures. Over these decades, the equipment and intellectual property shares of digital infrastructure have increased, while the structures share has fallen.

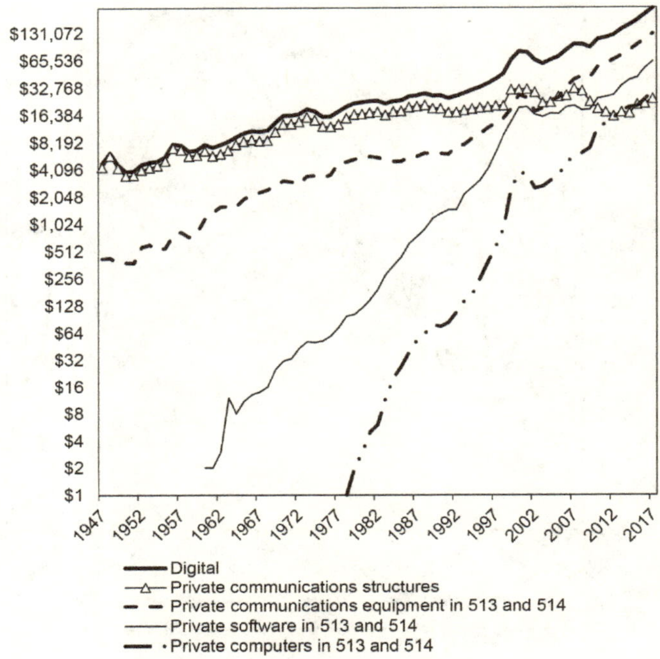


**Fig. 1.16 Real digital infrastructure investment, millions of chained 2012 dollars**

While the net stocks of these digital assets have increased substantially over time, as one would expect (table 1.1), the increase in the net stocks and the net stock shares of equipment, software, and computers is perhaps not as rapid as one might expect because depreciation rates for these assets are far higher than the rates for structures. Note that the assets we have classified as digital infrastructure have always been entirely private (table 1.3).

#### *1.4.1.5 Net Investment per Capita*

Gross investment gauges the resources devoted to infrastructure in a particular year. However, in terms of how much this investment is augmenting the stock of infrastructure, we must account for depreciation; a sizable slice of infrastructure investment simply covers depreciation. (Recall that to count as investment rather than maintenance and repair, spending must be for significant improvements rather than just for routine maintenance, which counts as a current expense rather than investment.) Moreover, as the population increases, demands on infrastructure would, all else being equal, likely increase. Accordingly, we pivot to examine real net infrastructure investment per capita.

For total infrastructure, depreciation is sizable, and, on a per capita

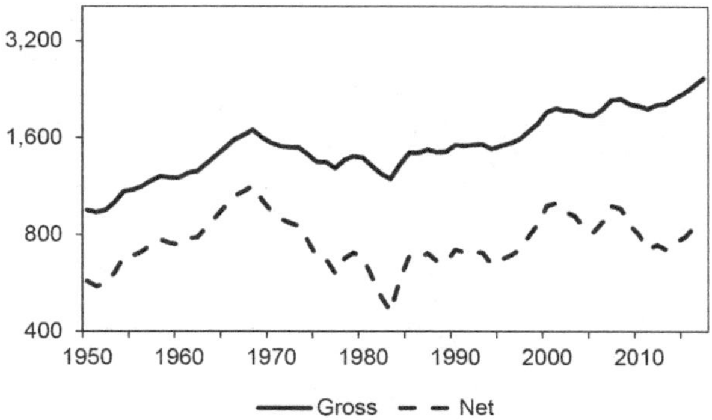


**Fig. 1.17 Real total infrastructure investment per capita, gross and net, ratio scale**

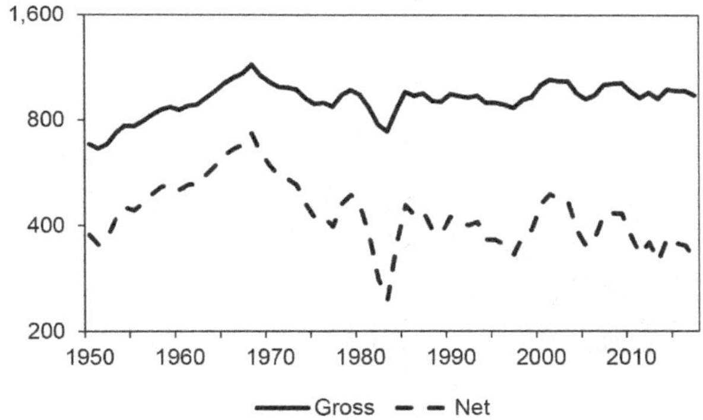


**Fig. 1.18 Real basic infrastructure investment per capita, gross and net, ratio scale**

basis, the gap between gross and net investment in overall infrastructure has widened during the past 20 years, as reported in figure 1.17. This gap had been growing slowly in earlier decades, but more recently the divergence has become more noticeable. Thus, despite gradual increases in real budget resources being allocated to infrastructure (as measured by real gross investment in infrastructure), actual additions to the real capital stock per capita have been considerably weaker.

In terms of the components of total infrastructure, for basic infrastructure (figure 1.18), real net investment per capita has drifted downward since the financial crisis and stands at its lowest level since the series hit bottom in 1983. For social infrastructure (figure 1.19), real net investment per capita trended up from the mid-1980s through 2007, but then dropped back considerably after the financial crisis (though with a slight pickup in recent years). For digital infrastructure (figure 1.20), real net investment per capita trended

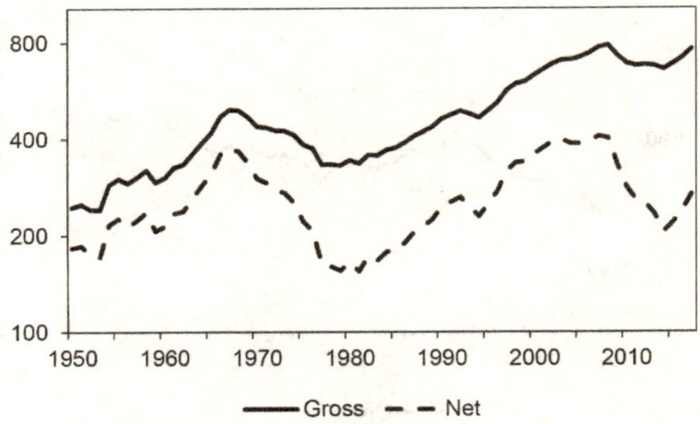


**Fig. 1.19 Real social infrastructure investment per capita, gross and net, ratio scale**

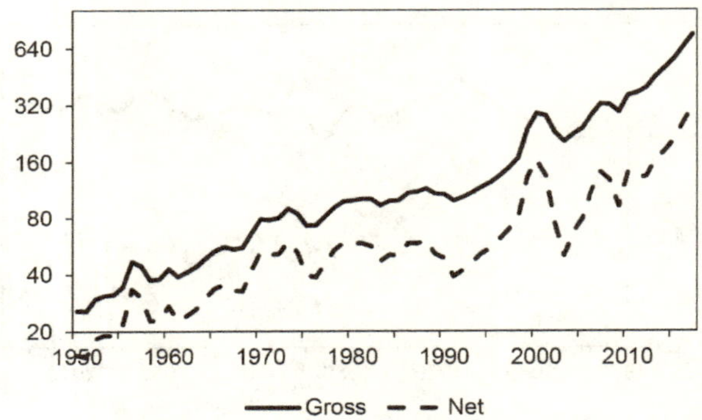


**Fig. 1.20 Real digital infrastructure investment per capita, gross and net, ratio scale**

up noticeably, on balance, since the 1950s, with a pickup in the second half of the 1990s (initial development of the internet), a drop back after 2000, and very rapid growth since then.

## 1.4.2 Real Net Capital Stocks per Capita

Another metric for assessing infrastructure is the growth rate of real net capital stocks per capita.

### *1.4.2.1 Overview*

Like net investment, this metric focuses on growth of infrastructure that is being used. This metric also can be linked to productivity outcomes. Such growth rates would feed directly into a growth accounting analysis that assessed contributions of infrastructure capital to productivity growth (perhaps adjusted by hours rather than population, depending on the question being asked). And, of course, a simple one-sector Solow growth model

**Table 1.4 Real net capital stock, by type of infrastructure (annual percentage change)**

| | 1997–2007 | 2007–2017 |
|---|---|---|
| Total | 1.2 | 1.0 |
| Basic | 0.6 | 0.6 |
| Social | 2.2 | 1.2 |
| Digital | 3.7 | 4.5 |
| Memo | | |
| Total factor productivity growth, private business | 1.5 | 0.4 |
| Real GDP per capita | 2.1 | 0.7 |

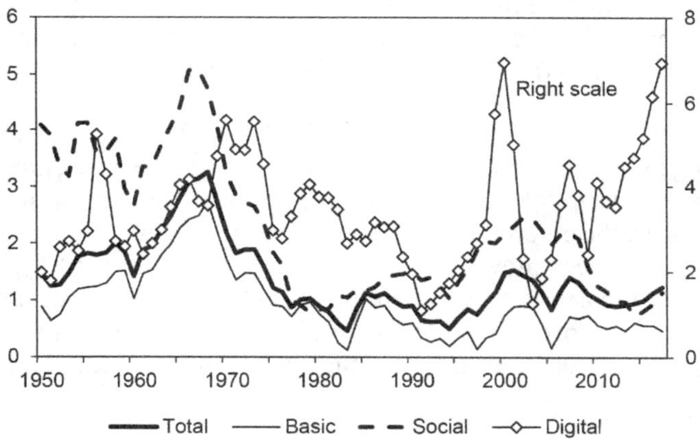


**Fig. 1.21 Real net capital stock per capita (percent change)**

would imply that capital per person should, at least in steady state, grow roughly in line with the growth rate of labor augmenting total factor productivity (TFP). (Multisector Solow models would have differential trends in capital stocks depending on trends in relative prices of different types of capital.) Thus, comparisons of the growth rates of real capital stocks per capita provide a very rough metric for thinking about whether infrastructure is growing rapidly or slowly relative to other economic trends, though such comparisons say nothing about the optimality of a particular growth rate of infrastructure.

Focusing on this metric, the growth rates of real net capital stocks by category are reported in table 1.4 over selected periods and in figure 1.21, with growth rates of TFP and real GDP per capita also shown in the table (from the BLS Multifactor Productivity database; Bureau of Labor Statistics 2019).

The growth rate of basic infrastructure has been steady at a sluggish rate, below that of TFP from 1997–2007 and just barely above the very slow rate of TFP growth that has prevailed since 2007. The growth rate of social infrastructure stepped down considerably since the financial crisis, though with growth rates well above TFP in both periods. Digital infrastructure continues to grow rapidly—even faster in the past 10 years than in the previous decade. (In figure 1.21, note the separate scale on right for digital infrastructure.) We do not draw powerful inferences from these comparisons with TFP growth rates, but it does appear that capital stocks of basic infrastructure have grown slowly over the past 20 years relative to other trends in the economy.

All told, these metrics seem consistent with underinvestment in some key types of infrastructure. While we have not developed a model of optimal infrastructure, we note that Allen and Arkolakis (2019) compare the benefits of additional highway construction to the costs and find large but heterogeneous welfare gains from additional highway construction.

### *1.4.2.2 Details for Basic, Social, and Digital Infrastructure*

Among the components of basic infrastructure (figure 1.22), growth rates of the real net capital stock per capita have been quite weak in the past 10 years, with the exception of the power category. Growth rates for water and sewer have been moving lower since 1970; over the past 10 years, they have dropped to about 0, after running at a bit less than 1 percent since the late 1990s. Transportation growth rates have also dropped to about 0, after running at less than 1 percent since the late 1980s. And, conservation and

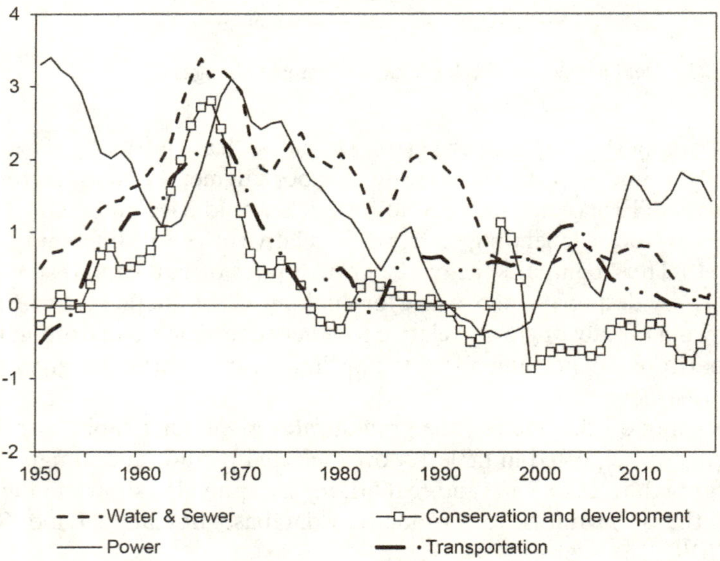


**Fig. 1.22 Real net capital stock per capita for components of basic, three-year average annual growth rate**

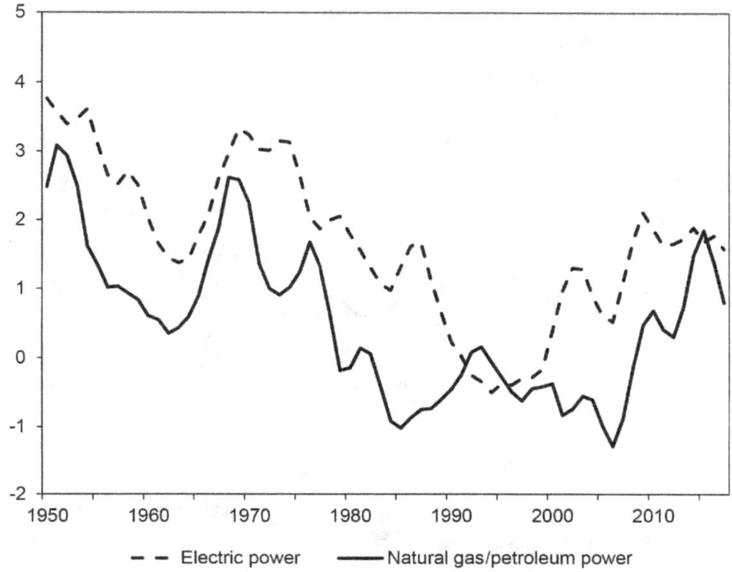


**Fig. 1.23 Real net capital stock per capita for components of power, three-year average annual growth rate**

development stocks have been falling since about 2000. In these categories, gross investment just has not been sufficient to keep up with depreciation and population growth.

Power infrastructure is the only category that has seen stronger growth since the financial crisis. Power infrastructure is now rising at about a 1.5 percent pace, well above its rather sluggish rate of growth during the 1990s and mid-2000s. Within the power sector (figure 1.23), growth rates of real net capital stocks per capita for electric power have picked up in recent years, reaching 1–2 percent, comparable to rates in the 1980s. Recent growth rates come on the heels of a period of essentially no growth from 1990 to 2000. Growth rates prior to the 1980s were, in general, more rapid, in the 2–3 percent range. Growth rates for natural gas and petroleum follow a broadly similar pattern to those for electric power, although the growth rates are, with just a couple of exceptions, uniformly lower.

Within the electric power category (figure 1.24), growth rates of real net capital stocks per capita for wind and solar power structures have been striking (separate scale on the right for this category). (The nominal capital stock of this category was 8.3 percent of the nominal stock of electric power capital in 2017.) These growth rates have been quite volatile, reaching as high as 45 percent over a three-year period in the late 2000s. Most recently, these rates have come down to about 5 percent. Electric power structures and electrical transmission equipment have remained quite sluggish in

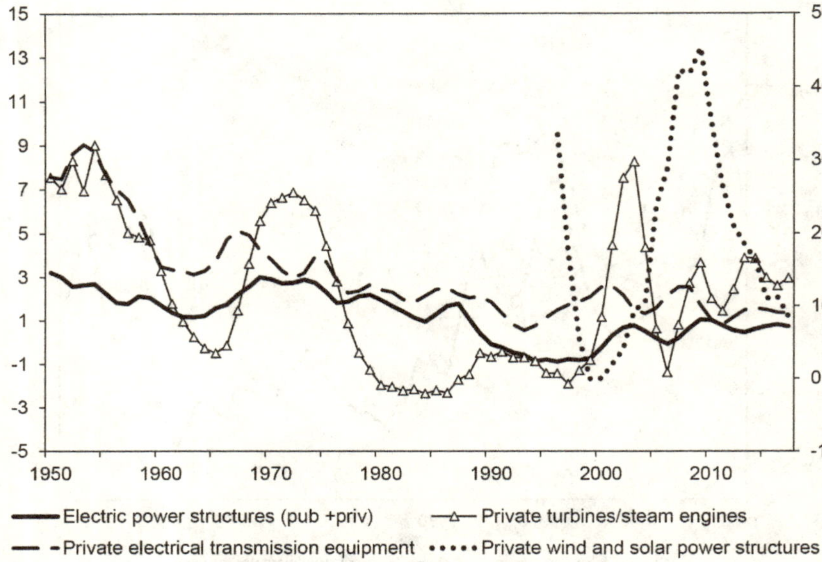


**Fig. 1.24 Real net capital stock per capita for components of electric power, three-year average annual growth rate**

recent decades. Growth rates for turbines and steam engines (equipment used within electric power plants to generate electricity) have risen to about a 3 percent pace in recent years, though growth has been more volatile than those for power structures and transmission equipment.

Within the transportation category (figure 1.25), the growth rate of the net capital stock per capita for highways and streets has moved down to about 0 percent years after rising at about a 1 percent pace from the late 1980s through the early 2000s.[28] Air transportation had been growing quite robustly from the late 1980s through the early 2000s, but its growth rate also has dropped back more recently to just above 0. Transit has been growing quite slowly since the time of the financial crisis. Real net capital stock per capita of the other category (including water, rail, and some other very small categories) has been falling over the entire period since 1950, dragged down by rail, with only a small offset from growth in water transportation infrastructure. On the whole, these patterns are consistent with narratives of aging transportation infrastructure that is not keeping up with demographic trends.

Growth rates of the real net stock per capita of social infrastructure are

28. For additional analysis of public spending on transportation and water infrastructure see Congressional Budget Office (2018). In addition, Barbara Fraumeni has done extensive work on highway infrastructure; see Fraumeni (1999, 2007).

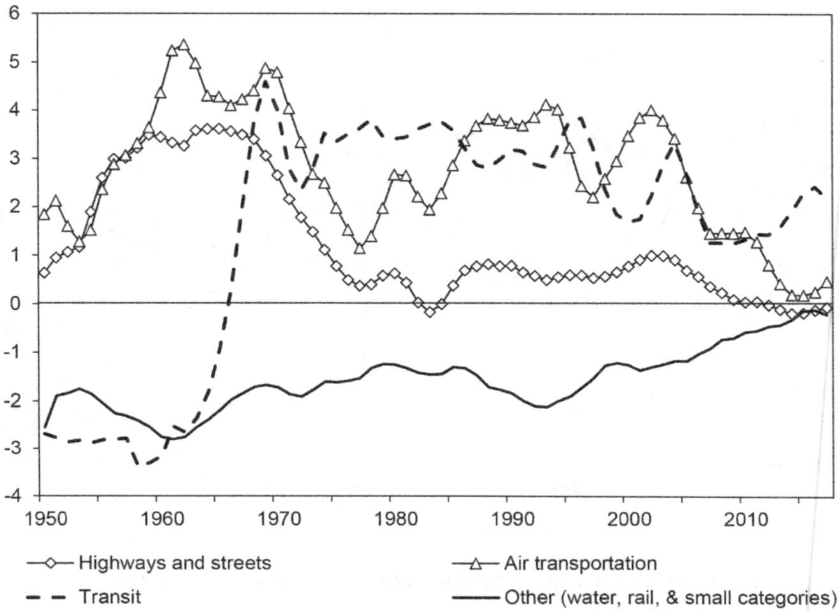


**Fig. 1.25 Real net capital stock per capita for components of transportation, three-year average annual growth rate**

reported in figure 1.26. Education, the largest category, has been growing very slowly in recent years following a surge in the early 2000s. This slow growth is perhaps not surprising given actual and projected declines in the school-age population. Within education (figure 1.27), growth rates for all of the major categories (state and local K-12, state and local higher education, and private) have followed similar patterns, driven in part by the size of the school-age population. Growth rates for these categories currently range from less than 1 percent to about 1.5 percent.

Health has been growing about 2 percent a year since the mid-2000s, a relatively slow pace relative to historical growth rates for this category of infrastructure (figure 1.26). Within health, growth rates of real net stocks of capital per capita have slowed for most major categories over the past 10 years (figure 1.28). Growth rates for private hospitals and state and local hospitals have slowed to below 1 percent, as has the growth rate of other health structures (doctors' offices and other nonhospital medical facilities). One exception to this pattern of relatively sluggish growth is in medical equipment (note the separate scale on right). The growth rates for this category have dropped back following a very strong pace in the 2000s but remain around 5 percent. Nominal capital stock shares have moved quite noticeably within the health category, as shown in figure 1.29. The share of

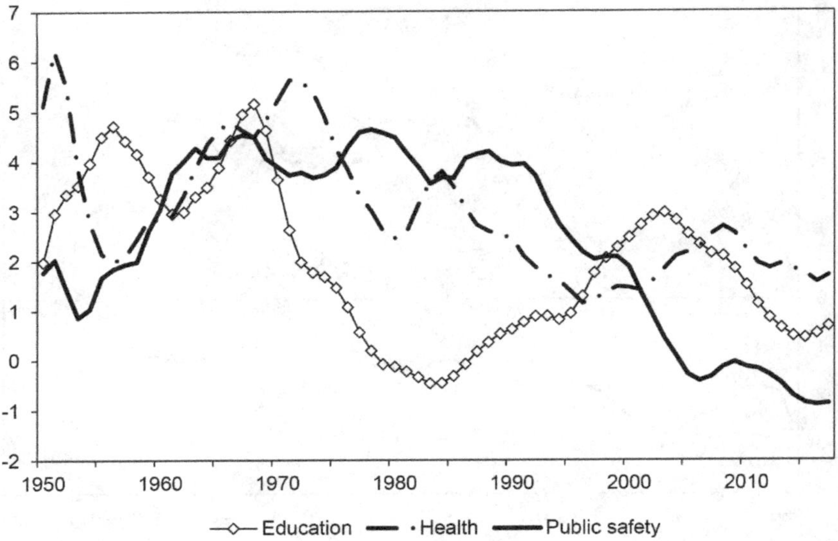


**Fig. 1.26 Real net capital stock per capita for components of social, three-year average annual growth rate**

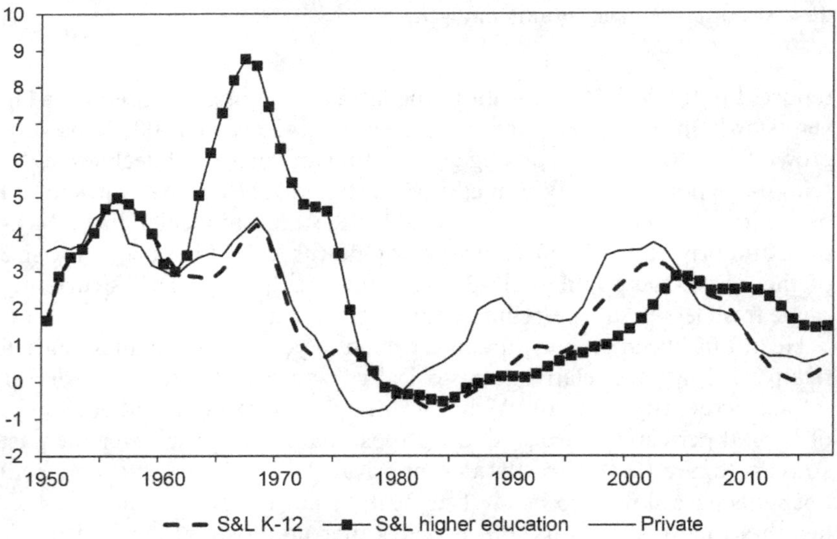


**Fig. 1.27 Real net capital stock per capita for selected components of education, three-year average annual growth rate**

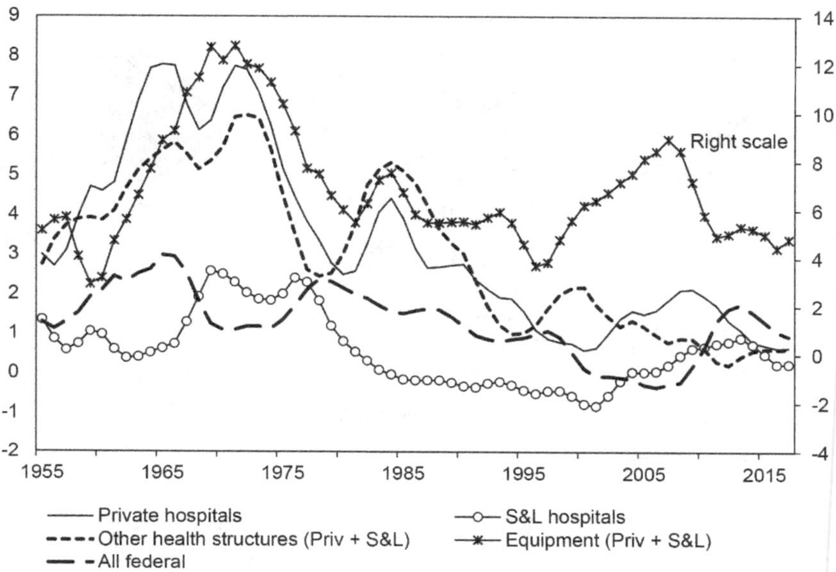


**Fig. 1.28 Real net capital stock per capita for selected components of health, three-year average annual growth rate**

private hospitals has risen considerably since 1957, while the share of state and local hospitals has dropped back. The other big shift is for the share of medical equipment, which now accounts for about one-quarter of the health infrastructure stock.

Public safety is a small share of social infrastructure, but perhaps one that looms large in the public's perception of state and local governments (share of nominal capital stock within social was 2 percent in 2017). The net capital stock for this category has fallen on a per capita basis since the mid-2000s (figure 1.26).

Turning to digital infrastructure, real net capital stocks per capita for most components of digital have grown very rapidly, as reported in figure 1.30. (Recall that our definition of digital infrastructure includes private, but not public, assets.) The one exception to rapid growth is private communications structures. After this category experienced 2–4 percent growth rates through the 1990s, growth rates have drifted down and have been near 0 in recent years (see left scale of figure). (Again, recall that this category includes both newer cell towers and also structures that once housed now-outdated telephone switching equipment.) Other categories in figure 1.30 capture infrastructure used for broadcast and telecom services and for cloud computing. The broadcast and telecommunications category is identified by BEA's industry code 513. Isolating cloud computing in the accounts is difficult because of the lack of complete granularity for key categories, but

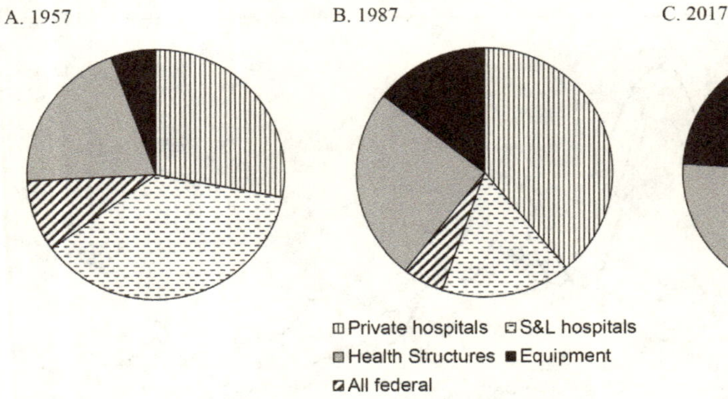


**Fig. 1.29 Nominal net capital stock shares, health**

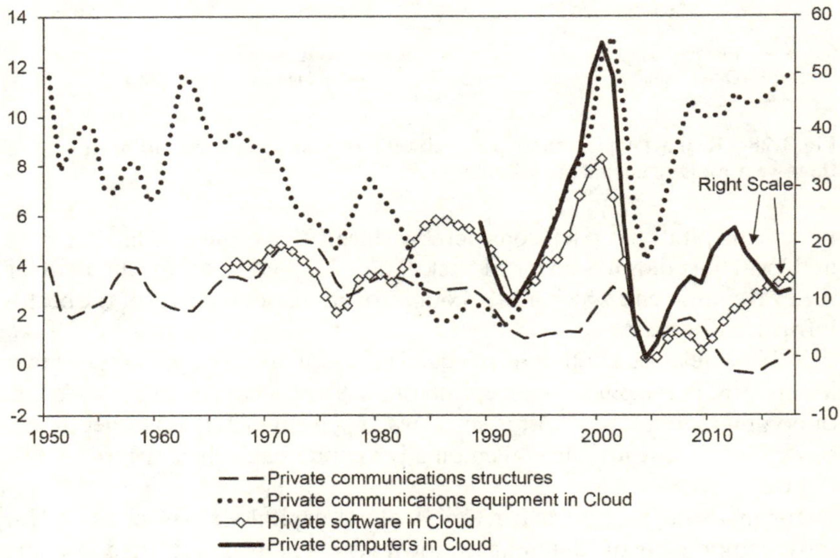


**Fig. 1.30 Real net capital stock per capita for components of digital, three-year average annual growth rate**

we focus on the BEA industry of data processing, internet publishing, and information services (industry code 514). Hence, to capture digital infrastructure we focus on computers, communications equipment, and software assets in these two industry groups.[29] Computers and software have grown

29. As noted, we ideally would include the structures containing data centers as well as the equipment and software in the data centers. Data centers are likely classified as office structures; however, the data are not granular enough to isolate data centers. Office construction within

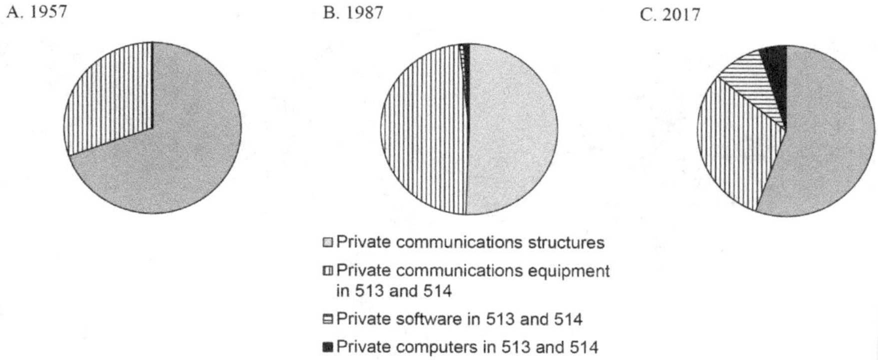


**Fig. 1.31 Nominal net capital stock shares, digital**

extremely rapidly in recent decades (note right scale in figure 1.30), and each category has been rising about 15 percent a year recently. Infrastructure for communications equipment within 513 and 514 also has increased quite rapidly in recent decades, increasing at a 10–12 percent pace in recent years.

Within the digital infrastructure category, shares of the nominal net capital stock have shifted notably during past decades, as reported in figure 1.31. In 1957, communications structures made up close to three-fourths of the category, with private communications equipment in 513 and 514 making up the rest. By 1987, the share of private communications equipment in 513 and 514 had grown to nearly half, with the share of communications structures dropping back to about half. And, by 2017, the explosion in computers and software in industry groups 513 and 514 is evident, with the share of equipment identified specifically as communications equipment in these industries dropping back.

### 1.4.3 New Prototype Measures of Highway Investment by State

BEA does not currently estimate fixed assets by state or region; however, for this chapter, we have developed new prototype estimates of highway and street gross investment (nominal and real) for each state for 1992 through 2017. Highways are a natural place to start developing regional data, given that the highway category is the single largest category of infrastructure in the US; we believe this effort could be a first step in developing additional regional data on infrastructure.

State shares were derived from state and local outlays of highway capital published in Government Finances Survey by the US Census Bureau for

industries acquiring digital infrastructure jumped after 2012 and has been robust recently, perhaps reflecting, in part, a surge in data center construction. These observations suggest that greater granularity to isolate data centers in the National Economic Accounts would be valuable.

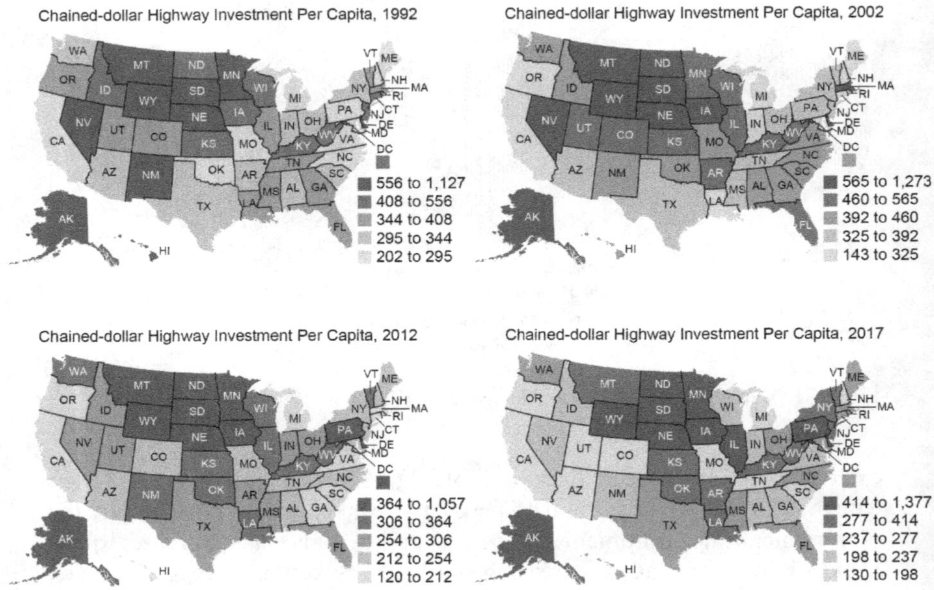


U.S. Bureau of Economic Analysis

**Fig. 1.32 Gross highway real (chained) investment per capita by state, 1992, 2002, 2012, 2017**

various years.[30] These shares were interpolated over missing years and then shares for each year-state pair were applied to current-dollar highway (regular and toll combined) gross investment to estimate investment for each state for each year. The price deflator for each state was set equal to the national deflator and chained-dollar real quantities were developed.

We summarize the estimates in state-by-state heat maps, with figure 1.32 reporting real investment per capita by state for 1992, 2002, 2012, and 2017, and figure 1.33 showing nominal investment as a share of nominal GDP by state for the same years. We draw the following conclusions from these data:

- The upper Midwest and north central states (including Iowa, Minnesota, Nebraska, North Dakota, South Dakota, and Wyoming) consistently ranked in the highest quintile for real gross investment per capita for all time periods shown; the same is true for nominal investment as a share of GDP. Perhaps not surprisingly, Allen and Arkolakis (2019)

30. As a result of measurement and timing issues, the Census Bureau's highway capital outlays do not equal BEA's state and local highway investment. Highway capital outlays from the Census Bureau were obtained for fiscal years 1993, 1996, 2002, 2009, 2013, and 2016.

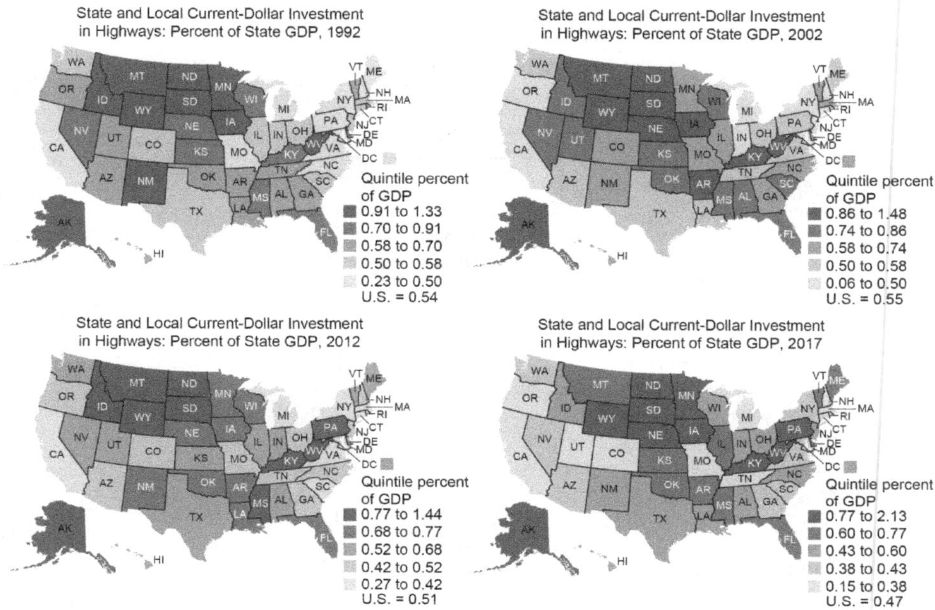


U.S. Bureau of Economic Analysis

**Fig. 1.33 Gross highway investment as share of GDP by state, 1992, 2002, 2012, 2017**

find relatively low welfare benefits from additional highway construction in these states.

- In contrast, many of the states in the western US—Arizona, California, Colorado, Oregon, and Utah—ranked in the lower quintiles for per capita investment in 2017, although this is a new development for some of these states (Colorado and Utah). Allen and Arkolakis (2019) find large welfare benefits from additional highway construction in California. (They also find very large benefits for additional construction in the greater New York City area.)
- While nominal investment as a share of GDP peaked in the early 2000s for most states, this metric continued to increase from 1992 to 2017 in three states: North Dakota, Pennsylvania, and Vermont.
- For most states, the rankings of real investment per capita by state and nominal investment per GDP by state are very similar; however, this was not the case for New York in 2017. Real highway investment per capita for New York exceeded the national average in 2017 based on a small decrease in population for the state compared to its highway investment; in contrast, nominal investment in these assets as a share of GDP fell below the national average for the year.

**Table 1.5** **BEA depreciation rates and service lives**

| | Depreciation rates | | Service lives | |
|---|---|---|---|---|
| | Fraumeni (1997) | BEA (current) | Fraumeni (1997) | BEA (current) |
| Government (federal, state, and local) | | | | |
| Buildings | | | | |
| Industrial | .0285 | .0285 | 32 | 32 |
| Educational | .0182 | .0182 | 50 | 50 |
| Hospital | .0182 | .0182 | 50 | 50 |
| Other | .0182 | .0182 | 50 | 50 |
| Nonbuildings | | | | |
| Highways and streets | .0152 | .0202 | 60 | 45 |
| Conservation and development | .0152 | .0152 | 60 | 60 |
| Sewer systems | .0152 | .0152 | 60 | 60 |
| Water systems | .0152 | .0152 | 60 | 60 |
| Other | .0152 | .0152 | 60 | 60 |
| Private structures | | | | |
| Educational | .0188 | .0188 | 48 | 48 |
| Hospitals (B) | .0188 | .0188 | 48 | 48 |
| Railroad replacement track | .0249 | .0249 | 38 | 38 |
| Railroad other structures | .0176 | .0176 | 54 | 54 |
| Communications | .0237 | .0237 | 40 | 40 |
| Electric light and power | .0237 | .0211 | 45 | 45 |
| Gas | .0237 | .0237 | 40 | 40 |
| Petroleum pipelines | .0237 | .0237 | 40 | 40 |
| Wind and solar | | .0303 | | 30 |
| Local transit | .0237 | .0237 | 38 | 38 |

*Source*: Fraumeni (1997) and Bureau of Economic Analysis (2013).

### 1.4.4 Depreciation Rates and Service Lives

Depreciation rates developed in Fraumeni (1997) largely were adopted by BEA at that time. Table 1.5 reports the depreciation rates and asset service lives from Fraumeni along with the latest updated estimates from BEA. Rates for infrastructure assets have been updated from Fraumeni for only two assets: (1) highways and streets and (2) solar and wind electric generation equipment (which was not included in the 1997 estimates). As can be seen by scanning down the table, depreciation rates for basic and social infrastructure assets are quite low, accompanied by long service lives. Typical depreciation rates are in the neighborhood of 2 percent or so a year, with service lives ranging from 40 to 60 years.

As noted, Fraumeni's estimates drew heavily on the work of Hulten and Wykoff. Their work was done in the late 1970s and early 1980s, and these estimates largely are still in use today. Accordingly, the information underlying depreciation rates for most infrastructure assets dates back almost 40 years. While it is possible that infrastructure assets depreciate at similar rates today as compared with 40 years ago, this time lapse also points to the desirability of revisiting estimates of depreciation rates.

Moreover, Hulten and Wykoff's estimates of depreciation rates for most infrastructure assets were based on a relatively thin information set. Hulten and Wykoff assigned assets to three categories depending on how much information the researchers had about age-price profiles for each asset type. For Type A assets, Hulten and Wykoff had extensive data available for estimating geometric depreciation rates. For Type B assets, Hulten and Wykoff had more limited data and so relied on a variety of other studies to estimate depreciation rates. For Type C assets, Hulten and Wykoff had no data available and obtained depreciation rates by using information from Type A or Type B assets for which the researchers had more information.

Except for privately owned hospitals, all infrastructure assets listed in table 1.5 are Type C assets. Accordingly, these estimates are pieced together based on a variety of estimates for other asset types. Put another way, depreciation rates for infrastructure assets reflect very little direct information about depreciation patterns for these asset types. On reflection, this observation is perhaps not so surprising, given that publicly owned infrastructure or privately owned infrastructure-like assets trade infrequently, so obtaining prices or valuations of these assets as they age is extremely difficult. Moreover, many of these assets have unique characteristics, also making valuation over time difficult.

#### *1.4.4.1 Cross-Country Comparisons of Depreciation Rates*

We can gain further perspective on US depreciation rates by comparing them to those in other countries for comparable assets. Table 1.6 compares US depreciation rates for three types of infrastructure assets (hospitals, schools, and roads) to those for six other countries that also use geometric depreciation rates. These comparisons are based on a Eurostat/OECD study from 2016, and the choice of categories reflects the coverage in that study. For all three asset types, US depreciation rates are at the lower end of the

**Table 1.6 Official depreciation rates for selected assets (for countries using geometric depreciation rates)**

| | Hospitals | Schools | Roads |
|---|---|---|---|
| US | .0188 | .0182 | .0202 |
| Austria | .021 | .020 | .030 |
| Canada | .061 | .055 | .106 |
| Iceland | .025 | .025 | .030 |
| Japan | .059 | .059 | .033 |
| Norway | .040 | .040 | .033 |
| Sweden | .0188 | .0182 | .0202 |

*Source*: Eurostat/OECD (2015), 12.

range. Indeed, other than for Sweden (where rates match those in the US), all other countries report higher depreciation rates. Depreciation rates in some countries are more than twice as high as those in the US.

Specifically, for hospitals and schools, Canada, Japan, and Norway use rates that are more than twice as high as those in the US. For roads, all other countries (except for Sweden) have higher rates than the US, with Canada's rate being nearly five times higher than the depreciation rate in the US.

A more detailed comparison with Canada highlights other assets in which Canada uses higher depreciation rates for infrastructure assets. Table 1.7 reports depreciation rates and service lives for a range of infrastructure

**Table 1.7 Comparisons of depreciation rates and service lives for selected infrastructure assets, United States and Canada**

| | Depreciation rates (%) | | Service lives (years) | |
|---|---|---|---|---|
| | USA | Canada[a] | USA | Canada[a] |
| Private structures | | | | |
| Educational | .0188 | .055[b] | 48 | 40[b] |
| Hospitals | .0188 | .061[b] | 48 | 36[b] |
| Railroad replacement track | .0249 | .053[b] | 38 | 27[b] |
| Railroad other structures | .0176 | .056[b] | 54 | 37[b] |
| Communications | .0237 | .128[b] | 40 | 20[b] |
| Electric light and power | .0211 | .058[b] | 45 | 38[b] |
| Gas | .0237 | .066[b] | 40 | 34[b] |
| Petroleum pipelines | .0237 | .078[b] | 40 | 29[b] |
| Water supply | .0225 | .057 | 40 | 39[b] |
| Sewer and waste disposal | .0225 | .078[b] | 40 | 29[b] |
| Wind and solar | .0303 | .065 | 30 | 34 |
| Local transit | .0237 | .075[b] | 38 | 29[b] |
| Government (federal, state, and local) | | | | |
| Buildings | | | | |
| Industrial | .0285 | .072[b] | 32 | 25[b] |
| Educational | .0182 | .055[b] | 50 | 40[b] |
| Hospital | .0182 | .061[b] | 50 | 36[b] |
| Other | .0182 | | 50 | |
| Nonbuildings | | | | |
| Highways and streets | .0202 | .106[b] | 45 | 29[b] |
| Conservation and development | .0152 | .076[b] | 60 | 29[b] |
| Water systems | .0152 | .057 | 60 | 39[b] |
| Sewer systems | .0152 | .078[b] | 60 | 29[b] |
| Other | .0152 | | 60 | |

[a] The figures for Canada reported for government infrastructure are for the corresponding category of private buildings and nonbuildings. Estimates for Canada are from Giandrea et al. (2018) unless noted otherwise.

[b] Estimates from Statistics Canada (2015).

*Source:* For Canada, Giandrea et al. (2018), table 1, and Statistics Canada (2015), appendix C; for United States, Fraumeni (1997) and Bureau of Economic Analysis (2013).

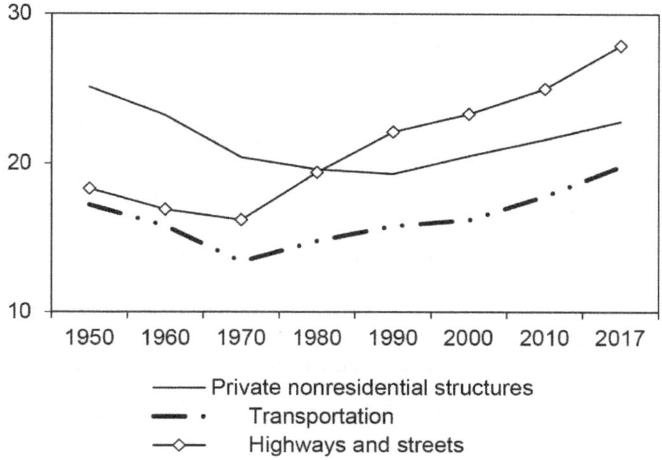


**Fig. 1.34 Average age of basic government infrastructure, current-cost basis (years)**

assets for the US and Canada. For both privately owned and publicly owned assets, the Canadian rates are uniformly higher. Again, for the assets listed in the table, the Canadian rates are at least more than double those used in the US.

### *1.4.4.2 Revisiting Depreciation Rate Estimates*

As noted earlier, the long amount of time that has passed since US estimates of depreciation rates for infrastructure assets were developed, the relatively thin information set on which these estimates were based, and the differences between estimated rates in the US and other countries all point to the desirability of revisiting estimates of depreciation rates for infrastructure assets in the US.

## 1.4.5 Age of the Infrastructure Capital Stock

Another way to assess trends in infrastructure is by reviewing the age of the infrastructure stock. Government infrastructure has aged very dramatically in recent decades, based on the average age of infrastructure, as reported in figures 1.34–1.36, on a current-cost basis.[31] Figures 1.34 and 1.35 highlight categories of basic infrastructure, with notable increases for highways and streets, power, and conservation and development. Figure 1.36 reports social infrastructure ages, showing the rise in average ages of health

31. Current-cost age is calculated by tracking for each dollar of each type of capital the amount remaining in the stock each year. With these figures, an average age for each type of capital can be calculated for each year. These ages are then combined for each year to get an overall average age using the current cost for each type of capital in that year.

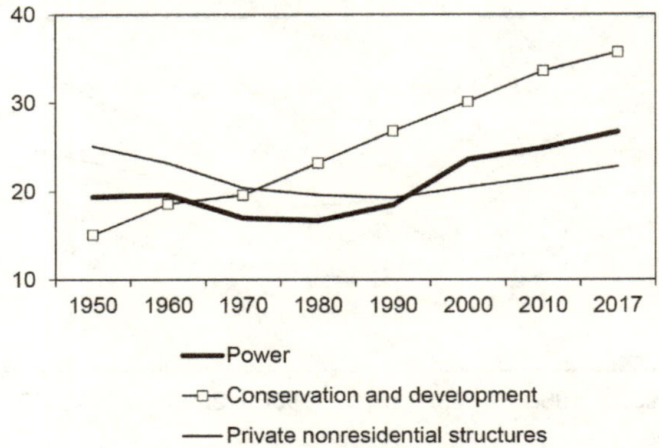


**Fig. 1.35 Average age of basic government infrastructure, current-cost basis (years)**

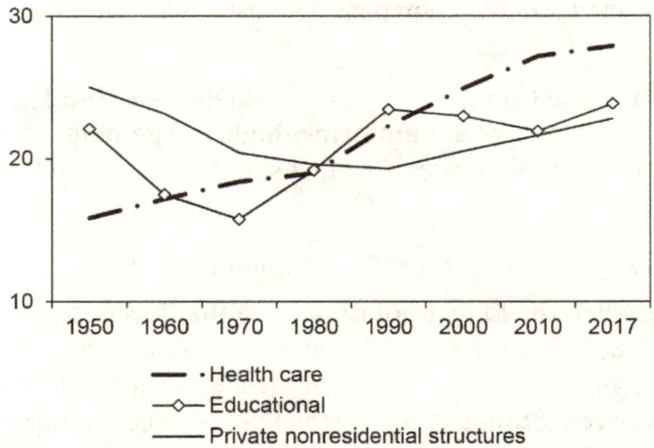


**Fig. 1.36 Average age of social government infrastructure, current-cost basis (years)**

care and educational infrastructure.[32] For comparison, the black dashed line in those figures plots the average age of private nonresidential structures. These assets have seen a gradual increase in age since about 1990, but to a lesser extent than the stock of government infrastructure.

Interpreting the increase in age for basic and social infrastructure is difficult without a model of optimal age, but the changes certainly are consistent with public narratives of aging infrastructure and investment not keeping up with growing needs as the population grows. To shed further light on

32. Private digital infrastructure has a short average age (in the neighborhood of two years recently for our definition). The average age moved lower from 1990 to 2000, moved back up by 2010, and has been mixed since then (with the age of computers rising and the age of software edging down).

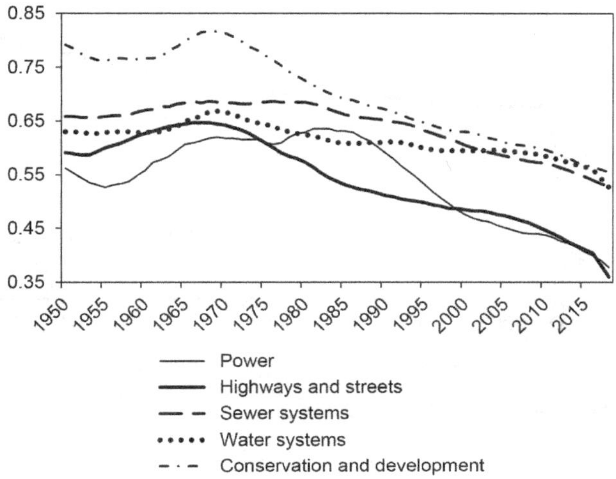


**Fig. 1.37 Remaining useful life ratios, state and local government infrastructure**

these issues, we turn to a metric introduced by Statistics Canada in 2017, a new measure referred to as "remaining useful life ratios." The remaining useful life of a given asset is the difference between the average age and the expected service life. The remaining useful life ratio is simply the remaining useful life divided by the expected service life. The resultant ratio indicates the percentage of the asset class that remains. The closer to zero, the older the asset relative to its expected service life.[33] We present this new metric for US data as another tool for assessing the overall state of infrastructure. Figure 1.37 presents remaining useful life ratios beginning with 1950 for basic infrastructure owned by state and local governments. The long-term trend shows that the remaining useful service lives for these asset types have all decreased.

Moreover, while average ages of US infrastructure generally have moved higher in recent decades, average ages of Canadian infrastructure have tended to move lower in the past 10 years. Figures 1.38–1.40 present comparisons for selected categories for which comparable categories and data were available on a historical-cost basis. As shown, for highways and communications structures, the average age of Canadian infrastructure has moved lower while the average age of US infrastructure in these categories has moved higher. In contrast, the average age of electric power structures is lower in the US than in Canada and has moved lower since the mid-2000s.

These graphs of average ages must be interpreted cautiously, because data limitations make feasible only a partial comparison to Canada. The

33. For information on Statistics Canada's remaining useful life ratios, see https://www150.statcan.gc.ca/n1/pub/13-604-m/13-604-m2017085-eng.htm.

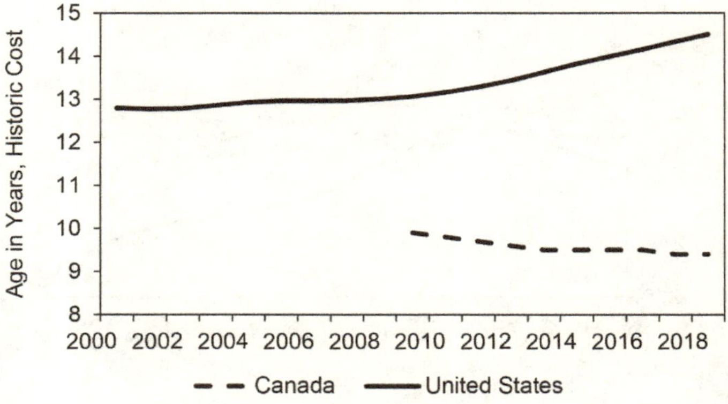


**Fig. 1.38 Average age, highways and streets**

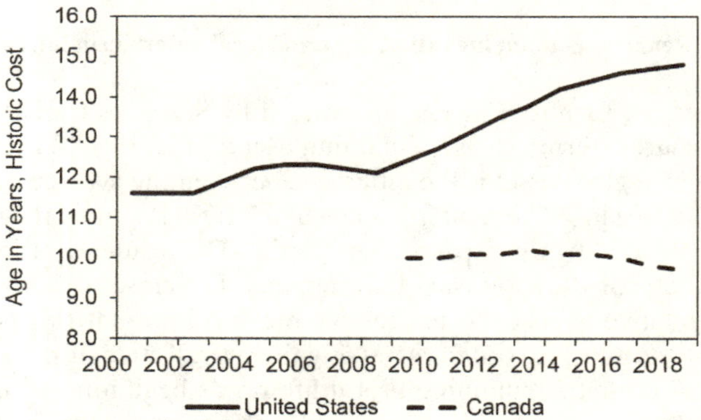


**Fig. 1.39 Average age, communications structures**

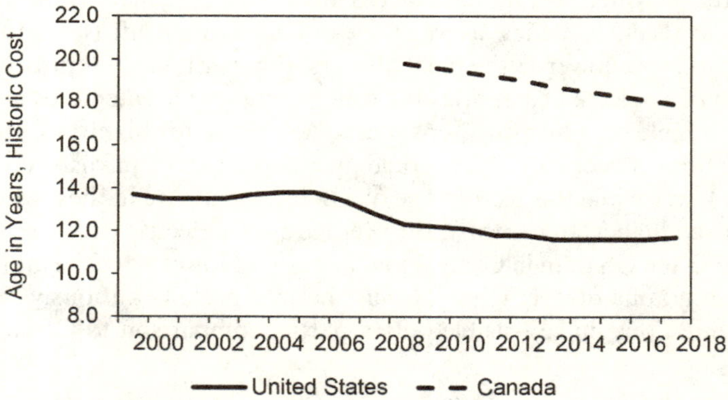


**Fig. 1.40 Average age, electric power structures**

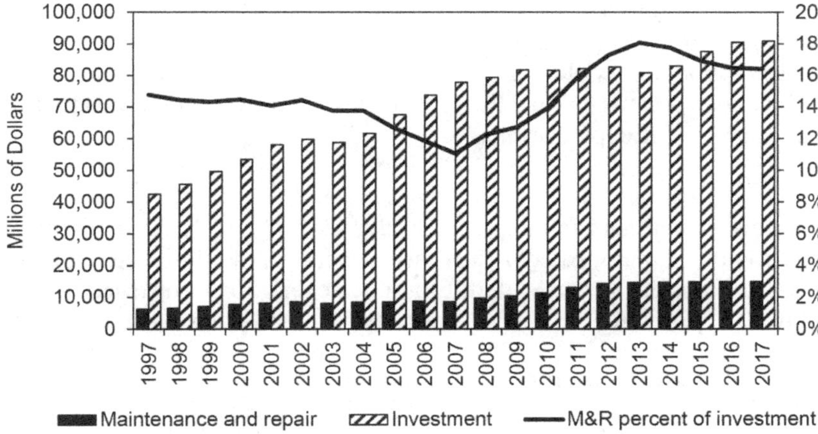


**Fig. 1.41 State and local highways and streets, maintenance and repair versus investment**

relevant Canadian data were available only starting in 2009 and only for select categories for which clean comparisons were possible. In addition, the Canadian data on average age are presented on a historical-cost basis, rather than the current-cost basis typically used for US data and reported in figures 1.34–1.36. Ages tend to be lower on a historical-cost basis because older assets still in service are aggregated up using purchase prices from long ago, which are lower than current prices for many assets.

### 1.4.6 Estimates of Maintenance and Repair

Trends in expenditures for maintenance and repair of infrastructure, while not part of infrastructure investment, may add useful detail to our portrait of infrastructure spending. Although estimates unique to specific infrastructure asset types generally are not available, estimates for state and local expenditures on maintenance and repair on highways and streets can be estimated from BEA's detailed benchmark supply-use tables. Figure 1.41 compares experimental estimates of maintenance and repair expenditures to total gross fixed investment for state and local highways and streets. The solid line in the chart is the ratio. This ratio declined from about 13 percent in 1997 to a little less than 10 percent in 2007; since then it has risen to a bit above 15 percent. In future work, we plan to explore the possibility of developing additional estimates of maintenance and repair for other types of infrastructure assets.

Estimates of maintenance and repair expenditures could be especially useful for developing richer models of depreciation. For example, Diewert (2005) develops a model in which maintenance expenditures can sustain the service flow from an asset. In his model, retirement decisions become endogenous (rather than a physical feature of an asset) and depend on how long an owner is willing to continue paying maintenance expenditures. Interestingly, Diewert's model still yields a geometric pattern of depreciation, though what lies behind that pattern would be more nuanced than in the standard application of geometric depreciation rates.

### 1.4.7 Prices

In this section, and in table 1.8 and figures 1.42 and 1.43, we highlight price trends for major categories of infrastructure. Additional figures show trends in some of the more interesting subcategories of infrastructure.

Overall, prices for infrastructure assets have trended more or less in

**Table 1.8 Infrastructure price indexes, average annual growth rates (percentage)**

| | 1947–2017 | 1947–1987 | 1987–2017 | 2000–2017 | 2000–2010 | 2010–2017 |
|---|---|---|---|---|---|---|
| GDP | 3.1 | 3.9 | 2.1 | 1.8 | 2.1 | 1.4 |
| Infrastructure | 3.6 | 4.8 | 2.1 | 1.2 | 2.2 | 0.0 |
| *Basic* | 4.0 | 4.6 | 3.1 | 3.4 | 4.6 | 1.9 |
| Water | 4.1 | 4.8 | 3.1 | 3.4 | 4.3 | 2.3 |
| Sewer | 4.1 | 5.0 | 3.1 | 3.4 | 4.3 | 2.3 |
| Conservation and development | 3.7 | 4.4 | 2.9 | 3.0 | 3.9 | 1.9 |
| Power | 3.8 | 4.8 | 2.6 | 2.5 | 3.3 | 1.6 |
| Electric power | 3.7 | 4.7 | 2.5 | 2.3 | 3.0 | 1.5 |
| Petroleum/natural gas | 4.1 | 4.6 | 3.6 | 4.0 | 5.4 | 2.3 |
| Transportation | 4.1 | 4.5 | 3.5 | 4.1 | 5.6 | 2.1 |
| Highways and streets | 4.0 | 4.2 | 3.7 | 4.3 | 6.1 | 2.1 |
| Air transportation | 4.0 | 4.2 | 3.6 | 3.8 | 4.8 | 2.6 |
| Water transportation | 4.0 | 4.2 | 3.7 | 3.9 | 5.3 | 2.3 |
| Rail transportation | 3.8 | 5.0 | 2.4 | 2.0 | 2.4 | 1.4 |
| Transit | . . . | . . . | 2.8 | 3.4 | 4.5 | 2.0 |
| *Social* | 3.7 | 4.8 | 2.2 | 1.9 | 3.2 | 0.2 |
| Public safety | 3.9 | 4.5 | 3.1 | 3.0 | 3.0 | 3.1 |
| Education | 4.1 | 4.7 | 3.4 | 3.6 | 4.9 | 2.0 |
| Health care | 3.2 | 4.6 | 1.3 | 0.1 | 1.0 | −1.1 |
| *Digital* | 1.8 | 4.2 | −1.2 | −3.7 | −3.9 | −3.5 |
| Communications structures | 3.1 | 3.4 | 2.6 | 2.9 | 4.3 | 1.1 |
| Communications equipment[a] | −1.1 | 2.3 | −5.3 | −7.6 | −8.3 | −6.8 |
| Communications software[a] | . . . | . . . | −2.0 | −1.6 | −2.3 | −0.7 |
| Computers[a] | . . . | . . . | −10.4 | −6.3 | −10.2 | −1.1 |

[a] Includes communications equipment, software, and computers used in the provision of digital services.

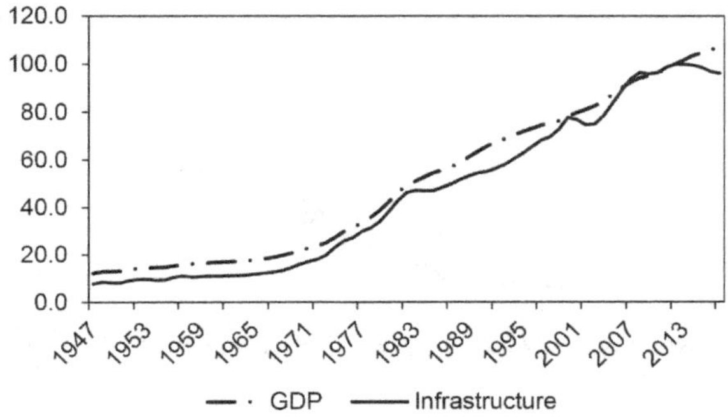


**Fig. 1.42 GDP and infrastructure, price indexes, 2012 = 100.0**

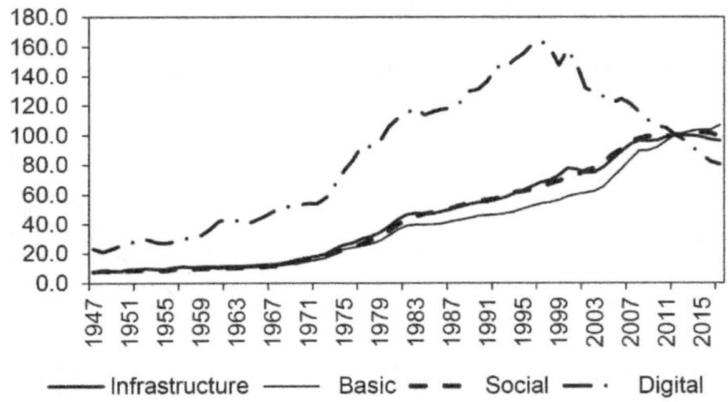


**Fig. 1.43 Total infrastructure, by type, price indexes, 2012 = 100.0**

line with GDP prices (figure 1.42) though infrastructure prices have risen somewhat faster. For the full period analyzed, 1947–2017, infrastructure prices increased at an average annual rate of 3.6 percent, while GDP prices increased 3.1 percent. Prices of infrastructure increased noticeably more rapidly than GDP prices in the first part of the sample (1947–1987) but about in line with GDP prices in the latter part of the sample. That being said, since 2010, overall infrastructure prices have changed little, a pace substantially below that for GDP prices. The softness in infrastructure prices since the financial crisis reflects a step-down in rates of increase for basic and social infrastructure. Within the social infrastructure category, prices for health care infrastructure actually have fallen since 2010, as a result of quality-adjusted price declines for medical equipment.

Table 1.8 and figure 1.43 disaggregate prices of total infrastructure into its basic, social, and digital components. Basic infrastructure accounts for most of total infrastructure, and its prices track overall infrastructure prices reasonably closely, especially in the first half of the period analyzed. In the latter part of the sample (especially since about 2000), prices of basic infra-

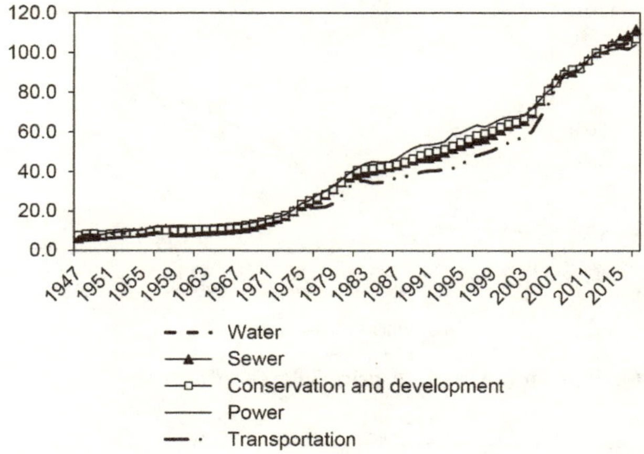


**Fig. 1.44 Basic infrastructure, price indexes, 2012 = 100.0**

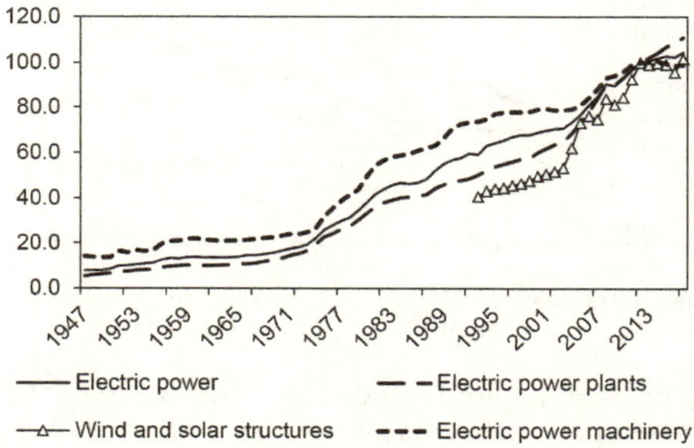


**Fig. 1.45 Electric power plants and machinery, price indexes, 2012 = 100.0**

structure have risen more rapidly than the overall price index. Because basic infrastructure consists mostly of structures, these price trends largely track trends in prices for construction.

Within basic infrastructure, transportation accounts for the largest share, and these prices grow steadily over all four periods analyzed (figure 1.46). Within transportation, highways and streets are by far the largest component; these prices became volatile and showed notable increases beginning in 1970 and continuing into the early 1980s, with an average annual price increase of about 10 percent from 1970 to 1982. Prices were generally more stable from the early 1980s until the latter half of the 2000s, when they began to increase notably again. Swings in overall construction costs and the price of petroleum by-products, which are inputs to the construction

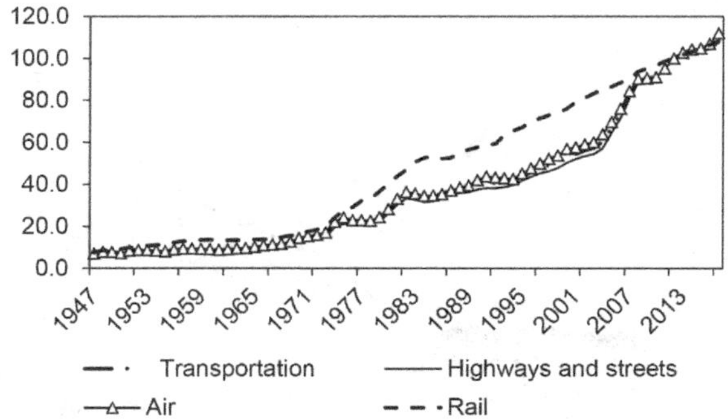


**Fig. 1.46 Transportation infrastructure, price indexes, 2012 = 100.0**

of highways and streets, could explain some of the variation in prices over time.

These relatively rapid price increases for highways and streets generally line up with those estimated by Brooks and Liscow (2019) for the cost per mile of Interstate Highway construction. They report that, in real terms, the cost per mile in 1990 was about three times higher than it was in the 1960s (from about $8 million per mile during most of the 1960s to $25 million per mile in 1990). Although Brooks and Liscow report moving averages over spans of years, if their time periods are converted to span, say, 1968 to 1990, the implied annual rate of increase is 5.3 percent. Over the same period, the price index in the National Economic Accounts for highways and streets exhibits an annual rate increase of 6 percent.

The second largest component within basic infrastructure is power, which primarily consists of private electric power plants and machinery (figure 1.45). Prices for electric power infrastructure were relatively flat from 1947 until the early 1970s but have grown quite a bit more rapidly since.

Within the power category, prices for electric power plants show relatively stable increases throughout these time periods, although we do observe a slowdown in price increases during the last few years.

Electric power machinery consists of turbines used to generate electricity as well as the equipment used for transmission and distribution. We observe relatively rapid increases in prices for this machinery from the early 1970s through the early 1990s. We also see an interesting trend in prices tied to increasing shares of imported machinery. In 1992, nearly 90 percent of this machinery was produced domestically, but by 2007 that figure had dropped to 60 percent, where it remains today. Over this period, prices for imported electric power machinery have been consistently lower than the price of competing domestic machinery, resulting in relatively modest price increases over this period.

Trends in prices for social infrastructure—mostly education and health

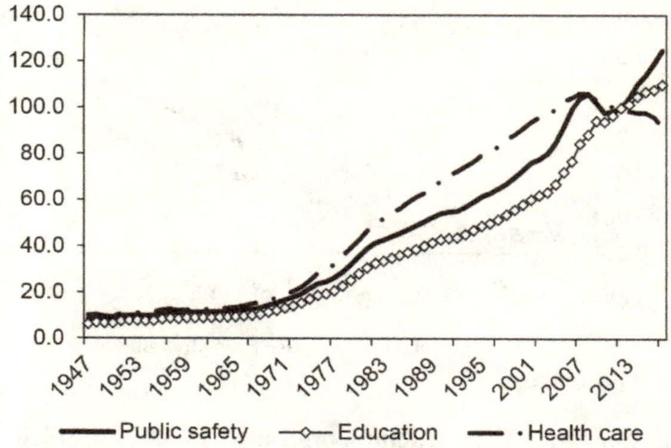


**Fig. 1.47 Social infrastructure, price indexes, 2012 = 100.0**

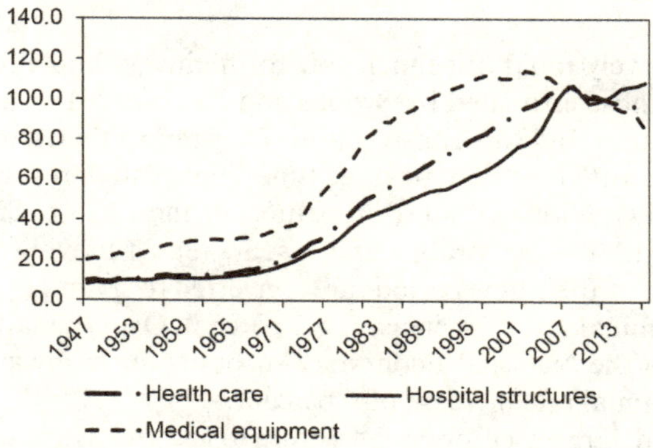


**Fig. 1.48 Health care infrastructure, price indexes, 2012 = 100.0**

care—are broadly consistent with trends in prices for all infrastructure prices (figures 1.43 and 1.47). Prices for health care infrastructure show a notable slowdown in the latter half of the period, falling from 4.6 percent average annual growth for the period 1947–1987 to 1.3 percent for the period 1987–2017; prices actually decline in the period 2010–2017 (figure 1.48). This slowdown and later downturn largely reflect declines in BEAs estimates of quality-adjusted prices for components of electro-medical equipment, including magnetic resonance imaging equipment, ultrasound scanning devices, and CT-scan machinery.[34]

Trends in prices for digital infrastructure—which consist of communications structures, equipment, and software, and computers—are roughly

34. For more information, see Chute, McCulla, and Smith (2018).

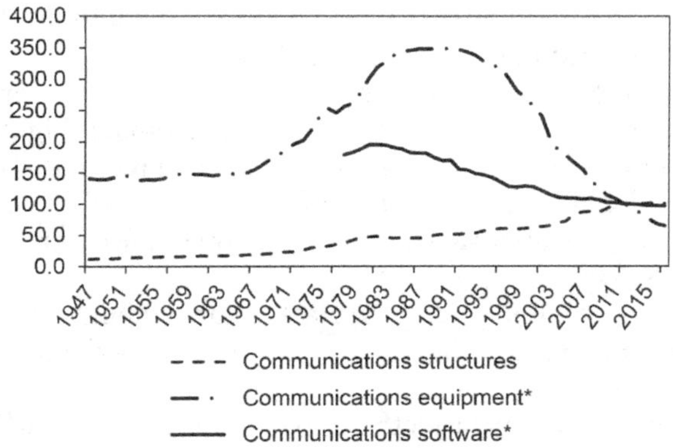


**Fig. 1.49 Digital infrastructure, price indexes, 2012 = 100.0**

consistent with trends in prices for all infrastructure until about the early 1990s, when prices for digital infrastructure began to fall markedly while prices for all infrastructure continued to increase (figure 1.43). In the 1947–1987 period, annual growth for digital infrastructure prices was 4.2 percent, primarily reflecting communications structures and equipment prices. From 1987 through 2017, prices declined at an annual rate of 1.3 percent (figure 1.49). During this period, prices of all asset types of digital infrastructure experienced slowdowns, with communications equipment (–5.4 percent) and computers (–10.4 percent) exhibiting the largest declines.

## 1.5 Conclusion

This chapter has provided a broad overview of data on US infrastructure from the National Economic Accounts, offering a definition of infrastructure that we have used to review the methodology underlying infrastructure data in the National Economic Accounts, to provide an overview of available data, and to assess the degree to which infrastructure investment has kept up with depreciation and a growing population. The chapter has also presented new prototype data on investment in highways and streets by state and on maintenance and repair expenditures for highways.

In terms of our analysis of trends, different stories and conclusions are appropriate for different categories of infrastructure. For important types of basic infrastructure, the trends in real net investment per capita and growth rates of real net stocks are consistent with narratives of infrastructure investment that has not kept up, or has only barely kept up, with depreciation and population growth. Social and digital infrastructure generally have come closer to keeping up on these metrics, with variation across categories.

Our state-level data highlight considerable variation in highway spending per capita (or as a share of GDP) across states. In addition, state-by-state rankings have tended to be relatively stable since 1992.

Another view of how well infrastructure investment is keeping up is to consider the average age of infrastructure. Our estimates highlight that for many important assets, the average age has risen in recent decades, and the remaining service life of these assets has fallen. These statistics are consistent with widespread narratives about aging and sometimes decrepit infrastructure in the US.

Our review of trends in prices of infrastructure highlights rapid increases in prices for some types of infrastructure for some periods (such as highways).

In terms of measurement methodology, we highlight that depreciation rates used in the accounts are based on estimates developed roughly 40 years ago and that these estimates are, for many categories, well below those used in some other countries. In addition, price indexes for infrastructure warrant additional attention, given that some are based on input-cost indexes rather than actual asset prices. Finally, for digital infrastructure, data classifications are sometimes not granular enough to identify relevant assets. Some additional work here also likely would pay dividends.

All of the data reported in this chapter are downloadable in a spreadsheet. We hope that our review and the availability of the data reported here will spur further research on infrastructure.

## References

Allen, Treb, and Costas Arkolakis. 2019. "The Welfare Effects of Transportation Infrastructure Improvements." NBER Working Paper 25487. Cambridge, MA: National Bureau of Economic Research.

Aschauer, David. 1989. "Is Public Expenditure Productive?" *Journal of Monetary Economics* 23 (2): 177–200.

Brooks, Leah, and Zachary Liscow. 2019. "Infrastructure Costs." Paper presented at the Summer Institute, National Bureau of Economic Research, Cambridge, MA, July.

Bureau of Economic Analysis. 2013. "BEA Depreciation Estimates." BEA memorandum. https://apps.bea.gov/national/pdf/BEA_depreciation_rates.pdf.

———. 2019. *NIPA Handbook of Concepts and Methods.*

Bureau of Labor Statistics. 2019. "*Multifactor Productivity Trends—2018.*" *News release,* March 20.

Chute, Jason W., Stephanie H. McCulla, and Shelly Smith. 2018. "Preview of the 2018 Comprehensive Update of the National Income and Product Accounts: Changes in Methods, Definitions, and Presentations." *Survey of Current Business* (April).

Cisneros, Henry. 2010. "America's Essential Infrastructure: A Key to Competitiveness." In *The Handbook of Infrastructure Investing,* edited by Michael Underhill. New York: John Wiley & Sons.

Congressional Budget Office (CBO). 2018. *Public Spending on Transportation and Water Infrastructure, 1956 to 2017.* Washington, DC: CBO.

Corrado, Carol, Jonathan Haskel, and Cecilia Jona-Lasinio. 2017. "Public Intangibles: The Public Sector and Economic Growth in the SNA." *Review of Income and Wealth,* series 63, supp. 2 (December): S355–S380.

Diewert, Erwin. 2005. "Issues in the Measurement of Capital Services, Depreciation, Asset Price Changes, and Interest Rates." In *Measuring Capital in the New Economy,* edited by Carol Corrado, John Haltiwanger, and Daniel Sichel. Chicago: University of Chicago Press.

European Commission, International Monetary Fund, Organisation for Economic Co-operation and Development, United Nations, and World Bank. 2009. *System of National Accounts 2008.* New York.

Eurostat/OECD. 2015. *Eurostat-OECD Compilation Guide on Land Estimation*, esp. chap. 6.5, "The Importance of Service Lives and Depreciation."

Fair, Ray. 2019. "U.S. Infrastructure: 1929–2017." Mimeo, Yale University.

Fernald, John. 1999. "Roads to Prosperity? Assessing the Link between Public Capital and Productivity." *American Economic Review* 89 (3): 619–38.

Fraumeni, Barbara. 1997. "The Measurement of Depreciation in the U.S. National Income and Product Accounts." *Survey of Current Business* (July): 7–23.

———. 1999. "Productive Highway Capital Stock Measures." Federal Highway Administration Department of Transportation report under subcontract to Battelle Memorial Institute, contract DTFH61-97-C-00010.

———. 2007. "Productivity Highway Capital Stocks and the Contribution of Highways to Growth in GDP: Volume 1." Federal Highway Administration Department of Transportation report under subcontract to Battelle Memorial Institute, subcontract no. 208937 to work order Bat-03-21.

Giandrea, Michael D., Robert Kornfeld, Peter B. Meyer, and Susan G. Powers. 2018. "Incorporating Canadian Capital Asset Depreciation Rates into US Capital and Multifactor Productivity Measures." Paper presented at Fifth World KLEMS Conference, Cambridge, MA, June 4–5.

Hulten, Charles R., and Frank C. Wykoff. 1981a. "The Estimation of Economic Depreciation Using Vintage Asset Prices." *Journal of Econometrics* 15 (April): 367–96.

———. 1981b. "The Measurement of Economic Depreciation." In *Depreciation, Inflation, and the Taxation of Income from Capital*, edited by Charles R. Hulten, 81–125. Washington, DC: Urban Institute Press.

Katz, Arnold J., and Shelby W. Herman. 1997. "Improved Estimates of Fixed Reproducible Tangible Wealth, 1929–95." *Survey of Current Business* 77 (May): 69–92.

Lally, Paul R. 2009. "BEA Briefing: How BEA Accounts for Investment in Private Structures." *Survey of Current Business* 89 (February): 11.

Munnell, Alicia H. 1992. "Policy Watch: Infrastructure Investment and Economic Growth." *Journal of Economic Perspectives* 6 (4): 189–98.

Statistics Canada. 2015. "An Update on Depreciation Rates for the Canadian Productivity Accounts." Canadian Productivity Review, catalogue no. 15-206-X (January 26). http://www.statcan.gc.ca/pub/15-206-x/15-206-x2015039-eng.htm.

Yamashita, Takashi. 2013. "A Guide to the Integrated Macroeconomic Accounts." *Survey of Current Business* 93 (April): 12–27. https://apps.bea.gov/scb/pdf/2013/04%20April/0413_macro-accts.pdf.

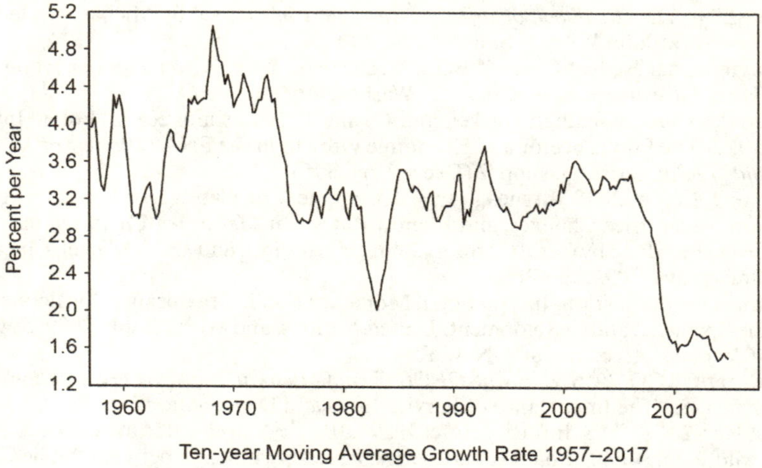


**Fig. 1C.1 Real GDP growth in the United States remains below pre–Great Recession rates.**
*Source:* Taylor (2017).

## Comment Peter Blair Henry

### Introduction

It is a pleasure to discuss this essay. There may be a few people in the country who know more about the Bureau of Economic Analysis' national income accounts than Bennett, Kornfeld, Sichel, and Wasshausen, but as I am not one of those people, my comments will be accordingly modest. I applaud the authors for taking on the issue of infrastructure measurement, and I thank the organizers for commissioning the piece. The topic of US infrastructure is an important one, but it tends to receive more heat than light, and this essay provides a step in the direction of correcting that imbalance.

Figure 1C.1 illustrates the proximate cause of the most recent instance of that imbalance. Even before the onset of COVID-19 and its cataclysmic impact on employment, incomes, and output, the growth rate of the US economy had been below its historical average since the Great Recession.

Peter Blair Henry is the W. R. Berkley Professor of Finance and Economics and Dean Emeritus at New York University Stern School of Business and a board member of the National Bureau of Economic Research.

For acknowledgments, sources of research support, and disclosure of the author's material financial relationships, if any, please see https://www.nber.org/books-and-chapters/economic-analysis-and-infrastructure-investment/comment-measuring-infrastructure-beas-national-economic-accounts-henry.

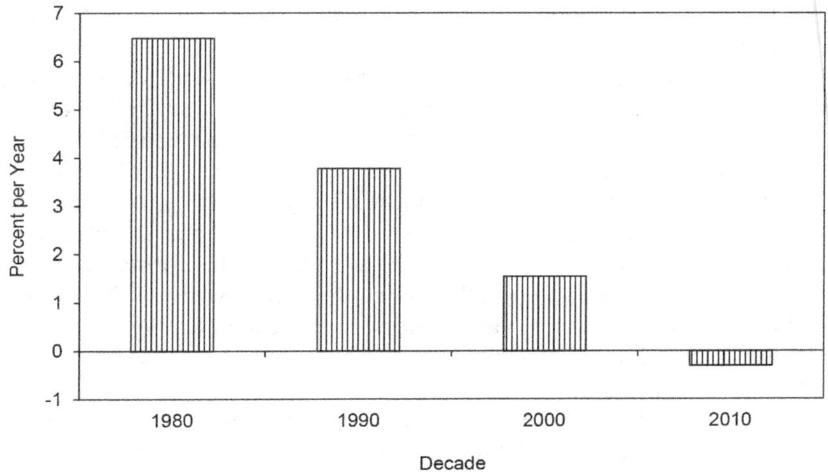


**Fig. 1C.2 The average five-year real Treasury rate has declined over the past four decades.**
*Source:* Hall (2017).

Declining productivity growth and the absence of structural reforms in the US have reduced expectations about the growth rate of potential output, reinforcing the slowdown in demand—especially for fixed investment—in spite of persistent, record-low real interest rates (figure 1C.2) and a reduction in corporate taxes, igniting fears of secular stagnation, and leading to advocacy for increased infrastructure spending as a way out of the slowdown (for example, Summers 2013).

Advocacy for greater investment in US infrastructure has a cyclical history dating back to a once-influential article by Aschauer (1989), which found that increases in the public capital stock (a proxy for infrastructure) had a large impact on output. Aschauer estimated that the elasticity of GDP with respect to public capital was 0.39, and argued that much of the US productivity slowdown in the 1970s was the result of reduced infrastructure investment. American policy makers seized on Aschauer's work as justification for higher levels of infrastructure spending (Rohatyn 1992; US Conference of Mayors 1992). Economists, in turn, pushed back.

Specifically, Munnell (1992) argues that Aschauer's estimates of the impact of aggregate infrastructure investment on output are implausibly large, even while acknowledging that investment in public capital has a positive and significant impact on growth. Gramlich (1994) is even more skeptical, finding, at best, mixed evidence that the US suffers from a shortage of infrastructure. Indeed, Gramlich's warning that the surfeit of interest in US infrastructure in the 1990s was out of proportion to its importance for long-run growth rings relevant at a time when talk of secular stagnation in this country has triggered yet another surge (Eichengreen 2015; Gordon 2015; and Summers 2015).

The central contribution of the chapter by Bennett, Kornfeld, Sichel, and Wasshausen is that it increases the ratio of facts to advocacy in the context of US infrastructure. The essay does so by breaking infrastructure into three types (basic, social, and digital), giving us three categories of observations (trends, adequacy, and methodology), reaching modest conclusions, and providing some suggestions for future research. The chapter is replete with tables (eight) and figures (49) that provide a wealth of information about infrastructure stocks and flows that researchers interested in this area will find valuable as they build on the authors' contribution. Rather than trying to cover everything the chapter does—and it does a lot—I will focus my discussion on two areas.

First, I will provide some context for the broad trends presented by the authors and explain why the data work in which they are engaged is so important, especially in a digital context. Second, I will evaluate the authors' definition of infrastructure "adequacy" and suggest a measure that may be more useful.

## Context and Broad Trends

In order to provide a useful guide to decision-making, debates about the wisdom of increased spending on infrastructure need to distinguish between cyclical arguments focused on a lack of aggregate demand and the impact of infrastructure stimulus spending on the growth rate of *actual output* in the short run, versus structural arguments about the impact that infrastructure spending has in the long run by raising the growth rate of *potential output*. Both of these issues are important, but we should not conflate them. There may be an argument for fiscal policy to stimulate growth in the short run, but that could take many forms to stimulate consumption rather than investment, including but not limited to direct payments to consumers and firms (to maintain employment). If we are going to spend resources on infrastructure, creating structures that are more or less permanent, then it is optimal to invest efficiently, to raise the trend rate of growth. Infrastructure stimulus enthusiasts will point out that there may be an intersection between the short-run and long-run arguments for infrastructure spending—that investment in infrastructure will both boost demand and raise the trend growth rate of output—but it is not clear that the data support this view, a point to which I will return later in my comments.

Turning to broad trends, the authors do a nice job of measuring and documenting important key facts about the changing composition of US infrastructure. The share of the US infrastructure stock comprising basic assets (such as roads) has decreased, while the share of social and digital assets has increased. In addition to the authors' documentation of these facts, it would be useful to know the extent to which investment in digital infrastructure—data centers, for example—is public versus private. Let me elaborate a bit.

When it comes to basic and social infrastructure, we think of assets that are largely owned by the federal, state, and local governments and that provide public infrastructure services. When it comes to the continuing evolution of the economy, however, and the ever-increasing provision of services—business to consumer and business to business—through platforms, it is natural to ask which, if any, digital assets in the world of the platform economy have similar qualities to basic and social infrastructure, and the extent to which maximizing aggregate productivity will require public investment. This line of inquiry raises a series of related questions.

Are there parallels between the provision of roads and the provision of digital infrastructure such as data centers and cloud computing? For instance, do the same laws of motion and attendant assumptions about depreciation rates and maintenance costs apply to digital infrastructure as apply to traditional fixed assets in the national income accounts? Also, my anecdotal sense is that the vast majority of construction of data centers suggested by figure 1.8 in the authors' paper has been the province of megasized tech firms such as Amazon, Microsoft, Google, and IBM, but it would be good to know definitively. More precisely, it would be useful to know, outside of the Department of Defense's Joint Enterprise Defense Infrastructure (JEDI), to what extent have cloud facilities been built by the federal government versus by private providers? Does it matter? And do we need to be concerned that the concentration of cloud infrastructure among the Big Four will lead to a suboptimally low provision of digital infrastructure? The falling prices and margins that indicate an increased commoditization of this space suggest not, but what kind of rules and refereeing of the digital ecosystem do we need to ensure efficient entry and competition by smaller-scale firms? All of these questions require more and better data, and I applaud the authors' initial efforts in this area, which lay the foundation for other researchers to join the hunt.

## Adequacy

Turning to adequacy, the authors provide three measures: (1) net investment per capita; (2) growth in the real net infrastructure capital stock per capita; (3) age of the infrastructure stock. Focusing on the second measure highlights an important issue. Figure 1.17 in chapter 1 shows that the average growth rate of net per capita transportation infrastructure over the past four decades appears to be about 0.5 percent per year, which is lower than in it was in the 1950s and 1960s, and is certainly lower than the growth rate of total factor productivity. Looking only at this picture, it is tempting to lean in the direction of the narrative that the United States is underinvested in transportation infrastructure. The problem, however, is that narrative does not consider whether a slower growth rate of transportation infrastructure is efficient. The central issue is whether, given a dollar of national savings, devoting that dollar to an increase in the stock of transportation infrastructure leads to a larger increase in GDP than allocating the dollar elsewhere, to private capital in particular.

If infrastructure is a public good that must be provided through state-funded investment, it is natural to define "adequacy" in terms of rates of return, and it would be useful to impose a little more structure on the data. In this case, the stock of infrastructure is "adequate" if the return on investing in an additional unit of infrastructure capital equals the rate of return on investing in an additional unit of noninfrastructure capital. If the return on investing in infrastructure is greater than the return on investing in an additional unit of noninfrastructure capital, then the stock of infrastructure is "inadequate." Similarly, if the return on infrastructure capital exceeds the return on noninfrastructure capital, there is an "excess" of infrastructure.

It is straightforward to capture these ideas succinctly using an aggregate production function that has two kinds of capital: infrastructure, $X$, and noninfrastructure, $K$, so that GDP, $Y = Y = AK^{\alpha}X^{\gamma}L^{1-\alpha-\gamma}$. Let $r_x = MPX/P_X$ be the (social) return on infrastructure, $r_K = MPK/P_K$ be the (private) return on noninfrastructure capital, and $= r_X/r_K$. Under these definitions, the stock of infrastructure is "inadequate" if $\rho > 1$, "adequate" if $\rho = 1$, and "excessive" if $\rho < 1$. Table 1C.1, constructed using data on $r_K$ and $r_x$ from Canning and Bennathan (2000), demonstrates the striking fact that at the time of

**Table 1C.1** **The rate of return on paved roads in advanced economies is less than the rate of return on private capital**

| Country | Rho |
|---|---|
| Australia | −0.02 |
| Austria | 0.00 |
| Belgium | 0.14 |
| Denmark | 0.4 |
| Finland | 0.68 |
| Germany | 0.55 |
| Ireland | 0.15 |
| Italy | 0.76 |
| Japan | 3.05 |
| Netherlands | 0.46 |
| New Zealand | 0.23 |
| Norway | 0.08 |
| Sweden | 0.21 |
| United Kingdom | 0.32 |
| United States | 0.26 |

*Source:* Canning and Bennathan (2000), table 7.

measurement, the stock of paved road infrastructure in 15 industrialized economies, including the United States, was excessive, in the sense that the rate of return to an additional unit of infrastructure capital was less than the return on an additional unit of noninfrastructure capital in every country except Japan. These numbers are consistent with the findings of Fernald (1999), who concludes that "the data seem consistent with a story in which the massive road-building of the 1950s and 1960s offered a one-time boost to the level of productivity, rather than a path to continuing rapid growth."

While there may be utility from investments that do not have an incremental impact on GDP, and the social rate of return to infrastructure does not capture such benefits, the advocates who want to ramp up infrastructure spending are focused on GDP. We need to think more carefully about the opportunity cost of increased public expenditure on infrastructure and the most efficient way to allocate national savings. Selective refurbishment of roads and other American hardscape may be in order and have a modest impact on national output, but figuring out the optimal role of public expenditure on digital infrastructure strikes me as a higher priority. If there is a compelling efficiency case to be made for the federal government to invest in digital infrastructure in a manner analogous to the way the government devoted resources to the construction of the Interstate Highway System, then that case should show up in measured social rates of return on digital infrastructure. The research required to properly calculate such rates of return is not for the faint of heart, but good public policy decisions require that we have these data. By initiating an ambitious and important effort to collect and measure data, the authors have pointed in us in the right direction. I look forward to their future contributions as well as the contributions of others inspired by their work.

## References


Aschauer, David A. 1989. "Is Public Expenditure Productive?" *Journal of Monetary Economics* 23 (2): 177–200.

Canning, D., and E. Bennathan. 2000. "The Social Rate of Return on Infrastructure Investment." World Bank Policy Research Working Paper 2390.

Eichengreen, Barry. 2015. "Secular Stagnation: The Long View." *American Economic Review* 105 (5): 66–70.

Fernald, John G. 1999. "Roads to Prosperity? Assessing the Link between Public Capital and Productivity." *American Economic Review* 89 (3): 619–38.

Gordon, Robert J. 2015. "Secular Stagnation: A Supply-Side View." *American Economic Review* 105 (5): 54–59.

Gramlich, Edward M. 1994. "Infrastructure Investment: A Review Essay." *Journal of Economic Literature* 32 (3): 1176–96.

Hall, Robert E. 2017. "The Role of the Growth of Risk-Averse Wealth in the Decline of the Safe Real Interest Rate." Working paper, Stanford University.

Munnell, Alicia H. 1992. "Infrastructure Investment and Economic Growth." *Journal of Economic Perspectives* 6 (4): 189–98.

Rohatyn, Felix. 1992. "What the Government Should Do." *New York Review of Books*, June 25.

Summers, Lawrence H. 2013. Remarks given at IMF Fourteenth Annual Research Conference in Honor of Stanley Fischer. http://larrysummers.com/imf-fourteenth-annual-research-conference-in-honor-of-stanley-fischer/.

———. 2015. "Demand Side Secular Stagnation." *American Economic Review* 105 (5): 60–65.

Taylor, John B. 2017. "Happy New Decade." https://economicsone.com/2017/12/31/happy-new-decade/.

US Conference of Mayors. 1992. *Ready to Go: A Survey of USA Public Works Projects to Fight the Recession Now*. Washington DC: US Conference of Mayors.

2

# Can America Reduce Highway Spending?
## Evidence from the States

Leah Brooks and Zachary Liscow

Infrastructure—capital investment in roads, water, schools, sewers, and many other facilities—is a key input into economic growth (Munnell 1992). Economic historians credit infrastructure investments with large increases in social welfare. For example, Beach et al. (2016) show that large-scale water purification in the US in the first part of the twentieth century decreased mortality and meaningfully increased human capital formation (see also Cutler and Miller 2005 and Ferrie and Troesken 2008). Duranton and Turner (2012) find that the large capital investment in the Interstate Highway System yielded broad-based increases in employment. And Allen and Arkolakis (2019) argue that large welfare gains are possible with improvements to selected segments of the Interstate System.

But these benefits are available only when we can build infrastructure at reasonable cost. Despite the importance of infrastructure, there is very lim-

Leah Brooks is an associate professor of public policy and public administration at the Trachtenberg School of Public Policy and Public Administration at George Washington University.

Zachary Liscow is an associate professor of law at Yale Law School.

We thank the editors of the volume for encouragement and Cliff Winston for helpful comments. We are very appreciative to Raven Saks (c. 2004) for excellent research assistance that yielded data on private residential construction costs, and to Nate Baum-Snow for sharing data on Interstate completion. We thank Jacob Waggoner and Mia Dana for excellent research assistance support throughout and to Peter Damrosch for an excellent literature review. Many thanks to Richard Weingroff, who provided consultation and advice at key points, and to Louise Sheiner for data advice and helpful conversations. For acknowledgments, sources of research support, and disclosure of the authors' material financial relationships, if any, please see https://www.nber.org/books-and-chapters/economic-analysis-and-infrastructure-investment/can-america-reduce-highway-spending-evidence-states.

ited evidence about overall infrastructure cost patterns and what drives those costs. While there is contemporaneous coverage of specific instances of very high spending on infrastructure—New York City's new subways, Boston's Big Dig, and California's high-speed rail have all received substantial media coverage—without systematic evidence it is hard to evaluate whether these projects are well-publicized outliers or typical expenditures (Barro 2019b; Goldman 2012; Varghese 2019).

The limited evidence in the literature suggests that per-unit expenditures are rising. Looking at the construction sector as a whole over the past 70 years, Swei (2018) finds limited evidence of real growth in materials prices but substantial growth in labor costs. Brooks and Liscow (2020) find that states spent three times as much to build a mile of Interstate Highway in the 1980s as they did in the 1960s. Mehrotra, Turner, and Uribe (2019) find that this trend continued for both new Interstate construction and Interstate maintenance from 1980 onward.

This increase in per-unit expenditures may explain the much-decried state of US infrastructure. There is a general belief that the quality of US infrastructure is low. The American Society of Civil Engineers consistently gives US infrastructure a failing grade (American Society of Civil Engineers 2017). The US spent about the same in real per capita terms in 2016 as it did in 1956. If per-unit infrastructure expenditure increases, even an equivalent amount of spending translates into less physical capital to facilitate the movement of people and goods.

In this project, we focus on infrastructure for which we can consistently measure per-unit expenditure over time and space: the US Interstate Highway System. Our goal is to highlight variation in spending. If some of this expenditure variation is the result of policy choices in low-spending states that are replicable in high-spending states, policy provides one route to lowering the cost of new infrastructure. New Interstate construction is particularly useful for analysis because a new mile of Interstate is at least fairly uniformly defined over time and space. While all highway miles are certainly not exactly comparable, comparisons across different types of infrastructure, or even the same type of infrastructure at different levels of depreciation, are even more fraught. We focus on the period from 1956 to 1993, which saw the construction of more than 90 percent of today's Interstate System.

We analyze total spending per mile, which is determined by the cost to build a constant-quality highway mile and the quality of that mile. If the quality of an Interstate mile is roughly constant over time, then changes in spending come exclusively from changes in cost, such as changes in the prices of labor or concrete. However, changes in highway quality can also increase spending—if, for example, states build Interstate Highways with more exit ramps, or higher-quality concrete. Our work in this chapter and in a related paper (Brooks and Liscow 2020) is a first step to providing evidence on the drivers of spending changes.

In our related work, we analyze the temporal variation in Interstate spending from 1956 to 1993 (Brooks and Liscow 2020). We show that the US spent roughly \$8.75 million 2016 dollars to build a new mile of Interstate for first decade and a half of the program, from 1956 to 1969. After this, however, Interstate spending per mile starts a steady increase. By the 1980s, states spent roughly \$25 million 2016 dollars to build a new mile of Interstate—roughly a tripling in spending. As neither labor nor materials prices increase in any meaningful way over the period, they do not explain the temporal increase.

Our related work also marshals multiple pieces of evidence to suggest that the rise of "citizen voice" drives at least some of these increased expenditures. We define "citizen voice" as an amalgam of changes in statutes, changes in judicial doctrine, and the rise of social movements, dating to the late 1960s and early 1970s, all of which combined to give individual citizens a greater ability to modify government behavior (Altshuler and Luberoff 2003; Glaeser and Ponzetto 2018). For example, the passage of the National Environmental Policy Act of 1969 gave individual citizens a cause of action to sue the government if they thought that the regulatory agency was not faithfully implementing the act. In addition, we find that correlates of citizen demand for higher-quality Interstates, such as income or education, are associated with higher costs only after the "citizen voice" tools for challenging government behavior appear.

In this chapter we focus on whether there is economically meaningful cross-state variation in per-mile Interstate spending. We find that there is—the interquartile range in spending per mile is an astonishing \$8.8 million, relative to the mean of \$10 million. If states spending over the median had limited their expenditure per mile to that of the median state, the Interstate system would have cost about \$260 billion to build, reducing the cost by 40 percent.

We then isolate Interstate spending subject to policy maker discretion, by conditioning on predetermined characteristics, such as changes in elevation along the route, that should drive costs.[1] When we restrict to spending subject to policy maker discretion, cross-state geographic variation falls but is far from eliminated. When we further limit analysis to the period after the rise of citizen voice, predetermined characteristics eliminate a smaller share of cross-state variation in spending.

We then look for clues as to the drivers of this cross-state variation by correlating Interstate spending and related private and public spending. We first show that the cross-state variation in Interstate spending is unusually large—considerably larger than any form of spending we study, other than highway maintenance—and this difference remains even conditional on predeter-

1. We deliberately use the phrase "policy maker" here to include both elected politicians and bureaucrats, both of whom have substantial power over spending decisions.

mined characteristics. We then test whether key types of spending covary with Interstate spending per mile. Of all the types of spending we analyze, including private construction and overall public spending, Medicare spending per enrollee is the most strongly statistically related with spending per new Interstate mile net of geographic covariates. Each additional $1,000 of Medicare spending per capita (mean $5,650) is associated with an additional $3.4 million dollars in Interstate spending, or about 20 percent of mean spending per mile. We do not think that senior citizen health care is driving greater expenditures on Interstate Highways. Rather, the same forces that yield high Medicare spending—possibly things like litigious citizens, or the social capital that allows people to pursue more medical care—may also yield more Interstate spending.

We then review the literature on the root causes of infrastructure costs. To help gain some insight, we examine the relationship between features of states and their Interstate spending per mile. In the period with more cross-state variation in the data (1970–1993), we find that states with a higher Democratic presidential vote share and (more tenuously) higher corruption have higher Interstate spending per mile. While these results are provocative, we interpret them with caution given that we do not limit to exogenous variation in spending.

Finally, we show that higher Interstate spending correlates both with higher subsequent maintenance expenditures and lower fatalities. The latter is possible evidence that higher initial spending yields higher-quality highways in the form of safer roads.

To undertake these analyses, we use novel data on the cost of the US Interstate Highway System from the Federal Highway Administration's *Highway Statistics* yearbooks that we assembled and cleaned in our related paper (Brooks and Liscow 2020). We combine these data with the date of mileage completion (Baum-Snow 2007) to calculate spending per mile. As in our related work (Brooks and Liscow 2020), we use multiple spatial data sources to calculate population density, slope, and wetlands and rivers by Interstate segment to control for the differential physical costs of constructing segments. Adding to our previous work, we also gather private spending on construction and health care, as well as public spending including Medicare, Medicaid, and state and local government general spending.

This chapter first presents background on the Interstate Highway System. We then discuss the data we use. We follow with an analysis of the variation in spending per mile and the variation in spending per mile subject to policy maker control, along with tests for the validity of this measure. We continue with the correlation between Interstate spending and other relevant private and public spending. We then review the literature on the root causes of infrastructure cost changes. In the final empirical section, we test whether some of these cost drivers are related to Interstate spending per mile. The final empirical section asks whether higher spending per mile is related to better Interstate outcomes; we then conclude.

## 2.1 Interstate Construction

Though planned since at least the 1940s, the Interstate System formally began with the Federal-Aid Highway Act of 1956. This act authorized a roughly 41,000-mile system with an estimated completion before 1970 at a projected cost of $25 billion 1946 dollars, or $192 billion 2016 dollars. In reality, Interstate construction was not proclaimed complete until the 1990s. The vast majority of miles were completed by 1993, the end of our study period. The total cost of the Interstate exceeded $504 billion 2016 dollars. (For details beyond this summary, see Brooks and Liscow 2020.) All states have at least some Interstate miles.

The Interstate construction program was a federal-state partnership. For each new mile of Interstate—our focus in this chapter—the federal government paid 90 percent of the cost; states bore the remaining 10 percent.[2] In return for federal funding, states were required to build roads up to "Interstate standards." These standards meant two lanes in each direction, full control of access, and a design that yielded a minimum speed of 50 miles per hour and that would support the projected traffic in 1975 (this requirement later changed to require support for projected traffic 20 years after completion). The government, although it mandated a minimum standard, would reimburse for quality above this minimum, subject to regulatory approval. The Interstate program was administered by state departments of transportation, which put projects out to bid. States varied in the bidding systems they used (Pietroforte and Miller 2002, 429).

In practice, states had broad latitude in ordering the segments they built and choosing how much to spend on each segment. However, the funding structure capped the amount states could spend in any one year. In each year of the program, the revenue available for highway spending came from the gas tax. The federal government split the gas tax revenue among states in proportion to the estimated cost of completion of remaining highway miles. Thus, states had to choose between constructing quickly at lower spending per mile or slowly at higher spending per mile.

In the years we study, the pace of construction slowed as the program aged. Most states built the bulk of their miles in the first two decades of the program; the 1950s and 1960s saw 60 percent of total miles constructed. States built another 30 percent of system mileage in the 1970s and the remaining 10 percent in the 1980s and early 1990s.

2. There were some exceptions to 90 percent reimbursement, as some states received modestly more reimbursement.

## 2.2 Data

To investigate the variation in Interstate spending per mile across states, we collect four types of data. These are Interstate spending per mile, measures of predetermined differences in construction costs, public and private spending by states, and key demographic covariates.

### 2.2.1 Spending per Mile

To construct Interstate spending per mile, we need both the numerator—spending—and the denominator—miles. For annual Interstate spending, we digitize state-level data from the US Department of Transportation's *Highway Statistics* yearbooks for years 1956 to 1993. These volumes report annual federal spending on new Interstate miles by state. The data appendix of our related paper (Brooks and Liscow 2020) details how we adjust these data to account for small anomalies and issues due to two special rules on apportionment. Here and throughout, we adjust all dollar figures to 2016 dollars using the Consumer Price Index for All Urban Consumers (CPI-U).

For the denominator of spending per mile, we measure miles constructed by year of completion from Baum-Snow (2007). For each roughly one-mile segment of Interstate, we observe the exact location of that segment and the year in which the segment was completed.

Because spending is counted when it occurs and miles are counted when completed, the timing of spending usually predates timing of completion of miles.[3] In this chapter, we focus on either the entire time period—in which case there is no temporal mismatch—or two long time periods, in which case this issue is substantially lessened.

### 2.2.2 Predetermined Features

To account for predetermined features that drive spending per mile and are outside of policy maker discretion, we rely on what researchers generally believe to be the three main drivers of physical construction costs (Alder 2019; Balboni 2019; Faber 2014). The first is population density, with data from the Decennial Census (specific files as noted in the data appendix). We measure population density for each one-mile segment as the population density of the census tract in which the largest part of the segment falls, when tract data are available, or the population density of the county, when tract data are not available.[4] We use population density from the census year

3. In addition, we adjust spending to be a weighted average of the year the segment opened and the two years prior. See details in Brooks and Liscow (2020). We omit Alaska, Hawaii, and the District of Columbia.

4. The entire country was tracted only in 1990; from 1950 to 1980, tract data are available only for selected areas.

closest to the opening of each segment.[5] We create a state or state-period measure by taking a segment-weighted average.

The second physical feature relevant to Interstate cost is the slope of terrain. We measure the average state slope by first finding the average slope of land within 50 meters of each segment using the US Geological Survey's National Elevation Map. We create a state or state-period measure of slope by taking the segment-length weighted average of all segment slopes for a state or state-period.

The final measure of predetermined features is based on the length of the segment, in miles, that intersects wetlands or rivers. We define wetlands as the any of water types in the Cowardin classification system from the US Fish and Wildlife Service (2018) National Wetlands Inventory. This definition includes rivers and any other large bodies of water. Our state or state-period measure is the average segment share in wetlands or rivers, weighted by segment length.

### 2.2.3 Public and Private Spending

We have several measures of private and public spending with which we correlate our Interstate spending measure. To compare Interstate spending to private spending, we use an index of private construction costs from R. S. Means, indexed to 100 in 1993, courtesy of Raven Molloy. Molloy collected these data for every five years from 1940 to 1980 and then annually 1981 to 2003. To measure construction wages, we use annual state-level construction payroll divided by number of construction employees from the County Business Patterns (available periodically in the 1950s and 1960s, then from 1971 to 1993) to measure average annual construction wages per state. We also include private health insurance expenditures per enrollee in 2001 (the earliest year available) from the Centers for Medicare and Medicaid Services' "Health Expenditures by State of Residence, 1991–2014" (see appendix for complete citation details). Private health insurance expenditures include expenditures by both the insurer and the insured.

We also compare Interstate spending to public spending. For Medicare and Medicaid, we use spending per enrollee from 1991, also from the Centers for Medicare and Medicaid Services' "Health Expenditures by State of Residence, 1991–2014."[6]

5. For example, we attribute the 1960 census characteristics to segments opening from 1956 to 1964, and the 1970 census characteristics to segments opening from 1965 to 1974.

6. In an appendix table we use a host of government spending measures from the Census of Governments (relying only on full censuses in 1967, 1972, 1977, 1982, 1987, and 1992). We use data on total statewide local government expenditures (the sum of state and all local expenditures) and rely on the time-consistent compilation from Willamette University (Pierson, Hand, and Thompson 2015). To avoid problems of differing state and local responsibilities, we aggregate all state and local government spending by state and year. These data do not include state-level accounts in 1967, so most of our data work relies on state-aggregate measures from 1972 onward.

### 2.2.4 Interstate Outcomes and Other Variables

To assess whether Interstate spending correlates with postconstruction outcomes, we collect the number of accidents and fatalities per mile from the oldest relevant *Highway Statistics*, which dates from 1995. We also collect 2015 state maintenance spending per mile, again from *Highway Statistics*. We use later measures of maintenance expenditures to assess the long-run quality of Interstate construction.

We also collect a variety of demographic and variables that measure other policies to see if they explain the cross-state variation. We describe these variables where we introduce them later.

See summary statistics for our main variables of interest in table 2.1.

## 2.3 Documenting Cross-State Differences

With these data in hand, we turn to documenting cross-state variation in Interstate spending per mile. We then create a measure of state spending per mile that reflects costs subject to policy maker discretion, omitting spending determined by preexisting features, such as the slope of the terrain. Finally, to look for clues about potential drivers of spending, we assess whether spending due to policy maker choice covaries with other relevant public and private spending.

### 2.3.1 Absolute Spending

We begin with absolute spending in figure 2.1, which shows how much states spend, on average, per new mile over the build-out of the Interstate system from 1956 to 1993. The average state spends $11.5 million per mile (all figures are in 2016 dollars). The bars in figure 2.1 present deviations from this average. Delaware spent the most per mile of any state, at just over $50 million dollars per mile; the top three spenders also include New Jersey at over $30 million per mile, and Connecticut at just under $25 million per mile. North Dakota spent the least of any state per mile, at roughly $3 million per mile. Even excluding the three top-spending states still leaves a difference of $30 million per mile between the highest- and lowest-spending states.

The figure demarcates the four census regions in shades of gray. Western states tend to spend the least per mile; northeastern states (and two states the Census denotes as part of the South but that may be more intuitively northeastern: Delaware and Maryland) are the highest-spending ones. There are no northeastern states in the bottom portion of the spending distribution.

This geographic variation is also visible in the top panel of figure 2.3, which maps spending per mile by state for the entire period of construction. Unconditional spending per mile is highest in the Northeast and on the West Coast; states in these regions are mostly in the top quartile of spending per mile (the darkest gray).

**Table 2.1** **Geographic variation in Interstate and other local spending**

| | Entire cross section | | | Period 1: 1956–1969 | | | Period 2: 1970–1993 | | |
|---|---|---|---|---|---|---|---|---|---|
| | Mean (1) | Standard deviation (2) | Diff: p75–25 (3) | Mean (4) | Standard deviation (5) | Diff: p75–p25 (6) | Mean (7) | Standard deviation (8) | Diff: p75–p25 (9) |
| Spending/mile, $ millions | 11.51 | 6.70 | 8.18 | 8.75 | 5.15 | 6.26 | 15.52 | 10.65 | 8.25 |
| Private spending | | | | | | | | | |
| Residential construction cost index | 31.53 | 4.93 | 5.83 | 19.83 | 1.70 | 2.12 | 48.55 | 5.66 | 5.84 |
| Health insurance/enrollee, 2001, $1,000s | 2.95 | 0.21 | 0.24 | . | 0.22 | . | 2.94 | 0.21 | 0.22 |
| Public spending, all $1,000s | | | | | | | | | |
| Medicaid per enrollee, 1991 | 6.01 | 1.93 | 2.17 | . | 1.93 | . | 5.97 | 1.91 | 2.44 |
| Medicare per enrollee, 1992 | 5.65 | 0.83 | 1.27 | . | 0.83 | . | 5.65 | 0.83 | 1.32 |
| Local government expenditure per capita | 6.50 | 1.31 | 1.80 | . | 1.30 | . | 6.94 | 1.34 | 1.58 |
| Interstate outcomes | | | | | | | | | |
| Fatalities per VMT, 1995* | 0.86 | 0.4 | 0.55 | . | 0.41 | . | 0.88 | 0.39 | 0.53 |
| Accidents per VMT, 1995* | 3.71 | 1.95 | 2.17 | . | 1.93 | . | 3.73 | 1.97 | 2.36 |
| Maintenance per mile, millions, 1995 | 5.73 | 4.27 | 4.92 | . | 4.20 | . | 5.92 | 4.35 | 5.52 |
| Potential root causes | | | | | | | | | |
| Share high school graduates | 52.24 | 7.56 | 9.40 | 46.28 | 7.39 | 9.47 | 60.92 | 7.54 | 10.17 |
| Median family income, $10,000s | 5.49 | 0.80 | 1.29 | 5.17 | 0.86 | 1.31 | 5.96 | 0.76 | 1.23 |
| Annual construction wages | 43.22 | 7.53 | 10.44 | 42.04 | 7.73 | 12.14 | 44.93 | 7.85 | 12.87 |
| Corruption index | 0.05 | 0.66 | 0.68 | 0.03 | 0.67 | 0.67 | 0.07 | 0.66 | 0.61 |
| Democratic presidential vote share | 44.93 | 5.57 | 6.22 | 48.38 | 6.72 | 8.02 | 39.91 | 4.68 | 6.08 |

*Note:* *Fatalities are per 100 million vehicle miles traveled (VMT). Accidents are per 10,000 vehicle miles traveled. All rows contain 48 observations, with the exception of accidents, which has 47. We omit Alaska, Hawaii, and Washington, DC. We weight all summary statistics by Interstate miles constructed in that state. For this reason, summary statistics for time-invariant variables, such as Medicaid spending in 1991, may vary slightly across the two time periods. In the "residential construction cost index," 1993 is 100. "Local government spending" is the total of all state and local government spending in the Census of Governments for all census years after 1967 (1967 does not report state-level information). The corruption index is from Boylan and Long (2003).

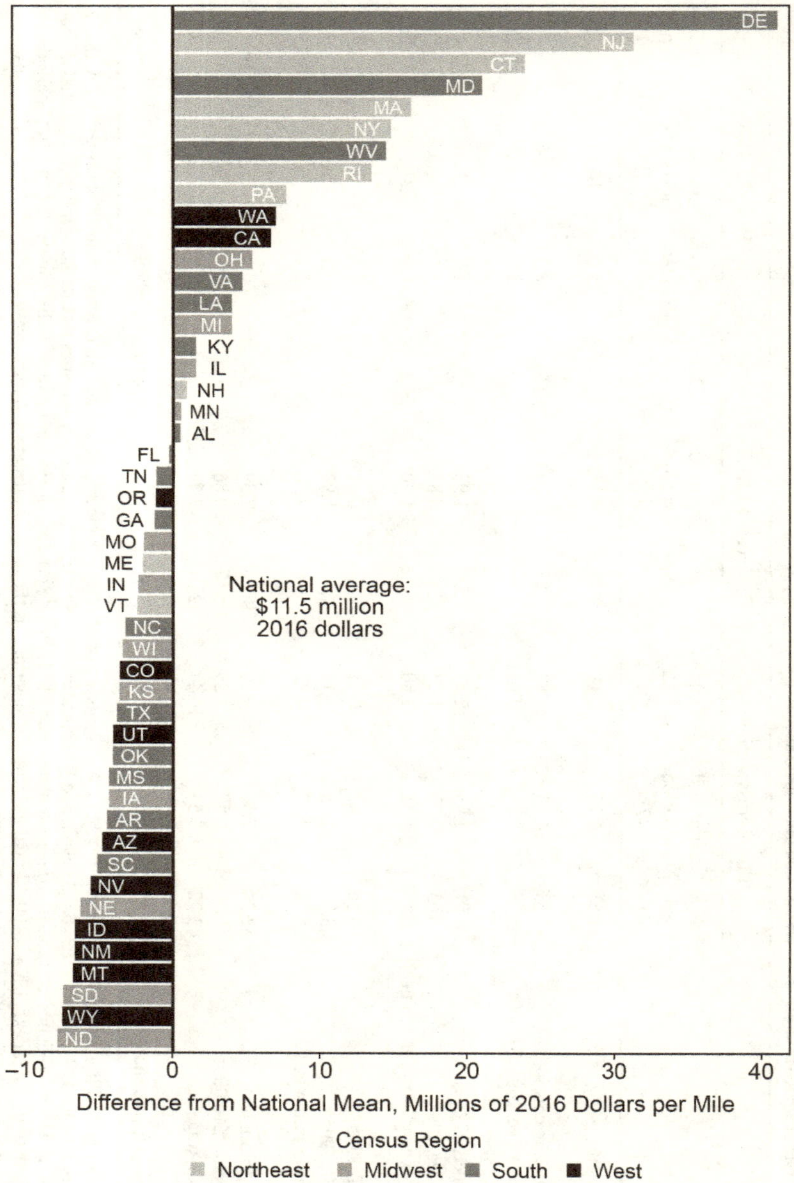


**Fig. 2.1 Interstate spending per new mile, absolute difference from national average**

*Note:* This figure presents deviations from national average Interstate construction spending per mile by state, 1956–1993. Here and everywhere else we omit Alaska, Hawaii, and Washington, DC.

### 2.3.2 Limiting to Spending Driven by Policy Maker Choices

Some of this spending variation is surely due to costs outside of state policy maker control. For example, construction costs in states with highways routed through more sloped land should be higher. Because we are interested in the scope of policy to potentially lower spending, our goal here is to isolate spending that is within the purview of state policy makers. In other words, for example, we cannot make Colorado less hilly, but we can suggest that Colorado change its procurement rules. Thus, we want to purge spending related to the former and keep only spending related to the latter.

To disentangle spending within policy maker choice from that determined by preexisting features, we regress spending per mile on three key covariates, denoted $G_s$: average population density, average slope, and share of miles in wetlands or rivers of segments constructed (see data section for more specifics on the calculation of these measures). Approximations of cost in the engineering literature rely on these three covariates (Alder 2019; Balboni 2019; Faber 2014). Recall that states were responsible for building highways on largely predetermined routes. Thus, the slope, the extent of wetlands and water, and the surrounding population density of segments were largely preexisting choices that constrained the actions of state policy makers.

While this is a useful exercise, these covariates may "overcontrol" for the amount of predetermined spending. For example, if areas with higher population density are more expensive places to build and also prefer more spending on Interstates, our method removes spending related to both of these causes. However, our goal is to remove only spending driven by population density itself. Thus, the covariates we use may contain elements of policy maker choice and may therefore yield residuals that understate the true variation in spending of interest. Alternatively, failure to control for omitted variables may yield residuals that are too big.

With these caveats in mind, we estimate

$$\text{spending per mile}_s = \beta_0 + \beta_1 G_s + \varepsilon_s, \tag{1}$$

where $s$ indicates state. The dependent variable is spending per new Interstate mile in 2016 dollars. We use the estimated residual, $\hat{\varepsilon}_s$, as our measure of spending within policymaker discretion. We weight all regressions by the number of Interstate miles built in a state so that the results approximate the average mile, rather than the average state.

Figure 2.2 presents these $\hat{\varepsilon}_s$ residuals. By construction, they average to zero. A comparison of figures 2.1 and 2.2 shows that the magnitude of the variation shrinks substantially. Instead of an almost $50 million difference between the highest and lowest spending states (as in figure 2.1), the difference falls to about $25 million. Notably, Delaware—the highest-spending

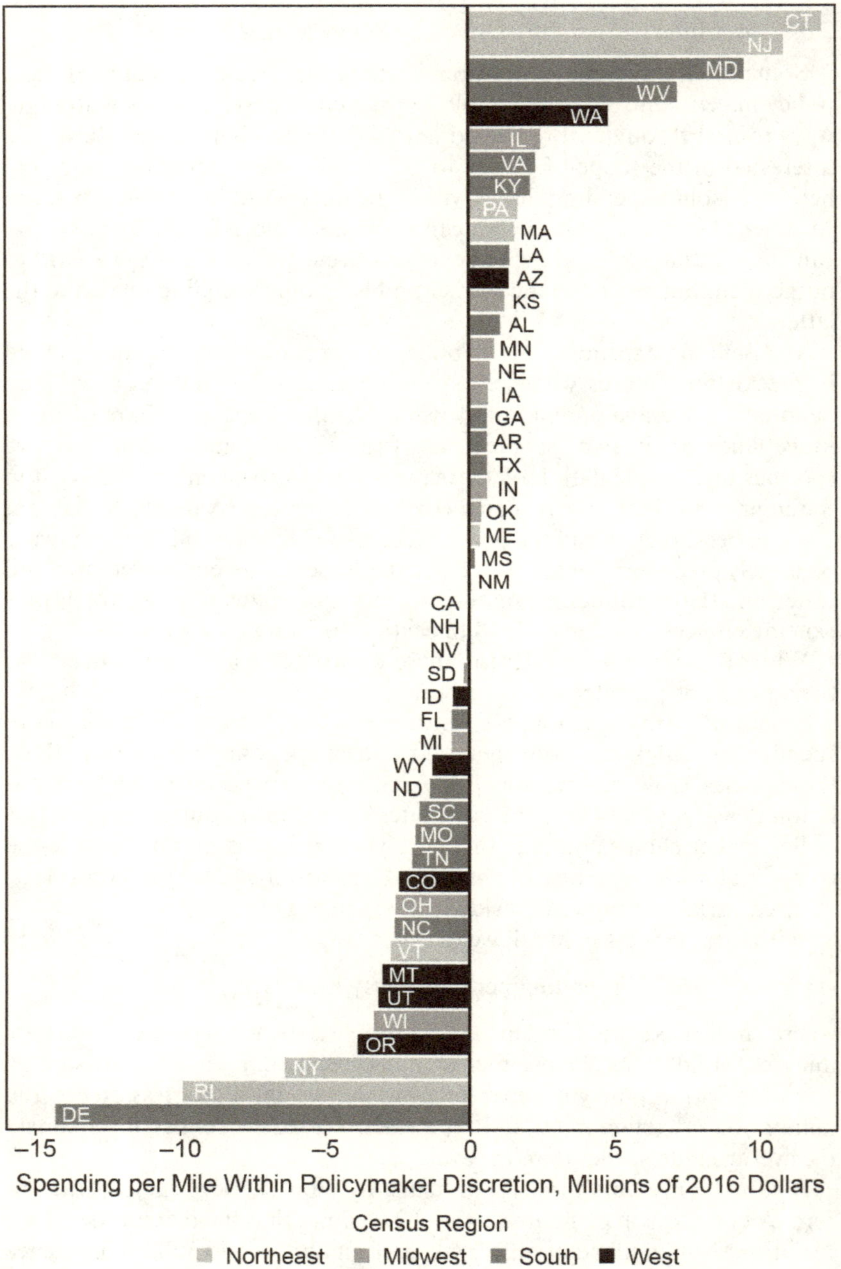


**Fig. 2.2 Interstate spending per new mile, spending within policy maker discretion**

*Note:* This figure reports residuals from a regression of Interstate spending per mile, 1956–1993, on population density, slope, and the extent of wetlands or rivers (see equation (1) and surrounding text for details).

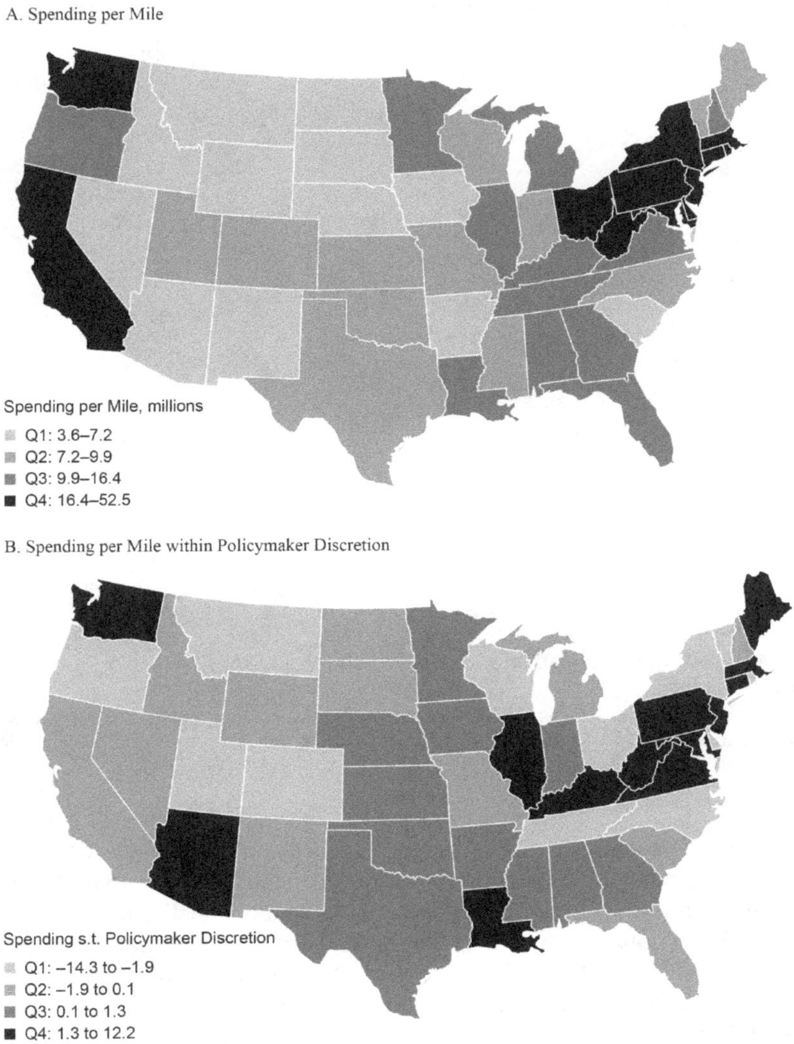


**Fig. 2.3 Geographic pattern of spending per interstate mile**

*Note:* Panel A maps quartiles of Interstate spending per mile from figure 2.1. Panel B maps quartiles of Interstate spending per mile subject to policy maker discretion as in figure 2.2.

state in the first figure—is now the lowest-spending state, spending almost $15 million fewer dollars per mile than the average state.[7]

The panel B of figure 2.3 shows this residual spending in a state map. While Washington State and parts of the mid-Atlantic region remain in the

7. Delaware has very few Interstate miles, and many of these miles are adjacent to or are over water.

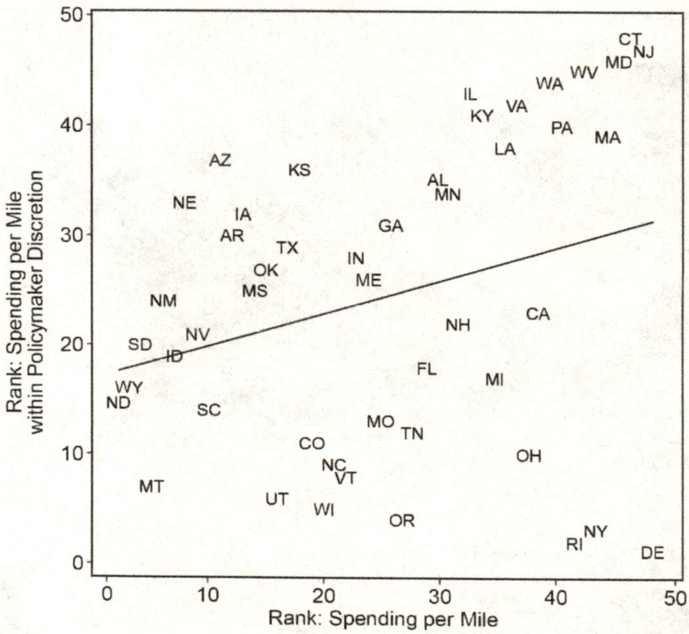


**Fig. 2.4 Rank-rank correlation, raw spending and spending within policy maker discretion**

*Note:* This figure shows each state's rank (from 1 to 48) in Interstate spending per mile on the horizontal axis versus the state's rank in Interstate spending per mile subject to policy maker discretion on the vertical axis.

top quartile of spending, much of New England and the Northeast moves out of the top quartile of spending. In addition, much of the South now falls into the second-highest quartile of spending per mile. The distribution also shows a fair amount of within-region heterogeneity in residual spending. For example, New York is in the bottom quartile, while most of its neighbors are in the top quartile. Louisiana is in the top quartile, while the rest of the South falls in lower quartiles.

We begin by considering the relationship between raw and residual spending. Figure 2.4 plots each state's rank in the raw spending per mile distribution on the horizontal axis and the rank of the residual from equation (1) on the vertical axis; points are the two-letter state abbreviation. The ranks are positively correlated, and the strength of the correlation is moderate ($\rho = 0.3$).

Interestingly, the controls $G_s$ change the ranks of high-spending states more than the ranks of low-spending states. There are virtually no states in the top left quadrant (unconditionally low and conditionally high spending), but quite a few states in both the top right (high conditionally and

**Table 2.2** **Estimates of spending conditional on predetermined characteristics robust to specification variation**

| | Full period | | | | Second period: 1970–1993 | | | |
|---|---|---|---|---|---|---|---|---|
| Covariates | $R^2$ (1) | Standard deviation (2) | Diff: p75–p25 (3) | Diff: p90–p10 (4) | $R^2$ (5) | Standard deviation (6) | Diff: p75–p25 (7) | Diff: p90–p10 (8) |
| Raw data | | 10.51 | 9.41 | 23.00 | | 16.08 | 14.32 | 35.43 |
| + Predetermined characteristics | 0.84 | 4.37 | 3.25 | 8.16 | 0.67 | 10.23 | 8.00 | 16.40 |
| + Characteristics squared | 0.87 | 3.62 | 2.77 | 8.58 | 0.71 | 9.81 | 7.51 | 15.94 |
| + Average number of lanes | 0.87 | 3.63 | 2.78 | 8.58 | 0.71 | 9.76 | 7.53 | 15.97 |
| + Without two highest observations | 0.88 | 2.98 | 2.66 | 4.91 | 0.79 | 5.66 | 6.98 | 14.04 |

*Note:* For variable definitions, please see note to table 2.1. Columns 1 to 4 report figures for 1956 to 1993 and columns 5 to 8 figures from 1970 to 1993 only. The first row of this table presents summary statistics for the residual from a regression of spending per mile on a constant. The second row reports summary statistics for the residuals from the estimation of equation 2.1. The third row reports summary statistics for the residuals from the previous estimation with the inclusion of a $G_s^2$ term. The fourth row reports summary statistics for residuals from an estimation that additionally includes the average number of lanes in a state. The final row has summary statistics from the same regression, but without the observations with the two highest values of spending per mile. All estimations have 48 observations except the last row, which has 46.

unconditionally) and bottom right (unconditionally high, conditionally low) quadrants.

### 2.3.3 Evaluating the Isolation of Spending from Policy Maker Discretion

These residual spending measures are of interest inasmuch as the variation we have isolated is truly just that spending within policy maker control. In this section, we stress-test the distribution of these residuals and assess their persistence over time.

If the residuals from figure 2.2 are spending within policy maker discretion, they should already omit predetermined spending variation. If this is the case, then changes in the specification should have little impact on the magnitude and distribution of their value. Table 2.2 tests this contention and reports the standard deviation, the interquartile range, and the difference between the 90th and 10th percentiles for the full period (first four columns) and the second half of our time period (1970–1993; last four columns). In the raw data (first row), the standard deviation in spending is 10.5 million 2016 dollars, or just slightly under mean spending over the entire period. The interquartile range and the 90-10 difference also reflect substantial variation.

These figures are even larger for the second period. The standard deviation of spending per mile across states from 1970 to 1993 is 16 million 2016 dollars, with an interquartile range of $14 million and 90-10 difference of $35 million.

The second row of table 2.2 shows our preferred measure of spending within policy maker control, or residuals from a regression of spending per mile on slope, population density, and water and wetlands. As we saw in the comparison of figures 2.1 and 2.2, these predetermined features do explain a substantial amount of the variation in spending; the standard deviation for the full period falls from $10.5 to $4.4 million. Interestingly, when we consider just the 1970–1993 period, in which we hypothesize that a new policy regime has taken hold, the standard deviation of the residual is substantially closer to the unconditional standard deviation of raw spending ($10.2 million for the residual versus $16.1 million). Relative to the full period, the interquartile range and particularly the 90-10 difference are larger.

The following rows test whether the residuals estimated in the second row change substantially as we include additional covariates. In the third row, we add controls for all the predetermined characteristics squared and report results for the resulting residuals. Regardless of the time period, the variation in the residual changes very little, suggesting that the linear specification soaks up the bulk of the variation related to the predetermined characteristics. In the next row we evaluate whether variation in the residual could be driven by variation in the number of lanes per highway across states. Ideally, our dependent variable would be spending per lane mile, but data on the initial number of lanes constructed are not available for the first part of our analysis period. Instead, we add a control for the average number of lanes per highway in a state. This adds no explanatory power to the regression—the $R^2$ does not change—and the variation in the residuals is also virtually identical to the previous specification. This holds both for the full period and for the second half.

Alternatively, one might be concerned that these results are driven by a few high outliers, visible in both figures 2.1 and 2.2. To assess the role of outliers, we drop the states with the two highest values of spending per mile and reestimate equation (1) using the covariates from the previous row. While the standard deviation and the difference between the 90th and 10th percentiles both decline, the interquartile range is little changed, suggesting that the residuals for most observations are not driven by a particular relationship between the covariates and the very largest observations.

Another way to test whether these residuals are driven by underlying state features or by temporal vagaries is to assess whether states' residuals persist over time. As we discussed earlier, in other work we argue that there was a regime shift in spending that takes place around 1970. Because of this, the correlation between pre- and post-1970 residuals may be small. However, if state-specific factors such as procurement practices or industrial composition determine costs in the post-1970 regime, we should expect persistence in residuals within this latter period.

A. 1956 to 1969 versus 1970 to 1993

B. 1970 to 1981 versus 1982 to 1993

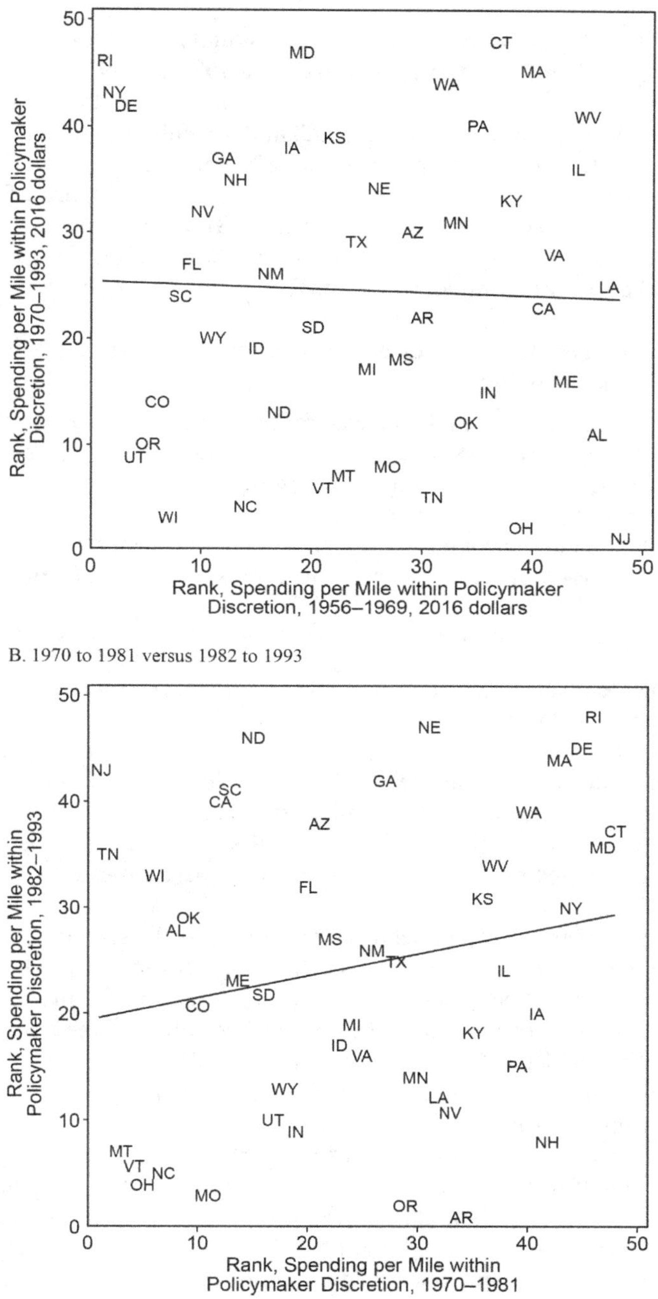


**Fig. 2.5 Correlation state rank, spending per mile subject to policy maker discretion**

*Note:* This figure presents state ranks in spending per mile, conditional on preexisting features. Panel A shows these ranks before 1970 (horizontal axis) and 1970 onward (vertical axis). Panel B shows these ranks between 1970 and 1981 (horizontal axis) and 1982 to 1993 (vertical axis).

Panel A of figure 2.5 plots each state's residual rank from 1956 to 1969; the vertical axis plots the residual rank from 1970 to 1993. We use ranks, rather than absolute magnitudes, to visually abstract from large outliers. As the figure shows, this correlation is small and actually negative ($\rho = -0.03$), consistent with a regime change in Interstate spending.

The pattern post-1970 is strikingly different. Panel B of figure 2.5 uses the same scheme but reports ranks from 1970 to 1981 on the horizontal axis and 1982 to 1993 on the vertical axis. Here the correlation is positive ($\rho = 0.2$), as we would anticipate if underlying state features drive spending.

### 2.3.4 Spending Due to Policy Maker Discretion and Related Private and Public Spending

Having created these residual measures of spending to reflect governance choices, we now turn to whether this residual variation is large or exceptional. We begin by comparing spending due to policy maker discretion with relevant private and public spending. The goal of this comparison is to illuminate possible common drivers of Interstate spending.

To make this comparison, we estimate regressions of the form

$$\text{spending per mile}_s = \beta_0 + \beta_1 G_s + \beta_2 C_s + \varepsilon_s . \tag{2.2}$$

The dependent variable is state Interstate spending per mile over either the entire 1956–1993 period or over the 1970–1993 period. As before, $G_s$ is the vector of the three key predetermined features as defined for equation (1). We denote additional covariates as $C_s$. As in table 2.2, we measure this residual variation in three ways: the standard deviation of the residuals; the difference between the 75th and 25th percentiles of the residual distribution; and the difference between the 90th and 10th percentiles of the residual distribution.

The first row in the top panel of table 2.3 repeats the second row of table 2.2 for comparison with the other results. The inclusion of predetermined features explains 84 percent of the variation in spending for the full period, as shown by the $R^2$ in column 3. The standard deviation of the residuals falls by more than half to \$4.4 million (column 4; relative to a raw mean spending of \$11.5 million per mile in table 2.1). The other measures of residual variation shrink by even larger shares.

The first row in the bottom panel of this table shows analogous figures for the second half of the period. The raw cross-state variation in spending for this period is larger: the standard deviation of \$16.1 for the second period is larger than the standard deviation of \$10.5 for the entire period. The predetermined covariates explain less of the overall spending in this later period ($R^2$ of 0.67 versus 0.84). The first row in each panel serves as the baseline to which we compare whether other spending explains a meaningful portion of spending due to policy maker discretion.

**Table 2.3** **Relationship between Interstate spending per new mile and public and private spending**

| | | | | Residual variation | | |
|---|---|---|---|---|---|---|
| | Coefficient (1) | Standard error (2) | $R^2$ (3) | Standard deviation (4) | p75 – p25 (5) | p90 – p10 (6) |
| Interstate spending per mile: entire period, 1956–1993 | | | | | | |
| Predetermined characteristics | | | 0.84 | 4.37 | 3.25 | 8.16 |
| Predetermined characteristics and | | | | | | |
| Private spending | | | | | | |
| Construction spending, 1993 = 100 | 0.03 | 0.10 | 0.84 | 4.34 | 3.18 | 7.99 |
| Health insurance per user, 2001, $1000s | −0.34 | 1.99 | 0.84 | 4.38 | 3.27 | 8.02 |
| Public spending, all $1,000s | | | | | | |
| Medicaid per enrollee, 1991 | −0.23 | 0.22 | 0.84 | 4.42 | 3.67 | 8.17 |
| Medicare per enrollee, 1991 | 1.29** | 0.47 | 0.85 | 3.93 | 3.2 | 7.86 |
| Local government expenditure per capita | −0.32 | 0.36 | 0.84 | 4.46 | 3.63 | 8.64 |
| Interstate spending per mile: second period, 1970–1993 | | | | | | |
| Predetermined characteristics | | | 0.67 | 10.23 | 8.00 | 16.40 |
| Predetermined characteristics and | | | | | | |
| Private spending | | | | | | |
| Construction spending, 1993 = 100 | 0.51** | 0.20 | 0.74 | 8.78 | 7.97 | 16.44 |
| Health insurance per user, 2001, $1000s | 8.66* | 4.99 | 0.70 | 9.68 | 7.27 | 14.62 |
| Public spending, all $1,000s | | | | | | |
| Medicaid per enrollee, 1991 | 0.46 | 0.46 | 0.68 | 10.06 | 8.08 | 16.56 |
| Medicare per enrollee, 1991 | 3.37** | 1.00 | 0.72 | 9.69 | 7.06 | 15.59 |
| Local government expenditure per capita | 1.13** | 0.57 | 0.69 | 10.06 | 7.67 | 14.13 |

*Note:* All rows contain 48 observations. ***Statistically significant at the 1 percent level. **Statistically significant at the 5 percent level. *Statistically significant at the 10 percent level. All regressions are weighted by Interstate miles constructed. The first row in each panel reports a regression of Interstate spending per mile on a constant and the three predetermined characteristics discussed in the text. All rows in each panel following "Geographic covariates and" report results from the estimation of Interstate spending per mile on geographic covariates and the named covariate (as in equation 2.2).

Our first additional covariate is private construction spending. This comparison to private costs tests whether Interstate spending per mile is higher in, for example, New Jersey or Connecticut because costs are generally higher in these states or because of other factors specific to the Interstates. If construction labor costs are generally higher in New Jersey, Interstate spending per mile should be related to private construction costs, as they both include these higher labor costs. Said differently, if construction costs matter to both, a control for private construction costs in equation (2) should substantially decrease the variation in the residual.

We measure construction costs via a constant quality index (see data section and appendix for more details). The second row of the top part of the table shows that there is virtually no relationship between the variation in private construction costs and Interstate spending per mile for the 1956–1993 period—despite the fact that both operate in similar markets. This is consistent with the result in Brooks and Liscow (2020) that cross-state variation in labor costs explains none of the temporal increase in Interstate spending per mile. The coefficient on residential private construction costs is small and very imprecisely estimated; the measures of residual variance are barely changed by the addition of this additional covariate.

This finding is somewhat different in the 1970–1993 period; here private construction costs are significantly and positively related to Interstate spending. A two-unit increase in the private residential construction index (about one-third of the interquartile range for this variable) is associated with $1 million additional Interstate spending per mile.

We can get at this same issue by evaluating whether, if highway spending varied across states in the same pattern as private construction costs, there would be any cross-state variation in Interstate spending left. We use a constrained regression to ask this question. We specify both the Interstate spending per mile and the construction cost index in logs so that no variation in excess of construction cost implies a coefficient of one. Estimating this log-log regression with the coefficient on private construction costs fixed at one, we find results very similar to the conclusions from table 2.3. This restriction has very little impact on the remaining variance in spending subject to policy maker discretion. Thus, the cross-state pattern of Interstate spending differs from that of residential private construction.

Another private cost that varies substantially across space is health care. If the regulatory environment that drives health spending also drives Interstate spending, we would expect to see a large drop in the residual with the inclusion of private health care costs. These private health care costs are expenditures by individuals and insurance companies for health care, including premiums and health care expenses, as well as administrative expenses by health insurers. For the full period, we find an imprecise correlation between private health insurance expenditures per user from 2001 (the earliest available year) and spending due to policy maker discretion. Costliness of private care may speak to the regulatory environment in the state. However, we see no strong relationship between highway spending and private health insurance expenses, as standard errors are large.

However, in the 1970–1993 period, this relationship strengthens substantially. An additional \$250 in private insurance spending—the magnitude of the interquartile range—is associated with slightly more than \$2 million more in Interstate spending per mile. This is about 14 percent of mean Interstate spending per mile. This is suggestive evidence that there may be common factors driving up both types of spending. However, the residuals change only modestly. For example, the standard deviation of the residuals falls from \$10.3 to \$9.68. Thus, there seem unlikely to be critical common drivers for these two types of spending.

With these mixed findings in hand, we now turn to public spending, which has different drivers than private spending does and which may therefore suggest different drivers in Interstate spending. We start with spending on Medicare per enrollee. Medicare funding decisions are almost exclusively federal. States have no control over what or how much the system covers, nor do they bear any fiscal liability for the program. Yet there is local variation: federal decisions manifest locally through the choices of patients, hospitals, and health care providers. In addition, Medicare reimbursement rates vary regionally.

Although there is a near vacuum in work on the geographic variation in highway costs, the geographic variation in Medicare has been studied intensely (see Cutler and Sheiner 1999; Martin et al. 2007; Wennberg and Gittelsohn 1973). The most prominent strand of the literature, led largely by researchers at Dartmouth, argues that there is substantial unexplained variation in Medicare costs. In implementing these studies, researchers usually adjust spending for Medicare prices, so that the effects are driven by the quantity of procedures, rather than the price of procedures (Skinner and Fisher 2010). Variation in prices is mechanical, because the federal government sets Medicare reimbursement rates. Quantity differences in health care, however, could be driven by, for example, different physician practice styles across the country.

The overview in Congressional Budget Office (2008) divides the drivers of Medicare spending into four main categories: prices; health and illness status; regional preferences about the use of healthcare services; and residual variation. The summary of the literature suggests unsurprisingly that price is not a major driver. While this literature argues that regional variation in individual preferences for care is generally not a large driver, the report acknowledges that it is very difficult to measure regional preferences and that demographics' ability to explain preferences may be limited. This literature points out that the unexplained variation is large and that addressing factors that cause the variation, such as physician practices, could yield large savings in the program.

A host of more recent work builds on these findings. For example, Gottlieb and colleagues (2010) analyze Medicare spending after adjusting for local price differences and find that utilization—not prices—drives Medicare spending. Finkelstein, Gentzkow, and Williams (2016) also find an important role for place-based variation. They use patient migration to show that "40 to 50 percent of geographic variation in utilization is attributable to demand-side factors, including health and preferences, with the remainder due to place-specific supply factors." Similarly, Molitor (2018) shows that physicians change practice styles after moving and estimates that place can explain between 60 to 80 percent of physician practice differences.

In contrast, Sheiner (2014) argues that using state-level Medicare spending data—like the data we use in this chapter—and a very limited set of state health status controls can explain a large amount of the cross-sectional variation in Medicare spending. She takes this as evidence that differing practice styles do not explain a large amount of variation in spending. Further, she is skeptical of the ability of geographic variation in Medicare spending to illuminate "inefficiencies in our healthcare system" (1). Our work addresses part of this concern. If spending of multiple types is consistently high in some states, it may suggest which factors are at work.

We correlate Interstate spending per mile with Medicare spending per enrollee in 1991, the earliest year with digitized costs. Interestingly, Medicare spending is statistically significantly related to Interstate spending; it is also the only variable in the table that yields a notable decrease in Interstate spending residuals. For each additional $1,000 of Medicare spending—an amount slightly smaller than the interquartile range for this variable—a state spends an additional $1.3 million dollars to build an Interstate mile. This $1.3 million is roughly 10 percent of the average state expenditure per mile. Comparing the final two columns of the table, it is clear that this stems from the explanatory power at the tails of the state spending distribution.

This relationship only strengthens in the second period. An additional $1,000 of Medicare spending—four-fifths of the interquartile range—is associated with an additional $3.4 million dollars in spending per mile, compared with an average of $15.2 million per mile. An additional $1,000 of local government spending—roughly three-fifths of the interquartile range—is associated with $1.1 million additional spending per mile. Medicare spending reduces the residual variation in the middle of the distribution (columns 4 and 5, standard deviation and interquartile range), whereas local government spending is more tied to reductions in residual variation at the tails of the distribution (column 6, 90-10 percentile difference).

Of all the variables we consider in this section, Medicare is the most strongly and significantly related to Interstate spending. To better understand the relationship with Medicare, figure 2.6 shows the raw correlation between Interstate spending per mile from 1970 to 1993 on the horizontal axis and Medicare spending per enrollee on the vertical axis. The two series are clearly related, particularly at the high end of spending. The distribu-

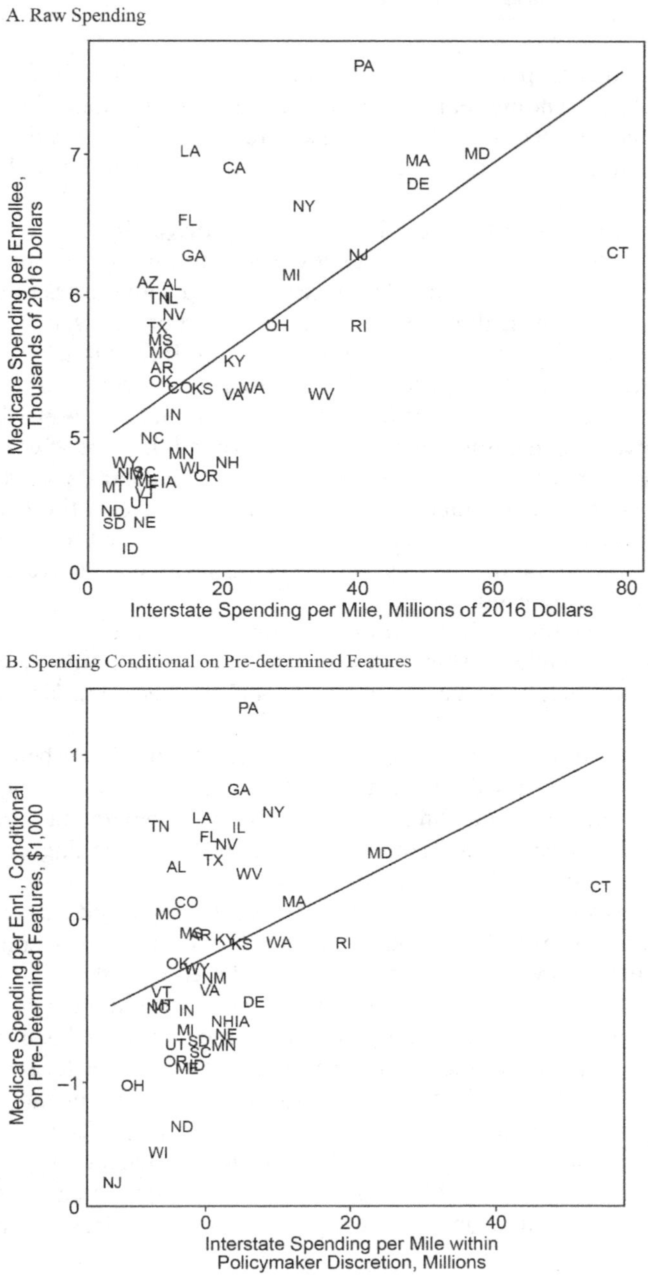


**Fig. 2.6 Correlation, Interstate spending per mile and Medicare spending per enrollee**

*Note:* Panel A shows the relationship between Interstate spending per mile after 1970 (horizontal axis) and Medicare spending per enrollee in 1991 (vertical axis; both in 2016 dollars). Panel B shows these two measures conditional on the three geographic covariates that we use throughout.

tion of Medicare spending is substantially less skewed than the distribution of Interstate spending. Panel B shows this relationship conditional on the geographic covariates; both axes present residuals.[8] The positive correlation remains, as does the much less symmetric distribution of Interstate spending.

We do not believe that Medicare spending drives Interstate spending. However, the correlation does suggest some common cost drivers. For example, the same institutional features that lead some states to consume large quantities of health services, such as second opinions, may also lead them to use more features, such as noise walls, on Interstates.

In contrast to Medicare, Medicaid decisions include substantial state discretion, subject to federal rules. States have some ability to choose who is covered, above certain minimum limits, and to expand the type of coverage. In form, the Interstate program is probably closer to Medicare, in the sense that states cannot limit coverage—if we analogize coverage to Interstate miles that the state must construct. However, states can provide Interstate quality above the minimum bar, as states can provide health care above a required minimum for Medicaid.

However, the Medicaid program, with substantially more state discretion, has virtually no relationship with Interstate spending and makes no meaningful change to the residual variance. This lack of a meaningful relationship holds for the second period as well.

We also evaluate whether general patterns of state fiscal behavior can explain Interstate spending. Perhaps states are high spending in all dimensions, and Interstate spending is a reflection of this general pattern. To test this hypothesis, we condition on overall state and local spending. To abstract from institutional differences in government organization across states, we use state aggregate spending.[9] This measure of total expenditure per capita is not statistically related to per mile Interstate spending; its inclusion actually slightly increases variation in the residuals. Therefore, if there is a common component that drives Interstate spending per mile and local government expenditure per capita, this component has little impact on local spending.

One might also hypothesize that particular categories of local spending, rather than public spending overall, might be related to Interstate spending and illuminate common cost drivers. In table 2A.3 we also consider the two key discretionary categories of local government: education spending and capital spending. Neither of these is statistically related to Interstate spending per mile, nor does either have any appreciable impact on the residual variation.

8. Because these regressions are weighted by miles constructed, the average of the points in the figures may not average to zero when not weighted.

9. Because the digital Census of Governments does not have state governments in 1967, we make an additional measure that uses data from Census years (ending in 2 and 7) from 1967 to 1992, but excludes state governments; this is "Local (no state) expenditure per capita, $1,000s." Results with this measure are in table 2A.3.

While we have considered each spending covariate independently, this may mask some interesting covariation across spending types and with Interstate spending. Table 2A.2 shows specifications with covariates standardized, so readers can compare their relative influence and specifications with all spending covariates entered jointly, both for the full period and the latter half. Regardless, Medicare per enrollee remains the category with the strongest and most precisely estimated relationship to Interstate spending per mile.

Finally, Interstate spending per mile has high cross-state variation. Table 2A.1 shows the coefficients of variation for all relevant variables. The only spending variable we analyze that has a higher coefficient of variation than Interstate spending per new mile is Interstate maintenance spending per mile. In particular, the coefficient of variation in Interstate spending is 0.58—about four times that of Medicare per enrollee and twice that of Medicaid per enrollee. This pattern remains even after controlling for predetermined features; dividing the residual standard deviation by the mean spending per mile produces 0.38,[10] considerably higher than forms of spending other than highway maintenance. This difference is even larger for the higher-variance 1970–1993 period.

In sum, there is substantial cross-state variation in Interstate spending per mile. When we restrict to the variation within policy maker control, the variation is somewhat diminished but still economically meaningful. The geographic pattern of spending subject to policy maker discretion is most related to Medicare spending per enrollee, potentially highlighting a common mechanism.

## 2.4 Root Causes of Variation in Interstate Spending

In this section, we review evidence on root cause drivers of infrastructure spending. Unlike the attention given to health spending, outside of some popular press profiles, there has been very limited work on the geographic variation in infrastructure spending. *New York* magazine profiled New York City's new transport infrastructure and found that for the same amount of money, New York gets "four new miles of tunneled LIRR (Long Island Rail Road) route and one new terminal station" while "London will get 14 miles serving seven stations" (Barro 2019b).[11] The article provides examples of high labor costs—many hours worked, if not necessarily high hourly wages—and high costs of coordination across governments.

In an equally eye-popping result, Gordon and Schleicher (2015) find that the US leads the world in the cost of building new rail. These authors rule

10. Recall that the coefficient of variation is simply the standard deviation of a distribution divided by its mean.

11. Rosenthal (2019) presents a similar example in the *New York Times*.

out a number of obvious suspects for these high costs: land, labor costs, and a decentralized system of infrastructure creation. The Reason Foundation also provides a state-level ranking of road spending, which highlights the declining quality of US road infrastructure, along with its increasing costs (see, for example, Feigenbaum, Fields, and Purnell 2019).

The General Accountability Office was recently tasked by Congress to undertake an assessment of what makes US infrastructure costly relative to other advanced economies. Taken as a whole, the report punts, suggesting that no comparisons are possible until agencies do a better job collecting cost information (Barro 2019a; General Accountability Office 2019). Indeed, at a November 2019 Transportation Review Board convening that Brooks attended, a top Federal Highway Administration (FHWA) official acknowledged that while FHWA monitors spending, it does not track costs on a per-project basis.

Broadly, there are many potential drivers of infrastructure spending. McKinsey Global Institute (2013) divides these drivers into seven categories. The first is technical explanations, including design standards, the type and location of projects, materials costs, and economies of scale. We choose the Interstate system in part to abstract from some of these technical concerns: design standards are set nationally and, to the extent that materials are a national market, our comparison is net of these costs. In Brooks and Liscow (2020) we find very little temporal variation in materials costs.

As the Interstate project drew to a close, fixed costs may have grown relative to variable costs. While this is an issue for a temporal analysis, it matters for cross-state variation only if these fixed costs were relatively larger in some states. This seems possible, but none of our data can speak to this question.

More generally, Flyvbjerg, Holm, and Buhl (2004) examined 258 rail, bridge, tunnel, and road projects from around the world, finding that projects have grown larger over time. For bridges and tunnels, they find that larger projects are associated with higher cost overruns, so a trend toward larger projects could be one reason that costs have grown. However, this only seems to hold true for bridges and tunnels. In their dataset, larger road projects (without bridges and tunnels) were not associated with higher cost overruns. In a study of cost overruns for Norwegian roads, Odeck (2004) found that overruns occur more frequently with smaller road projects. He attributes this finding to reduced economies of scale.

A second potentially important driver, also not relevant for our cross-state Interstate comparison, consists of the restrictions implicit in a funding source. Since the Interstate system follows a similar funding scheme across states, funding restrictions are unlikely to be a major driver of cross-state variation. In other types of projects, however, funding limitations or restrictions may limit some states' ability or incentive to make the long-term commitments that lead to low-cost projects. In addition, funding restrictions could increase costs across the board, without increasing cross-state variation.

A third potential driver is the market structure of the construction industry and the government's bidding and procurement practices. If the construction industry is more concentrated in some states, this could yield higher bids and therefore higher costs. For the state of Indiana, Kishore and Abraham (2009, 2) note a decline in the average number of bids on road projects, from 4.2 in 2001 to 3.6 in 2005. They attribute the decline in bids to consolidation among contractors, increased work with repeat contractors, and frequent delays that discourage contractors from bidding on state projects in the future. Many other bidding and procurement practices—such as the mandatory choice of the low-cost bid or Buy American provisions—are unique to US projects but constant across states, so they cannot explain the variation we document here (Davis 2017; Intueor Consulting 2016).

Fourth, labor costs are a potential driver of spending. Over the past 20 years, construction productivity has been flat as overall productivity has increased (McKinsey Global Institute 2013, 31). In the cross-state context, this could drive results if the change in productivity varies across state, which seems possible. Brooks and Liscow (2020) show that construction wages are roughly flat over time, so the price of labor does not explain the temporal increase in infrastructure cost. Further, labor's share of Interstate spending actually declines somewhat, suggesting that labor quantities are not a disproportionate cost driver.

All US states are subject to the Davis-Bacon Act of 1931, which requires the payment of "prevailing wages" on public projects. Findings on the role of Davis-Bacon in raising overall costs are mixed. In an early and influential study, Fraundorf, Norby, and Farrell (1984) found that Davis-Bacon adds about 26 percent to overall construction costs for new, non-residential buildings. Dunn, Quigley, and Rosenthal (2005) found that the California prevailing wage law led to an increase of between 9 and 37 percent in the cost of building subsidized housing.

However, this overall finding is not unanimous in the literature. Azari-Rad, Philips, and Prus (2003) criticized the early findings of Fraundorf, Norby, and Farrell (1984), pointing out that labor accounts for only a third of overall construction costs, making the 26 percent estimate seem implausible. The study of school construction costs by Azari-Rad, Philips, and Prus (2003) found no statistically significant difference between the cost of constructing schools across states with and without labor agreements.

Examining 10 years of Colorado road maintenance contracts, Duncan (2015) made similar findings. Duncan compared projects built with federal money, which are subject to both Davis-Bacon and Disadvantaged Business Enterprise (DBE) requirements, to locally funded projects. He found no difference in repaving costs, despite the different prevailing wage law and DBE requirements. He points out, however, that Colorado as a state has low rates of unionization in the construction industry, and thus Davis-Bacon may not substantially alter labor costs for highway contracts.

A fifth, oft-cited potential cause of high costs is the regulatory environment for large construction projects, including, but not limited to, environmental regulation, litigation threat, and eminent domain costs. While all Interstate projects are subject to review under the National Environmental Policy Act of 1969 (NEPA), regional variation in enforcement—or enforcement via threat of litigation—is likely.

More generally, Brooks and Liscow (2020) show that the rise of "citizen voice," which dramatically shifted the regulatory environment by allowing affected citizens more direct sway over government decision-making because of new statutes, judicial doctrine, and social movements, is consistent in timing and magnitude with the increase in infrastructure spending. In particular, proxies for economic and political power—income and housing prices—statistically explain much of the increase in Interstate spending, but only after 1970. Consistent with this, we see a pronounced rise, after the 1970s, in ancillary structures that reduce local impacts (for example, noise walls). We also see a notable increase post-1970 in politicians' joint discussion of environment and the Interstate, as measured by text from the Congressional Record.

By construction, environmental regulation is designed to raise project costs by forcing builders to internalize the negative externalities from their construction. The policy question is then whether these regulations increase costs above and beyond this internalizing of externalities. Hecht and Niemeier (2002) made use of the fact that many projects in California receive categorical exemptions from NEPA requirements to estimate the costs of completing an environmental impact statement. They found that the cost of completing an environmental impact statement can come close to matching the rest of the costs associated with the initial project design phase. In addition to the direct costs of litigation, Todorovich and Schned (2012) state that threat of litigation leads to expensive environmental impact statements that are overly technical.[12]

It is also possible that eminent domain costs could vary across states. Gordon and Schleicher (2015) identify the US, UK, Australia, and New Zealand as common-law countries with high infrastructure costs. They suggest that common-law countries may provide property owners with particularly strong protections that drive up the cost of eminent domain. However, the combination is not necessarily decisive. The authors note that countries such as Germany have strong property rights protections and per-unit infrastructure spending that is lower than in the US. Brooks and Liscow (2020) argue

12. Cordes and Weisbrod (1979) show that a requirement to better compensate those harmed by Interstate construction led to meaningful changes in program implementation.

that common law alone is insufficient to explain the rise in US per-unit infrastructure spending. During the period that per-unit infrastructure spending is rising, the US was (and is) a common-law country. Thus, common law alone, absent an interaction with some additional institutional feature, cannot be a sufficient explanation. Brooks and Liscow (2020) also suggest that land costs do not drive the increase in Interstate spending, since the share spent by states on land and planning declines over time.

In addition to these regulatory costs, other political institutions are a sixth potential driver of increased Interstate spending. Broadly, economists believe that institutions play a crucial role in determining state spending levels (see review in Besley and Case 2003). Ideology also plays a role in spending decisions, and empirical work suggests that ideology plays a greater role as income increases (Pickering and Rockey 2013). Brooks and Liscow (2020) find no relationship between changes in the specific institution of governmental fragmentation and increases in Interstate spending per mile.

Finally, project management is the seventh factor that could drive cost variation. There is a suggestion in the literature that management is very important, but work on quantitative classification is very limited. Many articles cite mismanagement as a major factor in delays and overruns. For example, Todorovich and Schned (2012, 5) attributes many delays in the NEPA process to "administrative process bottlenecks, project management failings, or a lack of capacity among the agencies involved in the process."

A large number of factors influence project management, including staff experience, institutional culture, and political will. Hecht and Niemeier (2002, 352) surveyed employees of the California Department of Transportation and found that fewer than 2 percent of employees felt that their agency would reward them for reducing the time or cost of a project—even with simple rewards like recognition.

And these are merely the major drivers in a retrospective sense. Looking prospectively, Winston (2013) highlights a number of technological innovations—most important among them the driverless car—that have the potential to decrease cost.

## 2.5 Interstate Spending: Evidence on Root Causes and Consequences

While our data do not afford relevant variation to identify causal effects, in this section we present correlations between some of the root causes from the previous section and Interstate spending per mile. We conclude by evaluating whether Interstate spending per mile is correlated with outcomes, such as accidents or maintenance spending.

### 2.5.1 Highway Spending and Potential Drivers

As our literature review covers more cost drivers than we have degrees of freedom—we have evidence from 48 states—we now turn to assessing the relationship between Interstate spending per mile and a few salient or well-measured potential cost drivers. As before, the dependent variable is spending per mile (in millions of 2016 dollars), and we condition on our three predetermined characteristics (slope, population density, and water and wetlands).

We focus here on the second period, 1970–1993, when Interstate spending variation is larger (the analogous table for the full period is table 2A.4). We focus on demand for Interstate quality and on wages and politics. In table 2.4 we report regressions where each variable enters individually (columns 1 and 3) and where all variables enter jointly (columns 2 and 4). To ease interpretation of levels, columns 1 and 2 show results for unstandardized variables; to ease relative comparisons, columns 3 and 4 report coefficients for standardized variables. In addition to the coefficient and standard error, we also report the standard deviation of the residuals and the interquartile range for the residuals, since we wish to understand how much cross-state variation remains.

The first two rows test the root cause that wealthier citizens prefer "more" highway, in the sense of having a safer, less physically disruptive, or less noisy main artery. We proxy for these demand factors with the share of people age 26 and above with at least a high school education and real median family income. While both variables have positive coefficients, indicating more spending in places with more educated populaces and higher income populations, neither of these factors is related in any sharp way with Interstate spending per mile.[13]

The evidence presented in Brooks and Liscow (2020) suggests that wages do not drive cross-state variation, consistent with our finding here in the third set of rows of the table. We use annual wages from the County Business Patterns data (see data appendix for details) and see a small, positive, and imprecisely related relationship between wages and cross-state spending.

As discussed later, management could play a significant role in cost containment. The second-to-last set of rows in this table use a measure of the most pathological form of mismanagement: corruption. We measure corruption via an index from Boylan and Long (2003), who surveyed statehouse reporters to generate a cross-state measure of corruption. This measure is a normalized average of reporter responses and ranges between −2 and 2. While this measure of corruption is not individually related to highway spending per mile, in the joint estimation, we do find that states where reporters perceive more corruption have higher spending. A change in corruption equal to the interquartile range (0.68) yields an additional $1.7 million dollars of spending per mile.

Political taste in willingness to spend public funds is another possibility. The final row in table 2.4 looks at the impact of the Democratic presidential

13. Some findings from the cross section here differ from results in Brooks and Liscow (2020). Here we rely on purely cross-sectional variation. Our related paper relies on within state changes, using a specification with state and period fixed effects. These two different sources of variation yield different conclusions.

**Table 2.4** **Spending per mile and potential explanations, 1970– 1993**

| | Unstandardized variables | | Standardized variables | |
|---|---|---|---|---|
| | Variables enter | | Variables enter | |
| | Individually (1) | Jointly (2) | Individually (3) | Jointly (4) |
| Share high school graduates | 0.10 | 0.16 | 0.79 | 1.24 |
| | (0.12) | (0.18) | (0.97) | (1.40) |
| Residuals: standard dev. | 10.10 | | 10.10 | |
| Residuals: Q75 – Q25 | 7.57 | | 7.57 | |
| Real median family income, $10,000s | 1.74 | 1.25 | 1.46 | 1.05 |
| | (1.30) | (2.18) | (1.09) | (1.83) |
| | 9.89 | | 9.89 | |
| | 8.85 | | 8.85 | |
| Real construction wage | 0.21 | –0.07 | 1.55 | –0.55 |
| | (0.13) | (0.20) | (0.96) | (1.48) |
| | 10.09 | | 10.09 | |
| | 8.25 | | 8.25 | |
| Corruption index | 1.79 | 2.51* | 1.27 | 1.79* |
| | (1.47) | (1.49) | (1.05) | (1.06) |
| | 9.96 | | 9.96 | |
| | 6.42 | | 6.42 | |
| Democratic presidential vote share | 0.44** | 0.55** | 2.39** | 2.95** |
| | (0.20) | (0.24) | (1.09) | (1.28) |
| | 9.82 | | 9.82 | |
| | 15.49 | | 15.49 | |
| Overall | | | | |
| Standard deviation of residuals | | 8.93 | | 8.93 |
| Diff: p75–p25 | | 6.62 | | 6.62 |

*Note:* All specifications contain 48 observations and condition on the three predetermined characteristics we discuss in the text. ***Statistically significant at the 1 percent level. **Statistically significant at the 5 percent level. *Statistically significant at the 10 percent level. All regressions are weighted by Interstate miles constructed and use data from the period from 1970 to 1993. The first column in the table reports results for separate estimations of equation 2.2. Below the standard error, we report the standard deviation of residuals and then interquartile range of the residual. The second column report results from a regression when we include all covariates together. The final two rows report summary statistics for the residual from this regression. Columns 3 and 4 have a parallel organization but report results for variables standardized to mean zero standard deviation one to ease cross-variable comparisons.

vote share from 1970 to 1993 (see appendix for construction details). Note that most of this period has a somewhat different political alignment than the present: the South was largely Democratic, and the Northeast substantially more Republican. With this caveat in mind, we see that a 5.6 percentage point increase in the Democratic presidential vote share, a change of one standard deviation, is related to a $3.1 million dollar increase in spending per Interstate mile (column 2).

Overall, most of these covariates have no substantive impact on the residual variation, measured as either the standard deviation of the residuals or the interquartile range of the residuals (the two rows below the coefficient and the standard error for each variable). Nevertheless, states that have a higher Democratic presidential vote share and (more tenuously) states that are rated as more corrupt seem to spend more on Interstates per mile. While we are cautious in our interpretation, given the lack of exogenous variation, these correlations may point the way for future research.

### 2.5.2 How Does Spending Relate to Outcomes?

If states are spending more on Interstate Highways but are in some sense "getting more"—safer or longer-lasting roads—the cross-state variation in governance choices may have fewer lessons for cost containment. In table 2.5 we assess whether state spending is correlated with measurable highway outcomes. As in the previous table, the top panel covers the entire period and the bottom panel the higher variance second period. The first two rows of each panel of the table repeat the first two rows of each panel of table 2.3 for reference. Over the entire period, controlling for fatalities per hundreds of millions of vehicle miles traveled (VMT) has no additional explanatory power for the variance in state spending—doing so in fact raises the residual variation at the tails of the distribution. Accidents per 100,000 of VMT have similarly no relationship with Interstate spending per mile.

States that spend more money to build a new Interstate mile also spend more to maintain those miles, as measured by per-mile maintenance costs per state in 2015. Over the entire period, each additional million dollars of maintenance per mile is associated with an additional $200,000 dollars of initial highway construction. Although this is a statistically significant relationship, the relationship accounts for very little of the residual variation in spending, either as measured by $R^2$ (84 to 85), or by the change in the standard deviation of the residuals (4.4 versus 4.5).

This pattern is similar when we limit the analysis to the second period, 1970–1993. States with higher highway maintenance expenditures are those that initially spent more per mile. This variation now does seem to explain some portion of the variation in the residual at the tails. However, unlike for the overall period, there is a negative and significant relationship between fatalities per vehicle mile traveled on Interstates and construction spending per mile. Reducing fatalities by the amount of the interquartile range—0.55 per 100 million vehicle miles traveled—is associated with $2.5 million dollars of additional Interstate spending per mile, or about 15 percent of the mean. This is some of the first statistical evidence of a positive outcome associated with increased highway spending.

## 2.6 Discussion and Conclusion

In this chapter, we show that the geographic variation in Interstate spending per mile is large. If states in the top half of the spending distribution had

**Table 2.5** **Relationship between spending per mile and highway outcomes**

| | Coefficient (1) | Standard error (2) | $R^2$ (3) | Residual variation: Standard deviation (4) | Residual variation: p75 – p25 (5) | Residual variation: p90 – p10 (6) |
|---|---|---|---|---|---|---|
| Interstate spending per mile: entire period, 1956–1993 | | | | | | |
| Predetermined characteristics | | | 0.84 | 4.37 | 3.25 | 8.16 |
| Predetermined characteristics and highway outcome | | | | | | |
| Fatalities per 100m miles of VMT | −1.39 | 1.04 | 0.84 | 4.23 | 3.64 | 8.38 |
| Accidents per 1m miles of VMT | −0.05 | 0.22 | 0.83 | 4.41 | 3.18 | 8.28 |
| Highway maintenance per mile, millions | 0.21** | 0.08 | 0.85 | 4.50 | 3.02 | 7.41 |
| Interstate spending per mile: second period, 1970−1993 | | | | | | |
| Predetermined characteristics | | | 0.67 | 10.23 | 8.00 | 16.40 |
| Predetermined characteristics and highway outcome | | | | | | |
| Fatalities per 100m miles of VMT | −4.51** | 2.20 | 0.69 | 10.29 | 7.64 | 16.81 |
| Accidents per 100,000 miles of VMT | 0.26 | 0.46 | 0.66 | 10.23 | 7.85 | 15.13 |
| Highway maintenance per mile, millions | 0.44** | 0.20 | 0.7 | 10.06 | 7.56 | 13.80 |

*Note:* All rows contain 48 observations, except for accidents, which has 47. ***Statistically significant at the 1 percent level. **Statistically significant at the 5 percent level. *Statistically significant at the 10 percent level. All regressions are weighted by Interstate miles constructed. The first row in each panel reports results from a regression of Interstate spending per mile on a constant and the three geographic covariates discussed in the text. All rows in each panel following "Predetermined characteristics and" report results from the estimation of Interstate spending per mile on predetermined characteristics and the named covariate (as in equation 2.2).

capped their spending at the median, the Interstate system would have cost 40 percent less to build. Furthermore, the coefficient of variation in Interstate spending is unusually large—considerably larger than for other forms of government spending. The high relative variance in Interstate spending per new mile remains even when we limit the analysis to spending within policy maker discretion—that is, spending net of predetermined route features. While we have done our best to control for features that determine spending and are outside of policy maker control, it is still possible that we have failed to control for all such determinants. However, the variation in Interstate spending per mile net of policy maker discretion we estimate is very large. It is at least as economically meaningful as the variation in other categories of spending, such as Medicare, to which economists have devoted reams of papers.

In addition, we show that the geographic pattern in spending per Interstate mile is related, surprisingly, to spending per Medicare enrollee. An additional $1,000 dollars of Medicare spending is associated with an additional $1.3 million dollars of Interstate spending per mile, or about 10 percent of the mean.

In Brooks and Liscow (2020), we show that temporal increases in the cost of constructing a new Interstate mile are driven by input quantities rather than prices. Our primary evidence for this conclusion is twofold: nationally, real prices for labor and materials change little from 1956 to 1993, and cross-state variation in labor prices is not correlated with Interstate spending. Our finding is very similar to the argument in the Medicare spending literature that it is quantities, rather than prices that drive variation in spending (see Finkelstein, Gentzkow, and Williams 2016; Gottlieb et al. 2010; and others). These results suggest that some common feature or features may drive "more" provision—both higher Medicare spending and higher infrastructure spending.

While we have no direct evidence on what these features are, we offer two speculative and related hypotheses. First, higher average incomes in a state, by increasing demand, could drive the provision of "more." This hypothesis is consistent with Brooks and Liscow (2020), in which we show that increases in incomes and housing values statistically explain the entire increase in Interstate spending per mile over the period. We also show that costly features that mitigate the local costs of the Interstate, such as noise walls, are substantially more common in the citizen voice period. In health care, "more" could be more additional health care screenings, more appointments with specialists, or more luxurious hospital surroundings.

Second, and relatedly, states may differ in culture, which could consist of the underlying preferences of state citizens, the institutions that aggregate those preferences, or both. This hypothesis is consistent with some of the Medicare spending literature, which argues that higher spending is driven by a "culture of practice" (Gottlieb et al. 2010; Molitor 2018). In the Interstate realm, this would be a "culture of production," where higher production costs could be due to state procurement practices, underlying preferences of state voters, or the state-specific market concentration of construction firms.

A central concern is whether additional spending delivers additional value. The Medicare spending literature generally finds that higher treatment spending is not associated with better health outcomes; see Chandra, Sabik, and Skinner (2011) and Fisher and colleagues (2003), among many others. The picture for Interstate Highways is more nuanced. We find that more Interstate spending per mile is associated with fewer fatalities, a finding that is consistent with more spending delivering higher quality. However, more initial Interstate spending is not associated with lower future highway maintenance. The reason could be that more initially expensive highway miles are also more expensive to maintain. Alternatively, the reason could be that states that initially choose high spending also spend more on maintenance. Of course, a full analysis of quality requires a more holistic analysis that extends beyond the three factors we consider here.[14]

Any increase in the quality of US infrastructure depends crucially on managing the amount we spend per unit. Understanding what drives Interstate spending and the extent to which costs justify benefits is crucial if we seek to spend more to improve the state of US infrastructure. What precisely drives infrastructure spending remains fertile ground for future research.

## Data Appendix

1. Interstate spending per mile
   See Data Appendix in Brooks and Liscow (2020).
2. Geographic features
   a. Population density
      We use tract population density, or county density when tract data are not available. See Brooks and Liscow (2020) for specific files.
   b. Slope
      We measure the average slope within 50 meters of a segment using the Digital Elevation Map from USGS, purchased in 2018.

14. While we find a correlation between Interstate spending per mile and Medicare spending per enrollee, we find no such relationship with Medicaid spending. This is consistent with an important role for income in generating spending. If higher income yields greater demand for spending, this means that it is the relatively wealthy who drive at least some of the spending increases. These relatively wealthy people are in the Medicare population. They are, however, by definition, not in the Medicaid population. This bolsters the case that part of the common driver of higher spending is higher income, or some institutional features that develop in the presence of higher-income people.

c. Wetlands

We use the length, in miles, that the segment touches wetlands, defined as any of the types of wetlands classified by the Cowardin system, from US Fish and Wildlife Service (2018) National Wetlands Inventory data set.

3. Public and private spending

a. Health care spending

We measure Medicare spending per enrollee, Medicare spending per enrollee, and private health insurance spending per enrollee from the Centers for Medicare and Medicaid Services' "Health Expenditures by State of Residence, 1991–2014." We specifically use tables 23 ("Medicare Per Enrollee State Estimates by State of Residence"), 26 ("Medicaid Per Enrollee State Estimates by State of Residence"), and 29 ("Private Health Insurance Per Enrollee State Estimates by State of Residence").

We download data from https://www.cms.gov/Research-Statistics-Data-and-Systems/Statistics-Trends-and-Reports/NationalHealthExpendData/NationalHealthAccountsStateHealthAccountsResidence.html.

The Centers for Medicare and Medicaid Services define private health insurance in the National Health Expenditure Accounts as follows: "Includes premiums paid to traditional managed care, self-insured health plans and indemnity plans. This category also includes the net cost of private health insurance which is the difference between health premiums earned and benefits incurred. The net cost consists of insurers' costs of paying bills, advertising, sales commissions, and other administrative costs; net additions to reserves; rate credits and dividends; premium taxes; and profits or losses." See https://www.cms.gov/Research-Statistics-Data-and-Systems/Statistics-Trends-and-Reports/NationalHealthExpendData/Downloads/quickref.pdf.

b. State and local expenditures

We use the 1967, 1972, 1977, 1982, 1987, and 1992 Censuses of Governments, as compiled by Willamette University researchers Pierson, Hand, and Thompson (2015).

These data do not contain state expenditures in 1967. Thus, to be time-consistent, we create a panel of spending per census year. Specifically, we include data on total local (nonstate) spending per capita per year, parks and recreation spending per capita per year, elementary and secondary education spending both per capita and per enrollee per year, and total education spending (which includes higher education and other small categories) per capita per year.

4. Other Interstate measures

a. Highway maintenance

We rely on the 2015 *Highway Statistics* data. We create highway spending per mile using maintenance spending from table SF-4 and maintenance mileage from table HM-10.

b. Fatalities per Interstate vehicle miles traveled, 1994

We use the oldest available digital data on highway fatalities from section 5 of *Highway Statistics, 1995*. Specifically, we use "Total Rural Interstate System Fatalities and Injuries," table FI-6, and "Total Urban Interstate System Fatalities and Injuries," table FI-7.

Both tables also include vehicles traveled and are available at https://www.fhwa.dot.gov/ohim/1995/section5.htm. Fatalities are expressed per 100 million miles of vehicle travel.

c. Lanes

Calculated from the Federal Highway Administration, Highway Performance Monitoring System, 2016.

5. Private construction spending

a. Private residential construction costs

These data were assembled by Raven Molloy, who has generously shared them. Molloy used city-level historical cost indexes from R. S. Means Company (2003). She matched the city names to Census place IDs, merged with city-level housing unit counts, and created statewide averages. We use these statewide averages. Costs are indexed and not in nominal dollars. Molloy uses these data in Saks (2008).

b. Private health insurance spending

We measure private health insurance spending per enrollee from the Centers for Medicare and Medicaid Services' "Health Expenditures by State of Residence, 1991–2014." We use table 29 ("Private Health Insurance Per Enrollee State Estimates by State of Residence").

We download data from https://www.cms.gov/Research-Statistics-Data-and-Systems/Statistics-Trends-and-Reports/NationalHealthExpendData/NationalHealthAccountsStateHealthAccountsResidence.html.

6. Demographics

We use data on population from the Decennial Census. Specifically, we rely on the Census of Population and Housing for 1950–2000. We use state median family income,[15] percentage of adults over the age of 25 who have graduated high school, and median home values. All final variables are state-period averages weighted by miles. We use data on population from the Decennial Census.

7. Inflation adjustment

We use the CPI-U from the Federal Reserve Bank of Minneapolis, downloaded from https://www.minneapolisfed.org/community/financial

15. Note that because of issues of data availability, we use mean family income for 1970.

-and-economic-education/cpi-calculator-information/consumer-price-index-and-inflation-rates-1913.

8. Democratic presidential vote share

We use data from 1956 to 1993. See Brooks and Liscow (2020) for full citation.

**Table 2A.1 Coefficient of variation: Interstate and other local spending**

| | Entire cross section | | | Second period: 1970–1993 | | |
|---|---|---|---|---|---|---|
| | Mean (1) | CV: standard deviation/ mean (2) | Residual standard deviation/ mean (3) | Mean (4) | CV: standard deviation/ mean (5) | Residual standard deviation/ mean (6) |
| Spending/mile, $ millions | 11.51 | 0.582 | 0.379 | 15.52 | 0.686 | 0.659 |
| Private spending | | | | | | |
| Construction cost index | 31.53 | 0.156 | 0.145 | 48.55 | 0.117 | 0.153 |
| Health insurance/enrollee, 2001, $1,000s | 2.95 | 0.072 | 0.072 | 2.94 | 0.070 | 0.078 |
| Public spending, all $1,000s | | | | | | |
| Medicaid per enrollee, 1991 | 6.01 | 0.320 | 0.311 | 5.97 | 0.321 | 0.320 |
| Medicare per enrollee, 1992 | 5.65 | 0.146 | 0.152 | 5.65 | 0.146 | 0.117 |
| Local government expenditure per capita | 6.50 | 0.201 | 0.208 | 6.94 | 0.193 | 0.187 |
| Interstate outcomes | | | | | | |
| Fatalities per VMT, 1995* | 0.86 | 0.469 | 0.543 | 0.88 | 0.445 | 0.408 |
| Accidents per VMT, 1995* | 3.71 | 0.525 | 0.478 | 3.73 | 0.529 | 0.403 |
| Maintenance per mile, $ millions, 1995 | 5.73 | 0.745 | 0.661 | 5.92 | 0.735 | 0.899 |

*Note:* For variables, please see note to table 2.1. This table presents coefficients of variation (standard deviation divided by mean, weighted by Interstate miles constructed) for Interstate spending per mile and other related or major public spending categories. The first set of three columns shows results for the entire period; the second set show results just for 1970 to 1993.

**Table 2A.2 Relative relationship of other spending to Interstate spending using standardized variables**

| | Full period | | Years 1970–1993 | |
|---|---|---|---|---|
| | Covariates enter | | Covariates enter | |
| | Individually (1) | Jointly (2) | Individually (3) | Jointly (4) |
| Construction spending, 1993 = 100 | 0.16 | 0.51 | 2.88** | 2.40** |
| | (0.47) | (0.53) | (0.86) | (0.86) |
| Health insurance per user, 2001, $1000s | −0.07 | 0.09 | 1.78* | 1.19 |
| | (0.50) | (0.51) | (1.00) | (0.90) |
| Medicare per enrollee, 1991 | 1.06** | 1.34** | 2.78** | 4.13** |
| | (0.49) | (0.64) | (1.07) | (1.27) |
| Medicaid per enrollee, 1991 | −0.44 | 0.29 | 0.88 | 2.19** |
| | (0.43) | (0.54) | (0.95) | (1.06) |
| Local government expenditure per capita | −0.47 | −0.81 | 1.39 | −1.14 |
| | (0.46) | (0.51) | (0.92) | (0.90) |

*Note:* All regressions contain 48 observations. ***Statistically significant at the 1 percent level. **Statistically significant at the 5 percent level. *Statistically significant at the 10 percent level. All regressions are weighted by Interstate miles constructed. All variables in this table are standardized to mean zero, standard deviation one. The first column reports results for the full period. Each row in the first column is the coefficient from a separate regression of spending per mile on the named covariate and the three predetermined characteristics. In the second column, covariates enter jointly. Columns 3 and 4 repeat this pattern, but for the period from 1970 to 1993.

**Table 2A.3** **Correlation between spending per mile and additional measures of public spending**

| | Coefficient (1) | Standard error (2) | $R^2$ (3) | Residual variation: Standard deviation (4) | Residual variation: p75 – p25 (5) | Residual variation: p90 – p10 (6) |
|---|---|---|---|---|---|---|
| Entire period: 1956–1993 | | | | | | |
| Predetermined characteristics | | | 0.84 | 4.37 | 3.25 | 8.16 |
| Predetermined characteristics and public spending | | | | | | |
| Local (no state) expenditure per capita, $1000s | −0.57 | 0.58 | 0.84 | 4.53 | 3.51 | 8.71 |
| Primary and secondary education per capita | −1.11 | 1.44 | 0.84 | 4.39 | 3.51 | 8.51 |
| Capital outlays per capita, $1000s | 0.07 | 1.88 | 0.84 | 4.37 | 3.23 | 8.11 |
| Second period: 1970–1993 | | | | | | |
| Predetermined characteristics | | | 0.67 | 10.23 | 8.00 | 16.40 |
| Predetermined characteristics and public spending | | | | | | |
| Local (no state) expenditure per capita, $1000s | 1.61* | 0.82 | 0.69 | 10.22 | 8.01 | 14.92 |
| Primary and secondary education per capita | 2.79 | 3.36 | 0.68 | 10.06 | 8.19 | 15.68 |
| Capital outlays per capita, $1000s | 5.36 | 3.51 | 0.69 | 10.18 | 7.99 | 14.97 |

*Note:* All rows contain 48 observations. ***Statistically significant at the 1 percent level. **Statistically significant at the 5 percent level. *Statistically significant at the 10 percent level. All regressions are weighted by Interstate miles constructed. The first row in each panel reports a regression of Interstate spending per mile on a constant and the three pre-determined characteristics discussed in the text. All rows in each panel following "Predetermined characteristics and" report results from the estimation of Interstate spending per mile on geographic covariates and the named covariate (as in equation 2.2).

Table 2A.4 **Spending per mile and potential explanations, 1956–1993**

| | Unstandardized variables | | Standardized variables | |
|---|---|---|---|---|
| | Variables enter | | Variables enter | |
| | Individually (1) | Jointly (2) | Individually (3) | Jointly (4) |
| Share high school graduates | −0.04 | −0.10 | −0.28 | −0.77 |
| | (0.05) | (0.09) | (0.41) | (0.69) |
| Residuals: standard deviation | 4.37 | | 4.37 | |
| Residuals: Q75 − Q25 | 3.48 | | 3.48 | |
| Real median family income, $10,000s | 0.14 | 1.00 | 0.12 | 0.87 |
| | (0.57) | (1.04) | (0.49) | (0.91) |
| | 4.34 | | 4.34 | |
| | 3.19 | | 3.19 | |
| Real construction wage | 0.02 | 0.01 | 0.13 | 0.06 |
| | (0.06) | (0.10) | (0.46) | (0.73) |
| | 4.32 | | 4.32 | |
| | 3.17 | | 3.17 | |
| Corruption index | 1.00 | 1.05 | 0.71 | 0.75 |
| | (0.64) | (0.70) | (0.46) | (0.50) |
| | 4.29 | | 4.29 | |
| | 3.04 | | 3.04 | |
| Democratic presidential vote share | 0.03 | 0.03 | 0.18 | 0.17 |
| | (0.09) | (0.11) | (0.61) | (0.70) |
| | 4.34 | | 4.34 | |
| | 8.26 | | 8.26 | |
| Overall | | | | |
| Standard deviation of residuals | | 4.05 | | 4.05 |
| Diff: p75–p25 | | 3.50 | | 3.50 |

*Note:* This table follows the same format as table 2.4 but uses data for the full 1956–1993 period.

## References


Alder, Simon. 2019. "Chinese Roads in India: The Effect of Transport Infrastructure on Economic Development." Working paper.

Allen, Treb, and Costas Arkolakis. 2019. "The Welfare Effects of Transportation Infrastructure Improvements." Working paper.

Altshuler, Alan A., and David E. Luberoff. 2003. *Mega-Projects: The Changing Landscape of Urban Public Investment*. Brookings Institution Press and the Lincoln Institute of Land Policy.

American Society of Civil Engineers. 2017. "2017 Infrastructure Report Card: A Comprehensive Assessment of America's Infrastructure." Technical report, American Society of Civil Engineers.

Azari-Rad, Hamid, Peter Philips, and Mark J. Prus. 2003. "State Prevailing Wage Laws and School Construction Costs." *Industrial Relations* 42 (3): 445–57.

Balboni, Clare. 2019. "In Harm's Way? Infrastructure Investments and the Persistence of Coastal Cities." Working paper.

Barro, Josh. 2019a. "Here's Why We've Failed to Figure Out Why Infrastructure Costs So Much." *New York*, July 24.

———. 2019b. "Why New York Can't Have Nice Things." *New York*, May 30.

Baum-Snow, Nathaniel. 2007. "Did Highways Cause Suburbanization?" *Quarterly Journal of Economics* 122 (2): 775–805.

Beach, Brian, Joseph Ferrie, Martin Saavedra, and Werner Troesken. 2016. "Typhoid Fever, Water Quality, and Human Capital Formation." *Journal of Economic History* 76 (1): 41–75.

Besley, Timothy, and Anne Case. 2003. "Political Institutions and Policy Choices: Evidence from the United States." *Journal of Economic Literature* 41 (1): 7–73.

Boylan, Richard T., and Cheryl X. Long. 2003. "Measuring Public Corruption in the American States: A Survey of State House Reporters." *State Politics and Policy Quarterly* 3 (4): 420–38.

Brooks, Leah, and Zachary Liscow. 2020. "Infrastructure Costs." Working paper.

Chandra, Amitabh, Lindsay Sabik, and Jonathan S. Skinner. 2011. "Cost Growth in Medicare: 1992 to 2006." *Explorations in the Economics of Aging*, edited by David A. Wise, 133–57. Chicago: University of Chicago Press.

Congressional Budget Office. 2008. "Geographic Variation in Health Care Spending." Technical report, Congress of the United States.

Cordes, Joseph J., and Burton A. Weisbrod. 1979. "Governmental Behavior in Response to Compensation Requirements." *Journal of Public Economics* 11: 47–58.

Cutler, David, and Grant Miller. 2005. "The Role of Public Health Improvements in Health Advances: The Twentieth-Century United States." *Demography* 42 (1): 1–22.

Cutler, David M., and Louise Sheiner. 1999. "The Geography of Medicare." *American Economic Review* 89 (2): 228–33.

Davis, Jeff. 2017. "The Trump Infrastructure Agenda—What Would 'Buy American, Hire American' Really Entail?" *Eno Transportation Weekly*, January 18.

Duncan, Kevin C. 2015. "The Effect of Federal Davis-Bacon and Disadvantaged Business Enterprise Regulations on Highway Maintenance Costs." *Industrial and Labor Relations Review* 68 (1): 212–37.

Dunn, Sarah, John M. Quigley, and Larry A. Rosenthal. 2005. "The Effects of Prevailing Wage Requirements on the Cost of Low-Income Housing." *Industrial and Labor Relations Review* 59 (1): 141–57.

Duranton, Gilles, and Matthew A. Turner. 2012. "Urban Growth and Transportation." *Review of Economic Studies* 79 (4): 1407–40.

Faber, Benjamin. 2014. "Trade Integration, Market Size, and Industrialization: Evidence from China's National Trunk Highway System." *Review of Economic Studies* 81 (3): 1046–70.

Feigenbaum, Baruch, M. Gregory Fields, and Spence Purnell. 2019. "24th Annual Highway Report." Technical report, Reason Foundation.

Ferrie, Joseph P., and Werner Troesken. 2008. "Water and Chicago's Mortality Transition, 1850–1925." *Explorations in Economic History* 45 (1): 1–16.

Finkelstein, Amy, Matthew Gentzkow, and Heidi Williams. 2016. "Sources of Geographic Variation in Health Care: Evidence from Patient Migration." *Quarterly Journal of Economics* 131 (4): 1681–726.

Fisher, Elliott S., David E. Wennberg, Thérèse A. Stukel, Daniel J. Gottlieb, F. Lee Lucas, and Etoile L. Pinder. 2003. "The Implications of Regional Variations in

Medicare Spending. Part 1: The Content, Quality, and Accessibility of Care." *Annals of Internal Medicine* 138 (4): 273–87.

Flyvbjerg, Bent, Mette K. Skamris Holm, and Søren L. Buhl. 2004. "What Causes Cost Overrun in Transport Infrastructure Projects?" *Transport Reviews* 24 (1): 3–18.

Fraundorf, Martha, John P. Norby, and Robert Mason Farrell. 1984. "The Effect of the Davis-Bacon Act on Construction Costs in Rural Areas." *Review of Economics and Statistics* 66 (1):142–46.

General Accountability Office. 2019. "Rail Transit: Federal Transit Administration Could Improve Information on Estimating Project Costs." Technical report, 19-562, General Accountability Office.

Glaeser, Edward L., and Giacomo A. M. Ponzetto. 2018. "The Political Economy of Transportation Investment." Special issue, "The Political Economy of Transport Decisions," *Economics of Transportation* 13: 4–26.

Goldman, Nate. 2012. "7 Things that Cost Less Than the Big Dig." *WBUR News*, July 12.

Gordon, Tracy, and David Schleicher. 2015. "High Costs May Explain Crumbling Support for U.S. Infrastructure." *Real Clear Policy*, March 30.

Gottlieb, Daniel J., Weiping Zhou, Yunjie Song, Kathryn Gilman Andrews, Jonathan Skinner, and Jason M. Sutherland. 2010. "Prices Don't Drive Regional Medicare Spending Variations." *Health Affairs* 29 (3): 537–43.

Hecht, Harry, and Debbie A. Niemeier. 2002. "Comparing Transportation Project Development Efficiencies: The California Department of Transportation and the California County Sales Tax Agencies." *Transport Policy* 9 (4): 347–56.

Intueor Consulting. 2016. "Report on Los Angeles County Metropolitan Transportation Authority Capital Project Construction Management Best Practices Study." Technical report, 16-AUD-01, Los Angeles County Metropolitan Transportation Authority.

Kishore, Varun, and Dulcy M. Abraham. 2009. "Construction Costs—Using Federal vs. Local Funds." Technical report, Indiana Department of Transportation, Federal Highway Administration, and US Department of Transportation.

Martin, Anne B., Lekha Whittle, Stephen Heffler, Mary Carol Barron, Andrea Sisko, and Benjamin Washington. 2007. "Health Spending by State of Residence, 1991–2004." *Health Affairs* 26 (supp. 2): w651–w663.

McKinsey Global Institute. 2013. "Infrastructure Productivity: How to Save $1 Trillion a Year." Technical report, McKinsey and Co.

Mehrotra, Neil, Matthew A. Turner, and Juan Pablo Uribe. 2019. "Does the US Have an Infrastructure Cost Problem? Evidence from the Interstate Highway System." Working paper.

Molitor, David. 2018. "The Evolution of Physician Practice Styles: Evidence from Cardiologist Migration." *American Economic Journal: Economic Policy* 10 (1): 326–56.

Munnell, Alicia H. 1992. "Policy Watch: Infrastructure Investment and Economic Growth." *Journal of Economic Perspectives* 6 (4): 189–98.

Odeck, James. 2004. "Cost Overruns in Road Construction—What Are Their Sizes and Determinants?" *Transport Policy* 11 (1): 43–53.

Pickering, Andrew C., and James Rockey. 2013. "Ideology and the Size of US State Government." *Public Choice* 156 (3): 443–65.

Pierson, K., M. Hand, and F. Thompson. 2015. "The Government Finance Database: A Common Resource for Quantitative Research in Public Financial Analysis." *PLoS ONE* 10 (6): e0130119.

Pietroforte, Roberto, and John B. Miller. 2002. "Procurement Methods for US Infrastructure: Historical Perspectives and Recent Trends." *Building Research & Information* 30 (6): 425–34.
Rosenthal, Brian. 2019. "The Most Expensive Mile of Subway Track on Earth." *New York Times*, 1.
R. S. Means Company. 2003. *Square Foot Costs*, 23rd ed. R. S. Means Company.
Saks, Raven E. 2008. "Job Creation and Housing Construction: Constraints on Metropolitan Area Employment Growth." *Journal of Urban Economics* 64 (1): 178–95.
Sheiner, Louise. 2014. "Why the Geographic Variation in Healthcare Spending Cannot Tell Us Much about the Efficiency or Quality of Our Healthcare System." *Brookings Papers on Economic Activity*.
Skinner, Jonathan, and Elliott Fisher. 2010. "Reflections on Geographic Variations in US Health Care." Technical report, Dartmouth Institute for Health Policy and Clinical Practice.
Swei, Omar. 2018. "Long-Run Construction Cost Trends: Baumol's Cost Disease and a Disaggregate Look at Building Material Price Dynamics." *Journal of Construction Engineering and Management* 144 (7): 04018058.
Todorovich, Petra, and Daniel Schned. 2012. "Getting Infrastructure Going: Expediting the Environmental Review Process." Technical report, Regional Plan Association.
US Fish and Wildlife Service. 2018. National Wetlands Inventory. Accessed July 2018. https://www.fws.gov/wetlands/data/data-download.html.
Varghese, Romy. 2019. "California's High-Speed Rail Cost Grows by About $2 Billion." *Bloomberg News*.
Wennberg, John, and Alan Gittelsohn. 1973. "Small Area Variations in Health Care Delivery: A Population-Based Health Information System Can Guide Planning and Regulatory Decision-making." *Science* 182: 1102–8.
Winston, Clifford. 2013. "On the Performance of the U.S. Transportation System: Caution Ahead." *Journal of Economic Literature* 51 (3): 773–824.

## Comment Clifford Winston

### Introduction

For several decades, a familiar refrain to motivate policy discussions about how to improve the performance of the nation's largest civilian public investment has been "America's road system is deteriorating, and urban traffic congestion is worsening." As early as Pigou (1920), economists have argued that efficient transportation infrastructure policy maximizes the difference between the social benefits and cost of its provision and use, including the

Clifford Winston is a senior fellow in the Economic Studies program at the Brookings Institution.

For acknowledgments, sources of research support, and disclosure of the author' material financial relationships, if any, please see https://www.nber.org/books-and-chapters/economic-analysis-and-infrastructure-investment/comment-can-america-reduce-highway-construction-costs-evidence-states-winston.

costs that users impose on one another, by specifying pricing guidelines to regulate demand and investment guidelines to specify design.

In a 1991 *Journal of Economic Perspectives* paper, I summarized the basic theory of optimal pricing and investment and the empirical evidence on the economic effects of the policy, which showed the potential for large annual welfare gains from more durable roads and reduced maintenance costs, less congestion and savings in travel time, and a significantly improved national highway budget balance.[1] Thirty years later, America's road system is still not being efficiently maintained, traffic congestion continues to worsen in more urban areas, and the federal Highway Trust Fund routinely runs deficits, while economists have provided more evidence that strengthens the case for using efficient transportation infrastructure policy to improve the system's performance.[2]

Despite the accumulating evidence, policy makers continue to eschew efficient pricing and investment. Instead, they have repeatedly claimed that the United States has been experiencing an infrastructure crisis that can be solved only by raising large amounts of revenue to fund repaving and expanding the road system. Large-scale infrastructure spending gained traction as a response to the impact of the coronavirus on the US economy, with President Trump calling for a $2 trillion package that would be used to restore the nation's roads, bridges, tunnels, and ports. Newly elected President Biden is proposing a $1.9 trillion infrastructure policy.

Beginning with Aschauer (1989) and Munnell (1990), the macroeconomics literature has supported policy makers' approach by producing evidence that increasing investment in the highway capital stock spurs productivity growth. Melo, Graham, and Brage-Ardao (2013) survey more recent literature.

Given that many microeconomists have remained dubious about repeated claims of large potential returns to increased spending on highway infrastructure because the glaring inefficiencies in current investment policy would reduce those potential returns, one would think that micro- and macroeconomists would have engaged in a debate on this issue.[3] However, direct engagement has not occurred, which has been a source of frustration for transportation economists like me, because we stress that efficient pricing is

1. The theory is applicable to all transportation infrastructure in addition to highways and has been applied to airports, air traffic control, and ports. I discuss only highways here.

2. Chapter 3 in this volume, by Giles Duranton, Geetika Nagpal, and Matthew Turner, concludes that the condition of the US road system is generally not deteriorating. However, roads may still not be in good condition in certain metropolitan areas with a large amount of traffic. In addition, as I discuss later, pricing and investment policies to keep roads in good repair have been inefficient for decades. Thus, to the extent that the condition of the US road system has been maintained or even improved, the increasing public expenditures to achieve this outcome have been excessive.

3. Chapter 4 in this volume, by Valerie Ramey, is a rare macroeconomic analysis that shows how inefficiencies can compromise infrastructure investment returns.

a vital prerequisite for making efficient infrastructure investments and we argue that analyses that neglect efficient pricing do not yield useful policy recommendations.

I mention this tension to disclose that I am not an impartial commenter on the chapter by Leah Brooks and Zachary Liscow, which focuses on explaining the variation across states in the cost per mile of new Interstate highway construction from 1956 to 1993 and concludes that while a large variation exists, it cannot be explained by any single influence among the subset that they consider. My perspective leads me to take immediate issue with the authors' chapter because it is not directed at making more efficient use of the current highway capital stock, valued at more than $3 trillion (Winston 2013), and it does not develop an efficiency benchmark from a transportation economics perspective to assess the historical construction of the highway capital stock.[4]

In what follows, I provide perspective on the challenges to improving the current road system by updating and expanding the components of an efficient transportation infrastructure policy that I discussed 30 years ago and by summarizing the critical inefficiencies in current transportation policy that reduce returns from highway spending. Against this background, I offer some comments on the Brooks and Zachary chapter that stress the importance of developing an efficiency benchmark to guide an assessment of the relative efficiency of states' construction spending. I then argue that the politics of highway infrastructure policy, which has generally prevented constructive policy reforms, may change in the future as autonomous vehicles gain widespread adoption and use by travelers and trucking companies. This watershed moment in the development of transportation is likely to create potentially large political costs for policy makers by making the costs of inefficient highway policies that have compromised nonautonomous road travel for decades much clearer to the public. Finally, I stress the importance of transportation economics as a fundamental approach for identifying ways to improve highway infrastructure.

## An Update of Efficient Transportation Infrastructure Policy

Small and Verhoef (2007) provide a rigorous theoretical overview of efficient pricing and investment policy for automobiles and trucks. Recent

4. According to the Federal Highway Administration, roughly 92 percent of current public road mileage and 90 percent of current Interstate Highway mileage had been completed by 1980. Weighted to account for road use, as measured say by vehicle miles traveled, those fractions of completed mileage would probably be even greater because roads for more heavily traveled routes were generally constructed earlier. I am grateful to Don Pickrell for providing the data that underlie the figures, which are contained in Federal Highway Administration, *Highway Statistics 2018*, table HM-220 (https://www.fhwa.dot.gov/policyinformation/statistics/2018/pdf/hm220.pdf), and "The Dwight D. Eisenhower System of Interstate and Defense Highways, Part VI— Interstate Status and Progress," final table (unnumbered) (https://www.fhwa.dot.gov/highwayhistory/data/page06.cfm#b).

empirical research has broadened our perspective on the policy's potential benefits and on the growing costs of its absence. Recent research has also quantified other critical inefficiencies in highway policy, including inflated input and project costs, misallocation of highway revenues, the protracted time to complete projects, and the slow adoption of technological innovations that could improve operations and safety.

### Efficient Highway Pricing and Investment

Highways provide the capacity to accommodate travel by cars and trucks, in the form of traffic lanes, as well as durability, in the form of pavement strength, to facilitate use by heavy trucks. Highway users impose costs on one another by contributing to congestion, which increases all users' travel time and reduces the reliability of trip times, as well as by wearing out the infrastructure, which necessitates maintenance expenditures to repair damaged pavement and vehicles.

Highway pricing and investment rules jointly constitute an efficient long-run policy, in which a user's full marginal cost is determined at the optimal levels of capacity and durability. The efficient pricing rule establishes congestion tolls and pavement wear charges so that users are charged for the social marginal costs of their trip. The technology available to set those prices more accurately and to charge highway users without disrupting their journey has greatly improved during the past 30 years.[5]

Today, a highway authority can set real-time congestion tolls by using data generated by travelers' use of GPS navigation services to determine traffic volume on a stretch of road during a given time interval and by drawing on plausible congestion-cost estimates available in the empirical literature and even available by experimentation. Singapore, for example, is well known for its sophisticated congestion-pricing scheme, which varies sharply by location, the extent of congestion, and time of day. Singapore's introduction of a global navigation satellite system will further improve the accuracy of road pricing.[6] Stockholm uses video analytics to identify the license plates of cars without transponders that facilitate automated congestion payments.

The extent of pavement damage depends on a truck's weight per axle, where the damage caused by an axle is defined in terms of the number of equivalent standard-axle loads (ESALs) that would cause the same damage; the standard is a single axle bearing an 18,000-pound load. Efficient road pricing encourages truckers to reduce their ESALs or weight per axle whenever possible by shifting to trucks with more axles (or by adding an axle to their truck), thus extending pavement life and reducing highway-maintenance expenditures and vehicle-repair costs (Small, Winston, and Evans 1989).

5. Vickrey (1963) outlined how congestion pricing could be implemented in practice using cameras at toll booths and sending motorists a bill by mail.

6. Lehe (2019) provides a recent review of urban congestion pricing schemes.

A highway authority can implement an axle-weight tax by estimating a truck's ESAL miles using high-speed weigh-in-motion technologies, which use sensors that are installed in one or more traffic lanes to identify a vehicle and record its number of axles, vehicle load, and location while the vehicle continues to travel in the traffic stream. The total charge would then be calculated as the product of the truck's ESAL miles and a plausible estimate of the resurfacing costs per ESAL mile, which would vary by road type indicated by location, and would be sent to the truck's owner.

The efficient investment rule calls for capacity and durability to be provided to the point where the marginal benefit from increasing investment in each dimension equals its marginal cost. Expanding highway capacity may be difficult in certain urban areas where land is not available to widen a road. And in cases where a congested area has expanded road capacity by adding a lane or even a new road, the new capacity is likely to be filled to a large extent in the long run by travelers who formerly avoided the congested thoroughfare, a phenomenon known originally as Downs's law (1962) and now widely referred to as "induced traffic."[7] Expanding road capacity will provide temporary benefits in travel time savings to current road users as well as benefits to new travelers drawn to the improved road, but the only way to reduce congestion permanently is to set an explicit price for capacity.

Optimal highway durability is achieved by minimizing the sum of up-front capital costs when the road is being built and the recurring maintenance costs that are necessary to keep it in good repair. Small and Winston's (1988) critique of the pavement thickness guidelines from the American Association of State Highway and Transportation Officials concluded that optimal thicknesses were significantly higher than those that the guidelines dictated for current and actual thicknesses, especially on heavily traveled Interstates. For example, Small and Winston estimated that the optimal thickness for heavily traveled rigid concrete pavements is 13.8 inches, compared with AASHO's estimate of 11.2 inches. Increasing thickness by 2.6 inches would more than double the life of the pavement. Greater road thicknesses would substantially reduce periodic maintenance expenditures and, because they would lower the marginal cost of an ESAL mile, would also soften the impact of efficient pavement wear charges on truckers.[8]

Finally, the different capacity and durability requirements of cars and trucks suggest that highway engineers unnecessarily inflated construction costs by designing freeways to accommodate both cars and trucks in the same lanes. Because cars account for the vast majority of traffic, they require several lanes but their weight does not require thick pavement, while heavy trucks require fewer lanes with thicker pavement. If policy makers designed

7. Duranton and Turner (2011) report evidence supporting Downs's law in their analysis of a cross section of US cities.

8. I am not aware of more recent evidence comparing optimal and current highway durability.

freeways that separated cars and trucks, they could have built fewer expensive lanes with thick pavement.

Recent empirical evidence identifies additional potential benefits that strengthen the case for efficient highway pricing and investment policies, including lower vehicle repair costs, greater reliability of travel, improved land use, and better public health. Smoother pavements would reduce the wear and tear on motorists' and truckers' vehicles. Driving on damaged roads is estimated to cost US motorists $130 billion in additional annual operating costs and repairs (The Road Information Program 2019), and to impose significant costs on truckers. Smoother traffic flows would result in more reliable travel that motorists would value approximately as much as they value reduced travel times (Small, Winston, and Yan 2005). By substantially reducing residential sprawl because the out-of-pocket cost of commuting would no longer be underpriced, taxpayers would benefit from improved land use patterns that increase residential density and lower the cost of public services (Langer and Winston 2008). And less congested travel would improve adults' and infants' emotional and physical health by reducing stress, whose costs include domestic violence, and pollution (see Winston and Karpilow 2020 for a survey of the evidence).

A less studied potential benefit from efficient pricing and investment, which I discuss below in the context of autonomous vehicles, is that reducing the cost and improving the speed and reliability of highway travel would also improve the efficiency of other major sectors of the US economy, including trade, labor, urban, and industry.

## Reducing Project Costs and Choosing Socially Beneficial Projects

Efficient highway policy calls for roads to be built and maintained at minimum cost and for policy makers to allocate highway funds to projects that yield the greatest social benefits. However, various regulations have increased the cost of the inputs used to build highways and the time required to do so. In addition, policy makers have not allocated highway funds to projects that produce the largest social benefits because projects are often selected for political or geographic "equity" reasons.

State and federal (Davis-Bacon) regulations have increased wages and expanded the labor force that is hired to manage and complete highway projects. Together, federal and state transportation departments currently employ roughly 200,000 workers in part just to ensure that projects meet all regulations. Winston (2013) surveys the evidence on those inflated labor costs. Buy America requirements for construction materials used in Federal-Aid Highway projects, such as bridge repairs, raise costs when less expensive foreign materials could have been used without sacrificing quality (Platzer and Mallett 2019).

The complexity of the planning process, regulations on highway design, and other factors may also increase the time costs to complete highway projects. Before highway authorities can begin actual roadwork, they must perform engineering analyses and obtain permits indicating that they have satisfied National Environment and Policy Act (NEPA) and, if applicable, state environmental quality reviews to ensure that projects are built in a safe and responsible manner and that they will not adversely affect the environment and communities. Gallen and Winston (forthcoming) summarize evidence that the average time to complete such a NEPA review has grown sharply over time and that the permitting process for major projects may take as long as 10 years.

Once roadwork begins, project managers may have to form work zones, which reduce capacity, slow travel speeds, and delay vehicles. A work zone is an area of a road where construction, maintenance, or utility-work activities occur, and it is typically marked by signs (especially ones that indicate reduced speed limits), traffic-channeling devices, barriers, and work vehicles. The Federal Highway Administration estimates that work zones accounted for nearly 900 million person-hours of traveler delay in 2014 (Work Zone Management Program 2016). Valued at even half the (private) average hourly wage (the US Department of Transportation's guideline for valuing most local travel) in 2014 of $24.50, work zone delays create an annual welfare loss of nearly $11 billion, and the losses persist even if a project is not delayed.[9]

There are many ways to spend highway funds to reduce the social costs of road travel, including congestion and traffic accidents. However, earmarked or demonstration projects, which have become a growing political cost of ensuring that multiyear federal transportation bills are passed, as well as highway funds that are allocated throughout the country generally do not satisfy those objectives. Money from the federal Highway Trust Fund for highway projects is distributed among states based on formulas that produce inefficient allocations because they include factors, such as a state's size, that are not accurate indicators of road congestion. Winston and Langer (2006) found that holding the level of spending constant, highway officials could reduce highway costs $13.8 billion per year, accounting for users' congestion costs and states' highway expenditures, if expenditures were explicitly targeted to those areas of the country with the greatest congestion. In addition, Metropolitan Planning Organizations often misallocate highway funds within urban areas because they target them to meet many objectives other than reducing social costs.

### Adopting the Latest Technologies

As noted, technological advance is an important part of an efficient infrastructure policy because it can enable policy makers to implement real-time

9. US Department of Transportation, "Revised Departmental Guidance on Valuation of Travel Time in Economic Analysis," December 2016 (https://www.transportation.gov/office-policy/transportation-policy/revised-departmental-guidance-valuation-travel-time-economic).

efficient prices for cars and trucks. Policy makers can also adopt the latest technologies to enable investments to improve highways' design characteristics and maintenance at modest cost and to enhance traffic safety.

To take some examples, Ng and Small (2012) pointed out that most highways in major metropolitan areas operate in congested conditions during much of the day, yet highway design standards are based on free-flow travel speeds. Highway authorities could effectively expand capacity during peak travel periods to reduce delays by adjusting the number and width of lanes on a freeway in response to real-time traffic volumes that are measured by GPS navigation services. To enable vehicles to move faster, heavy traffic volumes would call for more but narrower lanes, while lighter traffic volumes would call for fewer but wider lanes.

Technology exists to install lane dividers that can be illuminated so that they are visible to motorists, and so that they can also be adjusted in response to traffic volumes to increase or decrease the number of lanes that are available. As I pointed out previously, adding road capacity in dense urban areas where land is scarce is a very expensive proposition; however, installing variable lane widths could overcome prohibitive construction costs and benefit motorists.

The rapid evolution of material science (including nanotechnologies) has produced advances in construction materials, construction processes, and quality control that have significantly improved pavement design, resulting in greater durability, longer lifetimes, lower maintenance costs, and less vehicle damage caused by potholes. For example, Little et al. (1997) estimated that the SUPERPAVE effort in the late 1980s and 1990s (Transportation Research Board 2005), which developed new asphaltic binder specifications for repaving, produced roughly $0.7 billion (in 2020 dollars) in such benefits.

Other investments that apply recent advances in material science technologies are also possible, but they are often delayed because state departments of transportation try to minimize their expenditures—rather than the sum of their own and highway users' costs—and because departments of transportation award contracts on the basis of the minimum bid, not on the technological sophistication of the contractor (Winston 2010). Finally, state departments of transportation have been slow to implement advances in roadway structural monitoring technologies that would allow them to monitor the health of both pavements and bridges on a continuous basis, thus providing valuable information for optimal repair and rehabilitation strategies that could reduce the cost of highway services (Lajnef et al. 2011).

The large benefits of highway travel have been tempered by the recurring social costs of vehicle accidents, which, accounting for vehicle damage, injuries, and fatalities, run in the hundreds of billions of dollars (Winston and Karpilow 2020). Winston and Mannering (2014) summarized ways that technological advances could help improve road safety, including modernizing traffic signal control and basing it on real-time traffic flows; using

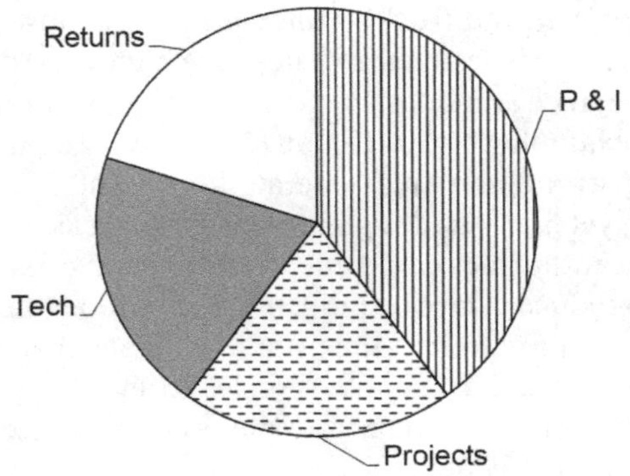


**Fig. 2C.1 Highway returns and policy inefficiencies**

photo-enforcement technology (roadside cameras) to enforce speed limits and other traffic laws, and to reduce dangerous high-speed police chases; and making much greater use of information technology to reduce the time to dispatch incident response teams to help accident victims and to advise motorists to avoid areas where incidents have recently occurred.

Summary

During the past 30 years, research in transportation economics has indicated that the cost of highway policy inefficiencies is substantially greater than was previously estimated from simple deadweight loss diagrams of the failure to impose congestion pricing and cost minimization calculations that found excessive maintenance costs. Inefficient pricing and investment, excessive production costs, misallocated funds, and slow technological advance have wasted hundreds of billions of dollars of the nation's expenditures on its highway capital stock, contributed to the decline in the road system's efficiency, missed opportunities to increase the pace of highway safety, and by doing so have reduced the efficiencies of other important sectors in the US economy.

Figure 2C.1 presents a pie chart to illustrate how the extensive waste generated by highway policy inefficiencies eats away at the potential returns from investments in the road system and leave at best a modest share in actual improvements for operators and users.[10] Shirley and Winston (2004) developed a theoretical argument that highway infrastructure investments generated benefits by lowering firms' inventories and estimated returns from those investments based on that mechanism. The authors found that annual

10. The divisions in the pie chart are hypothetical based on plausible assumptions that the largest source of inefficiency is attributable to suboptimal pricing and investment and that the inefficiencies related to technology adoption and project costs and selection are also significant.

returns have fallen over time to less than 5 percent by the 1990s, and they suggested that their finding could be partly explained by the cumulative impact of policy inefficiencies. Winston and Langer (2006) estimated that in a given year, one dollar of highway spending reduced users' congestion cost only 11 cents in that same year, and that those cost savings quickly dissipated in subsequent years because of road depreciation.

### Implications of the Discussion for Brooks and Liscow

The main implication from my extended discussion of efficient transportation infrastructure policies for Brooks and Liscow is that all highway policies, including but not limited to spending, should be evaluated against an economic efficiency benchmark. When assessing the construction of the Interstate Highway System, the optimal level of construction costs per mile should be determined as part of a dynamic welfare maximization investment problem where capacity and durability design solutions account for the expectations of demand (road use by cars and heavy trucks) and capital and maintenance costs, subject to regulatory, technological, and geographical constraints. States' actual construction costs should then be compared with their optimal construction costs—instead of compared with the median construction cost, as Brooks and Liscow do, or even with a minimum cost achieved by a particular state—to assess individual states' and the nation's construction cost efficiency.[11]

My discussion identified factors that are likely to exacerbate dynamic inefficiencies. For example, suboptimal prices lead to excessive road use and wear and tear, which may distort expectations of demand and costs, while regulations of labor and capital inputs, misallocated funds, protracted times to build road projects, and continued reliance on obsolete technology are likely to raise highway spending significantly. Brooks and Liscow report that the cross-state variation in labor costs explains none of the temporal increase in highway construction spending per mile. However, as I pointed out, labor expenditures have been inflated by state and federal (Davis-Bacon) regulations; reforming those regulations could produce at least a one-time permanent reduction in construction costs.

The authors' omission of an efficiency benchmark raises questions about comparing construction costs across states. Why is the median cost of construction a desirable benchmark for assessment? Perhaps higher construction costs reflect greater concerns with long-run efficiency and require better—but more costly—materials and design. States with lower construction costs may be sacrificing long-run efficiency, as has proven to be the case

11. Estimated construction costs for roads built to optimal capacity and durability can be determined from analyses by Keeler and Small (1977) and Small and Winston (1988), respectively, for completed US highways.

for states that underbuilt heavily used pavements and bridges. States with higher construction costs may be more efficient than other states because they are better prepared to provide highway services for large flows of traffic that include significant heavy truck operations, or they may have designed their roads to better withstand ice and snow, which can cause pavements to crack and become more susceptible to damage caused by heavy trucks. The authors' conclusion that the Interstate Highway System could have cost billions of dollars less to build if all states' construction costs were at the median value begs the question of whether such a state's road system would be more efficient in the long run than are other states' road systems. I am not aware of any evidence that states whose construction costs approach the median are known for their relatively efficient highway investment programs.

In sum, while the authors document cost disparities, they do not identify states that could possibly serve as a model for others in optimizing highway construction costs and they do not explain why those states, if any exist, were successful. It is quite possible that inefficiencies that have contributed to cost disparities were present at the start of the federal Interstate Highway System and have persisted for decades, and there is little reason to expect that policy makers are planning to pursue efficient reforms in the near future.

**Political Economy and the Potential for Future Improvements in the System**

The issue of why policy inefficiencies exist for so long is a challenging political economy puzzle for scholars and practitioners. Becker (1983) long ago asked rhetorically, Why can we not allocate resources so that an inefficiency is eliminated and that everyone shares in the efficiency improvement, with the gainers compensating the losers if necessary?

Inefficient highway policies have their roots in the 1950s, and policy makers have shown little interest in reforming them. In the absence of strong causal evidence, Winston (2021) concluded that status quo bias appears to be more consistent with the evidence on the persistence of policy inefficiencies than are other explanations. For example, New York City politicians have long expressed their opposition to congestion pricing on the grounds that it would place an undue burden on a large share of their constituents, who commute by car and do not have the option to use other modes to avoid a high peak-hour toll. Yet, Assemblyman David Weprin, the most vocal and a successful opponent of the 2018 New York City tolling plan, and the plan's sponsor, Robert Rodriguez of East Harlem, had the same share of constituents who would have to pay the new toll—a mere 4.2 percent.

One year later, a negative shock appears to have overcome the status quo bias that impeded congestion pricing in New York City—namely, the increasingly desperate financial situation of the city's transit system. Some form of congestion pricing is now likely to be implemented in Manhattan, with much of the toll revenue used to finance transit operations and improvements. However, the US Department of Transportation has not yet approved the city's congestion pricing project, and its implementation is expected to be delayed for a few years.

Highway budget deficits, attributable to a federal gasoline tax that has not been raised since 1993 while motor vehicle fuel economy has increased significantly, have caused some policy makers to consider a tax on vehicle miles traveled (VMT) as an alternative to a higher federal gasoline tax to raise highway revenues.[12] A VMT tax could be designed to vary by time of day and location and to charge vehicles for their contribution to congestion, pavement wear, emissions, and safety costs. Langer, Maheshri, and Winston (2017) present evidence that a hypothetical urban-rural differentiated VMT tax would be more efficient than raising the federal gasoline tax. Oregon and Utah are testing a VMT tax, and other states have indicated an interest in doing so, but such a tax has yet to be implemented anywhere in the country.

A different negative shock during the 1970s, high rates of inflation, arguably played a role in influencing policy makers to deregulate large parts of the intercity transportation system, which greatly improved its performance and benefited rail and truck shippers and airline travelers (Winston 2021). However, there has been very limited interest among policy makers in privatizing and deregulating US transportation infrastructure, and scholarly assessments have not suggested that widespread adoption of such a policy would produce significant social benefits.[13]

Looking further into the future, it is entirely possible that a positive shock—namely, the introduction and widespread use of autonomous vehicles—could spur policy makers to adopt more efficient highway infrastructure policies. Winston and Karpilow (2020) argue that autonomous vehicles represent a watershed moment in the development of transportation, which promises not only to vastly improve road travel and generate huge benefits to travelers, shippers, and delivery companies, but also to benefit major sectors of the US economy by reducing congestion and virtually eliminating vehicle accidents. The authors estimate that their overall impact on annual GDP growth is likely to exceed one percentage point.

To be sure, autonomous vehicles are still undergoing development and testing. However, Winston and Karpilow (2020) argue that policy makers

12. Some states have raised their gasoline taxes to help fund highway projects.

13. Public-private partnerships have a limited history in the United States. In recent years, investments have amounted to $20 billion to $40 billion, and the gains have been small; see Engel, Fischer, and Galetovic (2014) and their chapter in this volume. Winston and Yan (2011) simulated the effects on travelers of privatizing highways in Southern California and found that travelers could benefit from faster and more reliable travel in certain circumstances. However, in practice, the United States has no experience with highway privatization where the goal of the policy was to generate competition between highway providers that would improve the efficiency of road travel. It is uncertain whether policy makers could design a competitive private highway system effectively and that sufficient managerial talent exists to operate competing highway companies in the United States that would remain profitable and that would provide highway services that would raise motorists' welfare.

pose a greater risk than do industry participants to how soon US society realizes the huge potential benefits of autonomous vehicles, because policy makers could fail to remedy the inefficiencies in highway pricing, investment, and production policies that have compromised travel by nonautonomous vehicle for decades and that must be reformed to enable autonomous vehicles to operate efficiently and safely.

The global pandemic caused by the coronavirus has given new meaning to the familiar phrase "the whole world is watching." Taking a more positive perspective, the whole world will be watching in the future as countries, and cities and states within those countries, compete intensely to successfully develop and adopt autonomous vehicles. Given the enormous benefits at stake and the visibility and importance of global, interstate, and intercity competition, policy makers who weaken their jurisdiction's autonomous vehicle operations by failing to reform their highway policies may incur large political costs.

### Transportation Economics and Transportation-Related Issues

Scholars should be attentive to research in their field that is conducted by scholars in other fields, especially because such research may provide new insights and reveal shortcomings in a scholar's own field. However, in my less than objective view, research on transportation infrastructure by scholars in fields other than transportation economics has shown that transportation economics has a serious marketing problem within the economics profession.

I indicated in the introduction a major difference in the approaches of macroeconomists and transportation economists to improving transportation infrastructure and the absence of a debate to resolve that difference. More recently, I have become concerned that literature in other fields that addresses a transportation-related issue has neglected research in transportation economics on pervasive policy inefficiencies and its importance for drawing useful policy recommendations.

Perhaps transportation economics research is perceived as directed toward a small share of the economy. That is a misapprehension: Winston (2013) points out that pecuniary spending on transportation accounts for 17 percent of GDP, that time expenditures by travelers and shippers are comparable to pecuniary spending, and that both public and private investments in transportation capital are enormous. Given that transportation is an input into virtually all activities in an economy, using the insights of microeconomic transportation analysis as a foundation for understanding how to improve the productivity of the broader economy should be a key research priority.

My discussion of autonomous vehicles illustrated how transportation can have significant implications for major economic sectors and the US and global economy. Future research in transportation economics is likely to draw on big data and artificial intelligence to analyze autonomous vehicle operations in detail and to quantify with increasingly greater accuracy how that innovation affects many activities and sectors throughout an economy. The evolution of future research on autonomous transportation systems and their effects on the broader economy may help to overcome the perception of the field's narrowness. At the same time, I hope that the distinct features of transportation economics—specifically, its sound microeconomic foundations, disaggregated empirical work, and close attention to the efficacy of government policy—will gain greater appreciation by other economists and that the economics profession will give greater recognition to the field's contributions and importance.

## References

Aschauer, David Alan. 1989. "Is Public Expenditure Productive?" *Journal of Monetary Economics* 23 (2): 177–200.

Becker, Gary S. 1983. "A Theory of Competition among Pressure Groups for Political Influence." *Quarterly Journal of Economics* 98 (3): 371–400.

Downs, Anthony. 1962. "The Law of Peak-Hour Expressway Congestion." *Traffic Quarterly* 16 (3): 393–409.

Duranton, Giles, and Matthew A. Turner. 2011. "The Fundamental Law of Road Congestion: Evidence from U.S. Cities." *American Economic Review* 101 (6): 2616–52.

Engel, Eduardo, Ronald D. Fischer, and Alexander Galetovic. 2014. *The Economics of Public-Private Partnerships: A Basic Guide*. Cambridge: Cambridge University Press.

Gallen, Trevor, and Clifford Winston. Forthcoming. "Transportation Capital and Its Effects on the U.S. Economy: A General Equilibrium Approach." *Journal of Macroeconomics*.

Keeler, Theodore E., and Kenneth A. Small. 1977. "Optimal Peak-Load Pricing, Investment and Service Levels on Urban Expressways." *Journal of Political Economy* 85 (1): 1–26.

Lajnef, Nizar, Mohamed Rhimi, Karim Chatti, Lassaad Mhamdi, and Fred Faridazar. 2011. "Toward an Integrated Smart Sensing System and Data Interpretation Techniques for Pavement Fatigue Monitoring." *Computer-Aided Civil and Infrastructure Engineering* 26 (7): 513–23.

Langer, Ashley, Vikram Maheshri, and Clifford Winston. 2017. "From Gallons to Miles: A Disaggregate Analysis of Automobile Travel and Externality Taxes." *Journal of Public Economics* 152 (August): 34–46.

Langer, Ashley, and Clifford Winston. 2008. "Toward a Comprehensive Assessment of Road Pricing Accounting for Land Use." In *Brookings–Wharton Papers on Urban Affairs*, edited by Gary Burtless and Janet Rothenberg Pack, 127–75. Washington, DC: Brookings Institution.

Lehe, Lewis. 2019. "Downtown Congestion Pricing in Practice." *Transportation Research Part C: Emerging Technologies* 100 (March): 200–23.

Little, D. N., J. Memmott, F. McFarland, Z. Goff, R. Smith, C. V. Wootan, D. Zollinger, T. Tang, and J. Epps. 1997. "Economic Benefits of SHRP Research." College Station: Texas Transportation Institute.

Melo, Patrick C., Daniel J. Graham, and Ruben Brage-Ardao. 2013. "The Productivity of Transport Infrastructure Investment: A Meta-Analysis of Empirical Evidence." *Regional Science and Urban Economics* 43 (5): 695–706.

Munnell, Alicia H. 1990. "Why Has Productivity Growth Declined? Productivity and Public Investment." *New England Economic Review* (January/February): 3–22.

Ng, Chen Feng, and Kenneth A. Small. 2012. "Tradeoffs among Free-Flow Speed, Capacity, Cost, and Environmental Footprint in Highway Design." *Transportation* 39 (November): 1259–80.

Pigou, Arthur C. 1920. *The Economics of Welfare*. London: Macmillan Press.

Platzer, Michaela D., and William J. Mallett. 2019. *Effects of Buy America on Transportation Infrastructure and U.S. Manufacturing.* Washington, DC: Congressional Research Service.

Shirley, Chad, and Clifford Winston. 2004. "Firm Inventory Behavior and the Returns from Highway Infrastructure Investments." *Journal of Urban Economics* 55 (2): 398–415.

Small, Kenneth A., and Erik T. Verhoef. 2007. *The Economics of Urban Transportation.* Abingdon, UK: Routledge.

Small, Kenneth A., and Clifford Winston. 1988. "Optimal Highway Durability." *American Economic Review* 78 (3): 560–69.

Small, Kenneth A., Clifford Winston, and Carol A. Evans. 1989. *Road Work: A New Highway Pricing and Investment Policy*. Washington, DC: Brookings Institution Press.

Small, Kenneth A., Clifford Winston, and Jia Yan. 2005. "Uncovering the Distribution of Motorists' Preferences for Travel Time and Reliability." *Econometrica* 73 (4): 1367–82.

The Road Information Program (TRIP). 2019. *America's Surface Transportation System and Federal Funding: Key Facts.* Washington, DC: TRIP.

Transportation Research Board. 2005. *Superior Performing Asphalt Pavement: SUPERPAVE, Performance by Design*. Final Report of the TRB SUPERPAVE Committee. Washington, DC: National Academies.

Vickrey, William. 1963. "Pricing in Urban and Suburban Transport." *American Economic Review* 53 (2): 452–65.

Winston, Clifford. 1991. "Efficient Transportation Infrastructure Policy." *Journal of Economic Perspectives* 5 (Winter): 113–27.

———. 2010. *Last Exit: Privatization and Deregulation of the U.S. Transportation System*. Washington, DC: Brookings Institution.

———. 2013. "On the Performance of the U.S. Transportation System: Caution Ahead." *Journal of Economic Literature* 51 (3): 773–824.

———. 2021. *Gaining Ground: Markets Helping Government*. Washington, DC: Brookings Institution, forthcoming.

Winston, Clifford, and Quentin Karpilow. 2020. *Autonomous Vehicles: The Road to Economic Growth?* Washington, DC: Brookings Institution.

Winston, Clifford, and Ashley Langer. 2006. "The Effect of Government Highway Spending on Road Users' Congestion Costs." *Journal of Urban Economics* 60 (3): 463–83.

Winston, Clifford, and Fred Mannering. 2014. "Implementing Technology to Improve Public Highway Performance: A Leapfrog Technology from the Private Sector Is Going to Be Necessary." *Economics of Transportation* 3 (2): 158–65.

Winston, Clifford, and Jia Yan. 2011. "Can Privatization of U.S. Highways Improve Motorists' Welfare?" *Journal of Public Economics* 95 (7–8): 993–1005.

Work Zone Management Program. 2016. "Facts and Statistics—Work Zone Mobility." Federal Highway Administration, March 2.

# 3 Transportation Infrastructure in the US

Gilles Duranton, Geetika Nagpal, and Matthew A. Turner

We need major federal investments to rebuild our crumbling infrastructure and put millions of Americans back to work in decent paying jobs in both the public and private sectors.
—2016 Democratic Party platform

We propose to remove from the Highway Trust Fund programs that should not be the business of the federal government.
—2016 Republican Party platform

## 3.1 Introduction

Support for massive investments in transportation infrastructure, possibly with a change in the share of spending on transit, seems widespread. Such proposals are often motivated by the belief that our infrastructure is crumbling, that infrastructure causes economic growth, that current funding regimes disadvantage rural drivers at the expense of urban public transit, or that capacity expansions will reduce congestion. We provide an empirical and conceptual foundation for this important debate and highlight questions on which further research is needed.

We proceed in four stages. First, we document the quantity and quality of the Interstate Highway network, bridges of all types, public transit buses, and subways in each year over the past 20 to 30 years. Second, we investigate total expenditure and the unit cost for each of the four types of infrastructure over about the same time period. Third, we survey available estimates of

Gilles Duranton is the Dean's Chair in Real Estate Professor at the Wharton School at the University of Pennsylvania, a Centre for Economic Policy Research (CEPR) Research Fellow, a research affiliate of the International Growth Centre, and a research associate of the National Bureau of Economic Research.

Geetika Nagpal is a PhD student in economics at Brown University.

Matthew A. Turner is a professor of economics at Brown University, a research affiliate of the International Growth Centre, and a research associate of the National Bureau of Economic Research.

The authors gratefully acknowledge support from the Smith Richardson Foundation and the Zell-Lurie Center for Real Estate; valuable research assistance from Lin Fan, Margaux Kelley, Sunny Lee, and Julia Lynn; and helpful discussions and comments from Edward Glaeser, Erick Guerra, James Poterba, and Stephen Redding. For acknowledgments, sources of research support, and disclosure of the authors' material financial relationships, if any, please see https://www.nber.org/books-and-chapters/economic-analysis-and-infrastructure-investment/transportation-infrastructure-us.

the effects of infrastructure on economic growth and congestion. Finally, we propose a simple theoretical framework with which to organize this information and to think about whether current investments can be rationalized as a part of a socially optimal infrastructure policy.

On average, most US transportation infrastructure is not crumbling, except (probably) for our subways. Over the past generation, the condition of the Interstate Highway network improved consistently, its extent increased modestly, and traffic about doubled. Over about the same time period, the condition of bridges remained about the same, the number of bridges increased slowly, and bridge traffic increased modestly. The stock of public transit motor buses is younger than it was a generation ago and about 30 percent larger, although ridership has been about constant. The mean age of a subway car stayed about the same from 1992 to 2017, but at more than 20 years old, this average car is quite old. Subways carry about twice as many riders as they did a generation ago. Speed of travel by car, bus, and subway, all declined between 1995 and 2017, most likely as a consequence of large increases in road traffic and subway ridership. Like public transit, the Interstate system is largely organized around the provision of short trips in urban areas.

Expenditure on transportation infrastructure and its cost have both increased. Expenditure on the Interstate Highway network about doubled from 1984 to 2008, and building new highways has become markedly more expensive. Expenditure on bridges about tripled from 1984 to 2008. This expenditure resulted in modest expansions and maintained the condition of an aging stock of bridges. Expenditure on transit buses does not show any clear trend on a per rider basis. Subways also operate at about constant expenditure per rider. In 2008, total expenditure on the public transit bus fleet was about the same as the sum of capital and maintenance expenditure on the Interstate Highway System and about double total US expenditure on subway operation and maintenance.

To sum up, US transportation infrastructure is, for the most part, not crumbling, and expenditure is rising rapidly. However, still larger investment may make sense if such investment contributes to economic growth or reduces congestion. We review the recent literature estimating the effects of transportation infrastructure on economic activity. While this body of research strongly suggests that transportation infrastructure plays an important role in determining where economic activity takes place, it provides little compelling evidence about transportation infrastructure creating economic growth. We also review the recent literature relating capacity expansions to congestion. This literature points to demand management as the most effective policy to combat congestion. Capacity expansions typically meet with offsetting expansions in travel demand and do little to increase the speed of travel. Investments in transportation infrastructure intended to boost the overall level of economic activity or reduce congestion are risky at best.

The allocation of expenditure across modes of transportation requires scrutiny. That we spend about the same amount on public transit buses, which provide about two billion rides per year, as on the Interstate Highway System, which provides about 700 billion miles of vehicle travel per year, primarily for local travel, is a central and surprising feature of US transportation policy. To assess the reasonableness of this allocation, we imagine a planner whose object is to provide trips and who accounts for the public cost of capital and user inputs. This simple model suggests that the US federal government values a passenger mile of bus travel at about two and a half times as much as a passenger mile of car travel. Households are implicitly willing to trade the same two quantities at a rate of one and a half to one. The rationale for so strong a federal preference for transit over roads is unclear. It may be consistent with redistributive objectives or that bus miles in central cities are more valuable than car miles on exurban highways. Regardless, this policy preference merits further, careful consideration.

Massive investments in transportation infrastructure seem to draw support from across the political spectrum. These policies are often motivated by claims that our current infrastructure is crumbling or that such investments will spur economic growth. The available evidence does not support these claims. Expenditure on transportation infrastructure is growing and, for the most part, allows maintenance to match or outpace depreciation. Moreover, the available empirical evidence does not allow for much confidence in the claim that capacity expansions will lead to economic growth or reduce congestion. With that said, ongoing debates over the allocation of funds across modes seem justified. US spending on buses seems large relative to their ability to attract riders. Put another way, rationalizing current policy requires that the planner value travel by car much less than travel by bus. This relative valuation merits further debate and analysis.

Beyond this, we draw attention to the need for further research into the effects of transportation infrastructure on economic development, for the development of more and better data to monitor personal and truck travel, and for the development of even a rudimentary inventory of US water and sewer infrastructure. Finally, we discuss long-standing recommendations of transport economists for demand management as an alternative to capacity expansion for congested roads, and for "per axle weight" fees for trucks to incentivize the use of trucks that are less damaging to the highways and roads.

## 3.2 Usage, Stock, and Condition of Highways, Bridges, and Public Transit

### 3.2.1 Interstate Highways

The federal government bears some financial responsibility for roads in the Federal-Aid Highway System. This system is a subset of all roads but

**Table 3.1** **US roads and highways in 2008**

| | Rural | | | Urban | | |
|---|---|---|---|---|---|---|
| Highway statistics | Miles | Lane miles | VMT ($10^9$) | Miles | Lane miles | VMT ($10^9$) |
| Interstate | 30,196 | 122,825 | 243 | 16,554 | 90,763 | 476 |
| Federal-Aid System | 678,445 | 1,494,380 | 804 | 12,577 | 886,092 | 1,714 |
| Total | 2,977,222 | 6,091,943 | 990 | 1,065,556 | 2,392,026 | 1,983 |

*Note*: Extent and usage of rural and urban portions for different parts of the US road network as reported in various *Highway Statistics* tables for 2008.

strictly contains the Interstate Highway System. Table 3.1 provides some basic facts about the road system in the United States in 2008.[1] In rural areas, the Interstate Highway System accounts for about 1 percent of all mileage and about 2 percent of all lane miles, but about 24 percent of all vehicle miles traveled (VMT). Rural Interstate Highways are also important compared with the rest of the rural Federal-Aid Highway System. Rural Interstates account for less than 10 percent of rural Federal-Aid lane miles, but 30 percent of VMT in the Federal-Aid Highway System. The Interstate Highway System is similarly important in urbanized areas.

The urban portion of the Interstate consists of about half as many miles as does the rural portion. However, rural Interstates average about four lanes, while urban Interstates are almost six, so the urban Interstate consists of about three-quarters as many lane miles as does the rural Interstate. While the urban portion of the Interstate is network is smaller than the rural portion, it carries almost twice as much traffic in total, and almost 2.7 times as much on a per-lane-mile basis. In this sense, like transit, the Interstate primarily serves urban trips.

In what follows, we focus attention on the Interstate Highway System for three reasons. First, data availability is better. Second, the system is more extensively studied and so more is known about it. Third, the Interstate Highway System is an important part of the network. That said, the remainder of the network is understudied, and while we will not remedy this problem here, the rest of the network is an obvious subject for further research.

The federal government funds most Interstate Highway construction and maintenance and keeps a careful inventory of the roadways for which the federal government assumes financial responsibility. This inventory results in an annual database called the Highway Performance Monitoring System

1. The division of roads into "rural" and "urban" is pervasive in federal reporting on highways. Roads inherit their urban or rural status from the region they traverse. Urban roads lie in urbanized areas, rural roads do not. Given the importance of the tension between rural roads and urban public transportation in policy debates, we preserve the rural classification in table 3.1.

(HPMS). HPMS data are collected by various state highway authorities under the direction of the Federal Highway Administration, and these data describe the Interstate Highway network in detail. Mehrotra, Uribe, and Turner (2020) and Turner (2019) analyze these data and describe the evolution of usage, extent, and condition of the network from about 1980 until 2007.[2]

Figure 3.1 presents six figures based on data from Mehrotra, Uribe, and Turner (2020). Average annual daily traffic (AADT) per lane is defined as the number of vehicles traversing a given lane of roadway on an average day during the year. This is a common measure of the intensity with which a roadway is used. The solid line in panel A of figure 3.1 reports systemwide mean AADT (lane-mile weighted) for every year between 1980 and 2007 in thousands of vehicles per day. Thus, an average lane of the Interstate Highway System carried about 4,500 vehicles per day in 1980, and this figure more than doubled to about 10,000 vehicles per day by 2010. AADT on the Interstate Highway network increased by about 3 percent per year. The dashed and dotted lines in panel A of figure 3.1 report AADT on the urban and rural portions of the Interstate, respectively. AADT on the urban portion of the Interstate is about triple that on the rural portion; however, both parts of the network are following similar trends.[3]

Panel B of figure 3.1 reports a second measure of aggregate usage, total vehicle miles traveled (VMT) on the Interstate Highway System. We calculate this measure by multiplying segment-level AADT by segment length and again by 365. This gives an estimate of the number of vehicle miles of travel provided by a particular Interstate Highway segment. Summing over all segments gives an estimate of total VMT provided by the entire network in a year. The solid line in panel B of figure 3.1 reports aggregate Interstate VMT annually from 1980 until 2007. This figure shows that Interstate VMT increased from about 300 to 700 billion miles per year between 1980 and 2007. Over 27 years, this is an increase of about 3.2 percent per year. That VMT increased more rapidly than AADT reflects the fact that lane miles also increased during this time, even as AADT was rising. The dashed and dotted lines reflect urban and rural VMT. We see that most of the increase in VMT comes from the urban portion of the network. This partly reflects the increasing share of urban highways in the Interstate network.

In addition to tracking usage, the HPMS measures the extent and condition of the Interstate Highway System. Panel C of figure 3.1 reports lane miles of Interstate Highways in operation by year from 1980 until 2007.

2. HPMS data are not available for 2009 and are available for only a subset of states in 2008. HPMS data are also available from 2010 until 2016. However, a change in the format of the data in 2010 makes it difficult to compare post-2010 data with data from earlier years.

3. We note that the Interstate is becoming "more urban" over time as urbanized areas expand to include more of the network. Thus, the urban and rural AADT series in figure 3.1 do not reflect constant samples of roads.

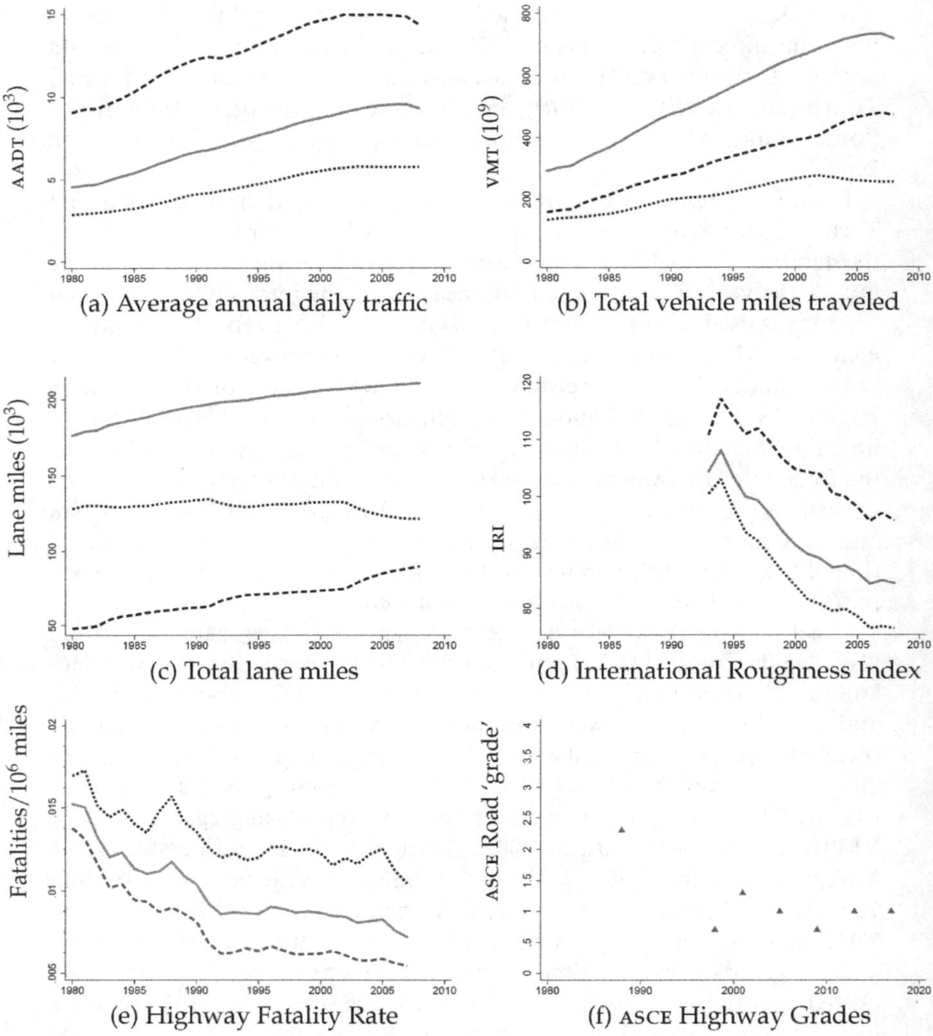


**Fig. 3.1 Interstate Highways: Usage, stock, and condition**

*Note:* Panels A–E are based on HPMS data. In A–E the solid line describes the national total, the dashed line describes the urban portion of the Interstate, and the dotted line describes the rural portion. A. AADT is lane-mile weighted. B. Total vehicle miles traveled on Interstate Highways. C. Total lane miles. D. Lane-mile-weighted international roughness index. E. Annual Interstate fatalities per million of VMT. F. American Society of Civil Engineers grades for US road infrastructure by year.

We see that lane miles increased from about 175,000 to about 210,000 over this period, an increase of about 20 percent, or 0.7 percent annually over 27 years. The preponderance of this increase reflects the widening of existing segments, not the construction of new mileage. The dashed and dotted lines in this figure describe urban and rural lane miles. We see that urban lane miles have increased, while rural lane miles are about constant. This partly reflects the reclassification of rural segments to urban.

Finally, the HPMS tracks the condition of the Interstate Highway System. To do so, the HPMS relies on annual measurements of the international roughness index (IRI). IRI measures the number of inches of suspension travel a typical car would experience in traveling a particular mile of roadway. As part of HPMS, state highway authorities measure IRI on every segment of the Interstate Highway System, more or less, every year.[4] Figure 3.1 reports lane-mile-weighted IRI for the Interstate Highway System from 1992 until 2007. The units of IRI are inches per mile, so a decline in IRI reflects an improvement in pavement quality.[5] The dashed and solid lines report IRI on urban and rural portions of the Interstate. Rural highways are in better condition than urban highways. Both rural and urban highways exhibit the same trend in condition. Both improve dramatically over our study period.

For reference, the Federal Highway Administration considers roads to be in *good* or *acceptable* condition when their IRI value is below 95 or between 95 and 170. Roads with IRI above 170 inches per mile are in *poor* condition (US Department of Transportation 2013). Panel D of figure 3.1 shows a decline in mean IRI from just under 110 inches per mile in 1992 to about 85 inches per mile in 2007—that is, from a little above the "good condition" threshold to a little below. The improvement in the condition of Interstate Highways has been almost monotonic. The only exception occurs between 1992 and 1993, when mean IRI increased slightly. As this was the first year when IRI reporting was required, we suspect that this increase reflects problems with initial reporting of IRI rather than actual deterioration of the network.

The two panels of figure 3.2 provide more detail about how IRI varies across the country. To make these figures, we divide each state into its rural and urbanized portions, adding the entirely urban District of Columbia, to get to 97 regions. We next construct mean IRI for the rural and urban portions of the Interstate in each state over the years 1993, 1994, and 1995. The range of these state-by-region IRI means is 37 to 175 inches per mile. We partition this range into six bins of equal width, 23 inches. Recalling that low values of IRI are good, in panel A of figure 3.2, we assign each bin a color ranging from light gray for the lowest and best bin to black for the

4. For more detail on the measurement and reporting of IRI, see Federal Highway Administration (2016) and Office of Highway Policy Information (2016).

5. HPMS has required IRI reporting for the universe of Interstate segments only from 1992 onward, so this measure begins later than those reported in other panels of figure 3.1.

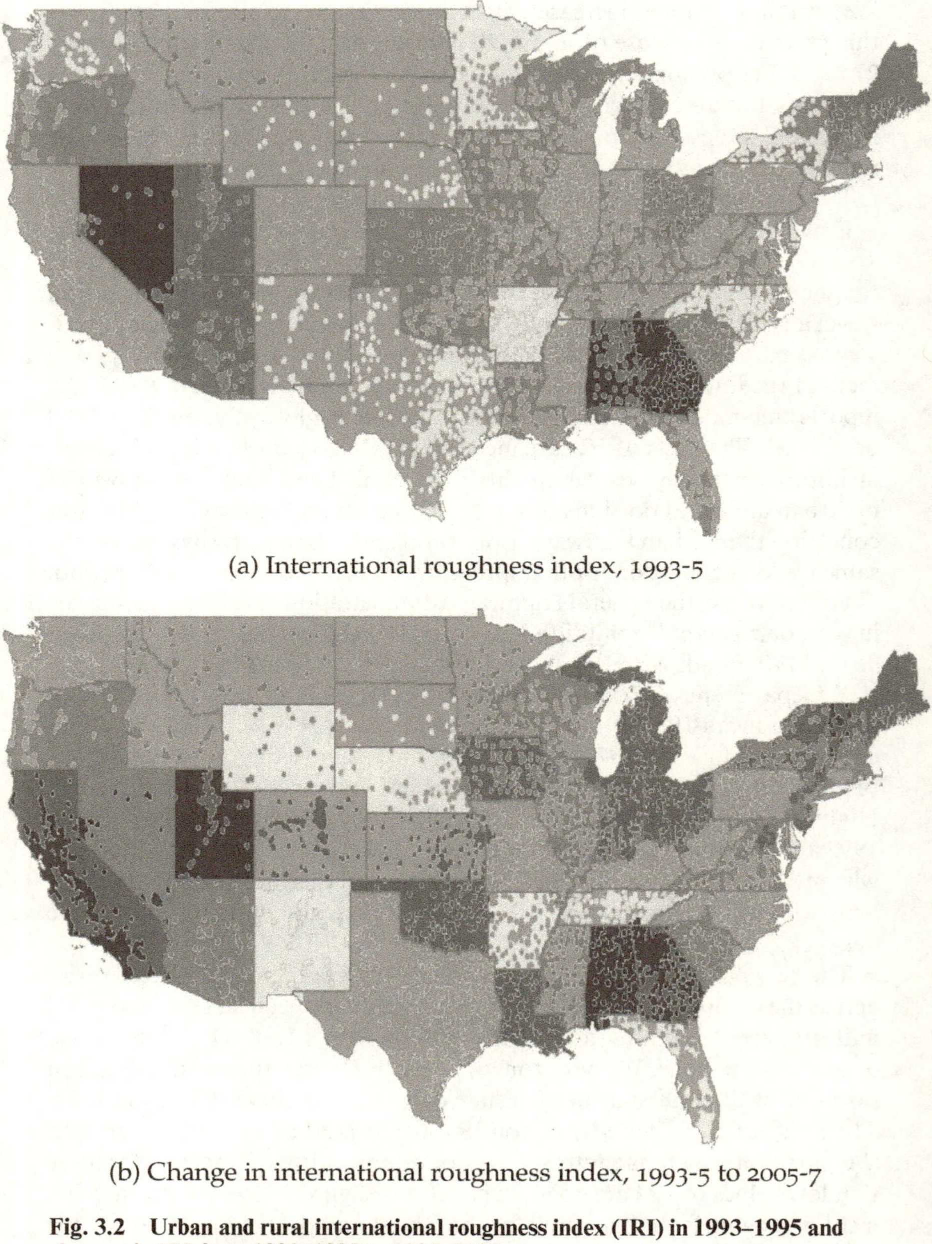

(a) International roughness index, 1993-5

(b) Change in international roughness index, 1993-5 to 2005-7

**Fig. 3.2 Urban and rural international roughness index (IRI) in 1993–1995 and changes in IRI from 1993–1995 to 2005–2007**

*Note:* Panel A shows the state mean IRI for rural and urban Interstate Highways averaged over 1993–1995. Panel B shows the state mean change in IRI for rural and urban Interstate Highways from 1993–1995 to 2005–2007.

highest and worst bin. For legibility, we exaggerate the size of the urbanized areas in each state.

Recalling Federal Highway Administration quality definitions, the good/acceptable threshold occurs at 95 inches, in the dark gray (like Oregon in both years) regions, while the acceptable/poor threshold occurs at 170 inches, in the dark gray and black regions. Therefore, this figure, while it reveals considerable heterogeneity in road quality, overwhelmingly indicates that in the 1992–1995 period, the Interstate was in pretty good shape, at least as indicated by the Federal Highway Administration's standards. Indeed, only Nevada, Alabama, and Georgia have Interstate conditions anywhere near the acceptable/poor threshold, and in Alabama and Georgia, only the rural portions of the Interstate approach this threshold.

Panel B of figure 3.2 is similar but reports on changes in IRI between the initial three-year period, 1993–1995, and the final three-year period, 2005–2007. The range of within-region change in IRI over this period was −77 to 20 inches per mile. We divide this region into six bins, each 17 inches wide. Recalling that decreases in IRI are good, in panel B of figure 3.2, we assign each bin a color ranging from light gray, for the largest decrease, to black, for the largest increase.

Medium gray describes the bin ranging from −9 to 8 inches—that is, the bin where mean regional IRI stays about constant. We assign black to the bin containing all regions where mean Interstate IRI increased between 9 and 20 inches over our period of about 12 years. From the figure, we see that only a handful of regions of the country experienced even such modest deterioration of their highways: urban California, urban Nevada, rural Utah, Alabama, rural Georgia, and urban Vermont. Most of the rest of the country saw reductions in IRI. Alabama and Georgia are striking in that the initial conditions of their roads were relatively poor and their deterioration relatively rapid.

Returning our attention to figure 3.1, in panel E we report Interstate fatalities per million vehicle miles traveled.[6] Panel E presents fatalities per million miles on rural Interstates (dotted line), urban Interstates (dashed line), and overall (solid line). The rural Interstate system is dramatically more dangerous than the urban Interstate, and this gap grows slightly over time. While much of the reduction in fatalities is surely a reflection of improvements in cars, at a minimum, any deterioration in the safety of the Interstates has not been sufficient to outpace improvements in vehicle safety.

Panel F of figure 3.1 reports the American Society of Civil Engineers (ASCE) annual grades for US road infrastructure, converted from letter grades to a four-point scale: A = 4.0, B = 3.0, C = 2.0 and D = 1.0.[7] These

6. Interstate fatalities are reported in US Federal Highway Administration (2019), tables FI210 and FI220.

7. Downloaded from https://www.infrastructurereportcard.org/making-the-grade/report-card-history/, January 2020.

Table 3.2 US travel speeds by mode and year from the NHTS

| Year | Car | Bus | Subway |
|---|---|---|---|
| 1995 | 26.35 | 15.70 | 15.00 |
| 2001 | 25.30 | 13.68 | 11.85 |
| 2009 | 25.46 | 12.63 | 10.42 |
| 2017 | 23.54 | 11.08 | 10.59 |

*Note:* Speed of travel (miles per hour) on an average trip by mode as reported in various years of the NHTS (called Nationwide Personal Transportation Surveys, or NPTS, prior to 2001). Trip speeds reported in 1995 and 2017 are adjusted to minor changes in survey questions and distance measurement introduced in these years.

highly publicized grades are constructed about every four years, starting in 1988. While the precise methodology used to calculate each year's score is not available, the report that accompanies each year's grade describes the factors that are reflected in the score. For roads in 2015, these factors were capacity, condition, funding, future need, public safety, innovation, and resilience. The ASCE grade for roads reflects conditions on all public roads. So while figure 3.1 invites a comparison of the ASCE road grade with various time series describing the Interstate system, we note that this is not really a fair comparison.

With that said, the difference between the ACSE measure of road condition and the IRI series is striking. The ASCE time series shows roads that are at best maintaining their D grade. The IRI series, on the other hand, shows almost monotone improvements in smoothness. Clearly, the ASCE infrastructure grades are not strictly about the physical condition of the Interstate, and a poor ASCE grade should probably not suggest that the Interstate network is crumbling.

Finally, table 3.2 reports the average speed of travel on an average trip by car, bus, or subway for each of the years in which the National Household Transportation Survey (NHTS) is administered, 1995, 2001, 2009, and 2017. Looking down the second column, we see an almost monotone decrease in the speed of travel by car over the 1995–2017 period. Given the well-known inverse relationship between speed and flow, this decrease seems consistent with the dramatic increase in VMT that we see in figure 3.1, again with the caveat that figure 3.1 describes the Interstate, while table 3.2 describes trips on all roads.

We note that the different waves of the NHTS on which table 3.2 is based define speed slightly differently, complicating cross-year comparisons. In particular, the 1995 wave uses a slightly different wording to elicit information about travel time, while the 2017 wave measures travel distance using a different methodology. Given this difference in definitions, the numbers we report for these years are based on (slight) statistical adjustments of reports for 1995 and 2017. We note that these sorts of inconsistencies compromise the usefulness of the whole NHTS program. Given the expense of this program and recent advances in using smartphones to measure travel behavior (for example, Akbar et al. 2020; Kreindler 2018), this suggests that phasing out the NHTS in favor of smartphone-based travel monitoring and surveys deserves serious consideration.

To sum up, an average segment of the Interstate carries about twice the traffic in 2007 as it did in 1980. This increase in the intensity of use occurs in spite of an about 20 percent increase in the extent of the network over this period. The increases to network extent, together with increased AADT, mean that the Interstate Highway System provided well over twice as much travel in 2007 as in 1980. Unsurprisingly, this increase in intensity of use is matched by a decrease in the average speed of travel by car, although our NHTS-based measure of speed reflects all car travel, not just travel on the Interstate.

For reference, the US population increased from about 226 million in 1980 to about 309 million in 2010, an increase of about 37 percent or about 1.0 percent per year. Thus, the lane miles of Interstate Highways grew at just above two-thirds the rate for population (about 0.7 versus about 1.0 percent), while the number of vehicle miles provided by the network grew about three times as fast as population.

In spite of the increased intensity with which the network was used during this period, the mean quality of the network, as measured by IRI, improved consistently from 1992 until 2007. Similarly, the rate of traffic fatalities on the Interstate falls over our study period. These two measures of service stand in contrast to the time series of grades given to US road infrastructure by the ASCE. This series indicates constant or deteriorating quality over the same period, although the ASCE "road grades" are based on the whole road network, rather than just the Interstate. It is, however, clear that the ASCE road grades should not be regarded as a measure of the physical condition of the US Interstate system.

Rural portions of the Interstate Highway System are used less intensively than the urban portions, and rural segments are in better condition than their urban counterparts. Perhaps more surprisingly, the basic trends are the same for both portions of the network. Usage increases and condition improves at about the same rate for both parts of the network. Figure 3.2 maps initial IRI and changes over our study period and does not reveal obvious patterns. Interstates in the rust belt and California deteriorate. Interstates improve from a high base in most of the mountain states. Interstates in Alabama and Georgia are noteworthy for deteriorating from relatively poor initial conditions.

### 3.2.2 Bridges

The federal government also maintains the National Bridge Inventory (NBI). These data are similar to the HPMS and are intended to serve a similar function, but for the nation's bridges rather than its highways. The NBI is available from about 1990 through to 2017.

For the purposes of the NBI, a bridge is defined as

> a structure including supports erected over a depression or an obstruction, such as water, highway, or railway, and having a track or passageway for carrying traffic or other moving loads, and having an opening measured along the center of the roadway of more than 20 feet between undercopings of abutments or spring lines of arches, or extreme ends of openings for multiple boxes; it may also include multiple pipes, where the clear distance between openings is less than half of the smaller contiguous opening. (Federal Highway Administration 1995)

For each bridge satisfying this definition, the NBI records a basic description of the structure, its location, its condition, and how it is used. Thus, the NBI allows a similar analysis of bridges as does the HPMS for highways.

Figure 3.3 provides a summary description of the state of US bridges. Our expenditure data will describe expenditure on Interstate bridges alone, so each panel of figure 3.3 reports the evolution of all bridges (solid line) and the evolution of the stock of Interstate bridges (dashed line).[8]

Panel A describes the stock of bridges. In order to weight large bridges more heavily than small bridges, we measure the stock of bridges by deck area (in square feet) rather than in the count of spans. In panel A, we see the deck area of US bridges increased from about three to about four billion square feet between 1990 and 2017, an increase of about 28 percent. Over the 27-year span of NBI data, this is an increase of about 0.9 percent per year. Thus, bridge area is growing modestly faster than Interstate lane miles and marginally slower than population. A caveat applies to these calculations: they are calculated over the slightly different time periods dictated by HPMS and NBI availability.

Panel B reports on the number of bridges over time. We see that the number of bridges in the NBI increased from about 570,000 to about 610,000. This is about a 7 percent increase, or an increase of about 0.25 percent per year over a 27-year period. This rate of growth is distinctly smaller than the rate of growth of lane miles of highways, which is itself less than the growth rate of population. Inspection of panel B shows that most new bridges were Interstate bridges.

The NBI does not report the number of lanes per bridge but does report the width of the bridge deck. We impute number of lanes per bridge by dividing by 12 feet, the width of a typical lane of Interstate Highway.[9] This done, we divide the reported value of AADT per bridge by imputed lanes, to arrive at an estimate of AADT per lane. This measure of AADT is comparable

8. The NBI identifies bridges as Interstate or not on the basis of their route signs. This will lead to a slight divergence from the HPMS, which reports on the legal status of the road.

9. See, for example, *Highway Statistics 2008*, table HM-33.

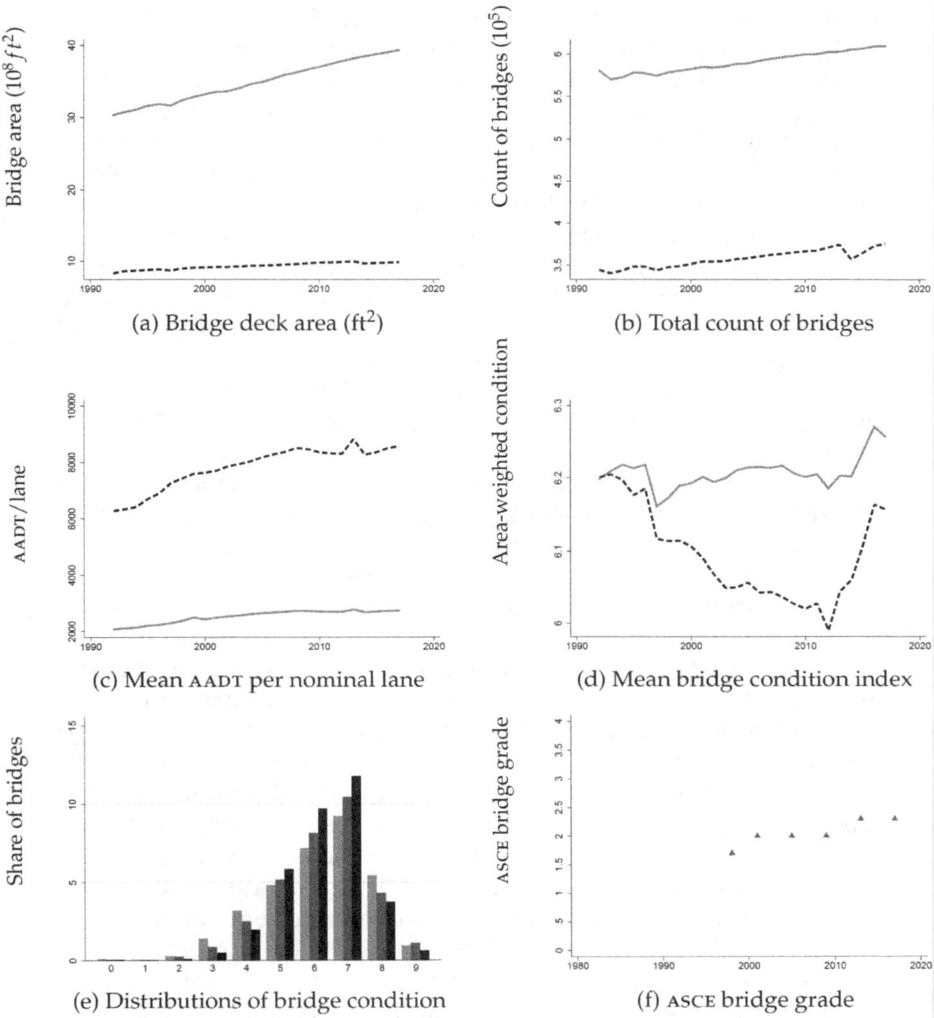


**Fig. 3.3 Bridges: Usage, stock, and condition**

*Note:* Panels A–E are based on NBI data. In A–D the dashed line describes the subset of interstate bridges while the solid line describes the universe of all bridges in the NBI. In panel D, bridges are weighted by deck area. Panel E shows a distribution of bridge condition in three years, 1992 (light), 2000 (medium), 2007 (dark). Panel F reports the ASCE bridge infrastructure grade by year.

to what we report in figure 3.1 for the Interstate Highway System, subject to the fact that bridge lanes are likely somewhat narrower than an average Interstate lane. Panel C of figure 3.3 reports the resulting measure of mean AADT. We see that AADT on an average lane of a bridge increases from about 2,000 to about 2,800, an increase of 40 percent or about 1.25 percent per year. This is rapid compared with the increase in the number of bridges, but this increase is also slightly more than the increase in bridge deck area. AADT on Interstate bridges is higher but grows at about the same rate.

Measuring the condition of a bridge is complicated, and the NBI reports on condition in some detail. In particular, for each of superstructure, decking, substructure, and channel, the NBI reports an ordinal measure of condition ranging from 0 to 9, with higher values indicating better repair.

To summarize these condition indexes, the NBI reports the minimum of the four as the "bridge condition index."[10] Panel D of figure 3.3 reports the deck-area-weighted mean bridge condition index. While this measure exhibits some variance, its range seems small, about 0.25 of a point or one quarter of a category on any of the component condition measures. More important, this index does not show a strong trend. The lighter dashed line shows the evolution of the condition of Interstate bridges. This index dips about 0.2 points between 1990 and 2010, before recovering to almost its initial level in 2017.

We experimented with variants of the condition index. We constructed an alternative condition index by summing each of the superstructure, deck, substructure, and channel condition measures, and we considered bridge-weighted (as opposed to deck-area-weighted) averages. Of these, only the bridge-weighted measure of the NBI index shows a downward trend; the others are either flat or increasing. In sum, "bridge condition" is difficult to describe. However, to the extent that the NBI allows us to measure bridge condition, the data do not indicate that the US stock of bridges is deteriorating but instead that maintenance is about offsetting deterioration.

Because bridge collapse is catastrophic, bridge condition codes indicating severe deterioration are of particular interest. These codes are: 0 for *failed condition*, out of service; 1 for *imminent failure condition*, bridge closed; 2 for *critical condition*, unless closely monitored closure may be required.[11] These three codes indicate a bridge that is badly deteriorated and in need of immediate repair, replacement, or closure. To track the prevalence of these badly deteriorated bridges, panel E of figure 3.3 reports histograms showing the share of bridges assigned each of the 10 possible bridge condition index values in 1992 (light gray), 2000 (medium gray), and 2007 (dark gray). These

10. See https://www.fhwa.dot.gov/bridge/britab.cfm#def for more detail on NBI bridge condition reporting.

11. More precise definitions for these codes and codes 3–9 are provided in US Federal Highway Administration (1995).

histograms show that the modal bridge condition is 7 (good condition) in all three years. Over time, the distribution of scores compresses as deteriorated bridges are improved and bridges in better condition deteriorate. The incidence of dangerous bridges is very low in all years and falling over time. Note that this figure describes all bridges in the National Bridge Inventory. This corresponds to the sample that generates the solid line of panel D of figure 3.3. Restricting attention to just Interstate bridges (not shown) leads to qualitatively similar conclusions: the modal bridge is in good condition, and the number of dangerous bridges has decreased over time.

Panel F of figure 3.3 reports the ASCE grades for US bridge infrastructure. These data are similar to those presented in figure 3.1 for highways and are the result of a similar process. Like the ASCE road condition index, the ASCE bridge grades are available about every four years, but the bridge grades start in 1998 rather than 1988. Thus, the ASCE bridge grades cover just about the same period as do the NBI data on bridge condition. Over the 1998–2017 period, the ASCE bridge condition improves from a C−, or 1.7 on our numerical scale, to a C+, or 2.3 on our scale.

Changes in the ASCE bridge index seem to match changes in the NBI bridge condition index more closely than the ASCE road grades match Interstate IRI. Neither fluctuates much over our study period. With that said, the ASCE seems to be grading bridges quite harshly. The modal bridge has an NBI index score of 7, or good, from 1992 to 2007, while the mean bridge has a score between 6 (satisfactory condition) and 7 throughout the period. Thus, as for the ASCE road condition grades, a poor ASCE bridge condition grade seems not to indicate pervasive disrepair, at least as measured by the National Bridge Inventory.

### 3.2.3 Transit

We now describe public transit service and capital stocks from about 1990 until 2017. This description is based on various data sets made available as part of the National Transit Database (NTD) available from the National Transit Administration. The unit of observation in these data is a transit district year. The number of transit districts covered by this database has increased over time, from 473 in 1992 to about 2,247 in 2017.

Public transit in the US consists of many different modes of travel, from jitney buses to cog railways to ferry boats, and the NTD is exhaustive. Table 3.3 reports on the numbers of riders, vehicles, service miles, and total expenditure by mode for 2017 and 2008 in the continental US. It aggregates the modes reported in the NTD somewhat. Our data on buses reflect three NTD modes: motor buses (mb), trolley buses (tb), and bus rapid transit (rb). Our data on light rail reflect two NTD modes, light rail (lr) and streetcar rail (sr). Subways report the NTD heavy rail (hr) data. Commuter rail is the NTD mode cr. Demand response aggregates both demand response buses

Table 3.3 Transit aggregate statistics by mode in 2008 and 2017 for the continental US

| | Bus | Light rail | Subway | Commercial rail | Van pool | Demand response |
|---|---|---|---|---|---|---|
| 2017 | | | | | | |
| Riders ($10^6$) | 4,679.4 | 554.7 | 3,808.9 | 497.8 | 35.24 | 157.2 |
| Vehicles | 68,972 | 2,553 | 11,671 | 7,121 | 15,174 | 57487 |
| Service miles ($10^6$) | 1,972.7 | 124.0 | 681.4 | 347.0 | 229.5 | 1186.1 |
| Passenger miles ($10^6$) | 16,843.3 | 2,690.3 | 17,555.5 | 12,250.7 | 1,254.6 | 933.2 |
| Expenditure ($10^6$) | 25,272.2 | 5,521.2 | 13,480.8 | 9,029.7 | 189.5 | 5,083.2 |
| # NTDs | 1,148 | 40 | 14 | 25 | 107 | 1,894 |
| 2008 | | | | | | |
| Riders ($10^6$) | 5,513.2 | 450.9 | 3,538.6 | 471.3 | 29.45 | 130.6 |
| Vehicles | 63,761.5 | 1,947 | 11,293 | 6,792 | 10,624 | 31,470 |
| Service miles ($10^6$) | 2,029.3 | 86.26 | 652.1 | 309.0 | 154.4 | 967.2 |
| Passenger miles ($10^6$) | 20,972.0 | 2,080.3 | 16,805.1 | 11,032.0 | 968.0 | 832.5 |
| Expenditure ($10^6$) | 21,396.4 | 4,344.4 | 12,107.9 | 6,919.8 | 137.3 | 3,168.4 |
| # NTDs | 500 | 28 | 14 | 22 | 59 | 466 |

*Note:* Riders and passenger and service miles are in millions. Expenditure is in millions of 2010 dollars and transit districts ("# NTDs") are counted only if they have a positive number of vehicles.

and taxis (dr and dt). By almost any measure, the preponderance of transit travel involves buses and subways. Given this, we focus our attention on these two modes of public transit.

The NTD classifies transit districts into two main categories: "full reporters" and "partial reporters." Transit districts are classified as partial reporters if they operate fewer than 30 vehicles during the year. About 20 percent of transit districts are partial reporters, and such districts are exempted from reporting certain data that is required of larger districts. In particular, partial reporters are not required to report "total passenger miles traveled," a quantity that we report on later.

Table 3.4 describes the way that public transit is distributed across transit districts on the basis of 2014–2017 averages of ridership and expenditure. Column 1 of the table reports the national percentage of transit riders across all modes for the six transit districts with the greatest ridership. New York accounts for about 40 percent of all transit rides in the entire country. Chicago is second, with 6 percent, followed by DC, Los Angeles, Boston, and Philadelphia. In total, these six districts account for about 60 percent of all transit rides in the country. Public transit usage is highly concentrated in a few large cities, particularly New York.

The rest of table 3.4 provides disaggregated information about bus and subway ridership and expenditure for these six transit cities and for the country as a whole. The concentration of transit into a small number of cities primarily reflects the dominance of the New York subway network. The

**Table 3.4** **Buses and subways in five biggest transit districts: Means 2014–2017**

| | All modes | Bus | | | | Subway | | | |
|---|---|---|---|---|---|---|---|---|---|
| | % riders | Riders | % | Expenditures | % total expenditures | Riders | % | Expenditures | % total expenditures |
| New York | 40.3 | 722.9 | 15.4 | 2,765.7 | 10.9 | 2,699.5 | 70.9 | 7,098.4 | 49.8 |
| Chicago | 5.6 | 249.2 | 5.3 | 836.3 | 3.3 | 230.2 | 6.0 | 884.9 | 6.2 |
| DC | 4.1 | 123.1 | 2.6 | 715.0 | 2.8 | 227.1 | 6.0 | 1,390.9 | 9.7 |
| Los Angeles | 4.0 | 290.0 | 6.2 | 1,254.0 | 4.9 | 45.6 | 1.2 | 792.3 | 5.6 |
| Boston | 3.3 | 118.9 | 2.5 | 527.0 | 2.1 | 164.1 | 4.3 | 499.5 | 3.5 |
| Philadelphia | 3.1 | 169.4 | 3.6 | 697.7 | 2.7 | 93.9 | 2.5 | 308.4 | 2.2 |
| Total | 100.0 | 4,679.4 | 100.0 | 25,412.0 | 100.0 | 3,808.9 | 100.0 | 14,266.7 | 100.0 |

*Note:* All counts of riders are given in millions per year. Expenditures are total capital and operating expenditures in millions of 2010 dollars. Second column gives total riders summed over all modes. The next four columns describe buses. The last four columns describe subways. Percentages describe the percentage of national totals in a city.

New York subway system carries about 71 percent of all subway riders and about 31 percent of all public transit riders in the entire country.

The remaining five of the top six transit districts account for another 20 percent of all subway riders, with the residual 9 percent distributed across eight smaller subway systems. Even excluding New York, subway ridership is still concentrated in a small number of places.

Unlike subway ridership, bus ridership is widely distributed. New York is also the biggest provider of bus trips but provides only 15 percent of the national total. The top six transit cities provide only about 36 percent of all bus trips.

Expenditure on buses and subways approximately tracks ridership, and, in particular, the share of total expenditure is closely related to share of ridership. A few points about expenditure are noteworthy. First, the New York subway system provides 70 percent of all subway rides but accounts for only about 50 percent of expenditure. This suggests that this system is relatively efficient. A caveat applies. Our data on expenditure reflect current capital and operating expenses. To the extent that subway systems are depreciating or augmenting their capital stocks, this is not reflected in our expenditure measures. Second, comparing bus and subway expenditure shares with ridership shares suggests that these large transit districts are providing public transit at a lower cost than smaller districts.

#### *3.2.3.1 Buses*

Panel A of figure 3.4 reports the total number of rides provided by the US bus fleet by year. The solid line gives national totals, the dashed line gives the annual total for the six transit districts listed in table 3.4, and the dotted line gives totals for the remaining smaller transit districts.

Total bus ridership ranges between about 4.5 billion and 5.5 billion but shows no clear trend. Both the large and small transit districts follow about the same path. Bus ridership is higher in the years following the 2008 financial crisis and lower otherwise. To put this number in perspective, with about 300 million people in the US, 5 billion rides per year implies about 17 bus trips per person per year. In contrast, by 2007, the Interstate Highway System was providing about 700 billion VMT per year, or about 2,300 miles per person per year.[12] Panel B of figure 3.4 reports total passenger miles traveled by bus. This figure tracks ridership closely but exhibits higher variance. Service miles increase and then decrease by about 50 percent over our study period, while ridership increases and then decreases by only about 20 percent. Both the large and small transit districts follow about the same path,

12. Note that we here report vehicle miles traveled. On average, each car in the US carries about 1.25 people (Couture, Duranton, and Turner 2018), so the figure for person miles traveled is about 25 percent larger.

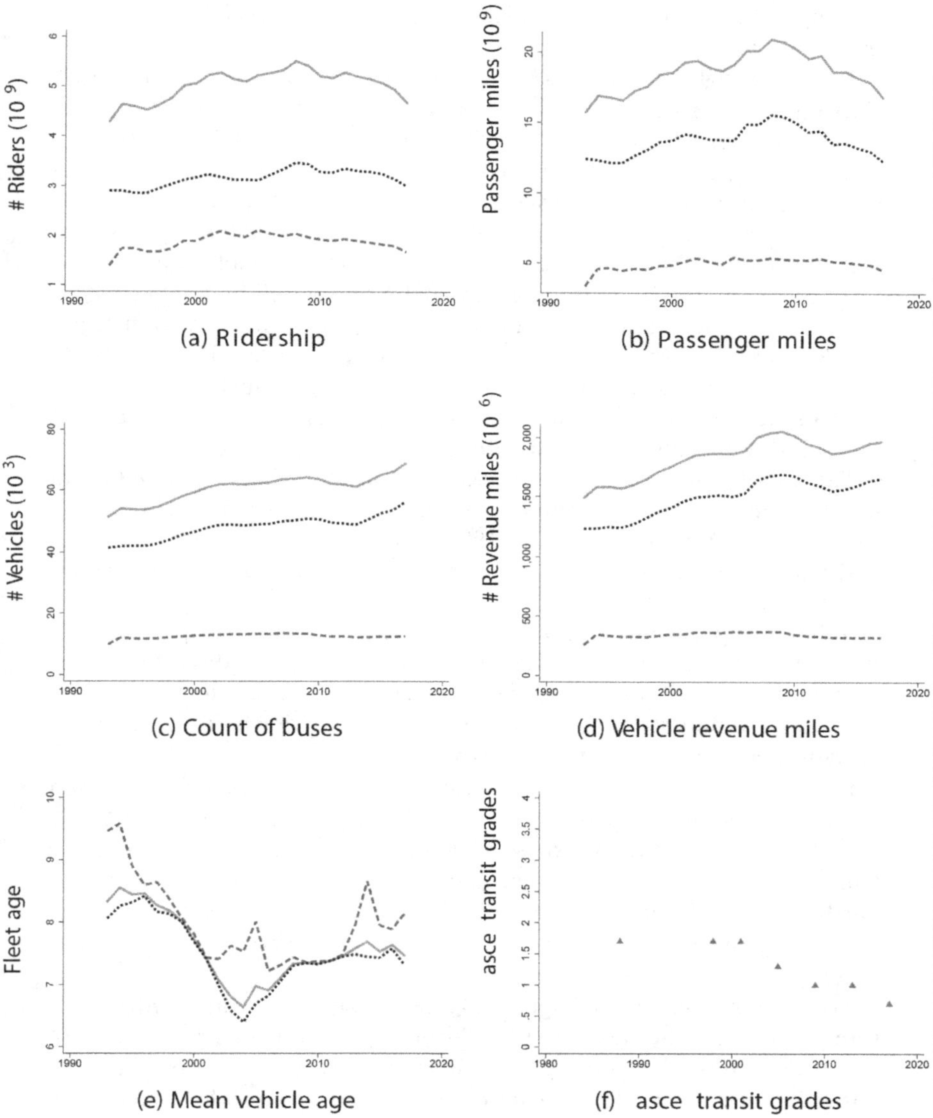


**Fig. 3.4 Buses: Usage, stock, and age of the fleet**

*Note:* Panels A–E are from the National Transit Database. In panel B, passenger miles traveled on buses are only for "full reporter" transit districts. In panels A–E, the solid line gives national totals, the dashed line gives the total for the six transit districts listed in table 3.4, and the dotted line gives totals for the remaining transit districts.

although more of the national variation in passenger miles comes from small transit districts.

Panel C of figure 3.4 reports the number of buses in service. Unlike ridership and passenger miles, the stock of buses increased monotonically over the study period, from about 50,000 in 1992 to about 68,000 in 2017, an increase of 36 percent, or about 1.4 percent per year. The count of buses in large districts is almost perfectly constant over this period, so that the increase in buses is primarily in small transit districts. Panel D reports total revenue miles for the bus fleet for each year. Like the count of buses, revenue miles increase fairly steadily, from about 1.5 to 2.0 billion, an increase of about 33 percent. This is an increase of about 1.2 percent per year, marginally less fast than the growth rate of the stock of buses. The divergence between large and small districts is even sharper for vehicle revenue miles than for vehicles. Revenue miles are about constant in large districts but increase dramatically in small districts.

Panel E of figure 3.4 reports on mean fleet age by year. We see that mean fleet age ranges between about 6.5 and 8.5 years, decreasing from about 8.5 to about 7.5 years over the period 1992–2017. The ages of vehicles in large and small districts track each other closely, although bigger districts generally have slightly older buses.

Table 3.2 reports the speed in miles per hour of an average trip on a public transit bus (excluding school buses) in years from 1995 to 2017. Like the corresponding speeds for car trips, these speeds are based on survey responses reported in different waves of the NHTS. Looking down this column, we see a dramatic decrease in the speed of an average bus trip over this period, from about 15 miles per hour to about 11 miles per hour. This is an even more dramatic decrease than we observe for the speed of trips by car. While one can imagine that this decrease reflects change in the composition of bus trips, toward more congested places, it seem likely that the decline at least partly reflects a decline in the speed of bus travel when routes are held constant and that this decline largely reflects the dramatic increases in AADT that we note in figure 3.1.

For reference, panel F of figure 3.4 reports the ASCE transit infrastructure grades. Like the ASCE road and bridge grades reported earlier, these scores are reported as letter grades that we convert to a four-point scale. Panel F shows a clear decline over the 1988 to 2017 period for which these scores are available, from a C– in 1988 to a D– in 2017. Comparing these scores to bus age seems problematic, both because bus age is clearly a partial measure of the state of bus infrastructure and also because the ASCE index aggregates information about all transit, not just buses. With that said, and recalling from table 3.3 that buses are the most important public transit mode, it is noteworthy that the ASCE transit index should show so clear a negative trend over a period when the count of buses is increasing monotonically and the mean fleet age is decreasing. Given this dramatic divergence, we probably should not regard the ASCE index as providing much information about the level or condition of bus-based public transit.

Unlike highways and bridges, aggregate bus usage is not increasing rapidly. Also unlike highways and bridges, the growth of the stock of buses is much more rapid than ridership. Like highways and bridges, the stock of buses, at least as measured by age, is not deteriorating over time. To the contrary, like highways, the condition of the US bus fleet seems to be improving. New bus capacity is dispersed among smaller transit districts. The stock of buses in the largest districts is about constant.

It is worth contrasting the relatively recent US experience with bus travel with that from 1935–1963. Meyer, Kain, and Wohl (1965) document that the number of riders carried by US motor buses peaked in 1945 at about 9.8 billion and began to fall in the postwar years, to 6.4 billion in 1960 and further to 5.8 billion in 1963, when the authors' data end. For comparison, in table 3.3 we see that bus ridership was about 5.5 billion in 2008 and 4.7 billion by 2017; US population in 1945, 1960, and 2008 was about 131 million, 151 million, and 304 million, respectively. Bus riding was a much more important part of American life during the postwar years than it is now. In part, this decline is attributable to the rising motorization of the poor (Blumenberg, Manville, and Taylor 2019).

### *3.2.3.2 Subways*

Figure 3.5 replicates figure 3.4 for subways. Panel A of figure 3.5 reports billions of riders. Between 1992 and 2017, ridership increased from about 2 billion to about 4 billion. This is an increase of about 100 percent, or about 2.8 percent per year. Panel B reports increases in passenger miles served by subways. This figure increases from about 10 billion to about 16 billion miles per year, an increase of about 60 percent. That this increase is smaller than the increase in riders indicates that the mean length of a subway trip declined over the study period. At about 2.8 percent per year, the growth rate in subway ridership is close to the 3.2 percent growth rate of VMT on the Interstate Highway System and significantly larger than the 1.2 percent growth rate of population.

Given the importance of the New York subway system, figure 3.5 reports separately on the New York subway, the dashed line, and all other subways, the dotted line. Panel A of figure 3.5 shows that almost all of the national increase in subway ridership over our study period reflects increases in ridership on the New York subway.

Panel C of figure 3.5 reports the stock of subway cars by year. We see that the number of subway cars in operation increased from about 10,000 in 1992 to about 11,500 by 2017. This is a 15 percent increase, or 0.6 percent per year. This is half the rate of national population growth and less than one-third the rate of ridership growth. Panel D reports aggregate revenue miles by year. Revenue miles increased from about 500 million to about

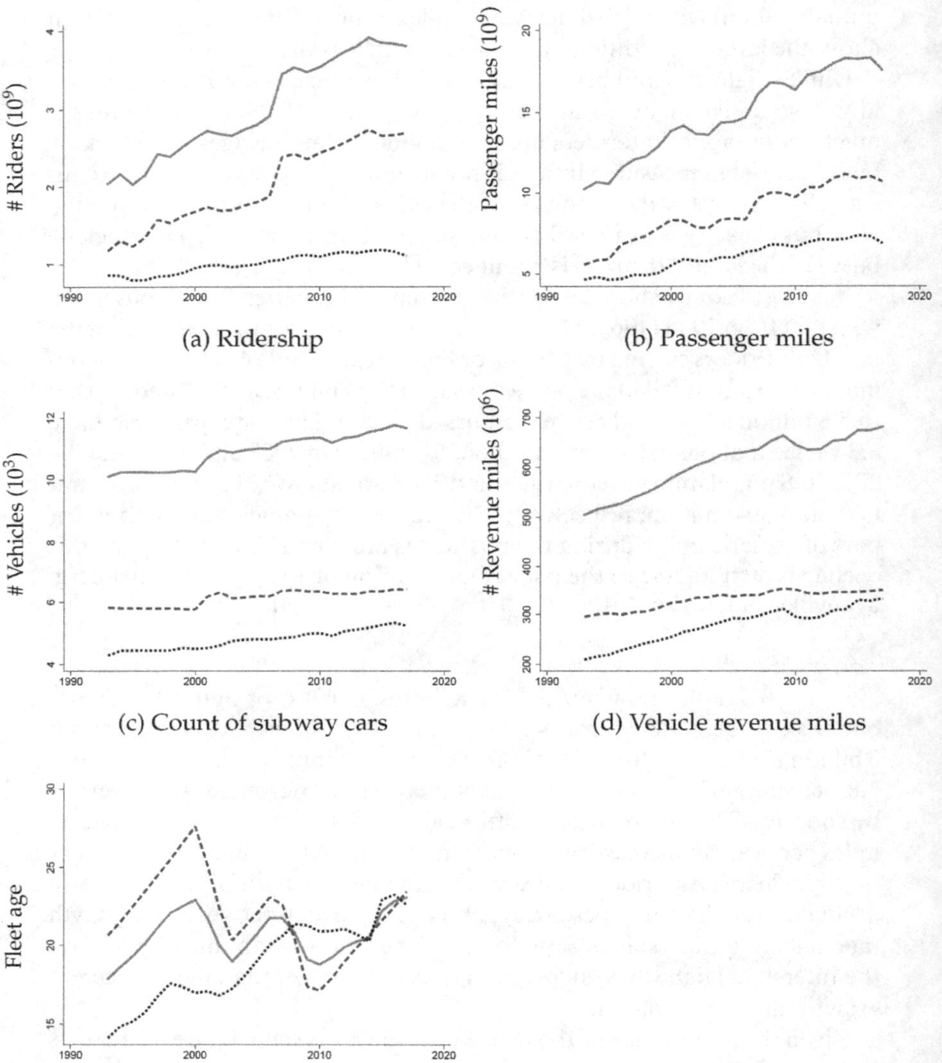


(a) Ridership

(b) Passenger miles

(c) Count of subway cars

(d) Vehicle revenue miles

(e) Mean age of subway car fleet

**Fig. 3.5 Subways: Usage, stock, and age of the fleet**

*Note:* All data from the National Transit Database. In all panels, the solid line gives national totals, the dashed line gives the total for the New York subway system, and the dotted line gives totals for the remaining transit districts.

700 million, an increase of about 40 percent. This is also much smaller than the increase in ridership. Since the number of subway cars increased by about 15 percent, this means that an average car is traveling farther. In all, over this period, the supply of cars and service miles increased much more slowly than did ridership. Smaller systems account for a much larger share of the increase in passenger miles than of ridership. This suggests that the New York subway is providing many more short trips, while the smaller systems are providing a small number of new trips, but trip length is increasing. As for trips by car and bus, we see in table 3.2 that the average speed of travel by subway is declining over our sample period.

Meyer, Kain, and Wohl (1965) report on subway ridership during the period between 1935 and 1963. Curiously, subway ridership was fairly stable throughout this period, at about two billion riders per year. Comparing their report to panel A of figure 3.5, we see that this is dramatically lower than current levels. While bus transit is failing to attract riders, we seem to be living in a golden age of subway ridership.

Panel E of figure 3.5 shows the mean age of the fleet of subway cars. We see that the mean age of the subway car fleet varies within about a four-year band, from 18 to 22 years, but without a clear trend. Investment seems to be approximately matching depreciation, although the fleet is quite old. Subway cars in smaller districts are clearly aging, while the mean age of the New York fleet is volatile but seems to be trending down slightly.

From panel F of figure 3.4 we see that the ASCE transit grades declined from a C– to a D– over the period 1988–2017. Again, this grade reflects all US transit infrastructure, not just subways. The monotone decline in the ASCE index is not matched by a corresponding increase in the age of subway cars. With this said, we regard our information about the condition of the subway capital stock to be quite incomplete, so this comparison should be regarded with some skepticism.

The NTD does not report information about subway track in a systematic way, and so we are not able to report on what is surely a far more important measure of physical capital. Anecdotal evidence suggests that, in fact, subway systems have been allowed to depreciate dramatically.[13] A more detailed examination of subway capital stocks remains an important topic for further research.

## 3.3 Expenditure and Cost of Services for Highways, Bridges, and Public Transit

We have so far described the level, condition, and usage of four of the primary stocks of physical capital involved in the transportation of people

13. For example, "How Politics and Bad Decisions Starved New York's Subways," *New York Times Magazine*, November 18, 2017.

and, for highways and bridges, goods. We now turn attention to the cost of these capital stocks.

Ideally, a measure of the "cost of infrastructure" would reflect capital costs, depreciation, and maybe externalities, probably on a per-trip basis. We are not able to provide such a calculation but can take some steps in this direction. In particular, for each of the infrastructure stocks described, we are able to measure total annual expenditure and to estimate the unit cost of service by year. Our measures are an improvement on what is currently available and reveal interesting trends. However, some distance remains between our estimates and the ideal.

### 3.3.1 Highways

Two recent papers describe the evolution of expenditure on the Interstate Highway System and of the cost to build this system, Brooks and Liscow (2019) and Mehrotra, Uribe, and Turner (2020). Before we discuss their findings, it makes sense to be explicit about what, exactly, they are describing.

As we saw in table 3.1, the Interstate Highway System serves a high fraction of VMT relative to its share in total US lane miles. However, about three-fourths of all vehicle miles driven in the US are not on the Interstate Highway System. We would like to consider the Interstate Highway System's share of the US road budget in light of this fact.

Total expenditure on roads and highways by all levels of government stood at $181.4 billion in 2008.[14] Of this total, the Interstate Highway System received $22.5 billion, including $20 billion for capital expenditure and $2.5 billion for maintenance.[15] The Interstate Highway System accounts for about 12.5 percent of all government expenditure on roads. Comparing with table 3.1, this is larger than the Interstate Highway System's share of lane miles and not far off from its share of all VMT.

Brooks and Liscow (2019) estimate the cost of building a mile of Interstate Highway in every year from 1956 through 1993. To do so, they rely on "PR511 data" to document the construction of Interstate mileage by state and year. These data, which also formed the basis for Baum-Snow (2007), were collected as part of the procurement of the Interstate Highway System. Brooks and Liscow match state-year level construction data to the state-year level expenditure data reported in the highway statistics series (for example, US Federal Highway Administration 1985), which are available from about 1956 through to the present.

Panel A of figure 3.6 reproduces figure 2 from Brooks and Liscow (2019). The figure shows the ratio of total expenditure on the Interstate Highway System to total miles constructed in five-year bins from 1960 to 1995. The

14. *Highway Statistics 2008*, table HF-2.

15. The larger Federal-Aid Highway System received $68.8 billion, including $59.2 billion for capital expenditure and $9.6 billion for maintenance (*Highway Statistics 2008*, table HF-12b).

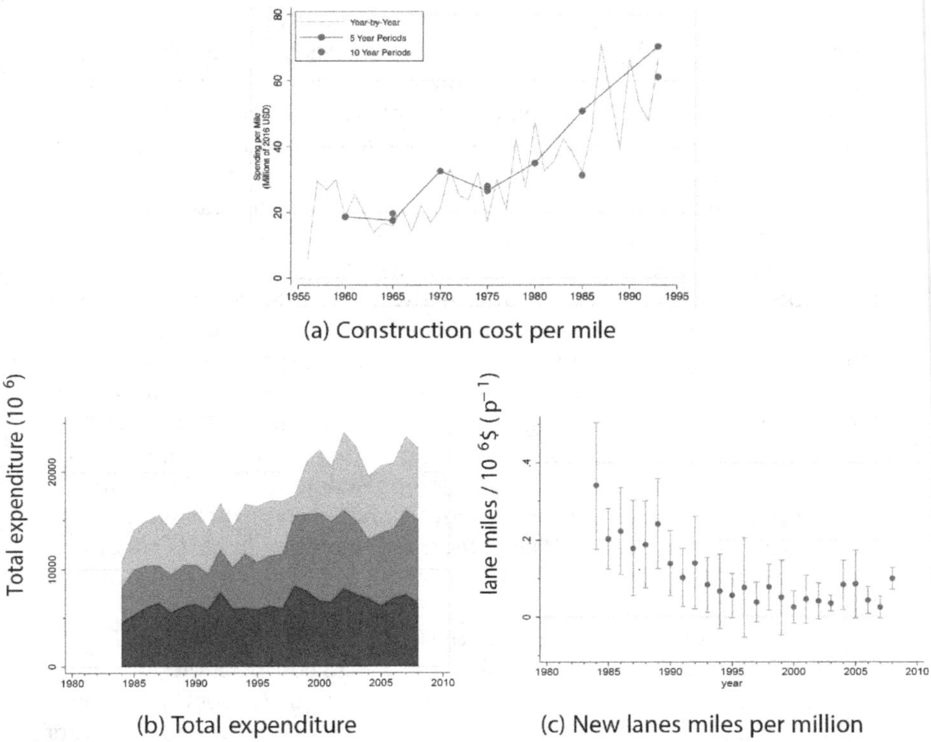


(a) Construction cost per mile

(b) Total expenditure

(c) New lanes miles per million

**Fig. 3.6 Total expenditure and construction cost per lane mile of Interstate Highway over time**

*Note:* A. Mean expenditure per mile of new Interstate Highway between 1960 and 1995. B. Total expenditure on the Interstate Highway System by year in three categories; construction, resurfacing, and maintenance. The height of each band gives expenditure in the category, and the upper envelope gives aggregate expenditure. C. Estimate lane miles of new construction per million dollars of expenditure over time. Panel A is reproduced from Brooks and Liscow (2019); panels B and C are from Mehrotra, Uribe, and Turner (2020).

figure shows a dramatic increase, from about \$20 million (2016) per mile, to about \$70 million per mile. This is about a 250 percent increase in real terms, or about 7 percent per year. Brooks and Liscow (2019) show that this increase probably reflects neither increases in input and labor costs nor changes in the location or terrain where highways were built.

Mehrotra, Uribe, and Turner (2020) also estimate the cost of Interstate Highway System but rely on the HPMS to measure changes in state-year level lane miles of the Interstate Highway System. As described earlier, the HPMS runs from 1980 through 2007, and so the study period in Mehrotra, Uribe, and Turner (2020) is more recent and shorter than that of Brooks and Liscow (2019). Like Brooks and Liscow (2019), Mehrotra, Uribe, and

Turner (2020) rely on highway statistics data for state-year level expenditure data. However, starting in 1984, highway statistics began to disaggregate state-year expenditure into construction, resurfacing, and maintenance. To exploit these more disaggregated expenditure data, Mehrotra, Uribe, and Turner (2020) begin their analysis in 1984, a few years after the beginning of the HPMS.

Panel B of figure 3.6 reports total expenditure on the Interstate Highway System over time in three categories: construction, resurfacing, and maintenance. The dark band on the bottom of the graph reports construction expenditure. This amount varies between about $5 billion and $7 billion (2010) per year and trends up only slightly over the study period. The intermediate band of the figure reports resurfacing expenditure. This varies between about $3 billion and $10 billion and trends up over the period. Unsurprisingly, as the system ages, resurfacing is progressively more important. The dark band at the top of the figure reflects other expenditure, for instance, snow removal, signage, and minor maintenance.[16] This amount trends up from about $3 billion to about $7 billion over the course of the study period. The upper envelope of the three bands gives total expenditure, and we see that this has trended up, from about $10 billion per year to about $21 billion per year.

Panel C of figure 3.6 is also reproduced from Mehrotra, Uribe, and Turner (2020). Like panel A, panel C describes the cost to construct the Interstate; however, it differs in three ways. First, it is inverted. It reports miles per million dollars instead of millions of dollars per mile. Second, it covers the period from 1984 to 2007. Third, it reports millions of dollars *per lane mile* rather than *per mile* of highway. Examining panel C, we see that in 1984–1990, $1 million of expenditure purchased about 0.2 lane miles. This fell to about 0.05 lane miles per million dollars in 2002–2007. Thus, the dramatic increase in construction costs documented by Brooks and Liscow (2019) continued at least through 2007.

One of the advantages of the HPMS is that it also tracks when Interstate Highways are resurfaced. Thus, Mehrotra, Uribe, and Turner (2020) are also able to track changes in the cost of resurfacing the Interstate Highway System. As for new construction, they find that resurfacing costs increase dramatically, although less fast than new construction.

It is well established in the engineering and economics literature that most of the damage to the Interstate is done by trucks, not cars. For the purpose of pavement engineering, the standard measure of usage is an "Equivalent Single Axel Load" (ESAL) of 18,000 pounds. This is about the equivalent of a single heavily loaded five-axel combination truck—in other words,

16. Because bridge expenditure does not affect system length or condition, we also include expenditure on bridges as "maintenance" in this figure. We analyze bridge expenditure separately.

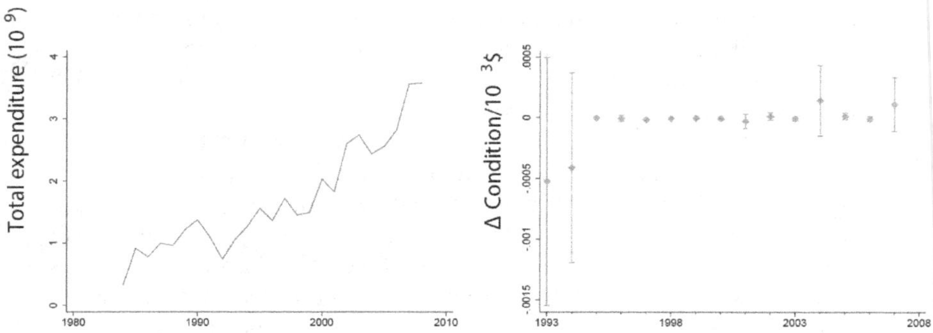


(a) Expenditure (b) Change in condition per dollar

**Fig. 3.7 Expenditure and mean change in condition per dollar over time**

*Note:* A. Billions of total expenditure by state and federal governments by year on all Interstate bridges, from *Highway Statistics* table SF12a. B. Mean change in condition per one thousand dollars spent by year, weighted by bridge deck area.

a typical tractor trailer rig (see, for example, Small, Winston, and Evans 2012; or Mannering, Kilareski, and Washburn 2007). A little more specifically, the damage done to a pavement surface increases approximately quadratically in axel weight (Small, Winston, and Evans 2012). On the basis of calculations available in Mannering, Kilareski, and Washburn (2007), and recalling that a single lane of Interstate Highway can carry about 2,200 cars per hour, a single combination truck causes about as much damage to a highway as about 2.1 commute hours of automobile traffic.[17]

This finding has two implications. First, as pointed out by Small, Winston, and Evans (2012), if user fees are to target the vehicles that cause damage to the roads, they must target trucks—in particular, trucks carrying heavy loads on a small number of axels. The HPMS reports crude measures of truck traffic such as mean truck AADT per hour. Given how sensitive pavement damage is to axel weight, data recording more detail about the portfolio of loadings carried by a highway segment is likely to be of considerable value to administrators, engineers, and social scientists alike.

### 3.3.2 Bridges

Panel A of figure 3.7 reports annual aggregate maintenance expenditure on Interstate bridges from highway statistics.[18] Total expenditure on Inter-

17. See Mannering, Kilareski, and Washburn (2007), example 4.1. A 2,000-pound car is about 0.0002 ESALs, while a typical combination truck is about 0.93 ESALs. The ratio of these two is about 4,600.

18. To be clear, expenditure on Interstate bridges is reported in highway statistics as part of capital expenditure in highway statistics. We here treat it separately. Since expenditure on bridges can have at most a trivial effect on the length or smoothness of Interstate Highways,

state bridges increased from about \$1 billion to about \$3.5 billion between 1984 and 2008. This is about a 9 percent rate of increase. Since the number of Interstate bridges increased only slightly from a base of about 350,000 over this period, this means that expenditure on an average Interstate bridge increased from about \$2.8 million to \$8.4 million per year over this period. Thus, the approximately constant mean bridge condition that we see in panel C of figure 3.3 reflects a dramatic increase in expenditure.

We can exploit state-year variation in the relationship between bridge maintenance and expenditure to estimate the cost of improving a state's bridge condition index over time. To accomplish this, let $t$ denote years, $s$ denote states, and $\Delta_{st}$BCI denote changes in the state mean bridge condition index between $t-1$ and $t$. Finally, let $y_{st}$ be state-year maintenance expenditure and $1_{st}(\tau = t)$ an indicator that takes the value one if $\tau = t$ and zero otherwise.

With this notation in place, we can estimate the following regression:

$$(1) \qquad \frac{\Delta_{st}\mathrm{BCI}}{y_{st}} = \sum_{\tau=1994}^{2016} \beta_{\tau} 1_{st}(\tau = t) + \varepsilon_{st}.$$

Panel B of figure 3.7 plots the resulting $\beta_t$ values together with 95 percent confidence intervals. These estimates reflect the change in state mean bridge condition index resulting from \$1,000 of expenditure. This figure is essentially flat, though a few years are estimated very imprecisely. Experimenting with different variants of the bridge condition index or with expenditure per square foot of bridge area leads to similar results.

This outcome is puzzling—the more so when we compare panel A of figure 3.7 to panel D of figure 3.3. Noting the differences in the range of the x-axis in the two figures, this comparison indicates that condition declined as expenditure increased by a factor of three. Thus, not only does panel B of figure 3.7 indicate that expenditure on bridge maintenance and construction has no measurable effect on mean bridge condition, it shows this result when the aggregate relationship is negative. We suspect that the estimated zero relationship between the bridge condition index and expenditure in panel B of figure 3.7 reflects the nature of the index construction. Expenditure that improves any aspect of a bridge other than the worst has no impact on the index. Given this fact, we expect the bridge condition to reflect maintenance expenditure very poorly. This is just what we see in panel B of figure 3.7. This outcome highlights the interest of using the more homogenous Interstate system as a laboratory in which to investigate changes in construction and maintenance costs, as in Brooks and Liscow (2019) and Mehrotra, Uribe, and Turner (2020).

in our discussion of the Interstate Highway System, we counted bridge expenditure as part of maintenance.

### 3.3.3 Public Transit

Like the NBI, the NTD reports information about the costs of providing public transit. In particular, the NTD reports operating and capital costs by transit district, year, and mode. Capital costs reflect capital expenditures on rolling stock, passenger stations, track, facilities, and administration.

Public transit in the US operates under two primary institutional arrangements. In one, the transit district owns and operates vehicles. In the other, the transit district contracts with a private firm to operate vehicles. Accounting for capital and operating costs in the second case is complicated, and the rules for this accounting changed in 1992, 1996, and 1997.

This caveat in place, the NTD permits us to calculate total expenditure by mode and year and to estimate total cost per rider by year and mode.

#### *3.3.3.1 Buses*

The solid line in panel A of figure 3.8 reports total expenditure on motor bus service in the US by year from 1992 until 2017. Total expenditure on buses increases from about \$15 billion to about \$26 billion over this period. This is an increase of 73 percent, or about 2.8 percent per year. The dashed line in this figure describes total expenditure on buses in the largest six transit cities, while the dotted line describes total expenditure in the smaller districts. Both series are trending up, although expenditure is rising somewhat more rapidly in smaller districts than in large districts.

US expenditure on buses, \$26 billion, is enormous: it is more than public expenditure on the Interstate Highway System. In exchange for this expenditure, motor buses provided about 20 billion passenger miles, versus 700 billion vehicle miles traveled on the Interstate Highway System. Obviously, this is not an entirely fair comparison. Interstate VMT also reflects considerable private expenditure that is not reflected in our expenditure data. We consider this issue in section 3.5.

To investigate trends in the cost of bus-based transit over time, we estimate a regression similar to the one we conducted for bridges (equation [1]). More specifically, we estimate the following regression separately for the six large transit districts and the remaining smaller districts:

$$\frac{c_{ist}}{y_{ist}} = \sum_{\tau=1992}^{2017} \beta_\tau 1_{ist}(\tau = t) + \varepsilon_{ist}. \tag{2}$$

Here, $i$, $s$, $t$ index transit districts, states, and years; $c$ denotes total expenditure on buses; and $y$ indicates a measure of output, here riders. Thus, this is a regression of district year level expenditure per trip on year indicators. The magnitudes of the βs indicate transit-district-weighted annual means of total expenditure per rider.

Panel B of figure 3.8 reports these fixed effects, along with confidence

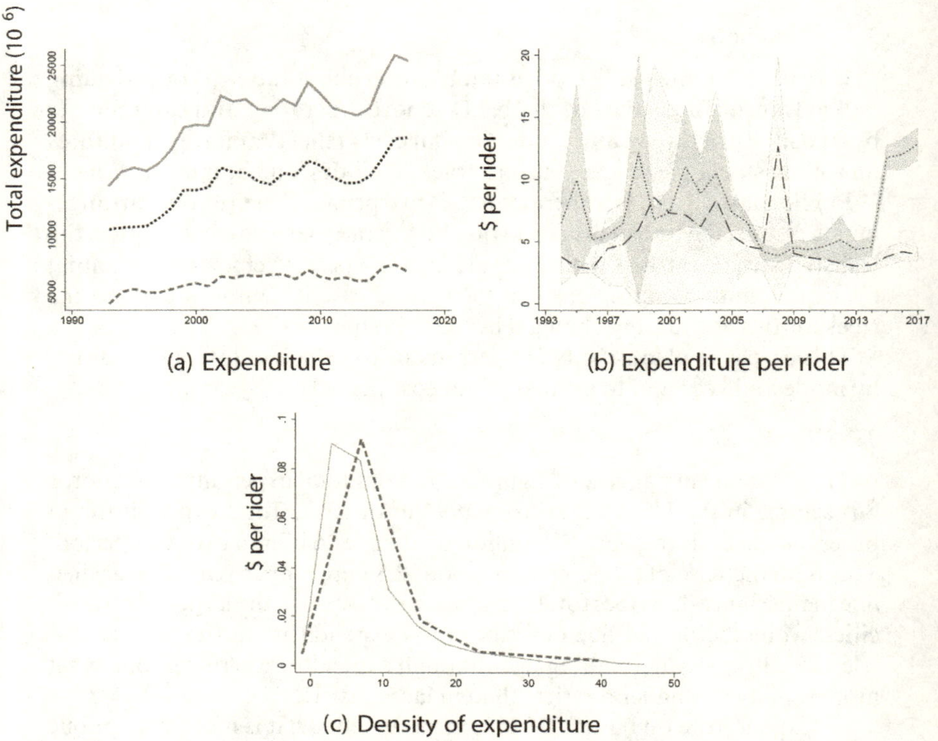


**Fig. 3.8 Total expenditure and unit cost for US bus service over time**

*Note:* A. Total expenditure on the US bus network in millions of 2010 dollars by year. Dashed line is total for six largest districts, dotted line is total for all smaller districts, and solid line is national total. B. Mean dollars of total expenditure per rider by year for large and for all districts. Dashed line is mean annual cost for large districts and light gray shading describes pointwise confidence bounds. Dotted line is mean annual cost per rider for all districts, and medium gray shading describes pointwise confidence bounds. C. Probability density function (PDF) of district mean cost per rider from 2014 to 2017. Dashed line gives the PDF of total expenditure per rider. Solid line gives the PDF of operating costs per rider.

intervals based on standard errors clustered at the state level. In this figure, the dashed line describes mean cost per rider in large districts, and the light gray area describes associated pointwise confidence bounds. The dotted line and medium gray shading provide the corresponding estimates for all districts. Several of the year means are estimated imprecisely. We suspect this is partly a result of the changes in accounting rules mentioned earlier. However, most year effects are estimated precisely, and the figure does not indicate a strong trend. Overall, the mean cost per rider is about five dollars in the large districts and a little higher on average, about what we would guess from table 3.3. There is a clear step-up in the average during the past few years, to about $12 per rider. Cost per rider in large districts is about constant over the whole course of the sample and has been trending downward since about 2000.

Panel C of figure 3.8 reports the density of mean cost per rider from 2014 to 2017, by transit district. The dashed line in this figure gives the density of total expenditure per rider. The mode of this density is about $9 per rider, but there is considerable variation around this mode. The solid line describes the density of operating costs per rider. Since operating costs are a portion of total costs, it follows that this density lies to the left of the density of total expenditure. The extent of cost dispersion across districts suggests that there may be considerable scope for inefficient transit districts to learn from efficient ones.

#### *3.3.3.2 Subways*

Figure 3.9 replicates figure 3.8 for subways. In light of the dominance of the New York subway system, we analyze New York and all smaller systems separately. In panel A of figure 3.9, we report total expenditure on subways by year. This amount rises from $8 billion to about $16 billion 2010 dollars from 1992 to 2017, an increase of about 100 percent.

This is striking for two reasons. First, this is close to the amount of public expenditure on the Interstate Highway System. Second, the increase is about proportional to the increase in ridership over this time.

In table 3.4, we saw that New York accounted for about half of all subway expenditure from 2014 to 2017. In panel A of figure 3.9 we see that this relationship has been about constant over the course of our study period. New York has accounted for about half of all US expenditure on subways, even as expenditure has doubled.

Panel B of figure 3.9 repeats the cost per rider exercise described in equation (2) for all subway districts and reports the cost per rider for the New York system. These estimates suggest that costs per rider have been trending up slowly on average even as cost per rider falls in New York. Costs per rider have increased from about $5.50 to about $7 on average and decreased from about $4 to about $3 in New York. As we mentioned earlier, our measure of total expenditure does not reflect capital depreciation or augmentation, so these estimates should be regarded with some caution.

## 3.4 Transportation Infrastructure and Economic Activity

Over the past generation we have seen US highways, bridges, and subways (but not buses) used much more intensively. Nevertheless, objective measures of condition improved or stayed constant (although our data for subways measure only subway cars and may thus be too partial to be really useful). This result has been achieved as a consequence of increases in expenditure on all four classes of infrastructure. This expenditure has allowed at least modest expansions of capacity and maintenance that at least matches

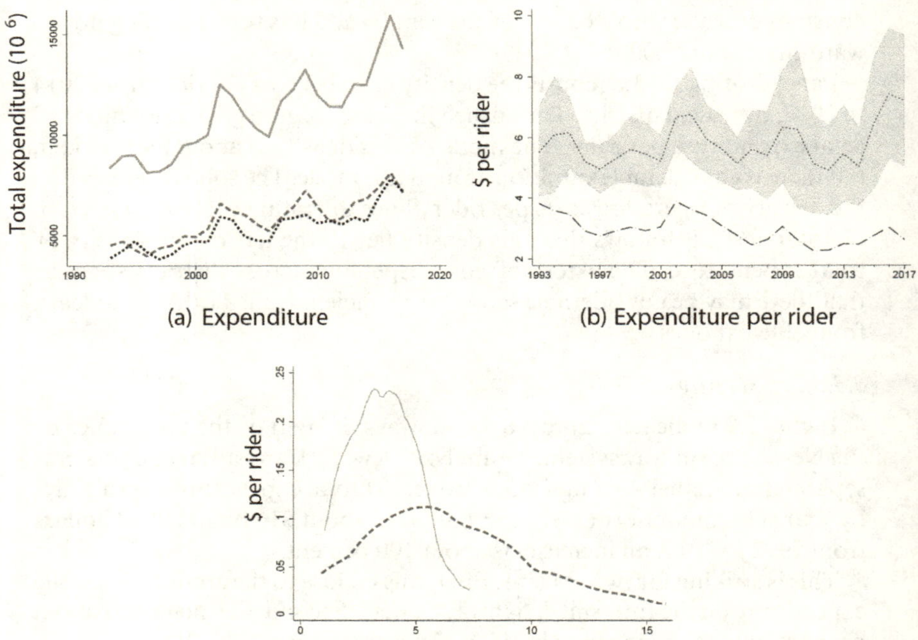


(a) Expenditure (b) Expenditure per rider

(c) Density of expenditure

**Fig. 3.9 Total expenditure and unit cost for US subway service over time**

*Note:* A. Total expenditure on the US subway networks in millions of 2010 dollars by year. Dashed line is total for New York, dotted line is total for all smaller districts, and solid line is national total. B. Mean dollars of total expenditure per rider by year for New York and all districts. Dashed line is mean annual cost for New York. Dotted line is mean annual cost per rider for all districts, and medium gray shading describes pointwise confidence bounds. C. Probability density function (PDF) of district mean cost per rider from 2014 to 2017. Dashed line gives PDF of total expenditure per rider. Solid line gives PDF of operating costs per rider.

depreciation. Massive increases in infrastructure are not required to reverse the decline of US transportation infrastructure. Not only is this infrastructure, for the most part, not deteriorating, but much of it is in good condition or improving.[19]

An alternative justification for increases in infrastructure spending relies on the existence of "wider economic benefits." Simply put, infrastructure investment may be an engine of economic growth through a range of spillover effects. We here provide a brief survey of what is known about how

19. We are aware that international comparisons suggest US transportation infrastructure lags behind that of a number of other developed countries (Schwab 2019). Addressing this issue is beyond our scope here. We nonetheless note that lagging behind does necessarily not mean that world leaders in infrastructure have invested their resources wisely nor that it would be worth emulating them.

transportation infrastructure affects the level and location of economic activity. A more exhaustive survey is available in Redding and Turner (2015).

Perhaps the most compelling of the available empirical results is that people and economic activity move in response to the availability of transportation infrastructure. Chandra and Thompson (2000) examine the effect of the Interstate Highway network on economic activity in rural counties that were traversed by Interstate Highways. They find that economic activity increased in these counties, but that these increases were about exactly offset by losses in neighboring counties that were just a little further from the new highways. Baum-Snow (2007) finds that almost all of the decentralization of US central cities between 1950 and 1990 can be attributed to radial Interstate Highways that facilitated travel between the old center and the new suburbs. A number of other papers find qualitatively similar results about highways—for example, Baum-Snow (2019); Baum-Snow et al. (2017); and Garcia-López, Holl, and Viladecans-Marsal (2015). A smaller literature finds qualitatively similar effects for public transit—for example, Gonzalez-Navarro and Turner (2018); Heblich, Redding, and Sturm (2018); and Tsivanidis (2019). To sum up, the empirical evidence is as clear as could be hoped: as transportation infrastructure reduces transportation costs, people and (usually) economic activity spread out.

Evidence that transportation infrastructure leads to increases in economic activity is less compelling. Duranton and Turner (2012) estimate the relationship between 1983–2003 changes in metropolitan area employment and the initial stock of Interstate lane miles. They find that a 10 percent increase in the stock of roads causes about 1.5 percent increase in employment over their study period. This effect is of about twice as large as the effect of an increase of one standard deviation in metropolitan-area mean educational attainment. Within their model, Allen and Arkolakis (2014) evaluate the effect of reductions in cross-metropolitan area transportation costs caused by the Interstate Highway System on aggregate economic output. They find that the Interstate Highway System increased economic output in the US by between 1 and 1.5 percent. Both Duranton and Turner (2012) and Allen and Arkolakis (2014) compare their estimated benefits to back-of-the-envelope cost estimates. Benefits of the Interstate Highway System estimated by Duranton and Turner are dramatically smaller than the costs estimated by either paper, while the Allen and Arkolakis estimate is above their cost estimate, but below the higher cost estimate of Duranton and Turner (2012).

On the other hand, Baum-Snow et al. (2017) compare 1990–2010 changes in employment and economic output in large Chinese cities to changes in their stock of highway lane miles and find no effect. Baum-Snow (2019) conducts a similar exercise on the 100 largest US metropolitan areas and also finds no effect. Note the difference between these two papers and Duranton and Turner (2012). The former two papers conduct a regression of changes on changes, whereas the latter regresses changes on levels. In a similar vein,

Duranton, Morrow, and Turner (2014) find that a metropolitan area's level of Interstate Highway miles has no measurable effect on the total value of its annual trade with other metropolitan areas though it affects their specialization.[20]

We have less evidence on the effects of subways and public transit on economic output. Gonzalez-Navarro and Turner (2018) examine population growth in every subway city in the world between 1950 and 2010 and find no relationship between population growth and subway system extent. They find a similar result for the relationship between subway system extent and the intensity of citywide lights at night. On the other hand, Ahlfeldt et al. (2015) and Heblich, Redding, and Sturm (2018) develop a theoretical framework to structurally estimate the effects of subways on Berlin and London. They infer large effects of transportation improvements on the population of cities. This said, in their framework, better transportation leads to a decrease in income per worker as agglomeration benefits are more than offset by the increased crowding of labor. What attracts workers to cities with better transportation are lower travel costs and the increased accessibility of locations with good amenities, not an expansion of economic activity.

Finally, we note a macroeconomic literature examining the effect of infrastructure expenditure on economic activity (e.g., Fernald 1999; Gramlich 1994; Leduc and Wilson 2013). This literature also does not suggest strong conclusions; however we refer the reader to the chapter by Ramey in this volume for an insightful review.

Following from Duranton and Turner (2011), there is also a literature relating capacity expansions to congestion. Redding and Turner (2015) survey the literature relating road expansions and traffic. This literature provides compelling evidence that a 1 percent expansion in a city's lane miles of highways causes a 1 percent increase in VMT over a fairly short horizon. Thus, as the history of Los Angeles clearly suggests, expanding road capacity to reduce traffic congestion is risky at best. A small recent literature examines the relationship between subway expansions and traffic—for example, Gendron-Carrier et al. (2018). This literature provides suggestive evidence that subways may have an effect on traffic congestion; however, this effect is likely fairly small. Duranton and Turner (2018) survey the literature evaluating various policy responses to traffic congestion and conclude that only policies to manage demand actually reduce traffic congestion.

To sum up, the evidence that infrastructure has important implications for how economic activity is organized is compelling. However, most of this evidence points to the importance of infrastructure as a determinant of where economic activity occurs. The evidence that infrastructure affects the

20. More precisely, the unit of observation in Duranton, Morrow, and Turner (2014) is a "commodity flow survey region." These regions are often somewhat larger than metropolitan areas but do not straddle state boundaries.

level of economic activity is mixed and is sensitive to econometric technique, and there is no clear basis for preferring one technique to another. Finally, the available evidence does not suggest that massive expansions of capacity are likely to provide a long-run solution to traffic congestion.

## 3.5 A Theory of Optimal Infrastructure Expenditure

We have now established the fundamentals of our ongoing allocation of resources to transportation infrastructure. We know the quantity and quality of three of the most important sorts of transportation infrastructure, particularly with regard to moving people.

It is not immediately obvious how we should think about the optimality of the observed program of expenditure. Can it possibly be rational to spend as much on buses as on the Interstate Highway system when the role of buses in national mobility seems so small relative to that of Interstate Highways? Does it make sense that subway cars are so old when subways seem to be attracting progressively more riders? In what follows we develop a simple framework in which to address these questions.

### 3.5.1 First Best

We consider the problem of a social planner providing transportation infrastructure by spending $K_i$ where $i = H, B, S$ stands for Interstate Highways (to which we aggregate Interstate bridges), buses, and subways, respectively. For each mode of transportation $i$, infrastructure expenditure $K_i$, measured in monetary amount, is combined with traveler inputs $L_i$, measured in time, to provide transportation services $Q_i$, measured in units of person distance:

$$Q_i = F_i(K_i, L_i). \tag{3}$$

Simply put, dollars of infrastructure expenditure and person hours combine to produce miles of travel.[21] Importantly, the production function of transportation $F_i(.,.)$ is homogeneous of degree $\nu_i$.

The social planner has the following social welfare (utility) function:

$$U = V\left(\sum_i Z_i Q_i\right) + C, \tag{4}$$

where the subutility $V(.)$ is increasing and concave and $C$ is the consumption of other goods. We call the parameter $Z_i$ the social weight of a mile traveled using mode $i$.

Our main objective is to recover the social weights in equation (4) from observable data about traveler inputs, infrastructure expenditure, and travel

21. Our framework is static. We implicitly view infrastructure expenditure as part of a steady state in a broader dynamic optimization. We leave this challenging extension to future work.

mileage by mode. This exercise allows us to assess the (relative) allocation of resources between modes. To assess the optimality of the (absolute) levels of expenditure, we would need to impose more structure on the demand for transportation and specify $V(.)$. Couture, Duranton, and Turner (2018) provide such a framework for a single mode of transportation.

Some further comments are in order. First, we consider a social planner weighting miles of travel differently across modes. There are several reasons why a social planner might do this. For instance, miles traveled with a subway in the central part of a large city may be economically more valuable than miles traveled on a highway in a rural area. A social planner may also have utilitarian motives and put a higher weight on bus miles, as buses are mainly used by the poor. Second, for simplicity and tractability, we treat travel distance as a good instead of an intermediate input that enables the earning of a labor income (though commute trips), the consumption of goods (through shopping trips), or various forms of leisure. See Couture, Duranton, and Turner (2018) or Duranton and Turner (2018) for further discussion of these issues. Third, we assume a quasi-linear social welfare function to avoid complications arising from income effects. Fourth, we also make the simplifying assumption that travel distances produced by different modes are perfect substitutes after accounting for their social weights. Fifth, we assume for simplicity that the returns to scale, measured by $\nu_i$, are "decreasing enough" to ensure the existence of a unique interior optimum for the allocation of resources across modes by the planner.

Without loss of generality, we normalize the price of consumption to unity so that the budget constraint for income $M$ is given by

$$C = M - \sum_i w_i^S L_i - \sum_i K_i, \tag{5}$$

where $w_i^S$ is the social cost of traveler inputs for mode $i$. We allow this cost to differ as modes differ in monetary costs, speed of travel, and externalities.

We now consider the social planner's program, choosing both $K_i$ and $L_i$ for all modes to maximize social welfare in equation (4) subject to the household budget constraint (equation [5]), keeping in mind that travel distance is produced according to the travel technology described by equation (3). This situation corresponds to an unconstrained first best.

The first-order conditions imply that, for each input, the social value of the marginal product of infrastructure expenditure should be equalized across any two modes $i$ and $j$:

$$Z_i \frac{\partial Q_i}{\partial K_i} = Z_j \frac{\partial Q_j}{\partial K_j} \text{ and } Z_i \frac{\partial Q_i}{\partial L_i} = Z_j \frac{\partial Q_j}{\partial L_j}. \tag{6}$$

The first-order conditions also imply that, for a given mode $i$, the last dollar spent on infrastructure should have returns equal to the last dollar spend on traveler inputs:

$$\frac{\partial Q_i}{\partial K_i} = \frac{1}{w_i^S}\frac{\partial Q_i}{\partial L_i}. \tag{7}$$

Then, recall that Euler's theorem for homogenous function implies

$$\frac{\partial Q_i}{\partial K_i}K_i + \frac{\partial Q_i}{\partial L_i}L_i = \nu_i Q_i. \tag{8}$$

After using this last expression to substitute for $\partial Q_i / \partial L_i$ in equation (7) and rearranging, we obtain $\partial Q_i / \partial K_i = \nu_i Q_i / (K_i + w_i^S L_i)$, which allows us to rewrite the first equality in equation (6) as

$$Z_i \frac{\nu_i Q_i}{K_i + w_i^S L_i} = Z_j \frac{\nu_j Q_j}{K_j + w_j^S L_j}. \tag{9}$$

This equation stipulates that, optimally, the amount of travel per dollar weighted by its social weight and the returns to scale should be equalized across modes.

### 3.5.2 Traveler Optimization and Decentralizing the First Best

There are several limitations to the analysis just set out. Foremost, we assume that the social planner chooses traveler inputs for each mode of transportation. In reality, the planner decides first on infrastructure expenditure for all modes before travelers individually choose their inputs by mode.

To model this, assume a representative traveler with utility,

$$u = V\left(\sum_i B_i q_i\right) + c, \tag{10}$$

where $q_i$ and $c$ are the traveler's travel distance and consumption of other goods, respectively. Summing travel and consumption across travelers recovers the aggregate quantities used above, $Q_i$ and $C$.[22] The traveler's objective function is like that of the planner, except that travelers may apply different weights, $B_i$, for the mileage by mode relative to the weights used by the social planner, $Z_i$.

The budget constraint of the traveler is given by

$$c = m - \sum_i (w_i^T + t_i)\ell_i - r, \tag{11}$$

where $t_i$ is a tax or subsidy for mode $i$, $\ell_i$ is traveler inputs, and $r$ is a lump-sum monetary transfer that satisfies the balanced budget condition of the planner. With $R$, the aggregate monetary transfer, we have $\sum_i t_i L_i + R = \sum_i K_i$. For the traveler, the private cost of travel inputs $w_i^T$ differs from its social cost $w_i^S$ since travelers generate externalities, including in particular pollution and accidents for highway travel. Importantly, we do not consider

22. To simplify notations and without loss of generality we assume a unit population of travelers.

congestion costs in $w_i^S$ as they appear through the production of travel, to which we now turn.

The representative traveler takes infrastructure investment and travel decisions by other travelers as given and faces constant returns to travel inputs. A traveler who devotes twice as much time to, say, highway travel will travel twice as far. More generally, travel distance is equal to the speed that a traveler experiences $Q_i/L_i$ multiplied by travel inputs of this traveler, $\ell_i$:

$$q_i = \frac{Q_i}{L_i}\ell_i. \tag{12}$$

Another way to think about equation (12) is to note that travelers receive the average and not the marginal return to their travel inputs, as they ignore the congestion they inflict upon other travelers.

The representative traveler maximizes the utility function (equation [10]) subject to the budget constraint (equation [11]) and the production of individual travel given by equation (12) for mode $i$. This yields

$$B_i\frac{Q_i}{L_i}V' = w_i^T + t_i. \tag{13}$$

We can first use this expression for mode $i$ and the analogous expression for mode $j$ to obtain the following:

$$\frac{B_iQ_i}{(w_i^T + t_i)L_i} = \frac{B_jQ_j}{(w_j^T + t_j)L_j}. \tag{14}$$

This equation indicates that the cost per mile faced by travelers weighted by the traveler's weight for that mode should be equalized across modes. As we show later, it is easy to compute the cost per mile faced by travelers for each mode and recover their relative weights. These weights can be compared to the social weights recovered from equation (9).

To reach the first best, the planner can set a tax (or subsidy) by mode $t_i^*$ so that the decentralized equilibrium coincides with the first best. To compute this optimal tax, we can use equation (13), divide it by the corresponding first-order condition for the planner, use equations (7) and (8) to substitute the term in $\partial Q_i/\partial L_i$, and rearrange to obtain

$$t_i^* = \frac{B_i}{Z_i}\frac{K_i + w_i^SL_i}{v_iL_i} - w_i^T. \tag{15}$$

This expression shows that the optimal tax should correct for the three different wedges: (1) between the utility weights $B_i$ used by travelers and those of the planner $Z_i$; (2) between the average cost in terms of travel input considered by the traveler and the marginal cost in the planner's calculation; (3) the private cost of travel inputs for travelers and the social cost of travel inputs. Finally, we note that, to decentralize the first best, the fiscal transfer $r$ is also needed to provide the optimal level of infrastructure expenditure since the taxes on travel inputs are needed to induce travelers to travel optimally.

While this framework makes it possible to compare the allocation of infrastructure expenditure across modes, it does not allow us to assess what the optimal overall expenditure on transportation infrastructure would be. For this, we would need to know more about the demand for transportation than we currently do. Our approach sidesteps the demand side by considering that miles across modes are perfect substitutes, so that we only need information about costs.

### 3.5.3 How Far Are We from the First Best?

We can now attempt to evaluate whether the marginal products of infrastructure expenditure are equalized between modes of transportation as described in equation (9). While we do not know the $Z_i$, everything else can be observed from the data or inferred from the literature. Hence, we can ask what the social valuations of different modes would need to be to justify the difference we observe if we were in a first-best world. Evaluating equation (9) requires knowing about $\nu$, $Q$, $K$, $L$, and $w^s$ for each mode.

Starting with the returns to scale parameter in the production of travel, $\nu_i$, Couture, Duranton, and Turner (2018) estimate a production function of travel by motorized vehicle for US metropolitan areas. While they restrict their estimation to a Cobb-Douglas case, they estimate slight decreasing returns to scale with $\nu_H = 0.96$ in their preferred regression. This implies about a 4 percent loss from congestion, consistent with the estimates reported by Parry, Walls, and Harrington (2007). Less is known about buses and subways. At the intensive margin, transit may enjoy increasing returns to scale as more traveler inputs in the form of more travelers can justify a greater transit frequency. Table 3.4 suggests that larger US transit districts provide transit services at a lower cost per rider. However, at the extensive margin, new transit lines are likely to serve less popular routes (Gendron-Carrier et al. 2018). To avoid biasing our calculations against transit, we assume $\nu_B = \nu_S = 1$. Obviously, knowing more about congestion and returns to scale in transit should be a priority for future research.

Turning to mileage by mode, $Q_i$, table 3.1 reports 243 billion vehicle miles traveled on rural Interstate Highways in 2008 and 476 billion on urban Interstate Highways for the same year. With 1.25 passengers per vehicle (Couture, Duranton, and Turner 2018), this corresponds to a total of 899 billion person miles. For transit, table 3.3 reports 21 billion person miles for buses in 2008 and 16.8 for subways in the same year.

For infrastructure expenditure $K_i$, section 3.3.1 reports an expenditure of \$22.5 billion dollars for the Interstate Highway System (inclusive of expenditure on bridges). For buses and subways in 2008, table 3.3 reports expenditure of \$21.4 billion and \$12.3 billion, respectively.

Obtaining measures of traveler inputs, $L$ is more involved. Starting with traveler inputs, $L$, we measure a mean car speed of 25.5 miles per hour from the 2008 NHTS in table 3.2. This is arguably a lower bound since travel on Interstate Highways is typically faster than on other roads and Interstate

Highways represent only about 25 percent of aggregate mileage. If we focus more realistically on trips longer than 10 miles, car speed increases to 31.8 miles per hour. Given the person miles of highway travel reported above, a speed of 31.8 miles per hour implies 28.2 billion person hours.

For transit, from the 2008 NHTS we calculate a speed of 12.6 miles per hour for bus travel and 10.4 miles per hour for subway travel.[23] Given the mileage for these two modes, we obtain 1.66 billion passenger hours for bus travel and 1.61 billion passenger hours for subway travel.

Finally, evaluating equation (9) requires measures of the cost per hour, $w^s$. Like traveler inputs, hourly costs cannot be read directly from the data. To compute the hourly cost for these three modes, we first consider the value of time. Existing estimates of the value of time traveled generally center around 50 percent of an individual's hourly wage (Small and Verhoef 2007; Small 2012). Although time in transit is typically valued at a higher cost and travel time on highways is valued at a lower share of the hourly wage, we retain this figure of 50 percent for our baseline calculation. We take the mean wage for 2008 to be about \$23 per hour, as in Couture, Duranton, and Turner (2018). This implies a cost of time of \$11.50 per hour.

For buses and subways, we assume a fare of \$1.50 per trip. Given the ridership figures reported in table 3.3, we get a fare of \$4.90 per hour for buses and \$3.30 per hour for subway. These figures imply a fare box recovery rate of about 40 percent, slightly above the figures reported by the NTD of about 25 percent for these two transit modes. Adding \$11.50 per hour for the cost of time, the cost of travel $w^S$ is thus \$16.48 per hour for buses and \$14.79 per hour for subways.

To compute the cost of car travel, we consider an operating cost of \$0.55 per vehicle mile, in line with federal guidelines for car travel reimbursement. At a speed of 31.8 miles per hour for 1.25 passengers, this implies a vehicle operating cost of \$14 per person hour. Adding \$11.50 per hour for the value of time of the travelers, we reach a total of \$25.50 per hour of highway travel. This calculation, so far, neglects the externalities associated with highway travel and represents only a private cost, not the social cost. Parry, Walls, and Harrington (2007) estimate the external costs associated with pollution, congestion, and accidents to be about \$0.10 per mile. This estimate is for all road travel. It is unclear what it implies for highway travel and for buses and subways. To be conservative, we can assume that highway travel has external costs of \$0.10 per vehicle mile due to worse accidents and more concentrated pollution for urban highways. This corresponds to about \$2.55 per hour. Hence, the social cost of travel, $w^S$, for cars is \$28.05 per person hour. Recall that congestion is taken into account through the scale parameter $\nu_i$.

23. These travel speeds may seem low but the travel time in the denominator of this calculation includes the whole duration of the trips, including waiting times or walking to a station. There are nonetheless worries regarding the quality of the information reported by travelers when using travel diaries like the NHTS.

To evaluate equation (9), we must be careful to avoid the double counting of the gas tax, which is included in the vehicle user cost of \$0.55 per mile used earlier. With a federal gas tax of 18 cents per gallon and a state gas tax at an average of 36 cents per gallon and with fuel economy of 20 miles per gallon, \$19.4 billion of traveler costs goes toward paying for highway expenditure.

Putting all these numbers together, for the marginal value product of infrastructure investment, $\partial Q_i / \partial K_i = v_i Q_i / (K_i + w_i^S L_i)$, we find 1.09 miles per dollar for Interstate Highways, 0.43 miles per dollar for buses, and 0.47 miles per dollar for subways. Using equation (6), these figures imply that implicitly the social planner puts two and a half times as much value on a passenger bus mile relative to a passenger highway mile and about 10 percent more value relative to a subway passenger mile. Alternatively, equating the marginal mileage per dollar of expenditure across modes, which corresponds to $Z_i = Z_j$ in equation (6), would require multiplying highway infrastructure expenditure by a factor of more than 40.

We can also use equation (14) to recover the traveler's (relative) weights, $B_i$, for the different modes directly from travel behavior. After noting that the taxes and subsidies are already included in the private costs we computed earlier, we find that the cost per mile faced by travelers for highway travel is obtained by simply dividing 899 billion miles traveled by 28.2 billion hours valued at \$25.50 each. This is 1.25 miles per dollar. The same calculation implies 0.77 miles per dollar for buses and 0.97 miles per dollar for subways. In turn, this implies the weight put on bus miles by travelers is just over one and a half times the weight they put on highway miles and about 20 percent less than the weight they put on subway miles.

We think there are two main reasons why the cost per mile that travelers are willing to incur for buses and subways is higher than for Interstate Highways. The first is that we imposed the same time cost for all modes, ignoring the fact that the hourly wage of highway travelers (generally by car) may be higher than that of transit users. If, instead of \$23 per hour, we assume \$30 per hour for highway travel and \$15 for bus travel, the relative weights between bus and highway travel are down to 1.9 instead of 2.5 in our benchmark calculation. It is also possible that travelers put a higher value on travel by bus or subway because it is more likely to take place in more highly urban parts of the country relative to highway travel, which may be more urban. Pushing in the opposite direction, we note that transit travel may have a higher time cost relative to the hourly wage than highway travel (Small and Verhoef 2007; Small 2012). While we can explain why travelers put a higher weight on transit relative to highway travel, this does not explain the gap with the social planner.

To explain why the planner appears to put a higher relative weight than travelers on transit miles, we can think of two second-best explanations. The first is that the planner may be constrained in ability to redistribute income. The planner may then increase infrastructure expenditure on transit to redistribute income given that transit, and buses in particular, is used primarily by the poor. Another possibility is that the planner cannot tax or subsidize modes of transportation as required by the first best. For instance, the gas tax in the US represents only a few cents per mile, much less than the externalities caused by highway travel. By increasing expenditure on highways, the planner lowers the cost of travel for travelers, which in turn, leads to an increase in travel inputs. As shown by Duranton and Turner (2011), this demand response is large, and because travelers neglect congestion and other externalities, the planner will want to restrain infrastructure expenditure relative to another mode like buses or subways, for which the demand response is less and the wedge between the social and private cost of travel is also less.

## 3.6 Conclusion

### 3.6.1 Policy

Perhaps our main conclusion is that, on average, US transportation infrastructure does not seem to be in the dire state that politicians and pundits describe. We find that the quality of Interstate Highways has improved, the quality of bridges is stable, and the age of buses and subway cars is also about constant. With this said, we suspect that subway car age is not a good indicator of systemwide state of repair and that subway systems are actually depreciating.

We also report on the cost of infrastructure. Our results here are mixed. For buses and subways, cost per rider has been fairly steady over time, except for a jump in the cost per trip of small district bus trips around 2014. The bridge condition index has stayed about constant in the face of a tripling of expenditure, although an analysis of state-year variation does not indicate a big increase in the unit cost of improvements to bridge condition. The cost of the Interstate, however, has increased rapidly and monotonically from about 1970 through to 2008.

Both the Interstate and public transit buses absorb about $20 billion of public expenditure each year, while the Interstate provides about 35 times as many person miles of travel but also uses dramatically more private inputs than do buses. It is difficult to evaluate the reasonableness of such allocation decisions (and the others we describe) without recourse to theory. Using a simple model, we find that public funds for transportation are, on a passenger-mile basis, disproportionately allocated to buses and subways rather than highways. A partial explanation for this is that travelers themselves prefer to devote a greater amount per mile to bus and subway travel. However, this preference does not explain fully the imbalance in government infrastructure funding between modes, as some redistributive concerns may be at play to explain this imbalance.

The condition of infrastructure has, for the most part, improved over the past generation. However, highways and subways per person have decreased, even as travel per person has increased. Thus, while the condition of the infrastructure has improved or stayed constant, it is serving much more demand, and so the speed of travel has decreased and the experience of drivers and riders is worse. We speculate that the sentiment that infrastructure is deteriorating derives from the fact that users' experiences are deteriorating with increased congestion and that this deterioration is largely independent of physical condition. Relatedly, public perceptions of infrastructure quality may also reflect the highly publicized infrastructure report card generated by the American Society of Civil Engineers. As we have seen, these reports cards provide little information about objective measures of physical condition.

While we find little evidence to support common justifications for increases to infrastructure spending, we note the importance of demand management as a policy response to traffic congestion and also of axel-weight-based user fees for trucks.

We have restricted attention to the Interstate Highway System, bridges, and public transit. We have neglected railroads, pipelines, subway tracks, local roads, and water and sewer systems. All are important. Administrative data describing pipelines, railroads, and subway track may be available, and an examination of these data should be a high priority for researchers. Much less is known about local roads, and systematic data describing US water and sewer infrastructure seem not to exist. The creation and interrogation of such data should also be a high priority for research.

### 3.6.2 Research

Our panorama of US transportation infrastructure, albeit partial, raises a number of questions for future research. First, policy would benefit from more precise cost estimates than the rough aggregates we present in this chapter. Estimates of the full cost of trips in various locations, broken down into fixed and variable components, would help to guide allocation and pricing decisions. Such estimates could rely on in part on the administrative data we exploit, but could also combine them with innovative new data sources to measure congestion and reliability for both highways and transit—for example, Akbar et al. (2020). Related to congestion, most economists have a strong presumption that congestion pricing must be the main policy response to congestion. Congestion pricing nonetheless begs two important questions. The first is how to make it less unpopular. The second is about how best to implement congestion pricing on a road network with different types of roads, vehicles, and interrelated congestion and environmental externalities.

This chapter suggests, but does not address, a number of interesting and important questions for further research. Catastrophic bridge collapses are economically important events. Does the bridge condition index provide information that is useful for predicting such collapses? Are we gathering the right information about bridge conditions? What is the value of further data collection? Pavement quality, as measured by the international roughness index, is relatively little studied. How does pavement quality contribute to travel speed and congestion? How does pavement quality contribute to depreciation of the vehicle stock? Such questions are understudied but are central to any formulation of an optimal maintenance policy.

Two of the findings we document in this chapter do not have a clear explanation. The first is the increase in the cost of Interstate Highways. Although recent literature has ruled out a number of explanations, there is still too much uncertainty about the cause of this increase for a solution to be designed. We need to know whether increasing costs reflect improvements in the quality of highways and environmental protection, or poor project management. The decline of buses also requires further diagnosis. Bus travel, as it exists, is likely to be an economically inferior good for travelers. This said, bus travel is not a good with fixed characteristics. The demand for bus travel may be sensitive to various dimensions of quality, including comfort, reliability, and the design of routes and connections.

Finally, our review of the literature suggests that transportation improvements lead to a displacement of economic activity while net growth effects are limited. This finding needs to be buttressed and refined. The balance between displacement and net growth effects is likely to differ greatly across projects depending on mode, spatial scale, whether the project serves a corridor between cities or is a transit improvement within, and so on. A better understanding of this heterogeneity is also a high priority.

## References

Ahlfeldt, Gabriel M., Stephen J. Redding, Daniel M. Sturm, and Nikolaus Wolf. 2015. "The Economics of Density: Evidence from the Berlin Wall." *Econometrica* 83 (6): 2127–89.

Akbar, Prottoy A., Victor Couture, Gilles Duranton, and Adam Storeygard. 2020. "Mobility and Congestion in Urban India." Working paper, University of Pennsylvania.

Allen, Treb, and Costas Arkolakis. 2014. "Trade and the Topography of the Spatial Economy." *Quarterly Journal of Economics* 129 (3): 1085–140.

Baum-Snow, Nathaniel. 2007. "Did Highways Cause Suburbanization?" *Quarterly Journal of Economics* 122 (2): 775–805.

———. 2019. "Urban Transport Expansions and Changes in the Spatial Structure of US Cities: Implications for Productivity and Welfare." *Review of Economics and Statistics* (forthcoming).

Baum-Snow, Nathaniel, Loren Brandt, J. Vernon Henderson, Matthew A. Turner, and Qinghua Zhang. 2017. "Roads, Railroads, and Decentralization of Chinese Cities." *Review of Economics and Statistics* 99 (3): 435–48.

Blumenberg, Evelyn, Michael Manville, and Brian D. Taylor. 2019. "Why Is Public Transit Use Declining? Evidence from California." Working paper, University of California, Los Angeles.

Brooks, Leah, and Zachary D. Liscow. 2019. "Infrastructure Costs." Working paper, George Washington University.

Chandra, Amitabh, and Eric Thompson. 2000. "Does Public Infrastructure Affect Economic Activity? Evidence from the Rural Interstate Highway System." *Regional Science and Urban Economics* 30 (4): 457–90.

Couture, Victor, Gilles Duranton, and Matthew A. Turner. 2018. "Speed." *Review of Economics and Statistics* 100 (4): 725–39.

Duranton, Gilles, Peter M. Morrow, and Matthew A. Turner. 2014. "Roads and Trade: Evidence from the US." *Review of Economic Studies* 81 (2): 681–724.

Duranton, Gilles, and Matthew A. Turner. 2011. "The Fundamental Law of Road Congestion: Evidence from US Cities." *American Economic Review* 101 (6): 2616–52.

———. 2012. "Urban Growth and Transportation. *Review of Economic Studies* 79 (4): 1407–40.

———. 2018. "Urban Form and Driving: Evidence from US Cities." *Journal of Urban Economics* 108 (0): 171–91.

Federal Highway Administration. 1995. *Recording and Coding Guide for the Structure Inventory and Appraisal of the Nation's Bridges*. Technical report, Office of Engineering, Bridge Division, Bridge Management Branch, Washington, DC.

———. 2016. *Measuring and Specifying Pavement Roughness*. US Department of Transportation FHWA-HIF-16-032.

Fernald, John G. 1999. "Roads to Prosperity? Assessing the Link between Public Capital and Productivity." *American Economic Review* 89 (3): 619–38.

Garcia-López, Miquel-Àngel, Adelheid Holl, and Elisabet Viladecans-Marsal. 2015. "Suburbanization and Highways in Spain When the Romans and the Bourbons Still Shape Its Cities." *Journal of Urban Economics* 85 (0): 52–67.

Gendron-Carrier, Nicolas, Marco Gonzalez-Navarro, Stefano Polloni, and Matthew A. Turner. 2018. "Subways and Urban Air Pollution." Technical report. Cambridge, MA: National Bureau of Economic Research.

Gonzalez-Navarro, Marco, and Matthew A Turner. 2018. "Subways and Urban Growth: Evidence from Earth." *Journal of Urban Economics* 108: 85–106.

Gramlich, Edward M. 1994. "Infrastructure Investment: A Review Essay." *Journal of Economic Literature* 32 (3): 1176–96.

Heblich, Stephan, Stephen J. Redding, and Daniel M. Sturm. 2018. "The Making of the Modern Metropolis: Evidence from London." Working paper, London School of Economics.

Kreindler, Gabriel E. 2018. "The Welfare Effect of Road Congestion Pricing: Experimental Evidence and Equilibrium Implications." Working paper, Harvard University.

Leduc, Sylvain, and Daniel Wilson. 2013. "Roads to Prosperity or Bridges to Nowhere? Theory and Evidence on the Impact of Public Infrastructure Investment." *NBER Macroeconomics Annual 2012* 27: 89–142.

Mannering, Fred, Walter Kilareski, and Scott Washburn. 2007. *Principles of Highway Engineering and Traffic Analysis*. Hoboken, NJ: John Wiley & Sons.

Mehrotra, Neil, Juan Pablo Uribe, and Matthew A. Turner. 2020. "Does the US Have an Infrastructure Cost Problem? Evidence from the Interstate Highway System." Working paper, Brown University.

Meyer, John R., John F. Kain, and Martin Wohl. 1965. *The Urban Transportation Problem*. Cambridge, MA: Harvard University Press.

Office of Highway Policy Information. 2016. *Highway Performance Monitoring Sys-*

*tem Field Manual*. Office of Management & Budget (OMB) Control No. 2125-0028.
Parry, Ian W. H., Margaret Walls, and Winston Harrington. 2007. "Automobile Externalities and Policies." *Journal of Economic Literature* 45 (2): 1335–53.
Ramey, Valerie A. 2021. "The Macroeconomic Consequences of Infrastructure Investment." This volume.
Redding, Stephen J., and Matthew A. Turner. 2015. "Transportation Costs and the Spatial Organization of Economic Activity." In *Handbook of Regional and Urban Economics*, volume 5B, edited by Gilles Duranton, Vernon Henderson, and William C. Strange, 1339–98. Amsterdam: Elsevier.
Schwab, Klaus. 2019. *The Global Competitiveness Report*. Geneva: World Economic Forum.
Small, Kenneth A. 2012. "Valuation of Travel Time." *Economics of Transportation* 1 (1): 2–14.
Small, Kenneth A., and Erik T. Verhoef. 2007. *The Economics of Urban Transportation*. New York: Routledge.
Small, Kenneth A., Clifford Winston, and Carol A. Evans. 2012. *Road Work: A New Highway Pricing and Investment Policy*. Washington, DC: Brookings Institution.
Tsivanidis, Nick. 2019. "The Aggregate and Distributional Effects of Urban Transit Infrastructure: Evidence from Bogota's Transmilenio." Working paper, University of California, Berkeley.
Turner, Matthew A. 2019. "Local Transportation Policy and Economic Opportunity." Hamilton Project Policy Proposal 3. Washington, DC: Brookings Institution.
US Department of Transportation. 2013. *Status of the Nation's Highways, Bridges, and Transit: Condition and Performance, Report to Congress*. Washington, DC: US Department of Transportation.
US Federal Highway Administration. 1985. *Highway Statistics, 1984*. Washington, DC: Federal Highway Administration.
———. 1995. *Highway Statistics, 1995*. Washington, DC: Federal Highway Administration.
———. 2019. *Highway Statistics, 2018*. Washington, DC: Federal Highway Administration.

## Comment Stephen J. Redding

One of the pieces of conventional wisdom about the US economy is its decaying infrastructure. On a recent report card, the American Society of Civil Engineers (ASCE) awarded US infrastructure a grade of D+. According to an article in the *New York Times* (John Holusha and Kenneth Chang,

Stephen J. Redding is the Harold T. Shapiro '64 Professor in Economics at Princeton University, a research fellow of the Centre for Economic Policy Research, and a research associate and director of the International Trade and Investment Program at the National Bureau of Economic Research.

I am grateful to Princeton University for research support. The usual disclaimer applies. For acknowledgments, sources of research support, and disclosure of the author's material financial relationships, if any, please see https://www.nber.org/books-and-chapters/economic-analysis-and-infrastructure-investment/comment-transportation-infrastructure-us-redding.

"Engineers See Dangers in Aging Infrastructure," August 2, 2007), "many of the nation's 600,000 bridges are in need of repair or replacement. About one in eight has been deemed 'structurally deficient,' a term that typically means a component of the bridge's structure has been rated poor or worse, but does not necessarily warn of imminent collapse." While these views are widely accepted in the public policy debate, they sit somewhat awkwardly with the empirical evidence presented in chapter 3, which suggests that if anything the condition of the US Interstate Highway System has improved over the past 20–30 years. These findings raise the important question of what explains this disconnect between the conventional wisdom and the empirical evidence in chapter 3. Is the conventional wisdom simply factually incorrect, in which case the evidence presented in this chapter will permit a better-informed public policy debate? Alternatively, is there a political economy explanation for the widely held perception of the poor state of US transport infrastructure? Or do the official metrics on the conditions of highways and bridges reported in chapter 3 provide an incomplete picture of its state of health? Can past values of these official measures, for example, predict known cases of bridge collapse or other failures of transport infrastructure?

More broadly, this chapter makes three main contributions to our understanding of US infrastructure. First, the chapter documents the quantity and quality of US roads, bridges, buses, and subways in each year in recent decades. Second, the chapter investigates total expenditure and unit cost for each type of infrastructure over this period. Third, it proposes a simple theoretical framework that can be used to compare actual infrastructure investments to alternative possible investments. In my view, all three of these contributions are hugely valuable. The authors are undertaking a tremendous public service in collecting together in one place comprehensive data on the performance of the US transportation network and providing a tractable framework for evaluating the provision of different types of transport infrastructure. As a result, I think that the chapter will be highly influential and widely cited. In the remainder of my comments, I focus on three main points. First, I review some of the evidence on infrastructure costs. Second, I consider the issue of market failures and the potential divergence between private and social marginal returns to alternative forms of transport infrastructure. Third, I examine the benefits of infrastructure investments.

Beginning with infrastructure costs, this chapter and Mehrotra, Uribe, and Turner (2019) replicate an earlier finding by Brooks and Liscow (2019) of a substantial rise in total expenditure and construction cost per lane mile of Interstate Highway since the early 1970s. When I first encountered this finding, I thought that it had a natural explanation in terms of the Balassa-Samuelson effect from macroeconomics. According to this explanation, productivity growth in the manufacturing sector raises worker wages, which bids up costs for nontraded sectors such as construction that use labor. However, this explanation is straightforward to rule out, because the rise in Interstate construction costs is not driven by a rise in labor costs. Another potential explanation could be that Interstate Highways today are more likely than in the past to be built in urban locations with a higher cost of land than rural locations. But the rise in Interstate construction costs is also not explained by higher costs of land or by a range of other controls for observable location characteristics relevant for construction costs, such as terrain and topography.

Resolving this puzzle ought to be a major objective for the research literature and the public policy debate going forward. There remain several plausible potential explanations on which further evidence is needed. For example, the timing of the construction of different segments of the Interstate is likely to be nonrandom, giving rise to a selection problem. The first segments of the Interstate to be constructed are likely to have been those with highest benefits relative to costs. If later segments have lower benefits relative to costs, and some of this decline in net benefits is explained by higher costs, this could explain a rise in construction costs per lane mile of Interstate Highways over time. Another potential explanation could be that a lane mile of Interstate today is not the same as a lane mile of Interstate in the past, so that we are not comparing like with like. For example, if there is greater provision of sound walls or other features today than in the past, and these features provide benefits such as lower noise or air pollution, these benefits should be taken into account and weighed against the higher construction costs.

A further possibility involves political economy considerations, such as greater representation of the concerns of local residents over time. While construction costs for some early segments of the Interstate were relatively low, this could have come at the cost of adverse consequences for the neighborhoods that they bisected. A famous example is the Cross-Bronx Expressway in New York, which was driven through the heart of the Bronx, with potential negative consequences for social and economic interactions within this neighborhood. As argued in Brinkman and Lin (2019), resistance to initial routes for Interstate Highways increased over time, and costly rerouting of highways to reduce the negative disamenities to local residents could in part explain rising construction costs over time. Again economic benefits to local residents in terms of neighborhood preservation should be offset against higher construction costs as part of a wider cost-benefit analysis of the impact of Interstate Highway construction.

Turning now to the issue of market failure, the authors compare relative expenditure and relative usage for different forms of transport infrastructure. They argue that the fact that we spend about the same amount on public transit buses, which provide about two billion rides per year, as on the Interstate System, which provides nearly a trillion miles of vehicle travel per year, should be central to the policy debate. I agree, and in drawing attention to relative levels of usage and government expenditure on different forms of transport infrastructure, the authors perform a valuable service. However, it would be useful to have more discussion earlier in the chapter about market failures and their relevance for government expenditure on alternative transport modes. This is a point of which the authors are well aware. Indeed, the divergence between private and social marginal returns to transport infrastructure features prominently in the theoretical model developed toward the end of the chapter. Nevertheless, it would be useful to emphasize up-front that the rationale for government intervention rests on market failures and externalities. For example, if congestion pricing is either technologically or politically infeasible, one could argue that the congestion externalities from private car use contribute in part toward the case for supporting public transit. Additionally, since public transit is disproportionately used by individuals with lower income, one could argue that income distributional considerations should also be taken into account in evaluating the implications of government expenditure on alternative forms of transport infrastructure.

In this context, although the authors have already undertaken an impressive amount of work in assembling such comprehensive data on US infrastructure, cross-country comparisons could be informative. For example, given the extensive provision of public transit in many European countries, one would conjecture that they devote relatively more government expenditure to public transit than the United States does. Does this imply that relative expenditure is even more out of line with relative usage in these countries than in the United States? Can the United States learn anything from the European experience? Or do these differences in levels of public and private transport provision between Europe and the United States reflect two alternative equilibria? What is the role of local economic conditions, such as population density, in influencing the case for government expenditure on alternative forms of transport infrastructure? More broadly, what are the implications of new technologies such as ride hailing (for example, Uber and Lyft) and autonomous vehicles for government support for these alternative transport modes?

Turning finally to the benefits of transport infrastructure, a growing empirical and theoretical literature concerned with evaluating these benefits has emerged in recent years. One of the key challenges in evaluating the causal effects of transport infrastructure is that its placement is likely to be nonrandom, such that locations that receive more transport infrastructure could have developed more rapidly than other locations, even in the absence of the transport infrastructure. To overcome this challenge, an important strand of recent research to which the authors have been influential contributors has exploited quasi-experimental variation in transport networks from, for example, strategic plans and historical exploration routes, including Baum-Snow (2007), Baum-Snow et al. (2017), Duranton, Morrow, and Turner (2014), and Duranton and Turner (2012).

Another key challenge is that transport infrastructure not only has direct economic effects on the locations through which it is constructed but also indirect effects on other locations, because of the reallocation of economic activity or general equilibrium interactions in goods and factor markets. To take account of these interactions and evaluate the real income effects of transport infrastructure investments, another strand of recent research has developed quantitative models of the spatial distribution of economic activity, including Ahlfeldt et al. (2015); Allen and Arkolakis (2014, 2017); Desmet, Nagy, and Rossi-Hansberg (2018); Donaldson (2018); Donaldson and Hornbeck (2016); Fajgelbaum and Schaal (2017); Redding (2016); Redding and Sturm (2008); and Tsivanidis (2018), as reviewed in Redding and Rossi-Hansberg (2017). These quantitative spatial models are rich enough to connect directly with central features of the observed data, such as gravity equations for goods trade and commuting flows, and yet remain sufficiently tractable as to permit transparent counterfactuals to evaluate the impact of alternative possible transport infrastructure investments on the spatial distribution of economic activity.

In the light of this recent research, it would be interesting to embed the demand for transport in the theoretical model developed by the authors in a richer quantitative structure that connects directly with the observed data. For example, one simple approach could be to view transportation as simply another economic activity that can be analyzed as a special case of Hulten's (1978) theorem. In particular, under the (strong) assumptions of a representative agent, no distortions and a closed economy, the change in aggregate real income ($d \ln W$) from a small shock to productivity ($d \ln A_i$) for an economy activity $i$ can be evaluated as

$$d \ln W = \sum_i \lambda_i d \ln A_i, \tag{1}$$

where $\lambda_i$ is the Domar weight (sales share) of economic activity $i$.

An advantage of this approach is that it can be used for either ex ante evaluation before transport infrastructure investments are made or ex post evaluation after these investments have been completed. A disadvantage is that for large changes in transport infrastructure, equation (1) holds only as a first-order approximation. More broadly, quantitative spatial models provide a framework for evaluating the impact of transport infrastructure investments on the spatial distribution of economic activity for both small and large changes. An example is provided by Redding (2016), which considers a model of trade in goods between locations connected by labor mobility. In this setting, the general equilibrium of the model can be summarized by two key equilibrium conditions: (1) goods market clearing such that income in each location equals expenditure on goods produced in that location; (2) population mobility such that workers receive the same real income across all populated locations.

An important property of these quantitative spatial models is that the equilibrium conditions for a counterfactual transport infrastructure improvement can be written solely in terms of variables that are observed in an initial equilibrium (such as income and trade shares) and the assumed impact of the change in transport infrastructure on goods trade costs (or in other contexts on commuting costs or migration frictions). For example, in Redding (2016), the counterfactual goods market clearing condition (from the first equilibrium condition above) can be written as follows:

$$\hat{w}_i\hat{\lambda}_i Y_i = \sum_{n\in N} \hat{\pi}_{ni}\pi_{ni}\hat{w}_n\hat{\lambda}_n Y_n, \tag{2}$$

where locations are indexed by $i$, $n \in N$; $w_i$ denotes the wage; $Y_i = w_i L_i$ is income; $L_i$ is population; $\lambda_i$ indicates the population share ($\lambda_i = L_i / \sum_{n\in N} L_n$); $\pi_{ni}$ is location $n$'s share of expenditure on goods produced by location $i$; and a hat above a variable denotes its relative change between the counterfactual equilibrium (denoted by a prime) and the actual equilibrium (no prime), such that $\hat{w}_i = w_i' / w_i$. The relative change in trade shares ($\hat{\pi}_{ni}$) satisfies

$$\hat{\pi}_{ni}\pi_{ni} = \frac{\pi_{ni}(\hat{d}_{ni}\hat{w}_i)^{-\theta}}{\sum_{k\in N}\pi_{nk}(\hat{d}_{nk}\hat{w}_k)^{-\theta}}, \tag{3}$$

where $\hat{d}_{ni} = d'_{ni} / d_{ni}$ is the relative change in the costs of trading goods between locations $i$ and $n$ as a result of the counterfactual changes in transport infrastructure.

Similarly, the counterfactual population mobility condition that equates real income across all populated locations (from the second equilibrium condition above) can be expressed as follows:

$$\hat{\lambda}_n\lambda_n = \frac{\hat{\pi}_{nn}^{-(\alpha\varepsilon/\theta)}\hat{\lambda}_n^{-\varepsilon(1-\alpha)}\lambda_n}{\sum_{k\in N}\hat{\pi}_{kk}^{-(\alpha\varepsilon/\theta)}\hat{\lambda}_k^{-\varepsilon(1-\alpha)}\lambda_k}. \tag{4}$$

Given observed data on income ($Y_i$), trade shares ($\pi_{ni}$) and population shares ($\lambda_i$) in an initial equilibrium and assumed changes in goods trade costs from a counterfactual transport infrastructure improvement ($\hat{d}_{ni}$), this system of equations (2), (3), and (4) can be used to solve for unique counterfactual changes in wages ($\hat{w}_i$), trade shares ($\hat{\pi}_{ni}$), and population shares ($\hat{\lambda}_i$) in response to the transport infrastructure improvement. Using these solutions for changes in wages, trade shares, and population shares, one can in turn recover the change in real income across all locations. Therefore, through embedding the demand for transport in the theoretical model developed by the authors in a richer quantitative structure, the authors would be able to connect more closely with the data used in the first part of the chapter and make richer quantitative statements about the impact of alternative forms of transport infrastructure on the spatial distribution of economic activity and real income.

Notwithstanding these comments and suggestions for future research, the authors already have written a great chapter. They have performed a hugely valuable public service in collecting together in one place comprehensive data on the performance of the US transportation network and providing a tractable framework for evaluating the provision of different types of transport infrastructure. The chapter should greatly enlighten the public debate about the current state of US infrastructure and the case for alternative forms of transport infrastructure investment.

## References

Ahlfeldt, G., S. Redding, D. Sturm, and N. Wolf. 2015. "The Economics of Density: Evidence from the Berlin Wall." *Econometrica* 83 (6): 2127–89.

Allen, T., and C. Arkolakis. 2014. "Trade and the Topography of the Spatial Economy." *Quarterly Journal of Economics* 129 (3): 1085–140.

———. 2017. "The Welfare Effects of Transportation Infrastructure Improvements." Dartmouth College.

Baum-Snow, N. 2007. "Did Highways Cause Suburbanization?" *Quarterly Journal of Economics* 122 (2): 775–80.

Baum-Snow, N., L. Brandt, J. Henderson, M. A. Turner, and Q. Zhang. 2017. "Roads, Railroads and Decentralization of Chinese Cities." *Review of Economics and Statistics* 99 (2): 435–48.

Brinkman, J., and J. Lin. 2019. "Freeway Revolts!" Federal Reserve Bank of Philadelphia Working Paper 19-29.

Brooks, L., and Z. D. Liscow. 2019. "Infrastructure Costs." Available at SSRN 3428675.

Desmet, K., D. K. Nagy, and E. Rossi-Hansberg. 2018. "The Geography of Development." *Journal of Political Economy* 126 (3): 903–83.

Donaldson, D. 2018. "Railroads of the Raj: Estimating the Impact of Transportation Infrastructure." *American Economic Review* 108 (4-5): 899–934.

Donaldson, D., and R. Hornbeck. 2016. "Railroads and American Economic Growth: A Market Access Approach." *Quarterly Journal of Economics* 131 (2): 799–858.

Duranton, G., P. Morrow, and M. A. Turner. 2014. "Roads and Trade: Evidence from the US." *Review of Economic Studies* 81 (2): 681–724.

Duranton, G., and M. A. Turner. 2012. "Urban Growth and Transportation." *Review of Economic Studies* 79 (4): 1407–40.

Fajgelbaum, P. D., and E. Schaal. 2017. "Optimal Transport Networks in Spatial Equilibrium." NBER Working Paper 23200. Cambridge, MA: National Bureau of Economic Research.

Hulten, C. R. 1978. "Growth Accounting with Intermediate Inputs." *Review of Economic Studies*: 511–18.

Mehrotra, N., J. P. Uribe, and M. A. Turner. 2019. "Does the U.S. Have an Infrastructure Cost Problem? Evidence from the Interstate Highway System." Brown University, mimeograph.

Redding, S. J. 2016. "Goods Trade, Factor Mobility and Welfare." *Journal of International Economics* 101: 148–67.
Redding, S. J., and E. Rossi-Hansberg. 2017. "Quantitative Spatial Models." *Annual Review of Economics* 9: 21–58.
Redding, S. J., and D. M. Sturm. 2008. "The Costs of Remoteness: Evidence from German Division and Reunification." *American Economic Review* 98 (5): 1766–97.
Tsivanidis, N. 2018. "The Aggregate and Distributional Effects of Urban Transit Infrastructure: Evidence from Bogotá's TransMilenio." University of California, Berkeley, mimeograph.

4

# The Macroeconomic Consequences of Infrastructure Investment

Valerie A. Ramey

## 4.1 Introduction

Public capital can play an important role in increasing long-run output and standards of living. Because of nonrivalry in consumption, nonexcludability in use, or both, the private sector will tend to underprovide key types of productive capital. Hence, there may be a role for government to raise social welfare by providing public capital, even when government must tax private resources for financing. Economic history is replete with examples of public capital, and infrastructure in particular, that had significant impacts on long-run GDP, welfare, or both. For example, Gordon (2017) highlights the contributions of publicly provided sanitation, clean water, and electrical infrastructure to both the rise in life expectancy and increase in productivity in the US during the first part of the twentieth century. In the period following World War II, the US Interstate Highway program has been linked

Valerie A. Ramey is a professor of economics at the University of California, San Diego, and a research associate of the National Bureau of Economic Research.

This is a revised version of a paper prepared for the NBER "Economics of Infrastructure Investment" conference that took place November 15–16, 2019. I am grateful for helpful comments from my discussant Jason Furman and co-editors Edward Glaeser and James Poterba, as well as from Hafedh Bouakez, Gabriel Chodorow-Reich, John Fernald, Christopher House, Per Krusell, Daniel Leff Yaffe, Garey Ramey, Johannes Wieland, and Sarah Zubairy; seminar participants at Duke University, NYU, Stanford, the University of Michigan, and the University of Texas at Austin; and NBER conference participants. I wish to thank Suzanne Golshanara for assistance in preparing the manuscript. Dan Wilson kindly provided supplemental data from his 2017 paper with Sylvain Leduc. I gratefully acknowledge financial support from National Science Foundation award number 1658796. For acknowledgments, sources of research support, and disclosure of the author's material financial relationships, if any, please see https://www.nber.org/books-and-chapters/economic-analysis-and-infrastructure-investment/macroeconomic-consequences-infrastructure-investment.

to significant increases in productivity and output (for example, Aschauer 1989; Fernald 1999; and Leff Yaffe 2020).

More recently, government infrastructure spending has also figured prominently in policy discussions regarding short-run stimulus. Government infrastructure spending is viewed by many policy makers as having advantages over government consumption spending for stimulating the economy during a recession. In a traditional Keynesian model, both productive and wasteful government spending stimulate the economy in the short run through standard income and multiplier effects and help push output back to potential output. Government investment spending such as infrastructure spending, however, has the additional advantage that it can change the path of potential output. In particular, if a short-run increase in government spending also raises the stock of productive public capital or long-run total factor productivity (TFP), then government spending provides two benefits: Keynesian demand stimulus in the short run and neoclassical supply stimulus in the long run. These lasting effects are particularly welcome since typically stimulus packages must be financed with an increase in distortionary taxes after the recession is over. If output remains higher because of the long-run effects of more public capital, then the tax base expands and the necessary increases in tax rates are less.

In this chapter, I examine the macroeconomic theory and empirical evidence on the benefits of infrastructure spending, both in the long run and the short run. Much of the theory and the empirical work suggests that even when there are substantial long-run benefits of infrastructure investment, the short-run benefits are probably lower than for nonproductive government spending. In the past few years, the macroeconomic theory literature has discovered that realistic features of infrastructure investment, such as the importance of time to build and sector-specific demand effects, can work to reduce the short-run aggregate stimulus effects, even when the long-run supply-side benefits are present. Moreover, much of the existing macroeconomic empirical evidence is consistent with the predictions of these theories. I conclude that infrastructure investment may not be the most powerful short-run stimulus.

On the other hand, theory and empirical estimates suggest that public capital and infrastructure spending in particular have had significant positive effects on long-run output and productivity. Whether current levels of infrastructure spending are above or below the optimal level depends on estimates of the production function output elasticity to public capital, as well as considerations of distortionary taxation and heterogeneity in the returns to different types of infrastructure.

The chapter proceeds as follows. Section 4.2 uses insights from both neoclassical and New Keynesian models to study the effects of government investment. The first few subsections present and calibrate both a stylized neoclassical model and a medium-scale New Keynesian model with lump-sum taxation. These sections discuss the economic mechanisms and intuition for how government investment can affect the macroeconomy. Section 4.2.4 simulates the models and compares the effects of increases in government consumption versus government investment and presents short-run multipliers. This section of the chapter shows that government investment and consumption have similar effects on output in the New Keynesian model, in contrast to the neoclassical model, in which government investment has weaker short-run effects. Section 4.2.5 amends both models to include realistic time-to-spend and time-to-build delays. The simulations from these versions of the model show that these delays dramatically reduce the short-run multipliers, so much so in the New Keynesian model that government investment offers no stimulus for the first few years.

Section 4.2.6 delves further into the multipliers at longer horizons. Both the neoclassical model and the New Keynesian model produce significantly higher multipliers at longer horizons. The size of these multipliers depends crucially on three key features: (i) the productivity of public capital in the aggregate production function; (ii) whether the increase in public capital moves the economy toward the social optimum or away from it; (iii) and how the public capital is financed.

Section 4.2.7 summarizes some of the models from the literature that analyzes the effects of government capital, and infrastructure in particular. Several of these models highlight other important features for the short-run effects of government investment, including the behavior of monetary policy.

Section 4.3 then moves on to the empirical evidence on the long-run effects of public investment in the US. After a brief overview of the empirical literature studying the elasticity of output to public capital, I use the stylized neoclassical model of section 4.2.1 to demonstrate the types of biases that can arise in estimating the output elasticity to public capital and discuss ways to reduce the bias.

Section 4.4 surveys the empirical estimates of the short-run effects of government investment spending. Much of the focus is on the American Recovery and Reinvestment Act of 2009 (ARRA) studies, and in particular on the infrastructure part of the ARRA. I offer new estimates of the effects of the ARRA on employment in highway construction.

Section 4.5 asks the question, Is the US underinvesting in public capital? The analysis compares past and current levels of government capital to the optimal levels implied by the stylized neoclassical model to shed light on this question. Section 4.6 summarizes some of the key results that emerge from the chapter and concludes.

## 4.2 Government Investment in Dynamic Macroeconomic Models

This section analyzes the short-run and long-run effects of government investment and public capital in both a stylized neoclassical model as well as a medium-scale New Keynesian model. The neoclassical model forms the underlying basis of the New Keynesian model, so the economic mechanisms of the neoclassical model continue to be key drivers of short-run results in New Keynesian models unless these mechanisms are specifically shut down. The neoclassical mechanisms are the drivers of the long-run benefits of public capital since the New Keynesian elements affect the economy only in the short run.

I use simulations of the models to illustrate several important insights from the recent literature studying the short-run effects of government investment. The first two are from Leeper, Walker, and Yang's (2010) analysis of government investment in an estimated medium-scale neoclassical model. First, if government investment is productive, then the negative wealth effect of increased taxation is muted by the positive wealth effect of future productive public capital. As a result, in the short run output may respond less to an increase in government investment than to government consumption. Second, government investment in public capital, and particularly infrastructure, typically involves implementation delays, and these delays severely mute the short-run multiplier. The third insight is from Boehm (2020), who notes that the long service life of private capital leads to a very high intertemporal elasticity of substitution in investment demand. Because investment rates are typically small relative to the capital stock, agents are very willing to intertemporally substitute investment, much more so than for consumption. The fourth insight is about the importance of the initial level of public capital relative to the socially optimal level. Long-run multipliers are higher if the economy is starting below the optimal level of public capital.

The models I study in this section treat all public capital the same and do not incorporate features that are unique to infrastructure. However, the basic mechanisms at work in the models apply to any type of public capital that appears in the production function. In section 4.2.7, I discuss some of the models that specifically incorporate the benefits of transportation infrastructure.

### 4.2.1 A Stylized Neoclassical Model

Most of the macroeconomic analysis of government investment builds on the pioneering work of Baxter and King (1993), who were the first to analyze both the short-run and long-run effects of government investment in a fully dynamic general equilibrium neoclassical macroeconomic model.[1] In the typical neoclassical model, government purchases have direct impacts on the economy in several ways. Let $G_t^C$ denote government consumption goods purchases in period $t$ and let $G_t^I$ denote government investment goods

1. Baxter and King's (1993) model considers only effects on steady-state levels, not on growth rates. Other strands of the literature have studied the growth consequences of public capital in endogenous growth models. See, for example, the important papers by Barro (1990) and Glomm and Ravikumar (1994, 1997).

purchases. The sum of government purchases has a direct impact through the economy-wide resource constraint:

(1) $$C_t + I_t + G_t^C + G_t^I \leq Y_t.$$

$C_t$ is private consumption, $I_t$ is private investment, and $Y_t$ is output. This resource constraint is key to the wealth effects that drive the labor and output response in neoclassical and benchmark sticky price New Keynesian models. A government that purchases goods and services extracts resources from the economy. Financing through current or future lump sum taxes adds no additional effects, so the resource constraint captures the key impacts. If there is no direct effect of government spending on the production possibilities of the economy, a rise in government purchases leaves the private sector with fewer resources. Households respond by lowering their own consumption and leisure and raising their labor supply. Employment rises not because the demand for labor has risen (since government spending does not directly affect the aggregate marginal product of labor) but because labor supply has risen. The rise in labor supply induced by the wealth effect is the key mechanism by which an increase in government purchases raises output in the neoclassical model and the benchmark New Keynesian sticky price model. In fact, as Broer et al. (2020) show, the benchmark New Keynesian model achieves higher multipliers than the neoclassical model by adding an additional negative wealth effect that stems from countercyclical markups and profits.

While government consumption and government investment enter symmetrically in the resource constraint in equation (1), they play different roles in the rest of the economic structure. Most modelers assume that government consumption enters household utility, but in a separable way, so that government consumption has no impact on the marginal utility of consumption.[2] In this case, there is no additional impact of government consumption on the economy, other than raising household welfare.

To be concrete, suppose that a representative household maximizes lifetime utility $U$:

(2) $$U = E_0 \sum_{t=0}^{\infty} \beta^t \left[ \ln C_t - \nu \frac{N_t^{1+\phi}}{1+\phi} + \Gamma(G_t^C) \right].$$

$\beta$ is the discount factor. This functional form is now widely used in macroeconomic models. Utility depends on the logarithm of consumption, $C_t$, and a constant elasticity of substitution (CES) function of hours worked, $N_t$. $\phi$ is the inverse of the Frisch elasticity of labor supply.

2. Important recent exceptions include Ercolani and Valle e Azevedo (2014) and Sims and Wolff(2018). Both papers incorporate public capital and also allow government consumption to affect the marginal utility of private consumption. Gallen and Winston (2019) argue that government investment in transportation infrastructure can also affect utility, because a higher stock of transportation infrastructure leads to time savings for the household by reducing time spent commuting to work and time spent traveling to shop.

Government investment, on the other hand, can have direct effects on the production function. Baxter and King (1993) specify a stylized Cobb-Douglas aggregate production function:

$$Y_t = A_t K_{t-1}^{\alpha} N_t^{1-\alpha} (K_{t-1}^{G})^{\theta_G}. \tag{3}$$

$A_t$ is the level of total factor productivity, $K_t$ is the private capital stock at the end of period $t$, $K_t^G$ is the public capital stock at the end of period $t$, and $N_t$ is the quantity of labor. Typical analyses assume constant returns to private inputs, which is also assumed here. The size of $\theta_G$, the exponent on public capital, plays an important role in the long-run impact of government investment, which can have consequences for its short-run impact as well. There are increasing returns to scale if $\theta_G$ is greater than zero. An important alternative allows for congestion effects in public capital that result in aggregate constant returns to scale in all three inputs (e.g., Glomm and Ravikumar 1994).

Note that virtually all of the short-run effect of government spending on output must operate through labor input, for the following reason. Both private and public capital are relatively fixed in the short run, so if government spending does not affect TFP ($A_t$) in the short run, government spending can raise GDP in the short run only to the extent that government spending raises labor input.

Finally, government investment and public capital are linked since government investment this period adds to the public capital stock available at the beginning of next period:

$$K_t^G = G_t^I + (1-\delta_G) K_{t-1}^G. \tag{4}$$

$\delta_G$ is the depreciation rate on public capital. Since government investment is typically a small fraction of the steady state stock of public capital, it takes numerous periods of elevated government investment to raise the public capital stock a noticeable amount. The capital accumulation equation for private capital is similar:

$$K_t = I_t + (1-\delta) K_{t-1}, \tag{5}$$

where $\delta$ is the depreciation rate on private capital.

Equations (3) and (4) capture the distinguishing characteristics of government investment relative to government consumption. A dollar increase in government investment raises the stock of public capital through equation (4), which has multiple effects on the production function in equation (3). First, for given TFP, private capital, and labor, the higher public capital stock leads to higher output. Second, the higher public capital stock, because it raises the marginal products of both private capital and labor, incentivizes firms to invest in more capital and hire more labor. In the neoclassical model, the only type of government spending that raises the demand for labor is government spending that directly raises TFP or public capital.

How the government spending is financed has first-order effects on the response of output and labor. The simplest assumption, and the one that gives the highest long-run multipliers, is that the government uses lump sum taxes. The government budget constraint is given by

$$G_t^C + G_t^I = T_t, \tag{6}$$

where $T_t$ is lump sum taxes. In the representative household, perfect financial markets, and rational expectations case, the timing of the lump sum taxes has no effect: deficit spending with later increases in lump sum taxes is equivalent to balanced budget lump sum taxes. In this case, the social planner solution is equivalent to the decentralized competitive equilibrium. In the more realistic case that the government must raise distortionary taxes, the timing of those taxes matters, and the positive effects of government spending on output can be severely muted.

In this benchmark economy, the social planner chooses sequences $C_t$, $N_t$, $I_t$, $Y_t$, and $K_t$ to maximize the lifetime utility of the representative household given in equation (2), subject to the economy-wide resource constraint in equation (1), the production function in equation (3), and the capital accumulation equations in equations (4) and (5), as well as exogenous processes for the two types of government spending. In principle, the social planner can also choose the level of public capital to maximize social welfare. Since the simulations involve exogenously varying public investment, public capital is taken as exogenous for now. As I will show in section 4.2.6, the multiplier depends on where public capital starts relative to the optimal level.

The first order conditions and steady-state conditions for this model are presented in the appendix.

### 4.2.2 A Medium-Scale New Keynesian Model

Many policy makers have advocated infrastructure spending to jump-start an economy during a downturn, so it is important also to consider the effects of public investment in a model that captures traditional Keynesian notions of slack resources and income multipliers in the short run. Therefore, I also construct and simulate a model that incorporates some key Keynesian mechanisms.

I do not use the benchmark New Keynesian model, which features sticky prices but flexible wages, because recent work on heterogeneous agent New Keynesian models has revealed that the sticky price assumption raises multipliers through a very implausible mechanism. Broer et al. (2020) demonstrate that labor supply rises more in response to demand shocks in a benchmark New Keynesian model than in a neoclassical model because of an additional negative wealth effect. In particular, sticky prices lead to countercyclical markups and countercyclical profits, causing households to raise their labor supply in response to the additional negative wealth effect. Adding noncompetitive labor markets and sticky wages causes labor to be demand-determined, so this implausible mechanism is shut down or at least muted even when the model also includes sticky prices.

The model I use expands on the influential study by Galí, López-Salido, and Vallés (2007) of the response of consumption and output to government consumption spending in a New Keynesian model. Their model includes capital adjustment costs, sticky prices, noncompetitive labor markets, rule-of-thumb consumers, monetary policy rules, and government debt feedback rules featuring lump-sum taxes.

I extend their model by (1) adding government investment spending and public capital; (2) adding sticky wages, following Colciago's (2011) extension of Galí, López-Salido, and Vallés (2007); (3) replacing private capital adjustment costs with investment adjustment costs; and (4) allowing variable private capital utilization. These last two features are now widely used in medium-scale New Keynesian models.

To be specific, the New Keynesian model used here superimposes the following features on the simple stylized neoclassical model presented in the preceding section.

- **Adjustment costs on investment**. This feature appears in many medium-scale New Keynesian models, but it can also be added to a neoclassical model.[3] For the typical government spending process used in most simulated models, adjustment costs on investment severely mute the short-run crowding-out effect on private investment and raise multipliers, an effect that has been overlooked by much of the literature.
- **Variable utilization of capital**. This feature allows firms to vary their utilization of capital (at a cost), so that capital services are more cyclical than the capital stock. The result is more elastic output supply, since variable utilization of capital mutes the diminishing returns to labor and prevents real marginal cost from increasing much when output rises. There is ample evidence that capital utilization varies significantly over the business cycle (for example, Shapiro 1993). This feature is not uniquely New Keynesian since it can also be added to a neoclassical model. It is a way to capture the more elastic supply curves that might characterize an economy with slack resources.
- **Sticky prices and noncompetitive product markets**. This feature characterizes even the simplest textbook New Keynesian model. In the simplest version of the New Keynesian model, this assumption is the only deviation from the neoclassical model (along with the accompanying monetary policy rule). It is assumed that firms are monopolistically competitive and face a Calvo-style (1983) adjustment cost on prices.
- **Sticky wages and noncompetitive labor markets**. Following Colciago (2011), I assume that households mark up wages over the marginal

3. See, for example, Leeper, Walker, and Yang's (2010) study, which I will discuss in more detail later. For various reasons, investment adjustment costs are generally favored over capital adjustment costs, though in many instances the two types of adjustment costs produce similar results.

rate of substitution and that they face Calvo-type (1983) adjustment costs. Most medium-scale New Keynesian models include both sticky wages and sticky prices.

- **Rule-of-thumb consumers**. In order to generate larger Keynesian effects of temporary income on consumption, I adopt the assumption of Galí, López-Salido, and Vallés (2007) that a certain fraction of consumers neither borrow nor save and simply consume all of their current income. More recent heterogeneous agent models use more sophisticated modeling and call the behavior "hand to mouth," but the effects are similar in many instances. The other consumers are assumed to be fully optimizing, forward-looking, and owners of all of the capital in the economy.
- **Elastic labor supply**. This feature is based not on an addition to the neoclassical model but rather on the calibration of a particular parameter. As I will discuss in more detail later, in both the neoclassical model and the New Keynesian model, I will allow the Frisch elasticity and the Hicks elasticity of labor supply to be significantly greater than implied by the micro estimates. This assumption facilitates a higher elasticity of supply, roughly mimicking the situation of an economy with slack and leading to higher multipliers for government spending.
- **Monetary policy and fiscal policy rules**. The monetary and fiscal policy rules follow Galí, López-Salido, and Vallés (2007). The monetary authority follows a Taylor rule that responds only to inflation. Lump-sum taxes respond to both the deviation of government debt and government spending from their steady-state values.

The appendix shows more details of this New Keynesian model.

### 4.2.3 Calibration of the Models

Even the simple neoclassical model presented earlier cannot be solved analytically unless the depreciation rate on capital is set at 100 percent, so we must analyze the models quantitatively.

Both the neoclassical and New Keynesian models are calibrated to be quarterly. The calibrated parameters with their descriptions are shown in table 4.1. Consider first the shared parameters. For utility in (2), the discount factor $\beta$ is set to 0.99, which implies an annual real interest rate of 4 percent. $\phi$ is set to 0.25, which implies a relatively high Frisch intertemporal elasticity of labor supply of 4. This high value is set both to match Baxter and King's (1993) calibration in the neoclassical model and to generate a high elasticity of labor supply for the New Keynesian model.[4] As I will show, a lower value of the Frisch elasticity implies a lower value of the multiplier.

In the production function equation (3), the capital share $\alpha$ is set to 0.36.

4. Baxter and King (1993) specify a utility function with the log of leisure rather than the direct hours term included above. Their calibration of the parameter on log leisure implies a Frisch elasticity of 4. See footnote 2 of Shimer (2009) for a demonstration.

**Table 4.1** **Baseline calibration of the models**

| Parameter | Value | Description |
|---|---|---|
| | | Parameters in both models |
| $\beta$ | 0.99 | Subjective discount factor |
| $\nu$ | 1 | Weight on disutility of labor |
| $\varphi$ | 0.25 | Inverse of the Frisch elasticity of labor supply |
| $\alpha$ | 0.36 | Exponent on private capital in production function |
| $\theta_G$ | 0.05 | Exponent on government capital in production function |
| $\delta$ | 0.015 | Depreciation rate of private capital |
| $\delta_G$ | 0.01 | Depreciation rate of public capital |
| $g_y$ | 0.175 | Steady-state share of total govt spending to GDP |
| $g_{iy}$ | 0.035 | Steady-state share of govt investment to GDP |
| $\rho_G$ | 0.95 | Autoregressive coefficient on appropriations process |
| | Additional parameters of the New Keynesian model | |
| $\kappa$ | 5.2 | Investment adjustment cost parameter |
| $\delta_1$ | 0.025 | Parameter on linear term of capital utilization cost |
| $\delta_2$ | 0.05 | Parameter on quadratic term of capital utilization cost |
| $\mu_P$ | 1.2 | Steady-state price markup |
| $\mu_W$ | 1.2 | Steady-state wage markup |
| $\theta_P$ | 0.75 | Calvo parameter on price adjustment |
| $\theta_W$ | 0.75 | Calvo parameter on wage adjustment |
| $\varepsilon_P$ | 6 | Elasticity of substitution between types of goods |
| $\varepsilon_W$ | 6 | Elasticity of substitution between types of labor |
| $\gamma$ | 0.5 | Share of rule-of-thumb consumers |
| $\psi_b$ | 0.33 | Debt feedback coefficient in fiscal rule |
| $\psi_g$ | 0.1 | Spending feedback coefficient in fiscal rule |
| $\psi_\pi$ | 1.5 | Monetary policy response to inflation |

I follow Baxter and King (1993) and Leeper, Walker, and Yang (2010) and set the parameter on public capital at $\theta_G = 0.05$. I will also consider higher values in the range produced by the meta-analysis by Bom and Ligthart (2014), who find a mean estimate of 0.08 in the short run and 0.12 in the long run. I set the depreciation rates to those implied by US Bureau of Economic Analysis (BEA) data in 2018, calculated as the ratio of current cost depreciation of fixed assets to the stock of fixed assets at the end of the previous year.[5] The ratio yields an estimate of quarterly depreciation rates of $\delta_G = 0.01$ and $\delta = 0.015$.

For the medium-scale model, I set the investment adjustment cost parameter and the utilization cost parameters similar to the values estimated by Leeper, Walker, and Yang (2010). The steady-state wage and price gross markups are set to 1.2 and the Calvo probability of not being able to adjust prices or wages is set to 0.75, which corresponds to an average price and wage duration of one year. Following Galí, López-Salido, and Vallés (2007), I assume a high fraction of rule-of-thumb consumers, 50 percent of the

5. The data are from the fixed asset tables at bea.gov.

population. More details on the calibration of the medium-scale model are provided in the appendix.

In the simulations, the economy starts from an initial steady state in which total government spending is 17.5 percent of GDP, the value in 2019. Of that, government investment spending is 3.5 percent of GDP, similar to the actual ratio in 2019.

Government spending is driven by appropriations shocks. As in Leeper, Walker, and Yang (2010), I assume that appropriations, *AP*, follow a standard first-order autoregressive (AR[1]) process:

$$AP_t = \text{constant} + \rho \cdot AP_{t-1} + \varepsilon_t. \tag{7}$$

Like Leeper, Walker, and Yang (2010), I assume an AR(1) process for government spending with a serial correlation parameter 0.95, which involves a very persistent increase. Since multipliers are higher the more persistent the change in government spending, the multipliers I report are higher than the ones that I would find for a less persistent increase in government spending.

The experiments are designed to compare the effects of government investment shocks to government consumption in both the stylized neoclassical model as well as the New Keynesian model and variations on those models. Most important, the experiments highlight the significant dampening of multipliers when there are implementation delays.

### 4.2.4 Experiments with No Implementation Delays

In this section, I compare the effects of an increase in government investment to an increase in government consumption in both the neoclassical and the New Keynesian models. With no implementation delays, government spending is equal to appropriations—that is,

$$G_t^J = AP_t \text{ for } J = C, I. \tag{8}$$

Figure 4.1 compares the effect of an increase in government consumption to an increase in government investment in the stylized neoclassical model. For both experiments, the path of government spending is the same, with only the type varying across experiments, so the two lines lie on top of each other in the upper left graph. The rest of the graphs show the endogenous response of key variables to an unanticipated increase in government consumption or government investment that is autocorrelated. Government spending, output, consumption, private investment, and public capital are expressed in deviations from their own steady-state values as a percent of steady-state output. Labor input and wages are percent deviations from their own steady-state values. The real interest rate is annualized-percentage-point deviations from its own steady state.

Consider first an increase in government consumption, whose effects are depicted by the solid line. As discussed earlier, the direct effect is a negative wealth effect on consumption and leisure. The government is extracting

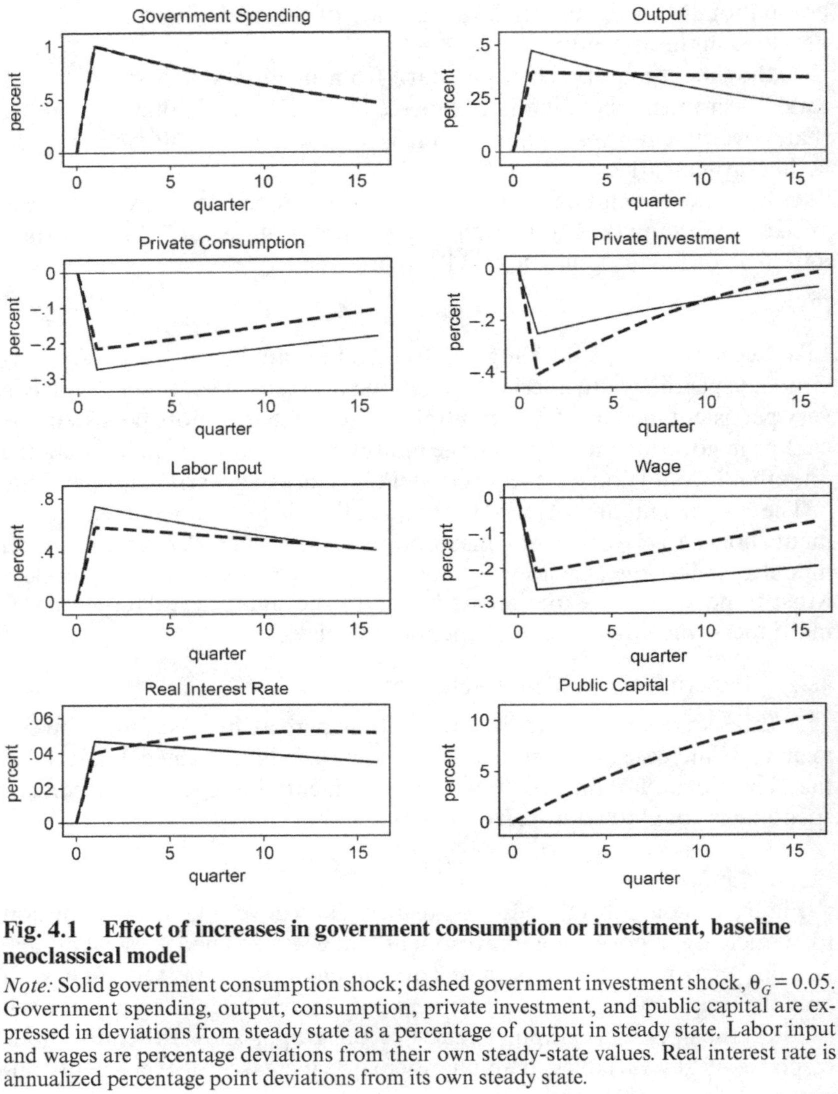


**Fig. 4.1 Effect of increases in government consumption or investment, baseline neoclassical model**

*Note:* Solid government consumption shock; dashed government investment shock, $\theta_G = 0.05$. Government spending, output, consumption, private investment, and public capital are expressed in deviations from steady state as a percentage of output in steady state. Labor input and wages are percentage deviations from their own steady-state values. Real interest rate is annualized percentage point deviations from its own steady state.

resources from the economy, so consumption falls and labor supply rises. This rise in the labor supply boosts output, with an impact multiplier of 0.47. Private investment spending is crowded out. There is no change to public capital. All values eventually return to their original steady-state levels since the government spending increase is not permanent.

The effect of an increase in government investment is shown by the dashed line. In this case, the impact effect on labor, consumption, and output is

**Table 4.2 First-year multipliers from simulated models**

| Model version ($\theta_G = 0.05$) | Government consumption AR(1) | Government investment AR(1) | Government investment delays |
|---|---|---|---|
| Neoclassical model | | | |
| Baseline | 0.47 | 0.40 | 0.37 |
| Frisch elasticity = 0.5 | 0.14 | 0.13 | 0.13 |
| Investment adjustment cost, capital utilization | 0.67 | 0.68 | 0.15 |
| New Keynesian model | | | |
| Baseline | 1.06 | 1.12 | 0.08 |
| No investment adjustment cost, no utilization | 0.19 | 0.16 | 0.06 |
| Frisch elasticity = 0.5 | 0.76 | 0.82 | −0.20 |
| No rule-of-thumb households | 0.68 | 0.73 | −0.05 |

*Note:* These estimates are based on the calibrated models described in section 4.2. The multipliers are equal to the ratio of the integrals of the impulse responses of output and appropriations.

somewhat less than for a government consumption increase. A muted negative wealth effect is key to this difference: the government is still extracting the same amount from current output but is now using that amount to build up wealth in the form of productive capital.

Private investment falls more during the first two years than in the government consumption case. The weaker wealth effect on labor means that output rises less in the short run, so more private spending must be crowded out by the government spending. The same weaker wealth effect means that households do not reduce their consumption as much, so the brunt of the crowd-out falls on private investment. The differential short-run response of consumption and investment is a key theme in Boehm's (2020) analysis of the short-run multipliers on government consumption versus government investment. The long service life of private capital leads to a very high intertemporal elasticity of substitution in investment demand.[6]

As the public capital stock is built up, output remains high. Labor input remains high and private investment recovers since the higher level of public capital raises the marginal products of both labor and private capital. Not shown in the figure are the results when the exponent on public capital, $\theta_G$, is 0.1 rather than 0.05. These effects are similar, though the muted wealth effect is a little more evident in the short run and the positive stimulus is more evident in the intermediate run.

Table 4.2 shows the undiscounted cumulative multipliers for the first year, since this horizon is relevant for stimulus spending. Following Mountford and Uhlig (2009), these multipliers are the integral of the impulse response

6. In Boehm's model there is even more crowding out, because consumption goods and investment goods are produced in different sectors and there is imperfect labor mobility between sectors.

of output divided by the integral of the impulse response of appropriations up to four quarters.[7]

The top panel of table 4.2 shows the short-run cumulative multipliers for this stylized neoclassical model ("baseline") as well as for two permutations. The first-year multiplier for government consumption in the baseline neoclassical model is 0.5 and for government investment is 0.4. Thus, the short-run multiplier is lower for government investment in the baseline neoclassical model. The lower multiplier is owing to the smaller negative wealth effect because households anticipate that their public capital will increase. I will discuss the last column later.

The second and third rows show multipliers for two variations on the stylized neoclassical model. The second row of the table shows that both the government consumption and investment multipliers fall dramatically when the Frisch elasticity is set to a value equal to the micro estimates of 0.5 rather than the baseline calibration of 4. On the other hand, the third row shows that adding investment adjustment costs and variable capital utilization to the baseline model raises the multiplier. The main effect comes from the investment adjustment cost, which hinders the crowding out effect on investment. In this version of the model, there is no difference in the first-year multipliers for government consumption and government investment.

Figure 4.2 shows the same experiments in the New Keynesian model. The solid lines show the effects of government consumption and the dashed lines show the effects of government investment. As discussed earlier, I included features and calibrated the model specifically to mimic slack in order to raise the short-run multiplier significantly.

The impact effect on output is almost 1.3 percent for an increase in government consumption. The combination of a high fraction of rule-of-thumb consumers with imperfect labor markets counteracts the negative wealth effect on the consumption of optimizing consumers and creates a rise in aggregate consumption, as first demonstrated by Galí, López-Salido, and Vallés (2007). Private investment is not crowded out because of the adjustment costs on investment. Labor input rises robustly since it is demand-determined. The rise in labor earnings increases the consumption of the rule-of-thumb consumers.

Labor input rises by the same amount when the shock is to government investment, as shown by the dashed line. The wealth effect mechanisms in the neoclassical model that dampened the labor supply response to government investment shocks relative to government consumption in the short run are absent in this model. The other variables have a slightly more positive response to government investment than to government consumption. Output, consumption, and capital utilization all have slightly higher impact responses. As public capital is built up, private investment rises and real wages recover.

7. Because of the short horizon, discounting has only a small effect. In a later section that looks at longer horizon multipliers, I present both integral and discounted multipliers.

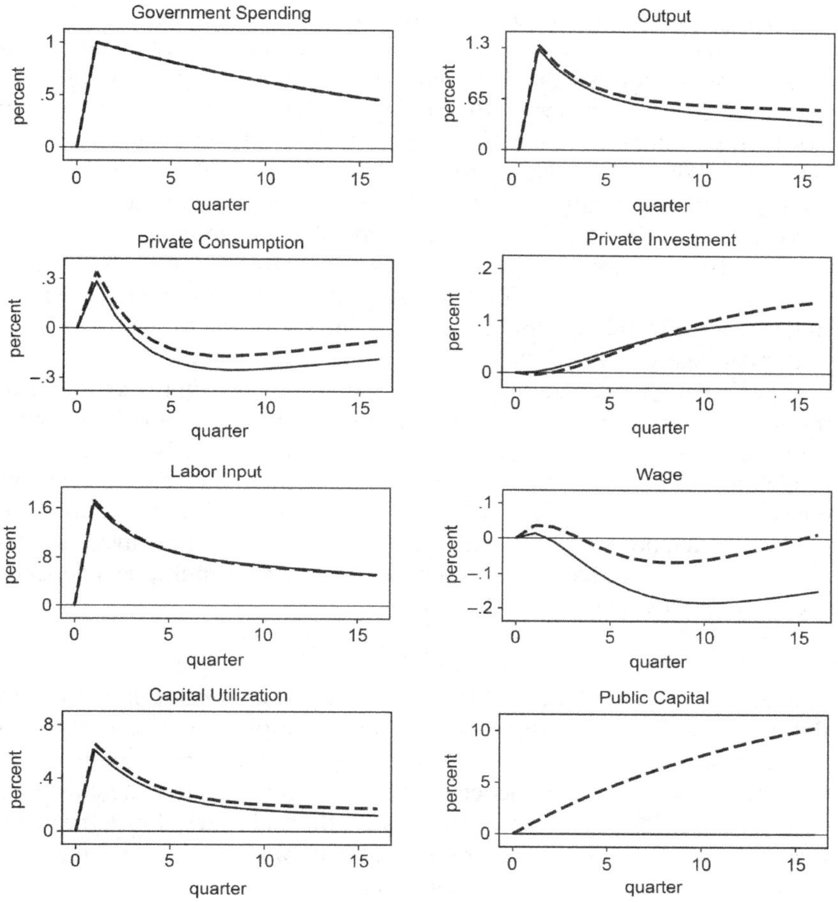


**Fig. 4.2 Effect of increases in government consumption or investment, New Keynesian model**

*Note:* Solid government consumption shock; dashed government investment shock, $\theta_G = 0.05$; Government spending, output, consumption, private investment, and public capital are expressed in deviations from steady-state value as a percent of output in steady state. Labor input and wages are percentage deviations from their own steady state values. Real interest rate is annualized percentage point deviations from its own steady state.

The bottom panel of table 4.2 shows the first-year multipliers for the New Keynesian model with $\theta_G = 0.05$. In the baseline New Keynesian model, the first-year multiplier for government consumption is 1.06 and for government investment is 1.12. The remaining rows show the multipliers for variations on the baseline New Keynesian model. Eliminating adjustment costs on investment and variable utilization significantly reduces both the government consumption and investment multipliers, so that they are even smaller than the baseline neoclassical model. I will summarize the mechanism since

I have not included graphs for these alternative parameterizations. Without adjustment costs on investment, investment is significantly crowded out on impact, much more so than in even the baseline neoclassical model. As a result, labor demand responds little on impact and thereafter rises only slowly. Real wages are approximately constant, so there is no increase in earnings to spur the consumption of the rule-of-thumb consumers. The multiplier ends up being less than in the neoclassical case because the New Keynesian model mutes the negative wealth effect on labor supply from the expected future taxes. The remaining rows show that using a lower Frisch elasticity or assuming no rule-of-thumb households also reduces the multiplier relative to the baseline case. All of the variations shown reduce the multiplier below unity.

There are three main findings from this analysis. First, in the neoclassical model the short-run government consumption multiplier is somewhat higher than the government investment multiplier. Second, in the New Keynesian model, government investment multipliers are slightly above government consumption multipliers. Third, both models are sensitive to the calibration of the Frisch labor supply elasticity and the presence of investment adjustment costs and variable capital utilization. The size of multipliers depends crucially on these features of the model.

### 4.2.5 Experiments with Time to Spend and Time to Build

Leeper, Walker, and Yang (2010) highlight two important limitations to the stimulus effects of government investment: implementation delays and future fiscal financing adjustments involving distortionary taxation. They estimate a more elaborate neoclassical model and consider the effects of these two additions. Each serves to diminish the multipliers. Since the negative effects of distortionary taxation are already well known, I will focus on the more novel feature of implementation delays.

As Leeper, Walker, and Yang (2010) point out, typically there are delays between appropriations and actual outlays. In addition, many infrastructure projects do not become part of productive capital stock until the project is completed (for example, a bridge). While routine maintenance of roads may involve delays of a year between appropriations and completion, new highways, roads, and bridges can involve delays of four years.

The American Recovery and Reinvestment Act (ARRA) illustrates how difficult it is to fast-track infrastructure project investment. The ARRA stimulus package specifically targeted "shovel-ready" projects because of the urgency for immediate government spending. Even then, there were significant delays between the appropriations, the outlays and the actual use of the new infrastructure.

Figure 4.3 shows the cumulative spending as a percent of Federal Highway Administration appropriations in the ARRA. These data are aggregated from Leduc and Wilson's (2017) state-level annual fiscal year

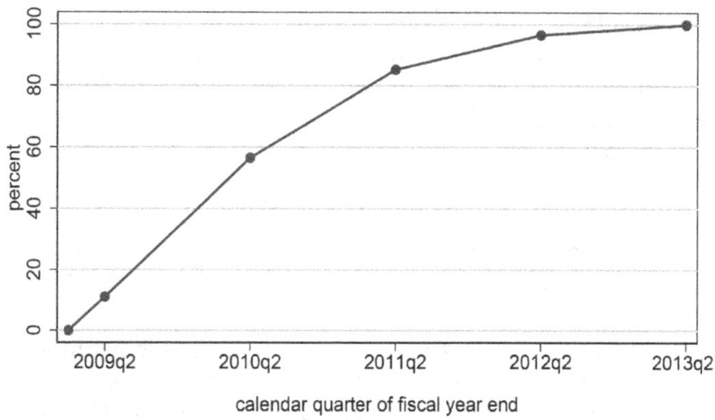


**Fig. 4.3 Federal Highway Administration outlays from the American Recovery and Reinvestment Act, cumulative percentage spent of total appropriation**

*Note:* These data are from Leduc and Wilson's (2017) replication files. I aggregated their state-level data to the national level.

data.[8] The ARRA was passed in February 2009, but by the end of June 2009 only 11 percent had been spent. By the end of June 2010, just over half had been spent. The cumulative spending did not approach 100 percent of appropriations until the end of June 2012. The mean (and median) duration of recessions in the US postwar period is 11 months, so most infrastructure stimulus would not be spent by the end of the recession. On the other hand, the unemployment rate often remains elevated for several years after a recession; for example, the unemployment rate was still 8.2 percent in mid-2012. Thus, it is possible that delayed spending might still be useful as a stimulus in a severe recession.

I now illustrate Leeper, Walker, and Yang's (2010) insight about implementation delays in the context of my models. I allow for both of the authors' delays: a delay between appropriations and outlays, which I call *time to spend*, as well as a time-to-build delay. The time-to-spend delay is captured by lags between appropriations and government investment spending as follows:

$$G_t^I = \sum_{n=1}^{N} \omega_n AP_{t-n}. \tag{9}$$

Note that because the summation begins at $n = 1$, there is a one-quarter delay between the appropriation and the start of spending. When the appropria-

8. All but four states have fiscal years that end on June 30. The remaining four states, which accounted for 18 percent of the appropriations, have fiscal years that end on September 30. Since the data are not available at higher frequency, I follow Leduc and Wilson and simply aggregate across the states and show dates on the graph that are the ending quarters for the fiscal years of the majority of the states.

tion is passed, households and firms have perfect foresight about the future path of government spending. Thus, these delays create "news" effects that can show up in behavior before government spending actually changes.

The time-to-build feature is modeled in the following replacement equation to equation (4):

$$(4') \qquad K_t^G = AP_{t-N} + (1-\delta)K_{t-1}^G.$$

I set $N = 6$ quarters and assume that $\omega_n = 1/6$ for each $n = 1, \ldots, 6$ to roughly match the peak and cumulative spending of the ARRA on government grants.[9]

Figure 4.4 shows the impact of government investment both with and without time to spend and time to build in the New Keynesian model. The dashed line repeats the no-delay case shown in figure 4.2. The dashed line with circles shows the responses when there are implementation delays. The impact of delays is dramatic. Rather than jumping 1.3 percent on impact, output now falls slightly for a quarter before rising to a peak of around 0.9 after almost two years. Rather than rising, private investment falls slightly during the first year because of the slower buildup of the public capital stock. Without the short-run increase in employment or real wages, rule-of-thumb households do not raise their consumption. As a result, the negative wealth effect on the optimizing households dominates and pushes down aggregate consumption. Thus, the time-to-spend delay knocks out the initial positive response seen in the no-delay case and the time-to-build delay slows down the positive effects of the eventual rises in public capital.

The last column of table 4.2 shows the multipliers for the case of delays. Recall that all of the multipliers are calculated relative to the integral of the appropriations response, which is identical to the no-delay government investment response but different from government investment spending when there are time-to-spend delays. In all variations of the neoclassical models and the New Keynesian models, the delay reduces the multiplier, dramatically in most cases. With delays, the neoclassical model produces greater multipliers than the New Keynesian model, though they are all still below 0.4. The features that helped the New Keynesian model produce high multipliers in the case of no delays produces zero or negative multipliers in the case of delays.

In short, in the presence of implementation lags multipliers fall to zero or even negative values.

### 4.2.6 More on Multipliers

This section covers three important additions to the discussion of multipliers from the last section. First, it presents the multipliers for longer

9. BEA NIPA series show quarterly ARRA capital grants-in-aid to states peaking in in 2010Q3 and cumulative spending at 50 percent of the total.

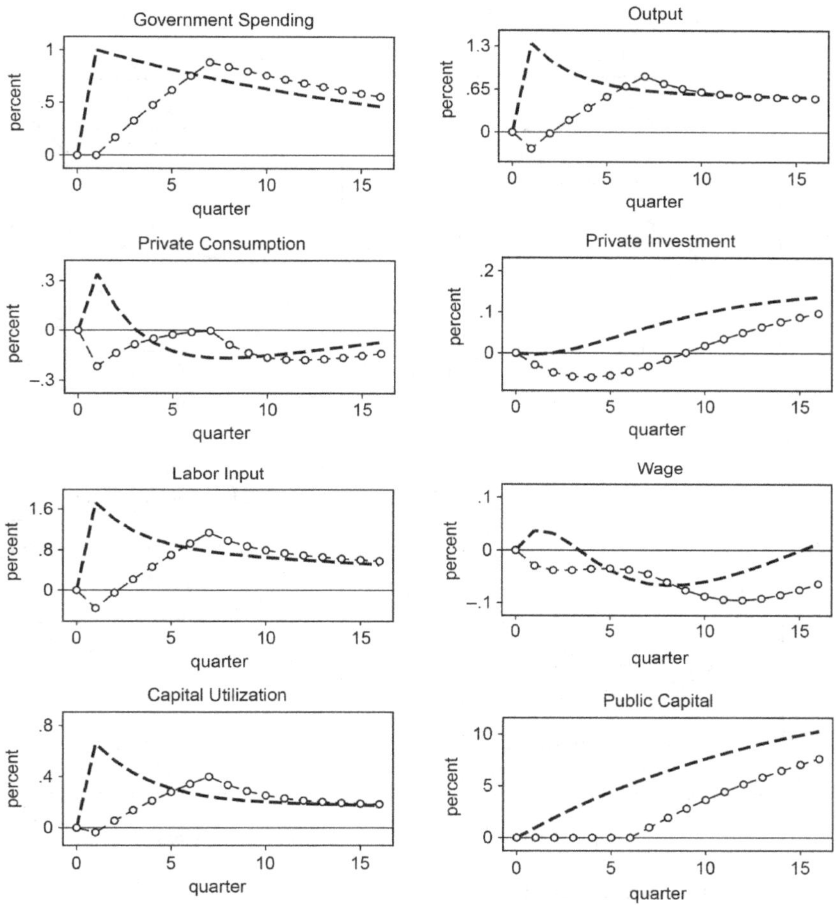


**Fig. 4.4 Effect of increases in government investment, New Keynesian Model, with time to spend and time to build**

*Note:* Dashed line government investment shock, no delays; dashed line with circles government investment with implementation delays. Government spending, output, consumption, private investment, and public capital are expressed in deviations from steady-state value as a percent of output in steady state. Labor input, utilization, and wages are percent deviations from their own steady state values.

horizons for the various models. Second, it discusses how multipliers depend crucially on the government investment-to-output ratio relative to the social optimum. Third, it adds a reminder of the importance of how public capital is financed.

Figure 4.5 shows the present discounted value cumulative multipliers for the first 20 quarters for government consumption, government investment when $\theta_G = 0.05$ (short dashed line) and when $\theta_G = 0.1$ (long dashed line).

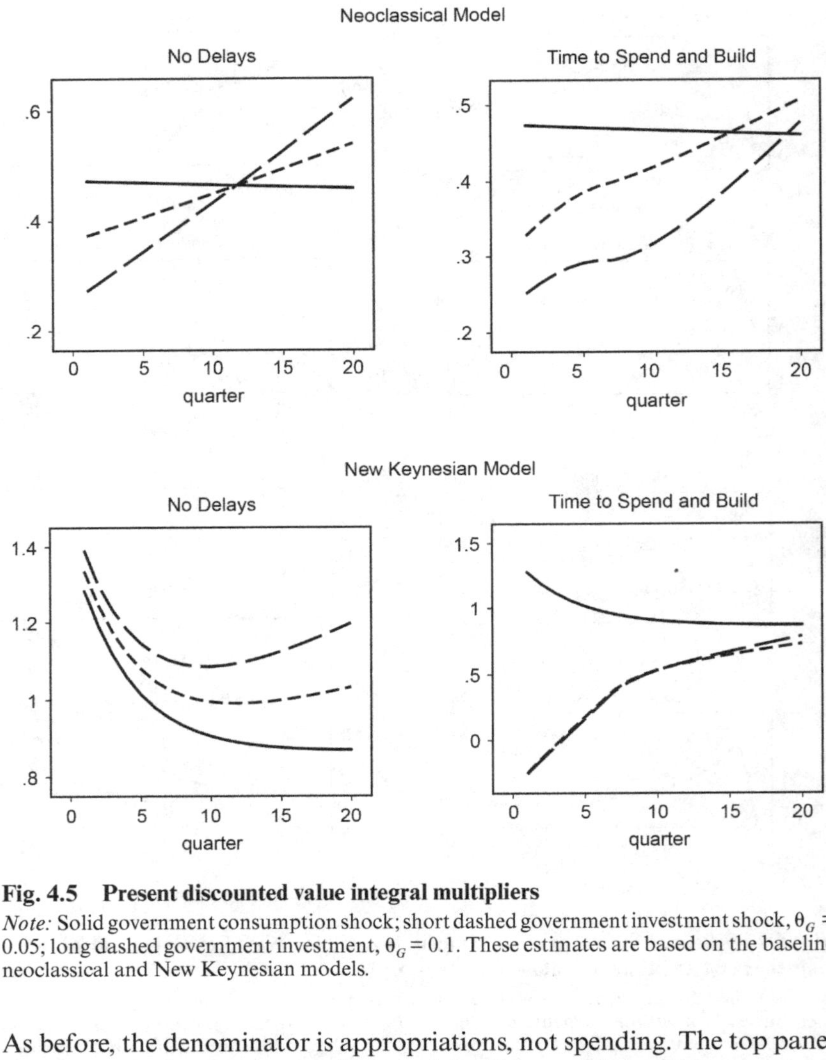


**Fig. 4.5 Present discounted value integral multipliers**

*Note:* Solid government consumption shock; short dashed government investment shock, $\theta_G = 0.05$; long dashed government investment, $\theta_G = 0.1$. These estimates are based on the baseline neoclassical and New Keynesian models.

As before, the denominator is appropriations, not spending. The top panel shows results for the neoclassical model. With no delays, the government investment multipliers are lower than the government consumption multipliers for the first 10 quarters, but then exceed them by increasing amounts as time goes on. The government investment multiplier is lower in the short run when capital is more productive (for example, $\theta_G$ is higher), since the negative wealth effect that raises labor supply is even more muted when that capital is more productive. With six-quarter time-to-spend and time-to-build delays in government infrastructure investment, the output multiplier for government investment is less than the multipliers for the government consumption for

**Table 4.3 Long-run multipliers from simulated models**

| | Present discounted value | | Undiscounted integral | |
|---|---|---|---|---|
| Model version | Neoclassical | New Keynesian | Neoclassical | New Keynesian |
| Government consumption | 0.44 | 0.89 | 0.43 | 0.90 |
| Initial steady state: government investment/GDP = 3.5% | | | | |
| No delays | | | | |
| Government investment, $\theta_G = 0.05$ | 1.3 | 1.8 | 2.4 | 3.0 |
| Government investment, $\theta_G = 0.10$ | 2.2 | 2.8 | 4.3 | 5.0 |
| 6-quarter time to spend and build | | | | |
| Government investment, $\theta_G = 0.05$ | 1.3 | 1.7 | 2.4 | 2.9 |
| Government investment, $\theta_G = 0.10$ | 2.1 | 2.5 | 4.3 | 4.9 |
| Initial steady-state: government investment/GDP = 1.5% | | | | |
| No delays | | | | |
| Government investment, $\theta_G = 0.05$ | 2.4 | 3.2 | 4.9 | 5.4 |
| Government investment, $\theta_G = 0.10$ | 4.4 | 5.4 | 9.3 | 9.8 |
| 6-quarter time to spend and build | | | | |
| Government investment, $\theta_G = 0.05$ | 2.3 | 2.9 | 4.9 | 5.3 |
| Government investment, $\theta_G = 0.10$ | 4.1 | 5.0 | 9.3 | 9.7 |

*Note:* These estimates are based on the calibrated models described in section 4.2. The multipliers are equal to the ratio of the integrals of the impulse responses of output and appropriations. PDV is present discounted value; integral is undiscounted. The top panel shows multipliers from simulations for which the steady-state government investment to GDP ratio is 3.5 percent, which matches the data. The bottom panel shows multipliers from simulations for which the steady-state ratio is 1.5 percent.

longer. Thus, evaluated only by the short-run multiplier, government infrastructure investment is inferior to government consumption investment in its potential to stimulate the economy.

The New Keynesian model results are reversed relative to the neoclassical model in the short run for the case in which there are no delays. Government investment multipliers are higher and more productive public capital leads to higher multipliers. However, delays work against the New Keynesian mechanisms and make the multipliers on government investment much lower than for government consumption for the first several years.

Table 4.3 shows the long-run multipliers for each of the cases. Here is where government investment spending has its great advantages. Consider only the top half of the table for now. While the present value long-run multiplier for government consumption ranges from 0.4 in the neoclassical model to 0.9 in the New Keynesian model, it ranges from 1.3 to almost 2 when $\theta_G = 0.05$ and from 2 to almost 3 when $\theta_G = 0.1$. Time-to-spend and time-to-build delays do not have much effect on the long-run multipliers. Discounting has noticeable effects, as illustrated in the last columns showing undiscounted integral multipliers. In those cases, the government investment multiplier is higher and the neoclassical multiplier is not as far below the New Keynesian multiplier.

All of the multipliers I have shown, however, are based on raising government investment spending relative to a steady state with the government investment-to-output ratio of 3.5 percent, which was calibrated to the value for the US in 2019. Leeper, Walker, and Yang (2010) calibrated their values similarly. It turns out that the multiplier depends significantly on whether the steady state value of the government investment to GDP ratio is above or below the socially optimal value of public investment.[10]

The expression for the optimal steady-state ratio of government capital and investment to GDP in the neoclassical model is as follows:[11]

$$\text{(10)} \qquad \frac{K_G}{Y} = \frac{1}{\beta^{-1} - 1 + \delta_G} \cdot \theta_G$$

$$\text{(11)} \qquad \frac{G^I}{Y} = \frac{\delta_G}{\beta^{-1} - 1 + \delta_G} \cdot \theta_G .$$

Recall that $K_G$ is public capital, $G^I$ is government investment, $Y$ is output, $\beta$ is the discount rate of the representative household, $\delta_G$ is the depreciation rate on public capital, and $\theta_G$ is the exponent on public capital in the aggregate production function. The economic intuition is straightforward: the higher is the intrinsic productivity of public capital, the greater should be the ratio of public capital to output and hence the higher the steady-state ratio of public investment to output to maintain that level. Using the calibration from the stylized model, the fraction multiplying $\theta_G$ in the capital ratio equation is equal to 49 (if output is measured quarterly) or 12.5 (if output is annualized), and in the investment ratio equation is 0.49. If $\theta_G = 0.05$, as in the baseline calibration of the model, the optimal public investment to output ratio is 2.5 percent; if $\theta_G = 0.1$, it is 5 percent. Thus, the simulations of the previous sections are all based on starting from a point at which the steady-state ratio of government investment to GDP is above the social optimum if $\theta_G = 0.05$ but below the social optimum if $\theta_G = 0.1$.

The bottom half of table 4.3 illustrates the impact on the multipliers if the simulations are re-run starting from a steady state in which the government investment to GDP ratio is much lower, 1.5 percent rather than the 3.5 percent of the top half of the table. Consider first the simulations for $\theta_G = 0.05$. The present discounted value multipliers in the bottom half of the panel are 60 to 80 percent greater, depending on the model. For example, with no delays the New Keynesian multiplier is 1.8 when the economy starts out at the higher government investment to output ratio, but 3.2 when it starts out at the lower ratio. The undiscounted multipliers are 90 to 110 percent higher.

10. I am indebted to Chris House for suggesting I explore this possibility.
11. See the appendix for the derivation of these equations.

The changes are even more dramatic when $\theta_G = 0.1$. The optimal ratio of government investment to GDP is 5 percent, so the starting point of the economy at 1.5 percent is very far below the optimum. In this case, present discounted value multipliers and undiscounted multipliers roughly double.

In sum, these results illustrate the importance of considering where the economy starts relative to the socially optimal amount of public capital in evaluating multipliers. In the long run, multipliers will be substantially higher if the economy starts from a steady state in which the government investment ratio to GDP is below the social optimum. In the short run, the effects are smaller and can be flipped if there is a wealth effect on labor supply.

Finally, it is important to remember that all of the simulations are based on the assumption of nondistortionary lump-sum taxes to pay off the government debt. This assumption was made in part to capture short-run multipliers relevant for stimulus programs that are financed by deficits in the short run. Adding more realistic distortionary taxation at longer horizons, however, dramatically lowers the multipliers. For example, Leeper, Walker, and Yang (2010) show that in the baseline no-delay case with $\theta_G = 0.05$ of their model, the present-value cumulative multiplier for government investment is 0.39 when taxes are distortionary but 0.93 when the authors assume counterfactually that taxes are lump sum.

### 4.2.7 Comparison to the Literature

This section gives an overview of some of the results from models in the literature. I first discuss reasons for any differences relative to the results of my simulations. I then briefly discuss the rich models from the transportation and trade literatures that incorporate more of the details of transportation infrastructure. Finally, I discuss the importance of monetary accommodation and the zero lower bound on interest rates for the size of short-run multipliers.

Table 4.4 summarizes multipliers from four neoclassical analyses of the effects of government spending. Baxter and King's (1993) long-run multipliers illustrate the amplifying effects of permanent increases in government spending and higher productivity of capital on multipliers. Leeper, Walker, and Yang's (2010) multipliers illustrate the dampening effect of distortionary taxation and lower Frisch elasticities on multipliers. Nevertheless, the result that the long-run multiplier for government investment is greater than for government consumption in a neoclassical model is robust to these details.

The third panel of table 4.4 shows details of the work of Ercolani and Valle e Azevedo (2014), who estimate a medium-scale model that has many features similar to a New Keynesian model (such as price and wage markups) but no nominal rigidities. Their paper is unique in its estimation (rather than calibration) of $\theta_G$. They estimate a value of $\theta_G = 0.09$, though they favor results from an alternative model in which they set $\theta_G$ to be 0, implying that public capital is unproductive.

Table 4.4 Summary of some neoclassical models from the literature

| Paper feature summary | Experiment | Government investment multiplier |
|---|---|---|
| Baxter and King (1993) | Permanent increase in $G$ | |
| Calibrated | Long-run multipliers | |
| Lump-sum taxation | $\theta_G = 0$ | 1.2 |
| | $\theta_G = 0.05$ | 2.6 |
| | $\theta_G = 0.40$ | 13.0 |
| Leeper, Walker, and Yang (2010) | AR(1) parameter 0.95 | |
| Estimated | Short run, no delays | 0.5 |
| Investment adjustment costs, utilization | Short run, 3 year delays | 0.1–0.3 |
| Distortionary tax response | Long run, across delay times | |
| Calibrated $\theta_G = 0.05$ or 0.10 | $\theta_G = 0.05$ | 0.3–0.4 |
| | $\theta_G = 0.1$ | 0.9–1.1 |
| Ercolani and Valle e Azevedo (2014) | AR(1) parameter 0.94 | |
| Estimated | Preferred estimate $\theta_G = 0$ | |
| Features similar to medium New Keynesian | 4-quarter | 0.8 |
| but no nominal rigidities | Long run | 0.4 |
| Distortionary tax, balanced budget | Unconstrained estim. $\theta_G = 0.09$ | |
| Nonseparable utility in C and G | 4-quarter | 0.8 |
| | Long run | 3.6 |
| Gallen and Winston (2019) | Multipliers calibrated to CEA | |
| Calibrated, transport infrastructure | Long-run US | 1.5 |
| Time to build | Long-run Japan | 0.9 |
| Short-run disruption from construction | | |
| Better transport saves household time | | |
| $\theta_G = 0.038$ | | |

The final panel of table 4.4 shows details of recent work by Gallen and Winston (2019), which represents an important step forward in the way it incorporates features unique to transportation infrastructure into a dynamic macroeconomic model. They include time-to-build delays, short-run disruptions of construction to the utilization of existing infrastructure, and the beneficial effects of improved transportation infrastructure on household time savings. Their model implies that infrastructure spending is not a good short-run stimulus, even when the long-run benefits are very positive.

Not shown in the table are the important models from the geography of trade literature, which takes transportation costs and spatial features seriously in modeling the potential benefits of transportation infrastructure. The quantitative analyses in these models directly model and measure the extent to which transportation infrastructure reduces trade costs between two points, opens access to markets, and allows for a variety of spillovers, agglomeration effects, and congestion effects. This literature, which is also known as "Quantitative Spatial Economics," has been surveyed recently by Redding and Turner (2015) and Redding and Rossi-Hansberg (2017). Recent

**Table 4.5 Summary of some New Keynesian models from the literature**

| Paper feature summary | Experiment | Government investment multiplier |
|---|---|---|
| Coenen et al. (2012) | 2-year stimulus, deficits | |
| Large-scale policy models | Instantaneous multipliers | |
| + 2 academic models | No monetary accommodation | 0.9 |
| US | 1-year monetary accommodation | 1.1 |
| | 2-year monetary accommodation | 1.6 |
| Drautzburg and Uhlig (2015) | ARRA, distortionary taxation later | |
| Estimated medium-scale model | Short-run multiplier | 0.2–0.5 |
| Distortionary taxes, respond to debt | Long-run multiplier | 0.3 |
| Calibrated $\theta_G = 0.023$ | | |
| Bouakez, Guillard, and Roulleau-Pasdeloup (2017) | AR(1) parameter 0.8 | |
| Calibrated | Impact multipliers | |
| No private capital (in baseline model) | Normal times, across delays | 0.8–0.9 |
| Lump-sum taxes | ZLB, no delays | 1.8 |
| Time to build, $\theta_G = 0.08$ | ZLB, 4-year time-to-build delays | 4 |
| Sims and Wolff (2018) | | |
| Estimated medium-scale model | AR(1) parameter 0.93 | |
| Distortionary taxes, respond to debt | 1- to 2-year multipliers | 0.7–0.8 |
| Nonseparable utility in C and G | | |
| Calibrated $\theta_G = 0.05$ | | |
| Boehm (2020) | AR(1) parameter 0.86 | |
| Calibrated model, 2-sectors (C, I) | Short-run multiplier (0 to 20 quarters) | 0.1–0.2 |
| Imperfect labor mobility | Long-run multiplier | 1.6 |
| Lump-sum taxes $\theta_G = 0.05$ | | |

contributions include those by Donaldson and Hornbeck (2016), who revisit Fogel's (1964) classic analyses of the contributions of railroads to US economic growth; Donaldson (2018), who studies the impact of railroads in India during the Raj; and Allen and Arkolakis (2019), who develop a new geographic framework and use it to study the welfare effects of improving each segment of the US highway system.

Table 4.5 summarizes several analyses from the New Keynesian literature. Many of these studies were conducted in response to the financial crisis and the stimulus programs adopted in response. I now highlight a key result from this literature that was not part of my experiments: the importance of monetary accommodation.

In New Keynesian models, the degree of monetary accommodation has important effects on short-run multipliers. As the Coenen et al. (2012) experiments show, the instantaneous multiplier for a two-year government investment stimulus is 0.9 for a standard Taylor rule but 1.6 if the stimulus is accompanied by monetary accommodation. When monetary policy is accommodative, the central bank does not raise nominal interest rates to combat inflation. As a result, real interest rates decrease.

The result that government spending multipliers are higher when monetary policy is accommodative is closely linked to the effects of government spending at the zero lower bound (ZLB) of interest rates. When interest rates are at their zero lower bound, the monetary authority cannot lower nominal interest rates. However, carefully timed fiscal spending stimulus that lasts no longer than the zero lower bound period can generate higher expected future inflation. These expectations lower the ex ante real interest rate and spur economic activity during the ZLB period. It is this mechanism, identified by Woodford (2011) and others, that can lead to high government spending multipliers at the ZLB.

This same mechanism leads to an unusual additional result, first highlighted by Eggertsson (2011). A negative supply shock, which in normal times would result in a fall in output, is predicted to stimulate output during a ZLB period. The negative supply shock generates higher expected inflation, which lowers the real interest rate and spurs demand.

Bouakez, Guillard, and Roulleau-Pasdeloup (2017, 2019) demonstrate that this mechanism can lead to a further reversal of New Keynesian results when the economy is at the ZLB. Recall from the earlier simulations that introducing time-to-build delays in public capital drastically lowered the short-run multiplier on government investment spending in the New Keynesian model during normal times. The authors show, however, that when the economy is at the ZLB, longer time-to-build delays lead to *higher* short-run multipliers. Time-to-build delays prevent increases in the public capital stock (which are a positive supply shock) from occurring during the ZLB period, which helps counter any deflationary pressures. Their impact multipliers are 1.8 for government investment with no time-to-build delay, and 4 for government investment when there is a four-year time-to-build delay.

The possible expansionary effects of negative supply shocks at the ZLB are not just a sideshow with respect to implications for optimal fiscal policy. The same mechanism also predicts that raising distortionary income taxes (a negative supply shock) at the ZLB is expansionary, as Eggertsson (2011), Woodford (2011), and Drautzburg and Uhlig (2015) demonstrate in both simple calibrated New Keynesian models and estimated medium-scale New Keynesian models. Thus, if ZLB effects generate higher government investment multipliers when there are time-to-build delays, ZLB effects raise government investment multipliers even more if the spending is financed by increases in current distortionary taxation rather than by deficits. This uncomfortable prediction is probably not understood by many who believe that spending multipliers are higher at the ZLB.

Some recent work has questioned this ZLB mechanism, however. First, Dupor and Li (2015) do not find evidence of the generated inflation effect, and Bachmann, Berg, and Sims (2015) do not find an impact of individual consumer inflation expectations on their spending propensities in the Michigan Survey of Consumers. Second, evidence contradicts the prediction that negative supply shocks are expansionary at the ZLB. For example, Wieland (2019) tests this prediction by studying the impacts of the earthquake and tsunami as well as the effect of oil price shocks in Japan, a country which has been at the ZLB for decades. He finds that these negative supply shocks were contractionary, contradicting the prediction of New Keynesian theory.

That said, there is some empirical support for higher multipliers being higher during ZLB periods. In Ramey and Zubairy (2018) we estimate multipliers around 1.4 at the ZLB in historical data if we exclude periods of World War II rationing. Miyamoto, Nguyen, and Sergeyev (2018) apply Ramey and Zubairy's methods to Japan and find higher multipliers at the ZLB, around 1.5 on impact. Further, as discussed later, Boehm (2020) finds some evidence for higher multipliers for government investment spending at the ZLB. Thus, whatever the mechanism, multipliers may be higher at the ZLB.

## 4.3 Empirical Evidence on the Long-Run Effects of Public Capital and Infrastructure

This section begins by reviewing some of the leading estimates of the elasticity of output to public capital, with a focus on the long run. It then uses the stylized neoclassical model to illustrate the two leading methodological challenges: (i) the distinction between production function elasticities and general equilibrium steady-state elasticities and (ii) the endogeneity of public capital. I illustrate the econometric problems by estimating the effects of public capital on artificial data generated by a simple extension of the model in section 4.2.1. Finally, I discuss a promising way to address the challenges and present some initial estimates that emerge.

### 4.3.1 An Overview of Existing Estimates

There is a long literature that seeks to measure the returns to infrastructure investment. An early example is Fogel's (1964) pioneering analysis of the contributions of railroads to US economic development. Several decades later, Aschauer's (1988, 1989) famous hypothesis that the productivity slowdown in industrialized countries was caused by reductions in infrastructure investment led to renewed research in this area. Aschauer estimated an aggregate production function and found an elasticity of output to public capital of 0.39 in US data. Munnell's (1990) extension of Aschauer's work found similar results, with elasticities between 0.31 and 0.39. Bom and Ligthart's (2014) excellent literature review discusses the variety of estimates of the production function elasticity of output to public capital and conducts an insightful meta-analysis. Their meta-analysis settles on a mean production function elasticity of output to public capital of 0.08 in the short run and 0.12 in the long run. They find that the elasticity is higher for public capital installed by local or regional governments and for core infrastructure. The mean estimate of the output elasticity for these latter types of public capital is 0.19 in the long-run.

Cubas (forthcoming) estimates the production function elasticity of output to public capital using information from the national income and product accounts combined with marginal product relationships. He finds an estimate of 0.09 for the US. Ercolani and Valle e Azevedo (2014) are perhaps the only researchers to estimate the production function elasticity of output to public capital in a medium-scale dynamic general equilibrium macroeconomics model. They find that when they incorporate both public capital and allow government consumption to be a substitute or complement to private consumption, the estimate of the production function elasticity to public capital is 0.09. Owing to significant uncertainty surrounding that estimate and other indications of model fit, however, the researchers' preferred specification is one in which the elasticity is constrained to zero.

The empirical macroeconomics literature tends to focus on estimates of output *multipliers*. Much of the recent macroeconomics literature has focused on short-run effects of general government spending, but several papers also provide estimates for long-run multipliers on government investment spending. For example, Ilzetzki, Mendoza, and Végh (2013) use structural vector autoregressions on a panel of countries to study the effects of government spending in a wide range of circumstances. They use standard Cholesky decompositions to identify shocks, and when the authors focus on government investment they find multipliers for public investment that range between 0.4 in the short run to 1.6 in the long run.

Some of the most convincing evidence of the productivity of public capital has used US regional or industry variation to estimate the output effects of road construction in the US. It is important to note that these estimates give only relative effects, because aggregate effects are typically taken out by constant terms or time-fixed effects. Fernald (1999) exploits the differences in benefits of the US Interstate Highway System across industries. He specifically models transportation services as an input into the production function, taking into account the complementarity between vehicles owned by the industries and roads and the difference in uses across industries. He finds that industries that rely more heavily on transportation experienced greater increases in productivity than other industries as a result of the building of the US Interstate Highway System. Using additional identifying assumptions, he translates his relative estimates into a production function elasticity of output to roads of 0.35, an estimate similar to Aschauer's (1989) estimate. However, Fernald argues that the effects are not large enough to be the principal explanation of the productivity slowdown.

Leff Yaffe (2020) uses state panel data and narrative evidence to estimate the output effects of the building of the US Interstate Highway System, accounting for anticipation effects and crowding in of state and local spending on roads. His multiplier estimates are significantly affected by the estimated "crowd-in" of state highway spending. In particular, an infusion of funds to a state (instrumented using Bartik-style instruments) typically led to additional road building to connect to the Interstate Highway System. When he includes the additional state and local spending in the government spending measure, Leff Yaffe's long-run relative multiplier estimate is 1.8.

Leduc and Wilson (2013) estimate the effects of federal highway grants to states during more recent times using annual state-level data starting in the 1990s. The authors report various long-run (10-year) multipliers. Their favored ones are just under 2.

The estimates are mixed for emerging economies. Cubas (forthcoming) studies the contribution of public capital across countries using a growth accounting framework that specifically incorporates its nonrival features. He finds some contribution of public capital to explaining cross-country income differences, but the magnitude depends on the degree of congestion of public capital. Henry and Gardner (2019) survey the evidence across numerous countries and conclude that in only a minority do infrastructure projects, such as paved roads and electricity, clear the required hurdles. On the other hand, Izquierdo et al. (2019) use a variety of identification methods and samples and find that the multiplier on public investment is very high in countries that start with low levels of public capital.

### 4.3.2 Production Function versus General Equilibrium Output Elasticities

Earlier sections illustrated the importance of the production function elasticity of output to public capital for the effects of government investment. In this section and the next, I highlight two major challenges associated with estimating this key production function parameter. The first is associated with the difference between the production function elasticity and the steady-state general equilibrium elasticity. The second is the problem of the endogeneity of public capital spending. I illustrate the challenges by comparing the approaches used in three leading sets of papers: (1) Aschauer's (1989) and Munnell's (1990) static production function estimates; (2) Pereira and Frutos's (1999) and Pereira's (2000) structural vector autoregression estimates; and (3) Bouakez, Guillard, and Roulleau-Pasdeloup's (2017) TFP and cointegrating relation estimates.

Aschauer (1989) and Munnell (1990) and much of the literature that followed estimated production elasticities using log levels of contemporaneous variables. These authors regressed the logarithm of aggregate output on the logarithms of contemporaneous values of labor, private capital, and public capital, or transformed the equation to regress productivity measures on public capital. Thus, temporarily leaving aside the endogeneity issues that I will discuss in the next section, these authors were estimating the production function elasticity, $\theta_G$ from the production function in equation (3) (section 4.2.1). In log form, that equation becomes

$$(12) \qquad \ln(Y_t) = \ln(A_t) + \alpha \cdot \ln(K_{t-1}) + (1-\alpha) \cdot \ln(N_t) + \theta_G \cdot \ln(K^G_{t-1}).$$

$\theta_G$ is the partial derivative of the log of output with respect to the log of public capital. To estimate the partial derivative, the regression must control for the contemporanous values of the private inputs.[12]

Let us now compare their method and results to the analysis by Pereira and Flores de Frutos (1999), denoted "PF" in the following exposition, who used structural vector autoregression (SVAR) to estimate the output elasticity to public capital.[13] PF noted several possible problems with the estimation method of Aschauer and Munnell, including issues of possible spurious regression (e.g. because the macroeconomic variables are nonstationary), omission of dynamic feedbacks, and possible simultaneous equation bias. PF sought to address all three of these issues by using an SVAR to estimate the elasticity of output to public capital. First, the authors tested and found unit roots in the logs of output, labor, and the two capital stocks. The authors could find no evidence of cointegration, so they estimated their system in first differences to avoid spurious regression. Second, PF's use of the SVAR allowed complete dynamics. Third, PF allowed for reverse causality from output and the other variables to public capital and identified exogenous movements in public capital as the innovation to public capital not explained by lagged values of the other endogenous variables; in other words, they used a Cholesky decomposition to identify the exogenous shock.

Pereira and Flores de Frutos (1999) fully recognized that they were estimating a different elasticity from the one estimated by Aschauer and Munnell. PF's headline number is a long-run elasticity of private output to public capital of 0.63.[14] This elasticity of output to public capital estimated by PF is not, however, the production function elasticity $\theta_G$. The production function elasticity of output to public capital, $\theta_G$, is the elasticity of output to an increase in public capital, holding TFP, labor, and capital constant. There is another elasticity of output to public capital, however, that includes the endogenous response of the private inputs to public capital in general equilibrium.

12. See Bom and Ligthart (2014) for a more detailed discussion.

13. Bom and Ligthart (2014) briefly survey the SVAR studies, but exclude them from their meta-analysis of output elasticity estimates. As I will demonstrate shortly, this was the correct decision given their focus on production function estimates. See Bom and Ligthart (2014) footnote 15 for a list of papers that use SVAR methods.

14. To obtain this number, PF first estimate the impulse responses of all the endogenous variables, including public capital, to their identified exogenous shock to public capital. The authors then calculate the long-run elasticity (shown in their Table 6) as the ratio of the impulse response of log output at 5 to 10 years to the impulse response of log public capital at 5 to 10 years, since both impulse responses have stabilized at their new levels by that time. Those impulse responses are shown in their figure 1.

The increase in public capital raises the marginal products of private inputs, which leads to incentives to accumulate more private capital. It is this elasticity that PF estimate. PF's impulse response function estimates show that private capital also rises permanently. (Employment bounces around in the short run but then returns to a level slightly above its former value.) Because private capital is allowed to respond, PF's elasticity is not the production function elasticity.

The relationship between the production function elasticity and the steady-state output elasticity can be derived from the neoclassical model presented in section 4.2.1.[15] In particular, the steady-state output elasticity to government capital, $\varepsilon^{SS}_{YK_G}$, is

$$(13) \qquad \varepsilon^{SS}_{YK_G} = \frac{1}{1+\Omega} \cdot \left[\Omega + \frac{1}{1-\alpha} \cdot \theta_G\right], \text{ where } \Omega = \frac{1}{1+\phi} \cdot \frac{\delta_G \cdot K_G}{C}.$$

$1/(1 + \phi)$ is the Hicks elasticity of labor supply, $\delta_G$ is the depreciation rate on public capital, and $K_G/C$ is the ratio of public capital to consumption.

If we use the calibration of the baseline neoclassical model from section 4.2.1, the relationship is given by

$$(14) \qquad \varepsilon^{SS}_{YK_G} = 0.043 + 1.49 \cdot \theta_G.$$

The constant term is positive because, even when public capital is not productive (that is, $\theta_G = 0$), labor supply increases and consumption falls relative to output because of the negative wealth effects. Thus, the steady-state elasticity of output to steady-state public capital is always greater than the elasticity of output to public capital in the production function. Most of this difference is due to the negative wealth effect raising labor supply, and part is due to the induced investment in private capital, which grows as $\theta_G$ rises.

We can use this relationship to calculate what Pereira and Frutos's (1999) estimated elasticity would imply for the value of $\theta_G$. Their long-run elasticity of 0.63, which allows private inputs to respond, is the general equilibrium steady-state elasticity. Equation (14) implies that $\theta_G$ is 0.39—exactly equal to Aschauer's estimate! Thus, Aschauer's (1989) production function output elasticity maps exactly to PF's long-run general equilibrium elasticity of output. According to the stylized model, the latter estimate should be larger because private inputs are also responding.

### 4.3.3 The Econometric Problem of Endogenous Capital

The endogeneity of public capital is a potentially serious problem, recognized by many researchers. Aschauer (1989) used ordinary least squares (OLS) for his main estimates but attempted to deal with possible reverse

15. This expression incorporates the assumption that the social planner also raises government consumption to maintain a constant steady-state government consumption-to-output ratio.

causality by using lagged endogenous variables as instruments. Using lagged endogenous variables as instruments was a common practice in the late 1980s but is now known to require implausible exclusion restrictions in most macroeconomic applications.

The simultaneity problem occurs because larger and more wealthy economies invest in more public capital. In fact, since a benevolent social planner should choose a level of public capital that maximizes the discounted utility of the representative household, it should respond to technological progress by increasing the amount of public capital.

We can make this point concrete by using what I have called a "DSGE Monte Carlo" (Ramey 2016). The idea is to simulate artificial data from a dynamic stochastic general equilibrium (DSGE) model for which we know the "true" parameters and then apply an estimation method to the artificial data to see whether it can recover the true parameters.

To be specific, I generalize the calibrated neoclassical model to allow the social planner to choose the optimal level of public capital, based on maximizing the discounted utility of the representative household.[16] I use the baseline calibration with $\theta_G = 0.05$. I then allow technology, $A$ in equation (3), to vary. Because an increase in $A$ raises the marginal product of public capital, a social planner will respond by raising public capital. Since I am interested in long-run effects, I calculate how steady-state values of the key variables change with changes in technology.

I estimate a regression similar to the one used by Bouakez, Guillard, and Roulleau-Pasdeloup (2017). In particular, rather than regressing output itself on the inputs, they use Fernald's (2014) measure of TFP as the dependent variable. Fernald makes very general assumptions and carefully measures TFP at the industry level using factor shares and then aggregates them to get aggregate TFP. He also adjusts it for cyclical utilization. In the context of the simple aggregate production function in my model, Fernald's measure is defined as follows:

$$\ln(\text{TFP}) = \ln(Y_t) - \alpha \ln(K_t) - (1 - \alpha)\ln(N_t). \tag{15}$$

Log TFP is defined as log output less share-weighted log private capital and labor.[17] This definition and the production function from equation (3) implies the following relationship between Fernald's measure of TFP and public capital:

$$\ln(\text{TFP}) = \ln(A_t) + \theta_G \cdot \ln(K_t^G). \tag{16}$$

16. Note that the social planner problem is not concave, since I assume constant returns in the private inputs, so existence and uniqueness are not guaranteed. See Glomm and Ravikumar (1994, 1997) for a thorough analysis of model in which the government chooses the public capital optimally. My explorations with the simple model suggest that there exists a unique maximum of the social planner problem, as long as $\theta_G$ is not too large.

17. Fernald (1999) performs the calculation in growth rates, as is standard for Solow residuals. However, these can be integrated to obtain log levels.

Thus, Fernald's (2014) TFP measure consists of both true level of technology, $\ln(A)$, and the effects of public capital.

Suppose we regress Fernald's log TFP measure on the log of public capital. Since true technology is not observed, it shows up in the error term of the regression—that is, the $\varepsilon_t$ in

$$\ln(\text{TFP}) = \theta_G \cdot \ln(K_t^G) + \varepsilon_t. \tag{17}$$

Bouakez, Guillard, and Roulleau-Pasdeloup (2017) estimate the regression as a cointegrating equation.[18] I will describe more details of their procedure later.

In the artificial data I generate from my model, I calculate the measure of TFP as the log of output minus the share-weighted logs of private capital and labor, just as Fernald does. I set the weights equal to the actual shares from the model. I then regress the log of TFP measure on the log of public capital using the artificial data generated by the model. Recall that I am focusing only on steady-state equilibrium values.

This regression produces an estimate of $\theta_G$ equal to 0.64, which is severely biased upward relative to the true value of 0.05. The reason for the upward bias is intuitive. When there is an increase in technology, $A$, the marginal product of all inputs increases. As a result, private agents increase private capital and the social planner increases public capital. Thus, the error term $\varepsilon_t$ in equation (17) is positively correlated with public capital.

One could in principle solve the problem by using instrumental variables, but it is difficult to find instruments for public capital in aggregate data. Bouakez, Guillard, and Roulleau-Pasdeloup (2017), however, employ a method that reduces the upward bias significantly. Although they do not discuss endogeneity issues, their method goes far to reduce this type of bias. I now describe their method.

In a short discussion section at the end of their quantitative model paper, Bouakez, Guillard, and Roulleau-Pasdeloup (2017) review the literature on the productivity of public capital and then present some independent evidence using US aggregate data. They use Fernald's (2014) TFP measure to avoid estimating a complete production function. They then add that "it is still important to account for the additional factors that may affect TFP in the long run" (Bouakez, Guillard, and Roulleau-Pasdeloup 2017, 75) but do not explain why it is important. The DSGE Monte Carlo analysis I developed earlier provides the perfect motivation: any changes in measured TFP (apart from public capital) are likely to lead the government to change public capital endogenously. Thus, in order to reduce the bias in the regression in equation (17), one should control for as many sources of TFP as possible in order to remove them from the error term, $\varepsilon$. Bouakez, Guillard, and Roulleau-Pasdeloup (2017) construct measures of the stock of

18. As surveyed by Bom and Ligthart (2014), several researchers have estimated cointegrating equations, but the applications were for other countries or panel data across sectors.

research and development spending and the stock of human capital. Their finding of cointegration between the log level of Fernald's TFP, log public capital, log R&D stock, and log human capital is strong evidence that they have identified the key drivers of TFP.

Pereira and Flores de Frutos (1999) estimated their model in first-differences because they could not find cointegration. Bouakez, Guillard, and Roulleau-Pasdeloup's (2017) analysis shows that more key variables needed to be included. By estimating the cointegration equation, Bouakez, Guillard, and Roulleau-Pasdeloup (2017) are picking up the long-run, presumably steady-state, relationships because the estimates are driven by the stochastic trends.[19] Bouakez, Guillard, and Roulleau-Pasdeloup's main estimates, shown in their table 2, imply a production function elasticity of output to public capital of 0.065.

We can shed light on the extent to which Bouakez, Guillard, and Roulleau-Pasdeloup's procedure reduces the upward bias in actual data. In particular, we can reestimate their equation, omitting the other determinants of TFP (the R&D stock and human capital stock), and see how the estimated coefficient on log public capital changes.

Using Bouakez, Guillard, and Roulleau-Pasdeloup's replication files, I estimate their equation on their data but omit their controls for TFP. The result is an estimate of the coefficient on the log of public capital of 0.33, in contrast to their estimate of 0.065. My estimate is much higher and is closer to the original estimates of Aschauer and Munnell. The difference between these two estimates is perfectly explained by the type of bias I just demonstrated in my DSGE Monte Carlo. Bouakez, Guillard, and Roulleau-Pasdeloup's controls for other factors affecting TFP go far to reduce the bias.

Using these variables as controls, however, may lead Bouakez, Guillard, and Roulleau-Pasdeloup's estimates to be *downward biased*. Government investment is likely a key driver of both the R&D stock and human capital—in other words, public capital affects $A$ in the stylized model—so it is not appropriate to simply include these two variables as controls. Thus, Bouakez, Guillard, and Roulleau-Pasdeloup's estimate is very likely a lower bound on the value of $\theta_G$.

These exercises have illustrated the difficulties in estimating the production function output elasticity to public capital. Obtaining unbiased estimates is difficult, because almost everything is endogenous.

## 4.4 Empirical Evidence on the Short-Run Effects of Government Investment in Public Capital

During the Great Recession, government infrastructure spending received much attention because of its possible role in stimulating the economy.

19. See King et al. (1987) for a discussion of the role of stochastic trends in long-run growth. The 1987 NBER working paper version is much more complete than the 1991 *American Economic Review* version.

The American Recovery and Reinvestment Act, enacted in early 2009 in the depths of the Great Recession, used both transfers and government purchases to try to stimulate the economy. Infrastructure spending was an important component of the purchases. "Shovel-ready" projects were specifically targeted because the need for immediate government spending was urgent. As shown earlier in figure 4.3, the delays in spending were nevertheless substantial.

As I discussed in section 4.2.5, the theoretical evidence suggests that, dollar for dollar, government investment spending has lower short-run stimulus effects than government consumption. The next sections review the empirical evidence.

### 4.4.1 Aggregate Evidence

Pereira and Flores de Frutos (1999), reviewed in detail in the discussion of long-run estimates in section 4.3, also studied the short-run effects. The authors found negative short-run effects of infrastructure spending on employment in all of their specifications. This fact, coupled with the recognition of the delays in investment, led the authors to recommend against using public investment for short-run stimulus. They argued that it could actually be counterproductive.

As discussed earlier, Ilzetzki, Mendoza, and Végh (2013) used structural vector autoregressions on a panel of countries to study the effects of government spending in a wide range of circumstances. When they focused on government investment they found multipliers for public investment around 0.4 in the short-run.

The work of Boehm (2020), which I discussed in the last section for its quantitative model predictions, tests those predictions using a panel of member countries of the Organisation for Economic Co-operation and Development (OECD). Recall that his key economic insight is that government investment should have a lower short-run multiplier than government consumption because the elasticity of intertemporal substitution for investment is much higher than for consumption. This feature means that government investment spending crowds out private investment spending to a much greater extent than government consumption spending crowds out private consumption. He tests this prediction of his model using a panel of OECD countries from 2003 to 2016. He identifies exogenous shocks to government consumption and investment using a Choleski identification, controlling for forecasts to avoid anticipation effects. He estimates multipliers near zero for government investment and around 0.8 for government consumption. He also finds evidence supporting the mechanisms he highlights in his theory. In particular, he finds that a government consumption shock does not crowd out private consumption, but a government investment shocks significantly crowds out private investment. Consistent with this evidence, he also finds little change in the real interest rate in the consumption goods sector after a consumption shock, but a significant increase in the real interest rate in the investment goods sector.

Boehm also offers some final evidence that provides some support to the models predicting higher multipliers at the zero lower bound (ZLB). When he estimates his model separately over ZLB periods and normal periods, he finds evidence of a slightly higher multiplier for government investment than government consumption during ZLB periods. Recall that Bouakez, Guillard, and Roulleau-Pasdeloup (2017, 2019) showed that at the ZLB, the New Keynesian model predicted a flipping of the ranking of multipliers, with government investment multipliers higher at the ZLB. Boehm's point estimates qualitatively support this prediction. The standard errors of the estimates are higher, though, so the estimates are not statistically different from each other.[20]

### 4.4.2 Cross-State Evidence

Many of the recent studies have estimated the effects of infrastructure by exploiting variation across states. This is especially true of the studies of the effects of the ARRA. These studies can estimate only relative effects because they exploit subnational data; that is, they answer the question, How much more employment or output occurs in State *A* when it receives $1 more in spending than the average state? Thus, the estimates do not provide direct evidence on aggregate effects because, by construction, they net out financing effects and do not measure the net effects of positive spillovers versus business-stealing effects. Moreover, most do not account for induced state and local spending, so the multiplier estimate may undercount the total government spending required to produce the result. Nevertheless, these estimates provide valuable insight into the underlying mechanisms.

The state employment data are typically much better than gross state product data. As a result, most studies focus on employment effects rather than gross state product effects. This focus is reasonable for short-run studies that are interested in the stimulus effects of government investment.

Leduc and Wilson (2013) estimate the effects of federal highway grants to states using annual state-level panel data from 1993 to 2010. The authors' long-run multipliers were discussed in a previous section. As noted by Ramey (2018), however, Leduc and Wilson's short-run estimated effects do not suggest much stimulus effect. Their figure 4 shows the effects of state highway spending on state total employment. The impulse response shows little effect or impact at year 1 but then a significantly negative effect on state employment at years 2 through 5. Thus, Leduc and Wilson's results suggest that highway spending is counterproductive as a short-run stimulus. These results echo those found by Pereira and Flores de Frutos (1999) in aggregate data. Gallen and Winston (2019) provide a possible explanation for the

20. In the smaller ZLB sample, the government investment multiplier estimate is 1.2 with a standard error of 0.66 for the first four quarters and 0.95 with a standard error of 0.72 for the first eight quarters.

short-run negative effects on total employment: highway construction can be very disruptive to the local economy.

Studies that focused all or in part on the infrastructure elements of the ARRA include Wilson (2012), Chodorow-Reich et al. (2012), Leduc and Wilson (2017), Dupor (2017), and Garin (2019). Chodorow-Reich (2019) synthesizes and standardizes the various studies of the ARRA for all types of spending and finds very similar employment multiplier estimates once they are standardized to calculate multipliers the same way. He finds that all of the leading instruments—whether they are Medicaid formulas, Department of Transportation factors, or a mixture of many factors—produce similar results. In particular, Chodorow-Reich estimates that two job-years were created for each $100,000 spent. As I point out in Ramey (2019), however, these estimates are based on unweighted data and do not take into account crowd-in of state and local spending. Once I make those adjustments, I find that each $100,000 spent led to 0.8 job-years created. These estimates are based on weak instruments, though, since the literature's instruments that are so strong for the ARRA grants are unfortunately weak for spending including additional state and local spending.

Leduc and Wilson (2017) used cross-state variation in ARRA appropriations for highways to study flypaper effects—that is, whether federal grants for highway construction crowd in or crowd out state and local spending on highways and roads. They found significant crowd-in, with each dollar in federal aid resulting in a total of $2.30 in state highway spending. The focus of their paper was the response of state and local spending and how that interacted with rent seeking, but in the appendix they showed regressions of the change in employment in the highway, street, and bridge construction industry on the instrumented appropriations. Leduc and Wilson were able to find a significant positive results in only one case of several. The failure to find positive results echoes my point that the earlier Leduc and Wilson (2013) analysis of highway spending before the ARRA did not find positive effects on total employment in the short run.

As Garin (2019) argues, a positive effect of highway spending on *construction* employment is a necessary condition for any further effects, such as local spillovers and Keynesian multipliers. Therefore, I examine in more detail the impacts of the ARRA highway grants on employment in highway, street and bridge construction, which I will call "highway construction" for short. I use Leduc and Wilson's (2017) data and a similar specification, which they describe in the text associated with their table B1. In particular, the regressions, which use cross-state variation for identification, estimate the effect of ARRA highway apportionments per capita in 2009 on the variables of interest in the succeeding years. I use the baseline sample of 48 states of Leduc and Wilson, and use their two road formula factors as instrumental variables for federal grant apportionments to states. I include their political variables as controls, though I lag them in my local projection specification

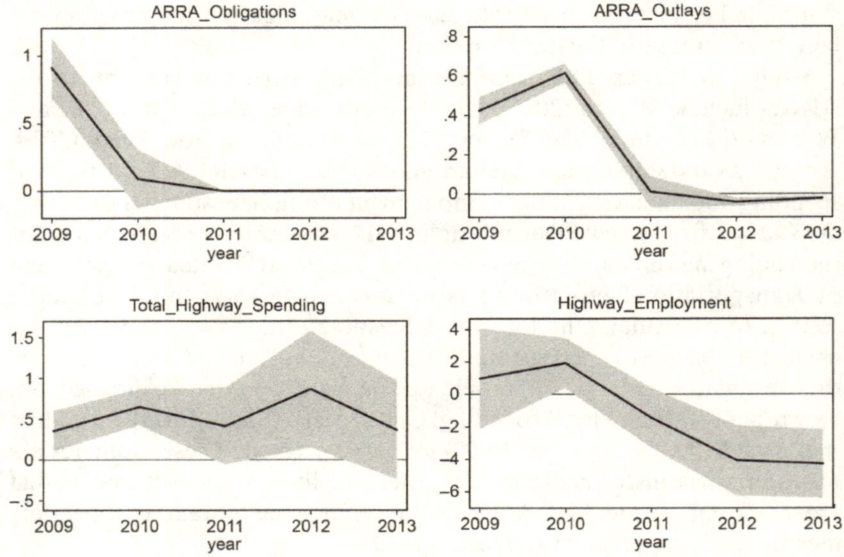


**Fig. 4.6 Estimated impulse responses to instrumented ARRA highway apportionments, no controls for log state population**

*Note:* The three spending graphs show the dollar impact per dollar of ARRA highway apportionments in 2009. The employment graph shows the employment impact in highway, road, and bridge construction employment for each $1 million of ARRA highway apportionments in 2009. In both cases, the ARRA apportionments are instrumented by Leduc and Wilson's (2017) two road factors. The confidence bands are 90 percent bands.

so that all right-hand side variables are dated 2009 or earlier. I include the change in per capita employment in highway construction between 2007 and 2008 as an additional control for pretrends. I estimate the impulse response in each year using a series of local projection regressions in which the left-hand side variable is the change in the variable of interest from 2008 and year $h$, where $h$ ranges from 2009 to 2013.

Figure 4.6 shows the impulse responses for the specification just described. The upper left graph accurately estimates that all of the ARRA obligations occurred in 2009. The upper right graph shows that the outlays occurred mostly in 2009 and 2010. The lower left graph supports the main result of Leduc and Wilson (2017), which is that total highway spending rose by more than the outlays. My new result is the impulse response for highway construction employment, shown in the lower right graph. According to the estimated impulse response function, highway employment barely responds in 2009 and 2010 but then falls significantly after that. These effects are clearly contrary to the intended effects of the ARRA.

Dupor (2017) in "So, Why Didn't the 2009 Recovery Act Improve the Nation's Highways and Bridges?" argues that the ARRA did not improve

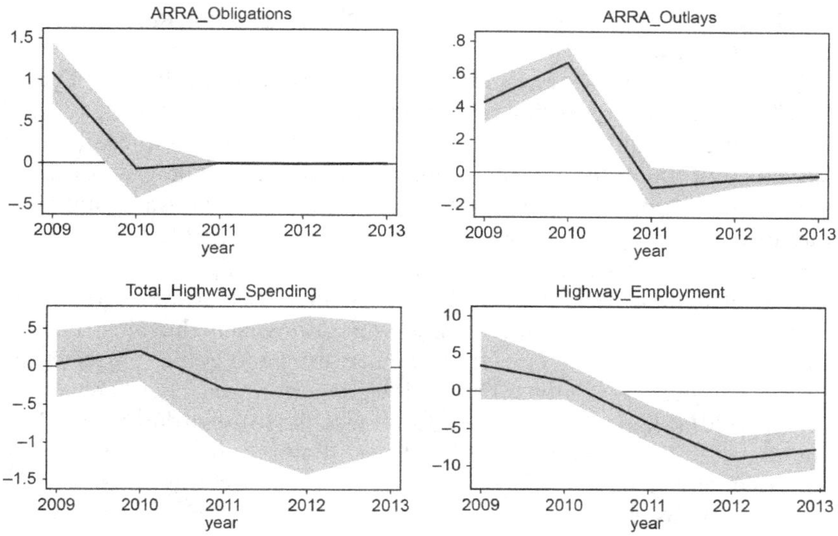


**Fig. 4.7 Estimated impulse responses to instrumented ARRA highway apportionments, controls for log state population**

*Note:* The three spending graphs show the dollar impact per dollar of ARRA highway apportionments in 2009. The employment graph shows the employment impact in highway, road, and bridge construction employment for each $1 million of ARRA highway apportionments in 2009. In both cases, the ARRA apportionments are instrumented by Leduc and Wilson's (2017) two road factors. The confidence bands are 90 percent bands.

highways and bridges because the federal grants completely crowded out state and local spending. Thus, Dupor argues for the opposite result of Leduc and Wilson (2017), who find significant crowding in. Dupor notes that the difference might be caused by his addition of the logarithm of state population as a control. He does not, however, make clear the econometric motivation for adding this control.

To determine how the results change when log population is included as a control, I add Dupor's log population control in the model I used to estimate the impulse responses shown in figure 4.6. The results when the population control is included are shown in figure 4.7. The top two graphs are similar to those from the previous specification, but the bottom left graph showing the impact on total highway spending is very different. In contrast to the analogous graph in figure 4.6, there is no change in total highway spending in figure 4.7. This result suggests complete crowd-out. The highway construction employment effects, however, are similar, with virtually no change in 2009 and 2010 but a significant negative effect in 2011 through 2013. The results obtained by adding Dupor's control variable no longer imply that increases in highway spending lower highway construction employment, but these results imply that no change in highway spending lowers highway construction employment.

Neither of the implied stories by Leduc and Wilson (2017) or Dupor (2017) is encouraging for highway grants as a stimulus. In the Leduc and Wilson results, total highway spending rises significantly as a result of the federal grants but results in a decrease in employment in highway construction. In the Dupor results, federal grants are ineffective in raising total highway spending, and still highway construction employment falls.

One possible explanation for the puzzling decline in highway construction employment might be a problem with the instruments. However, Chodorow-Reich (2019) tested the overidentifying assumptions using those instruments along with other leading ones from the literature and could not reject the overidentifying assumptions. Thus, this explanation seems less likely.

Garin (2019) finds slightly more positive results. He uses a database including almost 3,000 counties and ARRA spending on highways to estimate the direct effects on overall construction (not just highway construction) employment, as well as total employment. The biggest effect he finds is in total construction employment in 2010, with six jobs created per $1 million. He finds that each dollar of stimulus spent in a county led construction payrolls to increase by 30 cents over the next five years, an increase that is consistent with the labor share in the construction industry. However, when he tests for general equilibrium effects on local employment and payroll, he estimates effects that are close to zero. He finds no evidence of a local multiplier effect.

In sum, there is scant empirical evidence that infrastructure investment, or public investment in general, has a short-run stimulus effect. There are more papers that find negative effects on employment than positive effects on employment. The ARRA results are particularly negative, since the ARRA spending occurred at a time when interest rates were at the zero lower bound and the unemployment rate was 9 to 10 percent. Despite the slack in the economy and the accommodative monetary policy, the effects on construction employment were either slightly positive or negative.

### 4.5 Is the US Underinvesting in Public Capital?

Numerous commentators have argued that the US is underinvesting in public capital, and particularly in infrastructure. In this section, I shed light on this question with data on trends and insights from the models presented earlier.

Figure 4.8 shows government capital as a percent of GDP from 1929 to 2018. The data are current-cost net stock data on government capital and nominal GDP from the BEA. The figure shows long-run trends for all government capital, nondefense government capital, and transportation capital relative to GDP. All show significant swings over time. The total government

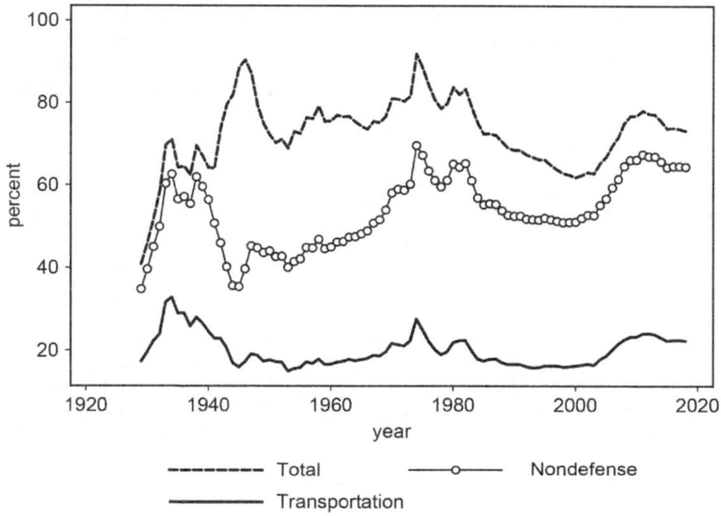


**Fig. 4.8 Government capital as a percentage of GDP in the US**

*Note:* Government capital is current-cost net stock from BEA fixed asset table 7.1. GDP is current-dollar GDP from the BEA.

capital ratio hit peaks in the 1940s and the mid-1970s. Both the nondefense and transportation government capital ratios hit peaks in the 1930s, the mid-1970s, and the early 2010s. The ratios have fallen only slightly since the early 2010s. Thus, current levels of public capital are comparable to those of some of the past high points.

Of course, this comparability does not mean that the level is optimal or that the allocation of government capital across types is optimal. We can shed light on this question by returning to the extension of the neoclassical model that allows the social planner to choose the optimal steady-state public capital, discussed in section 4.2.6. For reference, I repeat the equations for the optimal level of government capital and investment:

$$\frac{K_G}{Y} = \frac{1}{\beta^{-1} - 1 + \delta_G} \cdot \theta_G, \quad \frac{G^I}{Y} = \frac{\delta_G}{\beta^{-1} - 1 + \delta_G} \cdot \theta_G,$$

where $K_G$ is public capital, $G^I$ is government investment, $Y$ is output, $\beta$ is the discount rate of the representative household, $\delta_G$ is the depreciation rate on public capital, and $\theta_G$ is the exponent on public capital in the aggregate production function. Recall from section 4.2.6 that the calibration of the stylized model, converted to an annual basis to match the BEA data, implies that the fraction multiplying $\theta_G$ in the capital ratio equation is equal to 12.5 and in the investment ratio equation is 0.49.

With these formulas, we can compare the current state of public capital

**Table 4.6** **Comparison of actual to model optimum government capital and investment**

| | Government capital Percentage of GDP | Government investment Percentage of GDP |
|---|---|---|
| *BEA data, 2018* | | |
| Total government capital | 73 | 3.3 |
| Excluding defense | 64 | 2.6 |
| *Neoclassical model social optimum* | | |
| $\theta_G = 0.05$ | 63 | 2.5 |
| $\theta_G = 0.065$ | 81 | 3.2 |
| $\theta_G = 0.12$ | 150 | 5.9 |

*Note:* The data for government capital is current-cost net stock of government fixed assets from BEA fixed asset table 7.1. The data for investment and GDP is from BEA NIPA table 1.1.5. $\theta_G$ is the exponent on government capital in the production function. The model optimum is based on an annual depreciation rate of 3.9 percent and an annual discount factor of 0.96.

investment in the US to the optimal ratios implied by the stylized model. Table 4.6 shows the ratios of government capital and investment to GDP 2018 using BEA data, along with the model-implied optimal ratios for three values of $\theta_G$: the simulation baseline calibration of 0.05; Bouakez, Guillard, and Roulleau-Pasdeloup's (2017) estimate of 0.065; and the upper bound of Bom and Ligthart's (2014) range of 0.12.

The first two rows of table 4.6 show the ratios for the US in 2018, for both total government capital and nondefense government capital. Excluding defense capital, government capital is currently 64 percent of GDP and government investment in nondefense capital is 2.6 percent of GDP.

The next three rows of table 4.6 show the model-implied optimal ratios. If $\theta_G$ is equal to 0.05, then the socially optimal government capital-output ratio is 63 percent and the socially optimal government investment-output ratio is 2.5 percent. These model-implied ratios match the BEA data almost exactly. However, if the true $\theta_G$ is higher, then the socially optimal ratios are higher. For example, $\theta_G = 0.065$ implies a socially optimal capital ratio of 81 percent, and $\theta_G = 0.12$ implies a socially optimal capital ratio of 150 percent. Thus, viewed through the lens of this simple model, the current US levels of government investment are socially optimal only if $\theta_G$ is as low as 0.05. If $\theta_G$ is higher, then the US is underinvesting in public capital.

Clearly, the value of $\theta_G$ is crucial to the calculation. Obtaining more definitive estimates of this parameter is important for assessing whether US levels of government investment are too low.

Other assumptions of the model affect the optimal ratio calculation as well. The stylized model makes strong assumptions about elasticities of substitution between factors of production and returns to scale, both of which can affect the calculation. The model also incorporates the unrealistic assumption that public capital is homogeneous. If public capital is heterogeneous, then marginal products are not proportional to average products. For example, even if the overall level of transportation infrastructure is near the optimum, it may be misallocated: the current amount of transportation infrastructure might be too high in Detroit but too low in Seattle.

The stylized neoclassical model also assumes no distortions in the economy. The need to finance government spending with distortionary taxes might reduce the implied optimal government investment rate, since a unit of government capital would cost more than a unit of output because of the depressing effect of distortionary taxes on output. On the other hand, the New Keynesian-style product market and labor market distortions might lead to second-best results implying higher public capital.

In sum, the current range of plausible estimates of $\theta_G$ is too wide and the model used in this chapter is too stylized to give a definite answer to the question of whether the US is underinvesting in public capital. Nevertheless, the simple calculation offers a starting point for thinking about the issue in more general models and serves as an impetus to more research aimed at narrowing the range of plausible estimates of $\theta_G$.

## 4.6 Summary and Conclusions

This chapter has studied both the short-run and long-run macroeconomic effects of government investment. The theoretical analysis has considered both neoclassical and New Keynesian models. The empirical analysis has surveyed estimates at the aggregate and regional levels, illustrated the econometric challenges, and extended some existing empirical work. The following points summarize some of the key findings.

First, even when government investment has significant long-run effects, the short-run stimulus multipliers are less than those from government consumption in most situations. The two key reasons are (i) the effects of time-to-build delays and (ii) the propensity of government investment to crowd out private spending more than government consumption does. These results are supported by quantitative models, empirical panel studies across OECD countries, time series analysis in the US, and cross-state studies. The effects of time-to-spend and time-to-build delays, which appear to be inherent in infrastructure projects, work against the standard New Keynesian mechanisms and lower short-run multipliers.

Second, the long-run multipliers on government investment depend critically on both the production function elasticity of output to public capital and on where the economy begins relative to the socially optimal level of public capital. Higher production function elasticity raises multipliers, and starting far below the socially optimal level of public capital also raises multipliers.

Second, my review and small extension of the empirical literature on the long-run estimates suggests that the aggregate production function elasticity of output to public capital is probably between 0.065 and 0.12, similar to the range found by Bom and Ligthart's (2014) meta-analysis. However, this elasticity is very stylized and does not take into account possible differences in the marginal products of different types of government capital. Some studies find higher estimates for core infrastructure, and others do not.

Third, there is both theoretical support and some empirical support for the short-run multiplier on government investment being higher when interest rates are constrained by the zero lower bound. The theoretical mechanisms that lead to this effect, however, also imply that at the zero lower bound, financing government spending with distortionary income taxation rather than deficits leads to higher multipliers, a result contrary to most economists' priors.

Fourth, cross-section and panel evidence on US states or counties that focuses on bridge, highway, and road infrastructure spending suggests that the spending leads to either no change or a decline in employment in the first several years, even during ZLB periods. There is no obvious explanation for these puzzling results, though the disruptive effects of construction on existing infrastructure might play a role.

In sum, the macroeconomic approach to government investment provides strong support for the long-run benefits of infrastructure spending. However, the same approach raises questions about the suitability of investment in infrastructure and other public capital as a short-run stimulus.

## Appendix

The following provides the first-order conditions and steady-state conditions for the models presented in section 4.2.

### Stylized Neoclassical Model

The social planner chooses sequences $\{C_t\}$, $\{N_t\}$, $\{I_t\}$, $\{Y_t\}$, and $\{K_t\}$ to maximize the lifetime utility of the representative household given in equation (2), subject to the economy-wide resource constraint in equation (1), the production function in equation (3), and the capital accumulation in equations (4) and (5), as well as exogenous processes for the two types of government spending. The first-order conditions for the perfect foresight solution are as follows:

(1) $$\frac{(1-\alpha)Y_t}{C_t} = \nu N_t^{\phi} \text{ Marginal Rate of Substitution Condition,}$$

$$\frac{C_{t+1}}{C_t} = \beta\left[\alpha\frac{Y_{t+1}}{K_t} + 1 - \delta\right] \text{Consumption Euler Equation.} \tag{2}$$

If the social planner chooses government capital optimally, then we also have the first-order condition for that choice:

$$\frac{C_{t+1}}{C_t} = \beta\left[\theta_G\frac{Y_{t+1}}{K_t^G} + 1 - \delta_G\right].$$

The steady-state conditions are as follows:

$$\frac{K}{Y} = \frac{\alpha}{\beta^{-1} - 1 + \delta}, \tag{3}$$

$$\frac{C}{Y} = 1 - \delta \cdot \frac{K}{Y} - \delta_G \cdot \frac{K^G}{Y} - \frac{G^C}{Y}, \tag{4}$$

$$N^{1+\phi} = \frac{1-\alpha}{\nu C/Y}, \tag{5}$$

$$I = \delta \cdot K, \tag{6}$$

$$G^I = \delta_G \cdot K^G, \tag{7}$$

$$Y = AK^{\alpha}N^{1-\alpha}(K^G)^{\theta^G}. \tag{8}$$

If the social planner chooses public capital optimally, then in steady state,

$$\frac{K^G}{Y} = \frac{\theta_G}{\beta^{-1} - 1 + \delta_G}.$$

**New Keynesian Model**

I construct the model by modifying Galí, López-Salido, and Vallés (2007) to add government capital and sticky wages (using Colciago's 2011 assumptions). I also add variable capital utilization and replace capital adjustment costs with investment adjustment costs following Christiano, Eichenbaum, and Evans (2005) and Schmitt-Grohé and Uribe (2005). My model shares many similarities with Sims and Wolff's (2018) model extended with rule-of-thumb households.

Here I will highlight a few key details and refer readers for now to Galí, López-Salido, and Vallés (2007) for more details concerning the parts of the model that overlap. The full model equations will be made available in an online appendix, https://data.nber.org/data-appendix/c14366/.

Households

The general specification of households closely follows Galí, López-Salido, and Vallés (2007). There are two types of households, optimizing households and rule-of-thumb households. Both have the same utility function, identical to the one used for the neoclassical model, equation (2). Optimizing households maximize their lifetime utility subject to an intertemporal budget constraint. Sources of income include labor earnings, returns on the holding of government bonds, rental income from capital, and dividends. Uses of income are consumption, investment in physical capital, lump-sum taxes, and purchases of government bonds. Optimizing households own all of the capital in the economy and receive all profits. They also make decisions on the utilization of capital. Rule-of-thumb households consume their entire income each period, with their income consisting of labor earnings less lump-sum taxes.

### Labor Market

Both types of households supply $j$ types of labor, which firms use to create aggregate labor input through a CES aggregator. The elasticity of substitution between the different types of labor in this CES aggregator is $\varepsilon_w$. A fictitious labor union sets wages to maximize the weighted utility across the two types of households. The union can only reoptimize the wages with probability $1 - \theta_w$ and takes this into account when it is allowed to adjust the wage for type $j$ labor. Because wages are marked up over the marginal rate of substitution, households are willing to supply whatever labor is demanded. The labor supply of both types of households is always equal.

### Investment Adjustment Costs and Capital Utilization

The capital accumulation equation from the baseline neoclassical model is modified as follows:

$$K_t = (1 - \delta(u_t))K_{t-1} + I_t\left[1 - S\left(\frac{I_t}{I_{t-1}}\right)\right],$$

where depreciation depends on utilization,

$$\delta(u_t) = \delta_0 + \delta_1(u_t - 1) + \delta_2(u_t - 1)^2,$$

and investment adjustment costs are

$$S\left(\frac{I_t}{I_{t-1}}\right) = \frac{\kappa}{2}\left(\frac{I_t}{I_{t-1}} - 1\right)^2.$$

### Prices, Production, and Resource Constraints

The model follows Galí, López-Salido, and Vallés (2007) regarding competitive final goods firms and monopolistically competitive intermediate goods firms, which mark up price over marginal cost and face price adjustment costs. The elasticity of substitution parameter for the CES aggregator of intermediate goods to final goods is given by $\varepsilon_p$. The probability that a firm can adjust prices is $1 - \theta_p$.

The aggregate production function is modified in three ways relative to my neoclassical model:

$$s_t \cdot Y_t = A_t(u_t \cdot K_{t-1})^{\alpha}(N_t^d)^{1-\alpha}(K_{t-1}^G)^{\theta_G}.$$

In this version, output depends on capital services, which is the product of the utilization rate $u$ and the stock of capital. Wage stickiness leads to inefficient use of the types of labor (outside of steady state), so there is a wedge between the amount of labor supplied, $N_t$, and the effective amount of labor available for production, $N_t^d$:

$$N_t = \tilde{s}_t N_t^d, \text{ where } \tilde{s}_t \geq 1.$$

Similarly, the distortions caused by price stickiness imply a wedge (outside of steady state) between the amount of spending ($Y = C + I + G$) and the amount produced, so $s_t \geq 1$.

Monetary Policy and Fiscal Policy

The specification of the Taylor rule and the behavior of lump-sum taxes follows Galí, López-Salido, and Vallés (2007). According to Martín Uribe's notes, Galí, López-Salido, and Vallés implicitly assume that the deviation of lump-sum taxes from steady state is always equal for both types of households.

## References


Allen, Treb, and Costas Arkolakis. 2019. "The Welfare Effects of Transportation Infrastructure Improvements." NBER Working Paper 25487. Cambridge, MA: National Bureau of Economic Research.

Aschauer, David Alan. 1988. "The Equilibrium Approach to Fiscal Policy." *Journal of Money, Credit and Banking* 20 (1): 41–62.

———. 1989. "Does Public Capital Crowd Out Private Capital?" *Journal of Monetary Economics* 24 (2): 171–88.

Bachmann, Rüdiger, Tim O. Berg, and Eric R. Sims. 2015. "Inflation Expectations and Readiness to Spend: Cross-Sectional Evidence." *American Economic Journal: Economic Policy* 7 (1): 1–35.

Barro, Robert J. 1990. "Government Spending in a Simple Model of Endogenous Growth." *Journal of Political Economy* 98 (5 Part II): S103–25.

Baxter, Marianne, and Robert G. King. 1993. "Fiscal Policy in General Equilibrium." *American Economic Review* 83 (3): 315–34.

Boehm, Christoph E. 2020. "Government Consumption and Investment: Does the Composition of Purchases Affect the Multiplier?" *Journal of Monetary Economics* 115 (November): 80–93.

Bom, Pedro R. D., and Jenny E. Ligthart. 2014. "What Have We Learned from Three Decades of Research on the Productivity of Public Capital?" *Journal of Economic Surveys* 28 (5): 889–916.

Bouakez, Hafedh, Michel Guillard, and Jordan Roulleau-Pasdeloup. 2017. "Public

Investment, Time to Build, and the Zero Lower Bound." *Review of Economic Dynamics* 23: 60–79.

———. 2019. "The Optimal Composition of Public Spending in a Deep Recession." *Journal of Monetary Economics* 114 (October): 334–49.

Broer, Tobias, Niels-Jakob Harbo Hansen, Per Krusell, and Erik Öberg. 2020. "A Note on the Transmission Mechanism of Government Spending Shocks in the Basic Neoclassical Model." IIES working paper, Stockholm University.

Calvo, Guillermo A. 1983. "Staggered Prices in a Utility-Maximizing Framework." *Journal of Monetary Economics* 12 (3): 383–98.

Chodorow-Reich, Gabriel. 2019. "Geographic Cross-Sectional Fiscal Spending Multipliers: What Have We Learned?" *American Economic Journal: Economic Policy* 11 (2): 1–34.

Chodorow-Reich, Gabriel, Laura Feiveson, Zachary Liscow, and William Gui Woolston. 2012. "Does State Fiscal Relief during Recessions Increase Employment? Evidence from the American Recovery and Reinvestment Act." *American Economic Journal: Economic Policy* 4 (3): 118–45.

Christiano, Lawrence J., Martin Eichenbaum, and Charles L. Evans. 2005. "Nominal Rigidities and the Dynamic Effects of a Shock to Monetary Policy." *Journal of Political Economy* 113 (1): 1–45.

Coenen, Günter, Christopher J. Erceg, Charles Freedman, Davide Furceri, Michael Kumhof, René Lalonde, Douglas Laxton, et al. 2012. "Effects of Fiscal Stimulus in Structural Models." *American Economic Journal: Macroeconomics* 4 (1): 22–68.

Colciago, Andrea. 2011. "Rule-of-Thumb Consumers Meet Sticky Wages." *Journal of Economic Dynamics and Control* 343 (2/3): 325–53.

Cubas, German. Forthcoming. "Public Capital and Economic Development." *Economic Journal*.

Donaldson, Dave. 2018. "Railroads of the Raj: Estimation the Impact of Transportation Infrastructure." *American Economic Review* 108 (4/5): 899–934.

Donaldson, Dave, and Richard Hornbeck. 2016. "Railroads and American Economic Growth: A 'Market Access' Approach." *Quarterly Journal of Economics* 131 (2): 799–858.

Drautzburg, Thorsten, and Harald Uhlig. 2015. "Fiscal Stimulus and Distortionary Taxation." *Review of Economic Dynamics* 18 (4): 894–920.

Dupor, Bill. 2017. "So, Why Didn't the 2009 Recovery Act Improve the Nation's Highways and Bridges?" Second quarter 2017, Federal Reserve Bank of St. Louis Review.

Dupor, Bill, and Rong Li. 2015. "The Expected Inflation Channel of Government Spending in the Postwar US." *European Economic Review* 74 (C): 36–56.

Eggertsson, Gauti B. 2011. "What Fiscal Policy Is Effective at Zero Interest Rates?" *NBER Macroeconomics Annual 2010* 25: 59–112.

Ercolani, Valerio, and João Valle e Azevedo. 2014. "The Effects of Public Spending Externalities." *Journal of Economic Dynamics and Control* 46: 173–99.

Fernald, John. 1999. "Roads to Prosperity? Assessing the Link between Public Capital and Productivity." *American Economic Review* 89 (3): 619–38.

———. 2014. "A Quarterly, Utilization-Adjusted Series on Total Factor Productivity." Technical report, Federal Reserve Bank of San Francisco.

Fogel, Robert William. 1964. *Railroads and American Economic Growth*. Baltimore: Johns Hopkins Press.

Galí, Jordi, David López-Salido, and Javier Vallés. 2007. "Understanding the Effects of Government Spending on Consumption." *Journal of the European Economic Association* 5 (1): 227–70.

Gallen, Trevor, and Clifford Winston, 2019. "Transportation and its Effects on the

U.S. Economy: A General Equilibrium Approach." Technical report, Purdue University.
Garin, Andrew. 2019. "Putting America to Work, Where? Evidence on the Effectiveness of Infrastructure Construction as a Locally Targeted Employment Policy." *Journal of Urban Economics* 111: 108–13.
Glomm, Gerhard, and Balasubrahmanian Ravikumar. 1994. "Public Investment in Infrastructure in a Simple Growth Model." *Journal of Economic Dynamics and Control* 18 (6): 1173–87.
———. 1997. "Productive Government Expenditures and Long-Run Growth." *Journal of Economic Dynamics and Control* 21 (1): 183–204.
Gordon, Robert J. 2017. *The Rise and Fall of American Growth: The US Standard of Living since the Civil War*. Princeton, NJ: Princeton University Press.
Henry, Peter Blair, and Camille Gardner. 2019. "Global Infrastructure: Potential, Perils, and Framework for Distinction." Technical report, New York University.
Ilzetzki, Ethan, Enrique G. Mendoza, and Carlos A. Végh. 2013. "How Big (Small?) Are Fiscal Multipliers?" *Journal of Monetary Economics* 60 (2): 239–54.
Izquierdo, Alejandro, Ruy E. Lama, Juan Pablo Medina, Jorge P. Puig, Daniel Riera-Crichton, Carlos A. Vegh, and Guillermo Vuletin. 2019. "Is the Public Investment Multiplier Higher in Developing Countries? An Empirical Investigation." NBER Working Paper 26478. Cambridge, MA: National Bureau of Economic Research.
King, Robert, Charles Plosser, James Stock, and Mark Watson. 1987. "Stochastic Trends and Economic Fluctuations." NBER Working Paper 2229. Cambridge, MA: National Bureau of Economic Research.
Leduc, Sylvain, and Daniel Wilson. 2013. "Roads to Prosperity or Bridges to Nowhere? Theory and Evidence on the Impact of Public Infrastructure Investment." *NBER Macroeconomics Annual 2012* 27: 89–142.
———. 2017. "Are State Governments Roadblocks to Federal Stimulus? Evidence on the Flypaper Effect of Highway Grants in the 2009 Recovery Act." *American Economic Journal: Economic Policy* 9 (2): 253–92.
Leeper, Eric M., Todd B. Walker, and Shu-Chun Susan Yang. 2010. "Government Investment and Fiscal Stimulus." *Journal of Monetary Economics* 57: 253–92.
Leff Yaffe, Daniel. 2020. "The Interstate Multiplier." Manuscript, University of California, San Diego.
Miyamoto, Wataru, Thuy Lan Nguyen, and Dmitriy Sergeyev. 2018. "Government Spending Multipliers under the Zero Lower Bound." *American Economic Journal: Macroeconomics* 10 (3): 247–77.
Mountford, Andrew, and Harald Uhlig. 2009. "What Are the Effects of Fiscal Policy Shocks?" *Journal of Applied Econometrics* 24 (6): 960–92.
Munnell, Alicia H. 1990. "Why Has Productivity Growth Declined? Productivity and Public Investment." *New England Economic Review* (January): 3–22.
Pereira, Alfredo M. 2000. "Is All Public Capital Created Equal?" *Review of Economics and Statistics* 82 (3): 513–8.
Pereira, Alfredo M., and Rafael Flores De Frutos. 1999. "Public Capital Accumulation and Private Sector Performance." *Journal of Urban Economics* 46 (2): 300–22.
Ramey, Valerie A. 2016. "Macroeconomic Shocks and Their Propagation." In *Handbook of Macroeconomics*, vol. 2, edited by John B. Taylor and Harald Uhlig, 71–162. Amsterdam: Elsevier.
———. 2018. "Fiscal Policy: Tax and Spending Multipliers in the U.S." In *Evolution or Revolution: Rethinking Macroeconomic Policy after the Great Recession*, edited by Olivier Blanchard and Lawrence H. Summers, 71–162. Cambridge, MA: MIT Press.

———. 2019. "Ten Years after the Financial Crisis: What Have We Learned from the Renaissance in Fiscal Research?" *Journal of Economic Perspectives* 33 (2): 89–114.
Ramey, Valerie A., and Sarah Zubairy. 2018. "Government Spending Multipliers in Good Times and in Bad: Evidence from US Historical Data." *Journal of Political Economy* 126 (2): 850–901.
Redding, Stephen J., and Esteban Rossi-Hansberg. 2017. "Quantitative Spatial Economics." *Annual Review of Economics* 9: 21–58.
Redding, Stephen J., and Matthew A. Turner. 2015. "Transportation Costs and the Spatial Organization of Economic Activity." In *Handbook of Regional and Urban Economics*, edited by Gilles Duranton, J. Vernon Henderson, and William C. Strange, 1339–98. Amsterdam: Elsevier.
Schmitt-Grohé, Stephanie, and Martín Uribe. 2005. "Optimal Fiscal and Monetary Policy in a Medium-Scale Macroeconomic Model: Expanded Version." NBER Working Paper 11417. Cambridge, MA: National Bureau of Economic Research.
Shapiro, Matthew D. 1993. "Cyclical Productivity and the Workweek of Capital." *American Economic Review* 83 (2): 229–33.
Shimer, Robert. 2009. "Convergence in Macroeconomics: The Labor Wedge." *American Economic Journal: Macroeconomics* 1 (1): 280–97.
Sims, Eric, and Jonathan Wolff. 2018. "The Output and Welfare Effects of Government Spending Shocks over the Business Cycle." *International Economic Review* 59 (3): 1403–35.
Wieland, Johannes F. 2019. "Are Negative Supply Shocks Expansionary at the Zero Lower Bound?" *Journal of Political Economy* 127 (3): 973–1007.
Wilson, Daniel J. 2012. "Fiscal Spending Jobs Multipliers: Evidence from the 2009 American Recovery and Reinvestment Act." *American Economic Journal: Economic Policy* 4 (3): 251–82.
Woodford, Michael. 2011. "Simple Analytics of the Government Expenditure Multiplier." *American Economic Journal: Macroeconomics* 3 (1): 1–35.

## **Comment** Jason Furman

> Macroeconomists like infrastructure investment a lot more than the people who know something about it.
> —Ed Glaeser at some conference (according to the author's recollections)

Macroeconomists, myself sometimes included, have tended to see infrastructure investment as a solution to a wide range of economic concerns. What to do if the economy is in a recession and needs countercyclical help? Infrastructure. Worried about slower long-run growth? Infrastructure. Declining

Jason Furman is a professor of the practice of economics jointly at the Harvard Kennedy School and the Department of Economics at Harvard University. He is also a nonresident senior fellow at the Peterson Institute for International Economics.

I thank Wilson Powell for outstanding research assistance on this comment. For acknowledgments, sources of research support, and disclosure of the author's material financial relationships, if any, please see https://www.nber.org/books-and-chapters/economic-analysis-and-infrastructure-investment/comment-macroeconomic-consequences-infrastructure-investment-furman.

male employment rates? Infrastructure. Some of these same macroeconomists, who would otherwise never be caught citing an advocacy or lobbying group as an authority, have even been known to cite the American Society of Civil Engineers' (2017) grade of D+ for US infrastructure as, somehow, an authoritative assessment. In contrast, many economists who specialize in infrastructure often tend to stress a variety of downsides: the examples of cities with ample infrastructure but no growth (Glaeser 2008), the fact that transit may shift economic activity more than augment it (Gonzalez-Navarro and Turner 2018), and that the benefits of highway construction may be small relative to its costs (Duranton and Turner 2012).

Valerie Ramey steps into this debate with both of her feet firmly planted in macroeconomics; her analysis is grounded in aggregate production and demand functions with none of the texture afforded by the microeconomic literature (beyond including a more realistic "time to build" for infrastructure investment). But she approaches the debate with none of the wishful thinking and advocacy that have sometimes plagued macroeconomic pronouncements. Instead she has produced what should become the definitive assessment of both the theory and empirics of infrastructure, especially its short-run impacts.

In my original discussion of the conference draft, I used her paper as a launching point for a broader reflection on infrastructure, economic policy, and economic research, while also making some specific critiques of Ramey's models and analysis. Unfortunately, Ramey responded to and incorporated almost all of my critiques (for what they were worth), leaving me with just the broader reflections on infrastructure, economic policy, and economic research that I will make in the following four points:

1. US public investment is relatively low, but US infrastructure quality is relatively high.
2. The optimal level of public investment likely varies across types, and any assessment should factor in market failures and distortions.
3. A more granular production function may matter for assessing public infrastructure multipliers.
4. A full policy regarding countercyclical public investment needs to take into account more than multipliers.

## Low Public Investment, High Infrastructure Quality

*US public investment is relatively low, but US infrastructure quality is relatively high.* Gross government investment has fallen from its post–World War II peak of 7.1 percent of GDP in the 1960s to a near postwar low of 3.4 percent in 2019, as shown in figure 4C.1. Excluding defense investment, the trend is similar, with a peak of 4.3 percent in the 1960s to a near-postwar low of 2.6 percent of GDP in 2019. The United States is also below average

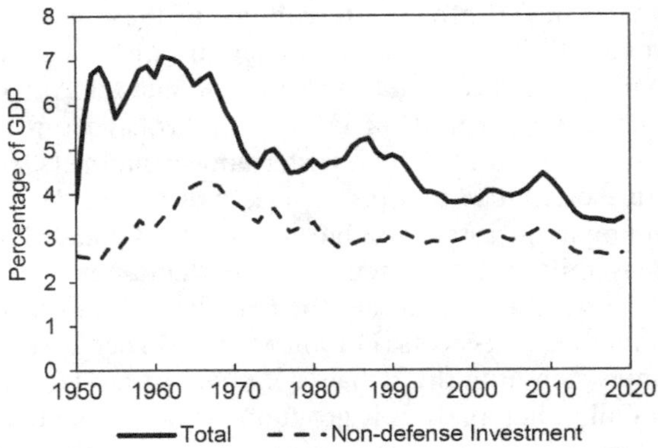


**Fig. 4C.1 US gross government investment**

*Source:* Bureau of Economic Analysis; Macrobond; author's calculations.

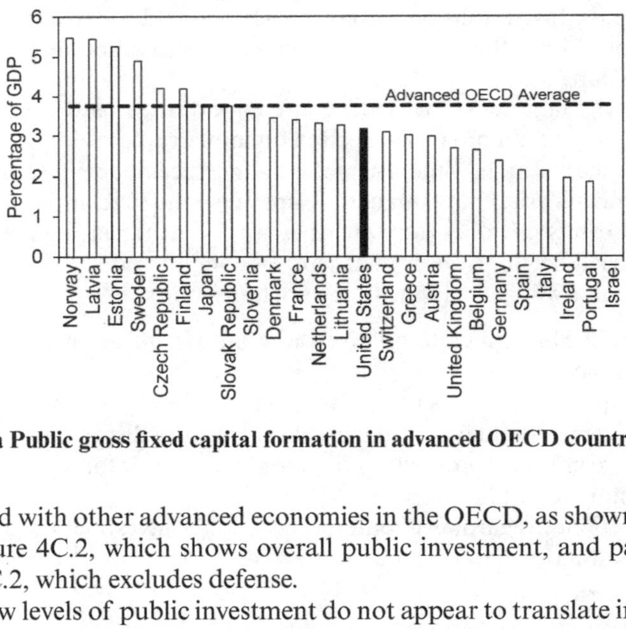


**Fig. 4C.2a Public gross fixed capital formation in advanced OECD countries, 2018**

compared with other advanced economies in the OECD, as shown in panel A of figure 4C.2, which shows overall public investment, and panel B of figure 4C.2, which excludes defense.

The low levels of public investment do not appear to translate into worse outcomes, at least in key measurable aspects of transportation infrastructure. Turner (2019) has shown that lane miles of Interstate Highway grew nearly continuously from 1980 to 2008 while the average smoothness of roads improved enormously over that period. The World Economic Forum rates US transportation infrastructure as better than the G7 average across multiple measures, except for railroad density, and ranks US road, air and liner shipping connectivity as the best in the world, as shown in table 4C.1.

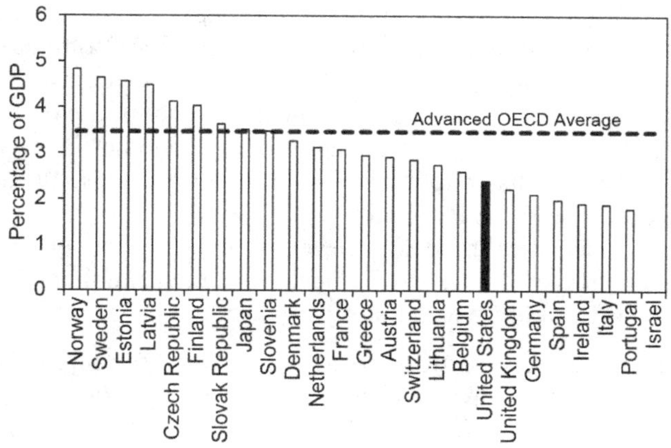


**Fig. 4C.2b Public nondefense gross fixed capital formation in advanced OECD countries, 2018**

*Source:* Organisation for Economic Co-operation and Development; author's calculations.

**Table 4C.1 Quality of transportation infrastructure in G7 countries**

| | Canada | France | Germany | Italy | Japan | United Kingdom | United States | G7 average |
|---|---|---|---|---|---|---|---|---|
| Overall | 66 | 83 | 84 | 73 | 88 | 81 | 80 | 79 |
| Road connectivity | 99 | 97 | 95 | 86 | 78 | 91 | 100 | 92 |
| Quality of road infrastructure | 67 | 74 | 72 | 57 | 85 | 64 | 75 | 70 |
| Railroad density | 13 | 100 | 100 | 100 | 100 | 100 | 41 | 79 |
| Efficiency of train services | 58 | 66 | 65 | 52 | 96 | 55 | 69 | 66 |
| Airport connectivity | 96 | 96 | 100 | 97 | 100 | 100 | 100 | 98 |
| Efficiency of air transport services | 72 | 75 | 75 | 65 | 87 | 72 | 80 | 75 |
| Liner shipping connectivity | 52 | 84 | 97 | 67 | 77 | 96 | 97 | 81 |
| Efficiency of seaport services | 68 | 69 | 71 | 61 | 80 | 69 | 76 | 71 |

*Note:* Scores are on a scale of 0 to 100, where 100 represents the frontier.
*Source:* Schwab (2019); author's calculations.

## Optimal Level of Public Investment

*The optimal level of public investment likely varies across types, and any assessment should factor in market failures and distortions.* Ramey does a simple, back-of-the-envelope assessment of the optimal level of the US public capital stock and finds that it is very dependent on the elasticity of output relative to the public capital stock. Unfortunately, Ramey's review and critique of the literature leads to more, not less, mystery on this parameter. With an elasticity of 0.05, the US public capital stock is a little higher than optimum, but with an elasticity of 0.11 found by Bom and Ligthart (2014), the public capital stock is well below optimal. More work is needed to identify this parameter, including taking into account the time frame for output, spillovers across regions, and a range of econometric problems that result from the fact that public investment is both a cause of and consequence of output and GDP growth.

The basic neoclassical model, however, provides a relatively small set of limits for this back-of-the-envelope calculation, and a number of additional considerations would be worth taking into account in future work:

- To the degree tax distortions are associated with funding public investment, that association would suggest even lower public investment. But to the degree that the funding of public investment addresses other distortions (for example, a gas tax addressing some externalities associated with gasoline use), then public investment would be higher.
- Private investment may be suboptimal as a result of distortions associated with capital taxation, monopoly power, and failure to take into account positive spillovers. All these considerations indicate more public investment than the simple Ramsey calculation would suggest.
- Public capital is highly differentiated and may not be exactly what one would think. Highways and streets, for example, are smaller than either intellectual property products or equipment, as shown in table 4C.2. All of these forms of capital should be accounted for separately, with their own output elasticities and optimal levels, in any more complete analysis.
- To the degree there are labor market failures that are reflected in the large long-term decline in non-college-graduate prime-age male employment rates, then additional infrastructure investments may shift the composition of aggregate demand, and these additional jobs should be reflected in any optimization exercise.

**Table 4C.2 Composition of US government investment in fixed capital, 2018**

| Type | Percent |
|---|---|
| Equipment | 22 |
| Intellectual property products | 30 |
| Structures | 47 |
| Highways and streets | 14 |
| Educational | 12 |
| Transportation | 4 |
| Offices | 4 |
| Other | 13 |

*Source:* Bureau of Economic Analysis; author's calculations.

- Finally, parameterizing any optimization exercise against historical data implicitly identifies the optimal quantity conditional on the historical average quality of infrastructure (as reflected in the output elasticity). Should the analysis explore and try to understand how improvements in quality would increase the optimum level and what those improvements might be?

I do not know what a more complete optimization exercise addressing these points would show, but based on a range of evidence and experience I would hazard the following guesses: (1) the composition of transportation investment matters much more than the level, including more user funding, shifting from rural to urban, more transit and less highway, and possibly more maintenance and less new construction. (2) If the composition can be improved, then a higher level could be justified. (3) The United States is underinvesting dramatically in research and development.

### More Granular Production Function

*A more granular production function may matter for assessing public infrastructure multipliers.* Ramey finds somewhat smaller multipliers than much of the previous literature, and much smaller multipliers than the roughly three found by Auerbach and Gorodnichenko (2012) for public investment. Ramey's multipliers, however, need not mean a large shift in priors for anyone who was more pessimistic about infrastructure as short-run fiscal stimulus (for example, Elmendorf and Furman [2008] wrote that infrastructure was "difficult to design in a manner that would generate significant short-term stimulus," and Furman [2020] wrote that "recent studies . . . find larger tax multipliers than spending multipliers").

Ramey mostly models public investment as an undifferentiated concept. In reality, there are many types of public investment, and they enter the production function in different ways. Econometric estimates of multipliers for each separate type of infrastructure are likely impossible, but the input-output matrix of the Bureau of Economic Analysis (BEA) provides some clues about the relative impact of different forms of infrastructure investment, with state and local transit being twice as large as water, sewage, and other systems, as shown in table 4C.3.

### More than Multipliers

*A full policy regarding countercyclical public investment needs to take into account more than multipliers.* Although the short-run multiplier is not an encouraging argument for public investment as fiscal stimulus, several other considerations are also important. The most important, as argued force-

Table 4C.3 **Input-output effects of infrastructure investment**

| Industry | Total multiplier |
|---|---|
| Government investment | |
| Federal nondefense | 1.5 |
| State and local passenger transit | 3.2 |
| State and local electric utilities | 1.8 |
| Core infrastructure investment | |
| Highways and streets | 2.0 |
| Electric power generation, transmission, and distribution | 1.8 |
| Water, sewage, and other systems | 1.6 |

*Source:* Council of Economic Advisers (2016).

fully by Haughwout (2019) is that infrastructure investment is currently *procyclical*. The reason is that 63 percent of state highway funding is through user revenues and other taxes and fees, while only 9 percent is funded by borrowing. With taxes and fees highly cyclical, this introduces a substantial procyclicality to state highway investment. Presumably the same logic implies that other forms of state investment are also very procyclical. As a result, introducing some countercyclicality into federal infrastructure investment (Haughwout 2019), or into federal financing for states more generally (Fiedler, Furman, and Powell 2019), could be thought of less as a way to get new stimulus in recessions and more as a way to smooth investment, preventing a precipitous decline that may otherwise occur.

I would love to see Ramey take her analytic machinery and employ it to answer the question of the optimal cyclical profile of public investment. It is unlikely that a procyclical profile is optimal. In fact, a number of considerations—unrelated to multipliers—suggest that a countercyclical profile may be preferable. Specifically, the fact that interest rates are lower, and material and labor costs may be lower, in recessions suggests that, if anything, shifting more investment into periods when the economy is weak could be desirable.

In particular, any cost-benefit analysis of a new public transportation program needs to reckon with how it accounts for the employment effects of the plan. As any student of economics learns, in normal times jobs should be disregarded, because even if the program is creating gross jobs, it is not creating them on net—it is just displacing some other form of employment. In a recession, however, net jobs are created and these have a social value to the extent that the marginal product of them exceeds the reservation wage. Net job creation could easily shift a project from failing a cost-benefit test to passing one. Understanding just how easily this shift could take place, however, depends on the number of net new jobs created—which can be benchmarked by the number of jobs per $100,000 of infrastructure spending. A range of estimates for this number is provided in table 4C.4.

Table 4C.4 **Estimates of number of new jobs created per $100,000 of infrastructure spending**

| | |
|---|---|
| Standard advocacy estimates | 2–4 |
| Chodorow-Reich (2019) | 2 |
| Ramey (2019) | 0.8 |
| Garin (2019) | 0.6 |

## Conclusion

Ramey brings much clarity to the aggregate analysis of public investment. She largely confirms that it should not be a major component of short-run stimulus and that it does have major long-run benefits, but the relationship between the overall level and social optimum remains far from clear. Extending her machinery to examine both the heterogenous varieties of public investment and the many distortions and market failures in both public and private investment would be an exciting next step to further increase the modeling's ability to yield concrete (so to speak) policy recommendations.

## References

American Society of Civil Engineers. 2017. "2017 Infrastructure Report Card."

Auerbach, Alan J., and Yuriy Gorodnichenko. 2012. "Measuring Output Responses to Fiscal Policy." *American Economic Journal: Economic Policy* 4 (2): 1–27.

Bom, Pedro R. D., and Jenny E. Ligthart. 2014. "What Have We Learned from Three Decades of Research on the Productivity of Public Capital?" *Journal of Economic Surveys* 28 (5): 889–916.

Chodorow-Reich, Gabriel. 2019. "Geographic Cross-Sectional Fiscal Spending Multipliers: What Have We Learned?" *American Economic Journal: Economic Policy* 11 (2): 1–34.

Council of Economic Advisers. 2016. "The Economic Benefits of Investing in U.S. Infrastructure." In *2016 Economic Report of the President*. Washington: US Government Printing Office.

Duranton, Gilles, and Matthew A. Turner. 2012. "Urban Growth and Transportation." *Review of Economic Studies* 79 (4): 1407–40.

Elmendorf, Douglas W., and Jason Furman. 2008. "If, When, How: A Primer on Fiscal Stimulus." Washington, DC: Brookings Institution.

Fiedler, Matthew, Jason Furman, and Wilson Powell III. 2019. "Increasing Federal Support for State Medicaid and CHIP Programs in Response to Economic Downturns." In *Recession Ready: Fiscal Policies to Stabilize the American Economy*, edited by Heather Boushey, Ryan Nunn, and Jay Shambaugh, 93–127. Washington, DC: Hamilton Project and Washington Center for Equitable Growth.

Furman, Jason. 2020. "The Fiscal Response to the Great Recession: Steps Taken, Paths Rejected, and Lessons for Next Time." In *First Responders: Inside the U.S. Strategy for Fighting the 2007-2009 Global Financial Crisis*, edited by Ben S. Bernanke, Timothy F. Geithner, Henry M. Paulson, with J. Nellie Liang, 451–88. New Haven, CT: Yale University Press.

Garin, Andrew. 2019. "Putting America to Work, Where? Evidence on the Effectiveness of Infrastructure Construction as a Locally Targeted Employment Policy." *Journal of Urban Economics* 111: 108–31.

Glaeser, Edward. 2008. *Cities, Agglomeration and Spatial Equilibrium*. Oxford: Oxford University Press.

Gonzalez-Navarro, Marco, and Matthew A. Turner. 2018. "Subways and Urban Growth: Evidence from Earth." *Journal of Urban Economics* 108: 85–106.

Haughwout, Andrew. 2019. "Infrastructure Investment as an Automatic Stabilizer." In *Recession Ready: Fiscal Policies to Stabilize the American Economy*, edited by Heather Boushey, Ryan Nunn, and Jay Shambaugh, 129–52. Washington, DC: Hamilton Project and Washington Center for Equitable Growth.

Ramey, Valerie A. 2019. "Ten Years after the Financial Crisis: What Have We Learned from the Renaissance in Fiscal Research?" *Journal of Economic Perspectives* 33(2): 89–114.

Schwab, Klaus. 2019. "The Global Competitiveness Report 2019." World Economic Forum.

Turner, Matthew A. 2019. "Local Transportation Policy and Economic Opportunity." Policy Proposal 2019-03. Washington, DC: Hamilton Project, Brookings Institution.

# 5

# Procurement Choices and Infrastructure Costs

Dejan Makovšek and Adrian Bridge

## 5.1 Introduction

For many countries around the world, building new infrastructure or repairing existing infrastructure stands near the top of the political agenda. On one hand, countries face the political challenge of securing more funding. On the other, potentially large efficiency gains could be achieved spending the funds that are available. One area for possible efficiency gains involves how we choose to procure projects—the procurement strategy.

In the past decades, contract theory yielded several Nobel laureates (such as Oliver Williamson and Oliver Hart). Their insights led to significant advances in various aspects of how we contract. In the case of infrastructure delivery, however, our understanding of the outcomes of different contractual models is very limited despite decades of use. There is a general lack of empirical data to test whether our theoretical comprehension is complete.

Available evidence from testing contract and auction theory propositions allows us to explain the performance of the most common and simplest

Dejan Makovšek is the procurement strategy lead at the Organisation for Economic Co-operation and Development's Infrastructure and Public Procurement Division in the Public Governance Directorate.

Adrian Bridge is an associate professor of Project Management at the Queensland University of Technology (QUT).

The authors would like to thank James Poterba, Edward Glaeser, Shoshana Vasserman, Arthur Antoine, Keith Molenaar, Ivan Damijanovic, and Alex Galetovic for their comments and help with earlier versions of this chapter. The analysis and the findings of this chapter do not necessarily reflect the views of the OECD or the QUT. For acknowledgments, sources of research support, and disclosure of the authors' material financial relationships, if any, please see https://www.nber.org/books-and-chapters/economic-analysis-and-infrastructure-investment/procurement-choices-and-infrastructure-costs.

procurement formats (a design-bid-build contract with a cost-plus payment mechanism, procured in an auction) relatively well.

This is not the case for other procurement formats or larger projects. For instance, in dimensions other than speed of delivery, it is still not fully clear whether contracts that bundle the design-and-build phase outperform the traditional design-bid-build contract, where the two phases are procured separately. Similarly, the implications of using high-powered incentives that lead to greater time and cost certainty in major projects are unclear. Any judgment on other dimensions is even more challenging. In the absence of evidence, industry perceptions need not match reality.

Furthermore, the fact that data on some dimensions of project performance are available and publicly observable can create a bias in procurement and contracting choices against those that are not. For example, cost overruns bear serious reputational concerns and are relatively easy to measure. It is far more difficult to determine whether a project was relatively "expensive." By implication, public clients today procure billions of US dollars of transport and other infrastructure around the world without a full view of the trade-offs between different project performance objectives.

To inform the process of procurement, contract and auction theory offered broad predictions with regard to three key procurement choices: bidder selection, delivery model, incentive power. Combined, the predictions suggest that, for example, a lump-sum contract that combines the phases of design and construction (or also operations and maintenance) procured through a negotiated process should outperform a cost-plus contract in which the design and construction were procured separately and the winning bidder was selected through an auction.

In this chapter, we find that the available evidence does not match the predictions well, especially when it comes to larger, more complex projects. Negotiation and bundling do not clearly lead to less renegotiation per se. An important cause for this result is the inability of the public clients to specify their full needs in advance. An investigation into the root causes behind this result is beyond the scope of this chapter.

We also show that high-powered incentives, requiring high certainty of on-budget and on-time delivery, carry a disproportionate cost premium even in the absence of renegotiations (complete contracts). We argue that this mismatch between predictions and evidence is best explained by the underappreciated role of uncertainty. Currently, uncertainty in contract theory is mainly recognized as a driver of postcontract renegotiations. Uncertainty, however, has an equally important role as a driver of risk contingencies, when bidders need to price the contract in the bidder selection phase.

As a result, efficiency gains in high-powered contracts may be more than offset by contingencies in the private supply chain, driven by uncertainties implicit to complex major infrastructure. The same consideration would apply to high-powered and long-term contracts such as road public-private partnerships (PPPs).[1]

The research and decision-making challenges listed here are a symptom of a larger issue: empirically we know relatively little about how procurement choices affect contract outcomes in (infrastructure) procurement. To make progress on this front we need to introduce systematic infrastructure cost and performance benchmarking, which will also include procurement choices as an explanatory variable. This point, however, is not yet recognized by policy makers. A consequence of this state of affairs is that the current approaches governments use to inform procurement strategies of projects leave a wide margin for further improvement.

Looking toward the future, we conclude the chapter by acknowledging that resolving the issues of bidder selection, project phase bundling, and incentive power still does not represent a comprehensive procurement strategy. The reason is that two essential choices precede these decisions. First is the make-or-buy question: Which capabilities should a procurement entity procure from the market and which should it build in-house? Second, aside from the question of bundling project phases, there is a question whether a project be procured through one or several parallel contracts and where the boundaries between them should lie. Both choices will importantly predetermine the competitive response, well before we start planning the bidder selection process. Both choices also require stepping outside of the purview of auction and contract theory, taking lessons from other new institutional economics theories and beyond.

In reviewing evidence, this chapter specifically focuses on the most advanced economies with competent public clients and institutions. Two reasons merit this choice. The first is that the availability of evidence for advanced economies is much greater. The second is that we can more easily focus on the interaction between procurement practices and project outcomes, without serious white noise from the issues of systematic corruption and underdeveloped institutions; these will have a far lesser significance in advanced economies than in the developing world. A great majority of the available evidence concerns road infrastructure.

Section 5.2 of the chapter begins with a brief historical overview of procurement and contracting, from Roman times until today. This overview serves to introduce basic infrastructure procurement or contracting concepts and reveals that many fundamental procurement problems remain relevant to this day.

1. In road PPPs, for example, both the construction and the maintenance aspects have very strict on-budget requirements—that is, they have to be almost fully priced ex ante. There are no ex post corrections resulting from competitive pressure or incentive regulation. In the case of seaport PPPs however, competition could be present for the same catchment area, providing persistent incentives for efficiency and eroding abnormal rents.

Section 5.3 takes the basic concepts introduced in the historical overview and explains in greater detail the main infrastructure procurement choices: bidder selection, delivery model, and incentive power. As most of the available evidence on our topics concerns road infrastructure, we outline the dominant options used in that market.

Section 5.4 captures what parts of economic theory relate to infrastructure procurement. The auction theory focuses on the bidder selection process and considers the choice of the delivery model or incentive power as a given. Contract theory takes the reverse view and considers the bidder selection choice as a given. Key predictions of auction and contract theory with regard to the main infrastructure procurement choices are distilled.

Section 5.5 lays out what empirical evidence is available to assess the accuracy of theoretical predictions. Predictions that can be assessed are selected. In terms of infrastructure most available evidence comes from transport infrastructure or road projects. To the extent possible, large sample quantitative research will be captured. Sections 5.6 through 5.8 then assess the match between three key theoretical predictions and available evidence.

In section 5.9 we outline how advanced economies approach the procurement of major transport infrastructure. The most developed aspect here is the process of bidder selection, where the rules are enshrined in legislation. Choices with regard to the delivery model and incentive power are left to operational guidance. Recent developments in the UK and Australia are also presented.

Concluding the chapter, section 5.10 highlights where the theoretical predictions and empirical evidence do not meet and stresses the importance for international infrastructure benchmarking to advance the theory and practice of procurement. Recent advances also suggest that an expanded concept of what a procurement strategy should entail is needed.

## 5.2 History and Procurement Choices

Today most, if not all, public infrastructure managers in advanced economies contract parts or all of design, construction, and maintenance activities to the market. Exceptions in advanced economies, however, existed until recently.[2] The beginnings of public works contracting are ancient. For example, the Roman Empire dealt with the make-or-buy question by having the first roads designed and built by the army with the aid of civilian or slave labor. Over time, these activities were contracted out to contractors—master builders (Adkins and Adkins 2014). The works were given away through a tender, and it is assumed that the lowest price was the winning criteria (Du Plessis 2004).

2. Prior to reforms that ended in 2003 the Norwegian Public Roads Administration planned and built 60 percent of the main roads itself (40 percent was subject to competitive tendering) (Odeck 2014).

The master builder was an all-in-one profile, responsible for the design and delivery of the project. It was not until the Middle Ages, when increasing complexity of projects and the broader availability of paper (used to make preconstruction plans) led to the establishment of a specialized profession, that a different person became responsible for the design of the project (the "designer" or architect), separating design from the function of the builder (Kostof 2000). By implication, the builder now got involved later in the project development process, when the design was (or should have been) already worked out in detail. This was also the birth of the oldest and to date dominant delivery model, called design-bid-build (DBB).

Aside from the delivery model, there are other contract dimensions that define performance incentives for the contractor. The earliest documented considerations of risk allocation and incentives in contracts go back to Roman Empire times. In his 10 books on Roman construction practices, Caesar Julius's chief engineer, Vitruvius, acknowledged the importance of construction risk allocation. In terms of incentives to the builders, for example, he proposed to Caesar Augustus the reintroduction of a practice from ancient Greece (Morgan 1960):

> When a [master builder] accepts the charge of a public work, he has to promise what the cost of it will be. His estimate is handed to the magistrate, and his property is pledged as security until the work is done. When it is finished, if the outlay agrees with his statement, he is complimented by decrees and marks of honour. If no more than a fourth has been added to his estimate, it is furnished by the treasury, and no penalty is inflicted. But when more than one-fourth has been spent in addition on the work, the money required to furnish it is taken from his property.[3]

This is an example of an early payment mechanism to incentivize performance that has some similarities with today's pain- and gain-sharing in contracts. The basic payment mechanisms widely used today were also documented around medieval times. Construction contracts from the Spanish city of Girona in the fourteenth century were observed to be applying three different formats, including unit price and lump-sum (Chamorro et al. 2018). Unit price (also known as admeasurement or bill of quantities) contracts define rates per unit of work.[4] Estimates of quantities are provided at the beginning, and a correction is applied at the end given the actually executed quantities. A lump-sum (or fixed-price) contract, on the other hand, would determine the cost of the contract in advance without a detailed cost breakdown.

Expert discussions on the performance of the two payment mechanisms

3. The oldest construction codes go back to Hammurabi, when the principle of an eye for an eye was observed. For example, for a collapsed building that killed its owner, the builder was to be put to death as well.

4. Another term used for this payment mechanism in economics is "scaling auctions."

were documented already between 1800 and1830 when the UK, exhausted by war with the French, wanted to be more careful about spending public money. The proponents of the lump-sum contract argued that this was the only way of keeping within cost estimates (Port 1967, 97):

> An architect before he can make a [lump-sum] contract must make a specification, in which he must set down everything that can possibly occur. . . Before a [lump-sum] estimate can be made he must digest his plan, and every part of it must be made out, and he must put down on paper every detail that will possibly happen; and therefore you are sure that the architect must do his duty in the first instance.

Against a much more varied procurement context, the same issues highlighted here are still of interest today. Our methods may have improved over time, but so has the complexity of what we are building. As we shall see in the review of theoretical and empirical work, many of the old dilemmas remain unresolved.

The history of procurement history has been dominated by the idea that competitive bidding yields the best results, inhibiting alternatives. Negotiations were allowed only when competition was not possible. In the US, for example, the construction of the federal Interstate Highway System began with the Federal-Aid Highway Act of 1956. Until the 1990s, this program was almost exclusively procured through competitive bidding based on the lowest price, using a design-bid-build delivery model. The primary payment mechanism was the bill of quantities approach, still dominant today (Federal Highway Administration 2016). The domination of competitive bidding was enshrined through legislation that favored competitive bidding (23 U.S. Code § 112, Pub. L. 85–767). Other methods were allowed only on a declarative level—that is, they could be considered only provided they "are effective in securing competition." Effectively, methods based on negotiation were not desirable.

In the twentieth century the projects became more complex, more expensive (Brooks and Liscow 2019), and larger (Flyvbjerg 2014). In recent decades, particularly for larger projects, procurement models in which negotiations need to play a stronger role are achieving greater penetration.

The next section broadly explains the general characteristics of the main procurement options that exist today and sets the scene for the review of theory and empirical evidence.

## 5.3 Broad Characteristics of (Infrastructure) Procurement Choices

After a public client makes a make-or-buy decision—that is, decides to procure from the market—our brief historical introduction highlights three key dimensions of procurement choices: selecting the contractor, determining the scope of work the contractor is hired to do, and deciding on what basis to compensate the contractor. Building on Kennedy et al. (2018), we define these choices in the following subsections.

### 5.3.1 Selecting the Contractor

**Bidder selection** concerns the process between the moment a call for proposals is published to the moment the contract is signed with the preferred contractor. Multiple options exist between a lowest price auction and a negotiation with a single bidder. Negotiations facilitate the exchange of pre-contract information that reduces uncertainty at the expense of competition. Negotiations also imply greater discretion in bidder selection.

Table 5.1 illustrates the procurement procedures described here as defined in European Union directives (European Union 2014a, 2014b). These pro-

**Table 5.1 Procurement procedures in the EU**

| Procedure | Description |
|---|---|
| Open procedure (Article 45) | In an open procedure, any business may submit a tender. The minimum time limit for submission of tenders is 35 days from the publication date of the contract notice. If a prior information notice was published, this time limit can be reduced to 15 days. |
| Restricted procedure (Article 46) | Any business may ask to participate in a restricted procedure, but only those that are preselected will be invited to submit a tender. The time limit to request participation is 37 days from the publication of the contract notice. The public authority then selects at least five candidates with the required capabilities, which then have 40 days to submit a tender from the date when the invitation was sent. This time limit can be reduced to 36 days, if a prior information notice has been published |
| Negotiated procedure with prior call for competition (Article 47) | In a negotiated procedure the public authority invites at least three businesses with which it will negotiate the terms of the contract. Most contracting authorities can use this procedure only in a limited number of cases—for example, for supplies intended exclusively for research or testing purposes. The contracting authorities in sectors such as water, energy, transport, and postal services may use it as a standard procedure. The time limit to receive requests to participate is 37 days from the publication of the contract notice. This can be reduced to 15 days in extremely urgent cases, or 10 days if the notice is sent electronically. |
| Competitive dialogue (Article 48) | This procedure is often used for complex contracts such as large infrastructure projects where the public authority cannot define the technical specifications at the start. After the publication of the contract notice, interested businesses have 37 days to request participation. The public authority must invite at least three candidates to a dialogue in which the final technical, legal, and economic aspects are defined. After this dialogue, candidates submit their final tenders. |

*Source:* European Union directives (2014/24/EU; 2014/25/EU).

**Table 5.2** **Frequency of basic bidder selection options in US road infrastructure procurement**

| Procurement procedure | DBB ($n$ = 134) | CM/GC ($n$ = 34) | DB/LB ($n$ = 39) | DB/BV ($n$ = 77) |
|---|---|---|---|---|
| Low bid | 80% | 0% | 100% | 0% |
| A+B (cost + time) | 13% | 0% | 0% | 18% |
| Best value | 1% | 47% | 0% | 61% |
| Qualifications-based | 1% | 41% | 0% | 0% |
| Other or not classified | 5% | 12% | 0% | 21% |

*Source:* Federal Highway Administration (2016).

cedures have counterparts in the US and other advanced economies that serve the same purpose.

Another aspect of the procurement procedure is to define the criteria based on which the bidders will be selected. Three common options are (1) the lowest price, (2) the economically most advantageous offer (a weighted combination of price and nonprice criteria), and (3) a nonprice or qualification-based competition.[5] Table 5.2 provides a snapshot of how frequently particular bidder selection criteria are used in US highway procurement across four main delivery models (these are outlined further later).

### 5.3.2 The Contractor's Scope of Work

**The delivery model** defines the stage of the project development (design maturity) at which a contractor is engaged and for what scope of work or services (for example, build-only, design and build, related risk allocation). Table 5.3 outlines common delivery models in use in advanced economies.

### 5.3.3 Compensating the Contractor

**Incentive (or contract) power** relates to the effectiveness of risk transfer and how strong the rewards or penalties are to manage performance metrics such as cost/time. The payment method is a key element of incentive power. Two polar opposites in this regard are cost-plus a fee or the lump-sum approaches. Table 5.4 outlines the common payment mechanisms in use. The frequency of different payment methods in US highway procurement is illustrated in table 5.5.

This overview illustrates a wealth of options procuring entities have in their arsenals today. In practice the combinations between the options in the three dimensions are not random.

The available literature shows that the workhorse of transport infrastructure procurement remains the design-bid-build model, procured through a low bid auction and a cost-plus (bill of quantities) payment mechanism (for

5. The criteria are defined based on measures of the bidders past performance or references. Qualifications could also be part of a two-stage process with preselection or included as one of the factors in the economically most advantageous offer.

**Table 5.3** **Commonly used delivery models**

| Delivery model type | Broad structure |
|---|---|
| DBB (design-bid-build) ("traditional delivery") | Design and construction separately and sequentially tendered to the private sector. Design either undertaken in-house or outsourced (for larger projects). Contractors engaged on basis of complete design (input-specified), with clients providing a design warranty. Contracts predominantly rely on bill of quantities payment mechanism. Lump-sum tends to be used only in smaller/simple contracts. |
| DB (design and build) | Design and construction are procured together from the private sector. At the time a request for proposal is issued, the design is developed up to an outline design level and the results are defined through an output specification (defines performance/end result) or a prescriptive specification (defines method and material). Contracts are predominantly fixed-price/lump-sum. |
| EPC (engineering-procurement-construction) | This option is similar to the DB variant with the two distinctions. Generally, there is no outline design available, only a specification of the functions the asset needs to perform. The contractual penalties for nonperformance (e.g. delay) can also be more severe than in a DB contracts. In PPPs, the project company (the SPV) contracts the design and construction through an EPC contract (and an operations and maintenance contract). |
| ECI (early contractor involvement) | Typically involves a two-stage process, with clients engaging a limited pool of contractors to work alongside designers, followed by a competed DB stage (with designers integrated into the contractor). Mostly used when conditions are highly uncertain or considerable innovation is required. |
| Construction manager/ general contractor (CM/GC) | The client procures professional services on a qualifications or best-value basis from a construction manager. During the design phase, the contractor acts as a consultant to the client to offer suggestions on innovations, cost and schedule savings, and constructability issues. Upon completion of the design or individual design packages, the contractor and client negotiate a price for the construction contract, and then the construction manager acts as a general contractor to complete construction. The contract can employ a guaranteed maximum price administered on a cost-reimbursable basis, unit price, or lump-sum contract (Federal Highway Administration 2016). This approach is gaining prominence in the US and is similar to ECI. |
| Alliancing | Clients and selected contractors jointly prepare project scope and target cost and agree on a shared risk/reward mechanism (cost incentive). Parties are bound by open-book accounting, no blame/no dispute policy, and unanimous decision-making. Project functions—transcending planning, design, and construction—are integrated through a joint project management board. Mostly used when conditions are highly uncertain and/or complex. |

*Source:* Kennedy et al. (2018), adapted by the author.

**Table 5.4** **Commonly used payment mechanisms**

| Payment mechanism | Broad structure |
|---|---|
| Remeasurement (also known as bill of quantities; unit price) | Using the remeasurement method (the measured or unit price contract), the works actually done are measured based on the individual rates and prices offered by the contractor in the bid in the bill of quantities (prepared by the employer). The bill of quantities contains particular items and gives a description of the work and quantity. Every individual item and the respective rate or price must beproperly contemplated and its content clearly understood to avoid disputes. The contractor will evaluate the rates and prices in the bill of quantities while keeping in mind prices for the materials, products, labor, equipment, plants, and so on (e.g., per cubic meter cost of the pit to be excavated). This process is called estimating and affords a means for the employer of comparing tenders received once they have been priced. |
| Cost-plus a fee (also known as cost reimbursable) | Under the cost-plus method, the contractor receives from the employer not only the payment for reasonable and properly incurred cost, but also a fee for overhead and profit. This method is more appropriate for high-risk projects where a lump-sum price (which takes all contingencies into account) would be too high. To encourage the contractor to perform the works for the lowest possibleprice, some additional mechanisms can be used—for example, the maximum guaranteed price or target price, described below. Under this arrangement, contractors are usually obliged to maintain comprehensive and contemporary cost records, and the employer usually reserves the right to audit the claimed costs to ensure they have been reasonably and properly incurred. The profit and overhead surcharge will be subject to competition in the tender period. This method is rarely used and is prohibited in some jurisdictions (Federal Transit Administration 2016). |
| Lump-sum (fixed-price) | Under the lump-sum method, a preagreed sum (regardless of actual cost incurred) is paid by the employer and the works actually done are not measured but paid against the schedule of payments, mostly once the predetermined sections (or milestones) are finished or when the project is fully completed. The lump-sum price is also influenced by claims, variations, and adjustments based on the particular contractual risk allocation, claims options, and variation (and adjustments) procedure. |
| Guaranteed maximum price | Employers sometimes want to cap the total contract price using the guaranteed maximum price to allocate all risks of potential price increases to the contractor. This approach is used and accepted, for example, in the United States using the construction management at risk delivery method. The main drawback of such a system is that it must be perfectly thought out in respect of risk allocation, insurance, securities, and financial reserves (or risk surcharges). Such a setup is not appropriate for projects in which numerous hazards with major risks are pending and it is not possible to price such risks transparently. |
| Target price contract | Under this regime, during the work two things happen in parallel. The contractor is generally paid actual costs plus a fee on a regular basis. The initial target price is adjusted during the work in accordance with claims and variations (compensation events) and their estimated cost. On completion, these two elements are compared. If there is a saving or a cost increase as against the target, thenthe parties share such savings or cost increases in the agreed proportions set out when the contract was agreed. A target price contract relies heavily on the ability of the procurement authority to competently engage with the private party in a collaborative fashion. It also assumes open-book principles—that is, the procuring authority should be able to monitor progress and actual costs incurred by the contract effectively. |

*Source:* Klee (2018).

**Table 5.5** **Use of payment mechanisms in US highway procurement**

| Payment method | Design-bid-build (*n* = 134) | Construction manager/ general contractor (*n* = 34) | Design and build (low bid) (*n* = 39) | Design and build (best value) (*n* = 77) |
|---|---|---|---|---|
| Lump-sum | 2% | 3% | 85% | 91% |
| Cost-plus fee* | 2% | 0% | 0% | 0% |
| Remeasurement* | 93% | 38% | 5% | 0% |
| Guaranteed maximum price | 0% | 56% | 0% | 4% |
| Other or not classified | 3% | 3% | 10% | 5% |

*Note:* Contract value ranged from $69,000 to $358 million with a mean of $27 million. *Description adjusted: cost-plus fee was originally "cost reimbursable" and remeasurement was originally "unit price."
*Source:* Federal Highway Administration (2016).

example, Federal Highway Administration 2016; Minchin et al. 2013).[6] This is true regardless of the project size. This procurement format is considered to be low-powered. Risk transfer to the contractor is minimal.

For major projects, ranging from several million to hundreds of millions of US dollars, other alternative contracting approaches have slowly started increasing in use since the 1990 in some advanced economies like the US, UK, Australia, Sweden, Netherlands (for example, for the US, see Federal Highway Administration 2016).

In US road infrastructure procurement, the introduction of alternative contracting approaches began more systematically with the initiation of the Federal Highway Administration's Special Experimental Project 14 (SEP-14) in 1990. Once cleared by the Federal Highway Administration (FHWA), the new approaches are no longer considered experimental; hence the state road agencies can use them on federal-aid projects without FHWA's approval. In 2004, the FHWA initiated SEP-15, which allowed contracting agencies to explore innovative approaches that address all phases of project development, such as PPPs.

The scope of this chapter does not extend beyond design-build (DB) and its close relative, the engineering-procurement-construction (EPC) contract, which is the default option for PPPs. Both alternatives are typically procured through negotiated procedures and rely on the lump-sum payment mechanism.[7]

6. The economics literature distinguishes between cost-plus and fixed-price contracts, whereas in construction contract law several formats could qualify. The cost-plus contract captures both the remeasurement and "cost-plus fee" payment mechanisms, while fixed-price contracts use the lump-sum payment mechanism. We note that cost-plus fee contracts are almost never used in infrastructure procurement and are prohibited in some jurisdictions (for example, the US; Federal Transit Administration 2016).

7. In the US, competitive bidding is used to secure a low bid or a best-value proposal (Federal Highway Administration 2016). That said, the Code of Federal Regulations (CFR; 23 CFR

A key distinction among the three delivery models involves at what point in the project development the contractor (that is, the winning bidder) is expected to price the project. A design-bid-build contractor would bid at a stage when the design is fully developed. In design-build, only an outline design will be available, where the engineering is typically 10–20 percent complete. An output specification will be available, though, describing what functions the asset should perform. For an EPC contract bidder there will be no outline design and only the output specification will be available. The DB and EPC bidders are expected to develop and price their solutions during the bidding process.[8]

Because the two alternatives also transfer design risk and ask for high cost certainty through the lump-sum payment mechanism and additional incentive mechanisms (such as liquidated damages for delays), these alternatives are considered to be high-powered procurement formats, with very high risk transfer.

In the next section, we look at the key predictions economic theory has made with regard to the three procurement choices. We do not deal with the make-or-buy question, as that topic deserves a separate paper, and instead focus on the three procurement choices just outlined.

## 5.4 Economic Theory Applications to Infrastructure or Construction Procurement

Two streams of economic theory deal with the basic procurement choices outlined earlier: auction theory and contract theory. Auction and contract theory have different focuses. Auction theory focuses on the bidder selection process and considers the project delivery model and incentive power as a given. Auction theory does not consider delivery models or incentive power. It does, however, yield insights or consequences for their application. Conversely, the main focus of contract theory has been the delivery model selection and incentive power. The results of the bidder selection process, i.e., the level of competition and price achieved are in this case a consequence of incentive power choices.

In both theories there is also a basic distinction between two types of contracts: complete and incomplete contracts. In complete contracts there are no ex post renegotiations. The winning bid fully reveals the bidder's revenue expectations ex ante. This could be the case for smaller and simpler contracts in infrastructure delivery.

§ 636) allows significant two-way information exchange activities between the proposal submission and bidder selection to reduce uncertainties or errors in the proposals. Recent research confirms this to be the case (Calahorra, Torres-Machi, and Molenaar 2019). For this reason, in economics this approach to bidder selection would qualify as "negotiations." The US variant of competitive dialogue—competitive negotiations—is applied in PPP procurement.

8. In practice these default options represent what is common, but they may not be always observed. For example, the level of outline design that the procuring entity makes available could vary.

In an incomplete contract, the bids no longer fully reveal the bidders' revenue expectations. Contracts are incomplete because writing comprehensive contracts is costly (Coase 1937; Klein, Crawford, and Alchian 1978; Williamson 1975, 1985), the project is too complex or the mere uncertainty of the future makes a complete contract impossible. The contractual incompleteness creates incentives for ex post bargaining and for good- and bad-faith renegotiation (Grossman and Hart 1986; Hart 1995; Hart and Moore 1990; Williamson 1979). The first is necessary because of unforeseen events, and the second is the result of strategic behavior to extract additional rents. The need to absorb changes leads to adaptation cost and what is more easily observable, cost overruns.[9]

### 5.4.1 Bidder Selection and Auction Theory Propositions

The traditional auction theory view has been that the benefits of competition always outweigh any other auction mechanism that involves fewer bidders (Bulow and Klemperer 1996). A key assumption behind this finding is that of complete contracts—that is, that the object of the auction can be well defined, which means the (lowest) price becomes the key determinant of the optimal result.

The more complex the object of procurement however, the less complete the contract. Therefore, auction theory adopted two main alternatives to auctions: negotiations and relational contracting. Both imply a trade-off with reduced completive pressure.

Goldberg (1977) suggested that competition for the contract stifles communication between the principal and the agent, which may lead to a suboptimal specification of the project. He argued that the bidders might have important information about construction practices, prices, or other aspects that might allow the client to prepare a better informed tender, reducing ex post adaptation cost. So far, theoretical has work tried to formalize the trade-off between ex ante information exchange (in negotiations) and ex post renegotiation in auctions (Herweg and Schmidt 2017).

In cases when the public clients repeatedly contract with a pool of the same firms, the issue of incomplete contracts could also be managed by long-term relations, or relational contracting—that is, through the use of reputational mechanisms (Spagnolo 2012).

Reliance on mechanisms other than competition at the same time implies greater discretion in bidder selection on the side of the procuring entity. As a result, there is greater scope for corruption, favoritism, or other practices that do not necessarily lead to best procurement results. Both adjustments to the traditional view, which prefers auctions, focus on contractibility and by implication uncertainty as a source of renegotiations and adaptation cost.

In a limited stream of auction theory literature (Goeree and Offerman 2003;

9. These two terms are not equivalent; the distinction is explained later in the chapter.

Milgrom and Weber 1982), uncertainty affects the bidders' ability to price the subject of the tender (or risk) efficiently rather than enable renegotiations. Specifically, bidders can lack information about the true cost of the object that is being tendered.[10] When this is so, bidders will also not be able to accurately assess potential ex post changes and in consequence additional ex post revenue opportunities. If bidders are risk averse, the perceived risk variance and the resulting risk premiums at a given level of competition will be higher.

Goeree and Offerman (2003) identify two effects of more information and lower uncertainty. First, if more information is made publicly available to the bidders, risk premiums will get lower, and bidding will become more aggressive.[11] Second, more public information may reduce the entry barriers for less experienced firms, increasing the number of competitors, which has a knock-on effect on the aggressiveness of the bidding again.

What this all implies is that contracts could be complete, a good level of competition could be present, and the most efficient bidder could win, but the procurement of a project would still be inefficiently expensive if the bidders did not have sufficient information about the true cost of the object procured. The theoretical prediction in this case does not explicitly extend to the question of when we can use bundled or high-powered contracts. Implicitly, though, it can be deduced that, especially in these cases, the exchange of precontract information will be a key requirement.

### 5.4.2 The Choice of the Delivery Model and Contract Theory Propositions

Contract theory consists of two streams, the principal-agent theory and the property rights theory. It is the latter that proposes it is possible to solve

10. As Goeree and Offerman (2003) explain, in private value auctions, bidders know their own value for the commodity but are unsure about others' valuations. In contrast, common value auctions pertain to situations in which the object for sale is worth the same to everyone, but bidders have different private information about its true value. The standard textbook example for a private value auction is the sale of a painting. A well-known example for a common value auction is the sale of oil drilling rights, which, to a first approximation, are worth the same to all competitors. In the real world, most auctions involve a mixture of both. If, for example, the competitors for the oil drilling rights used different technologies (so that their cost structures would be different), their private valuations of the rights would be different. Hence, if the common value of the object is uncertain, a bidder with a moderate private value and an overly optimistic estimate of the common value may outbid a rival with a superior private value but more realistic conjectures about the common value. If the common value were less uncertain, then bidders with superior private values (the most efficient bidders) would consistently prevail, leading potentially to an even higher auction result. Goeree and Offerman's (2003) proposition is similar but distinct from the principal-agent theory problem of adverse selection driven by information asymmetry between principal and agent and cannot be solved by a menu of contracts.

11. The same result in conventional financial economics would be attributed to improved risk pricing efficiency (Makovšek and Moszoro 2018) through a mechanism more straightforward than that of Goeree and Offerman (2003). This mechanism implies that risk premiums do not only arise as a result of reduced risk diversification possibilities. They also result from the inability to accurately assess risk. As investors are risk averse, disproportionate markups are added to accommodate the lack of information about risk.

the incomplete contract problem by bundling the contract phases (Hart 1995, 2003; Iossa and Martimort 2015).

In property rights theory, the appropriate assignment of ownership or residual control rights gives the owner of the asset bargaining power in situations beyond those defined in the contract. The logic of this approach is manifest in the design-and-build contract, in which any issues with incomplete design are internalized within a single contract. Going one step further, in PPP, the residual control rights are transferred to a private party.

In a stereotypical PPP, a dedicated project company (a special purpose vehicle) enters the contractual relationship with the public sector. The agreement between them defines an output specification—that is, what the project is meant to achieve, as opposed to what the project is (the input). The PPP is the bundling of project phases, from design to operations, in one long-term contract (for example, a design-build-finance-operate-maintain [DBFOM] contract).[12] The project company finances the project and recovers its investment either through a service-level agreement with the public client or by being granted the right to charge the users of the infrastructure (Engel, Fischer, and Galetovic 2014). The project company does not itself execute the project but organizes the execution through a network of contracts, passing the technical risks onto its suppliers (for example, construction risk to the construction contractor).

In such an arrangement the issues of incomplete contracts are internalized through two key incentives:

1. The output specification approach implies that the private sector partner obtains the residual control (ownership) rights to the infrastructure asset—that is, chooses the solutions to meet the predefined service standards. This approach is supposed to reduce contractual incompleteness issues, compared with the traditional approach, in which the input is defined by the public client.[13] The output specification also implies a full transfer of design, construction, and operations risk—a lump-sum/fixed-date contract.
2. The bundling of asset construction together with operation and maintenance into one single contract also incentivizes the private partner to invest in quality at the construction phase if such investments lower the project's life-cycle operating and maintenance cost.

12. While this is a common term to describe the broad contract arrangement in a PPP, the phase of design and build is contracted as the engineering-procurement-construction contract. As laid out in section 5.3, this format also bundles the design and build phases, but is generally tendered against an output specification. No outline design is made available.

13. The transfer of control rights also incentivizes investment into relation-specific assets (sunk with no or limited alternative use)—that is, infrastructure—despite the presence of an incomplete contract. In theory the transfer of control rights would also incentivize innovation.

Iossa and Martimort (2015)[14] formalized these propositions and found that the design-build-operate-maintain bundle provision beats traditional procurement if benefits from bundling are significant.[15] A key proposition that defines Iossa and Martimort's results is the assumption that the life-cycle cost optimization savings offset the (additional) risk premiums of a high-powered (PPP) contract, in which the private party bears the operations risk; hence Iossa and Martimort suggested that bundling and high-powered contracts go hand in hand.[16] An implicit assumption to the conclusion above is also that the bidder selection stage would not be affected by bundling and the high power of the contract.

Hence, the theoretical prediction is that through bundling project phases (that is, the transfer of residual control), we can eliminate or reduce contract incompleteness.

### 5.4.3 The Choice of Incentive Power and Contract Theory Propositions

In terms of how much risk one should transfer in a contract, the principal-agent theory defined the problem as a trade-off between incentives and insurance. Incentives are provided through transferring risk or making the agent's payoff dependent on the agent's effort. The agent's risk aversion implies there is a cost to risk transfer. Hence, lower risk aversion on the part of the agent allows the principal to provide more incentives by making the agent's payment depend on the agent's effort, while higher risk aversion increases the gains from insuring the agent and reduces the pay-for-performance sensitivity (Holmstrom and Milgrom 1987). In short, risk transfer should be executed at a level at which the risk premium does not offset the gains from increased effort.

On top of this basic relation, the principal-agent theory in a complete contract setting applies the issues of the opportunistic behavior of agents resulting from the information asymmetry between the agent and the principal. Two problems emerge: the adverse selection ex ante and moral hazard ex post contract signature (Laffont and Tirole 1993).

Adverse selection in the bidder selection process can occur because the principal does not know the true efficiency of the agents (the bidders). This makes it difficult for the principal to determine who will exert the most effort

14. In an earlier paper, Iossa and Martimort (2012) included uncertainty in user demand as a factor in the risk premium and noted that the PPP only makes sense if the private party can assess the risk well. Hence, bundled contracts would make sense for less complex contracts. This point was not transferred to the more recent paper or applied in the context of construction risk.

15. An analogous approach could be applied to a design-build contract only, arguing that contract incompleteness resulting from design issues would be internalized in this contract format.

16. They also acknowledge that the long-term nature of this contractual arrangement brings with it additional uncertainty (resulting from exogenous shocks), which may lead to renegotiation of the PPP contract itself (in other words, despite the property rights theory approach, contractual incompleteness remains an issue).

at a given incentive. If contracts are complete, however, the initial bid fully reveals the contractor's revenue expectations up front and there can be no ex post renegotiation. This means that when renegotiations are unlikely, a high-powered incentive—that is, a lump-sum (high-powered) contract—will ensure the best contractor is chosen in the competition (Bajary and Tadelis 2001).

When contracts are incomplete, the initial bid will not fully reveal the contractor's revenue expectations, and renegotiations will occur. Three theoretical solutions have been put forward.

Hart and Holmstrom (1987) sought to address the adverse selection problem in the context of incomplete contracts by offering the (potential) agents a menu of contracts, which allow them to be interested in the trade and reveal their true type.

McAfee and McMillan (1986) combined a bidding model with adverse selection and moral hazard challenges. These authors suggested that neither cost plus nor fixed-price contracts are desirable in an incomplete contract setting. The proposed solution is an incentive contract that makes the payment depend both on the bid and on realized costs: if realized costs exceed the firm's bid, the firm is responsible for some fraction of the cost overrun; if the firm succeeds in holding its costs below its bid, the firm is rewarded by being allowed to keep part of the cost underrun. A caveat to this result is that in McAfee and McMillan's model, cost-plus contracts give the contractor no incentive to bid aggressively; hence these contracts are never optimal.

A third option recommends low-powered incentives (Bajari and Tadelis 2001; Williamson 1985). Low-powered incentives have adaptability advantages. In construction, for example, this would be because cost-plus contracts involve a bill of quantities to which the bidders need to assign unit prices. If the actual quantities differ from the estimated ones the unit prices in the bill of quantities offer a reference price list to evaluate variation claims.[17] The lump-sum contract, on the other hand, involves only a general cost breakdown and it is not usual for it to contain a price/quantity breakdown as in the cost-plus (bill of quantity) contracts. Hence, the lump-sum contract is more rigid and involves greater transaction cost to renegotiate. A key driver behind this thinking is the assumption that the information asymmetry ex ante—the fact that the private party knows more than the public one, causing the adverse selection—is not the main issue. Both parties equally face future uncertainties.

Lastly, the moral hazard post contract signature manifests as quality shading. If the quality of the output is difficult to monitor, the contractor will reduce the quality to cut cost and increase profit margins. In this case

17. The contractor will still try to renegotiate the unit prices for the added work; however, the initial unit prices in the bill of quantities offer a reference point. This "anchor" is not available in the lump-sum arrangement.

high-powered incentives will exacerbate quality shading (Holmstrom and Milgrom 1991). If the quality is observable (at least after the job is finished), we can hold the agent financially accountable for his actions (Laffont and Martimort 2001), for example through performance guarantees.

The theoretical prediction of this part of contract theory is that in complete contracts we should rely on high-powered schemes, assuming ex post quality can be monitored. Thus, if bundling leads to greater contract completeness, bundling and high-powered incentives should go hand in hand.

If contracts are incomplete, several options are put forward. The obvious choice is to prefer low-powered incentives. More sophisticated propositions suggested the use a menu of contracts to ensure effective self-selection of the most efficient bidder. Lastly, McAfee and McMillan (1986) proposed a target price contract. In it, the public and the private party agree on a target in the competition phase and then share the savings or the losses at the end of the project.

### 5.4.4 What Does Theory Not Yet Address?

No economic theory would reconcile the perspectives of the auction and contract theory in a single model. One aspect that stands out in particular is the underappreciated role of uncertainty in contract theory, where it presently plays three roles:

1. A source of information asymmetry between the principal and the agent that interferes with the precontract identification and selection of the most efficient bidder
2. A source of information asymmetry between the principal and the agent, which ensures stronger incentives actually lead to greater postcontract effort
3. A postcontract source of renegotiations and adaptation cost

Uncertainty in contract theory, however, is not yet acknowledged as a source of less aggressive bidding or excessive contingencies ex ante. In short, it matters how well the bidders know the risks they are taking at the moment they need to price the contract.

A direct extension of this point is that the risk variance during contract execution is not just a question of choosing who will bear it but that of reducing or increasing it. A further unaddressed key question is whether it is more sensible to create the information to reduce the risk variance sooner in the project development cycle or later and who should do it.

Goldberg (1977) illustrated that if the bidders bore the cost of risk identification, it would be absorbed as overhead and included in future bids. Conversely, if the client fully compensated bidding cost, that would equal a cost-plus contract negotiated with a single bidder. In the precontract phase, it would be inefficiently costly, but these costs could well be offset by greater efficiency in the contract execution phase (more aggressive bidding and better contract specification or engineering solutions).

If bidders are to bear the cost of risk identification, is it efficient for all bidders (including the losers) to produce the same information (all detect the same risks separately)? Against the prospect that they might lose, do bidders invest sufficiently in information production? These are major issues for the procurement of complex projects that remain unaddressed in theory.

The next sections look at whether the empirical evidence matches theoretical predictions in the procurement of infrastructure.

## 5.5 Testing Theoretical Predictions and Available Evidence

Our review of auction and contract theory revealed a range of applications to infrastructure (or construction) procurement. The available empirical evidence allows us to further assess the following predictions, arranged according to three basic procurement choices:

1. Bidder selection
    - In complex projects increased exchange of precontract information should lead to more aggressive bidding and reduce the end cost of the project.
    - Negotiations should be preferred to auctions, because they allow an increased precontract information exchange and thus help reduce the need for costly renegotiations during contract execution.
2. Delivery model
    - Contracts that bundle project phases (for example, design and build) should also help reduce the incidence of renegotiations.
3. Incentive power
    - Fixed-price or lump-sum contracts are to be preferred in contracts in which there is little to no renegotiation—in other words, contracts that are complete. In all other cases cost-plus contracts should be used.

Other alternative propositions on how to inform incentive power in incomplete contracts in infrastructure procurement cannot be assessed because of lack of use in practice (the case for menus of contracts) or lack of evidence about the performance of the solution (the case for the target price contract).[18]

18. In practice this option is used in collaborative projects, in which the public and private parties jointly manage the execution. A high level of professional competence on the public side is required. Furthermore, the effectiveness of the method lies in the assumption that the public side can monitor the required cost of the contractor effectively. If that is not the case, the contractor is incentivized to bid with a high target and build on cost, maximizing private rents and essentially transforming this approach into a lump-sum contract.

With regard to the predictions that we can assess, ideally the evidence would allow us to secure a view of comparative statics—namely, how a change in a single procurement choice, keeping all else equal, affects the project outcomes. The outcomes would in their minimum configuration control for the trade-offs between cost certainty (that is, cost overruns), overall cost per physical unit of infrastructure, and quality. Since no piece of evidence meets this ideal, and since project outcomes can depend also on factors other than procurement choices, several explanations with regard to the interpretation of the evidence in this chapter are required.

Geographically, in its review of evidence this chapter specifically focuses on the most advanced economies with competent public clients and institutions. Two reasons merit this choice. The first is that the availability of evidence for advanced economies is much greater. The second is that we can more easily focus on the interaction between procurement practices and project outcomes, without serious white noise from the issues of systematic corruption and the quality of governance. Poor execution of procurement processes or contract management can be a substantial factor affecting project outcomes. For the same reason we do not pursue evidence that concerns regional or local authorities.[19]

We found that that the quality of infrastructure is not explicitly controlled in any of the studies. Fortunately, in general most of the available evidence concerns road infrastructure in advanced economies. Road design standards in this case are well established with a long tradition, and quality supervision by the procuring entities is considered to be effective—that is, quality shading is not considered to be an issue. No available evidence would suggest otherwise. The same assumption is adopted in several large-sample studies (for example, in Bajari, Houghton, and Tadelis [2014] or in Bolotnyy and Vasserman [2019]).

## 5.6 Does Increased Precontract Information Exchange Increase Bidding Aggressiveness?

Negotiations allow for more space to exchange precontract information than auctions. By definition, a negotiated process reduces the power of competitive pressure, since the number of bidders with which one can simultaneously negotiate and mutual transaction costs will imply participation restrictions. As a consequence, a negotiated process implies a trade-off

19. Evidence on the impact of increased discretion in bidder selection and rare attempts to compare the outcomes of negotiations versus auctions almost in the entirety come from this strata (for example, Baltrunaite et al. 2018; Chabrost 2018; Coviello, Guglielmo, and Spagnolo 2018; Palguta and Pertold 2017), mainly showing a negative impact of increased discretion. A single study of larger projects for road authorities in the US also exhibits a negative impact (Park and Kwak 2017)

between reduced competitive pressure and increased ex ante information exchange.

That said, increased ex ante exchange of information or the reduction of the uncertainties faced by the bidder can also be achieved in auctions. Procurement authorities have the possibility to share risk-related information on the object of procurement, regardless of the bidder selection approach. The theoretical prediction was that making more information available during the tendering phase (that is, reducing uncertainty) can lead to more aggressive bidding and also affect market entry (Goeree and Offerman 2003).

Kosmopoulou and Zhou (2014) show how removing an exogenous risk factor for the contractors reduces the price of the winning bids in road construction. Considerable time may pass between the actual bid submission and contract completion. If input prices (for example, for oil) are volatile, contractors need to be mindful of potential future price variations that affect the cost of their products (for example, asphalt). As contractors cannot do much to control these costs, they are a source of exogenous uncertainty. In the US, multiple institutions have applied pass-through formulas for inputs affected by considerable price variability. The Oklahoma Department of Transport (ODOT) applied such a formula for asphalt mixtures (an oil-related input). If the initial oil price grew by more than 3 percent, an automatic additional payment would be disbursed to the contractor. Between August 2006 and June 2009, ODOT granted a net additional payment to firms equal to 5.05 percent of the value of eligible contracted items, in return achieving an 11.7 percent reduction (on average) in the price of winning bids for the eligible items. The study relied on several empirical methods to confirm its findings, including difference-in-difference and discontinuity regression design.

In the case of De Silva et al. (2008) the procurement authority made additional information available, which led to a reduction in bid prices. The Oklahoma Department of Transport (ODOT) in the past published the bill of quantities without detailed internal estimates of unit prices. ODOT then changed its policy and started revealing its estimate for each component of the project.[20] The study compared the winning bids for asphalt pavements and bridge work. Asphalt paving projects are relatively straightforward as the job descriptions typically specify an area of roadwork to be surfaced, the depth of surfacing required, and the material to be used. In bridge work, there is more uncertainty. Soil conditions at a site may not be fully known until excavation work begins, and repairs may not be fully under-

20. ODOT released "a set of individual cost estimates for each quantity of material used and each important task involved. As a result, this policy change provides detailed information that can reduce substantially the uncertainty related to common components of the cost. For example, in one case, the state can reveal the cost of excavation which depends on soil conditions, and in another, the cost of a specific bridge repair which depends on the extent of the damage" (De Silva, Kosmopoulou, and Lamarche 2009).

stood until some demolition work is undertaken. The analysis included the state of Oklahoma, where the procurement protocol changed, and the state of Texas, where it remained the same (in other words, a difference-in-difference approach was used). In total, more than 13,000 bids submitted by construction firms were analyzed over the period 1998–2003. No change was recorded for asphalt projects, while the average bid for the bridge projects was reduced by 9.6 percent, with the average winning bid reduced by 9 percent. Unfortunately, no information is available on whether contract renegotiations were affected as well.

Using the same data, De Silva, Kosmopoulou, and Lamarche (2009) investigated bidder entry and survival. Entrants are typically less informed than incumbents; hence there is also a difference in efficiency. If an entrant wants to penetrate the market, the entrant must take greater chances in bidding. If the entrant does not become experienced (informed) within a reasonable period, the losses will force the entrant to exit. In this particular sample there were 322 incumbent firms and 109 entrants participating in over 2000 auctions. Using panel data regression, it was found that the information release reduced the bidding differential between entrants and incumbents attributed to information asymmetries. In addition, the median length of entrant presence in the Oklahoma procurement auctions increased by 68 percent.

The available empirical literature discussed here refers to auctions in cost-plus contracts using the design-bid-build delivery model—a detailed design is already available at the bidding stage.[21] The evidence concerns small and by implication simpler projects.[22] Yet even at this level significant and disproportionate impacts of uncertainty have been measured (for example, absorbing a 5 percent input price uncertainty led to an 11 percent reduction in winning bid price). In relation to the theoretical predictions, this section confirmed that reducing uncertainty for the bidders ex ante positively affects the winning bid price and competition. No empirical work investigates larger, more complex projects.

## 5.7 Do Negotiations and Bundling Lead to Less Renegotiation?

Following the exposition of economic theory, less renegotiation reduces adaptation cost. Bajari, Houghton, and Tadelis (2014), analyzing auction-

21. The delivery model or incentive power are not mentioned explicitly. The mentioning of auctions and the use of the bill of quantities imply however that these were cost-plus design-bid-build contracts.

22. Absolute bid size in US dollars is not mentioned. An approximate contract size can be inferred from Kosmopoulou and Zhou (2014). They reported that eliminating oil price fluctuation generated savings of 5 percent, amounting to US$23 million in over 600 auctions. Kosmopoulou and Zhou further report that these savings concern eligible items (related to oil price) that represent about 40 percent of the project value. These numbers together lead to an average project size of about US$1.5 million.

procured design-bid-build cost-plus road projects in the US with a mean size of US $2 million showed that these can be significant on a sample of 3,661 bids. Several models were used to break down the outcomes into separate effects. The adaptation cost represented 7–14 percent of the winning bid and ranged from 55 cents to two dollars for every dollar of change. The bidders could foresee where adaptation would be necessary, and the private rents are competed away (the average bidder could expect a profit margin of 3.5 percent). This is the case for small projects, however, where the uncertainty the bidders face is limited.

The theoretical prediction is that negotiations might facilitate increased precontract exchange of information and reduce the need for renegotiations. The more complex the project, the stronger the case.

Lessons from the private sector (Bajari, McMillan, and Tadelis 2009) show that in residential construction industry (private-private transactions), negotiated projects prevail and are generally awarded to more efficient or more experienced contractors. There is no analysis, however, that would test the impact on procurement outcomes. Caution is also necessary when trying to draw lessons from private-private contract relationships and transpose them to public-private relationships. Spiller (2009) proposed that third-party and governmental opportunism increase the incentives of public managers and private investors to raise contractual rigidity. In consequence public contracts are created with less flexibility than purely private contracts. Recent evidence confirms this is indeed the case (Beuve, Moszoro, and Saussier 2019). By implication, public managers in a negotiated process may be less flexible than private ones.

For infrastructure procurement, however, there is no evidence that would test the impact of the introduction of negotiations, keeping all else equal—for example in design-bid-build projects.[23] The use of negotiations in design-bid-build contracts has a limited function, since the solution to the engineering challenge is already defined (through a detailed design). What is left to be negotiated in public sector procurements is the interpretation of the specifications and the price. This means negotiations or competitive dialogue would have the greatest value in delivery models, where the bidders can also inform the solution—specifically, in our case, in design-build and engineering-procurement-construction contracts. Evidence is available that allows us to assess whether renegotiations in these cases are less significant than in auction-procured design-bid-build projects. To do so, we look at cost overruns on road projects.

Cost overrun evidence is spread over small and large projects, which may exhibit different levels of complexity and ultimately interfere with our inter-

23. A few studies exist that try to capture negotiation effects, but these studies do not do so in terms of procurement outcomes, or they refer to lower levels of the government, or both (for example, Baltrunaite et al. 2018; Chever and Moore 2017).

pretation of the evidence. Hence our first task is to get a view of how cost overruns develop with project size.

### 5.7.1 Cost Overruns in the Design-Bid-Build Delivery Model and Project Size

Cost overruns are not the same as adaptation cost. If cost overruns are high, however, adaptation cost will be high as well. Cost overruns represent the total value of changes to the initial contract. As explained in Bajari, Houghton, and Tadelis (2014), the first part of cost overruns comes directly from the additional work that was not anticipated (by the client). Adaptation cost (the second part) come in addition as the result of disruption to the normal workflow and the resulting haggling, disputes, and opportunistic behavior during renegotiations.[24] Put simply, it is the difference between the unit price for an item in the initial contract and the elevated unit price for the extra piece of work after renegotiation.

The number one direct reason for cost overruns that consistently appears in the construction management literature on transport infrastructure is scope creep, followed by errors and omissions in the design of the project (Makovšek 2013).[25]

Cost overruns are typically calculated as the difference between the total ex post cost of a contract and its initial reference value. In this section and in table 5.6, we are looking at the literature that measured cost overruns versus the award price. Most studies capture entire populations of projects over a select time period.

Table 5.6 does not show a stark difference between projects below US$5 million and projects that are tens of millions of dollars in size. Overall, the systematic cost overruns reach at most 9 percent.

Research on smaller project sizes showed that cost overruns do increase with project size.[26] Gkritza and Labi (2008), on a sample with an average project size of US$1 million, show a 1.55 percent growth in cost overrun for each 1 percent growth in contract award value. They acknowledge, however, that the relationship is nonlinear. This rate of growth does not extend to larger projects—at several US$10 million the systematic cost overruns would quickly exceed 50 percent or more. Very large projects of several US$100 million would have systematic cost overruns of several 100 percent.

24. As seen from Bajari, Houghton, and Tadelis (2014) and from Bolotnyy and Vasserman (2019), contractors can predict changes in simple contracts. These are included in their bids together with the expected earnings, which are then competed away (in their case) and represent a small part of the actual cost overrun. This is also why the cost overrun reported by Bajari, Houghton, and Tadelis (2014) is substantially lower (5.7 percent) than the adaptation cost.

25. The root cause of direct reasons is a different question. For example, the dominant explanation could be optimism bias or deliberate misrepresentation by the project's promoters, or more mundane reasons could be at work, such as inadequate risk management or ex post stakeholder pressure that could not be foreseen and managed ex ante.

26. The same has been determined for Navy construction projects (Jahren and Ashe 1990).

**Table 5.6** **Cost overruns in design-bid-build projects measured against contract value (at award) as the reference estimate**

| Source | Project type | Time period* | $N$ | Project size (mean in millions) | Average cost overrun (%) | Standard deviation (in %) | Geography |
|---|---|---|---|---|---|---|---|
| Ellis et al. (2007) | Roads and bridges | 1998–2006 | 1908 | US$2.8 | 9.36 | n/a | US, Florida |
| Bordat et al. (2004)* | Roads | 1996–2001 | 599 | Not directly reported (small) | 5.6 | n/a | US, Indiana |
| Bordat et al. (2004)* | Bridge | 1996–2001 | 621 | Not directly reported (small) | 8.1 | n/a | US, Indiana |
| Bhargava et al. (2010) | Roads | 1995–2001 | 1862 | US$0.9 | 6.1 | 24.4 | US, Indiana |
| Hintze and Selestead (1991)* | Roads | 1985–1989 | 110 | Not directly reported (small) | 9.2 | 1.22 | US, Washington |
| Bajari, Houghton, and Tadelis (2014)** | Roads | 1999–2005 | 819 | US$2.7 | 5.7 | 11.8 | US, California |
| Love et al. (2019)[a] | Roads | 1999–2017 | 18 | US$197 | 5.7 | 12 | Hong Kong |
| International Transport Forum (2018a)*** | Roads and bridges | 2008–2017 | 28 | €75 | 9.3 | 8.1 | Slovakia |
| Federal Highway Administration (2016) | Roads | 2004–2015 | 134 | US$21.6 | 4.1 | 9.1 | US |

*Note:* *Eighty-nine percent of projects were below US$2.5 million. **The authors do not report on cost overruns versus the winning bid but versus the in-house prebid estimate. Since the mean winning bid is 5.4 percent lower than the mean prebid estimate, the actual cost overruns measured against the winning bid in their sample would be marginally higher. ***The entire motorway program in the stated period.

[a] Shared by authors based on original data.

This is not confirmed in table 5.6 or by the Federal Highway Administration (2016), which found no relation between project size and cost overrun for larger projects in the size range up to US$357 million.[27] This is not to say, however, that for very large, mega projects above this range, cost overruns will not be substantially larger on average.

Based on this evidence, we cannot conclude that with the design-bid-build model larger contracts are more incomplete than smaller ones in ranges up to a few hundred million dollars.

*5.7.1.1 Further Evidence on Cost Overruns in Large Projects*

In addition to the studies in table 5.1, a body of evidence exists that measures cost overruns against the formal decision to build.[28] This evidence further corroborates the point that cost overruns (and by implication adaptation cost in contracts) in large projects are not disproportionately larger than in smaller ones.

As the formal decision to build occurs earlier in the project development, the estimates are less accurate, since the design documentation is not yet fully developed. The textbook example in figure 5.1 illustrates this point.

The evidence for road projects does not fully correspond to the textbook exposition. A consistent systematic cost overrun of around 20 percent ranging from several tens to several hundreds of million dollars has been shown. This is the case for advanced economies of the world (for example, Cantarelli et al. [2012] for the Netherlands; Flyvbjerg, Holm, and Buhl [2003] for Western Europe; Makovšek, Tominc, and Logožar [2012] for Slovenia).[29]

The early estimates are thus less accurate in terms of their dispersion

27. This analysis was not included in the original report and was confirmed by subsequent analysis of the data by the authors (personal communication with authors and Keith Molenaar).

28. This body of evidence is concerned with the presence of systematic errors in the cost (or benefit) estimates at the time, when a decision is formally made to proceed with the project development. If costs are systematically underestimated (or benefits systematically overestimated), then project appraisal may be affected. The formal decision to build is normally taken long before the project is mature enough to reach tendering. The studies do not observe contracts specifically, and a project may consist of many different contracts. The studies also do not report on any procurement dimension used in the contracts. Further review of available work in this domain is available in International Transport Forum (2018b) or Cantarelli et al. (2012).

29. Identification of the root cause of cost overruns measured against the decision to build (or the award price) is subject to ongoing work; the root cause is likely not the same for mega projects, which capture substantial political attention and so on. The explanations range from optimism bias or deliberate misrepresentation by the project's promoters (Flyvbjerg, Holm, and Buhl 2002) to technical explanations (Börjesson, Eliasson, and Lundberg 2014; Eliasson and Fosgerau 2013; Makovšek 2014) where the methods used to create inputs for project selection were imperfect, while the users had no ex post information to correct for errors. What is clear is that when projects get very large, the key determinant of cost overruns becomes the length of the project gestation period—the amount of time spent on project development before it reaches the tendering phase (Cantarelli et al. 2012; Flyvbjerg, Holm, and Buhl 2003). Hence, if a project requires a large number of years or decades to reach a decision to build, it is more likely to experience higher cost overruns. Very large projects are a case in point.

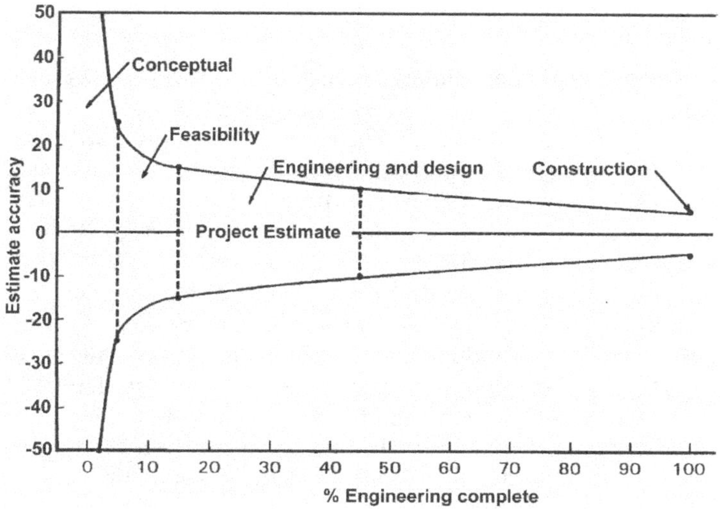


**Fig. 5.1 Cost estimation accuracy over the life of the project**
*Source:* Schexnayder, Weber, and Fiori (2003).

around the mean. The less developed the project design, the more costs are systematically underestimated. As the level of engineering becomes more complete, cost underestimation will decrease. The formal decision to build in the studies cited here is typically made at an outline design stage (10–20 percent of engineering complete).

For a design-bid-build (or any) contract to achieve a 20 percent cost growth against the award price, the winning bid on average would have to be made at a cost level that corresponds to a project's estimate very early in its development, and then the contract would need to consistently lead to a 20 percent cost overrun. This, however, is not what the evidence for larger project sizes in table 5.1 suggests.

In summary, the evidence discussed here further corroborates that design-bid-build road projects, ranging from 10 million to several hundred million dollars, experience average cost overruns well below 20 percent. An important stylized feature of cost overrun distributions measured against the contract award price or the decision-to-build estimate throughout almost all studies is a distribution asymmetric to the left with a tail to the right.

### 5.7.2 Do Bundled Delivery Models Lead to Less Renegotiation?

More complete contracts imply greater pressure on the bidders to express their revenue expectations ex ante and stress the importance of precontract information exchange. In transport infrastructure, bundled delivery models are commonly applied in large projects and in conjunction with high-powered incentives—the lump-sum payment mechanism.

#### *5.7.2.1 Design-Build Contracts*

The design-build model bundles design and construction phase in a single contract. Bidders in this case are commonly selected based on best value through a negotiated procedure.[30] The level of design provided to the bidders can range from 0 to 50 percent (Molenaar, Songer, and Barash 1999) of engineering but is commonly concentrated on the low end of the range. The payment mechanism applied is lump-sum (Chen et al. 2016; Federal Highway Administration 2016).

A rare example of a study that tried to control for complexity, bidder selection process, delivery model, and payment mechanism (but not cost per physical unit) was conducted by the Federal Highway Administration (2016).[31] Data for 291 projects were collected with a large share of bigger projects (mean US$27 million, standard deviation = 41 million); however, the results were statistically insignificant.[32] That said, the difference in cost overruns measured for design-bid-build and design-build projects was also very small.[33]

One of the key challenges for researchers of this topic was that the introduction of design-build delivery model is a relatively recent event, starting in the 1990s. As a result, most other studies faced the issues of small, unrepresentative samples, statistical significance issues, difference in project size magnitudes and therefore complexity, and so on (Federal Highway Administration 2006; Minchin et al. 2013; Park and Kwak 2017; Shrestha et al. 2007; Shrestha, O'Connor, and Gibson 2012; Warne 2005).

In summary, the evidence does not show that the design-build delivery model, in which the negotiated procedure is more commonly used, leads to greater contract completeness than auction-procured design-bid-build delivery model. How renegotiations can occur in the design-build model, however, is different from design-bid-build contracts. In the latter case a detailed design is made available to the contractor. This leaves the responsibility for design errors and omissions with the public client but at the same time also gives the public client control with regard to what exactly

30. In this case, the price is only one of the criteria for bidder selection, and bidders are not (primarily) selected on a lowest-bid basis.

31. One of the most cited studies on private sector vertical construction (residential or commercial/industrial buildings) contract performance (Konchar and Sanvido 1998, 102) also controlled for project complexity. The sample included 155 design-build projects and 116 design-bid-build projects. Facilities built were divided in six types. However, in multivariate linear regression neither the cost overrun differences nor the cost per physical unit (US dollars per square meter) for the two delivery models were statistically significantly different.

32. This is also a rare example of a study that included data on payment mechanism and procurement process.

33. DBB (bidder selection by lowest bid criterion) = 4.1 percent; DB (bidder selection by lowest bid criterion) = 2.8 percent; DB (bidder selection by best value criterion) = 4.0 percent. A similar result was found for 117 civil infrastructure DB projects (which included road projects) by Chen et al. (2016), who measured a systematic cost overrun of 5.8 percent.

the engineering solution is. In the design-build contract, an outline design is made available during bidding. In consequence most of the responsibility for design errors and omissions needs to be internalized by the contractor, leaving a much smaller scope for him to claim design error or omission. The public client no longer defines a detailed solution but provides a functional (output) specification, to which the asset needs to perform.

A logical conclusion would be that the cost overruns in design-build contracts are not smaller because the public client was not able to fully define ex ante what functions the public client wants the asset to perform. In consequence, changes are still required during construction. This point finds support in a study of 45 major design-build road projects in the Netherlands (Verweij, van Meerkerk, and Korthagen 2015),[34] with a mean project value of €190 million. The authors found that on average 50 percent of the cost growth could still be attributed to scope changes.[35] The root causes for this phenomenon are beyond the scope of this chapter, although the project management literature does offer some ideas, starting with Flyvbjerg, Holm, and Buhl's (2002) optimism bias or strategic misrepresentation.

*5.7.2.2 Engineering-Procurement-Construction Contracts*

In the design-build contract, an outline design is commonly made available during the bidding. This is not the case in the engineering-procurement-construction contract. The public client has even less control over what exactly the solution will be and defines expectations exclusively through an output specification. The lump-sum payment mechanism is the default option for this delivery model.

In transport infrastructure such contracts are primarily used because of the application of public-private partnerships (PPPs or P3 in the US).[36] A PPP is a project finance arrangement in which private debt and equity are used to finance the project and are paid back from the cash flow generated by the project. As lenders have no other recourse, they try to insure against risk that they cannot manage well or that is not part of their core business. Construction risk is transferred to the construction contractor through an engineering-procurement-construction contract alongside a range of incentives against nonperformance.[37] The bidders are normally selected through the negotiated process.

34. Thirty-eight of these were road projects. The study did not report the cost overrun against the contract award value. In addition, some projects were still in execution.

35. Of the rest, 12 percent could be directly attributed to incomplete contracts (incomplete, incorrect, conflicting contract terms); 35 percent of changes were due to technical necessities (for example, ground conditions turned out to be different from what was expected); 3 percent were due to changes in laws and regulations.

36. PPPs are also referred to through one of their many variants, most commonly as design-build-finance-maintain-operate (DBFMO) contracts.

37. The Natixis sample of major project finance projects (Blanc-Brude and Makovšek 2013) includes, for example, liquidated damages in case of delay (per day or per week), performance

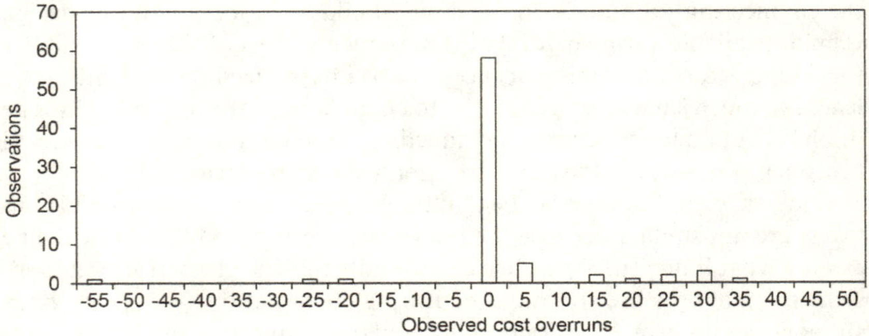


**Fig. 5.2 Cost overruns in project finance (NATIXIS dataset, $n$ = 75, 1993–2010)**
*Source:* Blanc-Brude and Makovšek (2013).

Blanc-Brude and Makovšek (2013) analyzed a database of 75 project finance schemes, ranging in size from US$24 million to US$13 billion. The sample is a mix of private-private transactions as well as PPPs.[38] The projects come from five continents and different sectors, including transport (14 roads and 12 other types). This dataset is unique in the sense that it represents the performance of the contractor as reported to the lenders and not the performance of the project company. Effectively, cost overruns in this case represent the construction risk exposure of the lenders and owners in the project company. The mean cost overrun of the sample is 2.6 percent (standard deviation = 11.4). With the median cost overrun at 0 percent, the risk is diversifiable; hence, project finance completely insulates the investors from the risk. However, unlike the rich distribution of cost over- and underruns around the mean in other (publicly financed) procurement options, in this case 18 projects were delivered with cost overruns, three with cost underruns, and 54 projects exactly on cost (figure 5.2).[39]

Raisbeck, Duffield, and Xu (2010) collected data on 21 PPPs and 33 traditionally procured projects (the procurement dimensions are not reported) from different sectors in Australia. The authors confirm that PPPs suffer almost no delays, compared to traditional procurement. The authors can-

guarantees, and full completion guarantees (a third-party guarantee that the project will be completed even if the main contractor defaults).

38. The data do not allow explicit identification. Nevertheless, the sector implies whether the projects were PPPs or private-private transactions. In total 43 projects were marked as to transport, social accommodation, and "environmental." In all these sectors, project finance arrangements would have to be PPPs (for example, roads, social housing projects, landfills). The average cost overrun of these projects was 1 percent.

39. Cost underruns do not imply that the contractor saved money and gave it back (it is a lump-sum contract), but that the project was canceled or the project scope was reduced. Conversely, cost overruns can be a result of scope increases introduced by (and paid for) by the client.

not, however, confirm with statistical significance that cost overruns measured versus the contract award stage are smaller (2.4 percent for PPPs versus 13.8 percent for publicly financed projects). Raisbeck, Duffield, and Xu include a review of literature commonly used in policy discussions, which are mainly industry studies suffering from a variety of sampling or representativity issues.

In this particular case the evidence does suggest that engineering-procurement-construction contracts are more complete and cost overruns are much lower than in other procurement alternatives investigated so far. Given that design-build projects represent a very similar procurement format, with the majority of the design risk transferred to the contractor, it is not immediately clear why the engineering-procurement-construction format or PPPs would perform substantially better. One possible explanation, however, is that the complicated financial and legal structure of PPPs makes changes prohibitively expensive for the public authorities.

## 5.8 Do High-Powered Incentives Mix Well with Complete Contracts?

Contract theory predicts that the cost-plus (bill of quantities) payment mechanism is more suitable for dealing with renegotiations than a lump-sum arrangement (Bajari and Tadelis 2001). Thus lump-sum contracts should be used when no or few renegotiations are expected. As noted during our review of theory, though, this proposition does not take into account uncertainties bidders face when pricing the contract. In our evidence review on the impact of precontract information exchange in auctions, substantial effects were measured in relatively small and by extension simpler projects.

In the following, we review evidence that provides some insights about how much uncertainty bidders face in contract pricing and what the impact of high-powered incentives on cost per physical unit could be.

### 5.8.1 Incentive Power and Performance in Small Contracts

In cost-plus design-bid-build contracts, bids are typically submitted through a bill of quantities, which lists expected quantities for the items and unit prices next to them. Bajari, Houghton, and Tadelis (2014), in their measurement of adaptation cost in such contracts, also revealed how much uncertainty bidders face. The authors found that bidders foresaw which items had quantities underestimated and strategically priced them. Bidders increased the prices for items for which quantities had been underestimated and reduced prices on quantities that had been overestimated to still achieve a lower total.

In an extension of the Bajari, Houghton, and Tadelis (2014) approach, Bolotnyy and Vasserman (2019) measured how risk averse bidders are in design-bid-build contracts. The authors simulated what would occur to project cost if the incentive power were to be increased. Their data build on Massachusetts Department of Transportation data on 440 bridge maintenance projects executed between 1998 and 2015 with an average contract value of US$2.7 million.

When bidders reduce their ex ante bid in the expectation of ex post adjustments, their main uncertainty is that they misestimate the adjustments. Bolotnyy and Vasserman (2019) demonstrated a substantial accuracy in the strategic behavior of bidders. The bidders could accurately foresee in the bill of quantities for which items quantities are underestimated. On average, for each 1 percent of quantity underestimation in an item, its unit price is increased by 0.085 percent.[40]

The same study also assessed what would happen with the price of the average winning bid had the procuring authority switched from a cost-plus to a lump-sum contract under which there would be no ex post adaptation. This condition implies that bidders would need to estimate well not only which items there will be quantity changes to but also what the changes in quantities will be. Bidders would have to express their full revenue expectations in the winning bid. Based on estimating bidders' risk aversion, the study showed that the switch would make an average winning bid in the sample 133 percent more expensive.

On the other hand, the results of Bolotnyy and Vasserman (2019) suggest that, even if the objective of contract completeness could be met, uncertainty interfering with the pricing of contract would still lead to significant additional cost. This result does not align well with the predictions of contract theory, which sees adaptation cost as the main challenge to incentive power selection.

This section observed small projects with an average size well below US$5 million. How does the level of adaptation cost develop for projects in the range of several tens or hundreds of millions of US dollars? What would happen if we applied bundled delivery models and lump-sum requirement on much larger projects, where the design is not necessarily complete at the time it needs to be priced?

### 5.8.2 Large(r) Projects and the Relevance of Incentive Power

The structural models in papers that tested contract theory propositions offer a precision view of how well bidders foresee ex post contract changes in the project, what part is the added cost of adaptations, and what part are the profit margins. Similar studies do not exist for larger, more complex projects. A single study to date investigated the relative performance of construction cost per physical unit for "traditional procurement" (design-bid-build

40. Bidders cannot push this approach to the extreme regarding the unit prices of underestimated items and discounts for the items for which they suspect the quantities are estimated accurately. When the procuring authority can detect a bid is materially imbalanced, a bidder could be disqualified. The advantage on the side of the bidders in practice is that it is difficult to determine with precision what "materially imbalanced" means.

contracts)[41] and PPPs (engineering-procurement-construction contracts) (Blanc-Brude, Goldsmith, and Välilä 2009). The sample is based on road contracts, tendered between 1990 and 2005 in the European Union. The study stands out from the others in that it targets large contracts, ranging from €20–300 million, consisting of 56 PPPs and 101 traditionally procured projects. Controlling for road type, terrain, economies of scale, portions of bridge and tunnel work,[42] size, and country (institutional environment), the study found that the ex ante (award) PPPs cost 24 percent more per lane kilometer.

An important characteristic of the Blanc-Brude, Goldsmith, and Välilä (2009) sample is also that the projects in question were supported by the European Investment Bank. This implies that the preparation and the execution of the bidder selection process benefited from the bank's advice, due diligence, and potential technical assistance. Thus, as far as quality of preparation or the execution of the bidder selection process is concerned, the performance of the sample is expected to be above average. There are no other indications in this study that the results (the difference between the PPPs and traditionally procured projects) could be affected by potential selection bias.[43]

As the Blanc-Brude, Goldsmith, and Välilä (2009) study captured contract cost at or close to award[44] and not ex post cost, further elaboration is necessary, and we cannot yet conclude that engineering-procurement-construction contracts carry a substantial cost premium over low-powered alternatives. As laid out in Makovšek and Moszoro (2018), two issues need to be acknowledged.

First, given all we know about cost overruns, the 24 percent cost premium for PPPs seems to be much higher than the average cost overrun observed in design-bid-build contracts. In addition, PPPs too exhibit cost overruns, albeit small. In table 5.1, cost overruns in design-bid-build projects reach at most 9 percent. As discussed in the previous section, engineering-procurement-construction projects have been recorded to reach cost overruns of 2 percent. Hence, indications are that even if Blanc-Brude, Goldsmith, and Välilä (2009) had ex post data on final contract cost, a significant premium would persist.

Second, a major argument why infrastructure would be more expensive in PPPs as opposed to traditional procurement is life-cycle cost optimization. Arguably, the long-term involvement in the project incentivizes the

41. According to the study, the majority of the "traditional procurement" sample are design-bid-build cost-plus contracts with a small presence of design-build lump-sum contracts.

42. Large bridges were separate projects and were excluded from the sample.

43. As noted in the beginning of the section, the study did control for numerous dimensions that would affect complexity and performed several robustness checks across several alternative subsample specifications.

44. The study's interpretation of ex ante cost estimate data was also addressed in greater detail in Makovšek (2013).

private owners to build a higher-quality infrastructure to save on maintenance cost later. While this may indeed be the case, there is no empirical evidence to show the observance of this principle is systematically worse in publicly financed infrastructure. Moreover, despite declarative embrace, there were practical obstacles to the introduction of these principles (Meng and Harshaw 2009). The UK National Audit Office (National Audit Office 2007) found that hospitals procured through PPPs were not built to a higher standard of quality. For roads specifically, the German Court of Audit (Bundesrechnungshof 2014) investigating German motorway PPPs came to the same conclusion.[45]

In summary, high-powered (that is, lump-sum engineering-procurement-construction) contracts procured through negotiation can lead to more complete contracts (greater cost certainty) but are substantially more costly than low-powered alternatives. In road infrastructure, limited available evidence suggests this premium is not a result of building to a higher standard.

Against our review of how economic theory informs procurement choices and the evidence on procurement outcomes, the next section looks at how governments procure in practice.

## 5.9 How Are Procurement Choices Informed Today?

Advanced public infrastructure clients ideally have a procurement strategy guidance defined, with more detailed support found in separate documents. The procurement strategy typically begins with a statement of objectives, a description of requirements, and an analysis of the market and client capability and then moves toward informing the delivery model (for example, Department of Infrastructure and Regional Development 2008; Federal Transit Administration 2016; HM Treasury 2016). Bidder selection process and incentive power are in most cases a result of the selected delivery model, whereby the first is strictly regulated by law.

### 5.9.1 Bidder Selection Choices Are Enshrined in Law

The bidder selection choice is subject to detailed description of the process (for example, Florida Department of Transportation 2015) and is broadly framed by the procurement legislation in any jurisdiction. In the European Union, directives on procurement negotiations for simpler projects are to be avoided, if competition can be secured. For more complex projects, when public authorities choose delivery models using an output specification (such as design-build), negotiations and competitive dialogue are allowed.

45. Two potential explanations were put forward. First, building to a different standard is inhibited by strict technical rules and regulations. Second, risk-averse lenders may prefer tried and tested methods rather than experimentation.

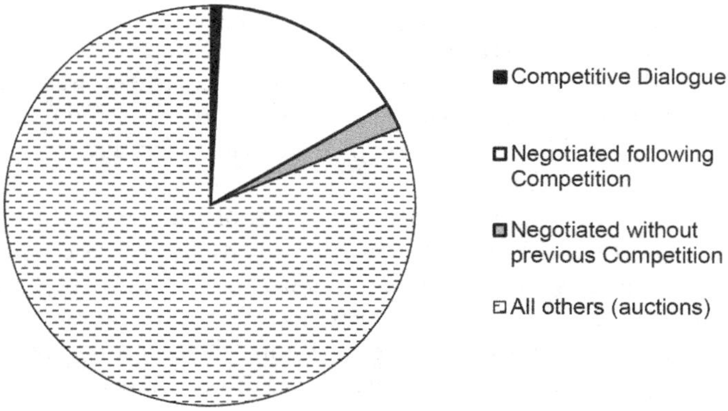


**Fig. 5.3 Procurement procedures in the EU market for rail and road projects above €50 million (2006–2016; *N* = 1520)**

*Note:* Sourced from TED electronic database, including all projects, where data on the procurement process were available.

*Source:* Based on data in Roumboutsos (2019).

Similar bidder selection options are now available in other jurisdictions (for example, in the US since 2004, Federal Acquisition Regulation [FAR], 48 CFR;[46] Scott 2006).

The use of negotiated procedures has been slowly increasing but is (at least in Europe) still limited (figure 5.3). In principle, the choice of procedure should be heavily related to the choice of the delivery model, but there may be other circumstances guiding this choice as well.[47]

### 5.9.2 The Delivery Model Is Chosen through MAUA

A common tool to inform the choice of the delivery model are simple descriptions of the pros and cons of various delivery models (for example, Federal Transit Administration 2016). Another widespread approach is the weighing of perceived attributes of individual approaches in pursuing project objectives (quality, being on time, cost, and so on). This method is

46. FAR in the US regulates procurement with federal funding (https://www.acquisition.gov/browse/index/far). The states themselves also developed procurement legislation, which follows similar basic principles.

47. For example, from the perspective of ex ante information exchange, where the delivery model requires a specification of needs such as with the design-and-build or engineering-procurement-construction models, the competitive negotiation (US)/competitive dialogue (EU) should be a necessity (Kennedy et al. 2018). That said, public clients could face impediments that affect their procedure choice related to, for example, available time to execute the tender, in-house capacity, or capabilities to run a competent negotiation. There is no systematic evidence showing whether there is a match between bidder selection procedures and delivery models.

called the multi-attribute utility approach, or MAUA (Chang and Ive 2002). Derivatives of this approach have been developed since the 1970s. Today, MAUA is enshrined in numerous government procurement practice guidelines (for example, Molenaar, Harper, and Yugar-Arias [2014] for highway infrastructure in the US; Department of Infrastructure and Regional Development [2008] in Australia).

MAUA is typically represented in the form of a table or a matrix (for example, Department of Infrastructure and Regional Development 2008). The first column lists the objectives or the desired outcomes of the project that the client considers important (such as speed of delivery, cost certainty, potential for innovation). In the second column the user attributes weights to these objectives (namely, decides which are more or less important). The remaining columns each represent one procurement option (such as traditional procurement, design and build, alliancing, PPP). For these, the user then scores how well the user believes a particular procurement option will satisfy the individual procurement objectives. In the end the weights of the objectives are multiplied by a utility factor representing the extent to which a procurement option satisfies each attribute. The most desirable procurement is the option with the highest score. The projects can also be subject to straightforward characterizations (for example, complex, simple) and procurement models designated as to which is best to match which type of project.

We should note that this approach asks many (research) questions on how well suited a particular procurement option is to meet a particular objective. As can be seen from this chapter so far, however, the performance of different procurement options is not well understood. Most available evidence is predominantly associated with cost overruns, delays, and construction speed. Aspects such as quality, value, or cost per physical unit are almost never captured. Empirically, as shown in this chapter so far, the trade-offs are not well understood. For more recent (collaborative) methods such as alliancing, there is practically no robust quantitative evidence available.

### 5.9.3 The Incentive Power Depends on the Delivery Model and Whether the Project Is Considered to Be "Simple"

The choice of incentive power to a large extent depends on the choice of the delivery model— by choosing the delivery model we also determine the payment mechanism. For the design and build or engineering-procurement-construction delivery models, the lump-sum payment mechanism is the default choice.

As regards the use of the lump-sum mechanism in relation to the design-bid-build delivery model, the guidance road agencies use tends to be prescriptive. Lump-sum contracts are allowed to be used only on very simple projects. For example, the Florida Department for Transportation (road) Design Manual specifically notes:

> Lump Sum Projects should be identified during the scope development process, rather than during or after the design process. . . . Lump Sum contracting should be used on simple projects. "Simple" is defined by the work activity, not by the project cost. (Florida Department of Transportation 2019)

The manual also provides examples of projects that may be good lump-sum contracting candidates: (1) bridge painting, (2) bridge projects, (3) fencing, (4) guardrails. Interestingly, design and build projects are also considered to be simple, because the manual assumes they have a well-defined scope for all parties and because such projects are thought to have a low possibility for change during all phases of work. As for the use of other payment mechanisms, when these are not a consequence of a particular delivery model, professional judgment is applied.

### 5.9.4 Recent Advances

In recent years, advances in the area of procurement in the UK and Australia signal a departure from the traditional perception of what a "procurement strategy" should entail. Specifically, important choices that will impact the outcomes of a procurement are made already before we start considering the questions of bidder selection, delivery model, and incentive power.

#### *5.9.4.1 Expanding the Concept of Procurement Strategy in the UK*

The UK has rolled out a series of initiatives with the aim of increasing the efficiency of procurement of infrastructure and in general. Specifically related to informing procurement choices, however, the new guidance moves beyond the core procurement choices pursued in this chapter. The newly deployed functional standards in relation to procurement identify the make-or-buy decision as the first choice to be made (HM Government 2019). The Project Initiation Route Map (HM Treasury 2016) explicitly introduces a step called project "packaging" alongside other, softer procurement dimensions (such as communication). The packaging concerns the question whether a (larger) project should be broken down into multiple contracts and where the boundaries between them should lie.

These two steps require a mindset that sees any project as a set of activities. These steps precede the procurement choices pursued in this chapter and importantly predetermine the procurement outcomes. For example, not insourcing an activity that we frequently need but that is available only from a single supplier will lead to an inefficient final procurement outcome, regardless of our choice of delivery model or incentive power. An example of bad "packaging" would be to procure a large project as a single contract in which, out of many, one activity has only two suppliers. As a consequence, two consortia would form around the two suppliers, and the competition benefits for all other activities would be reduced as well.

Both questions—the make-or-buy and packaging—go beyond the purview of auction and contract theory and move into the realm of the theory of the firm and new institutional economics. While the recent UK guidance asks that these questions be considered, it does not yet offer a tool to address them. To date, in infrastructure procurement such decisions have been left to professional judgment.

A tool that seeks to use economic theory to address the two questions discussed here and the three procurement choices we have dealt with in this chapter is currently being tried in Australia and is briefly explained next.

#### *5.9.4.2 A New Tool to Inform a Procurement Strategy in Australia*

The method proposed by Bridge and Tisdell (2004) and applied in Bridge and Bianchi (2014) and Teo (2014) rejects MAUA as tautological because it defines the cause—namely, procurement mode utility (for example, EPC contracts have better on-budget delivery)—in the same terms as the effect (for example, on-budget delivery for this project will be important). In consequence, MAUA simply points to the choice of the model that aligns with the buyer's preferred result. MAUA does not scientifically inform what the best procurement approach would be, given the nature of the project, when a simple broad description (for example, it is complex) is insufficient.

The first step in the Australian model is to identify the activities that concern the project's design, construction, maintenance, and operation. Each activity must be technologically bounded (distinct knowledge, skill set, or both) and correspond to the highest level of firm specialization available on the market. Table 5.7 represents an activity breakdown for a major road project case study.

In the second step, the model assesses each of the project-specific activities in terms of their transaction cost economics (TCE) attributes (frequency, asset specificity, uncertainty) and resource-based theory (RBT) attributes (rarity, cost to imitate). The assessment allocates the activities into eight brackets—competitive states (figure 5.4) that serve to predict which activities might lead to ex ante contract failures (low competition) or ex post contract failures (such as holdup).

Activities that are assigned a pattern 1 through 4 are considered most efficiently insourced, and so the remaining steps in the model focus only on the procurement of those activities assigned a pattern 5 through 8. For example, in pattern 8 the characteristics of variables are such that a firm (the supplier) could maintain a sustainable competitive advantage in the market. This would be because the activity is of large scale or size, or requires a rare technology, or both (Barney 2002). This limits the number of market firms that are capable of carrying out the activity, resulting in limited number of potential bidders (Teo 2014).

In the third step the model guides the user to explore bundling of activities—the model informs about whether the project should be split

**Table 5.7 Activity analysis**

| Design | Construction | Operations and Maintenance |
|---|---|---|
| *Design of construction*<br>1. Civil and structural engineering design<br>2. Civil and structural engineering design to the driven tunnel<br>3. Traffic engineering design<br>4. Mechanical and electrical engineering design, including air quality and ventilation<br>5. Fire safety design for tunnels<br>6. Landscaping and urban finishes design<br>*Design of performance, specification of maintenance*<br>7. Plan for routine maintenance, programmed maintenance, and rehabilitation of road pavement, road furniture, drainage maintenance, and ITS<br>8. Plan for reactive and programmed maintenance to specialist linings, mechanical and electrical and fire elements in driven tunnel | *Cut and cover tunnels*<br>9. Relocation of existing public utility plant, 10. Removal works, 11. Traffic management, 12. Bored piles, 13. Excavate and shotcrete, 14. Earthworks, 15. Structural, 16. Precast concrete, 17. Waterproofing, 18. Drainage, 19. Pavement, 20. Modifications to existing bridge and footpath, 21. Demolition, 22. Realignment of rail track<br>*Driven tunnel*<br>23. Excavation in tunnel and shotcrete, 24. Waterproofing, 25. Structural, 26. Precast concrete—barriers, kerbs, and wall, 27. Drainage, 28. Trimming and backfill of main tunnel, 29. Pavement, 30. Ventilation fan<br>*Road at grade*<br>31. Bulk excavation, 32. Subgrade preparation, 33. Drainage, 34. Concrete pavement, 35. Precast concrete: barriers, kerbs, 36. Retaining walls, 37. Asphalt pavement, 38. Realignment of existing busway, 39. Traffic management<br>*Bridge, ramps, median, walkway, and bikeway structure*<br>40. Traffic management, 41. Earthworks, 42. Pile foundation, 43. Structural works, 44. Precast concrete barriers, kerbs<br>*Bus stations*<br>45. Water and stormwater, 46. Electrical and communication, 47. Pile foundations, 48. Cast in situ concrete (lift wells, platforms, and bus bays), 49. Structural steelwork, 50. Roofing and draining, 51. Cladding and louvres, 52. Glazing, 53. Mechanical service, 54. Lift installation in bus stations | *Remaining construction activities in multiple parts of the project*<br>59. Intelligent Transport Systems and traffic operations<br>60. Inspections and data collection, including implementation of reactive routine and programmed maintenance to all parts of in project (including driven tunnel)—roads/pavement and furniture<br>61. Inspections and data collection, including implementation of reactive (emergency) maintenance |

*Source:* Teo (2014).

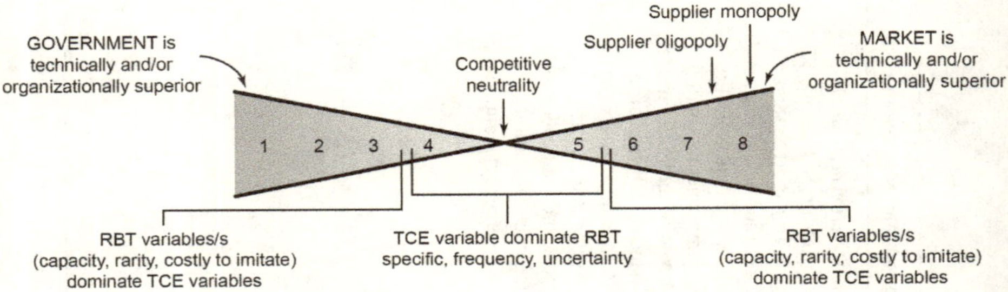


**Fig. 5.4 Make-or-buy analysis**

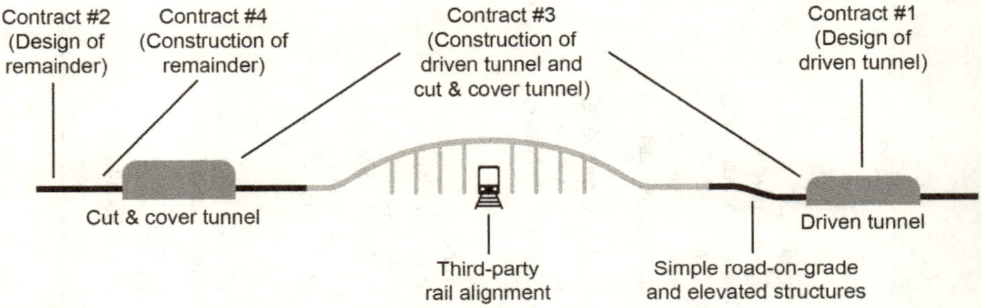


**Fig. 5.5 Bundling analysis**
*Source:* Based on Teo (2014).

into multiple contracts and which contract should particular activities be. At the risk of oversimplifying the process, the aim is to create bundles of activities that have a solid potential to attract many competitors and filter out those that do not, contracting them separately. This step corresponds to the "packaging" question in the recent UK procurement guidance introduced earlier. An actual major road project in Australia that was procured as a single alliancing contract was assessed by this model in figure 5.5 (Teo 2014).

The analysis showed that contracts 2 and 4 would have been most efficiently procured with a lowest price competition. Only for contracts 1 and 3 could alternative contracting methods such as alliancing, which rely on negotiations and do not derive their efficiency incentives from competition, be considered.

The model involves further steps to deal with other procurement dimensions, such as contract power. At time of the case study just discussed, the model did not yet acknowledge an important issue raised in this chapter: the role of uncertainty not only as a source of opportunistic behavior but also as a source of ex ante risk pricing failures.

In summary, the existing considerations of procurement in economic theory and construction management literature take the contract scope as a given and provide advice from that point on. For major projects, important decisions that will strongly affect procurement outcomes will have already been made by that point.

## 5.10 Discussion: The Opposing Forces in Contracts

The objective of this chapter is to provide an overview of what we know about how procurement choices affect procurement outcomes. Our scope was limited to a few well-established delivery models, which received most of the attention from the researchers; robust quantitative analysis that involves competent authorities in advanced economies is rare.

Where empirical evidence seems to depart especially vividly from the predictions of the economic theory is in the expectation that project phase bundling will reduce the need for renegotiation and that renegotiation is the primary challenge for the use of high-powered incentives or lump-sum contracts in our case. The available evidence does not support the expectation that negotiations and bundling lead to less renegotiation per se. This seems to be the case for road projects up to several hundred million US dollars. The issue is that cost overruns in design-bid-build projects are not very large; therefore, even if design-build projects could yield better results (and engineering-procurement-construction contracts actually do), the improvement would be a few percentage points. A marginal gain in cost (and time) certainty, however, yields a disproportionate cost premium.

In our discussion we first focus on this latter issue: why high-powered contracts are disproportionately more costly. Second, we stress that the same information that could help reduce uncertainty contractors face in bidding for infrastructure contracts would also help us better understand the performance of different procurement choices. Finally, recent developments suggest that the modern approach to procurement should be fundamentally revisited to optimally balance what the government is procuring from the market, in what contract sizes, and boundaries between contracts. These choices precede much of the discussion in this chapter, but will fundamentally codetermine procurement outcomes.

### 5.10.1 The Performance of High-Powered versus Low-Powered Contracts

Contract theory predicts low-powered contracts are a better solution for dealing with adaptation cost and suggests high-powered incentives should be applied, when contracts are sufficiently complete. This could be the case when a project is sufficiently simple or when the delivery model makes the contract "complete" by transferring property rights. Contract theory does not deal with the relevance of precontract exchange of information or when in the development cycle of the project its price must be established.

The evidence capturing projects with average sizes of US$1–200 million shows that all projects with cost-plus design-bid-build contracts will experience systematic cost overruns of a single-digit percentage and therefore adaptation cost.

Regarding the uncertainty the bidders face, for small projects, low profit margins and effective competition were demonstrated, and contractors had a reasonably precise grasp of the risks they are taking. When bidding, they could predict in the bill of quantities which items had been underestimated. Yet even in such simple settings, a risk premium of 133 percent was estimated (in Bolotnyy and Vasserman 2019) if the same projects were procured through a complete contract, where a detailed design is available and any remaining uncertainty must be fully priced in advance. The premium is disproportionate to the potential cost overrun of a few percentage points it has to absorb. Similarly, other cited examples also point to disproportionate responses of reducing precontract uncertainty (for example, Kosmopoulou and Zhou 2014).

In the bundled contract formats, the bidders must themselves develop a design during bidding. Construction risk is also comprehensively transferred and implies uncertainties much larger than guessing which items in the bill of quantities have been underestimated.

Moreover, contractors cannot assess risk in the same way as investors do.[48] Whereas investors could hope to rely on large time series of performance data, this is not the case for contractors. The pricing of design and construction risks relies heavily on expert risk workshops, in which experienced practitioners make informed guesses about the corresponding probabilities and impacts (Makovšek and Moszoro 2018). A further unhelpful factor is that governments have not fully exploited the possibilities of ex post analysis and performance benchmarking (OECD 2017).

In this context it is surprising that the actual premium for achieving cost certainty, such as in engineering-procurement-construction contracts in PPPs, is not much higher than the 24 percent measured in Blanc-Brude, Goldsmith, and Välilä (2009)![49] Although in the particular case there is

48. A more recent version of the approach also considers project-specific versus network-specific activities in cases where the design and construction pertain to the delivery of network infrastructure. In this case maintenance and operations can be performed network-wide, and thus economies of scale need to be considered as well.

Until recently, investors in infrastructure assets could not price risk efficiently because the adequate indices on the risk-return profiles of homogenous groups of infrastructure assets did not exist even after several decades of increased private investment into infrastructure. Recently progress was made toward establishing infrastructure as an asset class with a precise definition and benchmarks (https://edhec.infrastructure.institute/). Another G20 initiative is underway.

49. It is not straightforward to conclude that these premiums transform into abnormal profits for major contractors for a variety of reasons. For example, construction firms generally pursue multiple business lines, so the profitability of major projects would be drowned in the noise of other projects. Construction firms can be organized in several complementary profit centers. In the case of PPPs, for example, it is not uncommon to see an equity investor and a contractor being part of the same holding structure. The owners can choose when the profits will be expressed through the equity investment and when through the contractor. There is noise due to market cycles. Finally, construction firms can also dump risk down the supply chain,

only limited evidence to argue that the 24 percent premium is not the result of building to a higher standard, other evidence (as discussed earlier) corroborates that building on time and on budget alone will yield a disproportionate premium.

The order of magnitude difference with the 133 percent estimated in Bolotnyy and Vasserman (2019) can at least in part come from their approach, which involves the assumption of constant absolute risk aversion, an exponential function. It may not reflect real life. On the other hand, Nobel Prize–winners Kahneman and Tversky (1979) suggest that individuals tend to underweight larger probabilities but overweight those that approach zero. Thus the presence of low-probability, high-impact events could substantially affect contractors' risk perceptions and in consequence risk pricing. This is exactly what cost overrun distributions asymmetric to the left with a tail to the right imply. Indeed, in larger, more complex projects, the consequences of low-probability, high-impact events could be detrimental not just to the project but also to the contractor.[50] Hence, a small transfer of risk or uncertainty is still expected to yield a disproportionate premium.

Against these points, precontract information exchange will play a decisive role, but only limited empirical research on its impact has so far been pursued. Evidence on procurement of rail and road infrastructure in projects above €50 million in the EU suggests that less than a quarter relied on negotiated procedures and only a fraction of those on competitive dialogue (Roumboutsos 2019). The potential of these methods is not a given but must be exploited; public clients could significantly increase their efforts in identifying and sharing risk-related information (Kennedy et al. 2018).

Following our review of the relevance of procurement choices, the theory, and the evidence, we have to acknowledge that these lead to a nexus of opposing forces. Strengthening precontract information exchange through negotiation reduces uncertainty for the contractor at the expense of competition. Bundling design and build may reduce adaptation cost during project execution but implies greater uncertainty in risk pricing at the bidding stage. Finally, these choices interact with incentive power—how much cost certainty we want up front. Contract and auction theory have not yet reconciled these dimensions in a unified approach.

This discussion also implies that characteristics of PPPs, such as bundling and the high power of incentives, face trade-offs that could more than offset the potential benefits of the model. To date, though, no study has managed

which would imply that they are not necessarily the ones making money—their insurers and subcontractors could be the ones.

50. For example, in 1991 as the undersea Stoerebelt connection in Denmark was being constructed, water broke in through the face of the tunnel bore. Against the rules a worker forgot to close a bulkhead door, which flooded the tunnel and the Tunnel Boring Machine (TBM), resulting in massive delays and damage (Vincentsen and Smedegaard Andersen 2018).

to secure the data to allow a comparison of life-cycle cost with an adequate public counterfactual.[51]

In summary, at present public policy makers (or the industry) have no complete view of the consequences of their procurement preferences. Owners report simple reasons for why one procurement approach was preferred over another. For example, the primary reason for choosing the design-build delivery model is faster delivery (Songer and Molenaar 1996). Data on cost overruns are becoming more commonly available, and being on budget and on time involves reputational concerns. Comparative information on cost, however, is unavailable. The same is true for information about "value" or quality. These gaps in evidence could lead to suboptimal decision-making or, worse, create perverse incentives.

We turn to the issue of data availability, the role of governments, and what our review suggests for the future of procurement in the final subsection.

### 5.10.2 Reducing Uncertainty through Public Information

Our exposition so far has stressed the role of information in risk and procurement outcomes. Recently the International Transport Forum at the OECD (ITF) (Kennedy et al. 2018) mapped some of the best practices that are applied in reducing bidder uncertainty in major projects.

As noted earlier, however, one of the major challenges, especially in public infrastructure, is the absence of comprehensive and systematic benchmarking in terms of project outcomes. This has been a major inhibition also in the writing of this chapter, which has focused mainly on cost. Extending on categories of time and quality or adding maintenance on top would reveal even more scarcity of evidence.

To date, for example, it is not possible to compare infrastructure cost per physical unit in a robust (normalized) fashion. We are unable to say whether a kilometer of a 2×2 motorway built to a similar standard in, say, the UK is more or less expensive than in Germany, and if so why.[52] The same is true for railways and many other types of infrastructure. No international database that would with any confidence compare infrastructure project outcomes exists.

More recently however limited progress has been made. The UK committed in its Transport Infrastructure Efficiency Strategy (UK Department for Transport 2017) to pursue infrastructure benchmarking and issued the

51. In a comparison of a public road agency, which is funded from the general budget and dependent on annual budgetary discussions and a PPP, the latter would likely win. Such comparisons, however, are deceptive. The PPPs do not make road tolling possible. The introduction of tolling is a political challenge. If tolling can be introduced, the road infrastructure manager can be public or a PPP. Hence, an adequate comparison would involve a state-owned road company (such as those in Austria and Slovenia), which is funded through tolls and a toll-funded PPP.

52. The UK tried to benchmark with the Netherlands several years ago with very limited success (Infrastructure UK 2010).

first benchmarking principles in 2019.[53] Australia has been pursuing infrastructure benchmarking for several years.[54] A comprehensive road asset management standard has also been developed in multiple countries, though it does not yet extend to procurement choices and outcomes.[55] As project sizes increase, however, fewer potential observations become available. This makes it less likely that individual countries (unless they are among the largest economies) could successfully pursue a quantitative analysis.

The ITF (at the suggestion of the principal author of this chapter at the time) recently proposed an international transport infrastructure benchmarking initiative that would give a quantitative analysis the best possible chance, but countries have been slow to step forward (International Transport Forum 2018b). The benchmarking would begin with road infrastructure delivered in the recent past with the database updated on a periodic basis as the partnering organizations—the data owners—would deliver new projects. The data owners, the ITF, and potential research partners (such as universities) would have to agree on the data points per project collected and benchmarking objectives. Over time, the database could grow to include data preceding procurement (concerning planning and quality of project selection) and data on operations and maintenance (service levels and quality).

In conclusion, we do not argue that the lowest cost (at a given quality) is the only noble goal in infrastructure procurement. Other goals matter as well, depending on the context. We do argue, however that we do not have a sufficient empirical understanding of the trade-offs of procurement choices. While the majority of transport infrastructure budgets are spent on smaller and simple contracts, which are relatively well understood, potential suboptimal procurement choices on fewer but larger projects will have greater impact.

Benchmarking initiatives, such as those discussed in this chapter, could be an important step toward informing major procurement improvements. This is the state of the art in an era when a transition is slowly occurring from traditional procurement, in which the lowest price competition was the backbone to delivery models that forfeit price competition in favor of collaboration and are based on negotiation. Against the increased repertoire of different project delivery models, it seems to be even more pertinent to pursue decision support tools that comprehensively inform what we should buy from the market; how we should break down the projects into contracts;

53. UK Infrastructure and Projects Authority, *Best Practice in Benchmarking*, March 1, 2019, updated June 2, 2020, https://www.gov.uk/government/publications/best-practice-in-benchmarking.

54. Australian Government, Department of Infrastructure, Transport, Regional Development and Communications, "Cost Benchmarking for Infrastructure Investments," n.d., https://www.bitre.gov.au/data_dissemination/priority_projects/cost_benchmarking_infrastructure_investments.aspx.

55. The Australian example is available here: https://austroads.com.au/publications/asset-management/ap-t334-18.

and on which contract we should apply which bidder selection, delivery model, and incentive power choices.

## References

Adkins, L., and R. A. Adkins. 2014. *Handbook to Life in Ancient Rome*. Infobase publishing. https://doi.org/10.5860/choice.32-1097.

Bajari, Patrick, Stephanie Houghton, and Steven Tadelis. 2014. "Bidding for Incomplete Contracts: An Empirical Analysis of Adaptation Costs." *American Economic Review* 104 (4): 1288–1319.

Bajari, Patrick, Robert McMillan, and Steven Tadelis. 2009. "Auctions versus Negotiations in Procurement: An Empirical Analysis." *Journal of Law, Economics, and Organization* 25 (2): 372–99.

Bajari, Patrick, and Steven Tadelis. 2001. "Incentives versus Transaction Costs: A Theory of Procurement Contracts." *RAND Journal of Economics* 32 (3): 387–407.

Baltrunaite, Audinga, Cristina Giorgiantonio, Sauro Mocetti, and Tommaso Orlando. 2018. "Discretion and Supplier Selection in Public Procurement." Bank of Italy Working Paper 1178.

Barney, Jay. 2002. *Gaining and Sustaining Competitive Advantage*. 2nd ed. Upper Saddle River, NJ: Prentice Hall.

Beuve, Jean, Marian W. Moszoro, and Stéphane Saussier. 2019. "Political Contestability and Public Contract Rigidity: An Analysis of Procurement Contracts." *Journal of Economics and Management Strategy* 28 (2): 316–35.

Bhargava, Abhishek, Panagiotis Ch. Anastasopoulos, Samuel Labi, Kumares C. Sinha, and Fred L. Mannering. 2010. "Three-Stage Least-Squares Analysis of Time and Cost Overruns in Construction Contracts." *Journal of Construction Engineering and Management* 136 (11): 1207–18.

Blanc-Brude, Frédéric, Hugh Goldsmith, and Timo Välilä. 2009. "A Comparison of Construction Contract Prices for Traditionally Procured Roads and Public-Private Partnerships." *Review of Industrial Organization* 35 (1–2): 19–40.

Blanc-Brude, Frédéric, and Dejan Makovšek. 2013. "Construction Risk in Infrastructure Project Finance." Working paper, EDHEC Business School.

Bolotnyy, Valentin, and Shoshana Vasserman. 2019. "Scaling Auctions as Insurance: A Case Study in Infrastructure Procurement." Working paper 3887, Stanford Graduate School of Business.

Bordat, Claire, Bob G. McCullouch, Samuel Labi, and Kumares C. Sinha. 2004. "An Analysis of Cost Overruns and Time Delays of INDOT Projects." Publication FHWA/IN/JTRP-2004/07, Joint Transportation Research Program, Indiana Department of Transportation and Purdue University. https://doi.org/10.5703/1288284313134.

Börjesson, Maria, Jonas Eliasson, and Mattias Lundberg. 2014. "Is CBA Ranking of Transport Investments Robust?" *Journal of Transport Economics and Policy* 48 (pt. 2): 189–204.

Bridge, Adrian, and Robert Bianchi. 2014. *Major Infrastructure Procurement Research Project 2009–2013: Reforming the Procurement of Construction and Financing of Australian Infrastructure: Advancing Capacity, Competition and Investment*. Final report. Queensland University of Technology and Griffith University. https://eprints.qut.edu.au/76520/1/76520_Verification_Material.pdf.

Bridge, Adrian J., and Clem Tisdell. 2004. "The Determinants of the Vertical Boundaries of the Construction Firm." *Construction Management and Economics* 22 (8): 807–25.

Brooks, Leah, and Zachary D. Liscow. 2019. "Infrastructure Costs." *SSRN Electronic Journal*. https://doi.org/10.2139/ssrn.3428675.

Bulow, J., and P. Klemperer. 1996. "Auctions versus Negotiations." *American Economic Review* 86 (1): 180–94.

Bundesrechnungshof. 2014. "Bericht an Den Haushaltsausschuss Des Deutschen Bundestages Nach 88 Abs. 2 BHO Über Öffentlich Private Partnerschaften (ÖPP) Als Beschaffungsvariante Im Bundesfernstraßenbau." Technical report.

Calahorra, M., C. Torres-Machi, and Keith R. Molenaar. 2019. "Information Exchange in the Procurement Process of Design-Build Transportation Projects: Digging into the What, the When, the Who, and the How." University of Colorado Boulder.

Cantarelli, C. C., B. Van Wee, E. J. E. Molin, and B. Flyvbjerg. 2012. "Different Cost Performance: Different Determinants? The Case of Cost Overruns in Dutch Transport Infrastructure Projects." *Transport Policy* 22 (July): 88–95.

Chabrost, M. 2018. "Three Empirical Essays on the Impact of Discretion on Public Procurement Performance." Doctoral dissertation, Université Panthéon-Sorbonne-Paris I. https://tel.archives-ouvertes.fr/tel-01997216.

Chamorro, M. A., J. Soler, R. Ripoll, and E. Vilagran. 2018. "Building Contracts in the City of Girona from the 14th to the 18th Century." In *Building Knowledge, Constructing Histories: Proceedings of the 6th International Congress on Construction History (6ICCH 2018)*, edited by Nicolas Le Brun. London: CRC Press.

Chang, Chen Yu, and Graham Ive. 2002. "Rethinking the Multi-Attribute Utility Approach Based Procurement Route Selection Technique." *Construction Management and Economics* 20 (3): 275–84.

Chen, Qing, Zhigang Jin, Bo Xia, Peng Wu, and Martin Skitmore. 2016. "Time and Cost Performance of Design-Build Projects." *Journal of Construction Engineering and Management* 142 (2).

Chever, L., and J. Moore. 2017. "Negotiated Procedures Overrated? Evidence from France Questions the Commission's Approach in the Latest Procurement Reforms." *European Procurement & Public Private Partnership Law Review* 7 (4): 228–41.

Coase, R. H. 1937. "The Nature of the Firm." *Economica* 4 (16): 386–405.

Coviello, Decio, Andrea Guglielmo, and Giancarlo Spagnolo. 2018. "The Effect of Discretion on Procurement Performance." *Management Science* 64 (2): 715–38.

Department of Infrastructure and Regional Development. 2008. *National Public Private Partnership Guidelines*, vol. 1: *Procurement Options Analysis*. Canberra: Australian Government.

De Silva, Dakshina G., Timothy Dunne, Anuruddha Kankanamge, and Georgia Kosmopoulou. 2008. "The Impact of Public Information on Bidding in Highway Procurement Auctions." *European Economic Review* 52 (1): 150–81.

De Silva, Dakshina G., Georgia Kosmopoulou, and Carlos Lamarche. 2009. "The Effect of Information on the Bidding and Survival of Entrants in Procurement Auctions." *Journal of Public Economics* 93 (1–2): 56–72.

Du Plessis, Paul. 2004. "The Protection of the Contractor in Public Works Contracts in the Roman Republic and Early Empire." *Journal of Legal History* 25 (3): 287–314.

Eliasson, Jonas, and Mogens Fosgerau. 2013. "Cost Overruns and Demand Shortfalls: Deception or Selection?" *Transportation Research Part B: Methodological* 57: 105–13.

Ellis, Ralph, Jae-ho Pyeon, Zohar Herbsman, Edward Minchin, and Keith Molenaar. 2007. *Evaluation of Alternative Contracting Techniques on FDOT Construc-*

*tion Projects*. Final report, University of Florida, Gainesville, and Florida Department of Transportation. https://trid.trb.org/view/825920.
Engel, E., R. D. Fischer, and A. Galetovic. 2014. *The Economics of Public-Private Partnerships: A Basic Guide.* Cambridge: Cambridge University Press.
European Union. 2014a. "Directive 2014/24/EU of the European Parliament and of the Council of 26 February 2014 on Public Procurement and Union Repealing Directive 2004/18/EC." Accessed April 24, 2014. https://eur-lex.europa.eu/legal-content/EN/TXT/PDF/?uri=CELEX:32014L0024.
———. 2014b. "Directive 2014/25/EU of the European Parliament and of the Council of 26 February 2014 on Procurement by Entities Operating in the Water, Energy, Transport and Postal Services Sectors." Accessed April 24, 2014. https://eur-lex.europa.eu/eli/dir/2014/25/oj.
Federal Highway Administration. 2006. *Design-Build Effectiveness Study*. Final report to Congress, Federal Highway Administration.
———. 2016. *Quantification of Cost, Benefits and Risk Associated with Alternative Contracting Methods and Accelerated Performance Specifications*. Federal Highway Administration Project, Contract no. DTFH61-11-D-00009, 2013–2016.
Federal Transit Administration. 2016. *Best Practices Procurement & Lessons Learned Manual*. FTA Report 0105. Washington, DC: US Department of Transportation. https://rosap.ntl.bts.gov/view/dot/39038.
Florida Department of Transportation. 2015. "Design-Build Procurement and Administration."
———. 2019. "FDOT Design Manual."
Flyvbjerg, Bent. 2014. "What You Should Know about Megaprojects and Why: An Overview." *Project Management Journal* 45 (2): 6–19.
Flyvbjerg, Bent, Mette K. Skamris Holm, and Søren L. Buhl. 2002. "Underestimating Costs in Public Works Projects: Error or Lie?" *Journal of the American Planning Association* 68 (3): 279–95.
———. 2003. "How Common and How Large Are Cost Overruns in Transport Infrastructure Projects?" *Transport Reviews* 23 (1): 71–88.
Gkritza, Konstantina, and Samuel Labi. 2008. "Estimating Cost Discrepancies in Highway Contracts: Multistep Econometric Approach." *Journal of Construction Engineering and Management* 134 (12): 953–62.
Goeree, Jacob K., and Theo Offerman. 2003. "Competitive Bidding in Auctions with Private and Common Values." *Economic Journal* 113 (489): 598–613.
Goldberg, Victor P. 1977. "Competitive Bidding and the Production of Precontract Information." *Bell Journal of Economics* 8 (1): 250.
Grossman, Sanford J., and Oliver D. Hart. 1986. "The Costs and Benefits of Ownership: A Theory of Vertical and Lateral Integration." *Journal of Political Economy* 94 (4): 691–719.
Hart, Oliver. 1995. *Firms, Contracts, and Financial Structure*. Oxford: Clarendon Press.
———. 2003. "Incomplete Contracts and Public Ownership: Remarks, and an Application to Public-Private Partnerships." *Economic Journal* 113 (486).
Hart, O., and B. Holmstrom. 1987. "The Theory of Contracts." In *Advances in Economic Theory, Fifth World Congress*, edited by T. Bewley. New York: Elsevier.
Hart, Oliver, and John Moore. 1990. "Property Rights and the Nature of the Firm." *Journal of Political Economy* 98 (6): 1119–58.
Herweg, Fabian, and Klaus M. Schmidt. 2017. "Auctions versus Negotiations: The Effects of Inefficient Renegotiation." *RAND Journal of Economics* 48 (3): 647–72.
Hintze, J., and G. A. Selestead. 1991. "Analysis of WSDOT Construction Cost Overruns."
HM Government. 2019. "Government Functional Standard GovS 008: Commercial." London.

HM Treasury. 2016. "Improving Infrastructure Delivery: Project Initiation Routemap— Procurement Module." London. https://assets.publishing.service.gov.uk/government/uploads/system/uploads/attachment_data/file/529340/Prourement_Module.pdf.

Holmstrom, B., and P. Milgrom. 1987. "Aggregation and Linearity in the Provision of Intertemporal Incentives." *Econometrica* 55 (2): 303.

———. 1991. "Multitask Principal-Agent Analyses: Incentive Contracts, Asset Ownership, and Job Design." In "Papers from the Conference on the New Science of Organization, January 1991," special issue, *Journal of Law, Economics, & Organization* 7: 24–52.

Infrastructure UK. 2010. *Infrastructure Cost Review: Technical Report*. London.

International Transport Forum. 2018a. "Motorway Cost Estimation Review: The Case of Slovakia." *Case Specific Policy Analysis*. Paris. https://www.itf-oecd.org/motorway-cost-estimation-review-slovakia.

———. 2018b. "Private Investment in Transport Infrastructure: Dealing with Uncertainty in Contracts." Paris.

Iossa, Elisabetta, and David Martimort. 2012. "Risk Allocation and the Costs and Benefits of Public—Private Partnerships." *RAND Journal of Economics* 43 (3): 442–74.

———. 2015. "The Simple Microeconomics of Public-Private Partnerships." *Journal of Public Economic Theory* 17 (1): 4–48.

Jahren, Charles T., and Andrew M. Ashe. 1990. "Predictors of Cost-Overrun Rates." *Journal of Construction Engineering and Management* 116 (3): 548–52.

Kahneman, D., and A. Tversky. 1979. "Prospect Theory: An Analysis of Decision under Risk." *Econometrica* 47: 263–91.

Kennedy, Jonathan, Aris Pantelias, Dejan Makovšek, Klaus Grewe, and Julian Sindall. 2018. "Risk Pricing in Infrastructure Delivery: Making Procurement Less Costly." Paris. https://trid.trb.org/view/1565397.

Klee, Lukas. 2018. *International Construction Contract Law. International Construction Contract Law*. Wiley-Blackwell. https://doi.org/10.1002/9781118717868.

Klein, B., R. G. Crawford, and A. A. Alchian. 1978. "Vertical Integration, Appropriable Rents, and the Competitive Contracting Process." *Journal of Law and Economics* 21 (2): 297–326.

Konchar, Mark, and Victor Sanvido. 1998. "Comparison of U.S. Project Delivery Systems." *Journal of Construction Engineering and Management* 124 (6): 435–44.

Kosmopoulou, Georgia, and Xueqi Zhou. 2014. "Price Adjustment Policies in Procurement Contracting: An Analysis of Bidding Behavior." *Journal of Industrial Economics* 62 (1): 77–112.

Kostof, S. (Ed.). 2000. *The Architect: Chapters in the History of the Profession*. Berkeley: University of California Press.

Laffont, J. J., and David Martimort. 2001. "The Theory of Incentives : The Principal-Agent Model / Common Agency View Project Mechanism Design without Transfers and Constrained Delegation View Project." https://www.researchgate.net/publication/31737757.

Laffont, Jean-Jacques, and Jean Tirole. 1993. *A Theory of Incentives in Procurement and Regulation.* Cambridge, MA: MIT Press.

Love, Peter E. D., Michael C. P. Sing, Lavagnon A. Ika, and Sidney Newton. 2019. "The Cost Performance of Transportation Projects: The Fallacy of the Planning Fallacy Account." *Transportation Research Part A: Policy and Practice* 122 (April): 1–20.

Makovšek, Dejan. 2013. "Public-Private Partnerships, Traditionally Financed Projects, and Their Price." *Journal of Transport Economics and Policy* 47 (1): 143–55.

———. 2014. "Systematic Construction Risk, Cost Estimation Mechanism and Unit Price Movements." *Transport Policy* 35: 135–45.

Makovšek, Dejan, and Marian Moszoro. 2018. "Risk Pricing Inefficiency in Public–Private Partnerships." *Transport Reviews* 38 (3): 298–321.

Makovšek, Dejan, Polona Tominc, and Klavdij Logožar. 2012. "A Cost Performance Analysis of Transport Infrastructure Construction in Slovenia." *Transportation* 39 (1): 197–214.

McAfee, R. P., and J. McMillan. 1986. "Bidding for Contracts: A Principal-Agent Analysis." *RAND Journal of Economics* 17 (3): 326–38.

Meng, Xianhai, and Fiona Harshaw. 2009. "The Application of Whole Life Costing in PFI/PPP Projects." In *Proceedings of the 29th Annual ARCOM [Association of Researchers in Construction Management] Conference*, 769–78.

Milgrom, Paul, and Robert J. Weber. 1982. "The Value of Information in a Sealed-Bid Auction." *Journal of Mathematical Economics* 10 (1): 105–14.

Minchin, R. Edward, Xiaoxiao Li, Raja R. Issa, and Gary G. Vargas. 2013. "Comparison of Cost and Time Performance of Design-Build and Design-Bid-Build Delivery Systems in Florida." *Journal of Construction Engineering and Management* 139 (10).

Molenaar, Keith, Christofer Harper, and Ivo Yugar-Arias. 2014. *Guidebook for Selecting Alternative Contracting Methods for Roadway Projects: Project Delivery Methods, Procurement Procedures, and Payment Provisions*. Prepared for Next-Generation Transportation Construction Management Transportation Pooled Fund Program Study TPF-5(260). University of Colorado Boulder.

Molenaar, Keith R., Anthony D. Songer, and Mouji Barash. 1999. "Public-Sector Design/Build Evolution and Performance." *Journal of Management in Engineering* 15 (2): 54–62.

Morgan, M. H. 1960. *Marcus Pollio Vitruvius, The Ten Books on Architecture; with Illustrations and Original Designs Prepared under the Direction of Herbert Langford Warren*. New York: Dover Publications.

National Audit Office. 2007. "Improving the PFI Tendering Process."

Odeck, James. 2014. "Do Reforms Reduce the Magnitudes of Cost Overruns in Road Projects? Statistical Evidence from Norway." *Transportation Research Part A: Policy and Practice* 65: 68–79.

OECD. 2017. *Ex-Post Assessment of Transport Investments and Policy Interventions*. ITF Roundtable Reports. OECD.

Palguta, Ján, and Filip Pertold. 2017. "Manipulation of Procurement Contracts: Evidence from the Introduction of Discretionary Thresholds." *American Economic Journal: Economic Policy* 9 (2): 293–315.

Park, Jane, and Young Hoon Kwak. 2017. "Design-Bid-Build (DBB) vs. Design-Build (DB) in the U.S. Public Transportation Projects: The Choice and Consequences." *International Journal of Project Management* 35 (3): 280–95.

Port, M. H. 1967. "The Office of Works and Building Contracts in Early Nineteenth-Century England." *Economic History Review* 20 (1): 94–110.

Raisbeck, Peter, Colin Duffield, and Ming Xu. 2010. "Comparative Performance of PPPs and Traditional Procurement in Australia." *Construction Management and Economics* 28 (4): 345–59.

Roumboutsos, Athena. 2019. "Competition in Large Projects: PPPs vs Traditional Procurement." Presentation, International Transport Forum, Paris, June 22.

Schexnayder, Cliff J., Sandra L. Weber, and Christine Fiori. 2003. *Project Cost Estimating: A Synthesis of Highway Practice*. Washington, DC: Transportation Research Board.

Scott, S. 2006. *Best-Value Procurement Methods for Highway Construction Projects. Best-Value Procurement Methods for Highway Construction Projects*. Washington, DC: Transportation Research Board.

Shrestha, Pramen Prasad, Giovanni Ciro Migliaccio, James T. O'Connor, and

G. Edward Gibson. 2007. "Benchmarking of Large Design-Build Highway Projects One-to-One Comparison and Comparison with Design-Bid-Build Projects." *Transportation Research Record* 1994 (1): 17–25.
Shrestha, Pramen P., James T. O'Connor, and G. Edward Gibson. 2012. "Performance Comparison of Large Design-Build and Design-Bid-Build Highway Projects." *Journal of Construction Engineering and Management* 138 (1): 1–13.
Songer, Anthony D., and Keith R. Molenaar. 1996. "Selecting Design-Build: Public and Private Sector Owner Attitudes." *Journal of Management in Engineering* 12 (6): 47–53.
Spagnolo, Giancarlo. 2012. "Reputation, Competition, and Entry in Procurement." *International Journal of Industrial Organization* 30 (3): 291–96.
Spiller, Pablo T. 2009. "An Institutional Theory of Public Contracts: Regulatory Implications." In *Regulation, Deregulation, Reregulation: Institutional Perspectives*, edited by Claude Ménard and Michel Ghertman, 5–66. Northampton, MA: Edward Elgar.
Teo, Pauline. 2014. "The Effect of Procurement on Competition and Flexibility: Determining the Suitability of Public-Private Partnerships in Major Infrastructure Projects." PhD diss., Queensland University of Technology, Brisbane.
UK Department for Transport. 2017. "Transport Infrastructure Efficiency Strategy." London: UK Government. https://assets.publishing.service.gov.uk/government/uploads/system/uploads/attachment_data/file/664432/transport-infrastructure-efficiency-strategy.pdf.
Verweij, Stefan, Ingmar van Meerkerk, and Iris A. Korthagen. 2015. "Reasons for Contract Changes in Implementing Dutch Transportation Infrastructure Projects: An Empirical Exploration." *Transport Policy* 37 (January): 195–202.
Vincentsen, Leif, and Kim Smedegaard Andersen. 2018. *Risk Allocation in Mega-Projects in Denmark*. Paris: International Transport Forum.
Warne, Tom. 2005. *Design Build Contracting for Highway Projects: A Performance Assessment*. South Jordan, UT: Tom Warne & Associates.
Williamson, O. E. 1975. *Markets and Hierarchies: Analysis and Antitrust Implications*. New York: Free Press.
———. 1979. "Transaction-Cost Economics: The Governance of Contractual Relations." *Journal of Law and Economics* 22 (2): 233–61.
———. 1985. *The Economic Institutions of Capitalism: Firms, Markets, Relational Contracting*. New York: Free Press.

## **Comment** Shoshana Vasserman

It is quite clear from chapter 5 that not only are procurement practices ubiquitous and highly impactful for society, but they are also highly variable and comparatively understudied. The latter two conditions go hand in hand: there is such variety in conditions, restrictions, and requirements across procurement projects that the vast theoretical literature on contracts

Shoshana Vasserman is an assistant professor of economics at Stanford Graduate School of Business.

For acknowledgments, sources of research support, and disclosure of the author's material financial relationships, if any, please see https://www.nber.org/books-and-chapters/economic-analysis-and-infrastructure-investment/comment-procurement-choices-and-infrastructure-costs-vasserman.

and auctions (and, in fact, on models of procurement specifically) fails to generate many easily applicable rules of thumb.

A notable exception is "Auctions versus Negotiations" by Jeremy Bulow and Paul Klemperer (1996), which has become known as a "critique" of efforts to optimize auctions with clever incentive schemes rather than simply solicit the entry of additional competitors. Even this observation, however, relies on key modeling assumptions that rarely hold up in practice—complete contracts key among them—without which the validity of the conclusions is difficult to determine. What this means is that purely theoretical work is not enough: we need applied empirical work that can simultaneously speak to the validity of modeling assumptions in each setting and assess concrete policies that have been undertaken or proposed to the maximal extent possible.

Why then, are there so few empirical studies? Chapter 5 suggests a clear answer:

> To make progress on this front we need to introduce **systematic** infrastructure cost and performance **benchmarking**, which will also **include procurement choices** as an explanatory variable. This point, however, is not yet recognized by policy makers.

Why benchmarking, why include procurement choices, and what does it mean for all of this to be systematic? The nature of policy analysis is comparison. We wish to know how an existing procurement practice compares to a proposed alternative. As we can only ever try one variant at a time, we must rely on inferences of how an alternative would turn out on the basis of comparisons across existing examples. But comparisons require matching apples to apples. No two bridges are exactly alike, but a bridge in Massachusetts is similar to a bridge in Connecticut. Knowing precisely how similar they are is critical for determining how similar their construction costs and durations would be if conditions and procedures were the same—and if they were different.

There is no doubt that precisely what benchmarking standards should account for and include should be left for the experts to determine. But economists have a few requests that are worth listening to. It is generally insufficient to just record what work was done and how much was paid for it. In order to infer whether a project was done efficiently, there needs to be a record detailing how expectations for speed, cost, and quality were formed prior to completion of the project. This record must be as comprehensive and objective as possible. Crucially, it must be designed to be interpretable by any knowledgeable researcher.

A procurement manager in rural England may not know why a given railroad track near Berlin required the numbers of hours, screws, steel slabs, and so on that it did or why certain numbers wound up exceeding initial projections. But with enough examples to compare against, that procurement manager will be able to trace out patterns for which tracks are easier or cheaper to build and which features correspond to more efficiency or fewer surprises. Such insights are precisely what is needed to help determine the best procurement policy for each circumstance. For instance, variability between initial projections and ultimate usage suggests that there is contractual incompleteness. Consistency across many contractors is a sign of a competitive environment. The former observation suggests that careful negotiations may be preferable, while the latter suggests that barriers to eligibility for competing contractors may be unnecessarily prohibitive.

Moreover, these insights not only plug into established theoretical frameworks to suggest which rules of thumb are likely to apply, but they offer a path to more extensive empirical research. Bajari, Houghton, and Tadelis (2014) measured the cost of contractual incompleteness in California road pavement projects and found that while clearly relevant, it did not constitute a major loss. De Silva, Kosmopoulou, and Lamarche (2009) measured the impact of releasing internal cost estimates for highway construction projects in Oklahoma and found substantial improvements in the competition between incumbent and entrant firms. Detailed empirical studies of this sort can offer not just rules of thumb but also rigorous, tailored policy recommendations.

Impactful benchmarking is not impossible, but it requires explicit reporting requirements. It is no coincidence that the majority of existing empirical work on infrastructure procurement centers on projects with long-standing, detailed reporting standards like road paving and bridge construction. These types of projects are notably modular and formulaic, and so they are particularly suitable for comprehensive record keeping. But this is not the only reason for their unusual availability of detailed data. Absent explicit benchmarking standards, procurement agencies often keep only minimal records that are required for accounting purposes. When detailed records are not explicitly required, even the accounting that is done is often difficult to locate afterward. As a consequence, only projects whose procurement procedures require detailed cost delineation for public accountability have systematic records available.

The selected availability of detailed procurement data greatly limits researchers' ability to assess competing procurement policies, but it is not inevitable. For example, Luo and Takahashi (2019) compare procurement projects by the Florida Department of Transportation (FDOT) that use either a "unit-price" (UP) format or a "fixed-price" (FP) format. Unit-price procurement requires a comprehensive bill of quantities that details the amount of each input that FDOT engineers estimate will be needed for construction. Contractors submit unit bids for each input item and are ultimately compensated based on the actual quantity used. As such, detailed information regarding both estimated and realized costs is kept for these projects. By contrast, fixed-price contracts require only a single price bid for the entire project, and so no detailed delineation of costs and expectations is kept.

However, the distinction between projects that are procured with unit-price or fixed-price formats is hazy at best. As documented by Luo and Takahashi, FDOT managers choose which format to use for each project on the basis of heuristic guidelines. Thus, there is no inherent reason why projects procured with fixed-price contracts could not have records of a similar specificity to those procured with unit-price contracts; had a unit-price format been chosen instead, the records would have been made by default. Understandably, organizations like FDOT simply choose not to expend the additional effort (and cost) to create detailed records if they are not mandated to do so. As a consequence, even comparisons between similar projects procured with fixed-price and unit-price procurement formats are very difficult. Although Luo and Takahashi employ a number of clever econometric techniques to demonstrate the relationship between these formats in their paper, they are fundamentally limited in their ability to compare: there is no way to infer how a fixed-price contract would look in unit-price form.

It is precisely because different procurement projects are amenable to different forms of record keeping that standardized benchmarks are so important. Infrastructure projects come in all shapes and sizes; designing, planning, paying, and building come in many distinct forms. As such, it may not generally make sense to require item-level expectations and realizations for all inputs, as in the unit-price contract case. However, there is a tractable middle ground. In order to be maximally effective, benchmarks must be chosen to be systematic in the sense that they can be collected consistently across comparable infrastructure projects. For each category of project (perhaps grouped by scale and infrastructure type), there should be a set of meaningful metrics for uncertainty and performance of cost, speed, quality, and competition. Examples of metrics may include the composition of generic inputs (for example, commodities like fuel or concrete) and specialized inputs (for example, specially molded parts), the relationship between inputs and time to completion, and the extent to which the scope and cost of the project are likely to depend on contractor-chosen and unforeseeable developments during construction. In addition to these features, it is important for benchmarks to include metrics of competition: the number of contractors who contend for a project, the extent to which the procurer can impose quality control, and (crucially) the way the contractor is selected would go a long way.

Benchmarks do not need to be perfect. The variety of empirical papers discussed in chapter 5 (as well as a number of others) demonstrate how researchers can creatively extrapolate from partial data and natural quasi-experiments to build an understanding of which procurement practices work well, when, and why. To the extent that better, more comprehensive data become available, research will be faster and more convincing. This would be a welcome change.

## References


Bajari, Patrick, Stephanie Houghton, and Steven Tadelis. 2014. "Bidding for Incomplete Contracts: An Empirical Analysis of Adaptation Costs." *American Economic Review* 104 (4): 1288–319.

Bulow, J., and P. Klemperer. 1996. "Auctions versus Negotiations." *American Economic Review* 86 (1): 180–94.

De Silva, Dakshina G., Georgia Kosmopoulou, and Carlos Lamarche. 2009. "The Effect of Information on the Bidding and Survival of Entrants in Procurement Auctions." *Journal of Public Economics* 93 (1–2): 56–72.

Luo, Yao, and Hidenori Takahashi. 2019. "Bidding for Contracts under Uncertain Demand: Skewed Bidding and Risk Sharing." https://papers.ssrn.com/sol3/papers.cfm?abstract_id=3364708.

# 6 When and How to Use Public-Private Partnerships in Infrastructure
## Lessons from the International Experience

Eduardo Engel, Ronald D. Fischer, and Alexander Galetovic

## 6.1 Introduction

Public-private partnerships, also known as PPPs, P3s, and concessions, emerged in recent decades as a new organizational form to provide public infrastructure.[1] Even though public provision continues to be the dominant procurement option, investment in transport PPPs over the past 25 years has been considerable, adding investments of €203 billion in Europe and $535 billion in developing countries.[2] In some countries, investment via PPPs in other types of infrastructure, such as hospitals and schools, has also been significant. By comparison, PPP investments in the US have been relatively small.

PPPs are funded with a combination of user fees and government transfers. For example, a road in high demand can be funded entirely with tolls, while government transfers are usually the main funding source for schools and hospitals. In general, under a PPP the firm finances, builds, operates,

Eduardo Engel is a professor of economics at the University of Chile.
Ronald D. Fischer is a professor of industrial engineering at the University of Chile.
Alexander Galetovic is a senior fellow at Universidad Adolfo Ibáñez and a research fellow at the Hoover Institution.

We are grateful to Ed Glaeser, Keith Hennessey, James Poterba, and conference participants for their comments and suggestions. We thank Nicolás Campos for outstanding research assistance. Fischer gratefully acknowledges the financial support from the Complex Engineering Systems Institute (CONICYT-PIA-FB0816) and the Instituto Milenio MIPP IS130002. For acknowledgments, sources of research support, and disclosure of the authors' material financial relationships, if any, please see https://www.nber.org/books-and-chapters/economic-analysis-and-infrastructure-investment/when-and-how-use-public-private-partnerships-infrastructure-lessons-international-experience.

1. See Engel, Fischer, and Galetovic (2014a), Grimsey and Lewis (2004), and OECD (2008) for general introductions to PPPs.

2. Sources are the European Investment Bank (1990–2018) and Public-Private Infrastructure Advisory Facility (1990–2018).

and maintains the project. The contract term is long, usually between 20 and 40 years, and the facility reverts to the government when the concession ends. At that point the government can initiate a new concession, involving additional investments and revamping of the existing infrastructure, or manage the infrastructure itself.

### 6.1.1 Why Do Governments Choose PPPs? Political Economy Reasons

Governments choose PPPs mainly to spend more on infrastructure. First, and in contrast to public provision, most of the investment via PPPs is not counted as public debt, nor does it contribute to the fiscal deficit, at least in the short run. This is attractive for governments constrained by fiscal rules or international agreements, like the Maastricht Treaty, that limit their levels of debt and deficits.[3] The second reason PPPs allow governments to spend more is that these investments are usually not subject to congressional oversight and other budgetary controls. Therefore, PPPs allow incumbents more leeway for spending.

Nevertheless, the fiscal impact of a project in present value is the same, whether it is procured as a PPP or as a public work.[4] For example, by choosing a PPP to procure a toll road, the government does not pay for the up-front investment. However, these savings are equal, in present value, to the toll revenues that the government forgoes during the duration of the concession. This equivalence result also debunks the claim that PPPs free up government funds, an argument that ignores the fiscal impact of PPPs after the project is built.[5] It follows that investments in infrastructure via PPPs should be recorded in fiscal accounts in the same way as public investments (see Engel, Fischer, and Galetovic [2013] for a formal treatment).[6]

The preferential treatment of PPPs has led to higher deficits and to projects being provided as PPPs when traditional provision is more efficient.[7] Sometimes governments choose PPPs for ideological reasons: PPPs are a second-best option to replace an incompetent public sector with an efficient private

3. "Cynics suspect that the government remains keen on PFI not because of the efficiency it allegedly offers, but because it allows ministers to perform a useful accounting trick." *Economist*, July 2, 2009. PFI is the acronym for the UK's PPP program.

4. This argument omits any efficiency differences between these two procurement mechanisms.

5. "The boom [in PPPs] is good news for governments with overstretched public finances: many local and national authorities have found themselves sitting on toll roads, ports, and airports that they can sell for billions of dollars to fund other public services." *Financial Times*, July 5, 2007.

6. This recommendation does not rule out having a dollar of investment in public infrastructure count less than a dollar of other types of government expenditure as argued by Blanchard and Giavazzi (2004). It means that such a differential treatment should apply both to public provision and to PPPs.

7. "Some have argued that the structuring of Network Rail and the pursuit of PFI deals were influenced by the fiscal rules in place at the time. It is not for us to comment on the motivation behind these decisions, but it is possible to see why people might believe that their statistical treatment may have played a part." *Fiscal Risks Report*, UK Office of Budget Responsibility, 2017.

sector when privatization is not possible. This argument is incorrect. It overlooks that the private sector is already routinely involved in public provision of infrastructure as designers, builders, operators, and maintainers of public infrastructure. Moreover, stronger government capabilities are required to provide infrastructure services efficiently with PPPs. Finally, the financing of PPPs is more complex and there is more scope for opportunistic behavior because the contractual relationship between the firm and the government lasts for decades. These issues are at the core of PPP governance challenges.

### 6.1.2 Economic Reasons for Governments to Use PPPs

An economic argument for PPPs is that governments should use PPPs instead of public provision when they provide sufficient efficiency gains. Since private firms are already involved in building infrastructure projects under public provision, efficiency gains do not stem from private participation per se but from the different incentives.

*Narrow focus and dedicated management*: A PPP is a private specialized firm whose contracting relations with employees, other firms, and financiers are governed by private law. This improves incentives, because during the term of the PPP, the private firm can manage the infrastructure as a private entity. Moreover, by creating a specialized firm (called a special purpose vehicle, or SPV) to build and manage the infrastructure project, the scope of the firm is clearly defined and bounded, and the project gets a dedicated management team, which answers to the firm's board.

*Bundling*: PPPs provide incentives to make noncontractible investments during construction that may reduce maintenance and operations costs over the life cycle of the concession (Grout and Stevens 2003; Hart 2003). No such incentives are present under public provision, since different firms are in charge of construction and operations. This "bundling argument" in favor of PPPs requires that quality of service be contractible; otherwise, the concessionaire may lower costs by degrading the quality of service. Singh (2018) provides evidence that PPPs encourage investments that reduce life-cycle maintenance costs.

*Fewer and shorter construction delays*: Incentives to avoid delays are large if a PPP can begin charging user fees or receiving government transfers only after the project is operational.

The two efficiency arguments in favor of PPPs that follow apply when the project is funded mainly with user fees.

*Filtering white elephants*: PPPs filter white elephants since, in the absence of government transfers, no firm will be interested in a project in which user fees cannot pay for capital and operational expenditures. This insight goes back to Adam Smith.[8]

8. "When high roads are made and supported by the commerce that is carried on by means of them, they can be made only where that commerce requires them. . . . A magnificent road

*Avoiding the cost of bureaucracies*: PPPs allow users to pay the firm that builds and operates the infrastructure asset directly, avoiding the efficiency costs associated with spending money via government bureaucracies (see Engel, Fischer, and Galetovic [2013] for a formal model). These efficiency losses are caused by justifiable rigidities in public spending and by corruption.

*Advantages of private financing*: PPPs developed hand in hand with project finance, a technique based on lending against the cash flow of a project that is legally and economically self-contained. Banks, which are usually the main financiers during construction, mitigate moral hazard by exercising tight control over changes in the project's design and disbursing funds only gradually as project stages are completed. The oversight under public provision is weaker as a result of moral hazard.

*Better and less expensive maintenance*: In most countries, there is a bias to spend on new infrastructure and against maintaining the existing infrastructure. New infrastructure is more visible and can be used to increase an incumbent's reelection probability.[9] Also, the annual logic of public budgets makes it difficult to guarantee funding for future maintenance at the time the project is built.

Intermittent maintenance is very costly. Not only is the average quality of service much lower than with continuous maintenance, but the overall cost of intermittent maintenance is also higher. For example, in the case of highways, the cost of intermittent maintenance, which often involves costly rehabilitations, has been estimated to be between 1.5 and more than 3 times the cost of continuous maintenance.[10] Recent studies (see Leslie [2019] and references therein) suggest that PPPs may involve important efficiency gains from better maintenance for other types of infrastructure services, prominent among them hospitals.

PPPs solve the maintenance problem of public provision if the quality of the services provided by the infrastructure asset is contractible. It then suffices to set service quality specifications in the contract and enforce them on a regular basis. In the case of highways, which account for the largest fraction of investment in PPPs, the efficiency gains associated with better and cheaper maintenance are substantial. On the cost side, these savings are somewhere between 10 and 32 percent of initial investments.[11]

---

cannot be made merely because it happens to lead to the country villa of the intendant of the province." Adam Smith, *Wealth of Nations*, 1776.

9. Rioja (2003) estimates, based on social welfare criteria, that one-third of expenditures on new infrastructure should be allocated to maintaining existing projects.

10. See TRIP (2013) for the lower bound, which applies to the US. For the upper bound, see World Bank (1994, 4): "Timely maintenance expenditures of $12 billion would have saved road reconstruction costs of $45 billion in Africa in the past decade." The difference grows with the extent to which the road is allowed to deteriorate before it is rehabilitated.

11. We arrive at this range as follows: Annual maintenance costs of a typical highway are typically 2–3 percent of the initial investment. Over a 30-year period, discounted at 5 percent,

### 6.1.3 Governance and Renegotiations

Under a PPP there is more scope for opportunistic behavior than with traditional provision, because the contractual relationship between the firm and the government lasts for several decades. Therefore, efficient infrastructure provision under a PPP requires governance that prevents opportunistic renegotiations.

Contract renegotiations that modify the initial contract have been pervasive under PPPs, however. Even though incompleteness is to be expected in a complex contract that lasts several decades, the evidence suggests that renegotiations are often the result of poor project and contract design, opportunistic behavior by concessionaires, the desire of incumbents to increase spending in infrastructure, and outright corruption.

Renegotiations cancel the efficiency gains promised by PPPs. For example, if concessionaires expect to be bailed out when demand for the project turns out to be low, PPPs do not filter white elephants. Similarly, incentives for careful project and contract design are weak if lack of diligence at the design stage can be corrected by altering the project during construction. Even more worrisome, when contract renegotiations become central to the PPP business model, firms that are good at renegotiating and lobbying have an advantage, as they can bid more aggressively when the project is tendered, in the expectation of recovering profitability in renegotiations.

Renegotiations also allow incumbents to bring forward investment spending, to increase their probabilities of reelection. Because PPPs are kept off the balance sheet, additional spending does not go through the usual budgetary oversight process. Therefore, the incumbent can ask for additions to the initial project and pay for them with an extension of the concession term or payments that will be made by future administrations. Moreover, the new works are likely to be more expensive because they are usually not contracted in competitive tenders.

Recent evidence from Latin America shows a connection between renegotiations and corruption. Campos et al. (2019) consider all projects undertaken by the Brazilian conglomerate Odebrecht in eight countries over a 10-year period and find that the average renegotiation, as a fraction of the initial investment, was 71 percent for projects in which bribes were paid, compared with 6 percent for projects with no bribes. These percentages do not differ substantially between PPPs and public provision, suggesting that renegotiations are always problematic when providing public infrastructure.

The frequency and magnitude of costly renegotiations can be reduced by making them less attractive for concessionaires and public authorities.

this adds as much as 32–48 percent to the cost of the highway. Using the 3:1 ratio of maintenance costs under continuous and intermittent maintenance then leads to the 10–32 percent range for savings.

For example, the contract can include the requirement that any significant addition to the project must be assigned in a competitive auction, in which concessionaires cannot bid. Another helpful measure is to create an independent, specialized board that reviews and approves renegotiations to ensure that the SPV and its owners do not increase their profits in renegotiations.

Costly renegotiations can also be avoided by using contracts with better risk allocation. In the standard fixed-term highway PPP contract with tolls, the concessionaire bears all the exogenous demand risk. This risk is in general beyond the concessionaire's control, and low realizations of demand often trigger renegotiations. In contrast, a flexible-term contract, with the winning firm collecting a fixed amount in user fees (in present value), eliminates demand risk. By extending the contract term when the demand realization is low, these present-value-of-revenue (PVR) contracts have a built-in renegotiation, which is triggered automatically when demand falls. Therefore, it is unnecessary to modify the contract, avoiding this source of opportunistic behavior.

Chile began using PVR contracts for most transportation PPPs in 2007. The country reformed its PPP legislation in 2010 and created an independent technical panel that reviews and authorizes large renegotiations. Under the reformed law, the owners of the SPV are required to auction the works in all major additions to the initial project. The combination of both policy innovations was followed by a reduction in renegotiations of more than 90 percent, as a fraction of initial investment.

The remainder of this chapter is organized as follows. In section 6.2 we briefly review some data about global and regional PPP spending and show that PPPs represent a modest share of total infrastructure spending. Section 6.3 explains how current fiscal accounting practices stimulate the use of PPPs for the wrong reasons. Section 6.4 discusses the efficiency gains potentially brought about by PPPs. Section 6.5 deals with renegotiations, perhaps the main threat to the PPP model of procurement. Section 6.6 describes the PVR contract, which corrects many of the defects of fixed-term contracts. Section 6.7 concludes the chapter.

## 6.2 PPPs around the World

### 6.2.1 World Infrastructure and PPPs

Governments use PPPs to procure infrastructure.[12] Comprehensive figures of world infrastructure spending are notoriously difficult to obtain.

12. What is classified as infrastructure varies. Ports, airports, railroads, and roads are almost universally included in any list and are called "transport infrastructure." "Social infrastructure" includes government buildings and facilities, schools, jails, and hospitals. "Energy" includes electricity (generation, transmission, and distribution) and pipelines (oil and gas). "Sanitary infrastructure" includes waste management and water (production, distribution, sewerage, and

**Table 6.1** **World infrastructure spending and PPPs, 2008–2010, annual, billions of dollars**

| | Total | Private | | |
|---|---|---|---|---|
| | Public + private | PPP (project finance) | Non-PPP (project finance) | Corporate finance |
| Transport | 1,040 | [45–75] | — | n/a |
| Airports | 80 | | | |
| Ports | 110 | | | |
| Railroads | 400 | | | |
| Roads | 450 | | | |
| Social infrastructure | 490 | [12–20] | — | n/a |
| Water and waste | 160 | | — | n/a |
| Oil, gas (transmission) | 200 | | n/a | n/a |
| Electricity | 810 | [3–5] | [140–160] | n/a |
| Telecoms | 300 | | [42–48] | n/a |
| Total | 3,000 | | | |
| Total private | 1,000 | [60–100] | [180–220] | [680–760] |
| World GDP 2010 | 63,000 | | | |

Available estimates of global infrastructure and PPP spending come from a few studies by global consultancy firms and must be parsed from several studies. We now will see that available data suggests that PPP spending accounts for about 3 percent of global infrastructure spending and 8 percent of private infrastructure spending.[13]

According to Airoldi et al. (2013, exhibit 1), world public and private infrastructure spending, excluding telecoms, averaged about $2.7 trillion in 2008–2010.[14] As can be seen in the row labels of table 6.1, spending can be broken down into transportation ($1,040 billion), social infrastructure ($490 billion), water and waste ($160 billion), oil and gas transmission ($190 billion), and electricity ($810 billion). Transportation, in turn, can be broken down into ports ($110 billion), airports ($80 billion), rail ($400 billion), and roads ($450 billion). Moreover, according to the consultancy Infonetics, global capital expenditure spending in telecommunications was about $300 billion in 2011. Hence, yearly global infrastructure spending is about $3 trillion, around 5 percent of world GDP.

Also according to Airoldi et al. (2013, exhibit 1), private infrastructure spending is about one-third of total infrastructure spending. With some extrapolation to telecoms, this implies that private spending in infrastructure is about $1 trillion. Private infrastructure is funded through PPP project

treatment). Finally, sometimes telecom investments (cable or fiber optic transmission, towers, base stations, fixed line, and satellites) are included.

13. What follows is based on Engel, Fischer, and Galetovic (2014b).

14. This estimate includes 69 countries that account for about 96 percentage of world GDP.

finance, other project finance, and standard corporate finance. We have not found a breakdown of private infrastructure investment by type of infrastructure.

Estimates of PPP investment are rather sparse. We built the following estimate, reported in the first column of table 6.1, with information from Inderst (2013) and Blanc-Brude and Ismail (2013). Note that most PPPs are financed with project finance. According to Inderst (2013), who cites Dealogic (2012), total project finance around the world in 2012 was \$382 billion—total project finance for infrastructure projects varies between \$280 billion and \$320 billion. According to Inderst (2013, 24), PPPs represent between \$60 billion and \$110 billion per year of project finance.

It can also be seen in table 6.1 that around 75 percent of PPP spending is in the transport sector—that is, \$45–\$75 billion per year. Another 20 percent of PPP spending finances government services (\$12–\$20 billion per year), while the remainder (\$3–\$5 billion per year) is invested in the electricity, telecoms, and water and waste. It follows that PPP spending is only a small fraction of global infrastructure spending: around 3 percent of total world infrastructure spending and around 8 percent of private infrastructure spending.

### 6.2.2 PPPs in Europe and Developing Countries

PPP spending and the number of projects are relatively small. To gain some perspective about recent developments in PPP spending, we present some data from Europe and from developing countries.

#### *6.2.2.1 Europe*

In the European Union, infrastructure PPPs emerged in the 1990s and grew until the 2008 crisis, peaking at €26.8 billion in 2007 (see figure 6.1). There were 129 PPP projects in the EU that year, but since then their number and value has fallen, and in 2018 there were 39 projects worth €14.6 billion.

All in all, since the 1990s 1,841 PPP projects were undertaken in the European Union, valued at €383.2 billion, with an average project value equal to €480 million.[15] More than half of the investments (54.8 percent) were in roads (391 projects, €500 million on average), followed at a big distance by health care (393 projects, €129 million on average) and education (443 projects, €81 million on average).

However, these investments are a small fraction of EU investments in infrastructure. The European Economic Association (EEA) records investments in transport infrastructure.[16] Between 1995 and 2014, average annual EEA road infrastructure investment was €62.5 billion. Considering all transportation sectors (road, rail, inland water, sea, and air), this average increases

15. Source of the data in the paragraph: https://data.eib.org/epec/sector/all.

16. The European Economic Association includes all member countries of the EU plus Switzerland, Norway, Iceland, Lichtenstein, and Croatia.

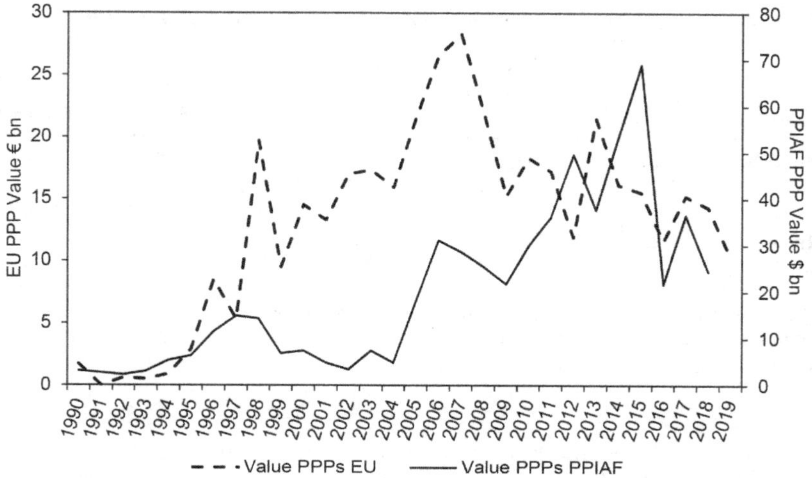


**Fig. 6.1 Value of PPP projects in the European Union and in developing countries**
*Source:* For the EU, https//data.eib.org/epec/sector/all. For developing countries, the PPIAF database 2019, processed by the authors.

to €111.5 billion. Therefore, transport PPPs represent 9 percent of transport investment in the EU. In Europe, PPPs are a complement and not the main source of transport investment.

Notwithstanding their small proportion of total expenditure in Europe, in some countries PPP projects represented substantial additions to the transport infrastructure. For instance, between 1999 and 2008 Portugal built 1,300 kilometers of highways using PPPs, which increased the stock of highway kilometers by two-thirds, from less than 2,000 kilometers before 1999.[17]

### *6.2.2.2 Developing Countries*

The Private Infrastructure Advisory Facility (PPIAF) keeps a database of PPP projects in developing countries, classified by type of investment (transport, energy, telecom, and water and sanitation). Between 1990 and 2018 there were 1,762 transport projects (railroads, roads, ports, and airports) with a combined investment value of $535 billion. The average road cost $287 million, close to the project average of $304 million. Figure 6.1 shows the evolution of these PPPs in value.[18]

Table 6.2 shows the sectoral composition of transport PPPs. About half of all the projects and amounts invested are road concessions. About a quarter of the projects, but only 13 percent of the investments, went to ports.

17. "Major Highway Growth in Portugal," *Highways Routes du Monde*, March 2010, http://www.worldhighways.com/sections/eurofile/features/major-highway-growth-in-portugal/.

18. We include projects only when they reach financial closure. The PPPIAF database includes projects with private participation that are not PPPs. These amount to 310 projects worth $46 billion—that is, less than 10 percent by value.

Table 6.2 Number and investment in PPPs by sector, developing countries

| Sector | Projects | Total investment ($ millions) | Average project size ($ millions) | % of PPP investment | % of projects |
|---|---|---|---|---|---|
| Airports | 142 | 95.085 | 670 | 17,8 | 8,1 |
| Roads | 921 | 264.219 | 287 | 49,4 | 52,3 |
| Ports | 469 | 69.839 | 149 | 13,1 | 26,6 |
| Railways | 228 | 105.601 | 463 | 19,7 | 13,0 |
| Total | 1760 | 534.744 | 304 | 100,0 | 100,0 |

*Note:* We exclude two projects that combine sectors: a US$79.5 million railway and port project in India and a US$17.7 million port and railway project in Mozambique.

*Source:* Private Infrastructure Advisory Facility.

Ports represent the smallest investment on average, because in most cases the PPP consists of an operational franchise and investments are mainly in equipment, but do not include new port infrastructure. The average size of an airport project ($670 million) is raised by two outliers, the $35 billion IGA airport in Turkey and the combined $20 billion of the Guarulos (São Paulo) and Rio de Janeiro airports, both in Brazil.

## 6.3 Why Governments Use PPPs: Fiscal Accounting

In many, if not most cases, PPPs have been attractive to policy makers because they promise to ease the fiscal constraints that limit resources for infrastructure projects. A PPP program allows governments to build schools, hospitals, roads, and airports without increasing the fiscal deficit.

### 6.3.1 PPPs as a Means of Evading Fiscal Spending Constraints

As mentioned in the introduction, there is no agreement on whether or how to include PPPs in the public accounts and in the government's balance sheet (see Grimsey and Lewis 2002; Heald 1997, 2010; Heald and Georgiou 2009; Heald and McLeod 2002; and Schwartz, Carbacho, and Funke 2008, part 4). In practice, PPPs investment is not considered government spending and therefore does not affect the fiscal deficit, even when the PPP is funded with periodic payments to the concessionaire. Governments use PPPs to circumvent fiscal constraints. In fact, this seems to have been the main incentive for the use of PPPs in Europe. For example, in the UK, the Private Finance Initiative (PFI) led to increases in public investment that were not recorded in the standard measures of public debt.[19] According to the National Audit Office (NAO) 2018 report on PFI and PF2:

19. As a signatory to the Maastricht Accord, the UK was required to keep its fiscal deficit below a maximum deficit.

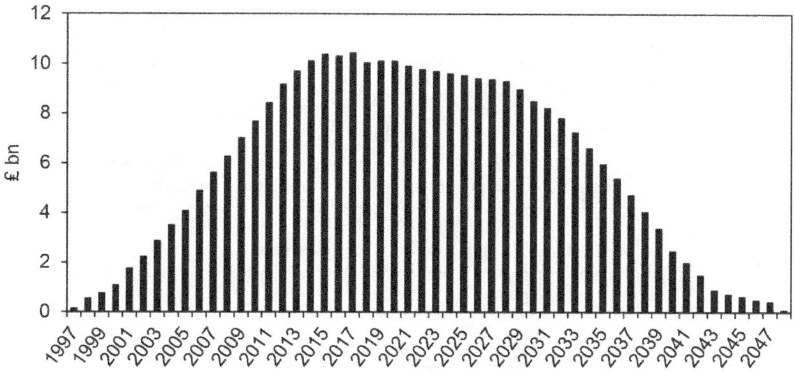


**Fig. 6.2 Private Finance Initiative past and forecast unitary charge payments**
*Source:* National Audit Office (2018).

> The Office for Budget Responsibility's (OBR's) July 2017 fiscal risks report cited the use of off-balance sheet vehicles like PFI as an example of a "fiscal illusion." . . . The debt is recorded as a financial liability but as noted by the OBR "most public and political attention, and the government's fiscal rules, still concentrate on the National Accounts measures of PSND (Public Sector Net Debt) and PSNB (Public Sector Net Borrowing)," which does not reflect fully PFI liabilities. PFI can be attractive to government as recorded levels of debt will be lower over the short to medium term (five years ahead) even if it costs significantly more over the full term of a 25–30 year contract.

These policies encumbered the UK with average annual payments of £7.7 billion for the 25 years beginning in 2017–2018, according to the NAO 2018 report. This represents 0.5 percent of the national budget until the 2030s (see figure 6.2).

Similarly, between 1995 and 2014, Portugal received €20 billion in PPP investments in roads, hospitals, and other projects. Ninety-four percent of the investment was in highways that used shadow tolls, and the annual minimum guaranteed payments were equal to 1 percent of GDP between 2014 and 2020, falling to 0.5 percent of GDP after 2020 and until 2030. In a study of Portuguese PPPs, Sarmento and Renneboog (2014) argue that the incentive to resort to PPPs was mainly to avoid budget constraints.

Another way in which PPPs can be used to increase current spending is by exchanging the future cash flows of existing infrastructure for an up-front payment. For example, the city of Chicago auctioned the operation of the Chicago Skyway, a 7.8-mile toll road linking downtown Chicago and the Indiana state line. The $1.83 billion bid for a 99-year lease allowed the city government to retire the remaining Skyway bonds, save some funds for the future, and use almost all of the remaining $475 million to increase current

**Table 6.3 Fiscal accounting: Funding from government transfers**

| | Public provision | PPP |
|---|---|---|
| Now: | Issue 100 in debt | "Save" 100 in debt |
| Now: | Spend 100 on infrastructure | Spend 100 on infrastructure |
| Future: | Collect 100 in taxes | Collect 100 in taxes |
| Future: | Pay bondholders 100 | Pay concessionaire 100 |

**Table 6.4 Fiscal accounting: Funding from user fees**

| | Public provision | PPP |
|---|---|---|
| Now: | Issue 100 in debt | "Save" 100 in debt |
| Now: | Spend 100 on infrastructure | Spend 100 on infrastructure |
| Future: | Collect 100 in user fees | Give up 100 in user fees |
| Future: | Pay bondholders 100 | Concession collects 100 in user fees |

spending. The efficiency gains of the contract were minimal, being at most a reduction in operating costs of $1 million per year (see Cheng 2010; Engel, Fischer, and Galetovic 2014a).

We have shown (Engel, Fischer, and Galetovic 2013) that the effects of PPPs on the intertemporal balance sheet are no different from those of public provision. Table 6.3 provides the intuition when the PPP is funded with government transfers. The first column shows the dynamics of debt and spending under public provision, the second column under a PPP. In both cases, the infrastructure is funded by a commitment to collect taxes in the future. Therefore the initial investment should count as public debt in both cases.

Table 6.4 considers the case in which user fees fund the project. Now, for both organizational forms, building the infrastructure entails a commitment to collect user fees in the future, in the same amount, to pay for the debt. It follows that the up-front investments should be counted as debt for a PPP as well.

### 6.3.2 Distorted Policy Choices

The choice between PPPs and public provision of infrastructure becomes distorted when PPPs are excluded from the fiscal accounts, because incumbents can then shift spending to future administrations. This distortion disappears if PPPs are included in toto in the balance sheet at the inception of the contract. As revenues accrue and the time at which the PPP contract ends comes nearer, the balance sheet incorporates these revenues on the revenue side. In that case, the choice between PPPs and traditional provision of infrastructure would depend only on which is more efficient to procure the infrastructure.

### 6.3.3 Eurostat and Fiscal Accounting of PPPs

In order to limit the use of PPPs to elude fiscal constraints, Eurostat introduced accounting rules for PPPs (Eurostat 2016). As a general rule, Eurostat considers that toll-funded PPPs are off the balance sheet, unless there exist significant government guarantees. In contrast, the treatment of government-funded PPPs seems to have been a compromise between the forces pushing for the exclusion of PPPs altogether from the government balance sheet and those finding that exclusion is unsound fiscal policy. Thus the classification of a particular government-funded PPP project as on or off the balance sheet depends on the answer to 84 yes-or-no questions divided into 11 sections.[20] Necessary conditions for the PPP to remain off the balance sheet are that there should be no government guarantee or early termination provisions that transfer risks back to the government.

Summing up, Eurostat guidelines are ineffectual in limiting the use of PPPs to circumvent budgetary controls, as the guidelines' main focus is on risk sharing, not on budgetary implications. There have been more effective rules in use in the past. In the 1980s the UK used the so-called Ryrie Rules for PPP projects.[21] These rules allowed private finance of public infrastructure only if public expenditure was reduced by the same amount. These rules were abandoned under the PFI program of the mid-1990s.

## 6.4 Economic Arguments for PPPs: Incentives, Risk, and Efficiency

### 6.4.1 Efficiency

PPPs are a response to the inefficiencies of traditional provision of government infrastructure. This implies that PPPs should be understood as an alternative way of procuring infrastructure and not as a mechanism for privatizing government assets and functions.

With traditional provision, incentives for efficiency tend to be weak. First, public agencies have multiple objectives and principals, exacerbating agency problems. Second, fiscal accounting practices are designed for budgetary purposes and not for monitoring performance. Third, in the public sector there are usually no bonuses associated with specific projects, and there are only career incentives for better performance. Fourth, the public sector is inflexible, because laws constrain hiring and firing, purchasing, and

20. For example, question 70 asks, "Does the [private] partner bear the construction risk and at least one of either the availability or the demand risks?" If the answer is no, the asset is classified on the government's balance sheet. If the answer is yes, additional conditions must be met for the asset to be kept off the government's balance sheet.

21. See Heald and McLeod (2002) for a discussion of the Ryrie rules. Maskin and Tirole (2008) provide a model for how PPPs are used to elude budgetary constraints.

contracting practices. Finally, the scale and scope of the organization that manages projects is constrained by the administrative structure of the state.

This lack of incentives has serious consequences. First, infrastructure assets are poorly maintained, because budgets are yearly appropriations and maintenance expenditures are a less visible use of resources than new or refurbished infrastructure. Often poor design and construction increase the cost of maintenance. The end result is often low service quality and higher costs. Second, the projects that are built are not always a good use of resources, because demand is systematically overstated, and costs and building times are underestimated (Flyvbjerg, Bruzelius, and Rothengatter 2003). In some cases, building pork barrel projects or poor planning leads to white elephants.

Historically one way of increasing efficiency has been to subcontract various building and design tasks to private firms, but the subdivision of activities between different firms leads to agency and coordination problems. PPPs represent an alternative organizational form that aligns the incentives of the various private parties in order to build, maintain, and operate a project. Under the PPP approach a single private entity—a so-called special purpose vehicle or SPV—is responsible for the finance, delivery, operations, and maintenance of the infrastructure project. The relation between the state and the SPV is governed by public law, but the SPV follows private law in its contractual relations with employees, other firms, and financiers. Finally, the scope of the SPV and its management team is clearly defined and limited to the project at hand, which focuses attention and incentives for efficiency.

Hart (2003) has shown that the theoretical benefits of PPPs arise in part from bundling design, building, operations, and maintenance into one contract. Since the concessionaire will operate and maintain the project, the concessionaire will design and build to minimize life-cycle costs. Provided that the quality of conservation can be measured and required by the contract, it is in the interest of the concessionaire to maintain the infrastructure continuously. Bundling, however, entails the risk that cost cutting may occur at the expense of service quality and user welfare. Thus, it is fair to say that PPPs work well when maintenance, quality, and performance standards can be defined and enforced. Roads are an example that satisfies these conditions.

The theoretical advantages of bundling have proved difficult to test, but the benefits in terms of improved maintenance are clear. As we have already mentioned, governments often do not perform regular, continuous maintenance. By contrast, a PPP owner benefits from routine maintenance if quality standards are enforced. The firm knows that reactive maintenance is more expensive and that there is the added cost of penalties for low service quality. As mentioned in the introduction, continuous maintenance of a highway not only provides better quality of service but is also less expensive.

There is some evidence that PPP projects tend to be delivered on time. For example, Raisbeck, Duffield, and Xu (2010, 352) found that, in a sample of

21 PPP projects and 31 traditional projects in Australia, the time "between the signing of the final contract and project completion, PPPs were found to be completed 3.4% ahead of time on average, while traditional projects were completed 23.5% behind time." The incentives for timely completion exist if the firm begins to receive revenues only when the project starts to operate. In the particular case of fixed-term contracts financed with user fees, this incentive is even stronger, because delays in construction cut into the revenue-generating period. Moreover, on-time delivery also requires good planning, project design, and execution—conditions that reduce cost overruns.[22]

As mentioned in the introduction, strong government capabilities are required for the success of a PPP program. The government is responsible for planning what to build (network planning and coordination), whether a particular project should be built (cost-benefit appraisal), and when it should be built. In addition, there are arguments for and against delegating project design to the SPV. The advantages lie in the creativity of the private sector and in the transfer of design risk to the concessionaire. The danger is that governments that delegate project design do not to have a full understanding of the projects they procure, nor of the risks involved. Thus there is no presumption that delegating project design to the concessionaire will lead to a better result.

When PPPs are financed with tolls, two additional sources of efficiency gains appear. First, the transfer of resources to the private firm is direct. In contrast, in a publicly funded project, the resources for construction, maintenance, and operations are collected through taxes and wend their way through the government bureaucracy until eventually they reach the SPV. The direct approach eliminates the costs associated with this bureaucracy. The second benefit is that tolling can reduce congestion and increase allocative efficiency, since the total marginal cost includes the congestion externality. Given that the taxes used to provide a free public highway create distortions, it might well be that a toll-funded PPP highway is more efficient than a congested toll-free public road.[23] A final advantage of PPPs is that the private firm will have stronger incentives to resist petitions for lower tolls than a publicly elected official.

### 6.4.2 Incentives and Risk Allocation

One of the challenges of a PPP contract is efficient risk allocation. Following Irwin (2007) we identify eight sources of risk: (1) construction, including design flaws, cost overruns, and delays; (2) operation and maintenance; (3)

22. A rule of thumb in construction states that if the project is delayed, overheads continue to be incurred. A second rule of thumb states that overhead is roughly one-third of the yearly as well as of the total cost of a project. Source: Klaus Grewe, personal communication.

23. In fact, a globally optimal fiscal policy would set tolls slightly higher than the optimal congestion toll, because by so doing the government can reduce distortionary taxation (see Engel, Fischer, and Galetovic 2013).

availability under the terms agreed in the contract; (4) residual value at the end of the PPP contract; (5) policy, ranging from macroeconomic uncertainty to government actions that affect the project; (6) demand; (7) financial factors (for example, interest rate and exchange rate fluctuations); and (7) political factors (for example, regulatory takings or expropriation).

Irwin (2007, 65) states the rule for efficient risk allocation:

> Each risk should be allocated, along with rights to make related decisions, so as to maximize total project value, taking account of each party's ability to: 1. Influence the corresponding risk factor. 2. Influence the sensitivity of total project value to the corresponding risk factor—for example, by anticipating or responding to the risk factor. 3. Absorb the risk.

Consider construction risk. The builder controls the time to complete and the cost of building the project. The concessionaire should thus bear these risks, perhaps with the exception of delays caused by disputes about the application of eminent domain and environmental certification. Similarly, because diligence during construction influences the availability of the facility during operation, it is efficient for the concessionaire to bear operation, maintenance, and service quality risks.

Bundling, control, and service standards are all required to ensure that these risks are effectively borne by the concessionaire. For example, it may be easier to hold the concessionaire who built the facility responsible for service quality—hence the importance of bundling. Likewise, without objective and measurable service standards, it is difficult to transfer service quality risk to the concessionaire.

Some risks are created by government policies and therefore should be borne by the government. For example, because the residual value of PPP assets depends on government planning decisions and the willingness to charge tolls in future concessions, it is reasonable to transfer the residual value risk to the government. This happens when the concessionaire recovers its initial investment over the term of the contract and then transfers the infrastructure value to the government.

Broadly speaking, policy risks fall into two categories. First, the government may implement policies that directly affect the project. For example, the government may change the rules to expropriate the concessionaire. Irwin's principle indicates that these risks should be borne by the government, to prevent opportunism. Second, actions by the government or the legislature may unintentionally affect the PPP. For example, currency devaluation may reduce a foreign firm's return, or a change in environmental standards may require additional investments. In these cases, the concessionaire is in the same position as any other private firm in the economy. Therefore, these are standard business risks. This principle is routinely overlooked.[24] For

24. García-Kilroy and Rudolph (2017) argue that governments should offer currency risk-sharing arrangements when financial markets fail to do so. García-Kilroy and Rudolph describe cases where this has been done, at a price close to what would have been a market price.

example, governments often grant foreign concessionaires insurance against devaluations. This practice discriminates not only against local investors but also against foreign firms in other sectors of the economy that have to bear this risk. More generally, policy risks that do not target the project specifically and that affect most firms in the economy (for example, those caused by monetary policy) should be treated as exogenous and allocated according to general principles of risk diversification.

Perhaps the main exogenous risk in a PPP funded with user fees is uncertainty about demand. As mentioned earlier, the general principle is that exogenous demand risk should be borne by the party best able to bear it. If the private firm assumes demand risk, taxpayers are in fact purchasing insurance against an exogenous risk (see Engel, Fischer, and Galetovic 2014a, chap. 5). As Hall (1998) notes, this is not cost effective. Demand forecasts are notoriously imprecise and future changes in policy may radically affect the usage of the facility, yet there is little that the firm can do. In those cases, either a present-value-of-revenue contract (see section 6.6) or an availability contract is appropriate, depending on whether the project is funded by user fees or government transfers.

The principle of transferring exogenous demand risk to the government admits of one important exception. When user fees are a PPP's only source of remuneration, the willingness of private firms to bid for the contract is a market signal that demand is sufficient (at least in expectation). This introduces a market test that is usually absent in infrastructure services. If there are no bidders at an auction, this suggests that the project is not privately profitable. Unless it has large positive externalities, there is a risk that the project is a white elephant.

As in the case of demand risk, financial risk is largely outside the firm's control. This does not mean, however, that the government should bear interest rate or exchange rate risk. Other firms in the economy do not receive this favored treatment, and firms can choose among alternative capital structures. More generally, governments are not particularly efficient at providing and selling financial insurance.

## 6.5 Governance and Renegotiations

Given the often unsatisfactory results of PPP programs in infrastructure, it is worthwhile to study whether these results are caused by defects in the governance of PPPs. At a minimum, a PPP-capable country requires institutions that allow private firms to receive a return after sinking a large investment. Furthermore, it must be possible to pledge the revenue stream generated by project to financiers and put them first in line if the PPP fails. These preconditions may preclude PPP investment in some countries.[25]

25. Or if it exists, it must be supported by multilateral financial institutions; see Engel, Fischer, and Galetovic (2014a).

However, even in countries that satisfy these minimal requirements, there is no guarantee that an infrastructure PPP will be successful. We deal with some of these problems in this section.

### 6.5.1 Renegotiations Are Pervasive

PPPs are routinely renegotiated. This has been well known since Guasch (2004) examined nearly 1,000 Latin American concession contracts awarded between the mid-1980s and 2000 and found that 54.4 percent of those in transportation (including roads, ports, tunnels, and airports) had been renegotiated. When Mexico privatized highways in the late 1980s, Mexican taxpayers had to pay more than US$13 billion after renegotiation of the initial contracts, on an estimated almost $13 billion in PPP investments. In Chile, 47 out of the 50 Chilean PPP concessions awarded by the Ministry of Public Works between 1992 and 2005 had been renegotiated by 2006, and one of every four dollars invested had been obtained through renegotiation (see Engel et al. 2009). More recently Engel, Fischer, and Galetovic (2019) analyzed 535 renegotiations of 59 highway PPPs in Colombia, Peru, and Chile. Renegotiations per concession/year average 9.5 percent of the initial investment in Colombia, 3.6 percent in Peru, and 1.3 percent in Chile. More than 45 percent of renegotiations (by dollar amount) occur during construction. Furthermore, in the case of Chile, at least 60 percent of the renegotiated spending increase falls on future administrations.[26]

One might think that renegotiations occur mainly in emerging economies, where governance is weak. Renegotiations are also pervasive in developed countries, however, as documented long ago by Gómez-Ibáñez and Meyer (1993). For example, three of the four highway concessions awarded in France in the early 1970s went bankrupt after the 1973 oil shock and were bailed out by the government. Similarly, several of the 12 highway conces-

26. Renegotiations are not only common in transportation infrastructure. An example from the sanitation sector is the two concessions for water utilities in Manila, Philippines, in 1997. As noted in Wu and Malaluan (2007), the state-owned utility was divided geographically into two companies serving the city, and auctioned as 25-year concessions. The two winning consortia offered tariffs that were 26 percent and 56 percent of the previous rates, respectively. However, by 2002 the consortia had managed to renegotiate their contracts and double the prices using the Asian crisis as an argument; the consortia then almost doubled prices again in 2005. Moreover, the companies invested less than specified in their contracts, at least until 2003, when Manila Water began to expand investment rapidly, perhaps because after the change in tariffs the implied rate of return on assets rose to 9 percent. Nevertheless, as a result of bad management, the other company, Manilad, went bankrupt (in 2003) after its petition for even larger tariff increases was denied. Regardless of the adverse effects of raising rates, there were compensating benefits from privatization: a massive expansion in connections, by 30 percent in the first five years of operation; and in Manila Water, nonrevenue water (lost to theft or because of leaking pipes) decreased from almost 58 percent to 35 percent, while the response to service complaints and the time to repair leaks improved substantially. We can conclude from this case that unless precautions are taken, companies' bids can be renegotiated to the advantage of the winners at the expense of the public—but even then the public may benefit. For a more critical evaluation, see Esguerra (2003).

sions awarded in Spain in the 1970s had higher costs than anticipated, while traffic was lower than expected, causing three highways to go bankrupt and the remaining contracts to be renegotiated. Spain seems to be a serial subsidizer of PPPs at the expense of the public: in November 2010, all political parties agreed that it was necessary to bail out, among others, the seven PPP highways running into Madrid, at a cost that could reach €4 billion (see Engel et al. 2018).

Industry participants often claim that circumstances change over the life of a concession. Because most PPP contracts last for several decades, renegotiations of inherently incomplete contracts are to be expected. Renegotiations thus provide the flexibility necessary to adapt to changing conditions. While there is some truth to this argument, it ignores two disturbing features of most renegotiations. First, they often occur shortly after contracts are awarded. For example, Guasch (2004, 14) finds that the average time to renegotiation was only 2.2 years after the concession was awarded, and 60 percent of all renegotiated contracts had been renegotiated within the first three years after the concession award. Engel et al. (2009) show that 78 percent of the amounts awarded in renegotiations of PPPs in Chile were brokered during construction, shortly after awarding the concession.[27]

Second, renegotiations tend to favor the concessionaire. For example, Guasch (2004) finds that two-thirds led to tariff increases, 38 percent to extensions of the concession term, and two-thirds to reductions in investment obligations. In the case of Chilean PPPs, we find that most renegotiations imply paying more for the works originally contracted. Thus, while in principle renegotiations may allow governments to expropriate concessionaires after they have sunk their investment, in practice it seems that the private partner benefits the most, at least in Latin America.[28]

### 6.5.2 The Origin and Consequence of Renegotiations

The prevalence of renegotiations suggests that they are not accidents, but an equilibrium outcome of the incentive structure in place. There are at least four economic mechanisms that produce systematic renegotiations.

First, in Engel et al. (2019) we show that the possibility of being ousted from office increases the effective discount rate of the incumbent, who values the future less than the social planner and wants to bring forward spending to increase the probability of winning an election. Because fiscal accounting rules keep PPPs off balance sheet, the incumbent can renegotiate the PPP contract to increase current infrastructure spending. The concessionaire, in turn, is willing to renegotiate the contract because he is backed by a long-term legal agreement that is binding on future administrations. This

27. For more on renegotiation of PPP contracts, see Guasch, Laffont, and Straub (2007, 2008).

28. For evidence on renegotiations of US PPPs that benefited private firms at the expense of taxpayers and users, see Engel, Fischer, and Galetovic (2011).

mechanism works independently of how the PPP is funded. With availability payments (as is the case, for example, with many highways in Europe), renegotiated payments will be borne by future administrations and constrain their ability to spend. If, on the other hand, the infrastructure is funded with tolls, future governments will forego revenues (see Engel, Fischer, and Galetovic 2013). Whatever the funding source, the incumbent can tie up resources that would have been available to future administrations, in exchange for current infrastructure spending by the concessionaire. In essence, therefore, in a renegotiation the concessionaire lends to the incumbent in exchange for payments by future administrations.

Even though there is no systematic evidence on the frequency of renegotiation of infrastructure provided under the traditional approach, this argument suggests that renegotiations should be less frequent in this case. Since the relation between government and the firm exists only during the construction period, there is less time for the firm to find arguments to renegotiate the contract. It is also more difficult to add additional works because they would lead to additional expenditures that must be approved by the legislature.

Renegotiations also generate adverse selection, by attracting firms skilled at lobbying but technically less proficient. Since renegotiations between the concessionaire and the government are bilateral, surpluses are split according to the relative bargaining abilities of each party. A better lobbyist should get a larger fraction of the pie in any renegotiation. Hence, if two firms are equally efficient, the firm with a better lobbyist can bid less at the competitive auction and win the concession, in the expectation of recovering up-front losses in later renegotiations.

The third mechanism at work is moral hazard. As we have seen, PPPs are appropriate when objective quality standards can be set, measured, and enforced. In that case, the concessionaire can be left to choose the production technology. Concessionaires foster the belief that PPP contracts should be adjusted to ensure the ex post financial equilibrium of the PPP, an argument that firms often produce to justify renegotiations (among many examples, this was the case for the bailout of Spanish PPPs mentioned earlier). This is not an acceptable argument for renegotiating the contract. If the firms' bids were prudent, the company should expect to receive the normal return on investment after adjusting for risk, as in all other sectors of the economy. Hence, the conditions of the bid should be preserved, and no renegotiation that results in a higher cost of providing the contracted service quality should be accepted. Renegotiations are not only unnecessary but also inefficient, because they weaken the incentives to control and reduce costs, thereby dampening the efficiency gains that PPPs can yield. Renegotiations meant to restore the concessionaire's financial equilibrium transform a fixed-price contract into a type of cost-plus contract. Even worse, since firms with strong renegotiation skills can extract more from the government, they can afford to exert even less effort to control costs. Thus, moral hazard increases the advantage held by good renegotiators even further and worsens the adverse selection problem.

Similarly, when the PPP agency has discretion to renegotiate, it feels less pressure to plan and design projects carefully, because it can renegotiate away its own mistakes. The problem is compounded when the costs of renegotiating can be shifted to future administrations and when the PPP agency is not accountable. Thus, when coupled with inadequate accounting or governance, the expectation of renegotiations generates moral hazard in the PPP agency.

Last, recent evidence from Latin America shows a connection between renegotiations and corruption. Campos et al. (2019) consider all projects undertaken by the Brazilian conglomerate Odebrecht in eight countries over a 10-year period and find that the average renegotiation, as a fraction of the initial investment, was 71 percent for projects where bribes were paid, compared with 6 percent for projects where bribes were not paid. The projects considered include both PPPs and traditional provision, suggesting that the connection between corruption and renegotiations is relevant when providing public infrastructure in general. Campos et al. (2019) also show that firms pay bribes to benefit from renegotiations.

### 6.5.3 Pervasive Renegotiations and Remedies

Pervasive renegotiations are caused by inadequate rules and governance. They encourage lowballing in the auction, in the expectation of recouping any losses by future bilateral bargaining. The remedies combine proper accounting rules, competitive tendering for additional works, and independent review of renegotiations.

As shown by Engel, Fischer, and Galetovic (2019), treating PPPs as regular government expenditure and debt eliminates the incentive to use renegotiations to increase current infrastructure spending and burden future administrations.

The remedy to adverse selection and moral hazard is to eliminate the possibility of increasing profits through bilateral renegotiations. This may be achieved by preventing the concessionaire from participating in the tenders for additions to the original works. In addition, renegotiations should be subject to review by an expert panel, ensuring that the concessionaire's net rents are not altered. Box 6.1 describes the role of expert panels in the UK and Chile. Finally, transparency suggests that all contract modifications be published in a web page, so that the public is informed about the changes and can question the reasons and the amounts. Active transparency, such as publishing project modifications and their cost, fosters accountability and hardens the negotiating position of the public authority.

Chile reformed its PPP law in 2010 and established a Technical Experts Panel (see box 6.1 for details). The panel helps in conflict resolution and

### Box 6.1 Dispute Resolution in the UK and Chile

In the UK, the framework for dispute resolution is set up in the HM Treasury "Draft Standardization of PF2 Contracts" of December 2012. The document sets up a tiered structure of procedures that starts with a consultation between the parties for a fixed period in an attempt to reach a mutually satisfactory agreement. If this consultation approach fails, the parties can put their case before an expert adjudicator selected from a panel or, alternatively, to mediation or conciliation. If either party believes the decision is not acceptable, they can appeal to an arbitration procedure or, eventually, the courts. Akinbode and Vickers (2017) show that these procedures can escalate and that badly defined contracts can close out reasonable options of solving the conflict.

In Chile, the 2010 reform to the PPP law established the Technical Experts Panel (TEP), a permanent, independent board of legal and engineering experts that reviews technical disputes between the Ministry of Public Works and a private party (usually an SPV). The TEP hears the parties in public audience and issues a recommendation within 30 days. Even though the recommendations are not binding, in approximately 40 percent of the cases the parties have agreed to the recommendation. The remaining cases proceed to mandatory arbitration, and the panel recommendation is considered in the decision.

**Table 6.5 Renegotiations in Chile: Before and after the 2010 reform**

| | Highways | | Transport | |
|---|---|---|---|---|
| | Number | Renegotiation (fraction of investment) | Number | Renegotiation (fraction of investment) |
| Before 2010 reform | 29 | 26.1% | 44 | 27.6% |
| After 2010 reform | 15 | 0.7% | 25 | 0.9% |

provides an opinion assessing the fairness of contract renegotiations above a threshold. In addition, the reform also makes it mandatory to put to tender additional works agreed on in a renegotiation and excludes the concessionaire or related parties from the ensuing contract.

Table 6.5 shows renegotiations as a fraction of initial investment for Chilean PPPs both before and after the 2010 reform of the PPP law. Since the time elapsed since the reform is relatively short, we present only renegotiations during the construction phase, both for highway PPPs and for all PPPs in the transport sector. The table shows that renegotiations during construction decreased by more than 90 percent following the reform.

## 6.6 PVR Contracts

The standard user fee PPP is a fixed-term contract that is awarded to the firm that bids the lowest fee, shortest term, or lowest subsidy. At the end of the fixed term, the infrastructure reverts to the state, which can award a new concession or provide the service either free or with user fees.

A fixed-term contract allocates most of the demand risk to the concessionaire. This makes sense when the infrastructure is a container terminal, where demand responds to service standards that are difficult to specify and monitor. But demand forecasts for roads are unreliable and depend mostly on exogenous factors such as macroeconomic activity. Moreover, quality of service for a highway is easy to specify and enforce. Thus, in a fixed-term contract the winning bid internalizes exogenous risk by asking for a higher return—that is, a user fee that generates enough expected income to compensate for demand risk. In order to make projects bankable, governments must pledge revenue guarantees. Also, as discussed in the previous section, fixed-term contracts tend to be renegotiated in times of severe economic stress.

In this section we argue that exogenous demand risk can be mitigated with present-value-of-revenue (PVR) contracts (see Engel, Fischer, and Galetovic 1996, 2001). This applies to infrastructure such as highways and airports, where quality of service is contractible and demand uncertainty is exogenous. Under a PVR contract, the regulator sets the discount rate and the tariff schedule. Firms bid the present value of the user fee revenue they require for financing, building, operating, and maintaining the infrastructure.[29] The firm that bids the lowest PVR gets the concession. The contract ends when the present value of user fees collected equals the winning bid. The term of the concession automatically adjusts to demand shocks, resulting in a substantial reduction of demand risk borne by the concessionaire. Since user fees are the main revenue source for the PPP, the contract attains the efficiency gains associated with PPPs discussed in section 6.4.

### 6.6.1 Advantages of PVR Contracts

PVR contracts reduce demand risk, because demand fluctuations and their associated revenue variations are reflected in a longer or shorter con-

29. User fees considered in the firms' bid are tolls in the case of highways. In the case of airports, only aeronautical revenues (passenger and airport fees) are considered; see Engel, Fischer, and Galetovic (2018) for details.

**Box 6.2 PVR and the Two Major Highway PPPs in the US during the 1990s**

The Dulles Greenway and Orange County's State Route 91 are the two main highway PPPs built in the US during the 1990s (see Engel, Fischer, and Galetovic 2011).[1] They both ran into problems that would have been avoided with a PVR contract.

**Dulles Greenway**

The Dulles Greenway is a 14-mile expressway that joins Dulles International Airport and Leesburg, Virginia. Investors put up $40 million in cash and secured $310 million in privately placed, taxable debt to finance the expressway. Loans were to be repaid with toll revenues. Tendered as a fixed-term, 42.5-year concession, the expressway was inaugurated in 1995. Demand turned out to be much lower than expected, with actual traffic equal to only one-fourth of projections. When the PPP defaulted in 1996, lenders restructured its debt and investors wrote off part of their equity. In addition, in 2001 the contract term was extended by 20 years, until 2056.

Despite a major forecast demand error, it was clear that even in low-demand scenarios the Dulles Greenway would eventually collect enough tolls to pay for capital and operational expenditures. Therefore, had the PPP been tendered using PVR, the contract term would have been extended automatically when demand turned out to be lower than expected, thereby avoiding losses for investors and bondholders. The contract renegotiation and debt restructuring that followed essentially turned the original fixed term contract into a PVR contract, yet this happened at a high cost.

**Orange County's State Route 91**

In 1995, the California Department of Transportation (Caltrans) awarded a 35-year concession of a 10-mile segment of the four-lane Riverside Freeway (also called State Route 91) between the Orange-Riverside County line and the Costa Mesa Freeway (State Route 55) to a private firm, California Private Transportation Corporation (CPTC). Motorists used the express lanes to avoid congestion in the nontolled lanes, paying tolls that could reach almost $11 for a round trip.

By the late 1990s, 33,000 daily trips brought the express lanes to the brink of congestion at peak time, turning the concession into a financial success. At the same time and for the same reasons, users in the nontolled public lanes were suffering congestion, and an expansion was urgently needed. Nevertheless, the contract included a noncompete clause that prevented Caltrans from increasing the capacity of the Riverside Freeway without CPTC's consent. Caltrans tried to elude the clause, arguing that expansions were necessary to prevent accidents, but CPTC filed a lawsuit. The verdict stated that noncompete clauses were meant to ensure the financial viability of CPTC and that they restricted Caltrans's right to adversely affect the project's traffic or revenues. Consequently, no new lanes could be built.

Protracted negotiations ensued, and eventually the Orange County Transportation Authority (OCTA) was empowered to negotiate the purchase of the tolled lanes. The value of the concession was not easy to determine, because it should have been the present value of profits from the State Route 91 express lanes, had the franchise continued as originally planned. Although the lanes cost \$130 million to build, initially the concession's value was set at \$274 million in a controversial (and ultimately unsuccessful) buyout attempt by a nonprofit associated with Orange County. After several years of negotiations, with frustrated commuters stuck in traffic in the meantime, OCTA bought the express lanes in January 2003 for \$207.5 million. Press reports suggest that CPTC received additional compensation.

Because this was a fixed-term PPP, demand risk was borne by the concessionaire. Therefore, this dispute was about the value of lost revenues and was unrelated to the cost of the infrastructure. Moreover, because the term was fixed, the value of lost revenues was inherently subjective. Not surprisingly, the concessionaire and OCTA disagreed. The disagreement had real economic cost: it delayed capacity expansion and prolonged costly congestion, In contrast, had this been a PVR contract with a clause allowing government to buy back the concession at any point in time, paying the difference between the winning bid and the amount collected (adjusting for savings in maintenance costs), no protracted renegotiation and dispute would have taken place.

## Note

1. This section is based on Gifford, Bolaños, and Daito (2014) and Engel, Fischer, and Galetovic (2014a). The State Route 91 project is also analyzed, from a financial valuation perspective, in Lucas and Montesinos (2021).

tract term. Since revenue is in present value, the duration of the PPP does not affect its profitability.[30] For the same reason, minimum traffic guarantees are no longer required to make the project bankable.[31]

The efficient assignment of demand risk lowers the overall cost of the project. On the one hand, Engel, Fischer, and Galetovic (2001) estimated that, relative to a fixed-term contract, the reduction in risk wrought by a PVR contract was equivalent to 30 percent of the cost of a highway. On the other hand, and as pointed out by Tirole (1997), bids are cost based, creating incentives to reduce costs.

In addition, PVR allow for more contractual flexibility, correcting a serious problem of fixed-term PPPs. In general, PPP contracts are designed to be inflexible, to limit the risk of creeping expropriation by the government. For this reason, fixed-term PPP contracts have a hard time incorporating early termination clauses in a way that avoids opportunistic behavior by the government. The reason is that the fair compensation is equal to the revenue that would have accrued had the original contract run until termination. Because future demand is random, that quantity cannot be calculated with verifiable information. In contrast, in the case of PVR, the government has the option to unilaterally buy back the concession, paying a "fair" price for the contract. This fair price is equal to the difference between the concessionaire's bid and the present value of toll revenue already collected (with a sum subtracted for savings in maintenance and operational costs). Because the concessionaire's winning bid determines the total amount of present value revenues it requests, the PVR contract is closer to a complete contract than a fixed-term contract, and a fair value for the early buyback option can be calculated at any moment with verifiable accounting information.

For the same reason, a PVR contract allows flexibility in setting user fees. This can be valuable, for instance by allowing adjustments of user fees to better manage the entire public transportation network of a city or to adjust congestion tolls in a highway. In contrast, flexibility to change user fees in a fixed-term PPP comes at the cost of a large increase in revenue risk for the concessionaire.

### 6.6.2 PVR in Practice

#### *6.6.2.1 United Kingdom*

The first present-value-of-revenue contract that we know of was awarded to Trafalgar House on September 29, 1986, to build the Queen

30. Given that damage to the road is driven mainly by usage (especially by heavy vehicles), maintenance cost is also related to demand. Hence a longer term is not reflected in higher maintenance costs. The contract does create some operation cost risk, but this is a small fraction of total costs.

31. Availability contracts also shield the concessionaire from demand risk. The government pays for both capital and operation costs. These contracts are useful when user fees cannot be charged.

Elizabeth II Bridge, crossing the Thames River at Dartford.[32] The proposal by Trafalgar was deemed the best among eight proposals.

The contract stipulated that Trafalgar would buy the two existing tunnels for £43 million, build a new 450-meter bridge, and operate all three for 20 years or until toll fees paid off the debt, whichever happened first. The project had four shareholders: Trafalgar House (50 percent), Kleinwort Benson (16.5 percent), Prudential (16.5 percent), and Bank of America (17 percent). The consortium financed the bridge with subordinated debt issued by insurance companies and term loans by banks. Project finance was used, and the shareholders invested only nominal equity. Interest on the syndicated loan was a floating rate, at a margin between 0.75 and 1.25 percentage points above the prime rate.

The bridge opened in 1991 and, after accruing the contracted toll revenue, the contract ended in March of 2002, almost 10 years before the maximum concession term of 20 years. The SPV in charge of the PPP was liquidated, the bridge reverted to public ownership and management, and the government began collecting tolls, now referred to as charges.

The Second Severn Crossing PPP on the Severn Estuary, which was tendered in 1990 and opened in 1996, also used a PVR contract. The contract stipulated a term of 30 years or until the concessionaire collected £995.8 million (in July 1989 prices), whichever occurred first. As with the Queen Elizabeth II Bridge, the PPP was financed fully with debt. Control of the crossing and the original Severn Bridge reverted to the UK government on January 8, 2018, after the required revenue had been collected. At that point responsibility for operating the bridge passed to Highways England, a public entity.

#### *6.6.2.2 Chile*

Figure 6.3 shows the cumulative investment in transport PPPs in Chile since the PPP program was launched in 1993 with the El Melón Tunnel.[33] As can be seen in the figure, initially all PPPs were fixed term. The first PVR contract was auctioned in 1998, and after 2006 PVR contracts became the norm. Note that a third type of contract—the so-called revenue distribution mechanism or MDI—appeared in 2002. These were five fixed-term PPPs that were renegotiated and turned into variable-term contracts in 2002, when their revenue plummeted following the Asian crisis of the late 1990s. By 2017, 29 of the 66 PPPs awarded were variable-term contracts. As figure 6.3 shows, by 2017 the cumulative investment in transport PPPs in Chile exceeded US$12 billion. Fifty-five percent of all investment had been made with (or turned into) variable-term contracts.

32. This section is based on Engel, Fischer, and Galetovic (2014a) and Levy (1996).
33. This section is based on Engel et al. (2019).

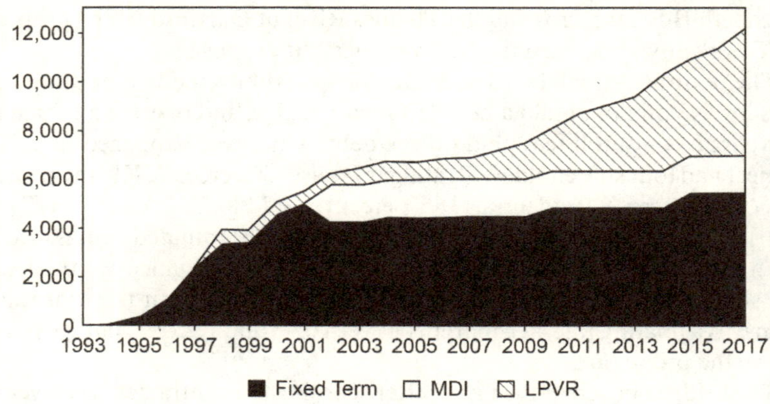


**Fig. 6.3 Value of PVR contracts in Chile**
*Source:* Authors with data from the Ministry of Public Works.

### 6.6.3 Financing and Renegotiations: Theory and Evidence

Flexible-term contracts have been used only in the UK, Chile, Colombia, and Portugal. Given all the advantages we described, this begs the question why they have not been used more. We can think of two reasons. First, there exists a belief that financing a PVR PPP is more difficult (see Klein [1997] for an early example).[34] We argue here that this belief is incorrect. Second, it is harder to renegotiate a PVR contract, which may explain why concessionaires sometimes oppose them.[35]

One reason why financing PVR contracts may be harder is that the contract term is not known in advance. This would seem to impose additional challenges on fixed maturity debt, and make financing more costly. Another concern is that the risk of debt prepayment by bondholders is higher under PVR contracts, since the PPP will pay its debt early when demand turns out to be high.

Many of the misunderstandings about PVR and debt contracts stem from ignoring that the per-period cash flows generated by a project depend only on demand realizations, not on the type of PPP contract. It follows that the main difference between a fixed-term contract and a PVR contract is that the latter lasts longer in low-demand scenarios and ends earlier in high-demand scenarios. When demand turns out to be low, the term is extended automatically, and the concessionaire receives revenues that are unavailable under a fixed-term contract. This implies that debt holders bear less risk with a PVR contract.

34. For financing of PPPs in general, and the important role of project finance, see, for example, Ehlers, Packer, and Remolona (2014), and Inderst (2010, 2013).

35. The PPP industry lobbied against PVR when it became the standard contract for highway and airport PPPs in Chile in 2007.

**Table 6.6** **Renegotiations in Chile: Fixed-term versus PVR contracts**

| | Fixed-term | | PVR | |
|---|---|---|---|---|
| Period | Number | Renegotiation (average) | Number | Renegotiation (average) |
| Construction | 20 | 32.0% | 15 | 3.6% |
| First eight years of operation | 20 | 25.2% | 15 | 2.5% |
| Total (construction + first eight years of operation) | 20 | 57.2% | 15 | 6.1% |

At the same time, the fact that the contract ends earlier in high demand scenarios implies a higher prepayment risk under PVR. However, the timing of prepayments is not correlated with periods of low interest rates. On the contrary, prepayment is triggered by an exogenous event—an unexpectedly high demand for the project. Moreover, because exogenous prepayments occur when demand for the project is high, they are likely to happen when the economy is booming and interest rates are high. By contrast, prepayment risk is usually costly for lenders when borrowers strategically prepay when interest rates fall. Thus with PVR, prepayment risk is low or even nonexistent. The Chilean experience with financing PVR contracts confirms this (see Engel et al. 2019).

Summing up, PVR contracts may be viewed as having an automatic renegotiation clause triggered by low demand realizations. Then the contract term extends automatically and the present value of total revenues is unaffected—no costly contract renegotiation is needed.

Table 6.6 compares the amounts renegotiated under fixed-term and PVR contracts for highway PPPs in Chile (similar results are obtained if airport PPPs are included). The table reports renegotiations as a fraction of the initial investment, both during construction and during the first eight years of operation.[36] Note that the percentage renegotiated fell by 90 percent with PVR contracts, both during construction and the first years of operation.

## 6.7 Conclusion

PPPs can deliver major gains in efficiency. However, successful PPPs require careful project and contract design by the government and good governance, both during the procurement and operation stages. The experience of the past 30 years and the analysis of this chapter suggest a set of best practices.

First, PPPs would not be used to circumvent fiscal restrictions if their link

36. Considering longer periods of operation reduces significantly the number of projects with PVR, since these contracts began being used on a regular basis only in 2007.

to the intertemporal fiscal constraint is acknowledged. This occurs if investment in PPPs is included in public accounts as if it were public investment, since the effect on the intertemporal budget constraint is identical. Second, careful planning, project design, and project management help PPPs to fulfill their promise. Careful planning reduces the frequency of costly mistakes and events that require modifications to the contract and thus renegotiations. Third, if renegotiations are reviewed and possibly approved by an independent expert panel, the incentives for opportunistic renegotiations are reduced. Fourth, there are fewer incentives to modify the project if additional works are tendered competitively. Finally, if concessionaires are not required to bear exogenous demand risk, the cost of the project is lower.

In 2010 Chile modified its PPP law, introducing an independent panel to review contract renegotiations and excluding concessionaires from building additions agreed in renegotiations. In addition, since 2007 Chile has routinely used PVR contracts, which shield the concessionaire from demand risk it cannot control. While we cannot prove causality, these reforms were based on sound economic analysis and were followed by a substantial decrease in renegotiations. This illustrates that governance and careful contract design are vital to reap the benefits from PPPs.

## References

Airoldi, M., J. Chua, P. Gerbert, J. Justus, and R. Rilo. 2013. *Bridging the Gap: Meeting the Infrastructure Challenge with Public-Private Partnerships*. Boston: Boston Consulting Group.

Akinbode, A., and P. Vickers. 2017. "Dispute Management: Peace in Our Pipeline." *Procurement & Outsourcing Journal*, March.

Blanc-Brude, F., and B. Ismail. 2013. "Who Is Afraid of Construction Risk?" Working paper, EDHEC-Risk Institute.

Blanchard, O. J., and F. Giavazzi. 2004. "Improving the SGP through a Proper Accounting of Public Investment." Centre for Economic Policy Research Discussion Paper 4220.

Campos, N., E. Engel, R. Fischer, and A. Galetovic. 2019. "Renegotiations and Corruption in Infrastructure: The Odebrecht Case." SSRN Working Paper.

Cheng, J. 2010. "The Chicago Skyway Concession." Senior essay, Yale University.

Dealogic. 2012. *Project Finance Review*. Full year 2012.

Ehlers, T., F. Packer, and E. Remolona. 2014. "Infrastructure and Corporate Bond Markets in Asia." In *Financial Flows and Infrastructure Financing*, edited by A. Heath and M. Read, 67–91. Sydney: Reserve Bank of Australia.

Engel, E., R. Fischer, and A. Galetovic. 1996. "Highway Auctions in Chile" (in Spanish). *Estudios Públicos* 61: 6–37.

———. 2001. "Least-Present-Value-of Revenue Auctions and Highway Franchising." *Journal of Political Economy* 109 (5): 993–1020.

———. 2011. "Public-Private Partnerships to Revamp U.S. Infrastructure." Discussion Paper 2011-02. Washington, DC: Hamilton Project, Brookings Institution.

———. 2013. "The Basic Public Finance of Public Private Partnerships." *Journal of the European Economic Association* 11 (1), 83–111.

———. 2014a. *The Economics of Public-Private Partnerships: A Basic Guide*. Cambridge: Cambridge University Press.

———. 2014b. "Finance and Public-Private Partnerships: A Roadmap." Background paper for the Global Financial Development Report of the World Bank.

———. 2018. "The Joy of Flying: Efficient Airport PPP Contracts," *Transport Research Part B* 114: 131–46.

———. 2019. "Soft Budgets and Renegotiations in Transport PPPs: An Equilibrium Analysis," *Economics of Transportation* 17: 40–50.

Engel, E., R. Fischer, A. Galetovic, and G. de Rus. 2018. "Public-Private Partnerships in Infrastructure: Reforming the Spanish Toll Road Concessions System" (in Spanish). *Cuadernos de Extensión Jurdica* 31.

Engel, E., R. Fischer, A. Galetovic, and M. Hermosilla. 2009. "Renegotiation of Concessions in Chile." *Estudios Públicos* (Summer): 151–205.

Engel, E., R. Fischer, A. Galetovic, and J. Soto. 2019. "Financing PPP Projects with PVR Contracts: Theory and Evidence from the UK and Chile." Paper presented at the Finance of Infrastructure Symposium, Hoover Institution, Stanford University, May 2019.

Esguerra, J. 2003. "The Corporate Muddle of Manila's Water Concessions." WaterAid and Tearfund.

Eurostat. 2016. *Manual on Government Deficit and Debt*. Brussels: Eurostat.

Flyvbjerg, B., N. Bruzelius, and W. Rothengatter. 2003. *Megaprojects and Risk: An Anatomy of Ambition*. Cambridge: Cambridge University Press.

García-Kilroy, C., and H. Rudolph. 2017. *Private Financing of Public Infrastructure through PPPs in Latin America and the Caribbean*. Washington, DC: World Bank.

Gifford, J., L. Bolaños, and N. Daito. 2014. "Renegotiation of Transportation Public-Private Partnerships: The US Experience." Discussion Paper 2014-16, International Transport Forum. Paris: OECD.

Gómez-Ibáñez, J. A., and J. Meyer. 1993. *Going Private: The International Experience with Transport Privatization*. Washington, DC: Brookings Institution.

Grimsey, D., and M. K. Lewis. 2002. "Evaluating the Risks for Public-Private Partnerships for Infrastructure Projects." *International Journal of Project Management* 20: 107–18.

———. 2004. *The Economics of Public-Private Partnerships*. Northampton, MA: Edward Elgar.

Grout, P., and M. Stevens. 2003. "The Assessment: Financing and Managing Public Services." *Oxford Review of Economic Policy* 19 (2): 215–34.

Guasch, J. L. 2004. *Granting and Renegotiating Infrastructure Concessions: Doing It Right*. Washington, DC: World Bank.

Guasch, J. L., J. J. Laffont, and S. Straub. 2007. "Concessions of Infrastructure in Latin America: Government-Led Renegotiations." *Journal of Applied Econometrics* 22 (7): 1267–94.

———. 2008. "Renegotiation of Concession Contracts in Latin America: Evidence from the Water and Transport Sectors." *International Journal of Industrial Organization* 26 (2): 421–42.

Hall, G. 1998. "Private Opportunity, Public Benefit?" *Fiscal Studies* 19 (2): 40.

Hart, O. 2003. "Incomplete Contracts and Public Ownership: Remarks and an Application to Public-Private Partnerships." *Economic Journal* 113 (486): C69–C76.

Heald, D. 1997. "Privately Financed Capital in Public Services." *Manchester School* 65 (5): 568–98.

———. 2010. "The Accounting Treatment of Public Finance Initiative Projects." In *The Budget Report*. London: House of Commons.

Heald, D., and G. Georgiou. 2009. "The Substance of Accounting for Public-Private Partnerships." *Financial Accountability & Management* 27 (2): 217–47.
Heald, D., and A. McLeod. 2002. "Public Expenditure." In *Constitutional Law, 2002. The Laws of Scotland: Stair Memorial Encyclopaedia*. Edinburgh: Butterworths.
Inderst, G. 2010. "Infrastructure as an Asset Class." *EIB Papers* 15: 70–104.
———. 2013. "Private Infrastructure Finance and Investment in Europe." EIB Working Papers 02.
Irwin, T. 2007. *Government Guarantees: Allocating and Valuing Risk in Privately Financed Infrastructure Projects*. Washington, DC: World Bank.
Klein, M. 1997. "Comments on the Proposal by Engel, Fisher, and Galetovic on Highway Auctions" (in Spanish). *Estudios Públicos* 67: 215–23.
Leslie, A. 2019. "Managing Hospital Assets under PPPs." Master's thesis, University of Chile.
Levy, S. M. 1996. *Build, Operate, Transfer: Paving the Way for Tomorrow's Infrastructure*. Hoboken, NJ: John Wiley.
Lucas, D., and J. Jimenez Montesinos. 2021. "A Fair Value Approach to Valuing Public Infrastructure Projects and the Risk Transfer in Public-Private Partnerships." This volume.
Maskin, E., and J. Tirole. 2008. "Public-Private Partnerships and Government Spending Limits." *International Journal of Industrial Organization* 26: 412–20.
National Audit Office. 2018. *PF1 and PF2*. Report by the Comptroller and Auditor General. London: House of Commons.
OECD. 2008. *Public-Private Partnerships: In Pursuit of Risk Sharing and Value-for-Money*. Paris: OECD.
Raisbeck, P., C. Duffield, and M. Xu. 2010. "Comparative Performance of PPPs and Traditional Procurement in Australia." *Construction Management and Economics* 28 (4): 345–59.
Rioja, F. K. 2003. "Filling Potholes: Macroeconomic Effects of Maintenance versus New Investments in Public Infrastructure." *Journal of Public Economics* 87: 2281–304.
Sarmento, J., and L. Renneboog. 2014. "The Portuguese Experience with Public-Private Partnerships." Tilburg University Discussion Papers 05-2014, January.
Schwartz, G., A. Carbacho, and K. Funke. 2008. *Public Investment and Public-Private Partnerships*. London: Palgrave Macmillan.
Singh, R. 2018. "Does Choice of Procurement Matter for Cost and Quality of Infrastructure?: Comparison of Quality and Cost of Roads." International Growth Centre Working Paper S-89209-INC-2.
Tirole, J. 1997. "Comments on the Proposal by Engel, Fisher, and Galetovic on Highway Auctions" (in Spanish). *Estudios Públicos* 67: 201–214.
TRIP. 2013. "Bumpy Roads Ahead: America's Roughest Rides and Strategies to Make Our Roads Smoother." Washington, DC: TRIP.
World Bank. 1994. *World Development Report 1994: Infrastructure for Development*. Washington, DC: World Bank.
Wu, X., and N. Malaluan. 2007. "A Tale of Two Concessionaires: A Natural Experiment of Water Privatisation in Metro Manila." *Urban Studies* 45(1): 207–29.

## Comment Keith Hennessey

Chapter 6 is excellent both as a primer on public-private partnerships (PPPs) and as a guide to effective PPP policy design.

Engel, Fischer, and Galetovic taught me some basic facts about PPP usage around the world:

1. Relative to total world infrastructure spending, the use of PPPs is quite small, on the order of 6–10 percent of total privately financed infrastructure and 2–3 percent of total infrastructure spending. I do not know whether this means that (a) there is significant upside potential and room for increased use of this tool, or (b) its use is small because it does not work well or is hard to do.
2. In Europe, PPP usage is almost entirely about transportation infrastructure, with a little health care thrown in. As the authors tell us, "For Europe, PPPs are a complement and not the main source of transport investment." They cite an example of a significant increase (65 percent) in Portuguese highway investment, but so far it seems that in Europe, too, PPPs have not caught on more broadly.
3. In developing countries, half the PPP dollars are going to roads, with the rest split roughly evenly among airports, railways, and ports. This makes intuitive sense, as each of these can generate a somewhat predictable revenue stream to justify private financing.

Having established some important facts, the bulk of the paper provides a helpful framework for how to think about whether and when to use a PPP. I would like to compliment the authors for their intellectual honesty. At the same time as they summarize policy design best practices and conclude that "PPPs can be a useful instrument of public policy," they are honest and direct about both the weaknesses in this policy tool and especially about the misconception that forms "the main motivation for their use." The misconceptions they describe are quite familiar to me from past American debates about PPPs, and if future debates were fully informed by this chapter, the likelihood of policy makers choosing wisely would increase substantially.

The authors emphasize that PPPs "have been attractive to policy makers because they promise to relax the fiscal constraints that limit resources for infrastructure projects." To me, the core lesson of the paper is that well-designed PPPs can make infrastructure spending more efficient, but they are usually pursued because policy makers mistakenly perceive them as a source of "free money."

Keith Hennessey is a lecturer in economics at Stanford Graduate School of Business.

For acknowledgments, sources of research support, and disclosure of the author's material financial relationships, if any, please see https://www.nber.org/books-and-chapters/economic-analysis-and-infrastructure-investment/comment-when-and-how-use-public-private-partnerships-infrastructure-lessons-international-experience.

At the federal level in the US, this misperception is common. US federal budgeting works with a fixed-length, short-duration budget window: 1, 5, or 10 years. Almost all federal budgeting is done on a cash-flow basis over one of those time frames, always measured in nominal dollars. Federal budget rules score and bind fiscal impacts on the federal fisc only, ignoring both state and private sector impacts. US legislators often have short time horizons, with members of the House of Representatives facing reelection every two years, and senators every six. A policy tool that purports to leverage federal tax dollars for greater total spending, with the lion's share of the spending and financing off budget, is tempting to legislators. Since their budgetary constraints apply to only a portion of the true accounting, their decision-making incentives are easily distorted.

This budgeting structure interacts with the chapter in three ways.

1. If you wanted to implement the authors' methodology at the federal level in the US, you would have to change budget scoring rules. The authors recommend an all-in, long-time-frame, expected-present-value accounting approach that would move onto the government balance sheet the private borrowing and subsequent revenue streams within a PPP. That makes good policy sense but would be difficult in terms of the federal budget process. Would legislators be willing to devote the time and legislative capital to setting up such intellectually honest budget process changes to limit the use of a rarely used policy tool that would be more attractive without the reforms?

2. The authors correctly point out that policy makers' desire to evade fiscal constraints is one reason PPPs have been attractive to policy makers outside the US. This is also true in the US. Some US legislators think they can "lever up" federal tax dollars to get more total infrastructure spending. Part of the reason is just that they do not understand the full accounting in this chapter. Part of the reason is that the forgone revenues would not have accrued to the federal government anyway, so federal policy makers ignore these revenues. And part of it is willful ignorance or, if you prefer, overoptimism—an intense desire for a magic wand that will generate free money for them to spend.

3. The problem, then, is that when these scoring difficulties combine with policy makers' desire to use PPPs to simply spend more, by far the most likely outcome is that, if budget rules are changed, they are changed in a manner that unfairly advantages PPPs so that more money can be spent without policy makers getting "charged" for it.

The project selection and avoid-the-white-elephants arguments cited by the authors have also been present in US PPP policy debates. The most common form of this argument is that legislators make poor decisions about which projects to finance, because they are either unwise or skewed by political concerns. As the authors correctly note, "pork barrel projects and poor planning often build white elephants." Allowing "the market to decide" which projects to finance will insert some discipline into the project selection process, advocates claim.

By "white elephant," it appears the authors mean projects with a low social return. Members of Congress look at this spending differently. Their focus is almost always limited by the geographic boundaries of the area they represent, and they are maximizing for some other measure of perceived benefit to the people and area they represent (weighted by their own preferences). Any effort to use PPPs to fight the desire of policy makers to allocate spending based first on geography would legislatively fail. If PPPs exclude projects with low social return in their districts, decision-makers will consider that a bug, not a feature.

The authors argue that government should use PPPs when they provide sufficient efficiency gains and that efficiency gains do not arise from private participation per se, but from the different incentives under both organizational forms. These may be the result of differences in risk allocation, contract design, financing, and political economy.

The authors describe seven efficiency claims for PPPs over public provision. I was convinced by the "narrow focus and dedicated management" claim, as well as the "bundling" and "fewer construction delays" claims, the latter of which I hope would be a high priority for US policy makers. As described earlier, I think the "filtering white elephants" argument is flawed because there are multiple legitimate criteria for deciding which projects are good. I found the "avoiding the cost of bureaucracies" and "advantages of private financing" arguments less persuasive. To me the most attractive potential efficiency gain associated with PPPs is "better and less expensive maintenance." In an American context, a policy tool that results in better-maintained transport infrastructure and addresses congestion externalities is exciting.

I also found the authors' principal policy design recommendation convincing: the use of present-value-of-revenue (PVR) contracts instead of fixed-term contracts. The US examples cited by the authors (the Dulles Greenway and Orange County's State Route 91) are good examples of the downsides of combining demand forecast uncertainty with fixed-term contracts. It would be interesting to see whether offering PVR contracts in the US would increase the number and quality of bids for a given set of transportation infrastructure PPP projects.

Despite good arguments made by Engel, Fischer, and Galetovic, I remain skeptical of the PPP as a tool for US infrastructure spending. Four questions merit further discussion.

1. How robust is the PPP design? This is the whiteboard problem. Suppose one begins a policy making process with an ideal PPP structure on a whiteboard, designed by the authors. Suppose further that design is modified by legislators, bureaucrats, and judges as it makes its way through the demo-

cratic process. Can the model still work, even though some of its features have been changed? It is of course impossible to answer this question in the abstract, but for a policy design to be worth pursuing, it should be legislatively and bureaucratically robust. It must work even when it is imperfectly implemented. There are a lot of moving parts in the design described by the authors and lots of points of potential failure. Is the PPP still worth pursuing if the implementation is only 80 percent faithful to the original design?

2. Managing the different elements of risk, the structure of the contracts, and the long-term relationships with private firms is, in the US context, the task of experts in the executive branch (specifically, the US Department of Transportation). The tasks described by the authors are conceptually challenging and may be bureaucratically even more so, especially if Congress is occasionally trying to interfere to "help." Is it worth developing the long-term expertise and skill set within the bureaucracy to effectively manage this when the aggregate size has so far been quite small?

3. Related to point 2 is the question whether it is worth the effort. Are the hypothesized efficiency benefits large enough, especially relative to just pursuing contracting reform?

4. Finally, does it make sense to improve and refine this policy tool if the "wrong reasons for PPPs" problem remains unsolved? That is, does it make sense to have a well-designed PPP tool if Congress is likely to use it for the wrong reason?

I thank the authors and NBER for the opportunity to comment and hope this input is helpful.

7

# A Fair Value Approach to Valuing Public Infrastructure Projects and the Risk Transfer in Public-Private Partnerships

Deborah Lucas and Jorge Jimenez Montesinos

## 7.1 Introduction

It is widely predicted that governments worldwide will invest tens of trillions of dollars in new infrastructure investments over the next decade. Which of the many candidate projects should be undertaken? Is entering a public-private partnership (PPP) cost-effective? How do alternative revenue and risk-sharing contracts affect government cost? What funding mechanisms should be used? The ability to accurately value projects and related contracts is vital for governments to give informed answers to such questions and to fulfill their responsibilities as stewards of public resources. Yet analyses of public infrastructure investments often rely on government accounting conventions and valuation approaches that significantly misrepresent the financial costs and benefits of both the projects and the associated contractual arrangements.

As a step toward providing public managers with practical tools designed to more closely align infrastructure valuation practices with financial principles, and to suggest the magnitude of the distortions arising from analyses that neglect the cost of risk, in this chapter we, first, briefly recap the theoretical and practical considerations surrounding the use of a fair value approach

Deborah Lucas is the Sloan Distinguished Professor of Finance at the MIT Sloan School of Management and director of the MIT Golub Center for Finance and Policy, and a research associate of the National Bureau of Economic Research.

Jorge Jimenez Montesinos is a research associate of the MIT Golub Center for Finance and Policy.

For acknowledgments, sources of research support, and disclosure of the authors' material financial relationships, if any, please see https://www.nber.org/books-and-chapters/economic-analysis-and-infrastructure-investment/fair-value-approach-valuing-public-infrastructure-projects-and-risk-transfer-public-private.

to assessing public investment projects; second, develop a framework consistent with that approach and with private sector practice for valuing public investment projects and the various claims associated with them, with an emphasis on PPPs; and, third, illustrate the implications of that approach versus popularly used alternatives for a hypothetical toll road project. While our main emphasis is on how valuation practices can be improved, we also discuss several related issues, including whether and when arrangements such as PPPs and infrastructure banks might legitimately alleviate government funding constraints; the implications of the availability of tax-exempt municipal bond funding in the US; and the incentives created by budgetary rules for US state and local governments. Engel, Fischer, and Galetovic (2021) provide a useful and complementary analysis of the effects of PPPs on efficiency, incentives, and governance.

The fair value approach posits that the cost of capital for any real or financial investment reflects the market price of the associated risks or the best available approximation thereof. Hence the cost of capital for a given project is essentially the same for governments and private investors. The government's borrowing rate, although frequently used by governments for discounting project cash flows, is not a full measure of the government's cost of capital for a risky investment. That conclusion rests on the observation that a risky investment can never be fully financed by low-risk government debt. Taxpayers and other government stakeholders are the residual claimants to any profits or losses; effectively citizens are conscripted equity holders in all risky investments undertaken by governments.

The fair value approach is largely good news for PPPs, as it suggests that a common concern about them—that they entail a higher cost of capital because private contractors have to "make a profit"—is misplaced. In fact, there is no necessary trade-off between the potentially greater operational efficiencies of PPPs and higher capital costs as long as the contracting process is sufficiently competitive to ensure that private partners earn a return that is commensurate with the risk they assume. However, because a fair value approach generally assigns a cost of capital that is higher than a government's borrowing rate, the approach tends to reduce the universe of projects that appear to be worthwhile investments. The exception is that projects that have countercyclical benefits will appear more valuable than under typical discounting practices (Gollier and Cherbonnier 2018). A fair value approach also tends to increase the assessed cost of contracts that shift risk from private partners to the government, which will make some PPPs arrangements appear significantly less attractive than under current valuation practices. Reliance on fair value principles suggests that a textbook approach to valuation—projecting associated net cash flows and assessing their risk, and then discounting by the corresponding cost of capital—applies to public infrastructure investments. While this is true, valuing public infrastructure investments entails complications that are usually absent from standard capital budgeting exercises that private firms would undertake. A contribution of the analysis here is to show how those nonstandard features can be incorporated into the valuation process on a consistent and comprehensive basis that avoids double counting and that clarifies the incidence of costs and benefits under alternative contractual arrangements.

To value public infrastructure investments, nonstandard considerations include how to incorporate public benefit flows that are in excess of revenue flows, and the cost of any negative externalities including tax distortions. It is also critical to assess the value of various types of subsidies and their incidence. Inferring the cost of capital can be tricky because of the limited availability of data on historical costs and revenues for most types of infrastructure projects and the less obvious choices for private sector firms with comparable risk exposures.

Subsidies to infrastructure investments take many forms. These include direct government payments; in-kind services; tax breaks to private partners; credit subsidies via preferentially priced direct government loans or credit guarantees; access to tax-advantaged municipal bond financing; minimum revenue guarantees in PPPs; and implicit guarantees such as those arising from the renegotiation of contracts when revenues fail to meet expectations. A number of these subsidies are contingent claims that can be valued most accurately using derivatives pricing methods, and a major contribution of the analysis is to show how some of these common contractual features can be valued using those methods.

A further consideration is that multiple levels of government may provide subsidies (for example, municipal bonds provide federal resources to state, local, and private entities). While it is natural that a local government, like a private firm, would treat federal subsidies as unambiguously increasing the attractiveness of undertaking a project, an analysis of social value requires taking into account the comprehensive cost of subsidies at all levels of government.

The analysis here is related to several distinct strands of literature. It builds most directly on Lucas (2012, 2014a) and references therein, which discuss the reasons for the systematic understatement by governments of the cost of their financial activities and develop and calibrate models to evaluate government financial costs more comprehensively for a variety of applications. More fundamentally, our analysis relies on the conceptual foundations of modern financial valuation and derivatives pricing techniques (among others, Arrow and Debreu 1954; Black 1976; Black and Scholes 1973; Merton 1973; Modigliani and Miller 1958; and Sharpe 1964). Our analysis also expands on themes developed in more recent analyses of infrastructure investments and PPPs, particularly Engel, Fischer, and Galetovic (2014a, 2014b, and 2021 and references therein). Finally, our analysis is related to fundamental issues in public finance and public choice. Those traditions typically place more emphasis than we do on distributional consequences and tax distortions, but they abstract from our main focus, which is the effects of risk on value.

The remainder of the chapter is organized as follows. Section 7.2 briefly recaps the theoretical and practical considerations associated with governments taking a fair value approach to valuation. Section 7.3 lays out a valuation framework for infrastructure projects and for the various contracts associated with them, including those that commonly arise in PPPs. Section 7.4 applies those ideas to compare the construction and operation of a hypothetical toll road via and PPP and via a more traditional financing structure and to illustrate the magnitude of the effects of alternative assumptions about capital costs. Section 7.5 discusses funding-related issues. Section 7.6 concludes.

## 7.2 Government Cost of Capital

The basic presumption that value of government investments should be evaluated using market prices rests on the logic that (i) the risk incurred is ultimately borne by taxpayers and other government stakeholders (henceforth referred to as citizens) and (ii) market prices are the best available measure of opportunity cost for most investments.[1] When a government assumes the risk of investing in an infrastructure project, any losses that are incurred eventually must be covered by increases in future taxes, or cuts to other spending. Similarly, any profits can be used to reduce future taxes or to fund other government spending. Effectively, then, citizens are equity holders in public infrastructure investments.

In a highly influential analysis, Arrow and Lind (1970) suggested that governments have a lower cost of capital than the private sector because they can spread project risk more widely and by doing so effectively eliminate it. However, as was recognized by many leading economists of the time, that line of reasoning does not apply to aggregate or undiversifiable risks. Furthermore, modern capital markets spread investment risk widely across investors, perhaps more broadly than governments typically do.[2] The evidence from the asset pricing literature suggests that diversifiable risk does not carry a risk premium. Hence, the undiversifiable risk associated with

1. For projects with very long-lived effects such as those to mitigate climate change, reference market prices may be unavailable, and other approaches to identifying value are necessary. The focus here is on valuation of the vast majority of infrastructure investments, which have at least loose analogues in private sector investments.

2. The degree to which the government is able to efficiently distribute risk relative to the private sector is ultimately an empirical question. For the state and local governments that undertake a large share of infrastructure investments, the tax base is likely to be narrow relative to the base of international investors that participate in global capital markets.

infrastructure investment represents a cost that is independent of whether the sponsor is a government or a private entity, and market risk premiums reflect that cost. (See Lucas [2014b] for a more complete discussion of these and related issues.)

Some might argue that the government can fund a project by issuing public debt that carries a low interest rate. However, issuing public debt can only alter the timing of when project cash flows are passed through to citizens. Adjustments in the size of the public debt do not in themselves affect the financial position of the government; rather, they are a means of financing. That is, if the government covers a negative cash flow by issuing additional debt, that debt eventually must be repaid with interest. Issuing the debt is value neutral because the amount borrowed equals the present value of future repayments. The interest rate on the debt depends on the strength of the government's promise to repay, and other features like whether the debt is tax-advantaged, but not on the risk of any particular project. Despite that logic, governments often identify their cost of capital with their own borrowing rate.

For revenue bonds whose payments are backed only by project cash flows, the riskiness of the debt and therefore the interest rate investors demand depend on project risk and the amount of debt issued. The obligation to pay debt holders from project cash flows adds leverage to the position of citizens in their role as equity holders or residual claimants. The more debt that is added to the capital structure, the riskier is the equity. Whatever the mix of debt and equity used for funding, the total risk is conserved and depends on the characteristics of the project; the famous Modigliani-Miller theorem holds for both government and private sector investments.[3]

The recognition that the value of a public infrastructure project depends on the market price of the associated risks, and that identifying the cost of risk can require approximations, suggests taking a fair value approach to evaluating project value. This approach measures the value of cash flows at market prices when possible but allows approximations when directly comparable market prices are unavailable or unreliable due to market conditions. A fair value approach generally entails applying the discount rates on expected future cash flows that private financial institutions would apply.

Along with aligning government valuations with economic principles, a fair value approach has the advantage of harmonizing the perspectives of the government and potential private partners. Understanding the value proposition for a private partner can improve outcomes, for instance, by helping governments avoid accepting unrealistically low bids that are likely to be renegotiated.

3. As for private sector investments, this abstracts from tax effects and the potential costs of financial distress when leverage is high.

## 7.3 Valuation Framework

The framework presented here takes an adjusted present value (APV) approach, which calls for first calculating the stand-alone value of a project as if it were entirely equity financed, and then separately adjusting for financing side effects such as the value of municipal bond tax exemptions or subsidized government guarantees (see, e.g., Brealey, Myers, and Allen 2019).

In this section we discuss the elements of an APV analysis as they pertain to infrastructure projects, starting with the basics of how to identify the relevant stand-alone cash flows and project discount rates. We also discuss how some of the most common financing side effects and subsidy arrangements can be valued using risk-adjusted discount rates and derivatives pricing techniques.

A popular alternative to APV is the weighted average cost of capital (WACC) approach, which adjusts the discount rate so as to implicitly take into account the value of financing side effects. In theory both approaches should yield identical results when correctly applied, and in practice the results tend to be similar for many private sector applications. However, APV is the only workable approach in this context because of the complexity of subsidies and contractual arrangements, as well as the need to understand how the value of various claims affects different project participants.

We take a textbook approach to valuation rather than a adopting more complicated academic model for several reasons. The workhorse APV model, implemented using the capital asset pricing model (CAPM) to identify discount rates, is relatively easy to understand and implement. Because it is widely used by firms in the private sector to evaluate investment opportunities, expertise and standard practices are available to help discipline the process, which promotes credibility and transparency. Furthermore, alternative models that have been proposed to estimate discount rates have so far not yielded sufficiently robust outcomes to be widely adopted in practice.[4]

### 7.3.1 Cash Flows

The first step in any net present value (NPV) analysis of project value is to estimate expected cash inflows and outflows over the life of the project. For long-lived projects, cash flows often are explicitly forecast through some terminal date, at which time a liquidating cash flow represents the net present value of any residual cash flows past that period. Cash inflows are composed of revenues from user fees, rents, and other charges. Cash outflows include capital expenditures, maintenance, salaries, and other expenses.[5]

4. Ammar and Eling (2013) estimate a Fama-French-style model to explain returns to infrastructure and find that returns covary positively with the market and also depend on the other Fama-French factors.

5. Depreciation is a noncash expense. Its cost is indirectly reflected in capital expenditure and maintenance costs.

An important consideration for public infrastructure investments is how to incorporate the value created for society beyond what is reflected in revenues. Significant differences between revenues and social benefits may arise for many reasons. For instance, a toll road may generate significant time savings for drivers on nearby highways by reducing congestion. Another example is that to increase access and encourage use, governments may choose to set user charges below cost and below the public's willingness to pay. Negative externalities, such as increased $CO_2$ emissions from a public power plant or the costs arising from the associated distortionary taxes needed to help pay for the project, also need to be incorporated.

In the APV framework presented here, the value of any such positive or negative externalities would be quantified and incorporated as a positive or negative cash flow. There are two possibilities for how to include them: (1) along with the cash flows for the stand-alone project; and (2) separately as an input into the adjustments to the base case value. The first option makes sense when the externalities are thought to be roughly proportional to the service flows net of cost from the project and when the perspective of interest is that of the government. As line items to be incorporated into the cash flows of the stand-alone analysis, the externalities might be described as "imputed additional revenues" and "imputed additional costs." The second option is preferred when the risk of the externalities is significantly different from the risk of the service flows net of cost, or when the project is being evaluated from the perspective of an entity like a private partner that does not care about the value of the externalities.

Although imputing the value of externalities requires judgment and involves considerable uncertainty, attempting to do so is unavoidable when the objective is to undertake a full and formal cost-benefit analysis of a project. The public finance literature provides some guidance on imputing the social value-added for public goods, but there is no general agreement on critical issues such as how to choose a social welfare function to use as an aggregator across different beneficiaries. Fortunately, for valuation objectives such as determining budgetary costs or for negotiating contracts with private partners, quantifying the value of externalities is often less critical.

Cash and in-kind subsidies also affect the cash flows associated with an infrastructure project. However, as for financing side effects, the present value of these subsidies can be evaluated separately from the calculations for the stand-alone project and then incorporated into the final APV calculation. One reason for treating all types of subsidies separately is that their effect on net value will depend on whose perspective is being considered. Another reason is that the risk characteristics of subsidies, and hence the appropriate rate to discount them, are often quite different from the risk characteristics for the project as a whole.

Several examples illustrate the complications associated with cash and in-kind subsidies. Imagine that a government agrees to perform certain maintenance functions for its private partner for free or at below its cost (for example, dredging a port). From the perspective of the government, the subsidy element of that service provision is an additional operating cost associated with the project; it adds to the present value of costs. From the perspective of the private partner, there is no need to track the annual cost savings. Rather, the benefit received will be implicit in its lower projected operating costs. Similarly, the free provision of land to a private partner should be treated as a capital expenditure for the government equal in value to what the land could be sold for to a private buyer, taking into account any use restrictions and other features that would affect its market value. For the private partner, the benefit from the free land use is implicit in reduced capital expenditures.

Another example is a contract obligating a government to make a constant annual payment to a private partner for some number of years to help defray fixed operating expenses. Clearly the contract in itself is positive NPV for the private partner and negative NPV by the same amount for the government. A further reason to value this contract separately is that the risk of the fixed contractual payments and hence the appropriate discount rate are likely to be considerably lower than for the project as a whole. Relatedly, we will see that a minimum revenue guarantee from the government, which also might be viewed in terms of its expected cash flows, actually is a package of put options whose value depends on the volatility of revenues. Because of that optionality, the associated cost of risk is higher than for the underlying project as a whole. That makes the guarantee more valuable to a private partner and more costly to the government than it would appear to be if the expected cash flows from the guarantee were rolled directly into the project valuation.

### 7.3.2 Cost of Capital

The approaches suggested here to identify the cost of capital (that is, the discount rate) for valuing infrastructure projects and their associated claims follows the logic of modern finance theory, as taught in business schools and widely adopted by large corporations and investment professionals. For completeness, we provide a basic description of some of these well-documented procedures. However, our main focus will be on considerations that are more specific to public infrastructure projects. Those include the greater difficulty of identifying private sector firms with comparable risk exposures; the limited availability of data on historical costs and revenues; and the pervasive use of financial and nonfinancial subsidies and guarantees that affect risk and hence capital costs. We emphasize that the relevant cost of capital will be different for the project as a stand-alone entity and for different claims related to the project, and we give examples of situations in which such distinctions typically need to be made.

### 7.3.2.1 *The Capital Asset Pricing Model*

The cost of capital for a project or financial contract reflects the pure time value of money plus the priced risk of the associated cash flows. The workhorse model for identifying a project's cost of capital is the capital asset pricing model (CAPM). It posits that investments whose risk can be inexpensively avoided through portfolio diversification will earn only the risk-free rate. However, investments exposed to "undiversifiable" or "market" risk on average earn a market risk premium in addition to the risk-free rate. Equivalently, expected cash flows from the projects with more market risk exposure, as measured, are discounted at higher rates.[6]

The CAPM quantifies undiversifiable risk for a stand-alone, all-equity-financed project through the idea of an "asset beta." Asset betas are estimated using historical data on stock returns on firms with similar risk exposures to the project under consideration. Specifically, stock returns on individual stocks or industry portfolios are regressed on the return to a broad market index like the S&P 500 to identify an equity beta. The equity betas are unlevered to remove the effects of debt financing on the risk of equity, yielding an "unlevered" or asset beta.[7]

The CAPM provides a discount rate for project's cash flows through the following equation:

$$(r_A) = r_f + ((r_m) - r_f), \tag{1}$$

where $(r_A)$ is the expected return on assets with similar market risk to the project and hence is the appropriate discount rate to apply to its expected cash flows; $r_f$ is the risk-free rate; and $(r_m)$ is the expected return on the market. $\beta_A$ is the asset beta. Note that the APV approach taken here requires discounting project cash flows as if the project is all equity financed and that asset betas are designed to do just that. The risk-free rate is generally taken to be the prevailing short-term (for example, three-month) Treasury rate, and a typical estimate of the market risk premium—that is, $((r_m)-r_f)$—would be 5–7 percent.

6. The intellectual appeal of the CAPM is that a similar story can be told in terms of utility functions and state prices, with higher values today for future payoffs that occur in high marginal utility states of the world. The CAPM equation can be derived from a general equilibrium pricing model under the assumption of quadratic utility and consumption that is equal to asset payoffs. Drawbacks include that the CAPM's predictive capabilities for asset returns are limited and that it abstracts from other factors likely to affect the cost of capital like liquidity and size. Despite those drawbacks, the CAPM is widely used because of its simplicity and because competing models are also poor at forecasting returns.

7. An adjustment can also be made for cash holdings, which are like negative debt. That adjustment tends to be small for most industries. Whether the adjustment for cash should be included depends on the cash needs of the project. If the project entails cash holdings at similar ratios to those of the comparison firms, no adjustment for cash is necessary.

**Table 7.1 Asset betas by industry and unlevered betas corrected for cash, over time**

Asset betas by industry

| Industry name | Number of firms | Beta | Unlevered beta corrected for cash |
|---|---|---|---|
| Air transport | 18 | 1.02 | 0.63 |
| Engineering and construction | 52 | 1.01 | 0.81 |
| Green and renewable energy | 21 | 1.62 | 0.80 |
| Homebuilding | 31 | 0.98 | 0.72 |
| Hospitals and health care facilities | 34 | 1.12 | 0.55 |
| Real estate (development) | 18 | 1.19 | 0.87 |
| Transportation | 19 | 1.14 | 0.90 |
| Trucking | 28 | 1.22 | 0.71 |
| Utility (water) | 19 | 0.42 | 0.32 |
| Total market | 7,209 | 1.12 | 0.80 |
| Total market (without financials) | 6,004 | 1.21 | 1.00 |

Unlevered betas corrected for cash, over time

| 2015 | 2016 | 2017 | 2018 | Average (2015–2019) |
|---|---|---|---|---|
| 0.61 | 0.85 | 0.76 | 0.67 | 0.70 |
| 1.19 | 1.07 | 1.01 | 1.13 | 1.04 |
| 0.68 | 0.84 | 0.47 | 0.72 | 0.70 |
| 0.92 | 0.81 | 0.77 | 0.89 | 0.82 |
| 0.59 | 0.44 | 0.45 | 0.51 | 0.51 |
| 0.82 | 0.93 | 0.47 | 0.61 | 0.74 |
| 0.77 | 1.19 | 0.83 | 0.80 | 0.90 |
| 0.92 | 1.03 | 0.76 | 0.81 | 0.84 |
| 0.77 | 0.33 | 0.47 | 0.27 | 0.43 |
| 0.70 | 0.73 | 0.65 | 0.72 | 0.72 |
| 0.87 | 0.9 | 0.85 | 0.90 | 0.90 |

*Source*: "Betas by Sector (US)," http://pages.stern.nyu.edu/~adamodar/New_Home_Page/datafile/Betas.html.

### *7.3.2.2 Estimation Approaches*

A relatively simple and transparent way to assign a cost of capital to a public infrastructure project is by associating an asset beta with it and using equation (1) to derive a discount rate to apply to the project cash flows. Estimates of asset betas by industry are readily available, for instance from the popular website of Professor Aswath Damodaran at New York University.[8] Table 7.1 shows cash-adjusted asset betas for selected industries from that source.

The most relevant comparison industry will depend on the project. For

8. "Betas by Sector (US)," January 2021, http://pages.stern.nyu.edu/~adamodar/New_Home_Page/datafile/Betas.html.

example, for a toll road, the industries in table 7.1 whose cash flows are likely to have a similar aggregate risk exposure include trucking (cash-adjusted asset beta of 0.71) and transportation (cash-adjusted asset beta of 0.9). One possibility would be to use the asset beta for trucking on the grounds that the transportation category is too broad and presumably includes firms like passenger airlines for which demand is more cyclical than highway usage. Alternatively, if trucking were viewed as too specific, another possibility would be to use an average of the two. The difference for the discount rate between those two choices is only about half a percentage point, assuming a 6 percent equity premium.

As another example, for a water treatment plant the natural choice from the table 7.1 industry list is "utility (water)" (cash-adjusted asset beta of 0.32). The much lower market risk for water than for toll roads, and correspondingly lower implied discount rate, reflects the fairly stable demand for water over the business cycle and perhaps the stabilizing effects of rate of return regulations on utility revenues.

For other public facility investments like ports or airports, it is less clear how one would impute an asset beta from the list of industries in table 7.1. A possibility would be to use a broad industrial average of asset betas. Another would be to handpick a list of comparison firms (for example, shipping companies for ports) and calculate asset betas from data on their historical returns.

Another possibility would be to try to infer asset betas from historical time series data on the returns to infrastructure funds. However, because infrastructure investments are generally privately held and trade infrequently, reliable information on returns is not available. Andonov, Kräussl, and Rauh (2018) analyze proprietary data from Preqin, a leading provider of data on alternative asset classes, and find that that the stream of cash flows delivered by private infrastructure funds to most institutional investors is very similar to that delivered by other types of private equity.[9] That suggests returns on private equity as another reference point for inferring asset betas.

There are several other options for estimating betas as inputs into constructing project discount rates. One is to collect cash flow data from similar projects and regress the data on overall market returns. A practical limitation is that for public infrastructure projects, time series data on cash flows are generally not publicly available, although some governments may have relevant information from past projects. Data may be available on revenues but not on costs.[10] A conceptual limitation to inferring betas from revenue data is that revenue data do not include any imputed additional revenues and may include the effects of certain types of subsidy payments. Furthermore,

9. The exception is US public pension plans, which receive lower returns on infrastructure than other institutional investors.

10. See a description of various PPP databases worldwide in Prats, Demaestri, and Chiara (2018).

estimates of asset betas based only on revenues are downward biased when fixed costs create operating leverage.[11]

Another possibility is to regress other variables likely to be associated with value on market returns. Again taking the example of toll roads, regressing detrended annual passenger miles driven on annual market returns gives an indication of the correlation between the value of road services and the overall market. Historical revenue data on toll roads and data on passenger miles driven are available from the US Department of Transportation. In section 7.4, we show how asset betas based on that data compare with those inferred from the stock return-based procedure using Damodaran's asset betas for related industries.

*7.3.2.3 Additional Considerations*

A fundamental question is whether the procedure of deriving asset betas from equity betas should be expected to reasonably capture the cost of market risk for public infrastructure projects. Our view is that for the evaluation of stand-alone, all-equity-financed projects, the answer is often yes. The procedure implicitly assumes that the earnings of the comparison firms have a similar exposure to market risk as the earnings—properly measured to include any imputed additional revenues discussed in section 7.3.1—of the infrastructure project. However, the cash flows associated with associated transactions, whose dynamics may differ significantly from the overall project, must be discounted at a cost of capital consistent with their risk, as illustrated in the example in section 7.4.

It is important to understand that assigning a cost of capital to a new project or associated claim is challenging even for the most sophisticated corporations and investors, and it always involves simplifications and approximations. A realistic goal is to identify discount rates that have no discernable bias, even when there is considerable uncertainty around any point estimate ultimately selected. And while identifying a point estimate may be necessary for purposes like budgetary accounting, sensitivity analysis that includes a plausible range of discount rates is useful for understanding and communicating the uncertainty related to the cost of capital.

If one accepts that market risk is a cost to the government, then the common practice by governments of equating their cost of capital to their own borrowing rate ensures a downwardly biased discount rate for all but the safest projects and claims. The size of the bias can differ significantly across projects and claims with different risk exposures. These observations run counter to the perception that using a government rate for discounting is somehow fairer to competing projects or more reliable because there is no

11. Revenue-based betas are appropriate for estimating the value of a revenue stream to a private partner and may be a useful input into the negotiation process.

judgment involved. Nevertheless, it is a legitimate concern that giving too much latitude to government analysts in choosing discount rates effectively gives them the ability to manipulate outcomes and that it is important to preserve transparency in the project evaluation and contracting process. Such concerns can be addressed in a variety of ways while staying true to fair value principles. For instance, governments can set clear guidelines and precedents for establishing discount rates, and the services of a professional valuation practice can be employed to participate in the selection of discount rates or to vet the rates that are chosen.

A further conceptual question is whether discount rates derived from market returns require a tax adjustment when applied to public infrastructure projects. The issue is that market returns are measured prior to personal tax payments on investment income and capital gains. Equilibrium market returns include compensation for the tax liabilities of the marginal investor in each asset class. The returns that accrue to citizens in their role as residual equity holders of public infrastructure projects are not taxable. That suggests a possible downward adjustment to discount rates when considering the project from the perspective of the government. However, the marginal investor in a given asset class is not directly observable. Because of the large market presence of tax-exempt investors such as pension funds, and because of the ability to offset capital gains with capital losses, the offset may be small (see Weber, Staub-Bisang, and Alfen 2016, 44). A different perspective is that the tax-free return to citizens as equity holders in infrastructure projects should be considered a tax expenditure for the government, so that the cost to the government of the tax-free return offsets its benefit to investors. In the example in section 7.4, we make no adjustment for this possible effect.

### 7.3.3 Summing Up: Valuing a Stand-Alone Project

We now have the ingredients for the first step of an APV analysis of a public infrastructure investment, which is to value it as a stand-alone, all-equity-financed project, leaving to the side the value of subsidies and financing side effects.

Expected project cash flows are estimated over a horizon of $T$. For each period $t$, we denote revenues $\rho_t$; augmented additional revenues $\rho_{\alpha,t}$; capital expenditures $\kappa_t$; periodic costs (for example, maintenance, salaries, marketing) $c_t$; augmented additional costs (for example, tax or pollution externalities) $c_{\alpha,t}$; and the present value of any cash flows beyond $T$, $\Gamma$. As earlier, $E(r_A)$ is the per-period discount rate that reflects the price of risk associated with the net cash flows. Then the NPV of the stand-alone project can be written as follows:

$$(2) \qquad \sum_{t=0}^{T} \frac{\rho_t + \rho_{\alpha,t} - c_t - c_{\alpha,t} - \kappa_t}{(1 + E(r_A))^t} + \Gamma.$$

### 7.3.4 Valuing Subsidies and Financing Effects

We now turn to methodologies to find fair values for subsidies and financing effects associated with public infrastructure investments. Those methodologies take into account that the risk characteristics of subsidies and financing effects, and hence the associated cost of capital, are often significantly different from those for the stand-alone project.

In assigning benefits from tax breaks and other subsidies in a PPP arrangement, it is important to take into consideration that the ultimate beneficiary may not be the private partner. For instance, if there is a competitive bidding process based on minimizing fees, fees plus subsidies will just cover costs, and any increase in subsidy on the margin will be offset by a lower fee for infrastructure users.

#### *7.3.4.1 Cash Subsidies, In-Kind Subsidies, and Externalities*

Future cash flows arising from cash subsidies, in-kind subsidies, or externalities that are roughly proportional to revenues or variable costs can be discounted at the same rate as the stand-alone project, on the logic that the associated market risk is roughly similar. However, when cash subsidies are set at contractually fixed levels, or when in-kind subsidies are delivered at a steady level that is independent of use rates, a lower discount rate that reflects the lower beta risk of those flows is appropriate. Other cash subsidies like minimum revenue guarantees are equivalent to put options, and we discuss how to value them with derivative pricing methods later. Similarly, risk properties of externalities determine the appropriate discount rate.

#### *7.3.4.2 Municipal Bonds*

A major source of funding for public infrastructure projects in the US is the municipal (muni) bond market. Outstanding municipal issuances totaled \$3.7 trillion in 2018, down from a peak of \$4.1 trillion in 2010. Annual issuances have fluctuated around \$400 billion in recent years, with revenue bonds comprising more than half of that total and general obligation bonds accounting for most of the rest of them.[12]

Tax-exempt munis are an attractive source of funds for state and local governments and PPPs that can access that funding because these bonds are subsidized by the federal government. The subsidy is in the form of a tax exemption on investors' interest income from federal income taxation that increases the value of the bonds and thereby lowers the cost of borrowing. The interest on most municipal bonds is also exempt from the state and local taxes of the issuing jurisdiction.[13]

12. Statistics from the Federal Reserve and Thompson Reuters, as reported by the Securities Industry and Financial Markets Association.

13. Pirinsky and Wang (2011) show how this feature creates a clientele effect that narrows the investor base and increases the cost of muni financing.

Those tax exemptions are most valuable to upper-income households with high marginal tax rates, which comprise the largest category of investors in munis. The annual reduction in interest costs associated with the tax exemption from the perspective of borrowers is related to the break-even tax rate, $\tau$. That tax rate equates the after-tax return on a nonexempt bond, $r_T$, with the return on a tax-exempt muni, $r_{TE}$, with similar credit risk, maturity, and liquidity:

$$r_{TE} = r_T(1 - \tau). \qquad (3)$$

Longstaff (2011) estimates an average break-even tax rate of 38 percent using muni swap data from 2001–2009, a rate that is close to the maximum statutory rate for that period and consistent with high net worth individuals being the marginal investors. Break-even tax rates for longer maturity munis have historically been much lower.

From a comprehensive government perspective, the APV of a public infrastructure project is reduced by the present value of all forgone revenues from tax exemptions. At each level of government, the cost depends on the counterfactual assumption about the effect on tax revenues, $E(\tau)$, had the exemption not existed. The annual cost is $P_t \times E(\tau) \times r_T$, where $P_t$ is the outstanding principal at time $t$. Discounting those annual flows over the lifetime of the bond at the rate $r_T$ gives the present value cost that can be incorporated into the APV.[14] The counterfactual for $E(\tau)$ traditionally was based on the high marginal tax rates of the wealthy households who are the main investors in munis. However, without the tax exemption, many muni investors would choose alternative investments with a more favorable tax treatment. To take that likelihood into account, one possibility is to assume a lower value for $\tau$, based on an average of ordinary income and capital gains rates or based on the observed investment behavior of wealthy households. Poterba and Verdurgo (2011) suggest that doing so could halve the estimated cost relative to basing it on the high marginal tax rates of the wealthy.

Note that the discount rate for muni bond cash flows is almost always lower than the fair value discount rate for the infrastructure project that the bonds are funding. Revenue bonds are much less risky because of equity or guarantee protections. The risk and required return on muni bonds will also depend on their priority in default and other features. As noted earlier, whereas payments on revenue bonds are funded out of project cash flows, general obligation bonds are backed by the taxing authority of the issuer and are generally safer for that reason.

Muni bonds issued at a project's inception may have a maturity that is shorter than the service life of the project. If the bonds will be rolled over into new muni bonds at maturity, the flow of forgone tax revenues and

14. Choosing the discount rate based on an equivalent taxable bond imposes consistency in the use of market rates before personal taxes.

subsidy benefits should be extended to the likely termination date for the final refunding. If refunding is not assured, the cash flows beyond the initial maturity date can be scaled to the probability of refunding.

For infrastructure projects involving PPPs, muni bonds may be issued on behalf of a private partner. When they are tax exempt, they are called qualified private activity bonds. The flow value of the tax advantage to the partner also can be approximated based on the difference between the taxable and tax-exempt interest rates times the outstanding principal: $P_t \times \tau \times r_T$. Discounting the flow value at $r_T$ and taking into account possible maturity extensions gives the present value benefit that can be incorporated into the APV from the perspective of the partner. In addition to conferring a tax advantage, being granted access to muni financing might signal implicit government credit support that further lowers the interest rate, and that additional advantage should also be quantified.

The ultimate beneficiary of the tax break or other subsidies may not be the private partner in a PPP arrangement. For instance, if there is a competitive bidding process over fees, fees plus subsidies will just cover costs (including capital costs), and any increase in tax subsidies will on the margin be offset by a lower fee for infrastructure users.

#### 7.3.4.3 *Debt Subsidies and Credit Guarantees*

Even when tax-advantaged funding is unavailable, governments may subsidize a partner's cost of funds by (i) guaranteeing loans or debt issues for the partner or (ii) issuing general obligation debt and lending the proceeds to the partner to help fund the project.

Government credit guarantees lower the cost of debt funding by transferring risk from a partner to the government. The value of credit guarantees can be estimated as the difference between the fair value of the promised payments on the debt absent the guarantee and the fair value of the promised payments with the guarantee. Congressional Budget Office (2011) describes that procedure and applies it to a federal guarantee of infrastructure investments in nuclear power plants. The value of debt absent a guarantee can be inferred from the market price of the partner's unguaranteed debt (also adjusting for maturity effects) or indirectly from its credit rating. Credit guarantees can also be valued as put options (Merton 1977), but that approach is often more complicated and not described in detail here.

A government may issue public debt and lend the proceeds to a private partner at a rate that is lower than what the partner could borrow at on its own. The subsidy value of such a concessional interest rate is found by discounting the promised cash flows on the concessional loan by the market interest rate available to the partner, and subtracting that present value from the principal of the loan. For example, say the government makes a one-year loan of $1 million to a private partner at a 5 percent interest rate. Based on the partner's credit rating, it is inferred that the partner would have borrowed at 6 percent in the market. Then the present value of the promised loan payment is (\$1.05 million)/1.06 = \$990,566, and the subsidy is \$9,423.

#### 7.3.4.4 Minimum Revenue Guarantees

PPP contracts sometimes include clauses that guarantee a minimum stream of revenues to the private partner for some time period (Rouhani et al. 2018). The guarantee's cost to the government and benefit to a private partner can be assessed most accurately by recognizing that the guarantee is a strip of put option on the stream of future revenues. Black's model for pricing commodity options is well suited to this application. The approach can also be used to estimate the ex ante cost of contract renegotiations that are triggered by profitability falling below some threshold, as discussed later.

Black's model, adapted here to value a minimum revenue guarantee, has the following inputs: $T$ is the time to maturity of the option (that is, the arrival time of the revenue flow); $F_T$ is the forward price of the revenue flow at $T$; $X$ is the minimum guaranteed revenue; $\rho_T$ is the risk-free rate on a continuous basis for maturity $T$; $\sigma_T$ is the standard deviation of time $T$ revenues; $N$ is the cumulative normal distribution; and $p_{0,T}$ is the value of the revenue guarantee for time $T$ as of time 0. Then

$$(4) \qquad p_{0,T} = e^{-\rho_T T}[XN(-d_2) - F_T N(-d_1)],$$

where

$$d_1 = \frac{\ln(F_T / X) + \sigma_T^2 T / 2}{\sigma_T \sqrt{T}} \text{ and } d_2 = d_1 - \sigma_T \sqrt{T}.$$

The forward price $F_T$ is found by calculating the present value of the expected cash flow at time $T$, discounting at the appropriate risk-adjusted rate, and then bringing that present value back to time $T$ multiplying by $e^{-\rho_T T}$.

The calculation also requires estimating the standard deviation of future revenues at each maturity. The standard deviation can be estimated from revenue data on similar projects when such information is available, or on estimates of demand variability. The time subscript on the volatility is included to suggest that there may be more uncertainty about revenues during certain periods, such as in the early years of a long-lived project when the start date of operation is uncertain.

The total value of a minimum revenue guarantee contract is the sum of the individual revenue payment guarantees $\Sigma_{t=1}^{T} p_{0,T}$.

#### 7.3.4.5 Renegotiation and Implicit Guarantees

It is widely recognized (for example, Engel, Fischer, and Galetovic 2011) that a major risk for governments engaging in PPPs is the high rate of renegotiation with private partners when revenues, costs, or time lines fail to meet expectations. The possibility of renegotiation can be viewed as a type of implicit guarantee that transfers value from the government to a private partner if a triggering event occurs. A rough way to incorporate the ex ante value of such protections is to use the method for valuing minimum revenue guarantees discussed earlier. The strike price $X$ could be set to the level of revenue below which additional compensation is likely to be received to top off realized revenues. Another approach would be to value renegotiation as a put option, where the partner would sell back the project to the government for some fixed price were the project's value to fall below some threshold level.

Private partners similarly bear the risk that the government will renegotiate or default on a contract, and they will require compensation for that risk that similarly can be valued using options pricing approaches. Ideally, contracts will be structured in a way that risk is shared optimally, taking into account the incentive effects of different arrangements (Rouhani et al. 2018). Engel, Fischer, and Galetovic (2011) note that having a partner firm face less risk to begin with reduces opportunistic renegotiations.[15]

### 7.4 Evaluating a Toll Road: An Example

An APV analysis of a hypothetical toll road project structured as a PPP illustrates the sensitivity of valuations to alternative assumptions about discount rates, risk-sharing arrangements, and funding sources. All cash flows and discount rates are in real terms unless otherwise noted.

#### 7.4.1 Cash Flows

The base case cash flows conform to the typical pattern of toll revenues net of capital expenditures and operating and maintenance costs. Here the project is assumed to start in 2018. The scale of the example project and some of its other features such as its duration are loosely based on projections that were made for the California State Route 91 Corridor Improvement Project. The appendix provides additional information about State Route 91, some general lessons from that experience, and other considerations for PPP investors.

In this stylized example, there are five years of large capital investments, followed by the typical S-shaped pattern of net toll revenues reflecting growing demand and profitability that plateau as capacity is filled (figure 7.1). The total project length is 40 years, including 5 years of construction and a 30-year concession to a private partner.

For simplicity, the residual value in the 40th year is set to zero. We also abstract from any lumpy capital expenditures beyond the fifth year, implic-

15. Engel, Fischer, and Galetovic (2011) advocate present value revenue contracts instead of taking the lowest fee bidder, as a way to make buying back a project when necessary easier, but also note the shortcoming that without upside revenue for partner there is no incentive to encourage demand

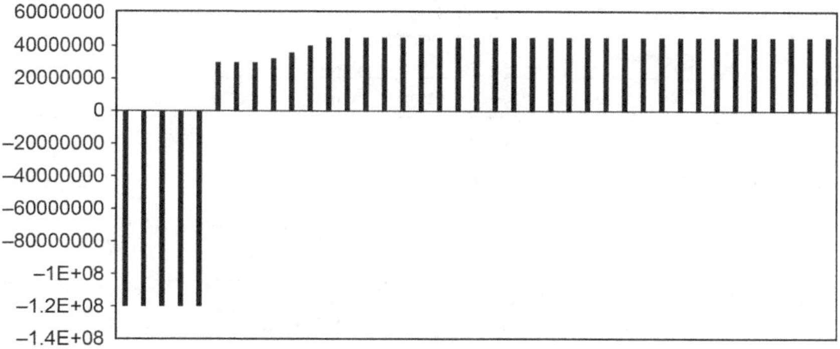


**Fig. 7.1 Toll road cash flows (annual)**

itly subsuming those costs into smoother operating and maintenance cost flows.

Estimates of the volatility of toll revenues or other components of cash flows are necessary to value minimum revenue guarantees and other options associated with the project. We calibrate volatilities using data from the US Department of Transportation (DOT) on 15 toll roads and bridges for which fairly complete toll revenue data are available from 1998 to 2016 (table 7.2).[16] For nominal (real) toll revenues, the coefficient of variation averages 0.30 (0.40), with a standard deviation of 0.14 (0.13). Whether the relevant variation is real or nominal depends on the terms of the contract being valued. From the perspective of the contracting parties, the variability for an individual project should be lower than what is estimated here because some of the variation is likely to be foreseeable, for example, because of projected growth in demand over time. The variability is also likely to be higher in earlier years and lower in later years when the road is at capacity and there is less uncertainty about the timing of the completion of construction.

### 7.4.2 Cost of Capital

We calculate the value of the stand-alone project using a discount rate based on an estimate of the asset beta for toll roads and returns data from 2018. For comparison we report the value of the stand-alone project discounting with a long-term muni bond rate of 1.72 percent (real), which in 2018 happens to be close to the median choice for the social discount rate of 2 percent (real), as reported in a recent survey of economists (Drupp et al. 2018). We also compare the results using the current 7 percent Office

16. Historical data on toll roads from the US Department of Transportation is the source of all data-based inferences on cash flows unless otherwise stated: https://www.fhwa.dot.gov/policyinformation/statistics.cfm.

**Table 7.2 Sample toll projects with DOT data**

| Facility name | State | 1999 | 2000 | 2001 | 2002 | 2003 | 2004 | 2005 |
|---|---|---|---|---|---|---|---|---|
| Toll revenues | | | | | | | | |
| Biscayne Key (Rickenbacker) Causeway | Florida | 5,067.00 | 5,302.00 | 5,649.00 | 5,805.00 | 6,938.00 | 6,627.00 | 5,418.00 |
| Cameron County International Toll Bridge | Texas | 7,697.00 | 8,942.00 | 11,541.00 | 12,398.00 | 13,595.00 | 15,124.00 | 16,086.00 |
| E-470 Beltway | Colorado | 3,169.00 | 12,612.00 | 24,657.00 | 36,266.00 | 37,121.00 | 59,855.00 | 73,733.00 |
| Eagle Pass-Piedras Negras International Bridge | Texas | 5,276.00 | 5,797.00 | 7,390.00 | 7,080.00 | 7,295.00 | 7,877.00 | 7,901.00 |
| Foothill/Eastern Toll Roads | California | 5,810.00 | 34,452.00 | 56,441.00 | 74,549.00 | 79,504.00 | 83,156.00 | 91,885.00 |
| Golden Gate Bridge | California | 58,124.00 | 58,453.00 | 59,369.00 | 59,180.00 | 59,289.00 | 79,427.00 | 86,393.00 |
| Laredo-Nuevo Laredo International Bridge | Texas | 21,917.00 | 26,147.00 | 28,748.00 | 28,548.00 | 31,342.00 | 32,436.00 | 33,272.00 |
| Lee County Toll Bridges | Florida | 24,234.00 | 26,321.00 | 27,763.00 | 29,162.00 | 30,235.00 | 31,924.00 | 33,581.00 |
| McAllen International Toll Bridge | Texas | 7,576.00 | 8,345.00 | 8,479.00 | 9,838.00 | 9,869.00 | 10,221.00 | 10,223.00 |
| Osceola Parkway | Florida | 4,871.00 | 6,120.00 | 7,255.00 | 7,529.00 | 6,586.00 | 7,056.00 | 2,253.00 |
| Richmond Expressway System | Virginia | 19,861.00 | 22,707.00 | 23,204.00 | 24,210.00 | 24,865.00 | 24,825.00 | 25,483.00 |
| San Joaquin Hills Toll Road | California | 35,009.00 | 42,032.00 | 46,582.00 | 51,634.00 | 57,734.00 | 63,379.00 | 70,145.00 |
| Tacony-Palmyra and Burlington-Bristol Bridges | New Jersey | 15,161.00 | 15,963.00 | 26,803.00 | 29,230.00 | 31,206.00 | 26,218.00 | 28,335.00 |
| Woods Hole, Martha's Vineyard and Nantucket Ferries | Massachusetts | 27,797.00 | 24,498.00 | 32,787.00 | 54,858.00 | 59,895.00 | 55,402.00 | 57,656.00 |
| Zaragosa Bridge | Texas | 11,539.00 | 11,472.00 | 12,377.00 | 12,152.00 | 10,130.00 | 10,766.00 | 11,651.00 |
| Operation Costs | | | | | | | | |
| Biscayne Key (Rickenbacker) Causeway | Florida | 2,976.00 | 1,216.00 | 1,878.00 | 1,743.00 | 2,841.00 | 2,951.00 | 2,388.00 |
| Cameron County International Toll Bridge | Texas | 1,442.00 | 1,896.00 | 2,587.00 | 2,869.00 | 3,062.00 | 3,112.00 | 3,485.00 |
| E-470 Beltway | Colorado | 5,194.00 | 9,536.00 | 8,412.00 | 14,715.00 | 18,476.00 | 14,820.00 | 23,563.00 |
| Eagle Pass-Piedras Negras International Bridge | Texas | 647.00 | 657.00 | 1,065.00 | 583.00 | 716.00 | 809.00 | 744.00 |
| Foothill/Eastern Toll Roads | California | 3,992.00 | 8,998.00 | 9,744.00 | 5,524.00 | 4,505.00 | 2,617.00 | 2,015.00 |
| Golden Gate Bridge | California | 8,380.00 | 8,789.00 | 9,703.00 | 12,669.00 | 11,736.00 | 16,365.00 | 17,603.00 |
| Laredo-Nuevo Laredo International Bridge | Texas | 13,961.00 | 12,853.00 | 21,518.00 | 18,193.00 | 24,265.00 | 19,601.00 | 19,911.00 |
| Lee County Toll Bridges | Florida | 8,266.00 | 2,044.00 | 4,269.00 | 3,459.00 | 4,039.00 | 4,539.00 | 4,444.00 |
| McAllen International Toll Bridge | Texas | 1,350.00 | 1,312.00 | 1,367.00 | 1,251.00 | 1,773.00 | 1,811.00 | 1,448.00 |
| Osceola Parkway | Florida | 1,318.00 | 1,717.00 | 1,287.00 | 1,766.00 | 1,240.00 | 1,678.00 | 327.00 |
| Richmond Expressway System | Virginia | 3,514.00 | 3,061.00 | 3,365.00 | 4,786.00 | 4,328.00 | 2,852.00 | 4,746.00 |
| San Joaquin Hills Toll Road | California | 1,096.00 | 1,003.00 | 470.00 | 1,092.00 | 1,376.00 | 1,466.00 | 994.00 |
| Tacony-Palmyra and Burlington-Bristol Bridges | New Jersey | 1,883.00 | 1,844.00 | 1,949.00 | 1,897.00 | 2,091.00 | 2,454.00 | 8,530.00 |
| Woods Hole, Martha's Vineyard and Nantucket Ferries | Massachusetts | 22,151.00 | 22,554.00 | 23,179.00 | 25,697.00 | 25,720.00 | 27,652.00 | 28,721.00 |
| Zaragosa Bridge | Texas | 655.00 | 918.00 | 1,039.00 | 1,694.00 | 1,645.00 | 1,862.00 | 1,776.00 |
| Maintenance costs | | | | | | | | |
| Biscayne Key (Rickenbacker) Causeway | Florida | - | 102.00 | 53.00 | 109.00 | - | - | 194.00 |
| Cameron County International Toll Bridge | Texas | - | - | - | - | - | - | - |
| E-470 Beltway | Colorado | - | - | - | - | - | - | - |
| Eagle Pass-Piedras Negras International Bridge | Texas | 27.00 | 27.00 | 44.00 | 146.00 | 202.00 | 228.00 | 210.00 |
| Foothill/Eastern Toll Roads | California | 631.00 | 1,304.00 | 1,239.00 | 1,818.00 | 3,326.00 | 3,053.00 | 3,402.00 |
| Golden Gate Bridge | California | 8,559.00 | 8,966.00 | 9,456.00 | 10,814.00 | 10,809.00 | 12,088.00 | 13,003.00 |

| 2006 | 2007 | 2008 | 2009 | 2010 | 2011 | 2012 | 2013 | 2014 | 2015 | 2016 |
|---|---|---|---|---|---|---|---|---|---|---|
| 6,040.00 | 8,083.00 | 8,582.00 | NA | 9,195.00 | NA | NA | 9,709.00 | 10,912.00 | NA | 7,943.00 |
| 15,814.00 | 17,867.00 | 17,369.00 | NA | 4,302.00 | NA | NA | 16,745.00 | 14,850.00 | NA | 14,700.00 |
| 78,943.00 | 91,730.00 | 95,435.00 | NA | 90,486.00 | NA | NA | 118,717.00 | 132,106.00 | 132,106.00 | 183,909.00 |
| 8,019.00 | 7,784.00 | 8,654.00 | NA | 8,115.00 | NA | NA | 7,838.00 | 8,043.00 | NA | 10,368.00 |
| 103,043.00 | 106,610.00 | 116,648.00 | NA | 103,907.00 | NA | NA | 123,945.00 | 129,005.00 | NA | 152,022.00 |
| 80,445.00 | 85,479.00 | 80,456.00 | NA | 93,077.00 | NA | NA | 103,779.00 | 106,977.00 | NA | 138,321.00 |
| 33,366.00 | 39,047.00 | 38,141.00 | NA | 40,644.00 | NA | NA | 45,068.00 | 44,735.00 | NA | 57,320.00 |
| 44,110.00 | 42,253.00 | 41,187.00 | NA | 37,483.00 | NA | NA | 37,765.00 | 39,174.00 | NA | 43,838.00 |
| 11,058.00 | 11,256.00 | 10,533.00 | NA | 11,187.00 | NA | NA | 12,977.00 | 13,232.00 | NA | 14,192.00 |
| 11,710.00 | 9,937.00 | 10,802.00 | NA | 10,356.00 | NA | NA | 11,632.00 | 11,550.00 | NA | 13,995.00 |
| 25,048.00 | 25,577.00 | 25,099.00 | NA | 33,191.00 | NA | NA | 36,307.00 | 36,551.00 | NA | 38,872.00 |
| 79,250.00 | 86,464.00 | 94,349.00 | NA | 91,812.00 | NA | NA | 102,508.00 | 109,938.00 | NA | 166,374.00 |
| 28,749.00 | 29,148.00 | 29,036.00 | NA | 30,455.00 | NA | NA | 33,545.00 | 33,567.00 | NA | 33,712.00 |
| 59,366.00 | 64,737.00 | 70,786.00 | NA | 71,033.00 | NA | NA | 75,697.00 | 79,787.00 | NA | 88,560.00 |
| 13,841.00 | 14,262.00 | 14,093.00 | NA | 14,551.00 | NA | NA | 15,983.00 | 17,581.00 | NA | 20,952.00 |
| | | | | | | | | | | |
| 3,055.00 | 3,630.00 | 3,723.00 | 3,988.00 | 4,301.00 | 4,114.00 | 4,002.00 | 3,613.00 | (1,132.00) | NA | 7,172.00 |
| 3,739.00 | 3,436.00 | 3,314.00 | 384.00 | 4,248.00 | 4,775.00 | 2,397.00 | 3,972.00 | 2,411.00 | NA | 3,700.00 |
| 16,676.00 | 19,805.00 | 28,989.00 | 22,968.00 | 25,937.00 | 28,270.00 | 25,974.00 | 23,823.00 | 27,806.00 | NA | 33,335.00 |
| 746.00 | 910.00 | 1,102.00 | 1,253.00 | 1,063.00 | 1,078.00 | 1,135.00 | 1,380.00 | 1,431.00 | NA | 1,115.00 |
| 2,959.00 | 15,364.00 | 14,154.00 | 17,190.00 | 15,572.00 | 13,169.00 | 719.00 | 12,910.00 | 12,507.00 | NA | 30,708.00 |
| 9,706.00 | 17,308.00 | 20,731.00 | 21,212.00 | 17,138.00 | 14,081.00 | 35,591.00 | 23,335.00 | 16,196.00 | NA | 122,606.00 |
| 25,735.00 | 29,726.00 | 31,837.00 | 34,086.00 | 31,975.00 | 33,236.00 | 32,983.00 | 34,028.00 | 34,380.00 | NA | 41,068.00 |
| 4,665.00 | 4,767.00 | 4,690.00 | 4,297.00 | 4,997.00 | 3,865.00 | 3,693.00 | 3,675.00 | 13.00 | NA | 3,725.00 |
| 1,711.00 | 2,246.00 | 2,727.00 | 2,542.00 | 2,300.00 | 2,774.00 | 2,899.00 | 3,351.00 | 3,083.00 | NA | 3,310.00 |
| 63.00 | 66.00 | 73.00 | 83.00 | 87.00 | 96.00 | 42.00 | 71.00 | 45.00 | 9.00 | 13.00 |
| 3,782.00 | 7,604.00 | 2,544.00 | 6,888.00 | 10,720.00 | 10,179.00 | 10,426.00 | 18,268.00 | 10,090.00 | NA | 9,617.00 |
| 1,302.00 | 9,943.00 | 10,260.00 | 10,729.00 | 10,485.00 | 10,119.00 | 9,869.00 | 10,499.00 | 9,878.00 | NA | 15,723.00 |
| 8,388.00 | 11,515.00 | 12,025.00 | 12,544.00 | 12,637.00 | 4,500.00 | 14,798.00 | 14,801.00 | 15,004.00 | NA | 14,617.00 |
| 28,611.00 | 29,498.00 | 31,099.00 | 36,112.00 | 29,438.00 | 31,289.00 | 34,138.00 | 32,148.00 | 32,490.00 | NA | 33,565.00 |
| 1,868.00 | 2,431.00 | 2,275.00 | 3,055.00 | 4,082.00 | 3,093.00 | 2,204.00 | 4,609.00 | 3,559.00 | NA | 5,749.00 |
| | | | | | | | | | | |
| 294.00 | - | 235.00 | 243.00 | - | - | - | - | - | NA | NA |
| - | - | - | - | - | - | - | - | - | NA | NA |
| - | - | - | - | - | - | - | - | - | NA | NA |
| 210.00 | - | - | - | - | - | - | - | - | NA | NA |
| 3,213.00 | 3,619.00 | 3,350.00 | 580.00 | 3,491.00 | 3,431.00 | 3,315.00 | 3,339.00 | 3,345.00 | NA | 1,566.00 |
| 13,853.00 | 14,025.00 | 14,632.00 | 16,221.00 | 15,301.00 | 17,589.00 | 18,277.00 | 19,226.00 | 20,006.00 | NA | 45,525.00 |

(*continued*)

**Table 7.2 (cont.)**

| Facility name | State | 1999 | 2000 | 2001 | 2002 | 2003 | 2004 | 2005 |
|---|---|---|---|---|---|---|---|---|
| *Maintenance costs (continued)* | | | | | | | | |
| Laredo-Nuevo Laredo International Bridge | Texas | - | - | - | 5,131.00 | - | 5,528.00 | 5,616.00 |
| Lee County Toll Bridges | Florida | 363.00 | 128.00 | 205.00 | 205.00 | 343.00 | 352.00 | - |
| McAllen International Toll Bridge | Texas | 79.00 | 77.00 | 80.00 | 353.00 | 501.00 | 511.00 | 408.00 |
| Osceola Parkway | Florida | 312.00 | 3,700.00 | 297.00 | 403.00 | 345.00 | 377.00 | 109.00 |
| Richmond Expressway System | Virginia | 2,523.00 | 2,785.00 | 3,181.00 | 6,068.00 | 1,267.00 | 2,005.00 | 1,761.00 |
| San Joaquin Hills Toll Road | California | 830.00 | 874.00 | 576.00 | 1,234.00 | 1,634.00 | 1,388.00 | 1,495.00 |
| Tacony-Palmyra and Burlington-Bristol Bridges | New Jersey | 3,503.00 | 2,100.00 | 2,313.00 | 2,335.00 | 2,556.00 | 2,635.00 | 4,047.00 |
| Woods Hole, Martha's Vineyard, and Nantucket Ferries | Massachusetts | 5,926.00 | 5,607.00 | 6,083.00 | 6,395.00 | 9,000.00 | 8,046.00 | 8,787.00 |
| Zaragosa Bridge | Texas | 36.00 | - | - | 478.00 | 464.00 | - | 501.00 |
| *Capital outlay costs** | | | | | | | | |
| Biscayne Key (Rickenbacker) Causeway | Florida | 97.00 | 90.00 | 1,001.00 | 83.00 | 1,243.00 | 1,418.00 | 1,964.00 |
| Cameron County International Toll Bridge | Texas | 6,263.00 | 4,028.00 | 541.00 | 1,155.00 | 1,275.00 | 1,652.00 | 1,470.00 |
| E-470 Beltway | Colorado | 98,479.00 | 60,602.00 | 48,376.00 | 134,694.00 | 115,520.00 | 28,604.00 | 14,865.00 |
| Eagle Pass-Piedras Negras International Bridge | Texas | 7,168.00 | 12,802.00 | 253.00 | - | - | - | 1,237.00 |
| Foothill/Eastern Toll Roads | California | 318,927.00 | 225,029.00 | 56,287.00 | 18,771.00 | 25,567.00 | 30,688.00 | 33,598.00 |
| Golden Gate Bridge | California | 8,910.00 | 20,395.00 | 33,307.00 | 29,281.00 | 32,029.00 | 53,972.00 | 67,209.00 |
| Laredo-Nuevo Laredo International Bridge | Texas | 2,346.00 | 32,847.00 | 24,940.00 | 8,963.00 | 1,514.00 | 2,717.00 | 3,090.00 |
| Lee County Toll Bridges | Florida | 13,254.00 | 8,615.00 | 2,773.00 | 1,675.00 | 6,010.00 | 2,189.00 | 11,170.00 |
| McAllen International Toll Bridge | Texas | 101.00 | 66.00 | 273.00 | - | - | 571.00 | 779.00 |
| Osceola Parkway | Florida | 3,128.00 | 32.00 | - | - | - | - | - |
| Richmond Expressway System | Virginia | 260.00 | 3,882.00 | 1,823.00 | 511.00 | 596.00 | 302.00 | 1,687.00 |
| San Joaquin Hills Toll Road | California | 21,040.00 | 9,340.00 | 11,231.00 | 5,202.00 | 8,226.00 | 9,852.00 | 3,688.00 |
| Tacony-Palmyra and Burlington-Bristol Bridges | New Jersey | - | - | - | - | - | 3,335.00 | 1,667.00 |
| Woods Hole, Martha's Vineyard, and Nantucket Ferries | Massachusetts | 5,796.00 | 9,283.00 | 6,632.00 | 5,270.00 | 2,429.00 | 1,985.00 | 4,513.00 |
| Zaragosa Bridge | Texas | 404.00 | 46.00 | 1,106.00 | 404.00 | - | 798.00 | 4,036.00 |

*Note:* *Capital outlay includes 17 improvement types. These improvement types are allocated among three broad categories: system
Administration, *Status of the Nation's Highways, Bridges, and Transit: Conditions & Performance*, chap. 6, https://www.fhwa.dot.gov

of Management and Budget (OMB) Circular A-94 guidance rate for federal investment projects.[17]

We choose the asset beta from table 7.1, using the 2018 average value between transportation (0.8) and trucking (0.81), which is 0.805. Setting the short-term risk-free rate at 2 percent and the equity premium to 6 percent implies a nominal discount rate of $.02 + .805(.06) = 6.8$ percent. We assume that expected inflation is 2 percent, which is consistent with the Federal Reserve's target. That implies a real fair value discount rate of 4.7 percent.

17. Circular A-94 allows for some flexibility to accommodate market rates that differ from the 7 percent real rate assumption but suggests that deviations should be rare. Although OMB has not adopted a full fair value approach, these changes can assist public infrastructure planners move in that direction.

| 2006 | 2007 | 2008 | 2009 | 2010 | 2011 | 2012 | 2013 | 2014 | 2015 | 2016 |
|---|---|---|---|---|---|---|---|---|---|---|
| - | - | - | - | - | - | - | - | - | NA | NA |
| - | - | - | - | - | - | - | - | - | NA | NA |
| 483.00 | - | - | - | - | - | - | - | - | NA | NA |
| - | - | - | - | - | - | - | - | - | NA | NA |
| 1,516.00 | 2,729.00 | 3,319.00 | 4,865.00 | 10,202.00 | 5,004.00 | 4,233.00 | 6,199.00 | 5,577.00 | NA | 3,922.00 |
| 1,397.00 | 517.00 | - | - | - | - | - | - | - | NA | 5,465.00 |
| 3,469.00 | 2,288.00 | 1,864.00 | 7,391.00 | 7,882.00 | 11,905.00 | 5,166.00 | 7,548.00 | 2,273.00 | NA | 7,120.00 |
| 9,283.00 | 10,985.00 | 10,085.00 | 11,756.00 | 12,087.00 | 9,530.00 | 9,123.00 | 10,165.00 | 14,744.00 | NA | 17,051.00 |
| 527.00 | - | - | - | - | - | - | - | - | NA | NA |
| | | | | | | | | | | |
| 1,105.00 | 582.00 | 2,104.00 | 1,812.00 | 4,725.00 | 8,089.00 | 7,193.00 | 5,566.00 | 6,364.00 | NA | 4,568.00 |
| 685.00 | 123.00 | 1,163.00 | 912.00 | 2,378.00 | 361.00 | 4,857.00 | 1,670.00 | 2,742.00 | NA | 685.00 |
| 34,952.00 | 20,583.00 | 12,360.00 | 5,033.00 | 15,076.00 | 2,599.00 | 3,120.00 | 12,237.00 | 4,237.00 | NA | 7,536.00 |
| 1,154.00 | 1,377.00 | 349.00 | 325.00 | 30.00 | 20.00 | - | 363.00 | 118.00 | 147.00 | 549.00 |
| 23,855.00 | 46,855.00 | 69,092.00 | 66,533.00 | 60,394.00 | 21,181.00 | 22,573.00 | 13,590.00 | 15,659.00 | NA | 38,095.00 |
| 41,009.00 | 20,812.00 | 39,395.00 | 18,179.00 | 29,704.00 | 51,612.00 | 47,550.00 | 63,206.00 | 37,395.00 | NA | 61,986.00 |
| 7,091.00 | 15,817.00 | 5,487.00 | 5,037.00 | 2,126.00 | 830.00 | 3,434.00 | 1,168.00 | 884.00 | NA | 1,665.00 |
| 69,260.00 | 58,096.00 | 49,489.00 | 11,242.00 | 5,799.00 | 3,594.00 | 6,256.00 | 5,207.00 | 2,760.00 | 453.00 | 283.00 |
| 1,763.00 | 380.00 | 5,483.00 | 18,755.00 | 17,062.00 | 1,798.00 | 742.00 | 8.00 | 1,651.00 | 235.00 | 984.00 |
| 1,085.00 | 279.00 | 164.00 | 248.00 | 36.00 | - | - | - | - | NA | NA |
| 4,442.00 | 3,393.00 | 8,901.00 | 7,622.00 | - | - | - | - | - | NA | NA |
| 996.00 | 1,392.00 | 2,440.00 | 2,362.00 | 6,497.00 | 8,865.00 | 563.00 | 520.00 | 1,215.00 | NA | 119.00 |
| 1,964.00 | 1,330.00 | 1,150.00 | 3,281.00 | 1,272.00 | 2,328.00 | 11,326.00 | 11,667.00 | 11,929.00 | NA | 8,516.00 |
| 20,158.00 | 26,585.00 | 15,653.00 | 17,604.00 | 12,831.00 | 15,583.00 | 8,905.00 | 10,949.00 | 6,370.00 | NA | 33,070.00 |
| 715.00 | 218.00 | 391.00 | 281.00 | 74.00 | 1,616.00 | 6,865.00 | 6,293.00 | 2,800.00 | 3.00 | 135.00 |

rehabilitation, system expansion, and system enhancement. See detailed notes in US Department of Transportation, Federal Highway
/policy/2010cpr/chap6.cfm#3.

We take this to be the correct rate for discounting net project cash flows and toll revenues.[18]

As discussed earlier, a government might incorrectly identify its cost of capital with its borrowing rate, which for the state and local governments sponsoring road projects is usually a municipal bond rate. Data from the Bond Buyer 20-Bond GO Index, which tracks rates on a portfolio of 20-year general obligation bonds rated AA by Standard & Poor's or Aa2 by Moody's, suggests that nominal rates averaged around 3.75 percent between

18. We attempted for comparison purposes to estimate betas based on the correlation of toll revenues with market returns from the 15 projects used to estimate volatility, but the data are insufficient to produce reliable estimates.

2010 and 2019. Adjusting for expected inflation implies a real long-term muni rate of 1.72 percent.

### 7.4.3 Value of Stand-Alone Toll Road Project

Discounting the figure 7.1 real cash flows at the real CAPM or risk-adjusted discount rate of 4.7 percent implies that the stand-alone project has a positive NPV of $36.7 million. As shown later, adding in any subsidies, financial side effects, guarantees, and externalities could reverse or add additional support for the conclusion that the project adds value.

The estimated NPV increases by an order of magnitude to $450.9 million using the real muni rate of 1.72 percent for discounting. (Using a social discount rate unadjusted for risk of 2 percent would lead to a similarly inflated conclusion.) Using the OMB rate of 7 percent implies an NPV of –$117.5. The very large differences in outcomes are attributable to the long life of the project and the low level of market rates.

A useful point of reference is the internal rate of return of the project, which is 5.703 percent. Any assumed discount rate lower than that will result in a positive NPV for the stand-alone project, and conversely for a discount rate that is below the internal rate of return.[19] Under our preferred discount rate the project in itself creates value. We turn now to how financing side effects might change that conclusion.

### 7.4.4 Incorporating Subsidy and Financing Cost Side Effects

We consider how minimum revenue guarantees, the cost of the municipal bond tax exemption, and the possibility of positive externalities from decreased congestion on other roads can be incorporated into the analysis to produce an APV for the toll road.

#### *7.4.4.1 Minimum Revenue Guarantees*

PPPs may include minimum revenue guarantees to protect partners against unanticipated shortfalls in revenues or increases in cost. An accurate estimate of the value of such guarantees is an important input into an APV analysis and also a useful bargaining tool for governments when negotiating a contract with private partners. We will see that the value of those guarantees can be considerable. The cost to the government may be justified when gains from improved operating efficiencies, faster construction schedules, lower toll charges, or other benefits that a private partner might deliver in return for the guarantee exceed its cost.

The value of a minimum revenue guarantee will vary with the floor revenue, revenue volatility, and the lifetime of the guarantee. In table 7.3 we report the results of using Black's model to calculate guarantee values for

19. The internal rate of return is unique in this example and can be used in this way because the cash flows change sign only once.

**Table 7.3** **Value of minimum revenue guarantee for toll road example ($ millions)**

| | A. Floor revenue = $15 million | | | | B. Floor revenue = $30 million | | | |
|---|---|---|---|---|---|---|---|---|
| | With risk adjustment | | No risk adjustment | | With risk adjustment | | No risk adjustment | |
| Guarantee duration | Declining volatility | Constant volatility | Declining volatility | Constant volatility | Declining volatility | Constant volatility | Declining volatility | Constant volatility |
| 5 | 12.8 | 5.3 | 10.2 | 3.5 | 46.9 | 31.0 | 40.0 | 23.5 |
| 10 | 15.7 | 13.2 | 11.7 | 8.4 | 67.4 | 64.8 | 51.8 | 47.6 |
| 20 | 26.3 | 40.5 | 15.6 | 25.6 | 121.4 | 152.1 | 78.9 | 109.7 |

*Note:* This table reports the minimum revenue guarantee (MRG) values obtained by applying Equation (4) for two different floor revenue levels ($15 million and $30 million). The calculation sequence is as follows: (1) Calculate revenue forward prices (fw = revenues*exp(rf*time)/(1+ra)$^{time}$; where rf = risk free rate; ra= real fair value discount rate). (2) Calculate d1 = (log(fw/strike) + time * (vol1$^2$)/2) / (vol1*sqrt(time)). (3) Calculate d2 = d1 – (vol1*sqrt(time)). (4) Calculate corresponding cumulative normal distribution values N(d1) and N(d2). (5) Finally, substitute the above calculated values for Fw, N(d1), and N(d2) in equation 4 as put = exp(–rf*time) * (strike * N(d2) – fw * N(d1)). In this part of the calculation, we substitute the corresponding floor revenues (i.e., strike = $15 million, or strike = $30 million) to obtain each component of our table. By adding up the first {5, 10, 20} put values, we obtain the corresponding value of the minimum revenue guarantees for {5, 10, 20} years duration. The calculations are made by assuming both (a) flat volatility of 0.3, and (b) a declining volatility vector [0.5, 0.5, 0.4, 0.4, 0.3, 0.3, 0.2 thereafter]. Steps 1–5 are then repeated, with the only difference that forward price of future revenues is calculated without risk adjustment (i.e., fw = expected future revenue flow). This will give us the corresponding "No risk adjustment" columns in our table. The code for these calculations can be followed and replicated in the following electronic notebook: https://github.com/moshemontesinos/guarantee_calculator_notebook/blob/main/BH_p3_calculator_R_v2.ipynb.

the toll road example, with and without risk adjustment, and for a range of assumed contract terms (see section 7.3.4.4 for formulas used). Specifically, we consider floors on annual revenues of $15 million and $30 million (versus the $64.8 million steady-state projected revenues) and guarantees with durations of 5, 10, and 20 years. To capture the greater uncertainty about revenues in early years, we consider a declining term structure of forward price volatilities ranging from a multiple of 0.5 for the first two years of operation ramping down to 0.2 for the sixth year of operation and beyond. We also consider a flat volatility of 0.3. The risk-free rate is fixed at 2 percent.

With risk adjustment, the estimated revenue guarantee values range from a low of $5.3 million for a 5-year $15 million minimum annual revenue with volatility of 0.3, to a high of $152 million for a 20-year $30 million minimum annual revenue with volatility of 0.3. The range of values is slightly narrower ($12.8 million to $121.4 million) under the assumption of declining volatility. Recall that the stand-alone NPV for the project is $36.7 million. These estimates demonstrate that minimum revenue guarantees can flip the APV of a project from positive to negative, even when the guarantees are far out of the money, as in the case of the $15 million floor relative to the $64.8 million in expected steady-state revenues.

The inputs for table 7.3 estimates without risk adjustment are identical to those with risk adjustment except for the forward prices of future revenues. Neglecting risk adjustment significantly biases down the estimated guarantee costs. For example, for a 20-year guarantee with a $30 million floor, under either volatility assumption, the guarantee value is more than $42 million higher when the cost of risk is taken into account. That difference is greater than the NPV of the stand-alone project.

#### *7.4.4.2 Subsidies from Municipal Bond and TIFIA Financing*

Debt has reportedly been used to fund approximately 70 percent of road construction projects in recent years. Subsidies are conveyed via tax advantages, credit support, or a combination of the two. General obligation, revenue, and private activity municipal bonds are the main sources of tax advantages. Direct or guaranteed loans made under the federal Transportation Infrastructure Financing and Innovation Act (TIFIA) program is the main source of federal credit support.[20] State and local governments may also provide credit support.

Here we assume that the $600 million in capital expenditures over the first five years of the project is funded with debt issuances that total $420 million and that the remaining $180 million of investment is funded with equity raised by the private partner at a fair market price. We assume that

20. TIFIA credit assistance is limited to 33 percent of eligible project costs (or up to 49 percent under compelling justification by sponsor). For a general overview see: https://www.transportation.gov/tifia/tifia-credit-program-overview.

TIFIA guarantees $120 million of the debt, a special activity muni bonds fund $230 million, and the balance of $70 million is covered by unsubsidized private partner debt.

A TIFIA guarantee provides full faith and credit backing from the US government on debt with maturities of up to 35 years, for qualifying projects that are substantially complete. With a TIFIA guarantee, the borrowing rate should be only slightly higher than the Treasury rate for a corresponding maturity (and may be lower if the debt is also tax exempt). The (nominal) market interest rate on the same debt without the TIFIA guarantee would depend on the underlying project risk, the priority of the debt in the project's capital structure and any recourse provisions, the total leverage, and a variety of other factors. A project's credit rating reflects those risk drivers and, when available, is a useful indicator of the market rate that would be attainable absent guarantees.

To provide a sense of the magnitude of a TIFIA subsidy, we assume that the TIFIA-backed debt is taken out in the fifth and last year of construction and amortizes over a 30-year maturity, with level payments of principal repayment and interest to investors. The interest rate is taken to be 2.25 percent, 25 basis points over the risk-free rate in this example. We further assume that the debt on the stand-alone project would be rated BB by Standard & Poor's, slightly below investment grade. In 2018 the spread over the Treasury rate for BB bonds was at a historically low level of approximately 2.25 percent. Adding this to the 2 percent risk-free rate implies an interest rate of 4.25 percent absent the guarantee. As described in section 7.3.4.3, we calculate the present value of the credit subsidy as the difference between the present value of the promised debt payments discounted at the subsidized borrowing rate of 2.25 percent (the principal value of the loan) and the estimated market rate of 4.25 percent. The resulting subsidy as of year 5 when the debt is issued is $27 million, or 22 percent of the $120 million of guaranteed debt. Discounting the subsidy to time 0 at the 4.25 percent rate implies a present value subsidy of $22 million.[21]

We assume that the $230 million of muni financing is issued at time 0 and that the principal will not be repaid until the 40th year. The initial maturity of the muni debt issued is likely to be shorter, but if the debt is rolled over at each maturity date then the tax advantage can continue over the life of the project. Because the debt will be outstanding over the riskier construction phase of the project, we assume that without the tax advantage it would carry an interest rate of 4.75 percent, which is higher than on the unguaranteed equivalent of the TIFIA bonds. We assume that the break-even tax rate is 20 percent, providing apparent annual interest savings of $230 mil-

21. This treats the risk of the subsidy over the first five years as equal to the risk of the debt issued in the fifth year. A more conservative assumption would be to treat the risk as similar to the risk of the project. Note too that in these calculations of debt subsidies we are discounting nominal debt payments at nominal rates rather than converting market data to real terms.

Table 7.4 Valuation of toll road project ($ millions)

| | Risk adjustment, full recognition of subsidy costs | No risk adjustment, no recognition of subsidy costs |
|---|---|---|
| Stand-alone NPV | 36.7 | 450.9 |
| Floor revenue guarantee (10 years, $30 million, declining volatility) | –67.4 | –51.8 |
| TIFIA guarantees | –22.0 | 0.0 |
| Municipal tax exemption | –39.0 | 0.0 |
| Positive externalities at 10 percent of revenues | 78.0 | 145.2 |
| APV | –13.7 | 544.3 |

lion (0.0475)(0.2). Discounting the flow savings at a 4.75 percent discount rate over 40 years gives a present value subsidy from the tax exemption of $39 million.[22]

The subsidies in this example are a cost to the federal government. A state or local government that is undertaking an APV analysis of the project might treat them as adding to the APV of the project. However, from a broad taxpayer perspective, the subsidies represent a transfer of value from federal to state and local taxpayers. Furthermore, to the extent that the subsidies are passed through to private partners in a PPP and the value is not recuperated through the bidding process or other contractual provisions, the subsidies have a net cost to taxpayers overall.

### 7.4.5 Incorporating the Value of Positive Externalities

The assessed value of the stand-alone project would be significantly higher if significant positive externalities were factored in. Users of nearby highways might also benefit from reduced congestion and travel times. Consumer surplus might exceed tolls paid. Those types of benefits are likely to be roughly proportional to revenues, and their value can be calculated by applying a multiplier to projected cash revenues and discounting at the stand-alone project discount rate of 4.7 percent. In this example, increasing revenues by 10 percent adds $78 million to the APV. That additional estimated value increases to $145 million if it is evaluated using the real muni rate of 1.72 percent as the cost of capital.

### 7.4.6 Adding It All Up

Table 7.4 summarizes the results of the APV analysis of a hypothetical toll road on a fair value basis, from a taxpayer perspective that includes financ-

22. A subtlety is that the apparent savings to the sponsoring government may exceed the cost to the federal government. As discussed earlier, the cost to the federal government may be lower than suggested by the breakeven tax rate because of asset substitution. The interest savings to the sponsor, however, is unaffected by asset substitution.

**Table 7.5** **Funding models for transportation projects**

| | PPP | Alternative project delivery | Project finance | Tolling and pricing | Value capture | TIFIA | Tolling, pricing, and value capture |
|---|---|---|---|---|---|---|---|
| All projects (= 191 projects) | | | | | | | |
| Total | 47 | 88 | 129 | 73 | 98 | 78 | 154 |
| Percentage | 24.6% | 46.1% | 67.5% | 38.2% | 51.3% | 40.8% | 80.6% |
| PPPs only (= 47 projects) | | | | | | | |
| Total | 47 | 8 | 35 | 30 | 17 | 24 | 39 |
| Percentage | 100.0% | 17.0% | 74.5% | 63.8% | 36.2% | 51.1% | 83.0% |

*Source:* DOT data and authors' tabulations.

ing subsidies as a cost. Table 7.4 also reports a cost estimate with the same elements, but without risk adjustment and treating credit subsidies as free. The results are starkly different: The APV on a fair value basis is –$13.7 million, whereas it rises to $544.3 million in the absence of risk adjustment and subsidy cost recognition.

The difference in estimated value is primarily the result of the higher discount rate used in the fair value analysis. It would be even larger if the minimum revenue guarantee were overlooked entirely in accounting for costs.

## 7.5 Funding and Budgetary Considerations

The analysis thus far has assumed that infrastructure investments are taking place in a well- functioning capital market and that subsidies are available for some forms of funding and not for others. Those assumptions are appropriate for the US, where most state and local governments have access to capital markets or banks, and where municipal bond financing is widely available. Probably in part because of those factors, PPPs have been less popular in the US than in other parts of the world where they may improve government access to capital. Table 7.5 shows the breakdown of funding and revenue models for a sample of US transportation projects, as reported by the DOT. PPPs are involved in 47 out of the 191 projects in the data set, but 35 out of the 47 also use project finance, and 24 of the 47 participate in TIFIA. In fact, a stated goal of TIFIA is to support private sector participation in infrastructure investments.

However, some view limited availability of funding to be a significant impediment to US investment in necessary infrastructure. To address that issue, proposals have been put forward to create a federal infrastructure bank to increase funding for and improve the selection of projects, particularly for surface transportation. Congressional Budget Office (2012a) analyzes a stylized version of the leading proposals and makes several important observations. A technical impediment to creating an infrastructure bank at the federal level is that a revolving fund structure is not feasible under US budgetary rules; funding would have to be reauthorized annually. More fundamentally, advocates for creating an infrastructure bank are often more concerned with increasing subsidies than with increasing funding access. CBO observes that subsidies could be increased by expanding TIFIA or through other credit subsidy programs. However, to understand the full cost of such expanding existing credit subsidy mechanisms, it is important to understand that under the Federal Credit Reform Act of 1990, reported credit subsidies do not take into account the cost of risk and hence understate the full value of the subsidies (Lucas 2012).

Relatedly, in an analysis of the effect of PPPs on transportation funding, Congressional Budget Office (2012b) finds that private financing will increase the availability of funds for highway construction only in cases in which governments restrict their spending by imposing legal constraints or budgetary limits on themselves. This highlights that restrictions such as balanced budget rules at the state level may impede infrastructure spending, particularly for major maintenance that is not classified as a capital expenditure that may have some additional budgetary flexibility.

The absence of capital budgets in some jurisdictions, notably at the federal level, is sometimes cited as a budgetary impediment to infrastructure funding. When budgeting is done entirely on a cash basis, the large up-front cost of many infrastructure investments may discourage lawmakers from authorizing the funds. Proponents of capital budgets or rules that would spread up-front expenditures over the service life of the project believe that such changes would reduce legislative impediments to funding large infrastructure projects. Opponents to such changes argue that budget transparency dictates that the full cost of spending be reported up front when the obligation is incurred. They also observe that, in the federal context, even very large projects have a negligible effect on federal budget totals, although that is less true at the agency level.

## 7.6 Conclusion

We have emphasized the importance of incorporating the effect of risk on value in assessing public infrastructure investments and associated financial contracts and subsidies, and shown how leading private sector valuation approaches can be adapted for public sector analyses. An extended example of a toll road project highlights a more general conclusion: the value of long-lived projects may be overestimated by an order of magnitude when the cost of risk is ignored, as is often the case in analyses of public infrastructure. The example also illustrates how investment decisions can be distorted significantly by applying a one-size-fits-all discount rate across a range of projects and contracts that have widely different risk characteristics.

An original contribution of this chapter is to establish that the ex ante or prospective cost of minimum revenue guarantees for private partners, and of contract renegotiations when profits fall below some threshold, can be estimated using Black's model for valuing commodity options. An options pricing approach accounts for the magnification of market risk associated with such guarantees and hence makes clear the significant value transfers that guarantees often entail. Adopting this approach would help governments to better understand the value proposition in PPPs and other arrangements with private partners. That information could improve governments' bargaining position and make it easier to avoid entering into contracts in which renegotiation is likely to be costly.

On the financing side, we note the prevalence of credit subsidies in the US that are delivered via the municipal bond market and to a lesser extent by federal credit programs. The wide availability of this "low-cost" funding may partially explain the lower incidence of PPPs in the US than in many other countries. Nevertheless, state and local governments rely heavily on private partners, and the analysis of contractual value transfers is relevant for many of those arrangements. From a cost-benefit perspective, it is important to account for the subsidy cost to federal taxpayers of credit subsidies, whatever the delivery vehicle. Those costs generally offset the financial benefit to state or local governments but are often neglected in the evaluation process by nonfederal project sponsors.

Finally, a major impediment to more accurate project evaluations is the lack of project-level historical data on cost and performance. Devoting additional federal resources to data collection, standardization, and dissemination could provide an important public good to support better decision-making by public sector project managers.

## Appendix

Here we provide additional information on the California State Route 91 (SR-91) project, some of the broader lessons illustrated by this example, and additional considerations for investors in PPPs.

Reference projections for SR-91 were prepared by Stantec, the authority's traffic and revenue consultant. A comparison of two of those preliminary studies reveals variations in toll revenue forecasts as large as 1.03x (average 0.18) from one estimation to the other.[23] This highlights an important lesson and persistent challenge in infrastructure projects as shown in Bain

23. Document 1: Orrick, Herrington & Sutcliffe LLP, "Riverside County Transportation Commission: Toll Revenue Senior Lien Bonds," June 26, 2013, p. 65, https://emma.msrb.org/EA546917-EA426056-EA822989.pdf. Document 2: Riverside County Transportation Commission, "SR-91 Corridor Improvement Project: Toll Revenue Bonds 2013, 2013 Series A and Series B," rating presentation, 2013, p. 20.

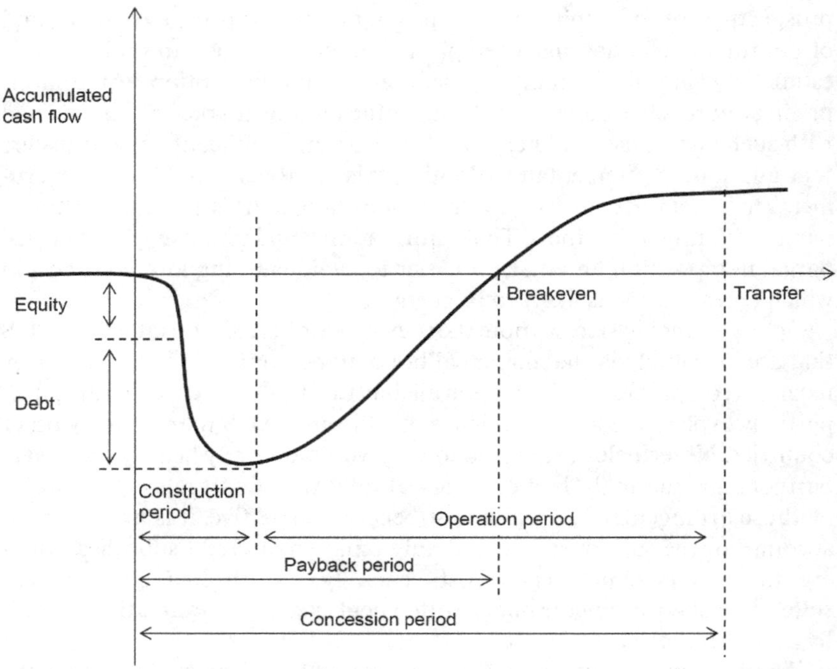


**Fig. 7A.1 Typical cash flow profile for a Department of Transportation project**
*Source:* Zhang (2009).

(2009) and Flyvbjerg, Holm, and Buhl (2005): the need to reduce uncertainty (and inaccuracy) in toll road traffic forecasts used for project valuation. In this type of deal, investors ponder whether the risks they might bear are compensated by the financial returns based on these analyses. In the case of SR-91, demand exceeded initial expectations in the project's first years of operation; however, it is noteworthy to mention that these preliminary forecasts defined the contract terms and risk allocation between private during the contracting process.

Typically, infrastructure PPP projects involve an initial amount of financial capital (debt and equity) set by the private partner to design, build, expand, upgrade, and/or operate the assets stipulated in the contract. This investment can be complemented with different types of public sector support (direct subsidies, guarantees, and so on). Construction costs tend to be large up-front investments, while operation and maintenance (O&M) represent a relatively smaller proportion of total costs. These costs are intended to be recovered (usually with a return) through payments in the form of user fees, public sector payments, or a combination of both. The risk profile, rights, and obligations assumed by each party vary from deal to deal and are determined by the type of project and PPP format chosen.[24] At the end of the contract, the assets are usually transferred back to public sector ownership.[25] When a project becomes operational (for example, the year a new toll road opens and starts to collect tolls), the demand is expected to go through a ramp-up period in its first years (usually with higher volatility). Demand fluctuations would be expected to stabilize, ceteris paribus, as the road matures and approaches physical capacity. Hence, we would expect an S-shaped growth profile as the asset reaches maturity (figure 7A.1).

## References


Ammar, Semir Ben, and Martin Eling. 2013. "Common Risk Factors of Infrastructure Investments." University of St. Gallen School of Finance, Working Papers on Finance 2013/7, Institut Für Versicherungswirtschaft (I.VW-HSG). https://www.unisg.ch/-/media/dateien/unisg/schools/sof/working-papers/13_7_eling-et-al_common-risk-factors-of-infrastructure-firms.pdf.

Andonov, Aleksandar, Roman Kräussl, and Joshua Rauh. 2018. "The Subsidy to Infrastructure as an Asset Class." NBER Working Paper 25045. Cambridge, MA: National Bureau of Economic Research.

Arrow, K., and G. Debreu. 1954. "Existence of an Equilibrium for a Competitive Economy." *Econometrica* 22 (3): 265–90.

Arrow, K., and R. Lind. 1970. "Uncertainty and the Evaluation of Public Investment Decisions." *American Economic Review* 60: 364–78.

Bain, R. 2009. "Error and Optimism Bias in Toll Road Traffic Forecasts." *Transportation* 36 (5): 469.

Black, Fisher. 1976. "The Pricing of Commodity Contracts." *Journal of Financial Economics* 3: 167–79.

Black, Fisher, and Myron J. Scholes. 1973. "The Pricing of Options and Corporate Liabilities." *Journal of Political Economy* 81 (3): 637–54.

Brealey, Richard, Stewart Myers, and Franklin Allen. 2019. *Principles of Corporate Finance*, 13th ed. New York: McGraw Hill Education.

Congressional Budget Office. 2011. *Federal Loan Guarantees for the Construction of Nuclear Power Plants.*

———. 2012a. *Infrastructure Banks and Surface Transportation.*

———. 2012b. *Using Public-Private Partnerships to Carry Out Highway Projects.*

Drupp, Moritz A., Mark C. Freeman, Ben Groom, and Frikk Nesje. 2018. "Discounting Disentangled." *American Economic Journal: Economic Policy* 10 (4): 109–34.

Engel, Eduardo, Ronald Fischer, and Alexander Galetovic. 2011. "Public-Private Partnerships to Revamp U.S. Infrastructure." Brookings Institution, Discussion Paper, February.


24. For instance, project size and maturity, stand-alone or network asset, urban infrastructure, and existing or potential competition can impact a project's risk profile. See a discussion on the relevance of these and other asset features in Fitch Ratings, "Toll Roads—10 Years in Infrastructure," 2017, https://your.fitchratings.com/Toll-Roads-10-Years-in-Infrastructure.html.

25. For a more detailed description of the life cycle of a PPP, including self-contained structures like project finance/SPVs see Engel, Fischer, and Galetovic (2014b).

———. 2014a. *The Economics of Public-Private Partnerships: A Basic Guide*. Cambridge University Press.

———. 2014b. "Finance and Public-Private Partnerships." In *Financial Flows and Infrastructure Financing*, edited by Alexandra Heath and Matthew Read, 193–222. Conference proceedings, Sydney, Australia, March 20–21. https://www.rba.gov.au/publications/confs/2014/pdf/conf-vol-2014.pdf.

———. 2021. "When and How to Use Public-Private Partnerships in Infrastructure: Lessons from the International Experience." This volume.

Flyvbjerg, B., M. Holm, S. Buhl. 2005. "How (In)accurate Are Demand Forecasts in Public Works Projects?" *Journal of the American Planning Association* 71 (2): 131–46.

Gollier, Christian, and Frédéric Cherbonnier. 2018. "The Economic Determinants of Risk-Adjusted Social Discount Rates." Working paper, Toulouse School of Economics.

Longstaff, Francis. 2011. "Municipal Debt and Marginal Tax Rates: Is There a Tax Premium in Asset Prices?" *Journal of Finance* 66 (3): 721–51.

Lucas, Deborah. 2012. "Valuation of Government Policies and Projects." *Annual Review of Financial Economics* 4: 39–58.

———. 2014a. "Evaluating the Cost of Government Credit Support: The OECD Context." *Economic Policy* July: 553–97.

———. 2014b. "Rebutting Arrow and Lind: Why Governments Should Use Market Rates for Discounting." *Journal of Natural Resources Policy Research* 6 (1): 85–91.

Merton, Robert. 1973. "Theory of Rational Option Pricing." *Bell Journal of Economics* 4 (1): 141–83.

———. 1977. "An Analytic Derivation of the Cost of Loan Guarantees and Deposit Insurance: An Application of Modern Option Pricing Theory." *Journal of Banking and Finance* 1 (1): 3–11.

Modigliani, F., and M. H. Miller. 1958. "The Cost of Capital, Corporation Finance, and the Theory of Investment." *American Economic Review* 48: 261–97.

Pirinsky, C., and Q. Wang. 2011. "Market Segmentation and the Cost of Capital in a Domestic Market: Evidence from Municipal Bonds." *Financial Management* 40 (2): 455–81.

Poterba, James, and Arturo Ramirez Verdugo. 2011. "Portfolio Substitution and the Revenue Cost of Exempting State and Local Government Interest Payments from Federal Income Tax." *National Tax Journal* 64: 591–613.

Prats, J., E. Demaestri, and J. Chiara. 2018. "Public Private Partnership Databases: Analytical Description and Comparative Analysis of National and International Databases." Discussion Paper IDB-DP-585. Institutions for Development Sector, Inter-American Development Bank (IDB).

Rouhani, O. M., R. R. Geddes, W. Do, A. Beheshtian, and O. H. Gao. 2018. "Revenue Risk- Sharing Approaches for Public-Private Partnership Provision of Highway Facilities." *Case Studies in Transport Policy* 6 (4): 439–48.

Sharpe, William. 1964. "Capital Asset Prices: A Theory of Market Equilibrium under Conditions of Risk." *Journal of Finance* 19 (3): 425.

Weber, B., M. Staub-Bisang, and H. W. Alfen. 2016. *Infrastructure as an Asset Class: Investment Strategy, Sustainability, Project Finance and PPP*, 2nd ed. Wiley Finance Series. Chichester, UK: Wiley.

Zhang, X. 2009. "Win-Win Concession Period Determination Methodology." *Journal of Construction Engineering and Management* 135 (6): 550–58.

## Comment R. Richard Geddes

### Overview

Is the social cost of bearing a fixed amount of project risk greater when borne by private investors or by taxpayers? That question was addressed by some of the twentieth century's greatest economists within the context of private versus government firm ownership. Noted contributions include Baumol (1968), Diamond (1967), Harberger (1968), Hirshleifer (1965, 1966), and Sandmo (1972), among others. Although the outcome of the intellectual battle can fairly be characterized as a stalemate, Arrow and Lind's 1970 contribution perhaps had the most lasting impact. They argued that, under certain conditions, the social cost of bearing a given amount of project risk approaches zero as risk is spread over an increasing number of taxpayers. Their analysis continues to influence the cost-of-capital (COK) debate today.

That debate waned after widespread economic liberalization in the late twentieth century but has recently resurfaced in the context of infrastructure delivery.[1] A poor record of on-time and on-cost delivery combined with constrained state and local budgets has increased scrutiny of large infrastructure projects. Moreover, accurate assessment of the relative public and private COK has gained renewed importance as governments turn to private partners to bear the risk of large infrastructure projects through public-private partnerships (PPPs).

Inaccurate or incomplete public-sector risk assessment has distorted infrastructure decision-making on at least two important margins. The first is the basic "go or no-go" decision, relevant for any project but particularly so for infrastructure megaprojects. If the assessed cost of taxpayer risk is below its true cost, then too many projects will pass benefit-cost muster, creating a social loss. That is critical not only for large projects but also for those with long design lives, where ignoring the cost of risk may overstate project value by huge amounts. Second, inaccurate public-sector risk assessment will distort the public-private delivery margin, with excessively low assessed taxpayer-risk cost driving too little private-sector participation. That distortion again generates deadweight loss.

Lucas and Montesinos (LM) make several important and timely contributions to the twentieth-century cost-of-capital debate, which when

R. Richard Geddes is a professor in the Department of Policy Analysis and Management at Cornell University and founding director of the Cornell Program in Infrastructure Policy (CPIP).

For acknowledgments, sources of research support, and disclosure of the author's material financial relationships, if any, please see https://www.nber.org/books-and-chapters/economic-analysis-and-infrastructure-investment/comment-fair-value-approach-valuing-public-infrastructure-projects-and-risk-transfer-public-private.

1. In the infrastructure community, the term "delivery" refers to a wide range of infrastructure-related activities, including project selection, design, construction, operations, maintenance, and financing.

implemented will help mitigate those distortions. LM incorporate strides in theoretical finance from the intervening decades to offer a new, general framework for assessing the social cost of risk bearing. In doing so, they harmonize public-sector risk assessment with sophisticated tools used to assess the cost of risk bearing in publicly traded corporations where careful assessments are crucial for efficiently allocating large amounts of capital.

LM's framework is also important because of its applicability to large, idiosyncratic infrastructure projects. A one-size-fits-all approach to assessing such projects is unhelpful and sometimes deceptive. State and local infrastructure owners often resort to using the observed tax-exempt bond rate, effectively ignoring the cost of taxpayer risk bearing altogether, *a la* Arrow and Lind (see Quiggin [1997] for one academic example). LM's approach is useful because of its generality and adaptability. They offer a menu of important project-specific adjustments, including for externalities, cash subsidies, and in-kind subsidies. They also provide examples illustrating the magnitude of the impact of various adjustments.

Moreover, LM contribute by reinforcing basic but overlooked risk-bearing concepts with a more institutional flavor. They state, "Taxpayers and other government stakeholders are the residual claimants to any profits or losses; effectively citizens are conscripted equity holders in all risky investments undertaken by governments." That statement's two key (but underexplored as applied to infrastructure) insights are that (i) taxpayers bear real risk from infrastructure projects in their capacity as residual claimants, similar to equity holders in private investment; and (ii) taxpayers do so involuntarily, in that they are "conscripted." That is, unless risk is properly accounted for, taxpayer capital is doing uncompensated risk-bearing "work." The analogous logic applied to labor suggests that the jurisdiction's residents would be legally required to work on infrastructure projects at below-market wages. A full accounting of such projects would include the true opportunity cost of that uncompensated work in any proper benefit-cost analysis.

LM use an adjusted present value approach through which they first calculate a project's all-equity-financed stand-alone value. They then make adjustments to that present value for externalities, tax distortions, and other project-specific considerations. This generates the project's adjusted present value (APV). When market prices are unavailable and approximations are needed for such adjustments, LM suggest using a "fair value" approach. That approach relies on using discount rates similar to what private financial institutions would apply to future cash flows. The APV model is operationalized using the capital asset pricing model (CAPM) to identify discount rates. LM argue that their framework's benefits include its relative ease of understanding and implementation.

LM then apply their approach to illustrate the risk cost of several common infrastructure delivery arrangements. This is where their work may be of greatest interest and value to infrastructure practitioners. The foremost example is a PPP that contains a revenue guarantee, under which a public-project sponsor promises the private partner a certain minimum level of revenue over the life of the contract. That is not uncommon in PPPs. The APV approach reveals such a high value of PPP revenue guarantees that it may change public owners' future decisions about the use of such guarantees. Using their illustrative example, LM state, "For example, for a 20-year guarantee of a $30 million floor, under either volatility assumption, the guarantee value is more than $42 million higher when the cost of risk is taken into account. That difference is greater than the NPV of the standalone project."

One can imagine exploring the application of the APV model to reveal other standard PPP arrangements' true risk cost. Although there are many, a particularly timely example was provided by Statement No. 94 of the Governmental Accounting Standards Board, entitled "Public-Private and Public-Public Partnerships and Availability Payment Arrangements," which was released in March 2020. The statement provides specific guidance for public infrastructure asset owners on how they should account for PPPs and availability payments (which are essentially performance payments promised by the public project sponsor) on public-sector balance sheets. It will require that public agencies begin accounting for PPPs and availability payment liabilities starting in 2022, so there is no time to waste. The APV approach offers an excellent framework for teasing out the impact of such arrangements on the cost of capital. Additional future applications of the LM approach include the public-sector comparator and value-for-money analysis when comparing PPPs with traditional infrastructure delivery, both of which are beyond the scope of this comment.

LM's analysis is not without its flaws, however. It repeats a common mistake in infrastructure policy analysis, which is to conflate the funding of infrastructure with its financing. Funding refers to the underlying source of dollars to pay for the infrastructure, while financing refers to the use of various financial instruments to generate the large up-front payments needed to design and construct an infrastructure facility once funding is in place. Funding can come from either some type of user fee (such as a toll or rate), or from a broad-based tax unrelated to facility use.

This concern extends beyond semantics, since the main policy challenge facing US infrastructure today is in securing adequate funding. The United States is fortunate in that, once adequate funding is in place (that is, if a deal is "bankable"), then developed financial markets, which can access a variety of financial instruments, exist to provide the necessary financing.

LM would also benefit from more careful and explicit recognition of the institutional differences between public and private-sector risk bearing. The terms "public" and "private" are introduced in LM's chapter (and indeed in most research papers) as though the terms are understood clearly without further elucidation. Although common, those terms are shorthand for a strikingly different set of institutional arrangements, including property rights, contractual arrangements, and social norms.

Two examples include limited liability and the transferability of residual claims. Although private investors benefit from limited liability (that is, their financial liability is in general strictly limited to the amount invested), taxpayers do not. In other words, when states or political subdivisions encounter fiscal difficulties, they can increase tax rates to raise revenues to meet obligations. Limited liability likely has an important impact on the cost of risk bearing.

Another example lies in the differing nature of public versus private residual claims. A defining feature of private-firm ownership is that ownership units are tradable or alienable on either public or private markets. Taxpayer residual claims in contrast are inseparable from residence in a particular jurisdiction, which precludes them from being traded in a market and thus rendering them unpriced.[2] That second difference also has profound implications for risk-bearing costs, which remain largely unexplored in the infrastructure and PPP literature. Indeed, the institutional differences may be so great that an added term in the CAPM model is needed to properly identify discount rates (for example, Geddes and Goldman 2020).

Finally, LM's view that the approach is easily understood and applied by public asset owners may understate the range of other responsibilities borne by those owners. There is rising awareness that the twenty-first century will require public owners to confront more complex delivery structures. Enhanced COK estimation is just one aspect of that new, more challenging delivery setting. Fortunately, rising awareness has engendered calls to formally assist asset owners in adopting new delivery techniques. Although just one tool, calls for the creation of state and regional "PPP units," which are small, expert groups within government that consult on delivery, have grown as a result (for example, Casady and Geddes 2016).

Such criticisms are, however, minor relative to the contribution made by this chapter to the cost-of-capital literature at a crucial time for infrastructure policy. Lucas and Montesinos are to be congratulated for skillfully bringing insights from modern finance, as well as the concept of residual claims, together to offer a new framework to properly account for the social cost of risk in major infrastructure projects. Their work, and the efforts flowing from it, is likely to improve infrastructure delivery in the coming decades.

## References

Arrow, K., and R. Lind. 1970. "Uncertainty and the Evaluation of Public Investment Decisions." *American Economic Review* 60: 364–78.

2. A third example, beyond the scope of this comment, is that tradability allows ownership concentration to change, which may also impact risk-bearing costs. See, for example, Demsetz and Lehn (1985).

Baumol, William J. 1968. "On the Social Discount Rate." *American Economic Review* 58: 788–802.
Casady, Carter B., and R. Richard Geddes. 2016. *Private Investment in U.S. Infrastructure: The Role of PPP Units*. Washington, DC: AEI Press.
Diamond, Peter. 1967. "The Role of the Stock Market in a General Equilibrium Model with Technological Uncertainty." *American Economic Review* 57: 759–76.
Demsetz, Harold, and Kenneth Lehn. 1985. "The Structure of Corporate Ownership: Causes and Consequences." *Journal of Political Economy* 93: 1155–77.
Harberger, Arnold C. 1968. "On Measuring the Social Opportunity Cost of Public Funds." In *The Discount Rate in Public Investment Evaluation*, conference proceedings of the Committee on the Economics of Water Resources Development, Western Agricultural Economics Research Council, Denver, Colorado, December 17–18, 1968: 1–24. Reprinted by the Institute for Defense Analysis as IDA Economic Paper, May 1971.
Hirshleifer, Jack. 1965. "Investment Decision under Uncertainty: Choice-Theoretic Approaches." *Quarterly Journal of Economics* 79: 509–36.
———. 1966. "Investment Decision under Uncertainty: Applications of the State-Preference Approach." *Quarterly Journal of Economics* 80: 252–77.
Geddes, R. Richard, and Joshua K. Goldman. 2020. "Institutional Economics and the Cost of Capital for Infrastructure Projects." *Journal of Economic Policy Reform*, published online June 2020. https://doi.org/10.1080/17487870.2020.1768856.
Governmental Accounting Standards Board. 2020. "Public-Private and Public-Public Partnerships and Availability Payment Arrangements." Statement No. 94, March.
Quiggin, John. 1997. "The Equity Premium and the Government Cost of Capital: A Response to Neville Hathaway." *Agenda* 4 (4): 475–88.
Sandmo, Agnar. 1972. "Discount Rates for Public Investment under Uncertainty." *International Economic Review* 13: 287–302.

8

# Digital Infrastructure

Shane Greenstein

## 8.1 Introduction

The deployment and adoption of the commercial internet in the 1990s brought about a major restructuring of digital infrastructure. Today digital infrastructure supports a range of innovative businesses in the sharing economy, social media, mobile information services, electronic retailing, and ad-supported media. All such activities were much smaller in the 1990s, and their operations have changed dramatically in a few decades. These digital services continue to grow and take on more importance in GDP. For example, in 2017 electronic retailing reached more than $545 billion for "Electronic Shopping and Mail Order Houses (NAICS 4541)." This category grew 65 percent from 2012. In 2017 online advertising contributed $105.9 billion among "Internet Publishing and Broadcasting and Web Search Portals (NAICS 519130)." This category grew 250 percent from 2012.

While many economic studies focus on the most visible parts of the digital economy, much remains unexamined behind the surface at the level of digital infrastructure. This oversight neglects essential economic activity and overlooks the source of important productivity advances. The internet was

Shane Greenstein is the Martin Marshall Professor of Business Administration at Harvard Business School, cochair of the HBS Digital Initiative, and a research associate of the National Bureau of Economic Research.

Thanks go to numerous audiences, Klaus Ackermann, Andre Boik, Tim Bresnahan, David Clark, kc claffy, Chris Forman, Ed Glaeser, Avi Goldfarb, Bradley Huffaker, Maggie Kelleher, John Laprise, Kristina McElheran, Abhishek Nagaraj, Frank Nagle, Tommy Pan Fang, Jim Poterba, Jeff Prince, Bill Rogerson, Greg Rosston, Alicia Shems, Scott Stern, Catherine Tucker, Pai-Ling Yin, and Ran Zhuo for conversations, editing, and comments. All errors are mine alone. For acknowledgments, sources of research support, and disclosure of the author's material financial relationships, if any, please see https://www.nber.org/books-and-chapters/economic-analysis-and-infrastructure-investment/digital-infrastructure.

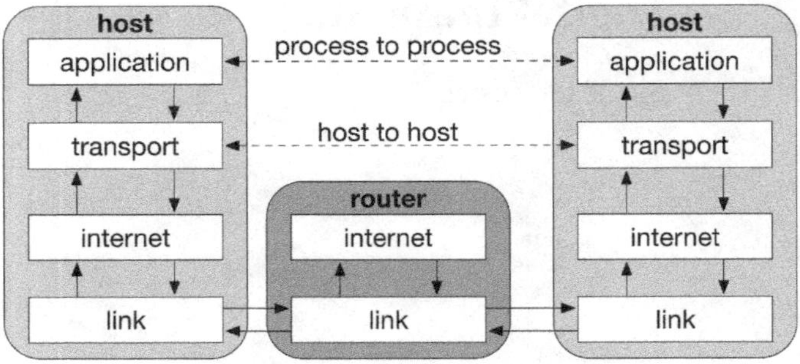


**Fig. 8.1 The four layers of the internet**
*Source:* Zhuo et al. (2019).

designed with a four-layer abstraction—application, transport, internet, and link (see figure 8.1)—so important parts of economic activity work with applications and are less visible. Processes in each layer handle requests from layers above and communicate with remote processes using layers below. This allows each layer to develop and operate independently. Thousands of independently owned, managed, and operated networks voluntarily exchange data via bilaterally negotiated agreements. These layers use many special types of equipment—root servers, fiber, broadband lines, networking switches and routers, content delivery networks, cloud facilities, and cellular towers. This equipment works with the privately owned investments of millions of content providers and user applications. Many organizations involved in digital infrastructure—such as data center operators, content delivery network specialists, data carriers, and access providers—perform this activity.

This chapter reviews studies from a number of areas, with an emphasis on innovation economics, industrial economics, growth accounting, and urban economics. The economic importance of these topics is almost self-evident. Even economists who are skeptical about public spending on traditional infrastructure still admit a role for large-scale public spending on digital infrastructure and on R&D to improve it. Among the salient questions examined in this chapter are the following: What determines variance in the supply of digital infrastructure, and how does that variance shape the performance of digital services? What does evidence suggest about the private incentives and economic returns to society from investment in broadband access and improvements in components of digital infrastructure? While statistical evidence documents considerable variance in the supply of digital infrastructure across regions of the United States, does that evidence show increasing or declining differences in the availability and use of the frontier over time, and why? Are the contributions of digital infrastructure to economic growth correctly measured, and, if not, what are the lessons for measuring prices, output, and quality?

This chapter seeks to inform research and policy analysis, not to advocate choices over policy. That goal focuses the discussion and limits its scope. While the review informs questions about alternative proposals for regulating access, I do not take a position on a specific proposal or regulatory design of, for example, "net neutrality." A curious reader can go to other sources for such analysis.[1] Relatedly, this review concentrates on economic research about the determinants of and returns from digital infrastructure in the United States and covers the global experience when possible. Again, a curious reader can go to other sources for international comparisons.[2] While the chapter assesses the economic justification for subsidizing infrastructure, once again, I refrain from performing an assessment of any specific proposal. Finally, the review does not provide a description of the minutiae of the engineering and operations of the internet. Again, other sources provide this.[3]

Section 8.2 discusses the legacy of the public origins of the internet and the adoption that followed after the internet privatized. Section 8.3 reviews the creation of value at homes and businesses and the role of innovation in creating value within the network. Section 8.4 reviews open questions about the governance of digital infrastructure. Section 8.5 concludes with observations about the unique boundaries between the public and private in today's digital infrastructure.

## 8.2 Origins

The internet arose from combining multiple inventions, which were created with government support and operated by government organizations for public purposes. That experience left an imprint on the organization of the network. It exploded in its scale and scope after privatization in the mid-1990s as a result of investments on a massive scale.

At a high level, the architecture for the internet today bears some resemblance to its government-operated predecessor. One set of firms provides access, while another partially overlapping set of firms provides long-

1. This literature has focused on theoretical and legal issues, supported by examples, and not econometric measurement. See, for example, Nuechterlein and Weiser (2005) for a thorough review of the origins of many regulatory rules at the outset of the internet; Greenstein (2015) for a history of the growth of the commercial internet; and Greenstein, Peitz, and Valletti (2016) for a review of economic research on the topic.

2. A curious reader can start with OECD (2014), World Economic Forum (2016), and Cirera and Maloney (2019).

3. On the architecture and its evolution, see Clark (2018). On the basic operations of the transport and internet layer today, and the origins of congestion, see Clark et al. (2014). On the basic economics of data networks, see Greenstein (2020). On the operations of the network interconnection, see, for example, Norton (2014).

distance lines, and still other organizations provide a range of additional services, such as name-serving, domain registration, and routing. Exchange of data still follows parts of the models established in the late 1990s, albeit today at a much higher level and volume of traffic and with a different composition of firms and negotiating agreements. The level of interconnectivity is also much higher and continues to grow (Zhuo et al. 2019).

Numerous activities have evolved. The type of data today supports a different set of applications than in the 1990s. Email and file transfer once dominated; today, data-intensive applications are more prominent, such as video, streaming, and gaming (Huston 2017). Applications today accommodate a mobile user, and firms operate towers and antennae to support that use case.

### 8.2.1 The Origins of Internetworking

No simple model can describe the origins of the internet and why its architecture evolved as it did after its commercial applications grew. A brief overview of the stages of development prior to the transition into commercial markets can provide an outline of the complex changes:

- *Initial prototyping.* The first set of frontier inventions took place during the 1970s and 1980s when the Defense Advanced Research Projects Agency (DARPA) was the sole funder. Prototypes for packet switching were first engineered. The network at DARPA grew beyond prototypes, although the result was not technically straightforward at the time. The name, TCP/IP (Transmission Control Protocol/Internet Protocol), the specific design for protocols, became the label for this network. Contemporaries built much more around TCP/IP to make it viable.
- *Refinement of the network by the National Science Foundation (NSF).* In the mid-1980s, parts of the TCP/IP-based network were transferred to the NSF.[4] Under NSF governance, the internet acquired a range of new refinements and new regional networks for supporting the shared use of resources.[5] Further innovation took place in the domain nameserver system (DNS). The Internet Engineering Task Force became established to guide further protocol development. These actions helped turn the internet into a living and evolving network, supported by a geographically dispersed organization.
- *Initiation of privatization.*[6] During the early 1990s, the focus was prag-

4. The reason is that many civilian participants were frustrated by the challenges of getting military clearances and so on, and the NSF leadership foresaw benefits to the US academic research community. See Abbate (1999).

5. Until the NSFNET came into existence, there was only one network and one backbone, and BBN operated it. Eventually the NSFNET introduced additional backbones and regional carriers. See Abbate (1999).

6. These events are described in more detail in Greenstein (2015), chap. 3.

matic and oriented toward issues with scaling operations. The most important invention supported routing between multiple networks.[7] A debate ensued about practices for data exchange in a privatized system in which, to achieve national interoperability of communications, competing firms had to cooperate. Independently, Tim Berners-Lee invented the World Wide Web and began to deploy it. It expanded the functionality of the internet in ways that made it more appealing to less technical users.

- *National deployment.*[8] In the middle of the 1990s, the internet backbone became a private asset, allowing private firms to build on top of it. At the same time, at the National Center for Supercomputing Applications (NCSA) at the University of Illinois, a team developed the Mosaic Browser. It became the source for Netscape and Internet Explorer, catalyzing the "browser wars," which occurred right after privatization. A related team at NCSA created a web server, which became the antecedent to Apache, the most popular web server for the next two decades.

To summarize, university researchers created many of these core inventions, and most received public funding from DARPA and NSF, with an exception for Tim Berners-Lee, whose funding came from CERN (the European Organization for Nuclear Research). The NSF and DARPA helped launch practices around standardization and network interconnection. Private markets inherited a reliable and operational network. While private firms had supplied some of the equipment used by NSF and DARPA, after the mid-1990s private investors picked up the bulk of operations and investment activity. While NSF-funded research into improvement in computing and networking continued after privatization, market forces took a more central role in determining the direction of innovation. The Web diffused on top of this infrastructure, and grew into the foundations for an enormous range of commercial applications.

### 8.2.2 Technological and Operational Legacy

At the outset, one key piece of the network infrastructure was visible to users, dial-up internet access. It built upon the existing telephone network, which was geographically ubiquitous prior to the diffusion of the internet as a result of public policies that encouraged universal availability of the phone network, even in high-cost areas. Dial-up services learned from existing Bulletin Board Services (BBSs), which provided experience with operat-

7. NSF switched from the routing protocol Exterior Gateway Protocol (EGP) and replaced it with Border Gate Protocol (BGP). BGP enables fully decentralized routing. Making this change was one of the early technical signs of the pending arrival of commercial network and the retirement of NSFNET. For extensive discussion, see Clark (2018).

8. These events are described in more detail in Greenstein (2015), chaps. 4, 5 and 6.

ing commercial services with dial-up technologies. The first generation of dial-up access was available almost everywhere in the United States within a few years after privatization.[9]

Not long after dial-up access demonstrated the viability of a national market, a variety of entrants aspired to provide faster speeds than delivered by dial-up. Today these access technologies go by the label "broadband."[10] Today, broadband providers dominate the supply of access services to the internet for both households and businesses. Broadband networks initially did not replicate the ubiquitous availability of dial-up. Broadband networks required physical investments. In low-density areas, the costs of building such lines were high, which necessitated high prices for access that some users were unwilling to pay. In addition, in recognition of a range of concerns, state and federal policy did not require universal geographic availability. Estimates of the population unserved by wireline broadband have varied from 15 percent to less than 5 percent of the US population, declining over time. Today about 10 percent of the US population does not use the internet, and surveys suggest the two prominent reasons for doing so are high prices and lack of availability (Anderson et al. 2019).

By historical standards, the switch from dial-up to broadband was swift. In 2001, only about one-half of US households had access to the internet, and virtually all access occurred over dial-up; today, approximately three-quarters of US households have broadband internet access in their homes. Most of that switch took less than a decade.[11] In its most common form, firms offer broadband as either DSL (digital subscriber line) over a phone line or through cable modems retrofitted to cable television systems. More recently, broadband over fiber has become available.

The experience today arose from three related diffusion trajectories. One, broadband access diffused to households. Two, broadband diffused to business, complemented by investment in advanced computing technologies. Three, different specialists offered activities, while a few large firms integrated into the infrastructure. Feedback loops moderated those trajectories. New application development encouraged more diffusion of broadband, which encouraged more application development. The uneven supply of

9. The reasons are discussed in detail in Greenstein (2015), particularly chaps. 5, 7, and 8.

10. The definition of broadband has undergone changes over time, as regulatory expectations change. For purposes of this discussion, the definition will be loose and encompass any wireline technology faster than the data rates of 56k dial-up, including ISDN, DSL, and cable modem service. Among wireless technologies, all Wi-Fi (IEEE 802.11b, g, n, and more); 3G, 4G, and 5G cellular services; and modern satellite service are broadband.

11. Greenstein and McDevitt (2011) provide data on the replacement of dial-up with broadband. For the diffusion of broadband, see Camille Ryan and Jamie M. Lewis, "Computer and Internet Use in the United States," *American Community Survey Reports*, September 2017, https://www.census.gov/content/dam/Census/library/publications/2017/acs/acs-37.pdf; and Pew Research Center, "Internet/Broadband Fact Sheet," June 12, 2019, https://www.pewInternet.org/fact-sheet/Internet-broadband/.

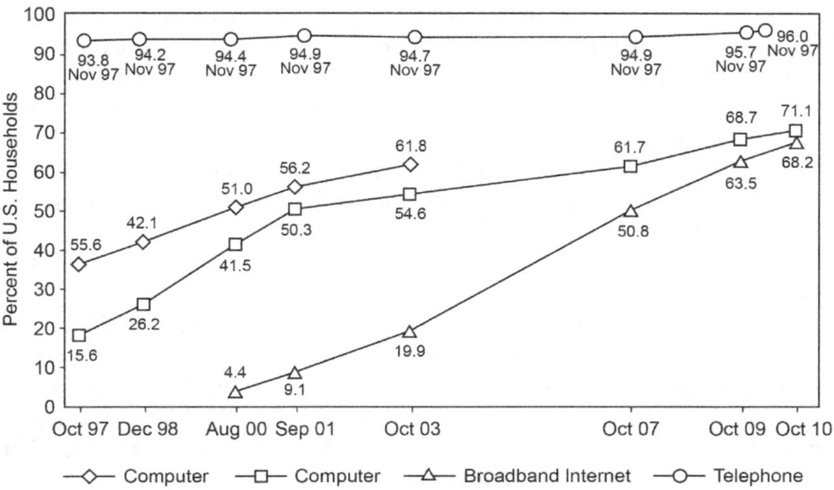


**Fig. 8.2 Internet adoption over time**
*Source:* National Telecommunications and Information Administration (2011).

networking created regional variance in the quantity and quality of digital infrastructure, and application development initially targeted areas and use cases favoring early adopters and, eventually, mass-market users. Uneven investment created variance in quantity and quality across countries, and different patterns of application development emerged within countries and across languages.

### 8.2.3 Adoption and Use

Adoption of the internet by households followed a standard S curve, with one-half of US households using dial-up by 2001 and one-half moving to broadband by 2007, continuing to grow thereafter. See figure 8.2, from a 2011 publication, for an illustration of both the S curves and the changing focus of US surveys.[12] At first they tracked personal computer use in homes, then dial-up, and finally broadband, ending the tracking of computer use.

Eventually, diffusion fell short of universal adoption as a result of lack of interest, lack of affordability, and lack of availability. Debates continue today over attributing nonadoption to different causes (see Horrigan 2020). Today, the adoption of broadband internet in the US hovers just below 80 percent of households, with the remainder of adopters using wireless

12. National Telecommunications and Information Administration, *Digital Nation: Expanding Internet Usage (NTIA Research Preview)*, February 17, 2011, https://www.ntia.doc.gov/report/2011/digital-nation-expanding-Internet-usage-ntia-research-preview.

access, either satellite or smart phones. In most developed countries, the percentage is higher. It is lower in underdeveloped countries, much lower in some. Worldwide, close to half of the global population uses the internet.[13]

The growing importance of digital infrastructure is also visible in other modes of access. For example, users of cellular telephony migrated from 3G to 4G, the latter entirely supporting digital communications.[14] Presently, more than three-quarters of US households own at least one smartphone, rising from virtually none in 2007.[15] Wi-Fi technology has diffused since its first deployment in 1999.[16] More than 86 percent of homes with access to broadband employ Wi-Fi.[17]

What role does competition play? Wallsten and Mallahan (2013) ask whether competition plays an important role in improving quality to households. They examine the effect of more entry on the quality of the broadband provided, measured by its bandwidth, and then exclude suppliers from the count unless those suppliers provide services to a minimum threshold of customers. The authors found that—after considerable data cleaning—the typical zip code contained one or two suppliers of broadband, and a small number had three or more. This analysis shows that the third entrant does not change pricing but does generate competitive pressures for qualitative improvement.

This agenda extends in many directions. Seamans (2012) examines whether perceived threats of municipal entry generate faster upgrades and finds evidence that it does. Skiti (2019) examines whether potential competitive entry generates any response and finds evidence that it does. Chen and Savage (2011) focus on the role of competition in shaping pricing. They match cable and DSL internet access providers in all the western states and compare pricing differences between monopolies or duopolies in many small cities. The authors find that variety of customers mediates pricing and, generally, reduces price declines from an additional supplier.

Diffusion of the internet created two investment trajectories at business establishments. Forman (2005) proposed a framework for understanding adoption among a sample of early adopters, and Forman, Goldfarb, and Greenstein (2005) applied the framework to the US economy. They compare the use of *basic* with *advanced* internet technologies at US businesses near

13. World Bank statistics: https://data.worldbank.org/indicator/IT.NET.USER.ZS?view=chart.

14. 4G is the fourth generation of broadband cellular technology, succeeding 3G. 4G uses only packet-switching technology, unlike 3G, which used both packet-switching and (in parallel) the (old) circuit-switching technology. As of this writing, 5G contains much more capacity than 4G and has only just begun to deploy in developed countries.

15. Ryan and Lewis, "Computer and Internet Use in the United States."

16. Wi-Fi is a standard defined by IEEE committee 802.11, operating over the 2.4 GHz and 5 GHz bands of spectrum.

17. NCTA, "Wi-Fi: How Broadband Households Experience the Internet," April 6, 2018, https://www.ncta.com/whats-new/wi-fi-how-broadband-households-experience-the-Internet.

the end of the first wave of investment after the commercialization of the internet. Basic investment involved developing access to support email and browsing for employees, and a large fraction of establishments (approximately 90 percent) had adopted this. Advanced investment involved altering processes to supply services for customers and to receive inputs from suppliers, and a much lower percentage (approximately 12 percent) had adopted it. These latter activities were costly and depended on coordinating with partners and many complementary investments to enable electronic commerce (McElheran 2015).

Forman, Goldfarb, and Greenstein (2005) show that almost every establishment (approximately 90 percent) adopted the basic internet, while advanced internet showed up more prevalently in some cities. Several factors played a role in the deployment of advanced internet technologies. Some locations contained data-intensive industries that had recently made capital investments in computing and business equipment, which raised the returns to complementary investments in digital infrastructure. More educated and more skilled labor could take advantage of digital infrastructure, again raising the returns. Finally, some businesses were more productive and more profitable than other firms and, thus, could make bigger investments in all capital equipment, including digital infrastructure.

### 8.2.4 Innovation within the Network: Content Delivery Networks

Any improvement within the network improved performance for both households and businesses. The creation of content delivery networks (CDNs) provides an illustration of growth in specialists. CDNs first became available in the late 1990s and began spreading after that. Geographically distributed networks of servers located close to users, CDNs (i) reduce data delay by rerouting user requests and (ii) provide a layer of reliability and security.[18] Today all but the smallest commercial content providers use CDNs. They have become an essential layer of digital infrastructure.

In the most common arrangement, a third-party commercial CDN negotiates with an internet service provider (ISP) or wireless access provider for the right to "colocate" a server close to users. The ISP may charge a "transit" fee to the CDN to take data over its network lines. Content providers pay the CDN to redistribute content to users from the CDN's servers, which the content provider "updates" at an arranged schedule (by the minute, hour, or day). Many content providers choose to update only timely and popu-

18. Even when servers have gone down, the cached content in a CDN may keep a firm's content available for users. In addition, CDNs can buffer content from a denial of service attack. For example, some CDNs, such as those operated by Cloudflare, have added security servers, such as protection against distributed denial of service (DDOS) attacks, which involve large numbers of queries to a server in a short time, exceeding the server's capacity and rendering it unable to provide any service. CDNs are one of several instruments that can provide buffers against such attacks.

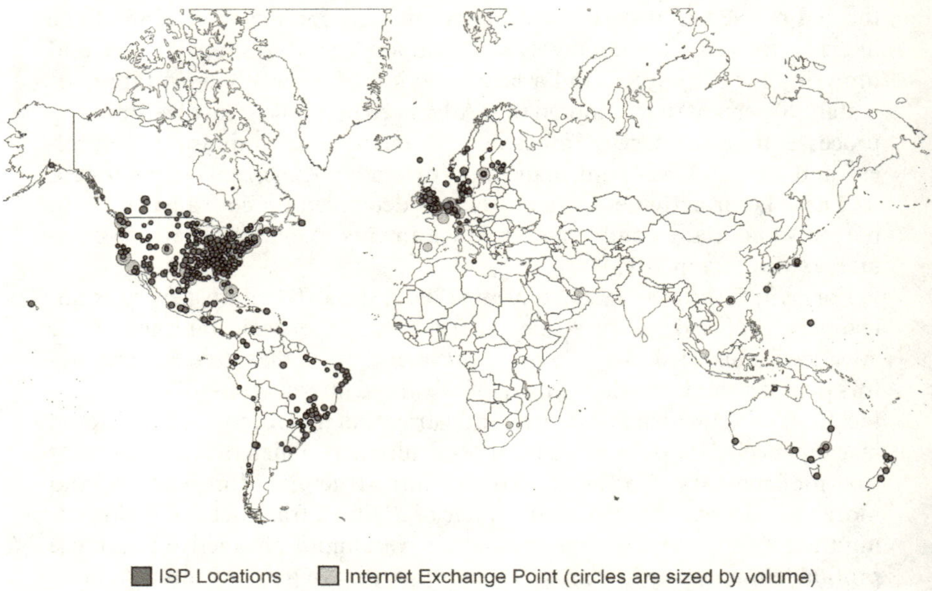


**Fig. 8.3 Netflix CDN network**

*Source:* Netflix Media Center, https//media.netflix.com/en/company-blog/how-netflix-works-with-isps- around-the-globe-to-deliver-a-great-viewing-experience, accessed February 2020.

lar content. Akamai is the largest provider of these CDN services in the US.[19]

Several large application firms have vertically integrated into operating their own CDNs. For example, Google, Apple, and Facebook operate CDNs and tailor the technical features of the CDN to their own needs. Again, they negotiate a price with ISPs for "colocation" in the network and sometimes pay fees for data transit. If negotiations with ISPs fail, the CDNs locate at internet exchange points (IXPs). In practice, only large firms opt for operating their own CDNs. It is usually less expensive to contract with a third-party CDN for small to medium volumes of traffic.

As illustration, figure 8.3 shows a map of Netflix's CDN network. As one of the largest sources of streaming content in the world, the firm's CDN network should be regarded as large. Netflix's CDN network comprises more than 4600 servers in 233 locations in 2016, according to Bottger et al. (2018)—primarily deployed within ISPs or at IXPs in the developed world.

The growth of CDNs coincided with the improvements in consumer experience, in lowering latency for the large data flows supporting video.

19. Akamai's revenues were $2.7 billion in 2018. The next largest providers of such services, Cloudflare and Limelight, had $192 million and $184 million in revenue in 2018, respectively.

When the data packets traveled to users over dial-up in the mid-1990s, users typically could tolerate delays. Later, data traffic reached users primarily through broadband lines and became composed of mostly streaming, video, and gaming applications, but with fewer delays.[20] A symbiotic relationship emerged between improvement in access, CDNs, and applications. Many new applications would have been infeasible without CDNs, such as "over-the-top" streaming services like YouTube, Netflix, Disney+, or HBO Go.

The spread of CDNs frames questions about the economic impact of innovation. The gains distribute widely, while CDN providers make the investment. Content providers experience faster delivery, users enjoy previously unobtainable content, and ISPs charge colocation fees and gain revenue. Understanding these gains and externalities shed light on incentives to improve. The contractual arrangement involving third parties arises in virtually any but the smallest ISPs in the United States, which suggests the arrangement serves the interest of ISPs. In contrast, it is more difficult to infer that CDNs owned by content providers serve all parties' interests. For a number of reasons—such as scaling issues, negotiating frictions, and the colocation expense—some firms prefer to locate some of their private CDNs at IXPs and not within ISPs. If application firms vertically integrate into their own CDNs and locate elsewhere, do others using third party CDNs get a different quality of service? As of this writing, no economic research has approached these questions.

### 8.2.5 Innovation: Data Centers and the Cloud

At the outset of the commercial internet, most firms housed their servers on company premises. That changed gradually (see, e.g., Byrne, Corrado, and Sichel 2018; Jin and McElheran 2018). Today third-party suppliers of data centers in the United States allocate assets worth at least several hundred billion dollars (Greenstein and Pan Fang 2019). Data centers lower latencies for business users, enable large-scale computing and innovative uses for that scale, consolidate managerial challenges and reap efficiencies from solutions to those challenges, enable flexible uses that previously were not possible, and remove frictions to accessing big-data applications. These abilities reduce the frictions supporting applications for a mobile labor force (see, e.g., DeStefano, Kneller, and Timmins 2019; Ewens, Nanda, and Rhodes-Kropf 2019). The largest agglomeration of data centers in North America is in Ashburn, Virginia, just outside Washington DC, near Metropolitan Area Exchange, East (commonly referred to as MAE-EAST), which is one of the oldest IXPs in the United States.

Just as with CDNs, the growth of data centers and the cloud illustrates an important question about the impact of investment in frontier digital

20. See, for example, the usage statistics in Nevo, Turner, and Williams (2016); McManus et al. (2018); and Huston (2017).

infrastructure. How do the gains distribute between cloud providers who operate the servers, the content providers who use them, and the users who enjoy previously unobtainable content?

Data centers contain rows of servers, which perform computation or storage. These buildings optimize for low energy use and optimal cooling, and they may contain expensive backup generators and structures to prevent flooding or reinforcements in floors to lower vibrations from passing vehicles. The inside wiring also may support a specific set of activities, especially in critical functions that support transactions with sensitive customer data.[21] These expensive features can matter. For example, because of built-in resiliency and smart site selection, the data centers in Houston continued operating without interruption during and after the flooding of Hurricane Harvey in September 2017.

Contracts for data centers cover every conceivable arrangement and option between ownership and rental markets. At one extreme, rental markets arise for just about any arrangement a buyer could want. There are plenty of firms that will take responsibility for the operations of the building and electronic equipment for a service fee. Many buyers with generic needs—such as storage for backup—rent space in data centers at various time intervals (for example, 5, 10, or 20 years), own the servers and program them, and let others manage the building. At the other extreme, firms with unique computing needs, such as Facebook, Apple, Microsoft, Amazon, Oracle, and Google, own everything. They operate the largest private data centers in North America and configure the building and servers to suit their applications. For example, if a firm has an essential operation within a data center, large CDN networks typically complement it, so the results deploy quickly to users. Sophisticated firms increasingly utilize complex architecture to balance the loads from user demands, such as using CDNs for rapid response to requests for timely content, cloud facilities for secondary response, and remote servers for requests of the least popular content.

Today a cloud service involves a data center that rents its services, with the additional feature that users can request any size and turn the service off and on at will. The providers increasingly offer software services for a nominal charge or for none at all. Demand for cloud services has grown as the services improve in quality and decline in price. For example, Amazon Web Services offers scores of cloud software services; Microsoft Azure supports many Microsoft products, such as Outlook, as a cloud service; and Google offers TensorFlow, a standard tool for machine learning, at no charge with Google's cloud service. The appeal of the cloud comes from its flexibility in capital commitment and scale and the option to substitute variable

21. The data center for the New York Stock Exchange, for example, permits many firms to access trading services at especially fast rates. As another example, a segment of business users in health, finance, and transportation require high security and high reliability, often referred to as the "five nines" of reliability—namely, 99.999 percent uptime.

costs for fixed costs on a balance sheet, which appeals to cash-constrained firms.[22]

The data center and cloud market have received some research attention. In the first paper on its productivity, Jin and McElheran (2018) examine the use of cloud computing in US manufacturing and find it predicts productivity growth among young firms and new units in established firms. Use of the cloud also predicts productivity, conditional on survival, in uncertain environments. The evidence is consistent with the highest gains accruing to firms that take advantage of the flexibility and lower costs of learning about IT needs in spite of uncertainty.

Tensions between the size of the investment and localization of demand shape the location of data centers. Greenstein and Pan Fang (2019) posit a framework that focuses on the "distaste for distance," which creates localization of demand, and different supply conditions across geography.[23] Facilities spread out to match local demand. These compete with facilities that "aggregate" the demand from many locations. The costs of supply reflect variance in economies of scale and variance in operational costs. Both fixed and variable costs vary with the cost of inputs, such as land, electricity, cooling, and technical labor. These lead to variance in costs across different locations, and firms respond to this tension with entry and capacity decisions. Greenstein and Pan Fang (2019) forecast a "minimum threshold" of local users under which no entry occurs and find evidence consistent with this model. That suggests data centers and cloud services have an urban bias, favoring bigger and denser cities.

If buyers perceive shorter distances between users and the data centers for cloud services as an important attribute of cloud services, then that will create further potential for tension around the localization of supply. The first evidence about the demand for cloud services suggests users will place value on distance (Wang, LaRiviere, and Kannan 2019). While ubiquitous frontier infrastructure confers large societal benefits, such frontier infrastructure tends not to be available in low-density regions.

## 8.3 Creating Value

How and why did digital infrastructure produce value? How is that measured? The internet grew and diffused to households and businesses more rapidly than the telephone, electricity, and other technologies, so the ques-

22. See, for example, Coyle and Nguyen (2018). Byrne, Corrado, and Sichel (2018) estimate the quality-adjusted price decline between 2009 and 2016 at 17.3 percent per annum for Amazon Web Services.

23. "Distaste for distance" arises from a mix of three factors. The first two—user dislike for latency and user desire to avoid congestion—look alike in reducing distances between users and facilities. A third factor, "server hugging," arises from managerial preferences for nearby physical facilities, which facilitates monitoring.

tion informs understanding of the causes of economic growth (see, e.g., Comin and Hobijn 2010).

### 8.3.1 Creating Value at Households

At first glance, internet access adoption would seem to follow the classic model of adoption, whereby those with the greatest willingness to pay adopt earliest and those with lower willingness to pay adopt later, as a result of declines in price, increases in quality, or both. In this model, the value to consumers provides the value of access in terms of consumer surplus. This model has considerable appeal because it provides a path toward valuing improvements from access infrastructure.

The model would appear to be a good approach for measurement. After all, just contrast the price and quality of internet access to households in 2001 with 2016. Around 2001, dial-up dominated access to the internet, and approximately half of US households were online. Web traffic dominated the internet, and wireless access had just entered a new era with the introduction of Wi-Fi and 3G cellular service, which ran a data service in parallel with voice services on cellular towers and handsets. By 2016, broadband access dominated all modes of access, and three-quarters of US households maintained connections online. In 2016, the predominant applications leading to data traffic were streaming, video, and gaming; Wi-Fi 5 and 4G served as the predominant wireless modes of transmission. This 15-year history suggests a large and valuable increase in access networks that should manifest in price declines, quantity increases, and qualitative improvement.

One positive symptom of improvement shows up in GDP (especially after the Census reclassified activities to track activity). From 2012 to 2017, payments for access to wireline forms of internet access reached \$88.7 billion, growing more than 30 percent in those five years. In addition, payments for access fees to wireless service reached over \$90.0 billion, an increase of 57 percent.[24]

An estimate for user adoption by income, shown in figure 8.4, also seems to fit the model.[25] While adoption grows across all demographic groups, the variance in adoption across income is visible. The persistent pattern—with lower-income groups adopting less frequently—motivates hypotheses that high prices deter low-income households from purchasing internet access. Yet, other parts of the measured record contain more ambiguous indicators. The growth displayed in figure 8.4 ought to arise from either a decline in prices or an increase in quality or both. The consumer price index (CPI) for access covers only access. Proper accounting of user costs involves both a charge for telephone calls and a separate charge for internet access. For

24. Statistics of US Business, US Census.

25. These graphs aggregate periodic surveys (not smoothed) conducted by the Pew Internet and American Life Project.

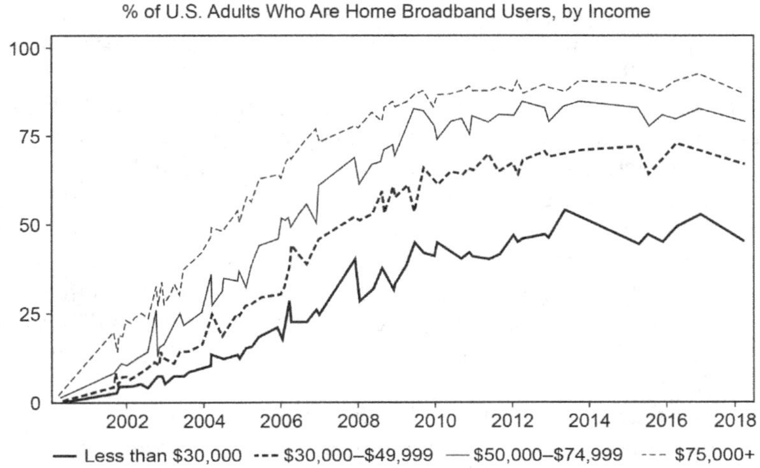


**Fig. 8.4 Broadband adoption by income level**

*Source:* See Pew Research Center, "Internet/Broadband Fact Sheet," June 12, 2019, https://www.pewresearch.org/internet/fact-sheet/Internet-broadband/, under "Who Has Home Broadband?," with income as the primary sorting variable.

some users the user cost included an additional expenditure for a second line. Many users sought to avoid the cost of an additional line, and those users employed the existing lines more intensely.[26]

As broadband diffused, the CPI for internet access has covered broadband delivery, and the charges for telephony have become less relevant. That price series for internet access has remained flat for an extended period of time after a one-time drop in the middle of the decade. For example, in 2007, the CPI was at 73.2, and more than a decade later in 2018 it was at 76.0.[27] In other words, the consumer price of broadband has *increased* by 3.8 percent. The puzzle does not disappear with a comparison with other indices. The closest comparable CPI—that for wireless services, which also includes the price of telephone calls—displays a drop from 64 to 46 (a 28 percent decline in prices).[28]

Simple alternative explanations do not provide an answer. Increased adoption cannot account for the rise in revenue in the face of no price change. From 2011 to 2018, approximately 3–5 percent of US households first began using broadband internet, depending on the survey. That is too

26. See Greenstein and McDevitt (2011) for the details.

27. See the series for internet services and electronic information providers in US city average, all urban consumers: US Bureau of Labor Statistics, "CPI for All Urban Consumers (CPI-U)," https://data.bls.gov/PDQWeb/cu.

28. See wireless telephone services in US city average, all urban consumers: US Bureau of Labor Statistics, "CPI for All Urban Consumers (CPI-U)," https://data.bls.gov/PDQWeb/cu.

small a number to account for a 30 percent growth in revenue.[29] Expenditure per household must have gone up, but how did that happen without a nominal price decline?

One explanation stresses that quality must have improved, but it went unmeasured. Some evidence suggests this is the case. For example, there is evidence of increasing speeds over time for all major wireline networks.[30] There are several potential reasons that the speed increase went unmeasured. First, as with many other consumer services, the CPI for broadband compares the prices of contracts for a given service.[31] The procedure reduces measuring qualitative improvement if contracts do not reflect those improvements. That could happen because better caching, buffering, and other features do not factor into pricing in contracts. These features are hard to impute.

More subtle, contracts measure bandwidth and appear as part of a tiered menu of quality and price. If households do not use the same contract over the entire period, it is possible for them to increase expenditure on access without any measured price increase in a CPI. Hence, existing procedures also create an upward bias in the price index that fails to account for users switching to better contracts. That is exacerbated by the lack of measurement of savings, as noted earlier, when households dropped incurring expenditures for a phone line in order to move to broadband access.

A related explanation stresses issues with definitional boundaries between complements in use. The price measurement system treats access as a distinct service from content. Changes in the quality of content play no role in the price index for access. Stated another way, the standard measurement framework focuses on transactions for access, but not freely available services that users obtain along with their access. Standard procedures ignore the new goods—such as search, social media, and advertising-supported news and entertainment—even though content has improved. While those could motivate more adoption over time, as well as purchases of more bandwidth, we see only a constant price and more expenditure; not the cause, which is more quality.

There is secondary evidence to support these explanations. It draws from outside of price measurement and stresses the heavy evolution of applica-

29. More adoption did not produce the revenue increase. See Pew Research Center, "Internet/Broadband Fact Sheet," June 12, 2019, https://www.pewInternet.org/fact-sheet/Internet-broadband/, and Ryan and Lewis, "Computer and Internet Use in the United States" (see n. 11).

30. See, for example, the Netflix comparisons of measured speeds over 2012–2018 yields a doubling of realized speeds for most networks (Netflix, "United States: Leaderboard," https://ispspeedindex.netflix.com/country/us/, accessed April 2019).

31. The CPI is constructed from a weighted average of contracts for ostensibly similar services, where the weights come from household surveys and the contracts come from suppliers. This procedure necessarily underestimates the introduction of new goods—here, experienced as higher speeds—and qualitative improvements not reflected in common measures, such as bandwidth.

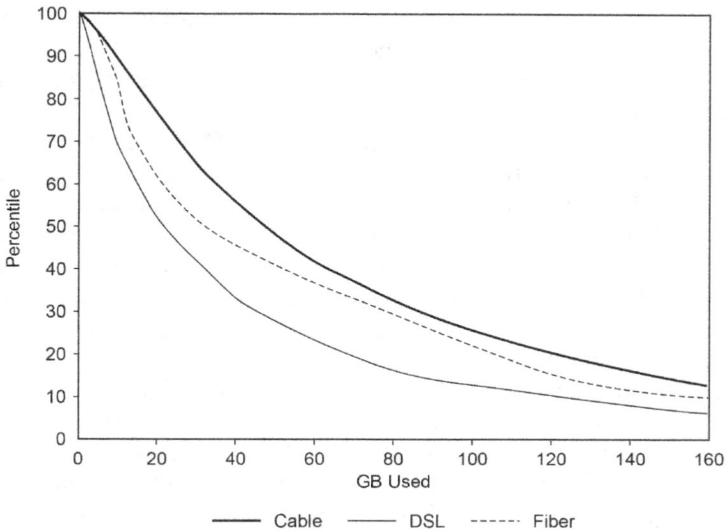


**Fig. 8.5 Cumulative distribution of user traffic, by technology (highest users removed)**

*Source:* Federal Communications Commission, September 2013, https//www.fcc.gov/reports-research/reports/measuring-broadband-america/measuring-broadband-america-2014, accessed March, 2020.

tions of the internet and the traffic that supports them. In the earliest days of the internet, text dominated traffic, either in the form of email or passive browsing. In contrast, more recently households have been adopting streaming services and receive increasingly many more magnitudes of data than they send (Huston 2017). For example, streaming a standard- to high-definition movie generates one to three gigabytes (GBs) per hour. To appreciate that size, examine figure 8.5, which shows a typical household's activity of data in 2013. The median household uses 20–60 GB a month. Netflix has increased its subscribership in the US from 20 to 60 million over the second decade of the millennium. Merely binge-watching a streamed series could massively increase data use. Netflix is far from the only streaming service. In short, as household streaming of television and movies rises, the capacity of access and underlying infrastructure also had to rise considerably. That could result in more intensive use of existing bandwidth and could motivate households to switch to more bandwidth at a higher price. That would register as more expenditure, not necessarily as a higher price in a price index.

Such considerations motivate research about heterogeneity in user demand for access. Rosston, Savage, and Waldman (2010) examine the demand for more speed as one of many attributes consumers choose to pay for. They find that a small set of users pay for higher speeds at any point in time. That user (un)willingness to pay for more speed acts as a fundamental brake, slowing investment in upgrades in the short run. In other words, households act as if they prefer to migrate to higher speeds gradually, and firms respond accordingly.

Building on these estimates, Greenstein and McDevitt (2011) analyze the returns to households from upgrading to broadband from dial-up access. Despite the low valuations for frontier speeds, the authors show that the broadband upgrade over dial-up conferred a large consumer surplus on the economy. The consumer price index for access underestimated those gains, which would have generated at least a 2–3 percent decline in prices each year. Most conservative estimates of quality adjustment suggest an underestimate in standard economic measurement of access pricing.[32]

Another informative research agenda analyzes both the contracts between users and access firms and subsequent user behavior. Usage-based pricing and data caps in wireline access contracts are more common, but only a little research has modeled the adoption and use decision in the presence of these contracting constraints. Nevo, Turner, and Williams (2016) provide a framework for understanding these decisions. They analyze usage data for a set of customers of a single ISP. These users face three-part tariffs, which impose a shadow value on the price of data as users approach their monthly allowances.[33] Users are sensitive to the charges affiliated with reaching a data cap, but they also endogenously select into capacity consistent with their own use, especially for those who are heavy users of streaming (as Nevo, Turner, and Williams observe, where 60 percent of data use relates to streaming applications). Variation in user behavior permits an analyst to recover variation in the willingness to pay for broadband, which provides insight into the gaps between private and social incentives to build or upgrade broadband. The estimates of Nevo, Turner, and Williams (2016) suggest that the gap is substantial, once again consistent with the presence of insufficient private incentives to upgrade quality at a rate in line with society's broader interest.[34]

Byrne and Corrado (2019) focus on valuing the missing free complements. Borrowing insights from the measurement of capacity utilization, the authors argue that some consumers use access technologies for free goods more intensively than others.[35] The complementarity between paid

32. It is important to note an additional implication. The gains should result in a reallocation of household time, which will generate restructuring in many other industries that also bid for household time, such as television, radio, news, and entertainment.

33. See Burnham et al. (2013) for an early census of the use of tiered pricing and caps based on the usage of data in wireline and wireless forms.

34. Malone, Nevo, and Williams (2017) also examine the willingness to pay for more bandwidth, based on usage data from one ISP. They focus on the trade-offs for different ways to approach congestion of networks. The authors show that peak load pricing along with caching more effectively deals with congestion than does throttling of traffic.

35. This approach follows numerous studies that examine the time spent online as a possible avenue for valuing digital goods. See, for example, Boik, Greenstein, and Prince (2019); Bryn-

access services and network use leads to an unmeasured quality adjustment for the price of access. Looking across cable television, cellular telephony, and the internet, the authors calculate a nearly $1,800 boost to consumer surplus per connected user, which amounts to a one-half percentage point addition to US real GDP for 2007–2017. That suggests the derived demand for access infrastructure is large, and so is its underlying value. None of the free services could provide such satisfaction without employing digital access and relying on nearly ubiquitous access.

The progress in understanding the experience outside the US has tended to take advantage of idiosyncratic institutional details that create opportunities for insights. An early paper comparing international experiences is Wallsten and Riso (2010), which shows a wide variance in access prices and availability across countries. Yet that has not stopped naive approaches that reduce the nuances in prices to one statistic to facilitate comparisons.[36] Wallsten and Riso's findings suggest that single statistics heighten the potential for unobservable factors in cross-country regressions.

One set of studies examines the deployment of broadband in the United Kingdom. As a result of the UK's underlying switch network, broadband deployed in a somewhat random geographic pattern, creating similar neighboring areas with different broadband experiences. This quasi-randomness creates plausible exogeneity. One line of research looks at the consequences of uneven broadband deployment on property prices for homes (Ahlfeldt, Koutroumpis, and Valletti 2017). Better broadband has an impact on local prices for real estate, evidence that homebuyers value broadband.

### 8.3.2 Creating Value at Business

The experience within business in the 1990s creates challenges for measurement. The deployment of email and browsing cannot generate insight into whether adoption of novel digital technologies had an impact because these basic internet technologies became available *and adopted* almost everywhere in the US within a few years, leaving almost no variance from which to infer the gains. At best, this diffusion would show up in general gains in productivity, though growth accounting would not be able to attribute the growth to any specific investment.

What can be inferred? It is possible to examine changes consistent with the adoption of advanced internet technologies, which required broadband and complementary investments as well as skilled labor, and for which there is variance in supply across regions and industries. This is the approach in Forman, Goldfarb, and Greenstein (2012), which considers whether the investment in advanced internet technologies became associated with alleviating

jolfsson, Collis, and Eggers (2019); Brynjolfsson and Oh (2012); Goldfarb and Prince (2008); Goolsbee and Klenow (2006); and Hitt and Tambe (2007).

36. Most commonly used are OECD (2014) or World Economic Forum (2016), which get their broadband prices from the same source: data from the World Bank.

or acerbating regional inequality. Building on research linking information technology use to productivity gains,[37] an optimistic view forecasts that digital infrastructure potentially could reduce distances and aid those who lived at a distance from areas with higher incomes. The authors find, in contrast, that the first wave of the investment boom exacerbated regional inequality. Using an instrumental variable approach and a battery of additional tests, the authors relate wage growth to investment in advanced internet technologies. They find that business adoption of the internet makes regions with higher income richer in some places, but not everywhere. The largest divergences occur in major urban areas with skilled workforces and prior investment in IT. In short, the high-income locations experienced the most wage growth.

Note the large open question: Has subsequent regional growth altered the pattern of additional investment in digital infrastructure by business? Has additional investment continued to produce wage dispersion? Have regional IT wages diverged from other skilled wages, or have skilled wages diverged in a similar pattern? Relatedly, why has IT investment continued apace while real productivity gains have stayed close to 2 percent per annum after the much higher rates of productivity growth during the dot-com boom? How has that productivity growth been distributed across the country, and does it bear any relationship to the regional variance in the first generation of advanced internet equipment?

Inadequacies in data also make it challenging to infer the productivity effects of broadband. A researcher typically has access only to either (i) available supply of broadband or (ii) purchased supply of broadband. Each suffers from a distinct form of endogeneity bias and measurement error. There are additional challenges to measurement. At one time, the Federal Communication Commission (FCC) ostensibly tracked the former at the geographic level of the zip code but counted any firm as a supplier if it had one customer in that zip code. By including satellite suppliers, the FCC came to numbers that reached maximal levels. At best, less availability—when measured as zero or one supplier—indicates a setting with limited supply and little competitive pressure. It is challenging to find an econometric escape from such limited data. Today the federal government provides a broadband map of availability; more availability does not tell us about adoption or use.[38]

One approach to these challenges, taken by Kolko (2012), examines different indicators of economic change affiliated with broadband—growth in information industries, wages, employment, telecommuting, and home-based work—and focuses the investigation on medium-sized cities where

37. For a recent review, see, for example, Cardona, Kretschmer, and Strobel (2013).

38. Federal Communications Commission, "Fixed Broadband Deployment," https://broadbandmap.fcc.gov/#/.

exogenous instruments might be plausible, such as the topography of an area. This approach does not lean heavily on any single finding, because of suspected measurement error. The approach looks for robust patterns. Kolko finds that many indicators of a relationship between more broadband and improved economic activity, though not the key ones affiliated with taxes, such as wages and employment.[39]

The experience outside the US has some parallels but also generates new insight. DeStefano, Kneller, and Timmins (2018) take advantage of the uneven rollout of DSL in the UK and link that to information about firm productivity. They find that the impact of broadband on business productivity is modest at best. They do see, however, that broadband is associated with restructuring the location and scale of activity. These results suggest complementary investments can play a significant role in fostering restructuring organizations, even when no short-term productivity improvement is visible.[40]

Using detailed information about wages and workers, Poliquin (2020) finds another parallel experience with business adoption of broadband at Brazilian firms, where broadband became geographically available in a quasi-random way to firms. Overall, wages increased 2.3 percent on average at establishments following the establishment's adoption of broadband, consistent with a productivity gain. Consistent with the theory of biased technological change, wages increased the most for workers engaged in nonroutine cognitive tasks, while returns were negative for routine cognitive tasks. There was no effect of broadband adoption on wages for either routine or nonroutine manual tasks. Poliquin also finds skill bias arises from changes within an existing labor force, not additions to it through recruiting.

The economic impact of access extends to topics around the globe. For example, one set of studies examines the impact the global spread of digital infrastructure spread had on trade, such as Fernandes et al. (2019). They examine export behavior in China during the period 1999–2007 and link firm participation in export markets to the rollout of the internet. They combine firm-level production data with province-level data on internet availability. Manufacturing rose during this period, and they find evidence of improvements in communication with buyers and input suppliers coincident with a more visible virtual presence. Like other studies, this one finds that improvements depend on the availability of broadband, but broadband alone is insufficient to explain all the increases in manufacturing. The authors stress

39. In spite of concerns about measurement, this continues to be a popular approach for measuring availability, particularly on the margin for lack of availability. For example, see Falck, Gold, and Heblich (2014).

40. This is in line with other work on the impact of broadband on the productivity of business, which also find modest effects on productivity but measurable changes in other firm attributes in the presence of complementary investments (see also DeStefano, Kneller, and Timmins 2019; Haller and Lyons 2015, 2019).

the role of numerous complementary investments to implement productive uses for broadband in firm processes.

Deployment of broadband access also generates symptoms of economic growth, especially in locations that previously lacked any wireline access. Hjort and Poulsen (2019) examine the gradual laying of fiber along the African coast, which enables wireline access where it previously was only possible by satellite. This experience is exogenous to potential adopters and creates many points of comparison between the served and underserved areas, including improved adoption (see also Cariolle 2019). Hjort and Poulsen's estimates show large positive effects on employment rates, with especially large increases in high-skill occupations. Remarkably, the authors also find smaller gains in employment for less educated workers.

An important open topic concerns the effect of digital infrastructure on entrepreneurship. In the developed economies, digital infrastructure has played a role in fostering a test bed for frontier application development by a range of entrepreneurial business. The size and importance of such externalities remain elusive to quantitative methods. Comparison of worldwide experience holds potential to identify the role of infrastructure in fostering technology-led entrepreneurial effects.

### 8.3.3 Value from Improving Protocols

A key piece of network infrastructure is its protocols and protocol stacks, intended to make digital equipment universally compatible.[41] Although complex, the protocol stack design for sending data packets along the least congested route was, and continues to be, an essential feature of the digital infrastructure inherited from the NSF/DARPA era. Many improvements continue to be added to this design.

Protocol development today does not reside exclusively with governments. Several nonprofit organizations design and upgrade the protocol stack used for global internet infrastructure. Many stakeholders contribute to improvements. For example, the Internet Society oversees the Internet Engineering Task Force (IETF), which designs protocols behind TCP/IP (Transmission Control Protocol/Internet Protocol), BGP (Border Gateway Protocol), and other protocol stacks. The Internet Society and other organizations subsequently charge little for their use.[42]

An improvement in the protocols of the internet benefits households,

41. Protocols are the set of rules and regulations that determine how data makes it through the network. A networking protocol defines conventions for processes, which includes definitions for both the format of data packets and also for recovery in the event of transmission errors. Protocol stacks are composed of a family of related protocols assembled together; they act as a reference model for designers, who largely aspire to make compatible equipment. For longer descriptions, see, for example, Clark (2018), Greenstein (2015), or Knieps and Bauer (2016).

42. The Institute of Electronic and Electrical Engineers (IEEE) maintains 802.11, the standard underlying Wi-Fi. The Internet Corporation for Assigned Names and Numbers (ICANN)

businesses, carriers, and application developers. Nonrivalry in use, combined with de facto lack of excludability, gives software protocols a set of properties isomorphic to classic public goods. This implies that improvements in protocols could confer large gains to society, and failures to design well could have negative consequences. Hence, similar to the questions for CDNs and cloud computing, developments in protocols raise questions about estimating externalities in an interdependent system.

The estimation of these gains or consequences is challenging because every user and supplier has access to the same improved protocols at the same time. Relatedly, as is true for many public goods, there is no competitive alternative, and users cannot opt out of the protocol stack if the relevant institutions make poor decisions. That (typically) results in no meaningful variance in adoption with which to make estimates of impact.

An important example of research about protocols is Simcoe (2012). The author examined the speed with which the IETF generated new protocols for the internet before and after privatization. He traces variance in speed to its underlying determinants, such as the composition of the committees making new protocols. He focuses on the role of disagreements between participants with varying interests, stressing the importance of multistakeholder institutions that (do or do not) become slower as the private costs and commercial risks become concentrated in the efforts of a few experts, who either come from universities or firms. Their interests may not align as their designs touch a wider breadth of the economy, resulting in a greater breadth of voices developing conflicting stakes in the details.[43]

Other research focuses on the growth of standardized and large-scale (and mostly invisible) digital processes for collecting and reselling a user's data and for supporting auctions to place online advertisements (Goldberg, Johnson, and Shriver 2019). Market incentives have not produced a system that transparently informs users about which aspects of their private data will be collected and sold to others after use of an application. Obtuse terms of service have proliferated, and every user must possess nearly an advanced degree in computer science and legal scholarship to figure out how to answer basic questions about whether their data will be resold. Attempts to design a standard infrastructure for privacy, such as P3P, failed to be adopted (Cranor et al. 2008). It is a remarkable state for a feature with such public importance.

That example illustrates an open avenue for research. What are the incentives for and gains from improvement in protocols, as designed by quasi-

governs assignment of domain names and updates the routing tables used by every switch and router on the internet. See, for example, Clark (2018).

43. Research with this focus has also begun to explore the workings of committees who govern other important elements of equipment. For a variety of perspectives about standards in wireless communications, see, for example, Bar and Leiponen (2014) or Baron, Gupta, and Roberts (2018).

public organizations or private firms? How do these incentives align with the incentives to adopt such protocols? How large are the shared benefits of improving protocols? More broadly, today a mix of publicly subsidized and privately funded research finances protocol development. How large are the contributions from members in relation to those benefits? Government users no longer act as the major test bed for protocol development as they did in the past. Whose experience has the most salience for the direction of improvement?

One approach to these questions focuses on estimating the size of the externalities from the deployment of a key piece of infrastructure. For example, Nagle (2019) takes a novel approach to this topic by examining a set of externalities in protocol improvement that *were not* global. Counterintuitively, he focuses on quite the opposite: externalities from software in which the spillovers were particularly *localized* in scope. He focuses on the spillovers from a French government mandate to use Linux, a program adopted as part of general policies to encourage the use of open-source software. Nagle finds the mandate had consequences for the rate of new business formation in complementary digital areas. The analysis takes advantage of a natural placebo test in events, in which the Italian government did not enforce a similar decree within its own borders. Nagle's estimates suggest that the externalities can be substantial if governments enforce their policies. The study frames a big open question: What conditions lead the local supply of talent to respond, and what limits that response?

Another approach to this topic examines an episode of the recent past, in which, with the benefit of hindsight, the economics were comparatively simple. The costs of R&D were defrayed against the benefits affiliated with meeting the mission of a federal agency (at DARPA and NSF), and professional recognition among research peers provided motivation for most of the efforts. While these costs were concentrated, the external benefits to society were widely shared. That sets up a question: What were the economic gains from the public investments in the historical R&D that supported protocol development? Greenstein and Nagle (2014) employ a method for estimating the value of unmeasured web servers in the United States in 2011. The authors show that these inputs make a positive contribution to economic growth in the United States. The authors further show that the returns from web servers alone generated enough economic gains to equal the US government's R&D internet investment. That is an important conclusion, because the authors do not make a full account for all gains from the invention of the internet (which is still an open question).

A third approach analyzes evolving market-based events using economic lessons from outside digital infrastructure. For example, the exhaustion of the Internet Protocol address space markets for trading IP addresses. Edelman and Schwartz (2015) consider alternative principles for organizing the design for the new and resale market and the properties affiliated with different proposals.

### 8.3.4 Uneven Geographic Deployment

Much research focuses on understanding the causes behind and consequences from the uneven supply of access and related network components. In developed countries, users in most suburban locations saw many options, with occasional overbuilding leading to more. Businesses in high-density settings could experience even more supply (see, e.g., Connolly and Prieger 2013; Wallsten and Mallahan 2013). Beyond those simple statements, the actual experience with entry and adoption depended on a host of factors, such as regulatory rules for pole attachments and ease of interconnection.

Variance in supply potentially creates the type of variance that econometricians like to exploit. The primary challenges are measurement. Many of these variations cannot be seen except at a fine level of geography, such as a neighborhood. Attempts to measure availability at this fine-grained level have encountered numerous challenges. For example, an attempt to create a National Broadband Map began in 2011, went through several revisions, was regarded as accurate in some but not all locations, and was discontinued in December 2018. As of this writing, the FCC is developing a new mapping program.

Government subsidies for high-speed access networks arise partly from analogies with local telephony, in which many providers received building and operational subsidies from universal service programs.[44] For example, the 1996 Telecommunications Act established the E-Rate program, which taxed telephone calls to finance subsidies for rural broadband. Today the program raises more than $4 billion dollars annually, focusing on developing broadband internet access in costly locations and making it available to organizations with public missions, such as libraries, schools, and hospitals. As another example, the 2009 stimulus package included $7 billion of subsidies for rural broadband. At a local level, many local governments also try to shape supply. Many insist through cable franchise agreements that cable providers build out into low-income or less dense areas.

Programs to address demand also exist but are less common. With this motivation, Rosston and Wallsten (2020) examine the impact of the Internet Essentials program, sponsored by Comcast to foster adoption of broadband by lowering prices for qualified low-income households in the parts of the US where Comcast provides service. This program provides information to test the proposition that low-income households are reluctant to adopt

44. There were many proposals for rural subsidies of broadband as part of the 2009 stimulus package, and they built on a previous set of subsidies in the E-Rate program, which were established by the 1996 Telecommunications Act.

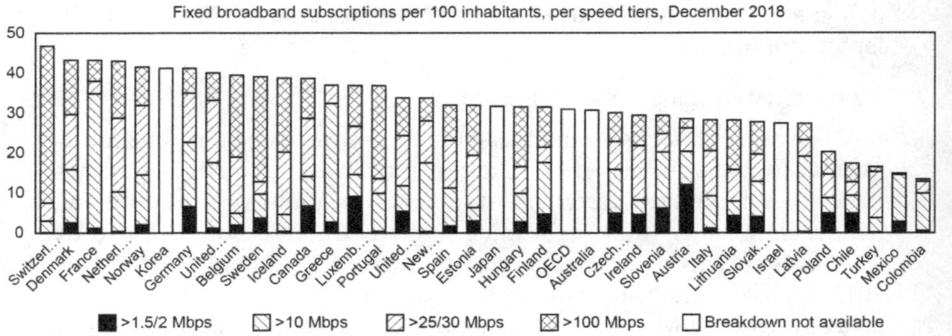


**Fig. 8.6 Broadband across the globe**

because of high prices. The measurement challenge requires clever statistical approaches. Rosston and Wallsten estimate *new* adoption in comparison to the counterfactual—that is, some households who qualify for the program would have adopted at the regular higher price. By comparison with adoption among similar households in similar areas that lack such programs, demand does grow among the target population in areas where the Internet Essentials program operates, suggesting the program supports hundreds of thousands of users who would not have adopted otherwise.[45]

Another type of study focuses on rural broadband (see, e.g., Whitacre, Gallardo, and Strover 2014). An interesting fact complicates inference: broadband satellite has been available in virtually every location, and for many years. For many uses, such as email, browsing, and noninteractive internet services, satellite broadband is technically sufficient, albeit more expensive than broadband in a typical suburban location. With such facts as motivation, Boik (2017) investigates a specific situation to understand the micro-mechanisms shaping behavior. He examines low-density North Carolina and studies willingness to pay for satellite broadband versus wireline broadband. He finds considerable willingness to pay for wireless access, which, in turn, limits the potential welfare gains from subsidies for building out wireline access. This willingness renders uneconomic most subsidies for wireline services in low-density locations.

Many open questions remain. Considerable data exists to measure variance across the globe (OECD 2014; World Economic Forum 2016). Figure 8.6 illustrates broadband capabilities across the globe. Why does this variance arise? What economic outcome does the variance produce in dif-

45. Rosston and Wallsten also show that a fraction of current nonadopters (potential users) are insensitive to price—in the sense that a large number of nonadopters do not change their behavior in spite of these massive price reductions. This suggests nonadoption among laggards does not have economic causes and requires policies not focused on price.

ferent countries? Studies of micro-mechanisms could illuminate the causes and consequences.

There is also need for analysis of the experience outside of developed economies. For example, Björkegren (2019) examines the demand for and benefits from mobile digital infrastructure in Rwanda. Using a year of phone calls, he provides estimates of the value of belonging to a network, as well as of the value of the infrastructure that supports it. Here he finds evidence of network effects in demand, which suggests the externalities from new networks can be substantial.

Further estimates of demand for wireless access in developing countries are needed. Unlike other innovative products in the modern economy, all innovative digital services do not first arise in developed countries before migrating to the markets of developing countries. A set of innovative services—and new to the world!—have begun to appear in the developed world where wireless devices have become the primary tool for accessing the internet. Many fundamental economic activities, such as payments and banking, have developed atop this ubiquitous wireless infrastructure. For example, China's most popular payments application for wireless devices, WeChat, has more than one billion users and has become an electronic substitute for cash. Such innovation has become increasingly common in developing economies and merits further study.

## 8.4 Open Research Questions

Two distinct views animate open questions about digital infrastructure supply. An outlook that could be labeled as "optimistic" anticipates experimentation in a few places, followed by more diffusion to more users, more regions, and a larger set of applications. This view interprets the state of digital infrastructure at a point in time as temporary, transient, and in the midst of wider diffusion. In contrast, an outlook that might be labeled as "pessimistic" stresses that digital infrastructure has achieved higher productivity in dense locations. That arises because of economies of scale in equipment, increased productivity from the colocation of many related activities, and the availability of skilled labor in urban areas in developed economies.

The two outlooks make different predictions and, accordingly, base policy on different premises. In the optimistic outlook, differences in supply melt over time as once expensive infrastructure, which incubated in a few cities, spreads to new users and new locations. The most important open question concerns the determinants of the speed of diffusion, which then determines how fast laggard regions catch up to frontier regions. In this view, policy intervention focuses on speeding up diffusion to laggard locations by removing deterrence to adoption. The pessimistic outlook perceives persistent large differences. In the most pessimistic views, a few locations enjoy the benefits of the frontier. The role of public policy aims at reaching a societal ideal—orienting toward ameliorating unequal economic outcomes caused by unequal supply.

### 8.4.1 Informing Open Questions about Subsidies

Differences in these two views animate many open research questions today about optimal subsides for digital infrastructure. Examples discussed in this chapter illustrate why debates examine the same fact base but point in different directions. The experience with CDNs supports the optimistic view, because of the wide geographic dispersion of supply and the presence of third parties. In contrast, the experience with data centers supports the less optimistic view, because of the concentration of supply around urban cities and the persistent demand for local supply. The two views also differ in their interpretation of the diffusion of broadband, with one side stressing the speed with which it reached a high percentage of households, and the other lamenting the slowing rate of adoption. These examples suggest no general answer will emerge, because analysis depends on specific cost conditions and use cases, and these are moving targets.

Deeper research can address some of the tension. For example, though users prefer a local supply of infrastructure when it is available, it may be possible to use remote data centers, cloud storage, and/or satellites. A similar trade-off faces users choosing between satellites and wireline broadband. These topics would be, and could be, informed by estimates of demand.

Another challenge arises from government efforts to employ infrastructure for noneconomic outcomes, such as informing citizens, furthering the education of children, contributing to the public health of a local population, or guaranteeing its safety. How much does society want to spend to encourage those goals? How much should it pay to build out the internet in low-density places to organizations with public missions, such as libraries, schools, hospitals, and public dispatchers? It can be challenging to translate these demands into pecuniary terms. As with the demand for many public goods, it is naive to presume an easy answer. With a moving frontier of acceptable quality, the measurement issues are especially vexing.

These challenges animate debates about government support for digital infrastructures, which tend to divide into one of three categories. The first category has to do with services at schools, hospitals, libraries, or governmental organizations such as police, fire, and other government services. The second concerns services for business. The third focuses on households.

The first category contains the most difficult issues to measure but, ironically, has tended to contain the least vociferous debate. Political systems in developed countries tend to view these investments as urgent. It is common for the entities in a locality to coordinate their purchases. Considerable federal funding has been redirected from universal services funds toward these use cases. That said, there is a largely open research question related to the economic benefits of such investment. Analysis similar to Athey and Stern (2002) is exemplary, and there could be much more.

The second category, subsidies to business, also contains difficult measurement issues because of externalities. The effects from building new broadband, for example, may shape wages and employment of the local populace, and the building may shape the accumulation of additional services built on top of digital infrastructure. These debates are particularly fraught because of issues inferring causation—that is, does cheaper or better broadband *cause* better economic outcomes? The answers to those questions depend on counterfactual analysis. On the one hand, how would business behave in its procurement of services in the absence of subsidy? If business would have paid for broadband, why should the government subsidize it? On the other hand, what if the purchases take place in a location that faces eroding economic growth prospects? Would more, cheaper, or better broadband slow the erosion of the underlying economic value of economic activities performed in nearby areas or prevent an economic decline in the absence of such subsidy?

Such counterfactual questions frame difficult challenges for policy assessment. In the context of a backward-looking assessment of subsidies to broadband build-out in low-density settings, the analyst asks, What would have happened to wages, employment, and other indicators of economic prosperity in the absence of subsidy? An ideal empirical experiment would compare two otherwise similar locations which differ in only one respect: one received a subsidy and the other did not. Historical circumstances rarely produce such comparisons, however, so research has to find clever ways to exploit the minutiae of such situations, as in Boik (2017) or Skiti (2019).

Forward-looking policy assessment requires even more information. Analysis needs to understand the accumulation of business activities in the same location, which are more likely to generate large regional gain. For example, many localities and state development agencies grant tax abatements to build data centers, hoping to foster more development in a locale. While that might generate construction jobs for a short period, it is less obvious that such structures make a location inviting for further development on the digital frontier. Even a moderately large data center does not employ many people. What are the spillovers for the local service economy? What is the evidence about accumulation and spillovers after such tax abatements? These are open questions.

The third category, subsidies for access to households in low-density settlements, tends to focus on settings in which the costs of access are high and incremental gains go to a small number of households. This situation arises often in areas experiencing spotty housing settlement, such as rural areas. What would the households do with or without subsidy? What are the incremental gains in one situation compared with the other? Once again, the analysis of gains depends on counterfactual questions, and these are not easily answered.

All these questions lack general answers because analysis depends on achievable aims, which vary over time. The costs and capabilities for satellite service, for example, have changed considerably over the past two decades, and so too have the capabilities of both fixed-wireless and mobile wireless communications over long distances. Economic circumstances and prospects also vary considerably across the thousands of low-density counties of the US, so the marginal potential adopter can and will vary for any specific proposal, and so too will the cost-benefit calculation.

In developing countries, all three categories of questions arise in different forms, once again preventing the emergence of any durable general answer. For example, a developing country may consider subsidies for capital expenditures for wireless infrastructure, which provides a foundation for further building of public services, business, and household activities. The counterfactual questions are especially challenging because investments in infrastructure alone may be insufficient to generate economic growth—that is, in the absence of complementary physical and human capital, particularly digital infrastructure and related firm investments in commercialization (Cirera and Maloney 2019). At the same time, the presence of network effects in wireless devices (Björkegren 2019) implies that subsidies might be beneficial well beyond the gains affiliated with satisfying the initial demand. Building wireless use could jump-start the use of digital infrastructure, which can become the basis for the development of further applications, such as in basic household finance and microloans for small entrepreneurs. Once again, the open question is fundamental: What is the evidence about accumulation and spillovers after building wireless digital infrastructure?

### 8.4.2 Open Questions about Governance

Historical studies of success and failure to innovate could illuminate understanding about how governance shapes the evolution of digital infrastructure. For example, the supply of infrastructure has supported the growth of valuable, standardized, and large-scale communications, such as texting, email, and a browser-supported advertising-oriented media market. That growth has fostered availability on multiple devices, supported by both wireline and wireless access. Any supplier can find the relevant technical standards and build a component that interoperates with the existing system. Why did that emerge, and what pitfalls were avoided? Similar questions arise about privacy standards. Why does this system work well for some attributes and not others?

The examples presented here will suggest that the boundary between public and private is in flux across a wide set of activities. Some software is private, some is open-source, and some employs a mixed model. Some software comes from consortia, other software from standard-setting organizations, and still other software from private suppliers. Government policy plays a variety of roles—for example, in subsidizing research and invention, in workforce training in higher education, in providing some services, and in defining legal boundaries for different types of organizations. The precise boundaries are open to debate and differ substantially across countries. Do those boundaries matter for economic outcomes? Answering that question could inform policy debates in many countries.

The governance of ubiquitous software requires attention, though such activity falls far outside the scope of (traditionally) regulated markets or public goods. Concrete examples can illustrate the open questions. Contrast two starkly different models. Some privately supplied software has achieved ubiquitous use, such as the Microsoft Operating System, Oracle Server, and Android/iPhone smartphone operating systems. Private firms supply this software, upgrade it, service requests, and exclude those who fail to pay an appropriate price. Another model also yields ubiquitous software. The World Wide Web Consortium is one example. Managed by a not-for-profit consortium, which regularly upgrades the software, the Web achieves ubiquity through nonexclusion, making upgrades available without restriction. The continuing success of the Web illustrates a model that leads to widespread use. What economic factors lead to a match between these governance models and market settings? How much difference does the governance model make to outcomes?

Web server software raises similar questions and offers different insights. Different users today largely employ three different servers: Apache, IIS, and Nginx. The first one descended from earliest experiments with web servers at the University of Illinois, organized as an open-source project. Microsoft offers IIS, generally as part of a range of the enterprise software it offers and certifies. The third, Nginx, comes in a freemium form, with a fast but limited version available at no charge. An enterprise version requires payment for services. Apache and IIS had a large impact on the market in the first two decades, but Nginx has enabled large gains in high-volume servers. The trade-offs between each of these organizational forms defy easy characterization.

As an example, Athey and Stern (2015) ask why some countries use more pirated operating system software. Their framework contrasts two broad determinants: (1) variation in willingness to pay for software, which shapes economic incentives to pirate software, and (2) institutional enforcement of property rights, which shaped incentives for private actors to invest in software. Athey and Stern measure the former with economic variables, such as per capita income, while they measure the latter with country-specific histories of respecting property rights. If the former is important, then sellers of proprietary software could potentially change their pricing strategies. If the latter is important, then pricing is unlikely to address the challenge, and better enforcement of legal regimes for property rights could have a larger effect.

Their framework provides a pathway forward. Two differences between operating systems and other internet infrastructure potentially shape the economics of other digital infrastructure. In most settings, infrastructure must be available for continuous operations and compatible with other parts of the internet. Continuous operation and compatibility requires the range of complementary operations mentioned previously.

The definition of infrastructure remains fluid in widely used software tools as well. For example, consider software repositories, such as GitHub, which has become common. GitHub aids the sharing of code and reduced frictions in large-scale projects. Making collaboration across distance easier, GitHub's creation had a well-known productivity impact; and Microsoft recently purchased the entire platform for $7.5 billion in stock. It is essential infrastructure for many software projects. How Microsoft's purchase shapes GitHub's productive impact remains an open question.

Mapping software offers an example of the new frontier of the public-private boundary. The fundamental work was once thought to be solely a government function, and private firms merely repackaged the information in more accessible format for general consumption. At present, however, digital mapping has passed to either proprietary or open-source projects, which draw input from crowds, and these compete with one another. These platforms vary in their governance and source of input, as well as in response to new opportunities (see, e.g., Nagaraj 2019; Nagaraj and Piezunka 2018). The next generation of mapping for autonomous vehicles has moved to private sources. Different firms use distinct models of how to use input from users. All mapping depends critically on government-funded satellites that provide GPS (Global Positioning System) coordinates, so public support is never far away. Are the incentives to develop digital maps too low or too high, and do they result in too few or too many development projects? What are the incentives to share results, once they are developed?

A different and important insight comes from research focused on nowcasting in developing countries—that is, using present economic activity to forecast events over a short time horizon, particularly where GDP measurement apparatus is absent or primitive. Near ubiquitous digital infrastructure can offer a way forward in measurement. For example, Indaco (2020) uses Twitter activity (as measured through GPS-labeled photos) to determine whether geo-located IP addresses give as much information as light from satellite photos. The study correlates Twitter use with other measures of economic activity, such as the light from satellite photos, because the same types of advanced investments support both—namely, continuous electrical supply, skilled labor, and a range of complementary investments. Ackermann and Angus (2014) provide a similar exercise when they examine the distribution of IP addresses. Once again, this provides evidence of economic activity.

To close, consider this provocative question: Is Wikipedia digital infrastructure? Its ubiquity suggests it ought to be treated as such. It receives more than 15 billion pages views per month.[46] At the time of this writing, over 5.9 million articles grace its web pages in English alone, with more than 500 new articles added each day. Volunteers built the entire corpus of text. More to the point, because of its not-for-profit status, aspiration toward a neutral point of view, and minuscule storage and transmission costs, the scale economies appear virtually limitless. Wikipedia has become a focal site on which many others depend, including many search engines and Q&A sites. Many software firms also use it to complement their documentation efforts on GitHub, providing longer explanations and links.

The Wikipedia example epitomizes the open questions of this topic: What is and is not infrastructure when public funding is absent? Where are the boundaries of public and private when the private infrastructure contains properties similar to public goods? Can something be called infrastructure merely if it is shared, inexpensive, nonexclusive, and seemingly essential? Is the source—either public or private—relevant to the economics or virtually irrelevant?

To finish, note that Wikipedia remains unavailable in China, where the government firewall blocks access. That is but one example of many that illustrates the "splintering" of the internet. That occurs as a result of the erosion of compatibility of complementary equipment and software, resulting in distinct regions of the globe pursuing their own direction of technical developments, each internally consistent within national boundaries, yet inconsistent and incompatible across borders. Splintering has begun to arise as different governments censor content and impose limits on the operations of applications consistent with local preferences for privacy, security, copyright, and other government policy. Some of these actions have begun to migrate into the infrastructure layers, where governments impose, for example, distinctly different packet-inspection processes in routers or different back-door designs within operating systems. These actions and policies frame open questions about the consequence for seamless interoperability.

## 8.5 Conclusion

Long before it spread across the globe, it was fashionable to call the internet an "information superhighway." The label arose from a combination of observation and aspiration. The *observation* contained a grain of truth about the physical layout of the internet. Many backbone lines followed existing rights-of-way for roads, bridges, and highways. The *aspiration* channeled a proposed vision for the future, with the government subsidizing the capital expenditure and leaving the assets unpriced—as with a freeway. The

46. "Wikimedia Statistics," https://stats.wikimedia.org/v2/#/all-projects.

aspiration advanced an ideal in which information remained unpriced and subsidized by government support.[47]

With the benefit of decades of hindsight, we can see that both the observation and aspiration about highways bear only partial resemblance to the present state of commercial digital infrastructure. One can gain insight from understanding the merits and shortfalls of the comparison.

Begin with the similarities. In the past few decades economic actors shared the use of the long-lasting capital of digital infrastructure, like much other infrastructure, and many economic actors employed digital infrastructure as an intermediate input in the production of goods and services. As an intermediate input, digital infrastructure acted much like a new road connecting two areas with previously poor connections, lowering frictions between potential transactions in different locations (Goldfarb and Tucker 2019). At a high level of abstraction, lowering of frictions created two types of new economic opportunities, either fostering cooperative agreement between suppliers of complementary inputs or encouraging competition from suppliers who serve new customers in new areas. New supply chains and applications built on these, such as those that employed more personalization; these would not have emerged or deployed in the absence of the low-cost and reliable network infrastructure.

The metaphor goes only so far in illuminating the core of the economic challenges, however. The building of digital infrastructure was not a one-time event, and the continued improvement changed transactions along many dimensions. The volume and type of traffic grew, and the degree of personalization increased, which, in turn, changed the viability of different services and the prospects for the firms offering services. The contrast with roads and highways could not be sharper: Roads typically do not undergo improvements in their key attributes every few years, while in digital infrastructure innovations accumulated, from many different suppliers, producing a system with capabilities that no central planner or brilliant designer could have specified in advance. New digital infrastructure supported frequent reassessments; in turn, these encouraged more experiments to expand service. That pace of improvement also heightened disagreements among distinct views about how to make valuable use of opportunities enabled by improved infrastructure. That enabled "innovation from the edges" (Greenstein 2015), which raised the importance of bringing frontier applications to market to settle the unresolved question about how to create value.

More pointedly, digital infrastructure *does not* resemble roads and highways in its pricing or governance. Building and operating roads and highways are largely government functions, and, relatedly, most highways and surface

47. The aspiration became associated with a range of policy initiatives that subsidized the internet for research in the late 1980s and, eventually, with the specific aspirations of a presidential candidate, Al Gore. See, for example, Greenstein (2015), chaps. 2 and 3, for a discussion of these policies.

streets remain unpriced and nonexcluded, with the possible exception of some toll roads and bridges. Questions about design and enhancement become decisions in the public sector. In contrast, while the role of public funding was once important, today private funding lags behind investment in the vast majority of digital infrastructure. Public funding continues to play a role in R&D activities, and the economic justifications for those subsidies are strong as a result of the externalities for suppliers and users. Beyond that, however, the degree of government intervention in digital infrastructure differs substantially from the typical practices with roads. The level of tax subsidy is much lower for digital infrastructure and more haphazard, affiliated with local tax abatement for large projects, zoning for new access services, or subsidies for internet access in costly areas. Modern suppliers face minimal mandates to become ubiquitous, reliable, and inexpensive beyond what market forces incentivize them to build and perform, whether governments accommodate those incentives or not. Despite the societal importance of fostering widespread use of frontier services, providers have unfettered discretion over price and other aspects of service. Failure by users to pay the minimal price leads to denying service to users. Altogether that situates the boundary between public and private at a substantially different place.

As of this writing, many of the most fundamental economic questions still remain unanswered. As this chapter has stressed, variance in the supply and use of innovative digital infrastructure arises within every developed country, as well as between developed and developing countries. Much of that variance arises because of differences in commercial incentives—quite unusual for infrastructure with such recognized importance for economic outcomes. That sets the stage for numerous research questions about the rate and direction of those incentives, as well as whether infrastructure's performance achieves societal goals.

## References

Abbate, Janet. 1999. *Inventing the Internet*. Cambridge, MA: MIT Press.

Ackermann, Klaus, and S. D. Angus. 2014. "A Resource Efficient Big Data Analysis Method for the Social Sciences: The Case of Global IP Activity." *Procedia Computer Science* 29: 2360–69.

Ahlfeldt, Gabriel, Pantelis Koutroumpis, Tommaso Valletti. 2017. "Speed 2.0: Evaluating Access to Universal Digital Highways," *Journal of the European Economic Association* 15 (3): 586–625.

Anderson, Monica, Andrew Perrin, Jingjing Jiang, and Madhumitha Kumar. 2019. "10% of Americans Don't Use the Internet. Who Are They?" Pew Research Center, April. https://www.pewresearch.org/fact-tank/2019/04/22/some-americans-dont-use-the-internet-who-are-they/.

Athey, Susan, and Scott Stern. 2002. "The Impact of Information Technology on Emergency Health Care Outcomes." *Rand Journal of Economics* 33 (3): 399–432.

———. 2015. "The Nature and Incidence of Software Piracy: Evidence from Windows." *Economic Analysis of the Digital Economy*, edited by A. Goldfarb, S. Greenstein, and C. Tucker. Chicago: University of Chicago Press.

Bar, Talia, and Aija Leiponen. 2014. "Committee Composition and Networking in Standard Setting: The Case of Wireless Telecommunications." *Journal of Economics & Management Strategy* 23 (1): 1–23.

Baron, Justus, Kirti Gupta, and Brandon Roberts. 2018. "Unpacking 3GPP Standards." *Journal of Economics & Management Strategy* 27 (3): 433–61.

Björkegren, Daniel. 2019. "The Adoption of Network Goods: Evidence from the Spread of Mobile Phones in Rwanda." *Review of Economic Studies* 86 (3): 1033–60.

Boik, Andre. 2017. "The Economics of Universal Service: An Analysis of Entry Subsidies for High Speed Broadband." *Information Economics and Policy* 40: 13–20.

Boik, Andre, Shane Greenstein, and Jeff Prince. 2019. "The Persistence of Broadband User Behavior: Implications for Universal Service and Competition Policy." *Telecommunications Policy* 43 (8): 101820.

Bottger, Timm, Felix Cuadrado, Gareth Tyson, Ignacio Castro, and Steve Uhlig. 2018. "Open Connect Everywhere: A Glimpse at the Internet Ecosystem through the Lens of the Netflix CDN." *ACM SIGCOMM Computer Communications Review* (CCR) 48 (1).

Brynjolfsson, Erik, Avinash Collis, and Felix Eggers. 2019. "Using Massive Online Choice Experiments to Measure Changes in Well Being." *PNAS* (Proceedings of the National Academy of Sciences) 116 (15): 7250–55.

Brynjolfsson, Erik, and Joo Hee Oh. 2012. "The Attention Economy: Measuring the Value of Free Digital Services on the Internet." 33rd International Conference on Information Systems.

Burnham, Brad, Shane Greenstein, Neil Hunt, Kevin McElearney, Marc Morial, Dennis Roberson, and Charles Slocum. 2013. *Issues in Data Caps and Usage-Based Pricing*. Report, Federal Communications Commission, Open Internet Advisory Committee, Economic Impacts Working Group, May 5. https://www.hbs.edu/faculty/Pages/item.aspx?num=49733.

Byrne, David, and Carol Corrado. 2019. "Accounting for Innovation in Consumer Digital Services: IT Still Matters." NBER Working Paper 26010. Cambridge, MA: National Bureau of Economic Research.

Byrne, David, Carol Corrado, and Dan Sichel. 2018. "The Rise of Cloud Computing: Minding Your P's, Q's and K's." NBER Working Paper 25188. Cambridge, MA: National Bureau of Economic Research.

Cardona, M., T. Kretschmer, and T. Strobel. 2013. "ICT and Productivity: Conclusions from the Empirical Literature." *Information Economics and Policy* 25 (3): 109–25.

Cariolle, Joel. 2019. "Telecommunication Submarine-Cable Deployment and the Digital Divide in Sub-Saharan Africa." CESifo Working Paper 7415. https://papers.ssrn.com/sol3/papers.cfm?abstract_id=3338769##.

Cirera, Xavier, and William Maloney. 2019. *The Innovation Paradox: Developing-Country Capabilities and the Unrealized Promise of Technological Catch-Up.* Washington, DC: World Bank Group.

Chen, Yongmin, and Scott Savage. 2011. "The Effects of Competition on the Price for Cable Modem Internet Access." *Review of Economics and Statistics* 93 (1): 201–17.

Clark, David. 2018. *Designing an Internet.* Cambridge, MA: MIT Press.

Clark, David, Steven Bauer, William Lehr, kc claffy, Amogh Dhamdhere, Bradley

Huffaker, and Matthew Luckie. 2014. "Measurement and Analysis of Internet Interconnection and Congestion." TPRC Conference Paper, September 9.

Comin, Diego, and Bart Hobijn. 2010. "An Exploration of Technology Diffusion." *American Economic Review* 100 (December): 2031–59.

Connolly, Michelle, and J. E. Prieger. 2013. "A Basic Analysis of Entry and Exit in the US Broadband Market, 2005–2008." *Review of Network Economics* 12 (3): 229–70.

Coyle, Diane, and David Nguyen. 2018. "Cloud Computing and National Accounting." ESCoE Discussion Paper, December. Office of National Statistics, UK.

Cranor, Lorrie Faith, Serge Egelman, Steve Sheng, Aleecia M. McDonald, and Abdur Chowdhury. 2008. "P3P Deployment on Websites." *Electronic Commerce Research and Applications* 7 (3): 274–93.

DeStefano, Tim, Richard Kneller, and Jonathan Timmins. 2018. "Broadband Infrastructure, ICT Use and Firm Performance: Evidence for UK Firms." *Journal of Economic Behavior & Organization,* 155(C): 110–39.

———. 2019. "Cloud Computing and Firm Growth." Working paper presented at NBER Winter Digitization Meetings.

Edelman, Benjamin, and Michael Schwarz. 2015. "Pricing and Efficiency in the Market for IP Addresses." *American Economic Journal: Microeconomics* 7 (3): 1–23.

Ewens, Michael, Ramana Nanda, and Matthew Rhodes-Kropf. 2019. "Cost of Experimentation and the Evolution of Venture Capital." Working Paper 15-070, Harvard Business School.

Falck, Oliver, Robert Gold, and Stephan Heblich. 2014. "E-lection: Voting Behavior and the Internet." *American Economic Review* 104 (7): 2238–65.

Fernandes, Ana, Aaditya Mattoo, Huy Nguyen, and Marc Shiffbauer. 2019. "The Internet and Chinese Experts in the Pre-Ali Baba Era." *Journal of Development Economics* 138: 57–76.

Forman, Chris. 2005. "The Corporate Digital Divide: Determinants of Internet Adoption." *Management Science* 51 (4): 641–54.

Forman, Chris, Avi Goldfarb, and Shane Greenstein. 2005. "How Did Location Affect Adoption of the Commercial Internet? Global Village vs. Urban Leadership." *Journal of Urban Economics* 58 (3): 389–420.

———. 2012. "The Internet and Local Wages: A Puzzle." *American Economic Review* 102 (1): 556–75.

Goldberg, Samuel, Garrett Johnson, and Scott Shriver. 2019. "Regulating Privacy Online: The Early Impact of the GDPR on European Web Traffic and E-Commerce Outcomes." https://ssrn.com/abstract=3421731.

Goldfarb, Avi, and Jeff Prince. 2008. "Internet Adoption and Usage Patterns Are Different: Implications for the Digital Divide." *Information Economics and Policy* 20 (1): 2–15.

Goldfarb, Avi, and Catherine Tucker. 2019. "Digital Economics." *Journal of Economic Literature* 57 (1): 3–43.

Goolsbee, Austan, and Peter Klenow. 2006. "Valuing Consumer Products by the Time Spent Using Them: An Application to the Internet." *American Economic Review* 96 (2): 108–13.

Greenstein, Shane. 2015. *How the Internet Became Commercial: Innovation, Privatization, and the Birth of a New Network*. Princeton, NJ: Princeton University Press.

———. 2020. "The Basic Economics of Internet Infrastructure." *Journal of Economic Perspectives* 34 (2): 192–214.

Greenstein, Shane, and Ryan McDevitt. 2011. "The Broadband Bonus: Estimating Broadband Internet's Economic Value." *Telecommunications Policy* 35: 617–32.

Greenstein, Shane, and F. Nagle. 2014. "Digital Dark Matter and the Economic Contribution of Apache." *Research Policy* 43: 623–31.
Greenstein, Shane, and Tommy Pan Fang. 2019. "Where the Cloud Rests: the Economic Geography of Data Centers." Working paper, Harvard Business School.
Greenstein, Shane, Martin Peitz, and Tommaso Valletti. 2016. "Net Neutrality: A Fast Lane to Understanding the Trade-Offs." *Journal of Economic Perspectives* 30 (2): 127–50.
Haller, Stephanie, and Sean Lyons. 2015. "Broadband Adoption and Firm Productivity: Evidence from Irish Manufacturing Firms." *Telecommunications Policy:* 1–15.
———. 2019. "Effects of Broadband Availability on Total Factor Productivity in Service Sector Firms: Evidence from Ireland." *Telecommunications Policy* 43 (1): 11–22.
Hitt, Lorin, and Prasanna Tambe. 2007. "Broadband Adoption and Content Consumption." *Information Economics and Policy* 19 (3–4): 362–78.
Hjort, Jonas, and Jonas Poulsen. 2019. "The Arrival of Fast Internet and Employment in Africa." *American Economic Review* 109 (3): 1032–79.
Horrigan, John. 2020. "Measuring the Gap: What Is the Right Approach to Exploring Why Some Americans Do Not Subscribe to Broadband?" National Data Inclusion Alliance. https://www.digitalinclusion.org/measuring-the-gap/.
Huston, Geoff. 2017. "The Rise and the Rise of Content Distribution Networks." Presentation at Workshop on Information Economics, Center for Applied Internet Data Analysis, University of California, San Diego, December 2017. http://www.caida.org/workshops/wie/1712/slides/wie1712_ghuston.pdf.
Indaco, Augustin. 2020. "From Twitter to GDP: Estimating Economic Activity from Social Media." *Regional Science and Urban Economics* 85 (November): 103591. https://www.sciencedirect.com/science/article/pii/S0166046220302763.
Jin, Wang, and Kristina Steffensen McElheran. 2018. "Economies before Scale: Learning, Survival, and Performance of Young Plants in the Age of Cloud Computing." Rotman School of Management Working Paper 3112901. https://papers.ssrn.com/sol3/papers.cfm?abstract_id=3112901.
Knieps, G., and J. M. Bauer. 2016. "The Industrial Organization of the Internet." In *Handbook on the Economics of the Internet*, edited by M. Latzer and J. M. Bauer, 23–54. Cheltenham, UK: Edward Elgar.
Kolko, Jed. 2012. "Broadband and Local Growth." *Journal of Urban Growth* 71 (1): 100–113.
Malone, Jacob, Aviv Nevo, and Jonathan W. Williams. 2017. "The Tragedy of the Last Mile: Economic Solutions to Congestion in Broadband Networks." NET Institute Working Paper 16-20. https://ssrn.com/abstract=2849869.
McElheran, Kristina 2015. "Do Market Leaders Lead in Business Process Innovation? The Case(s) of E-Business Adoption." *Management Science* 61 (6): 1197–216.
McManus, Brian, Aviv Nevo, Zachary Nolan, and Jonathan W. Williams. 2018. "Steering Incentives and Bundling Practices in the Telecommunications Industry." NET Institute Working Paper 18-12. https://ssrn.com/abstract=3267060.
Nagaraj, Abhishek. 2019. "Information Seeding and Knowledge Production in Online Communities: Evidence from OpenStreetMap." Paper, UC Berkeley Haas School of Business. http://abhishekn.com/files/nagaraj_seeding.pdf.
Nagaraj, Abhishek, and Henning Piezunka. 2018. "Deterring the New, Motivating the Established—The Divergent Effect of Platform Competition on Member Contributions in Digital Mapping Communities." http://abhishekn.com/files/nagaraj_piezunka_competition.pdf.

Nagle, Frank. 2019. "Government Technology Policy, Social Value, and National Competitiveness." Working Paper 19-103, Harvard Business School.

National Telecommunications and Information Administration. 2011. "Digital Nation: Expanding Internet Usage." February 2011. https://www.ntia.doc.gov/files/ntia/publications/ntia_internet_use_report_february_2011.pdf.

Nevo, Aviv, John Turner, and Jonathan Williams. 2016. "Usage-Based Pricing and Demand for Residential Broadband." *Econometrica* 84 (2): 411–43.

Norton, William B. 2014. *The Internet Peering Playbook: Connecting to the Core of the Internet*. Palo Alto, CA: DrPeering Press.

Nuechterlein, Jonathan, and Philip Weiser. 2005. *Digital Crossroads: Telecommunications Law and Economics in the Internet Age*. Cambridge, MA: MIT Press.

OECD. 2014. *Measuring the Digital Economy: A New Perspective*. Paris: OECD Publishing. https://doi.org/10.1787/9789264221796-en.

Poliquin, Chris. 2020. "The Wage and Inequality Impacts of Broadband Internet." Working paper, University of California, Los Angeles. https://poliquin.xyz/files/poliquin_jmp.pdf.

Rosston, Gregory, Scott Savage, and Donald Waldman. 2010. "Household Demand for Broadband Internet Service in 2010." *B. E. Journal of Economic Analysis & Policy* 10 (1): 79.

Rosston, Gregory L., and Scott J. Wallsten. 2020. "Increasing Low-Income Broadband Adoption through Private Incentives." Stanford Institute for Economic Policy Research Working Paper 20-001. https://siepr.stanford.edu/research/publications/increasing-low-income-broadband-adoption-through-private-incentives.

Seamans, Robert. 2012. "Fighting City Hall: Entry Deterrence and Technology Deployment in the Cable TV Industry." *Management Science* 58 (3): 461–75.

Simcoe, Timothy. 2012. "Standard Setting Committees: Consensus Governance for Shared Technology Platforms." *American Economic Review* 102 (1): 305–36.

Skiti, Tedi. 2019. "Strategic Technology Adoption and Entry Deterrence in Broadband." *Industrial and Corporate Change* 29 (3): 713–29.

Wallsten, Scott, and Colleen Mallahan. 2013. "Residential Broadband Competition in the United States." In *The Economics of Digitization*, edited by Avi Goldfarb, Shane Greenstein, and Catherine Tucker. Cheltenham, UK: Edward Elgar.

Wallsten, Scott, and James Riso. 2010. "Residential and Business Broadband Prices, Part 2: International Comparisons." Policy paper, Technology Policy Institute. https://techpolicyinstitute.org/policy_paper/residential-and-business-broadband-prices-part-2-international-comparisons/.

Wang, Shuang, Jacob LaRiviere, and Aadharsh Kannan. 2019. "Spatial Competition and Missing Data: An Application to Cloud Computing." Working paper presented at NBER Winter Digitization Meetings.

Whitacre, Brian, Roberto Gallardo, and Sharon Strover. 2014. "Broadband's Contribution to Economic Growth in Rural Areas: Moving towards a Causal Relationship." *Telecommunications Policy* 38 (11): 1011–23.

World Economic Forum. 2016. *The Global Information Technology Report*. https://www.weforum.org/reports/the-global-information-technology-report-2016.

Zhuo, Ran, Bradley Huffaker, kc claffy, and Shane Greenstein. 2019. "The Impact of the General Data Protection Regulation on Internet Interconnection." NBER Working Paper 26481. Cambridge, MA: National Bureau of Economic Research.

## Comment Catherine Tucker

Chapter 8 is a very useful summary of the existing literature on digital infrastructure. There are some key highlights to the piece. You learn a lot about the history and technology underlying the internet such as root servers, fiber, broadband lines, networking switches and routers, content delivery networks, cloud facilities, and cellular towers. There are also intriguing pieces of data, such as that in 2018, 2 percent of US households still use dial-up. In general, chapter 8 highlights two factors that have held up the literature. First is the lack of convincing sources of exogenous variation that would allow an economist to measure the effects of digital infrastructure on outcomes. Second is that the literature has focused on broadband without much thought about additional technologies such as content distribution networks, cellular technologies, and cloud computing. The cloud added approximately $214 billion in value-added to US GDP in 2017. The cloud added approximately 2.15 million jobs in 2017. In approximately 15 years since 2002, the cloud economy has nearly tripled in size. And yet it has been vastly understudied in economics. This useful summary helps frame and guide the forthcoming literature on this topic.

However, I want to focus my discussion on a passage in the chapter that reads as follows:

> To close, consider this provocative question: Is Wikipedia digital infrastructure? Its ubiquity suggests it ought to be treated as such. . . . The Wikipedia example epitomizes the open questions of this topic: What is and is not infrastructure when public funding is absent? Where are the boundaries of public and private when the private infrastructure contains properties similar to public goods? Can something be called infrastructure merely if it is shared, inexpensive, nonexclusive, and seemingly essential? Is the source—either public or private—relevant to the economics or virtually irrelevant?

This strikes me as a very useful framing of a potentially large and looming question. Economists studying digital infrastructure have tended to focus on the wires, and physical manifestations of that infrastructure. However, a novel question that the chapter highlights is that perhaps platforms have actually become one of the most pressing digital infrastructure issues.

This topic is already being discussed in the popular press. For, example, a recent article in the *New York Times Magazine* reads:

Catherine Tucker is the Sloan Distinguished Professor of Management and a professor of marketing at MIT Sloan, chair of the MIT Sloan PhD Program, and a research associate of the National Bureau of Economic Research.

For acknowledgments, sources of research support, and disclosure of the author's material financial relationships, if any, please see https://www.nber.org/books-and-chapters/economic-analysis-and-infrastructure-investment/comment-digital-infrastructure-tucker.

> All this is to say that a sufficiently successful social platform is experienced, much like Uber, as a piece of infrastructure. Except, instead of wrapping its marketplace around a city's roads, Facebook makes a new market around communication, media and civil society. This, from a founder's perspective, is an electrifying outcome. But this cultural metastasis has led to a swift and less-than-discriminate backlash. Already, calls for regulating the largest internet platforms are growing louder while remaining tellingly vague.[1]

The 2020 pandemic has also led journalists to argue that Amazon fulfilled the role of a public utility and so should be treated like one.[2] However, it is notable that much of this discussion of infrastructure and public utilities with relationship to large technology platforms is really a call for either more regulation or antitrust action. This is already a debate among law scholars. Rahman (2018) has argued that digital platforms such as Google, Facebook, and Amazon are the core infrastructure of our twenty-first-century economy and public sphere.

It strikes me that economists have much that is useful to say about this debate that we have not yet engaged with. In particular, our research can help answer key questions:

- Do platforms meet the definition of infrastructure as economists use the term?
- What does our experience with making various parts of infrastructure public and then returning them to the private sector teach us about optimal conditions for public or private governance of digital infrastructure?

Are economists' definitions of infrastructure useful for this task? My impression is that the answer is no. Instead, most definitions have a "you know it when you see it" flavor, and focus on the idea that it is self-evident that something is infrastructure, as highlighted in chapter 1 in this volume, by Bennett, Kornfeld, Sichel, and Wasshausen:

> We begin with the challenging question of how to define "infrastructure." Defining the economic boundaries of infrastructure is imprecise and somewhat subjective. We consider three broad categories of infrastructure that can gauge different aspects of infrastructure from a National Economic Accounts standpoint. "Basic" infrastructure (such as transportation and utilities) reflects a traditional definition of infrastructure. From there, we expand that core to include additional economic activity

1. John Herrman, "What If Platforms Like Facebook Are Too Big to Regulate?," *New York Times Magazine*, October 4, 2017.

2. See, for example, Wendy Liu, "Coronavirus Has Made Amazon a Public Utility—So We Should Treat It Like One," *Guardian*, April 17, 2020.

that would potentially be included in infrastructure, including social and digital infrastructure.

Therefore it is not clear to me that economists are going to be helpful for determining a precise definition and whether something like the Amazon or Uber platform would qualify. Economics is helpful, however, in understanding the underlying characteristics that digital platforms share with entities that are commonly thought of infrastructure and understanding them through an economics lens.

Initially in the language of network effects or two-sided platforms, economists viewed the key challenges for businesses as being able to attract sufficient numbers of users. This is the focus of the early literature on digital platforms and allowed us to understand that essentially the key property of what may or may not be a digital platform is whether or not there are significant network effects. Given this early focus, it might be simple to dismiss the argument that platforms resemble infrastructure such as utilities or railroads as being related to arguments surrounding natural economies of scope or scale, which suggest that there will be only one platform that succeeds at any one point in the market.

However, I would argue that this analogy is not particularly accurate. Increasingly, digital markets are not characterized by there being only one platform or means of achieving a certain goal. If I am an advertiser, I have multiple platforms to choose to use, for example, to reach a potential consumer. As a ride-sharing user, I also have multiple platforms to choose between. Instead, in this essay I argue that the temptation to claim that digital platforms reflect digital infrastructure instead reflects the degree of governance platforms themselves impose on their users.

To initiate some of this debate, I want to introduce a term from the classroom that we use to describe one of the key challenges of building a platform and relate it back to the infrastructure debate. In the classroom, I introduce students to the idea of "coring" of platforms. "Coring" was initially introduced as a term to describe the idea that platforms need to ensure that their technology is at the "core" of interactions. The idea was that if a platform-controlled technology was not at the "core" of the interaction within the platform, then the platform risked losing control of that transaction. For example, if a real estate platform could not ensure that buyers and sellers used its technologies to execute real estate transactions, then it would risk losing control of the market (Gawer and Cusumano 2008).

However, since the early 2000s when this concept was introduced, the nature of digital platforms has changed. As a result of all the shifts documented in chapter 8, hardware and its technological manifestations have become less important. As a result, if platforms are to ensure that transactions or interactions take place on the platform, they have to erect steps around governance that provide incentives for transactions to stay on the platform. The way I describe this in the classroom is that ultimately as a platform your major job is to make sure interactions on your platform do not just happen but also go well. This requires relinquishing a technical mindset and adopting the mindset of a government or police officer to put into place the right incentives for successful interactions. And it is the mindset that these platforms have to take on governance tasks that I think has led commenters to argue that the platforms are infrastructure.

Examples of "coring" are the erection of huge and complex rating systems that give insight into the likely unobserved quality of platform participants. These have been a key part of the literature on the underlying infrastructure of digital platforms in digital economics. Notable examples include Fradkin et al. (2015); Nosko and Tadelis (2015); and Tadelis (2016). As well as being notable in general, these examples are notable in particular for the fact that they reflect the work of economists at large technology platforms trying to set up optimal incentive systems for reputation systems using the classic tools of economics. Other examples of coring are constraints on who can use the platform and attempts to make sure that antisocial behavior by one user of the platform does not have negative spillovers for other users.

It is useful to recognize that just because something is "infrastructure" does not imply that governments should control that infrastructure or regulate access to this infrastructure. There are parallels here too with the early development of internet infrastructure that chapter 8 highlights. That digital infrastructure has "happened" swiftly, with very little government intervention. Furthermore, the US pathway for decentralized digital infrastructure has dominated worldwide. This has led to cries from non-US governments to have more control over underlying internet protocols. Similar, the recent increase in the importance of platforms have led non-US governments to seek to potentially intervene and gain more control.[3] In other words, chapter 8's question, whether digital platforms are infrastructure, sets up one of the most crucial technology policy debates of our time.

## References

Bennett, J., R. Kornfeld, D. Sichel, and D. Wasshausen. 2021. "Measuring Infrastructure in BEA's National Economic Accounts." This volume.

Fradkin, A., E. Grewal, D. Holtz, and M. Pearson. 2015. "Bias and Reciprocity in Online Reviews: Evidence from Field Experiments on Airbnb." In *Proceedings of the Sixteenth ACM Conference on Economics and Computation*, 641.

3. See, for example, the Australia Competition and Consumer Commission, *Digital Platforms Inquiry: Final Report*, July 26, 2019, https://www.accc.gov.au/publications/digital-platforms-inquiry-final-report.

Gawer, A., and M. A. Cusumano. 2008. "How Companies Become Platform Leaders." *MIT Sloan Management Review* (Winter): 68–75.
Nosko, C., and S. Tadelis. 2015. "The Limits of Reputation in Platform Markets: An Empirical Analysis and Field Experiment." Technical report, National Bureau of Economic Research.
Rahman, K. S. 2018. "Regulating Informational Infrastructure: Internet Platforms as the New Public Utilities." *Georgetown Law and Technology Review* 2: 234.
Tadelis, S. 2016. "Reputation and Feedback Systems in Online Platform Markets." *Annual Review of Economics* 8: 321–40.

# Contributors

Jennifer Bennett
Bureau of Economic Analysis
4600 Silver Hill Road
Suitland, MD 20746

Adrian Bridge
Queensland University of Technology
2 George Street
Brisbane QLD 4000, Australia

Leah Brooks
Trachtenberg School of Public Policy and Public Affairs
George Washington University
805 21st Street NW
Washington, DC 20052

Gilles Duranton
The Wharton School
University of Pennsylvania
3733 Spruce Street
Philadelphia, PA 19104

Eduardo Engel
University of Chile
Department of Economics
Diagonal Paraguay 257
Santiago, Chile

Ronald D. Fischer
Centro de Economia Aplicada (CEA)
Departamento de Ingenieria Industrial
Universidad de Chile
Republica 701 Santiago, Chile

Jason Furman
Harvard Kennedy School
79 John F. Kennedy Street, Box 82
Cambridge, MA 02138

Alexander Galetovic
Adolfo Ibáñez University
Diagonal Las Torres 2640
Peñalolen, Santiago, Chile

R. Richard Geddes
Department of Policy Analysis and Management
Cornell University
Ithaca, NY 14853

Edward L. Glaeser
Department of Economics
315A Littauer Center
Harvard University
Cambridge, MA 02138

Shane Greenstein
Technology Operation and Management
Harvard Business School
Soldiers Field
Boston, MA 02163

Keith Hennessey
Graduate School of Business
Stanford University
655 Knight Way
Stanford, CA 94305

Peter Blair Henry
New York University
Leonard K. Stern School of Business
Kaufman Management Center
44 West 4th Street, 11-160
New York, NY 10012

Robert Kornfeld
Bureau of Economic Analysis
4600 Silver Hill Road
Suitland, MD 20746

Zachary Liscow
Yale Law School
127 Wall Street
New Haven, CT 06511

Deborah Lucas
MIT Sloan School of Management
100 Main Street, E62-640
Cambridge, MA 02142

Dejan Makovšek
OECD
2 rue Andre Pascal
Paris F-75775, France

Jorge Jimenez Montesinos
MIT Golub Center for Finance and Policy
One Broadway, Suite 1375
Cambridge, MA 02142

Geetika Nagpal
Department of Economics
Brown University
Box B
Providence, RI 02912

James M. Poterba
National Bureau of Economic Research
1050 Massachusetts Avenue
Cambridge, MA 02138

Valerie A. Ramey
Department of Economics, 0508
University of California, San Diego
9500 Gilman Drive
La Jolla, CA 92093-0508

Stephen J. Redding
Department of Economics and School of Public and International Affairs
Princeton University
Princeton, NJ 08544

Daniel Sichel
Department of Economics
Wellesley College
106 Central Street
Wellesley, MA 02481

Catherine Tucker
MIT Sloan School of Management
100 Main Street, E62-533
Cambridge, MA 02142

Matthew A. Turner
Department of Economics
Brown University
Box B
Providence, RI 02912

Shoshana Vasserman
Stanford Graduate School of Business
655 Knight Way
Stanford, CA 94305

David Wasshausen
Bureau of Economic Analysis
4600 Silver Hill Road
Suitland, MD 20746

Clifford Winston
The Brookings Institution
1775 Massachusetts Avenue, NW
Washington, DC 20036

# Author Index

# Subject Index

Note: Page numbers followed by "f" or "t" refer to figures or tables, respectively.